A CENTURY *of the* MADISON SYMPHONY ORCHESTRA

J. MICHAEL ALLSEN

LITTLE CREEK PRESS
MINERAL POINT, WISCONSIN

Copyright © 2025 J. Michael Allsen

All rights reserved. No part of this publication may be reproduced, distributed, or transmitted in any form or by any means, including photocopying, recording, digital scanning, or other electronic or mechanical methods, without the prior written permission of the publisher, except in the case of brief quotations embodied in critical reviews and certain other noncommercial uses permitted by copyright law. For permission requests or other information, please send correspondence to the following address:

Little Creek Press
5341 Sunny Ridge Road
Mineral Point, WI 53565

ORDERING INFORMATION
Quantity sales. Special discounts are available on quantity purchases by corporations, associations, and others. For details, contact info@littlecreekpress.com

Orders by US trade bookstores and wholesalers.
Please contact Little Creek Press or Ingram for details.

Printed in the United States of America

Cataloging-in-Publication Data
Names: J. Michael Allsen, author
Title: A Century of the Madison Symphony Orchestra
Description: Mineral Point, WI Little Creek Press, 2024
Identifiers: LCCN: 2025902950 | ISBN: 978-1-955656-95-5
Classification: MUSIC / Genres & Styles / Classical
MUSIC / History & Criticism
HISTORY / United States / State & Local / Midwest
(IA, IL, IN, KS, MI, MN, MO, ND, NE, OH, SD, WI)

Book design by Little Creek Press

CONTENTS

Preface XIII

Acknowledgments XVII

Foreword (by MSO executive director Robert Reed) XX

1 Prelude: Classical and Orchestral Music in Madison Before the Founding of the Madison Civic Music Association 1

Classical Music in Madison, ca. 1850–1926:
Amateur Choirs 1

The Madison Musical Union 3

Professional Touring Musicians in Madison 4

Madison's Own Musical Celebrities .12

Opera, Operetta, and Musical Comedy in Madison 16

Summer Music for Edification and Pleasure:
The Monona Lake Assembly 18

Local Conservatories and the University
School of Music 20

Amateur and Professional Orchestras in
Madison Before 1926 23

The Madison Orchestral Association 34

Notes to Chapter 1 40

2 The Madison Civic Music Association and the Founding of the Madison Civic Symphony and Madison Civic Chorus: 1925–1940 46

From the Madison Community Music Committee
to the MCMA, 1920–1926 46

The Beginnings of the Madison Civic Symphony 50

The Madison Civic Chorus 56

Sidebar: Town and Gown:
The University Versus Civic Music 57

MCMA and the Madison Vocational School 59

Concerts of the 1930s 62

Civic Music Festivals and Other Extravaganzas 67

    Sidebar: Concerts in the "Red Gym" and
    the "Cow Barn" 71

MCMA-Sponsored Opera in the 1930s 79

    Sidebar: The Madison Opera Guild. .82

Civic Music and the Local Press 82

Musicians of the Orchestra and Chorus: Selected Profiles

    Marvin Hartman 84

    Alexius Baas. 87

    Florence Bennett 88

    Grace Schumpert 89

Marie Endres: Concertmaster, 1927– 1960 91

Notes to Chapter 2 97

3 Founding Father: Dr. Sigfrid Prager, Music Director 1926–1948 101

Early Life: From Berlin to Service in World War I 101

Argentina and New York, 1919–1925. 106

Madison and New York, 1925–1926 110

Madison's Maestro: The MCMA, Vocational School, and
Other Work in Madison 113

Work in Chicago, Sheboygan, and Beyond the Midwest 120

WPA Conductor: The Madison Concert Orchestra
and Wisconsin Symphony Orchestra 123

Prager as a Performer 131

Prager as a Composer and Arranger. 132

Prager as a Writer and Lecturer 134

Prager's Retirement and Final Years. 135

Personality and Legacy 141

Notes to Chapter 3 145

4 A Tale of Two Maestros: The Madison Civic Symphony in the 1940s and 1950s 151

The War Years 151

The Kunrad Kvam Affair 157

Civic Music After the War 159

The End of the Beginning: The Retirement of Sigfrid Prager 162

A New Music Director: Walter Heermann 164

Concerts of the 1950s 169

Publicity and Program Books 174

    Sidebar: From the Women's Committee to the
    Madison Symphony Orchestra League, 1956–1980 176

The Orchestra and the Community 178

Toward a Professional Ensemble 179

Performances and Recordings of the 1950s 180

Musicians of the Orchestra and Chorus: Selected Profiles

    The Kirkpatricks 184

    James and Ann Crow 185

    Robert Tottingham 188

    Betty Bielefeld 189

Notes to Chapter 4 191

5 Walter Heermann, Music Director 1948–1961 196

Hugo Heermann 197

Walter Heermann: Early Life and Emigration to America 204

The Cincinnati Symphony Orchestra and Military Service 206

Conducting the Cincinnati Symphony Orchestra and
Solo Appearances 212

Other Musical Work in Cincinnati: Chamber Music,
Conducting, and Teaching 218

Life in Cincinnati 224

Summer Performances and Teaching in
Interlochen and Madison 226

Conducting in Charleston and Springfield 229

Work in Madison 231

Retirement 233

Legacy 234

Notes to Chapter 5 237

6 A Time of Changes: The Orchestra, Chorus, and Opera in the 1960s and 1970s 245

A New Music Director: Roland Johnson 246

Concerts of the 1960s and 1970s 250

Youth and Neighborhood Family Concerts 255

Pops Concerts 258

Opera Returns to Madison 259

  Sidebar: The Quest for a Civic Auditorium and
  the "Auditorium Wars" 264

The MCMA Board Evolves 269

Professionalizing the Orchestra 270

The End of Free Concerts and a New Name:
The Madison Symphony Orchestra 271

The Madison Symphony Orchestra in the 1960s and 1970s 274

Concertmasters of the 1960s and 1970s 276

The Madison Civic Chorus in the 1960s and 1970s 280

Celebrating a Half Century 282

Toward a Professional Staff 283

Musicians of the Orchestra and Chorus: Selected Profiles

  Richard (Dick) Lottridge 286

  George and Nancy Shook 289

  Ann Stanke 290

Notes to Chapter 6 294

7 Roland Johnson, Music Director 1961–1994 298

Early Life: Johnson City. 298

Cincinnati. 301

Navy Service and a New Career Path 303

Graduate Study and Teaching at the College of Music of Cincinnati. . . 305

Johnson as a Composer 309

Studies with Hermann Scherchen. 313

Alabama. 314

    Sidebar: Arline Hanke Johnson. 318

Madison 321

Retirement 324

Legacy. 327

Notes to Chapter 7. 329

8 Passing the Baton: The Orchestra, Chorus, and Opera in the 1980s and 1990s 333

Opening the Oscar Mayer Theatre. 334

Concerts of the 1980s and Early 1990s 336

Changing Course. 339

Shining Brow 343

The Retirement of Roland Johnson and
the Search for a Successor 346

Passing the Baton 351

John DeMain and the MSO 352

DeMain's Inaugural Season and the Close of the 1990s 357

    Sidebar: Innovative Auxiliary: The Madison Symphony
    Orchestra League, 1980 to present. 359

Musicians of the Orchestra: Selected Profiles

    Tyrone and Janet Greive. 363

    Marc Fink 366

Paul Haugan 368

Notes to Chapter 8 371

9 John DeMain, Music Director 1994 to present. 375

Early Life in Youngstown 376

Juilliard and the Kenley Players 378

Julius Rudel and Exxon/Affiliated Artists Awards:
From New York City to St. Paul. 380

Houston and Porgy and Bess 382

Moonlighting and Marriage:
Work in Omaha and Elsewhere 387

Madison and Beyond 389

Retirement and Legacy 390

Notes to Chapter 9 393

10 The Madison Symphony Orchestra in a New Millennium 395

Marking a New Millennium and Celebrating 75 Seasons 395

From the Oscar Mayer Theatre to Overture Hall 398

The Overture Concert Organ 406

The Musicians of the Madison Symphony Orchestra 409

Administrative Changes 414

The Madison Symphony Chorus 419

MSO Concerts of the Past Quarter Century 420

Musicians of the Orchestra and Chorus: Selected Profiles

Greg Zelek 427

Rose Heckenkamp-Busch 428

Naha Greenholtz and Kyle Knox 429

A Katrin Talbot Gallery 433

Notes to Chapter 10 442

11 The Madison Symphony Orchestra and the Future......445
Robert Reed..............................445
Challenges and Opportunities..................447
Looking Toward the 100th Season................451
Notes to Chapter 11........................453

Photos and Images: Sources and Permissions..............454
Bibliography................................459
Index of Composers and Musical Works..................477
General Index................................490

PREFACE

I have been involved continuously and in various ways with the Madison Symphony Orchestra since 1983—nearly all of my adult life. I think that I can claim a uniquely multifaceted perspective on the MSO. First and foremost, I was a longtime member of the orchestra. My wife and I arrived in Madison in 1982, and I started graduate work in musicology at the University. However, at the beginning of that school year, I actually skipped my first musicology seminar to take an audition for the Madison Symphony Orchestra. I didn't make it into the orchestra, but in the fall of 1983, I auditioned again—successfully this time—and played second trombone during the 1983–84 season. I stepped away after that season to concentrate more fully on my graduate coursework, and eventually to spend a few years as a stay-at-home dad to our son. However, I did remain on the MSO's substitute list and played with the orchestra several times during the late 1980s. Then in 1990, there was an opening on bass trombone. Principal trombonist Joyce Messer encouraged me to audition—I've jokingly referred to this as the moment that I "came out of the closet" as a bass trombonist—and I won the position. I remained the orchestra's bass trombonist until my retirement in 2018, including a term on the orchestra committee and taking part in contract negotiations. Those 29 seasons included some of the most significant bits of the MSO's recent history: the premiere of the opera *Shining Brow*, the retirement of Roland Johnson and the arrival of John DeMain, the Mahler cycle, the opening of Overture Hall, a dramatic expansion of the season, and the tremendous growth in the quality of the orchestra's performances over the last couple of decades. I am very grateful to have been part of it.

Though I had stepped away from playing regularly in the orchestra for a few years beginning in 1984, I began writing program notes for the MSO in the 1984–85 season. I asked general manager Bob Palmer if I could write notes for the opening concert of the season. He agreed and said that if they liked what I wrote, I could keep doing it—the only agreement I've ever had with the MSO regarding program notes. As I write this preface in June of 2024, I am preparing to work on my 41st season of MSO program notes. As its longtime annotator, I have a deep connection with most of the repertoire performed by the MSO over the last four decades.

MSO Low brass and Maestro DeMain, 2014. L-R: Joyce Messer, Benjamin Skroch, John DeMain, Mike Allsen, Josh Biere

Another perspective on the MSO came from working in its administration. I spent the 1995–96 season as a full-time employee, working as the MSO office manager, where my job(s) included everything from managing databases and volunteers, helping with marketing campaigns, editing and mailing fundraising letters, and organizing board meetings, to finding ways of salvaging and drying out the MSO's archives and historical photographs after our storage room in the basement of the Madison Area Technical College (MATC) building was flooded in the spring of 1996. In the summer of 1996, I left to take a teaching job at UW–Whitewater, but that season left me with a deep appreciation of what goes on behind the scenes to put an orchestra on stage in front of an audience. A very different perspective has come in the last few years: I became a member of the MSO board in the fall of 2022. As a board member, I've had to start thinking about budgets, marketing campaigns, branding, and many other things that I paid no attention to when I was a musician on stage. It has been particularly exciting to work as part of a couple of committees looking for ways to expand the orchestra's mission, the diversity of its offerings, and its outreach to a broader audience, all of these fundamental to the MSO's *next* hundred years.

Finally, the MSO has been one of my historical interests for the last quarter century. In 2000–2001, the orchestra celebrated its 75th season and commissioned me to write a short history. The results were four historical chapters published in the four program books that year, and a complete chronicle and index of the orchestra's performances from 1926 to 2001. Though I am not in any way ashamed of those four short chapters, I've always been aware that they had been a rush job: I had to do nearly all of the writing and much of the research during the course of about a month during my 2000 summer break from UW–Whitewater. I have always wanted to go back and "do it right"—incorporating information from a much larger range of sources. My retirement from the orchestra and from UW–Whitewater in the spring of 2018 gave me the time to do it right, and this book has been one of my major retirement projects. This much more comprehensive history of the orchestra incorporates extensive work on materials from the archives of the Wisconsin State Historical Society, the Wisconsin Music Archives, and the archives of the Madison Symphony Orchestra itself. (Indeed, part of this project involved completely reorganizing and creating a rough catalog of the MSO Archives.) It draws upon hundreds of articles in Madison newspapers and newspapers and other sources from around the country, as well as from Germany and Argentina, and the personal papers of Walter Heermann and Roland Johnson. I have also had the opportunity to correspond with librarians, orchestra personnel, and other historians in several different cities. Most enjoyable of all has been the opportunity to do oral history interviews with the musicians, board members, administrators, volunteers, and others who played roles in creating the MSO's history.

The history of the Madison Symphony Orchestra is similar in many ways to the histories of other orchestras in medium-sized cities across America. Like many comparable groups, it was originally a largely amateur community orchestra that evolved over time into a fully professional ensemble. However, the cast of characters and the cultural backdrop of Madison make the MSO's story unique. This history begins with a prelude (Chapter 1), setting the stage for the founding of the Madison Civic Symphony in 1926 and concluding with a short history of orchestral music in Wisconsin's capital city from the 1850s through 1925. The five main historical chapters (Chapters 2, 4, 6, 8, and 10) divide the narrative into segments of about 20 years each. Each of these deals with the evolution of the orchestra, the Madison Symphony Chorus, and eventually the Madison Opera: the types of programs they performed, repertoire, and soloists, as well as discussing venues and the development of the governing board and administration. Each historical chapter closes with short profiles of a few players and singers who were active during that period. One remarkable aspect of the orchestra's history is the fact that in the course of 100 years, there have been only *four* music directors. Chapters 3, 5, 7, and 9 are biographies of these men: Sigfrid Prager, Walter Heermann, Roland Johnson, and John DeMain. The conclusion, Chapter 11, includes a bit of speculation about the future of the MSO.

In earlier drafts, I spent a great deal of time talking about the history of Madison itself, as background to the musical history that is my main concern. However, I eventually realized that (a) David Mollenhoff, Stuart Levitan, and other nonmusical historians have already covered this ground far better than I could, and (b) I was creating an unwieldy and overcomplicated book that was well on its way to becoming an 800-page doorstop. This final version is concentrated on the growth of the MSO as a musical institution. However, I have retained a few pertinent excursions outside of this main story, presented in the text as sidebars. Another major detour was the initial "prelude" chapter, in which I originally tried to tell the *entire* story of classical music in Madison before 1925, including a massive appendix listing some 950 performances between 1850 and 1925. This had ballooned to over 45,000 words before I decided to limit my focus. Much of the 30,000-word part of this exposition that does not appear here is really fascinating history, and I do not consider it to have been wasted effort: I hope to publish that material in another form at some point.

ACKNOWLEDGMENTS

Many people have provided assistance and support over the last six years. I'll begin by thanking Robert Reed, executive director of the MSO, who agreed to cover the production costs of this book. (I'll note that all proceeds from sales will go to support the MSO.) Robert has also very kindly contributed a foreword. The administrative staff of the MSO, particularly Ann Bowen, Peter Rodgers, orchestra librarians Kathy Taylor and Jennifer Goldberg, and office manager Alexis Carreon, have been unfailingly helpful: allowing me to set up shop in the MSO office for months at a time, granting unlimited access to the orchestra's archives, photos, music library and other files, letting me make innumerable copies, and supporting my work in many other ways. I also thank Katrin Talbot for generously digging up and sharing the wonderfully expressive portraits she has taken of MSO players.

Thanks also go to the folks at Little Creek Press: to Kristin Mitchell for her excellent design work, for her unflagging enthusiasm for this project, and for her patience with innumerable questions from its author; and to Kevin Campbell for his eagle-eyed editing and for his work on the bibliography and general index.

Oral history has been an important part of my research, and I was able to draw upon several interviews that I did back in 1999 and 2000 for the 75th anniversary chapters: interviews with Roland Johnson, John DeMain, Grace Schumpert, Gerald Borsuk, Jim and Ann Crow, Ted Iltis, and Helen Hay, as well as written remembrances by Marilyn Ziffrin and Otto Festge. Most of them have passed away over the last quarter century, but having their memories of the orchestra's earliest days has been particularly useful. I'll also thank my interviewees from the last few years, including John DeMain, Betty Bielefeld,

Dick Lottridge, Marian Bolz (since deceased), Fred Mohs, Terry Haller, Joel Skornicka (since deceased), Beverly Taylor, Bob Palmer, Sandy Madden, Rick Mackie, Samuel Hutchison, George and Nancy Shook, Wally Douma, Ann Bowen, Marc Fink, Tyrone and Janet Greive, Sharon Stark, Jeff Bauer, Robert Reed, Elaine Mischler, Greg Zelek, Rose Heckenkamp-Busch, Kyle Knox, and Naha Greenholz.

In working on Sigfrid Prager, one very fortunate contact was with Prof. Silvia Glocer of the University of Buenos Aires. She happened to be working on a biographical article on Prager for an Argentinian online dictionary at the same time that I was working on my biographical chapter. Our correspondence was invaluable: Silvia was able to share details of his career in Argentina in the 1920s and after 1948, material that I would simply not have been able to access. In return, I was able to help her with information on his early life in Germany and his work in New York City and Madison.

In writing about Walter Heermann and Roland Johnson, I have had the privilege of working closely with their families. Heermann's grandson, Peter Neal, contacted me several years ago after finding the 75th anniversary chapters on my website. During the Covid lockdown, Peter arranged for an extended Zoom interview with his mother, Heermann's 93-year-old daughter Paulita. In July 2021, Paulita invited me to come for a visit at her summer home in Interlochen, Michigan. Over the course of three busy days, during which I had free reign of a rather posh "cabin" owned by the Heermann family in Interlochen, I was able to work with an extraordinary set of scrapbooks documenting over 60 years of Walter Heermann's musical life. I also met Peter Neal and other members of the extended family in Interlochen. Similarly, I worked closely with Johnson's children, Carl Johnson and Karen Kretschmann, and their spouses, Barbara Westfall and David Kretschmann. I conducted formal interviews with them, but they also granted me virtually unlimited access to Johnson's papers, photographs, and a fragmentary memoir sketched out by Roland after his retirement. In the case of John DeMain, John himself has a soon-to-be published memoir: an engaging and well-written double narrative of his life combining a biography by the late Greg Hettmannsberger with John's own recollections. I have done my best, in Chapter 9, to provide a fairly concise biography that does not conflict with that book. Contributions from additional contacts in Madison, Cincinnati, Springfield (Ohio), Charleston (West Virginia), Key West (Florida), and Freiburg (Germany) are acknowledged in the chapter endnotes.

I also thank my family. One of my inspirations in writing a piece of local history is my dad, Ken Allsen, who, after his retirement from IBM, became one of the mavens of architectural history in Rochester, Minnesota, publishing five books and four monographs (to date!). He and my mom Nancy have been my biggest cheerleaders, reading and commenting on each draft chapter as I finished them. My son Jeff has also been encouraging throughout this project. My wife Diann was, among many other good things, a great editor, purging pomposity and pointing out things that would be confusing to a general reader. (She also tried—with limited success—to cure my excessive fondness for the em dash!) Diann read and improved drafts of the first three chapters before her death from Covid in December 2020. I think that having a large, long-term project like this was an important part of maintaining my sanity during the lockdown and the years following her death. I can't help but wish that she could have seen the completed product.

My most important inspiration has been the Madison Symphony Orchestra itself. As a player, annotator, and, more recently, as a member of the audience, I have found the MSO to be an unending source of fulfillment, deep emotion, and wonder. *A Century of the Madison Symphony Orchestra* is respectfully dedicated to the musicians of the MSO, past and present.

Madison, Wisconsin
June 2024

FOREWORD

by Robert Reed, executive director,
Madison Symphony Orchestra

One of the reasons why the Madison Symphony Orchestra is a leading U.S. regional symphony orchestra preparing to celebrate its 100th anniversary season is the amazing people associated with it. The orchestra musicians, choir members, and music directors over the years have created inspiring musical programs and have raised both the artistic profile and respect for the organization. The Madison community has a love for the arts and has supported the organization over the course of a century through its generous donations, fundraisers, special events, and ticket sales. The board members and advisors, administrative staff members, and many volunteers continue to execute plans to ensure its financial viability to ensure the next 100 years. Dr. J. Michael Allsen (Mike) is one of those special people who have made the Madison Symphony better and more relatable.

A few years ago, the Madison Symphony Orchestra (MSO) made an important decision. For its centennial season, the MSO knew it would present many dynamic performances for a diverse group of music lovers and people who wished to experience high-quality concerts. That is good and dandy, but we also wanted something that would be more permanent and could easily be referred to in the coming years. The leadership of the MSO decided to ask Mike to write a detailed book on the 100 years of the Madison Symphony Orchestra. Why Mike? Because he is the perfect person given both his expertise and his extensive history with the Madison Symphony Orchestra.

Mike Allsen served as bass trombonist of the Madison Symphony Orchestra from 1990 to 2018. He was a member of the orchestra under two of the four music directors. In addition, Mike has written the MSO's program notes since 1984 (41 seasons and counting) and has led Prelude Discussions prior to our concerts for many seasons. He even served as a full-time member of the staff back in the 1990s. If anyone has any questions about the MSO's programs, venues, or people, the best person to contact is Mike; he is certainly the first call for MSO staffers with any questions about our history. His knowledge of the MSO is immense. As you will find out reading this book, Mike has plenty to say about the MSO, and we are honored that he can tell our story so well.

This book is the result of six years of research and writing. It was important to us that every period of the MSO's history be presented. There may be a few patrons reading the book whose memories stretch back to concerts conducted by Dr. Sigfrid Prager at the Stock Pavilion. A few more patrons will remember performances in the postwar era conducted by Walter Heermann. Many will remember the MSO's long-standing relationship with Madison Area Technical College. Some will remember the dedication of the Oscar Mayer Theatre in 1980 with Beethoven's *Symphony No. 9*, conducted by Roland Johnson, or the world premiere of Daron Hagen's opera *Shining Brow*. Many will remember the opening performance of the Overture Center for the Arts in 2004 conducted by Maestro John DeMain. Mike recalls all of these (and much more!) in entertaining detail.

Many orchestras celebrate their hundredth anniversary with a glossy "coffee table"–style book, heavy on photos and light on details. Mike has chosen instead to write a piece of real history, highly detailed and meticulously documented. Mike's writing becomes understandably more personal as he reaches the period of the MSO's history of which he was a part.

I hope everyone reading this book will find it fascinating. Some may feel like sections of the book will transport them back to the live performances that took place. Some may find it educational as they learn something new about the Madison Symphony Orchestra. The one thing I can guarantee is that you will come away better informed about the origins of the Madison Symphony and the highlights of our first 100 years.

The last thing I wish to mention is that Mike truly loves the MSO. He has decided to donate all proceeds from sales of the book to the orchestra. We at the Madison Symphony Orchestra are fortunate to have someone so qualified and enthusiastic to write this book. I am also happy that I can honestly call Mike my friend and someone I enjoy spending time with.

Robert Alan Reed, Executive Director, Madison Symphony Orchestra
December 2024

CHAPTER 1

Prelude: Classical and Orchestral Music in Madison Before the Founding of the Madison Civic Music Association

In a June 1920 article in the *Wisconsin State Journal*, University of Wisconsin music professor Peter Dykema asserted that 70% of Madison's 8000 homes had pianos, and he went on to praise the variety of classical music being performed in the town, from visiting artists and orchestras to homegrown choirs, chamber music, and bands.[1] Clearly, the Madison Civic Symphony, founded in 1926, did not arise in a musical vacuum, but in a city that already had a tradition of consuming and performing classical music. I have opened this account of the orchestra's history with a "prelude"—a chapter that sets the scene for the history of the orchestra.

Classical Music in Madison, ca. 1850-1926: Amateur Choirs

Musicmaking in Madison during this period was dominated by local amateur groups. Choral music was the first form to thrive in frontier Madison. Church choirs were established by most congregations, and by the turn of the century, these groups would often perform public "sacred concerts" of choral music, vocal quartets, and organ music, typically on Sunday evenings. In the decade 1901 to 1910, for example, sacred concerts were staged by several Madison congregations: St. Patrick's, St. Raphael's, and Holy Redeemer Catholic Churches, and First Congregational, Christ Presbyterian, First Methodist

Episcopal, Methodist Episcopal Baptist, and Unitarian Churches.

Music was an important part of expressing cultural solidarity in immigrant populations in 19th- and early 20th-century America. Though Madison's founding settlers had been largely Yankees, who retained political control of the city through the late 19th century, the population was increasingly becoming dominated by more recent immigrants: Germans, Norwegians, Irish, and later Italians were Madison's leading ethnic minorities in the late 19th and early 20th centuries. Germans were the first to arrive in large numbers in the early 1850s. Virtually every American city with a sizable German population could boast of a Singverein or Liederkranz (singing society), or Maennerchor (men's chorus), devoted to performances of German classical choral works and folk music. The Madison Maennerchor—among the oldest continuously existing musical groups in Wisconsin—was founded in 1852 by a group of 12 German immigrants under the leadership of Francis (Franz) Massing. It was joined in the 1860s by a Liederkranz mixed chorus, though this mixed group does not seem to have lasted long. It is clear that throughout the late 19th century and into the early 20th century, the Maennerchor was Madison's leading choral group, and its concerts were a source of tremendous community pride.[2] In 1925, Madison's Norwegian community founded a similar men's choir, the Grieg Chorus. This group, like the Madison Maennerchor, is still performing today. Yet another, more broadly community-based men's chorus, the Mozart Club, was founded in 1901 under the leadership of local organist Elias Bredin and was initially directed by the University professor Fletcher Parker. This group was active well into the 1950s.[3]

The largest choral organization in Madison in these years was the University's Choral Union, founded in 1893. The choir, under the direction of Prof. Fletcher Parker, was open to both University students and community members. (It remained a successful university/community group until 2023, when it was ended by the University

1.01 Program for the University Choral Union's May Festival of 1898, with soloist Johanna Gadski pictured.

School of Music.) Their first concert, on February 5, 1894, at the newly opened University Armory, featured Handel's *Messiah*, sung by a choir of 102 to an audience of 1800. Its two concerts each year became major musical events in Madison.[4]

The Choral Union staged a particularly impressive program on May 19, 1897, bringing in a professional orchestra, the Boston Festival Orchestra, to accompany, and several prominent guest soloists: soprano Rose Stewart, mezzo-soprano Jennie Mae Spenser, contralto Katherine Bloodgood, tenor J. H. McKinley, baritone Giuseppe Campanari, bass Heinrich Meyn, and pianist Minnie Little. The chorus, now 175 singers, performed the first part of Mendelssohn's oratorio *St. Paul*. The baritone Campanari was a particularly big star at the time; he sang the prologue to Leoncavallo's *I pagliacci* and, with the other singers, the sextet from Donizetti's *Lucia di Lammermoor*. Orchestral selections included the Tchaikovsky *1812 Overture*, one of Litolff's *Concertos symphoniques*, and Liszt's *Les préludes*.[5] Buoyed by the success of this program, Parker and the Choral Union staged even more ambitious May Festivals in years to come.

The Madison Musical Union

There were several musical associations in Madison during the course of the late 19th century that sponsored concerts by "local talent." In early 1867, there was a series of three "parlor concerts" at City Hall, featuring local musicians in programs of short instrumental works, operatic arias and duets, and parlor songs.[6] The success of these programs seems to have led to the formation of Madison's first local musical society, the Madison Musical Union, whose inaugural meeting, involving about 25 people, took place at the Congregational Church on March 16, 1867. The group met regularly over the next few years, formally incorporating with the State of Wisconsin in 1869.[7] Its meetings, open to the public, included musical performances by its members, and by 1870, the Madison Musical Union was also organizing more ambitious public concerts. In July 1870, members of the group performed three concerts, all featuring 12-year-old Madison soprano Helen Hastreiter, at the Belvidere Jubilee, a large music festival in Belvidere, Illinois.[8] On August 25, 1870, the Union staged its first local public concert in City Hall, featuring several operatic arias, duets, and quartets, a few works for piano, and five choral works. The featured singer, Agnes Staines, was a former Madison resident. The *State Journal* enthused the next day:

> We feel to congratulate the Union on its perfect success in this, its

first effort to please the public, and we firmly hope it will not be the last time that our citizens will have the pleasure of attending one of its very enjoyable concerts. We are glad so many of our music loving people availed themselves of the privilege extended to them last evening, and were in attendance. The presence of so large an audience was a great encouragement to the members of the Musical Union, and stimulated them to do their best. We like to see home talent sustained and liberally encouraged.[9]

They followed this on September 26, 1870, with a concert billed as "A Grand Festival of the Madison Musical Institute," featuring "a drama, songs and choruses by the Madison Musical Union, and instrumental music by a full brass band."[10] On June 24, 1871, the Madison Musical Union presented a costumed and partially staged version of George F. Root's 1857 "operatic cantata" *The Haymakers* at Hooley's Opera House. This performance was successful enough that it was repeated in October 1871 as a benefit for victims of disastrous forest fires in northern Wisconsin.[11] The Madison Musical Union continued its weekly meetings and gave occasional public concerts throughout the 1870s, though it seems to have faded away as a formal organization after 1880. However, it set a pattern for several civic-minded musical groups to follow, culminating in the 1910s and the 1920s with the Madison Orchestral Association and the Madison Civic Music Association.

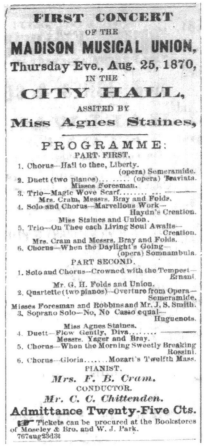

1.02 Madison Musical Union program of August 25, 1870.

Professional Touring Musicians in Madison

Most touring professional musicians who came to Madison in the earliest days were part of minstrel shows or musical variety acts: the Green Mountain

Boys and Swiss Bell Ringers were popular acts in the 1840s and 1850s. However, the *Wisconsin Argus* of July 9, 1850, includes a brief review of what may be the earliest documented classical concert by visiting artists in Madison:

> Concert.—Mr. W. D. Hillis, assisted by his Lady and Brother, favored our citizens with concerts of vocal and instrumental music on the evenings of the 4th and 5th. They are well worth hearing. Their trios and duets are performed in good taste and with thrilling effect [and] power. Their voices all possessed great compass and power, but Mrs. Hillis is the gem of the trio. A female voice of such compass and yet so pure and liquid in its tones, we never before heard. To hear her sing the Bird of Passage, accompanied by the flute, is worth the ticket.[12]

The review does not tell us where the concert took place—though either Lewis's Hall[13] or the State Capitol would have been the most likely venues—nor does it tell us much about what was performed or about the performers themselves. However, it is possible to identify Mr. and Mrs. Hillis. William D. Hillis (1821–1896) was a singer, music teacher, and church musician who spent most of his career in Illinois.[14] His wife, who was 15 years old at the time of this concert, was Lois E. (Newhall) Hillis (1835–1919), a member of the Newhall family of musicians, who traveled throughout Illinois in the late 1840s and 1850s. While touring with her family, she seems to have had a brief—and entirely innocent—teasing flirtation with Abraham Lincoln in 1849.[15] An 1855 parlor song titled *Were I But His Own Wife* is subtitled "Ballad as sung by Mrs. W. D. Hillis of the Newhall Family."[16] In 1855, William and Lois joined the faculty of the newly founded Berean College in Jacksonville, Illinois, but sometime soon thereafter settled in Elgin, Illinois.[17] The *Wisconsin Argus* writer's one reference to an actual song at the end of this review seems to confirm the at least partially "classical" nature of this concert—the writer was almost certainly referring to Mendelssohn's *Abscheislied der Zugvögel*, op. 63, no. 2 ("The Passage-Bird's Farewell"), a vocal duet for two sopranos published in 1844—with one of the vocal parts performed on flute, by either William or his brother.

The single most important change for Madison's musical life in the 1850s was the arrival of the railroad in 1854. Now easily connected to Milwaukee, Chicago, St. Louis, and beyond, Madison became an attractive stop for musicians and opera companies who were touring in the Midwest. Beginning in 1855, there were regularly two or three events each year featuring star vocal or instrumental performers. The first of these "post-railroad" concerts was on June 8, 1855, at Fairchild's Hall, a program featuring three prominent opera

1.03a,b,c Three of the performers who appeared in Madison in 1855: Teresa Parodi (pictured ca. 1851), Amalia Patti (ca. 1860), and Maurice Strakosch (in 1871).

singers, soprano Teresa Parodi, contralto Amalia Patti, and tenor Giovanni Leonardi, with Maurice Strakosch accompanying on piano. Tickets were priced at a premium $1.00, at a time when most theatrical and musical events in Madison were priced at 25¢ or less. The program opened with a piano version of Mendelssohn's *A Midsummer Night's Dream* (undoubtedly the overture) and a series of operatic arias and duets by Balfe, Verdi, Meyerbeer, Donizetti, Rossini, Mozart, and Bellini. It also included three original works by the pianist Maurice Strakosch and a pair of popular ballads.[18] This sort of "package" program, featuring two or three vocalists, sometimes combined with an instrumental soloist, seems to have been the norm for touring musicians at the time, and there were many more concerts of this kind from the 1850s onward.

Appearances by star performers continued through the Civil War, and one remarkable singer who appeared in Madison during these years was Elizabeth Taylor Greenfield (ca. 1819–1876), who sang at City Hall on May 19, 1863. Greenfield, one of the first widely known African American singers, was born into slavery, but she moved to Philadelphia with her mistress when Elizabeth was still a child. She began touring the United States, Canada, and England in the 1850s, billed as the Black Swan, and she also began a close association with the abolitionist Harriet Beecher Stowe. Greenfield reportedly had a particularly powerful and lovely soprano voice, often

1.04 Elizabeth Taylor Greenfield, the "Black Swan."

compared favorably to leading operatic sopranos—even to the greatest soprano of the day, the "Swedish Nightingale" Jenny Lind.[19] Though it was generally complimentary about Greenfield's performance, the *State Journal*'s review of her performance also reflects the casual racism of the day:

> The concert, by the "Black Swan," last evening was not largely attended. In point of musical excellence it was superior to any concert in the city for many months past. Miss Greenfield has a voice of wonderful range, power, and sweetness. If some tolerably good-looking white girl had her voice and musical talent she would create a *furore*. It was certainly very remarkable to hear the finest music of German and Italian composers exquisitely rendered by a woman who, in form and general appearance, might have been taken for an obese black cook, dressed in opera costume.[20]

Among the first great concert artists to visit Madison was the Norwegian violin virtuoso Ole Bull (1810–1880). Bull toured extensively in the United States and first made it to Wisconsin in 1853, when he performed a concert in Milwaukee. His concerts, typical for virtuosos touring America at the time, included his own compositions but also solo singers performing both operatic arias and popular songs. He returned to Milwaukee in 1854, when an enthusiastic review in the *Milwaukee Democrat* included the following charmingly awful bit of doggerel:

> Io Paean! Io sing!
> Honor to the Fiddle King!
> King by right divine and holy,
> All the world has crowned thee, Ole![21]

Bull's many American tours took him to the large cities of America, but he seems to have had a special fondness for Wisconsin, where he performed concerts in much smaller cities like Milwaukee, Madison, and even small towns like Janesville and Stoughton—all places where this fervent Norwegian patriot felt at home among large Norwegian immigrant communities.[22] Bull first appeared in Madison on July 1, 1856, performing at the Baptist Church with "Adelina Patti, the Extraordinary Young Prima Donna, [Vincenzo] Morino, The Eminent Baritone, [Louis] Schreiber, the Celebrated Cornet Player, and [Franz] Roth, the Distinguished Pianist."[23] This was in fact an all-star lineup: Patti and Morino were already internationally known opera singers, and Patti in particular would go on to become one of the 19th century's great *prima donnas*. Schreiber, a German immigrant, was one of America's leading brass virtuosos, and he later became a successful manufacturer of cornets. Roth served as Ole Bull's accompanist in several American tours. Bull returned exactly a year later, with concerts on July 1–2, 1857, now with a pair of English singers, Harrison George and Henry Horncastle, and an English pianist/composer, William Dressler.[24]

Bull spent much of the next decade at home in Norway, but he returned to the United States after the Civil War in 1867, eventually performing in Madison on January 20, 1868. On this tour his concerts included American soprano Charlotte Varian, baritone Ignaz Pollak, and pianist/composer Edward Hoffman.[25] This was a sensationally successful event, packing Madison's 900-seat City Hall, and he scheduled four more concerts in Madison over the following week, earning some $1775.[26] A hyperbolic notice in the *Madison Advance* the following day was typical of the response:

> This king of violinists was at the city hall last night. He whom no man can criticize because no man understands his skill and acquirements, is above our weak comments, above our praise. The task even to speak of him would be to gild fine gold. He believes the violin is the greatest of all instruments, and all believe him, if Ole Bull holds the instrument. Those who were with him only suffered as stars suffer by the noonday sun, no less brilliance though lost in the floods of greater light.[27]

However, Bull's visit in January 1868 would also have an important impact on him and on Madison's musical life over the next decade. Bull, then a 58-year-old widower, met 18-year-old Sara Chapman Thorp (1850–1911) at a reception following the opening concert. She was the daughter of a wealthy Eau Claire lumberman, Joseph G. Thorp, who had recently moved his family to Madison upon his election to the State Senate. A romance between Bull and Sara Thorp seems to have been encouraged by Sara's formidable mother, Amelie Thorp, who was then Madison's leading society matron. Bull engineered a fairly quick return to Madison and gave another pair of concerts later that same year, on November 17 and 18, this time with "Miss Barton," soprano, baritone Gustavus Hall, and pianist Egbert Lansing.[28] Two years later, Bull returned to Madison for a concert on March 26, 1870, now accompanied by soprano Hattie Safford, tenor William MacDonald, and again Edward Hoffman.[29] Rumors of a romance between Sara Thorp and Bull were already widespread, and during this visit he stayed as a guest at the Thorp home. Though Senator Thorp apparently disapproved of the relationship, he seems to have been overcome by his wife's promotion of the match and genuine affection between the couple. At Bull's invitation, Sara and her mother traveled to Norway later that spring. Sara Thorp and Ole Bull were privately married at the American consulate in Christiana in June. A formal wedding ceremony followed when they returned to Madison, on September 22, 1870. (Amelie Thorp was careful to spread the story of the June "private ceremony" to avoid scandal: Sara was already three months pregnant when the couple returned to Madison.) Two days later, the *State Journal* gave a detailed account of the lavish reception at the Thorpe home.[30] Bull gave a solo recital a few days later before he and his new bride left on tour.

1.05b,a Sara Chapman Thorp Bull and Ole Bull.

For the rest of his life, Ole and Sara Bull would reside in the Thorp home when he was not on tour or summering on his private island in the North Sea. The Bulls also had a house in Cambridge, Massachusetts, where they would spend increasing amounts of time—it would become Sara's home for decades after her husband's death. While in Madison, Bull seems to have done everything possible to avoid his in-laws, however, spending much of his time socializing with Norwegian friends, or in a "billiard house" he had built behind the Thorp home.[31] It is worth noting that the Thorp home at 130 East Gilman St. still stands today. Known for years as the Knapp House, it is now the Governor's Mansion Inn, a bed and breakfast. It served as Wisconsin's executive residence from 1883 until 1950, housing 18 of Wisconsin's governors, until the current executive residence in Maple Bluff was acquired by the state.

Despite a whiff of scandal about the difference in age between the Bulls, Madison seems to have adopted Ole Bull as a native son: local papers in the

1870s include many accounts of his concert tours in Europe and stunts like playing from the peak of the Great Pyramid of Giza on his 66th birthday in 1876.[32] More importantly to Madison's musical life, he made sure that his American tours made stops in Madison, and he also gave many informal recitals and benefit concerts when he was in town. On May 12, 1872, for example, he gave a benefit concert in the Assembly Chamber of the State Capitol to help fund the Norwegian library at the University.[33] Before leaving for Norway in May 1873, he invited all Norwegians in Madison to a free concert at the courthouse.[34] He also made stops in Madison on two of his last American tours. On February 16, 1877, he played at the Congregational Church with American soprano Clara Falk and her German-born husband, pianist/composer Louis Falk.[35] His last formal concert appearance in Madison was on January 28, 1879, at the Congregational Church, again with the Falks.[36] However, he did play an informal concert at the Thorp home in October 1879 at a reception that was part of the annual congress of the American Association for the Advancement of Women. The famed abolitionist and women's suffrage activist Julia Ward Howe was at the reception as well, and she did a dramatic reading of her poem *The Battle Hymn of the Republic*.[37] Shortly afterward, the Bulls left for their home in Cambridge. Ole Bull fell ill that winter, and they returned to Norway where he died on August 17, 1880.

There are four Madison-related postscripts to the story of Ole Bull. (1) On June 26, 1855, a year before Bull's first visit, a young violin virtuoso billed as "Le Petit Ole Bull" appeared at Fairchild's Hall. This violinist, whose real name was Nicholas Goodall, toured briefly under this pseudonym in the 1850s, clearly intending to capitalize on the reputation of the great Norwegian.[38] (2) One of Ole Bull's sons by his first marriage, Alexander Bull, also had a career as a touring violin virtuoso. He made two appearances in Madison: on January 10, 1893, at Christ Presbyterian Church and on January 10, 1901, at the Baptist Church. (3) In 1879, Bull's nephew, 23-year-old Storm Bull, was appointed as professor in the Engineering department at the University of Wisconsin, at least partly with a little help from his famous uncle. He had a distinguished career at the University as a researcher and as a teacher—David Mollenhoff notes that he was Frank Lloyd Wright's geometry teacher during the architect's brief time as a University student. Storm Bull was elected Madison's mayor in 1901, the first University professor to hold the post.[39] (4) Lastly, there is a Madison Symphony Orchestra–related postscript. Pianist Storm Bull appeared as a 16-year-old prodigy with the Madison Civic Symphony on May 29, 1929, playing the Grieg concerto. Storm Bull was related to the mayor of the same name and was the great grand-nephew of Ole Bull, but also a distant cousin to Edvard Grieg. The Chicago-born pianist would go on to a successful career as a soloist and composer in the 1930s, and after service in World War II, he had a 30-year tenure as a professor at the University of Colorado, Boulder.[40]

The opening of the Fuller Opera House in 1890 was a landmark moment in Madison's music history. The Fuller remained Madison's flagship performing venue into the 1920s (when it was renamed the Parkway Theatre). It hosted hundreds of traveling opera, operetta, and musical comedy performances. It also hosted performances by visiting soloists, ensembles, and orchestras, though many of those concerts were being held in new venues at the University: Music Hall and the University Armory.

There were several truly spectacular programs in Madison during the period 1890 to 1926. The leading contralto of the day, Ernestine Schumann-Heink, appeared in Madison five times: in 1908 (Fuller Opera House), 1910 (University Armory), 1912 (Fuller Opera House), 1924 (Parkway Theatre), and 1925 (Christ Presbyterian Church). Schumann-Heink was apparently a great favorite in Madison, and her programs, including those at the large Armory and Fuller/Parkway, nearly always sold out. On November 7, 1906, composer Ruggero Leoncavallo conducted a program of excerpts from his operas at the University Armory. The concert featured seven singers from Milan's Teatro alla Scala accompanied by the 50-piece La Scala Orchestra. The finale, after an evening of singing, was Leoncavallo's *March Viva l'America*, which he dedicated to President Roosevelt. The *State Journal* review called this "the best version of 'Yankee Doodle' ever made."[41] On May 21, 1923, soprano Amelita Galli-Curci, one of the leading *prima donnas* of the day, gave a concert at the University Stock Pavilion, which was sponsored by the University School of Music. Galli-Curci, performing with flutist Manuel Berenguer and her husband, pianist Homer Samuels, sang to an enormous crowd of 4000. The audience applause at her first appearance was described as "deafening," and the singer apparently took it in stride when students in the audience set off skyrockets during a couple of these ovations.[42]

1.06 Amelita Galli-Curci and Homer Samuels, ca. 1923.

Madison's Own Musical Celebrities

There were a few Madison natives in this period who went on to prominent national and international musical careers. Three of them, bass George Walker, baritone Lawrence Salerno, and tenor Karl Fischer-Niemann, will make appearances in later chapters. In this chapter, I will briefly introduce three more Madison-born musical celebrities, beginning with soprano Bertha Waltzinger (1867–1927). Her parents, German immigrants, were among Madison's pioneer families, arriving in 1859 and running a local confectionary and catering business for decades. Bertha, the youngest of 11 children, was already well-known as a singer locally when she was still quite young. At some point in the early 1880s, when she was still "scarce more than a child," she sang the lead role in a production of the "comic opera" *King Alfred* at Madison's Fourth Ward School. According to a recollection published nearly 50 years later, May De Voe, who frequently appeared as a vocal soloist in Madison, reportedly told young Bertha afterwards that "you have the voice."[43] In May 1882, at age 15, Waltzinger also sang a small role in a local production of William Bradbury's popular sacred cantata *Esther, the Beautiful Queen*. She studied in Connecticut and New York City in 1885–87, working with

1.07 Bertha Waltzinger in the 1890s.

distinguished teacher Frederick E. Bristol before returning to Madison. Over the next few years, there are several notices of her concerts in Madison, as a soloist in church and other community concerts, and as a solo recitalist. By 1890, she had returned to New York City, where she continued her studies with Bristol. (Even after beginning her professional career, she would continue to work occasionally with him until at least 1895.) Waltzinger supported herself by singing as a soloist at several churches, and she appeared twice as a soloist in Carnegie Hall. Beginning in 1892, Waltzinger was a lead singer in several prominent opera companies, making her professional debut with Henry Clay Barnabee's Bostonians in Albany, New York, on October 10, 1892, singing the role of Annabel in Reginald De Koven's *Robin Hood*. She later sang with the companies of DeWolf Hopper, Reginald De Koven, Jefferson de Angelis, and Thomas Seabrooke. She performed in Madison while on tour with the DeWolf Hopper Company on April 10, 1895, at the Fuller Opera House, where she sang the lead role in Woolson Morse's operetta *Dr. Syntax*. Her return to Madison as a star of one of the country's premiere touring companies was front-page news in the *Wisconsin State Journal*. That summer, Waltzinger sang to an enormous crowd of 8000 at the Monona Lake Assembly on July 29, 1895.

She continued to tour with opera companies in the late 1890s, but she also found success on Broadway. Among her credits was originating the role of Isabel in John Philip Sousa's popular operetta *El Capitan* during its tryout run in Boston, and opening at the Broadway Theater in 1896. That same year, she sang the lead in Reginald De Koven's *The Mandarin* at the Herald Square Theater. One of her greatest Broadway successes was the lead role of Dolores in the wildly successful musical comedy *Florodora* at the Casino Theater in 1901 and 1902. (She was the fifth singer to play the role in this British import's run of 552 performances between 1900 and 1902, and she then sang the role on tour.)

Waltzinger also returned to perform in her hometown on a few occasions. On January 18, 1897, at Christ Presbyterian Church, she gave what was described as "the last and only appearance of Miss Waltzinger, previous to spending five years in study abroad." (She may have intended to spend time in Europe, and was indeed urged to do so by Nellie Melba and other prominent musicians, but it seems unlikely that she ever left America for any significant time.[44]) She later turned to vaudeville, touring for several years with her husband, comedian and actor George C. Boniface, Jr., often appearing on stage with their French bulldog Snooze! She later toured as a solo headliner after Boniface became ill and was forced to retire. On February 7–11, 1910, she headlined a vaudeville bill at Madison's Majestic Theater. Her repertoire included a set of popular songs sung in German (one of her signatures on the vaudeville stage) and a song written for her in 1909 by Egbert Van Alstyne and Harry Williams, *My Sunbeam*. A glowing review of the first performance hailed Waltzinger as "the Madison girl whose theatrical success is a pride to us all." After George Boniface died in 1917, Waltzinger married Thomas Ward, assistant manager of New York's St. Regis Hotel. She died in New York City in 1927 but was interred at Madison's Forest Hill cemetery.[45]

Mezzo-soprano Olivia Monona (1888–1976) apparently took her stage name from one of Madison's lakes. She was born Olivia Goldenberger, a member of one of Madison's pioneering Jewish families, and graduated from the University School of Music in 1909. In 1910, she moved to Chicago to join the newly formed Chicago Grand Opera Company. She performed as one of the members of the company's chorus, and she married Oscar Hanke, one of the violinists in the orchestra, in 1919. In 1929, Monona moved to New York City to join the Metropolitan Opera chorus, where she sang until her retirement in 1945. Over the course of her career, she performed in over 200 operas. She was a lead member of the chorus in both companies and developed a reputation as a dependable *comprimaria*—a female supporting character—backing prominent *prima donnas* Kirsten Flagstad, Lily Pons, and others. Monona retired to Little Rock, Arkansas, but eventually returned to Madison in 1972, just a few years before her death.[46]

1.08 Olivia Monona in costume, 1912.

Violinist Gilbert Ross (1903–1993) was the son of University of Wisconsin–Madison sociology professor Edward Alsworth Ross and Rosamond Ross. He was born in Lincoln, Nebraska, where his father was then teaching at the University of Nebraska, but E. A. Ross took the position in Madison in 1906, and his son grew up in the city.[47] Gilbert Ross began studying violin at the age of seven, and his family arranged for him to study at the Chicago Musical College. At age 13, he won the school's highest prize, the Diamond Award, which offered an opportunity to perform with the Chicago Symphony Orchestra. Ross, accompanied by his mother, moved to New York City in August 1918, where he began musical studies with the great Hungarian violinist and teacher Leopold Auer. Auer spent most of his career in Russia but fled following the 1917 revolution, and he had recently settled in the United States. Nearly 50 years later, Ross published an extended reminiscence of his work with the rather intimidating Auer, whom he clearly considered to have been a prime influence.[48] Ross had heard Mischa Elman, a student of Auer's, perform in the Fuller Opera House in January 1913, and already at age 10 had decided that he wanted to study with the same teacher. Ross studied with Auer for nearly two years, and he would frequently return

1.09 Gilbert Ross and his mother, 1923.

for lessons and advice over the following several years, until shortly before Auer's death in 1930. While still in his teens, Ross had a successful concert tour in Germany, including a solo performance with the Berlin Philharmonic.

Ross would continue to tour in the United States, Canada, and Europe throughout the 1920s, and his career was avidly reported in the local press. In April 1924, for example, both local papers reported on his purchase of a rare 1751 Guadagnini violin.[49] Ross also continued to perform in Madison during his visits home. He seems to have had a friendly relationship with Prof. Cecil Burleigh, violinist and composer at the University, and he performed several of Burleigh's works. On February 26, 1926, Ross played the premiere of Burleigh's *Violin Concerto*, op. 60, with the Minneapolis Symphony Orchestra at the University Stock Pavilion, on one of the last programs sponsored by the Madison Orchestral Association. (He had earlier performed the first movement of the Tchaikovsky *Violin Concerto* with the Minneapolis Symphony Orchestra in the Armory on November 27, 1923.) It is also clear that he had a close musical relationship with Sigfrid Prager after Prager settled permanently in Madison in 1926. Ross would play as concertmaster in the first performance of the Madison Civic Symphony on December 14, 1926.[50] He then appeared as a violin soloist in each of the orchestra's first three seasons:

- Saint-Saëns, *Violin Concerto No. 3* (3/8/1927)
- Bruch, *Violin Concerto No. 1* (11/15/1927)
- Beethoven, *Violin Concerto* (10/31/1928)
- Mendelssohn, *Violin Concerto,* second movement (5/28/1929: a children's concert)

Ross and Prager also performed chamber music together in at least two concerts in early 1929 (January 1 and May 28). The January program included Burleigh's *Fairy Sailing* and two transcriptions of songs by Granados that were prepared by Ross and Prager and later published.[51]

After extensive solo work and touring in the 1920s, Gilbert Ross spent most of his remaining career in academia. He taught at Cornell University and Smith College from 1931 to 1942. In 1942, Ross joined the faculty of the University of Michigan. He was the founding first violinist of the Stanley Quartet in 1949, the University of Michigan's first resident chamber ensemble, and performed with the quartet until his retirement in 1971. Ross continued to perform and research, and in 1976 he issued a recording of the fiddle works of the 19th-century American composer William Sidney Mount. On the recording, he performed on a rare surviving example of Mount's own invention, the hollow-backed "cradle of harmony" fiddle.[52] Ross died in Michigan in 1993.[53]

Opera, Operetta, and Musical Comedy in Madison

The first performance of something resembling an opera in Madison seems to have been the staged spectacle *Forest Festival* of October 1857 (discussed later in this chapter). Though it would be another eight years before Madison saw a full-length staged opera production, local audiences were clearly aware of operatic music. Opera arias, ensembles, and choruses were featured heavily in locally produced concerts from the 1860s onward. When touring package shows, beginning with the concert headlined by Teresa Parodi and Amalia Patti in June 1855, began to arrive in Madison via the new railroad connections, vocal soloists were largely drawn from the world of opera. A typical concert might include popular American songs of the day, but most of the repertoire sung by these vocalists would be drawn from opera, and occasionally the performers would stage selected scenes or acts, as on July 23, 1863, when the English soprano Anna Bishop, her daughter Louisa, and a male singer, A. Sedgewick, performed the final scene of Bellini's *La sonnambula* in costume.

The earliest professionally staged opera productions in Madison were in August 1865, performed at City Hall by Campbell and Castle's English Opera Troupe. The company was led by baritone S. C. Campbell and tenor William Castle and featured sopranos Rosa Cooke and Mrs. M. E. Burrows, contralto Adelina Motte, tenor Charles Virrecke, baritone Edward Seguin, and basses Warren White, William Skaats, and Otto Lehman, with a total of "forty artists of acknowledged ability." S. C. Campbell was the stage name of Sherwood Abraham Coan (1829–1874). Campbell was first successful as a minstrel show performer in the 1850s and early 1860s; among several songs written for him was the familiar sentimental ballad *Aura Lea* (1861). After 1864 he turned exclusively to opera, making his debut in early 1864 in a production of Michael William Balfe's *The Bohemian Girl* in Brooklyn, New York. He first worked with the English tenor William Castle during this production, and in 1865 they organized an opera company with the purpose of touring and presenting operas exclusively in English.[54] Their run in Madison opened on August 19 with *The Bohemian Girl*. Though seldom heard today, this 1843 opera was a durable favorite in the late 19th and early 20th centuries, and it became a staple of touring opera companies: there would be 10 more

1.10 S. C. Campbell in the 1860s.

professional productions of this opera in Madison over the next 60 years.[55] Their selection on August 20 was almost certainly Bellini's *La Sonnambula*.[56] They had planned to finish their run on August 21, with William Vincent Wallace's 1848 opera *Maritana*, but had to cancel due to a storm that night, and because Castle was ill. They stayed in Madison for an additional night and performed Donizetti's *Don Pasquale* on August 22.[57] The Campbell and Castle company's brief stay in Madison reflected a pattern that would be repeated many times into the 1920s, where touring opera companies would perform from a repertoire, presenting a different piece every night in order to fill the hall as much as possible. Given the limitations of City Hall, their performances, like those of many later companies—at least until the opening of the Fuller Opera House in 1890—must have been distinctly bare-bones productions. Grand operas performed in Madison were, not surprisingly, works from the then-current standard repertoire. The enduring popularity of Balfe's *The Bohemian Girl* has already been noted, but other works heard multiple times in Madison in the late 19th century through 1925 include Flotow's *Martha* (three staged productions, and several concerts that presented an act of the opera), Gounod's *Faust* (four staged productions, and three concert versions of Act III), Auber's *Fra Diavolo* (three staged productions), Donizetti's *Lucia di Lammermoor* (three staged productions), and Bizet's *Carmen* (four staged productions).

Beginning in the 1880s, lighter operettas began to dominate the repertoire of touring companies coming to Madison. For example, Gilbert and Sullivan arrived in Madison in a big way during the 1885–86 season, which saw *three* productions of *The Mikado* by three different companies: the Sydney Rosenfeld Opera Company (October 8), the Burton Opera Company (December 10), and the Chicago Opera Company (on the evening of May 15, with a performance of *H.M.S. Pinafore* as a matinee). There was actually a fourth professional performance—of sorts—of *The Mikado* that season: on December 17, Haverly's Minstrels included a burlesque version, titled *The Ci-gar-do* as the finale of their show.[58] Clearly caught up in Gilbert and Sullivan fever, a group of Madison amateurs from Grace Episcopal Church staged *H.M.S. Pinafore* on December 7, 1885.[59] Operetta ruled Madison's stages until the first decade of the 20th century, when even lighter musical comedy and vaudeville dominated.

Madison's amateur musicians were also active in staging opera, operetta, and musical comedies. What seems to have been the earliest amateur staged opera performance in Madison was mounted by Madison's German citizens, less than a year after the professionally staged productions by the Campbell and Castle English Opera Company ... and it was, remarkably, written by a Madison

1.11 Francis Massing and family, 1857.

musician. The three-act opera *Der Peter in der Fremde (Peter on his Travels)* was premiered at Turner Hall on April 24, 1866. According to a newspaper notice: "It is arranged and composed by our townsman Francis Massing, who is well-known to have musical and comical genius, and illustrates in a piquant and comic style, village life in Germany."[60] The libretto for this work seems to have been based upon a well-known German folk poem of the early 19th century. The composer, Francis (Franz) Massing (1829–1876), was born in Prussia but had settled in Madison by the early 1850s. By 1866, he was among Madison's leading citizens, a prominent local attorney and an active figure in local politics. The musical side of his life is not as well documented, but he was one of the charter members of the Madison Maennerchor in 1852, serving as the chorus's first director, and was later active in the Mozart Club.[61] *Der Peter in der Fremde* is the only musical work by Massing to which I have found a reference.[62] I have not found references to locally produced opera or operetta for nearly 20 years following this, but Table 1.1 lists several more productions from the 1880s onward.

Summer Music for Edification and Pleasure: The Monona Lake Assembly

During this period, public musicmaking in Madison typically slowed during the summer months, though there were regular concerts by the always-busy band led by John Lueders and other local bands. By the 1890s, there were summertime band concerts nearly every night of the week in one of Madison's parks or on the capitol square. Madison's churches also provided "sacred concerts" by their choirs and hosted organ recitals. However, one annual summertime musical focus was the Monona Lake Assembly—an annual Chautauqua-style encampment on the southwestern shore of Lake Monona held each July from 1879 until 1908. From 1881 onward, the encampment served as the main annual event of the Wisconsin Sunday School Assembly—designed to provide training and enrichment for Protestant Sunday school teachers. Though the 1881 Assembly lasted 10 days, it was later a more concentrated two- to four-day program of lectures, debates, and devotional services. The Assembly always included concerts, often including the Lueders Band, and

Table 1.1: A List of Local Opera and Operetta Performances in Madison 1866 to 1922[63]

Date	Venue	Work	Comments
4/24/1866	Turner Hall	Massing, *Der Peter in der Fremde*	Discussed above.
12/7/1885	Turner Hall	Gilbert and Sullivan, *H.M.S. Pinafore*	Mostly a local production, though the role of Ralph was sung by Chicago-based Charles Barnes.
4/23-24/1890	Fuller Opera House	Planquette, *The Chimes of Normandy*	Local singers.
4/3/1893	Turner Hall	Flotow, *Martha*	Madison Maennerchor.
4/18/1895	Turner Hall	Lortzing, *Czar und Zimmermann*	Madison Maennerchor.
6/6/1895	Grace Episcopal Church	Spenser, *The Little Tycoon*	Sponsored by the Grace Church Guild.
12/8/1899	Fuller Opera House	Flotow, *Martha (concert version)*	Madison Opera Club. This program was accompanied by a full orchestra, directed by Charles Nitschke.
7/7/1900	Grace Episcopal Church	Gilbert and Sullivan, *H.M.S. Pinafore*	Joint production by Grace Episcopal (Madison) and St. James Episcopal (Chicago); accompanied by a full orchestra, directed by Charles Nitschke.
4/22/1902	Fuller Opera House	Gilbert and Sullivan, *Pirates of Penzance*	Local singers and the St. Patrick's Catholic Church Choir.
11/22/1902	Fuller Opera House	Planquette, *The Chimes of Normandy (Les cloches de Corneville)*	Local singers and the St. Patrick's Catholic Church Choir.
5/4/1905	Fuller Opera House	Gilbert and Sullivan, *Patience*	Local singers; staged as a benefit for the building of a hospital in Madison.
11/9–10/1909	Fuller Opera House	Stothart, *The Cancelled Cook (premiere)*	Local singers; held as a benefit for the local Attic Angels charity.
5/20/1916	Fuller Opera House	Gilbert and Sullivan, *H.M.S. Pinafore*	Local singers; directed by Fletcher Wheeler.
2/25/1922	Parkway Theatre	Gilbert and Sullivan, *The Mikado*	Sponsored by Grace Episcopal Church. Local singers; directed by Fletcher Wheeler.

local soloists and church choirs, but occasionally featuring nationally known musicians—particularly well-known sacred vocal ensembles such as the Boston Stars in 1891. One program, on July 29, 1895, featured Madison-born star soprano Bertha Waltzinger. The same program featured Hungarian violin virtuoso Edouard Reményi, who appeared several times in Madison in the 1880s and 1890s, and pianist Henry Eames. Opera star Achille Alberti appeared at the Assembly in 1898, and the Chicago-based Spiering String Quartet was featured in 1902. In 1904, to mark the Monona Lake Assembly's 25th anniversary, the organizers engaged the band of Giuseppi Creatore, one of the period's greatest professional touring bands, to perform concerts at Assembly grounds for an entire week surrounding the event. The response to the Creatore Band was so enthusiastic that the Assembly brought in another famous band, led by Henri Morin, for a week in 1905. However, attendance at the Assembly had already begun to decline in the early 20th century, and the 1908 Assembly would be the last. The Assembly's property was eventually acquired by the city in 1912 and converted to a public park: Monona Park, later renamed Olin Park.

Local Conservatories and the University School of Music

From the 1860s onward, there were private music teachers in Madison—primarily of piano and voice—who maintained studios to teach children and adults. Evidence of this comes from the 1860s though the 1920s, when local newspapers were unfailingly generous in their coverage of student recitals, carefully listing performers and repertoire and even publishing encouraging reviews of student performances. However, the first private music school teaching multiple subjects in Madison was founded by the remarkable Ada Bird (1859–1914). Born in nearby Sun Prairie, Bird initially studied piano in Chicago before traveling to Europe, where she studied at the Royal Conservatory in Leipzig and at the Paris Conservatory.[64] In 1887, Bird settled in Madison and founded the Wisconsin Conservatory of Music. (This is not to be confused with the Milwaukee school of the same name, which was founded in 1899 and is still in operation today.) Initially, she worked with two female teachers of voice, Nettie Gale and Norwegian immigrant Valborg Stub, but by 1890, the faculty had expanded to at least seven teachers and offered a wide variety of lessons, training in music theory and composition, elocution and dramatic reading, and language study in French and German.[65] The conservatory seems to have been disbanded sometime after 1891, and in 1895 Bird joined the faculty of the University's newly organized School of Music. However, in 1909, she left to organize a new private conservatory, the Wisconsin School of Music (not to be confused with the UW–Madison School of Music), which would remain in operation until the 1960s. Bird and her successor Elizabeth Buehler built the school into a Madison institution that educated thousands of local music students. They also assembled a large faculty, with several piano teachers and instructors of voice, strings, woodwinds, and brass. An advertisement for the conservatory in September 1916 listed two dozen faculty members in several areas—including interpretive dance—and several student ensembles.

1.12 Elizabeth Buehler (seated at the piano), posed with the Wisconsin School of Music's female faculty in 1933.

Ada Bird led the Wisconsin School of Music until her death in 1914,[66] when Elizabeth Buehler (1878–1967) took over as director of the conservatory. Another Wisconsin native, born in Monroe, Buehler studied piano with Bird at the University before traveling to Vienna for further study.[67] She was one of the conservatory's instructors when it opened in 1909 and served as its director from 1914 until her retirement in 1965. The conservatory did not survive her retirement: it seems to have disbanded after 1965. However, it was an important Madison musical institution for over half a century, and it was particularly closely connected to the Madison Civic Symphony. It was the Wisconsin School of Music that sponsored the first visits to Madison by Dr. Sigfrid Prager, the orchestra's first conductor, in the summers of 1925 and 1926. In each of those summers, Prager and the singer George Walker came to Madison from New York City to give a series of lecture-recitals sponsored by the conservatory. Prager taught conducting there as well in the summer of 1926, and he continued to teach composition and conducting at the Wisconsin School of Music for a few years after he became the Madison Civic Symphony's music director in the fall of 1926. He obviously maintained a close relationship with Buehler: When Prager was naturalized as an American citizen in 1930, she and her brother Fred stood as witnesses. Many of its faculty performed with the Madison Civic Symphony and Chorus in the 1920s, 1930s, and 1940s, most notably the orchestra's concertmaster Marie Endres, who joined the faculty in 1920 and eventually led the string department until 1965. Throughout its early years, the orchestra's string section was also heavily populated by her Wisconsin School of Music students.[68]

Another local private conservatory was founded in 1908 by Fletcher Wheeler (1860–1929). Wheeler grew up in Ohio and Iowa and trained as an organist at the Paris Conservatory under the eminent Alexandre Guilmant. He moved to Madison in 1908 to become the organist and music director at Grace Episcopal Church, but he also opened a conservatory that fall, initially named the Wisconsin College of Music, but soon thereafter known as the Wheeler School of Music and Dramatic Arts.[69] Though not quite as large and certainly not as long-lasting as the Bird/Buehler Wisconsin School of Music, the Wheeler conservatory was similarly able to attract excellent musicians to Madison to instruct its students—for example, Milwaukee-based violinist Willy Jaffe joined the faculty in 1908, and flutist Florence Bennett (later a member of the Madison Civic Symphony) began teaching there 10 years later. An advertisement of September 1916 lists a faculty of 17—including Wheeler's wife and son—teaching piano, organ, voice, woodwinds, brass, strings, percussion, banjo, mandolin, music theory, and "normal methods" (that is, training for music teachers).[70] In addition to public recitals by its students, the Wheeler conservatory also sponsored occasional guest artist concerts, and regular programs by its faculty members. In the early 1920s, for example, there were frequent performances by the Fine Arts Trio, a faculty piano trio from the conservatory. Wheeler continued to work at Grace Episcopal Church, but he also led local choirs and directed at least two local productions of Gilbert and Sullivan operettas, *H.M.S. Pinafore* in 1916 and *The Mikado* in 1922. He died unexpectedly in February 1929, and the music school he founded does not seem to have lasted very long after his death.

Of course, the largest and most enduring local music school in Madison is the University of Wisconsin–Madison School of Music. The founding of the University of Wisconsin was one of the stipulations in the state constitution of 1848, and the first classes met in early 1849. Amateur, student-led musicmaking occurred from the very beginning: the inauguration of the first chancellor, John A. Lathrop in 1850, was accompanied by a student brass band. Though there had apparently been an informal "Music Academy" associated with the campus in the 1860s, most formal instruction in music into the 1870s was offered through the University's Female College, and most of the music made on campus was by its female students. Music instruction became more coeducational after the arrival of Prof. Fletcher A. Parker in 1878. During the 1880s and 1890s, concerts by the Glee Club and other University groups also became popular draws on and off campus. For example, the very first musical program hosted by the newly completed Fuller Opera House in 1890 was a joint concert by the University Glee Club and Banjo Club. In 1895, after a campaign by University President Charles K. Adams, the regents approved the organization of the School of Music and authorized it to grant bachelor's degrees. Parker was named the University's first professor of music, and he initially led a faculty of six, including Ada Bird and local band and orchestra leader and violinist John Lueders.[71]

1.13 Prof. Fletcher A. Parker, the University's first professor of music, 1902.

The 800-seat auditorium in Assembly Hall (dedicated in 1880, and renamed Library Hall in 1884) became the venue for most of the School of Music's recitals. The School of Music formally took over the space in 1900, and it was renamed again as Music Hall in 1910. University student and faculty recitals there became an important part of the musical scene in Madison as a whole. In the 1910s and 1920s, faculty recitals by Charles H. Mills, Leon Iltis, Cecil Burleigh, and other faculty received every bit as much coverage in the *Wisconsin State Journal* and *Capital Times* as most visiting classical stars: each paper frequently published two or three articles leading up to the program, with details on repertoire and comments from the performers, and they usually published detailed reviews as well.

Amateur and Professional Orchestras in Madison Before 1926

There were several attempts to organize orchestras in Madison prior to the founding of the Madison Civic Symphony. The earliest locally created orchestra was led by Henry Pellage, a violinist, bandleader, and music store proprietor who was active in Madison between 1856 and 1860. While in Madison, he led a military brass band that was extremely active in the city from 1857 to 1860,

1.14 Music Hall auditorium ca. 1914.

frequently performing outdoor concerts and accompanying dances. Pellage seems to have moved to Janesville (35 miles south of Madison) in late 1860 or 1861 and then joined the Union Army as a volunteer during the Civil War, leading a military band attached to the Third Wisconsin Cavalry. Pellage died in Kansas on October 6, 1863, during what is generally known as the Battle of Baxter Springs. He was part of a Union detachment that was attacked and defeated by the Confederate guerilla group led by William Quantrill. Nearly 100 Union soldiers were massacred—including Pellage and 10 of his bandmates—after most had tried to surrender.[72]

In happier days in Madison, Pellage directed what was billed as a "full orchestra" and performed a violin solo during a local musical extravaganza, the "Fairy Operatta of *Forest Festival*," staged at Van Bergen's Hall on October 12 and 13, 1857. The "operatta" was led by Chicago-based musician Chandler Robbins, who began to recruit local musicians in late September 1857, inviting "all the young ladies in the city between the ages of nowhere and anywhere," as well as "adults who are vocalists."[73] I have found nothing specific about the music, nor about Robbins himself, but he apparently toured widely with his *Forest Festival* in the late 1850s: in addition to the Madison production, it was produced in Detroit, Michigan (October 1855), Rock Island, Illinois (June 1856), Janesville, Wisconsin (August 1857), Milwaukee, Wisconsin (September 1857), Bangor, Maine (July 1858), and others.[74] In each case there was a similar pattern: Robbins would appear in town a few weeks ahead of time to recruit and rehearse local vocalists and instrumentalists, and a large group of local girls—as many as 400 for some performances. He seems to have traveled with a small group of professional singers and dancers as well. Just what all the young girls did, aside from filling the stage and looking charming (and, undoubtedly, inducing their parents to buy tickets) is unclear. But the effect was certainly spectacular, as reported in the *State Journal*:

> The Forest Festival at Van Bergen's Hall, last evening, was the most beautiful spectacle, to say nothing of the exquisite music, that our citizens ever, we venture to say, enjoyed. About two hundred young ladies, so arranged with respect to height and size as to form a deep crescent, the centre of which was the fairy queen upon a raised dais of evergreens and flowers, with the subsequent introduction of shepherdesses, naiads, dancing flower girls, and Highland Maids in costume, presented a scene of bewildering and gorgeous beauty, taste, and elegance that can hardly be surpassed, the more especially as the ladies composing the operatta are the fairest that the city affords. The stage was beautifully fitted up with evergreens and flowers, garlands, and artificial trees, among the boughs of which were hung cages of singing birds. The orchestra, under the direction of Mr. Pellage, was admirably conducted and arranged and was equal, if not superior to any thing of the kind in the state.

Though the review does not say anything else about the orchestra, it does note that "Mr. Pellage, in a difficult and beautiful violin solo, drew down the applause of the house, which he richly merited."[75]

In 1860, Pellage directed concerts sponsored by the short-lived Madison Philharmonic Society, one of several civic-minded community groups that arose in Madison in the late 19th and early 20th centuries that promoted performances by local and touring musicians. The group seems to have sponsored only three concerts, all in 1860: at the Baptist Church on April 12 and July 3, and at City Hall on September 11.[76] All three concerts were given "for the benefit of Mr. Pellage"—meaning that all proceeds went to him. Pellage organized an orchestra and chorus of local musicians for at least the September concert, which opened with an orchestral overture and closed with a chorus from Haydn's *The Creation*, and it is likely that he led small orchestras at the other two concerts as well.

A few years later, a new sponsoring group, the Euterpean Society—loftily named for the Greek muse of music—was organized in Madison. In this case, concerts were led by William Burke, a violinist and entrepreneur who opened a music store on Carroll Street in 1862. Burke's initial public appearance in Madison was a successful "gift concert" at City Hall on July 22, 1862. There were several of these events in Madison in the early days: concerts that featured a raffle, with the entertainment culminating in a drawing for "gifts" (prizes). In the case of Burke's concert, he recruited "the best musical talent in the city" to perform, and the top prize was a new piano.[77] The Euterpean Society seems to have been organized by early 1862 when it hosted a ball at Atwood's Hall on February 4. The Society's first concert, at City Hall on August 20, 1863, was more ambitious than the earlier Madison Philharmonic Society programs, and together with several instrumental and vocal solos, duets, and trios, included at least four orchestral selections, played by a 13-member orchestra:

- Mozart, *Overture to "The Marriage of Figaro"*
- Godfrey, *Waterloo Polka*
- Verdi, *Anvil Chorus*
- Boieldieu, *Overture to "The Caliph of Bagdad"*

The orchestra may also have played on Burke's own choral composition *God Bless Our Country*, which was "composed for this occasion."[78]

A second, equally ambitious Euterpean Society program was staged at City Hall on February 25, 1864, this time featuring a guest soloist, the Chicago-based soprano Anna Main. This program, primarily vocal music, did include at least two orchestral pieces conducted by Burke.[79] The Euterpean Society sponsored or took part in four more concerts that year before disbanding in the fall of 1864: March 16 at Van Bergen's Hall, July 16 on the capitol square, July 7 in Van Bergen's Hall (in support of a locally organized stage comedy), and August 2 at City Hall.[80] The August program also included a new local chorus, the Concordia Society. Though Burke was involved with all four concerts, it is unclear whether or not they included orchestral works. On September 17, 1864, the *State Journal* published a complimentary open letter from some two dozen Madison men to Burke, asking for another concert—if possible by the end of the month—and pledging financial help. The paper also printed Burke's polite response, which assured that "I shall immediately set about making the necessary arrangements, so as to have the Concert take place as nearly as possible at the time you desire."[81] However, the promised "grand benefit concert" did not take place until April 7, 1865. This program in City Hall featured a pair of vocal soloists from Milwaukee, the Orphean Brothers (a men's chorus), the Madison Brass Band, and "other musical talent of the city," but not an orchestra. It was successful enough that the entire program was repeated on the next evening.[82] Though Burke appeared as a violin soloist in a couple of local concerts in 1865, the April program seems to have been the last that he organized. William Burke left Madison for Harrisburg, Pennsylvania, in October 1865, and several of his students and friends put on a farewell concert for him at City Hall on October 2, 1865, with an opening violin solo by Burke himself.[83]

There are scattered mentions of orchestras comprised of local musicians over the next decade: for example, a concert featuring "Mozart's Twelfth Mass, [with] Full Chorus, Assisted by Large Orchestra," on August 1 and 2, 1865, at City Hall, a program led by H. R. Palmer of the University's Madison Musical Academy.[84] These were orchestras brought together to perform on local variety concert programs or to support large choral performances like the one in August 1865. However, in 1874, there was an attempt to create a standing professional orchestra in Madison, organized by a pair of recent German immigrants, pianist and conductor August Bareuther and violinist John (Johann) Lueders. The group formed under the auspices of the Madison Musical Society, apparently an organization distinct from the contemporary Madison Musical Union.

1.15 Advertisement for the Madison Musical Society orchestra that ran in local newspapers for three months in 1874.

The formation of an orchestra was announced publicly on March 9, 1874, and it gave its inaugural concert on May 11 in Hooley's Opera House, in combination with the Madison Maennerchor and several local vocal soloists. In addition to the vocal works and chamber performances by members of the orchestra, the concert included five full orchestral pieces:

- Conradin Kreutzer, *Overture to "Das Nachtrager in Granada"* (*The Night-Camp in Granada*)
- Hans Christian Lumbye, *Drømmebilleder* (*Dream-Pictures: Fantasy for Orchestra*)
- Christian Gottlieb Müller, *Potpourri ("Gay Fellows")*
- Franz von Suppé, *Overture to "Dichter und Bauer"* (*Poet and Peasant*)
- Johann Strauss II, *An der schönen, blauen Donau* (*On the Beautiful Blue Danube*) with chorus

Response to the concert, which was heavily attended by Madison's German citizens, was very enthusiastic, and one unsigned review offered some (rather faint) praise to the orchestra:

The orchestra, numbering 15 performers, acquitted itself most handsomely, and showed how valuable to Madison would be such a company of musicians, if they could be encouraged to the training necessary to perfect them in playing. The first piece, a difficult one, went a little hard in one or two places, but the others were most admirably played throughout, and gave entire satisfaction.[85]

The orchestra performed twice more that summer, playing outdoor concerts on July 4 and July 15. However, despite a determined advertising campaign, the Madison Musical Society's orchestra seems to have faded away by the end of 1874. One contributing factor may have been competition from the Milwaukee-based orchestra led by Christopher Bach, a larger, professional group that performed frequently in Madison during this period. August Bareuther seems to have moved permanently to Oshkosh soon thereafter, where he had a long tenure as a professional musician.[86] For his part, John Lueders remained in Madison until his death in 1911, and he had a career as a violinist, violin teacher, and leader of a successful concert band. He would also continue to organize small orchestras in the 1880s and 1890s to accompany touring opera companies and occasional oratorio performances.

In the years around the turn of the 20th century, another, longer-lasting local professional orchestra was led by a prominent Madison musician: violinist and conductor Charles Nitschke. Born in Bavaria in 1846, he emigrated initially to St. Louis, and then moved to Philadelphia, where in 1876 he led an orchestra at the Centennial Exposition. Nitschke spent most of the next two decades in Chicago, where at various points he led theater orchestras, performed in the Theodore Thomas Orchestra, and taught at the Chicago Academy of Music. At the World's Columbian Exposition in Chicago in 1892–93, Nitschke performed in the Exposition Orchestra and was assistant conductor to the orchestra's director, Theodore Thomas.[87] He first appeared in Madison in the fall of 1894 when he was hired to conduct the National Guard's First Regiment Band, though he returned to Chicago in May 1895 for work in a theater orchestra.[88] Nitschke returned to Madison in August 1898, now as a member of the University faculty and director of the orchestra of the Fuller Opera House, and he would spend the next several years as one of the city's most high-profile musicians. Almost immediately after his arrival, Nitschke put out a call to the "best talent of the city" to play in a band and an orchestra under his leadership.[89]

Dozens of newspaper notices over the next seven years document the busy schedules of Nitschke's Military Band and Nitschke's Orchestra. The orchestra performed most frequently at dances and receptions but occasionally gave formal concerts as well. The first of these seems to have been on May 3, 1900, at Turner Hall. Nitschke led an orchestra of 27 players, including his sons Charles, Jr., as concertmaster and Richard on viola and drum, in a program that included eight orchestral pieces and solos by soprano Jeanette Daggett Weber and violinist Minnie Kelly.[90] Over the next few years, the orchestra played concerts with the Madison Maennerchor, played outdoor summer concerts in Madison's parks, accompanied a local production of *The Mikado*, and even made appearances at some of Madison's earliest vaudeville performances in 1901 at

1.16 Prof. Charles Nitschke, 1903.

the Madison Summer Theatre, a popular tent show located at the corner of Pinckney and Doty Streets. For reasons that are not clear, however, Charles Nitschke seems to have left Madison rather abruptly before the start of the school year in 1906, and by December 1906 he had opened a music school in Guthrie, Oklahoma.[91]

During his tenure at the University, Nitschke also directed the University Orchestra, Madison's oldest continuously existing orchestra, predating the founding of the Madison Civic Symphony by over 30 years. It was officially founded in 1894, a year before the institution of the University School of Music, though it would be 10 years before the group began to give regular public performances. By the 1910s, membership in the orchestra was regularly 40 players, though its musical quality remained irregular, perhaps in part because there was a revolving set of conductors during the decade, some of whom led the orchestra for only a single academic year. This changed with the arrival of Prof. Edwin Morphy in 1920. Morphy, who directed the orchestra until 1934, expanded the number of rehearsals and focused on high-quality performances of first-rate orchestral literature. He also focused on outreach, arranging for early radio performances and out-of-town tours by the University Orchestra. By the mid-1920s, its concerts were moved from Music Hall to the University Armory in order to accommodate a larger audience.[92]

Another place Madisonians heard orchestral music was in the city's theaters. In the first few decades of the 20th century, Madison's larger theaters had concert organs and staff organists, mostly to provide musical backing for silent movies. The Fuller Opera House had maintained a small orchestra from

1.17 UW-Madison Symphony Orchestra, early 20th century.

the 1890s onward to support traveling opera, operetta, and musical theater companies, and later, movies. By the 1920s, the Fuller (Parkway after 1922), Strand, Orpheum, and Majestic, and later the larger New Orpheum (1927) and Capitol (1928) theaters all maintained small orchestras of local musicians who could be called upon to accompany vaudeville acts and touring musical comedy productions, and to provide backing to silent films, including playing between shorts and features. These theater orchestras were small ensembles of primarily woodwind and brass players, usually combined with a few string players. Though they were there primarily to serve as accompaniment for musical acts and movies, these groups would occasionally present independent concert programs as well. On May 4, 1924, for example, the Parkway Concert Orchestra, "augmented by extra musicians, a total of eighteen, seated upon the stage with special scenic settings and lighting effects," presented a classical concert under the direction of the theater's conductor and violinist George Cervenka. The program opened with Mendelssohn's *Ruy Blas Overture* and closed with Sousa's *Stars and Stripes Forever* and included works by Beethoven, Godard, Moszkowski, Herbert, Drdla, and Massenet, with "popular airs as encores."[93]

Theater orchestras were a valued source of income for Madison's resident professional musicians. For example, flutist Florence Bennett, who also performed with the Madison Civic Symphony in the late 1920s, made her living in Madison by teaching lessons and playing in and conducting local theater orchestras.[94] Another musician who worked in Madison's theaters was Bernard "Bunny" Berigan (1908–1942), who would later be one of the most prominent trumpet soloists of the Swing era in the late 1930s and a successful bandleader in his own right. At age 16, Berigan moved from his native Fox Lake (about 50 miles northwest of Madison) to Madison to live with his uncle, a professional drummer, and to play in several local bands. In 1927–28, he played regularly with the orchestras of the New Orpheum and Capitol Theaters, before leaving for the East Coast in April 1928.[95]

Though much of the repertoire Madison's theater orchestras played was classical, the orchestras themselves seem to have been heavily populated by gigging musicians like Berigan, who were also part of Madison's burgeoning jazz scene—a situation that led to controversy at least once in the 1920s. In January 1926, Emil Flindt, pianist and leader of the Strand Theater's orchestra, performed *Sonatique*—a jazz-style version of Beethoven's *"Pathetique" Sonata*, arranged by Louis Katzman—as part of the music prior to a movie. Laurence Powell, a faculty composer at the University, heard this and was upset enough to gather a petition with 100 signatures protesting the "jazzing" of classical works by the Strand's orchestra. Flindt wrote directly to Katzman, a New York–based composer, arranger, and bandleader, who would work closely with George Gershwin later in the 1920s when Gershwin started his own nationwide radio show.[96] Katzman's reply was shared with the *Wisconsin State Journal*, which published a column-length article describing what it called "Madison's Jazz War" in early February. Katzman mounted a spirited defense of jazz as a sophisticated style in itself and as a tremendously popular form of the day. He concluded with a challenge:

> In conclusion I want to say that at sometime in the future I hope to have the pleasure of appearing in Madison personally and will gladly let the public decide whether they want to attend a concert arranged and edited by Laurence Powell, the noted critic, or whether they would like to hear some of the classics jazzed. I am sure Mr. Powell will be overwhelmed by the results.[97]

Nothing came of this throwdown, and the "Jazz War" seems to have ended as merely a war of words. However, this amusing little tempest in a teapot does show that in the 1920s, which saw the founding of the Madison Civic Symphony, many in Madison saw the preservation of classical music as a "cause."

1.18 The Parkway Theatre Orchestra, May 1926.

Though theater orchestras had existed in Madison well before the 1920s, this decade seems to have been the peak of their prominence, as Madison's movie palaces competed to put on the most opulent showings of their feature films. On March 17, 1926, for example, three of the city's theaters advertised special musical programs connected with their main features. Flindt's Strand Orchestra, billed as "11 Kings of Syncopation," offered an Irish-themed musical program in honor of St. Patrick's Day. Then, following the feature, a comedy, and a newsreel, Lytta Lynn played an organ solo. The Majestic also advertised a jazz band, the six-piece Sid's Serenaders, playing in support of a western, *Two-Fisted Jones*. At the more classically oriented Parkway, a stage play was preceded by "a twenty-five minute concert opening with *Poet and Peasant*."[98] The tradition of theater orchestras did not last long into the Great Depression, however. The city's two largest theaters, the New Orpheum (opened 1927) and the Capitol (opened 1928), were able to maintain instrumental groups into the early 1930s, but the advent of "talkies" with recorded soundtracks and the economics of the Depression seem to have combined to put an end to resident theater orchestras.

Larger touring productions—operas, musical comedies, and ballet companies—would often travel with their own small orchestras, a fact that would always be trumpeted in local advertising. The groups were small, but even an orchestra of a dozen players warranted special notice in advertising. The same was true with some of the more extravagant movies of the day. For example, in February 1917, the Fuller hosted a weeklong run of *A Daughter of the Gods*, a big-budget fantasy film starring the Australian actress and champion swimmer Annette Kellerman. (Like many movies of the 1910s and early 1920s, before the institution of the Motion Picture Production Code, *A Daughter of the Gods* courted controversy—in this case, for brief flashes of nudity during a couple of Kellerman's underwater scenes.) The Fox company sent its own "Symphony Orchestra of 15" on tour with the movie, a fact noted prominently in the Fuller's advertising. This orchestra played a score written for the film by Robert Hood Bowers.[99] Given the high cost and prestige of the production, the theater also charged premium prices for admission to the show, significantly higher than the usual 5¢ to 15¢ for its typical movie offerings.

1.19a/1.19b (Rather risqué!) advertisements in the *Wisconsin State Journal* of February 1917 for *A Daughter of the Gods*.

Touring theater and movie orchestras would occasionally play public concerts outside of the orchestra pit. For example, on January 6, 1919, after news of Theodore Roosevelt's death broke, the orchestra traveling with *Hearts of the World* (a World War I propaganda film directed by D. W. Griffith) offered a special memorial concert in the Wisconsin State Assembly Chamber.[100]

In addition to homegrown attempts to create an orchestra and theater orchestras, Madisonians heard orchestral music performed by professional touring ensembles from the 1860s onward. Christopher Bach's Orchestra, based in Milwaukee, was organized in the late 1850s by German immigrant Christopher Bach (1835–1927), a conductor, composer, and cornetist. The orchestra was a focus of German cultural pride in Milwaukee, and by the 1890s it was a thoroughly professional ensemble of more than 70 players. It continued to perform well into the 20th century, conducted after 1907 by Bach's son Hugo.[101] Christopher Bach's Orchestra appeared frequently in Madison, beginning as early as August 27, 1866, when the orchestra performed in Madison's Turner Hall at a festival jointly sponsored by the Turn-Vereine of Madison and Milwaukee.[102] This program included several orchestral works by Suppé, Flotow, and a few works by Bach himself, including a newly composed *Turner March*. It also included choral and operatic numbers, performed by Madison's Maennerchor and Liederkranz, and "gymnastic exercises and acrobatic feats" performed by the Milwaukee Turn-Verein.[103] Bach's Orchestra performed in Madison dozens of times over the next 40 years, most often called in to accompany large choral programs by the University Choral Union and others, but occasionally giving independent concerts of its own.

Several other touring chamber orchestras and full-size symphony orchestras appeared sporadically in Madison as well, as shown in Table 1.2, listing 19 performances during this period. The most frequent visitor, appearing six times in Madison, was the Theodore Thomas Orchestra, which would become the Chicago Symphony Orchestra in 1913. However, a few additional famous orchestras appeared in Madison after the turn of the century as well, most notably Milan's La Scala Orchestra, the New York Symphony Orchestra, the London Symphony Orchestra, and the Minneapolis Symphony Orchestra.

The Madison Orchestral Association

There was clearly an audience for orchestral music in Madison, and in 1912, a group of Madison citizens formed the Madison Orchestral Association to support Madison performances by America's great symphony orchestras. The directors of the Association included both Ada Bird and Fletcher Wheeler, directors of Madison's rival private conservatories, but also included local figures who would later be involved in supporting the Madison Civic Music Association (MCMA). On July 24, 1912, the *Wisconsin State Journal* announced that the first season of concerts sponsored by the Association would include three programs by the Theodore Thomas Orchestra—soon to be renamed the Chicago Symphony Orchestra—in November, February, and April, with concerts to be held at the University Armory. The Armory clearly had drawbacks as a concert space—it was designed primarily as a gymnasium. However, it had a much larger seating capacity than Madison's premiere performance space, the Fuller Opera House, and as a University venue, it was also available at a much lower cost than the Fuller. The Armory would host all of the Association's programs until 1926. The group announced that a guarantee fund of $1700 had already been secured from donors, and that more funding was expected as season tickets went on sale.[104] On October 19, the Association published a formal advertisement for the concerts, noting that season tickets could be purchased for $3.00. This ad also included a manifesto of sorts, headed by "A

Table 1.2: Concerts by Touring Professional Orchestras in Madison, 1871 to 1912

Date	Ensemble	Venue
12/20/1871	Vienna Lady Orchestra (all-female chamber orchestra)	Hooley Opera House
2/28/1873	Theodore Thomas Orchestra (predecessor of the Chicago Symphony Orchestra)	Hooley Opera House
12/11-12/1875	Vienna Lady Orchestra, with soprano Elisa Deverient	Hooley Opera House
6/20/1885	Theodore Thomas Orchestra	Turner Hall
3/8/1893	Theodore Thomas Orchestra	Fuller Opera House
5/7/1896	Clara Schumann Orchestra (Chicago-based all-female chamber orchestra)	University Armory
5/19/1897	Boston Festival Orchestra, appearing with the Madison Choral Union and several opera soloists	University Armory
11/13/1897	Clara Schumann Orchestra	First Methodist Episcopal Church
5/16-17/1898	Boston Festival Orchestra, appearing with the Madison Choral Union and several opera soloists	University Armory
11/13/1900	Theodore Thomas Orchestra	Fuller Opera House
10/21/1901	Hungarian Court Orchestra (chamber orchestra)	First Methodist Episcopal Church
5/8/1903	Boston Festival Orchestra, appearing with the Madison Choral Union and several opera soloists	University Armory
11/7/1906	La Scala Orchestra, appearing with several opera soloists and conducted by composer Ruggero Leoncavallo	University Armory
1/18/1909	Theodore Thomas Orchestra	Fuller Opera House
10/20/1909	New York Symphony Orchestra, appearing with dancer Isadora Duncan	University Armory
11/30/1909	Theodore Thomas Orchestra	Fuller Opera House
5/3/1911	St. Paul Symphony Orchestra, appearing with several opera soloists	Fuller Opera House
4/20/1912	London Symphony Orchestra	University Armory
7/19/1912	Minneapolis Symphony Orchestra	Monona Park Auditorium

few facts about the Madison Orchestral Association," noting that "1. It aims to unite all musical interests in Madison; membership in the association is open to everybody. 2. Its only object is to secure for Madison the best orchestral music at the lowest price," and listing members of the executive committee.[105] The Association clearly considered part of its mission to be educational: just a few days later, it published a list of books on "how to listen" for the benefit of Madisonians who planned to attend concerts,[106] and it later arranged for lectures to precede each concert. The group also arranged for children's matinees on the afternoons before most of the concerts, and its members volunteered to give preconcert talks in local schools beforehand. Community interest was clearly very high: At the first concert on November 26, 1912, the Thomas Orchestra played a program of Bach, Beethoven, Franck, and Wagner to an audience of 1700 in the University Armory. An account published the next day reported that only nine tickets went unsold.

The Chicago Symphony Orchestra performed 15 more concerts over the next six seasons under the sponsorship of the Madison Orchestral Association, to equally large audiences, though the Association began to report deficits at the close of each season. An urgent "appeal for guarantors" in September 1917[107] was apparently successful, and the Association announced another season of three orchestral concerts, with the Minneapolis Symphony Orchestra performing the second program. There was a hiatus in 1918–19, with the Association announcing on October 14, 1918, that "because of the exigencies of the war" it was planning to "cancel all its arrangements for concerts during the coming season."[108] This would also have coincided with the outbreak of the influenza pandemic in Madison. In fact, aside from concerts of the University Orchestra, the only live orchestral music heard in Madison during the 1918–19 season was an appearance by the touring 50-member Russian Symphony Orchestra at the Fuller Opera House on November 18, 1918. Apparently still beset by financial problems, the Association did announce an abbreviated season of two concerts for 1919–20, one by the Minneapolis Symphony Orchestra in January 1920 and one by the Chicago Symphony Orchestra in April 1920, but the April concert was apparently canceled.[109] The following season included concerts by the Minneapolis Symphony Orchestra, the Detroit Symphony Orchestra, and the New York Philharmonic, all of whom appeared in early 1921. The New York Philharmonic's appearance on May 23, 1921, seems to have stirred particularly intense interest in the local press, with several notices describing the repertoire beforehand, and detailed reviews in both newspapers on the following day. The Association was able to secure only one orchestra for its 1921–22 season, the Cincinnati Symphony Orchestra, on November 1, 1921. This program was led by Eugène Ysaÿe, who had appeared in Madison in 1905 and 1913 as a violin soloist. Later in his career, however, he turned increasingly to conducting, and he became the music director of the Cincinnati Symphony Orchestra in 1918. Two aspects of this concert are notable. First, this was apparently the first attempt at a nationwide broadcast of an orchestra concert. The broadcast was noted briefly in the local Madison papers, but the *Cincinnati Enquirer* provided more extensive coverage, describing the broadcast as a kind of experiment by the University Physics Department and noting that the concert broadcast was heard clearly as far away as North Dakota and Pennsylvania.[110] Secondly, this concert was probably the first visit to Madison by a future conductor of the Madison Civic Symphony, Walter Heermann, who was then performing as a cellist in Cincinnati.

On November 22, 1922, the *State Journal* published an appreciation of the Association's 10 years of work, including hundreds of talks about music given to local schoolchildren and clubs. The article noted that, given increasing traveling costs during the war years and afterwards, the Association had had to cut back on the number of concerts it sponsored, but it concluded on a hopeful note that the season would once again expand.[111] Initially only the Cincinnati Symphony Orchestra was scheduled for 1922–23, but an influx of money from donors allowed the Association to bring in the Minneapolis Symphony Orchestra as well. In 1923–24, the group brought the Minneapolis Symphony Orchestra for two programs—both of which included children's matinees—and the Chicago Symphony Orchestra for one program. The Association was able to host the Minneapolis Symphony Orchestra for three programs in 1924–25. In 1925–26, the Association moved its two planned concerts from the Armory to the more acoustically sound University Stock Pavilion. The first program, by the Minneapolis Symphony Orchestra on February 26, 1926, included University of Wisconsin composer Cecil Burleigh's *Violin Concerto*, op. 60, played by local violinist Gilbert Ross.[112] The second program, which would be the last concert sponsored by the Association, was the Chicago Civic Orchestra on March 23. Table 1.3 provides a complete list of the performance that the Association sponsored.

Following its 1925–26 season, the Madison Orchestral Association disbanded. In part, the problem was money. In the first few seasons, ticket receipts had covered the bulk of the sizable cost of bringing full-size professional orchestras to Madison. Audience interest remained strong throughout, but costs rose substantially during the war years. After its first few years, the Association had almost always ended each season with a deficit, and it was increasingly dependent on donors. However, an equally important reason for the Association's dissolution was the prospect of a local orchestra founded by a new community group, the Madison Civic Music Association. A *State Journal* article of September 5, 1926, announcing the beginning of rehearsals for the new Madison Civic Symphony included the following:

> Many members of the Madison Orchestral Association, which is now disbanded, are giving their support to the new civic symphony orchestra, according to Dr. H. P. Greeley, recent president of the board of directors of the association, "We do not wish to stand in the way of the full development of a Madison symphony organization," he declared. "The orchestral association is now disbanded, and will not attempt to bring outside orchestras to the city at least until Madison has a suitable auditorium. Consequently guarantors will not be asked for contributions to finance activities which have now been discontinued."[113]

The Madison Orchestral Association was an unqualified success in bringing fine orchestral performances to Madison audiences: During its 14-year run, it sponsored 33 concerts in Madison—most of these including additional student matinees—by six of America's great orchestras. While the Madison Civic Symphony, an almost entirely amateur community ensemble, would be a very different sort of group than the professional orchestras sponsored by the Association, these programs proved that Madison could and would support orchestral music. More than any other group, the Association set the stage for the Madison Civic Music Association and the founding of Madison's own symphony orchestra.

Table 1.3: Concerts Sponsored by the Madison Orchestral Association, 1912 to 1926

Date	Ensemble	Venue
11/26/1912	Theodore Thomas Orchestra (= Chicago Symphony Orchestra)	University Armory
2/18/1913	Theodore Thomas Orchestra	University Armory
4/15/1913	Chicago Symphony Orchestra	University Armory
11/25/1913	Chicago Symphony Orchestra	University Armory
1/20/1914	Chicago Symphony Orchestra	University Armory
3/10/1914	Chicago Symphony Orchestra	University Armory
11/17/1914	Chicago Symphony Orchestra	University Armory
2/16/1915	Chicago Symphony Orchestra	University Armory
3/16/1915	Chicago Symphony Orchestra	University Armory
11/16/1915	Chicago Symphony Orchestra	University Armory
1/25/1916	Chicago Symphony Orchestra	University Armory
3/14/1916	Chicago Symphony Orchestra	University Armory
12/5/1916	Chicago Symphony Orchestra	University Armory
2/13/1917	Chicago Symphony Orchestra	University Armory
3/27/1917	Chicago Symphony Orchestra	University Armory
11/29/1917	Chicago Symphony Orchestra	University Armory
1/19/1918	Minneapolis Symphony Orchestra	University Armory
4/2/1918	Chicago Symphony Orchestra	University Armory
1/17/1920	Minneapolis Symphony Orchestra	University Armory
2/7/1921	Minneapolis Symphony Orchestra	University Armory
3/29/1921	Detroit Symphony Orchestra	University Armory
5/23/1921	New York Philharmonic	University Armory
11/1/1921	Cincinnati Symphony Orchestra	University Armory
11/28/1922	Cincinnati Symphony Orchestra	University Armory
2/6/1923	Minneapolis Symphony Orchestra	University Armory
10/23/1923	Minneapolis Symphony Orchestra	University Armory
11/27/1923	Chicago Symphony Orchestra	University Armory
4/1/1924	Minneapolis Symphony Orchestra	University Armory
10/28/1924	Minneapolis Symphony Orchestra	University Armory
2/2/1925	Minneapolis Symphony Orchestra	University Armory
5/9/1925	Minneapolis Symphony Orchestra	University Armory
2/20/1926	Minneapolis Symphony Orchestra	University Stock Pavilion
3/23/1926	Chicago Civic Orchestra	University Stock Pavilion

Notes to Chapter 1

1. *WSJ* 6/6/1930, 8. [In citations, *WSJ* = *Wisconsin State Journal*; *CT* = *Capital Times*]
2. The most comprehensive history of the group was published to celebrate its sesquicentennial in 2002: Paul Essert, Richard Layman, Eric Walke, et al., *Madison Maennerchor: 150 Years* (Madison, Wisconsin: Madison Maennerchor, 2002). This booklet includes several earlier historical articles on the group, as well as membership lists and recent history.
3. Local musician and journalist Alexius Baas later published a retrospective appreciation: "Madison's Mozart Club Provided Top Choral Music for 58 Years," *CT* 6/29/1960, 33.
4. *WSJ* 2/28/1896, 1; Susan C. Cook, ed., *A Century of Making Music: A Documentary Scrapbook of the University of Wisconsin–Madison School of Music* (Madison: University of Wisconsin–Madison School of Music, 1995): 8.
5. *WSJ* 4/24/1897, 1.
6. *WSJ* 1/28/1867, 1.
7. *WSJ* 3/20/1867, 4; *WSJ* 3/2/1869, 2.
8. *WSJ* 7/16/1870, 4.
9. *WSJ* 8/26/1870, 4.
10. *WSJ* 9/23/1870, 1.
11. *WSJ* 6/25/1871, 4; *WSJ* 10/17/1871, 4. Though billed in Madison newspapers as a "grand opera," *The Haymakers* is better described as a secular cantata, depicting an idealized rural American scene. It was quite popular in the United States during the 1860s and 1870s. See Dena J. Epstein, H. Wiley Hitchcock, and Polly Carder, "Root, George Frederick," *Grove Music Online*, www.oxfordmusiconline, accessed 9/1/2021.
12. *Wisconsin Argus* 7/9/1850, 2.
13. Henry C. Youngerman, "Theatre Buildings in Madison Wisconsin 1836–1900," *The Wisconsin Magazine of History* 30/3 (July 1947): 273–74. One of the first venues built expressly for public events was run by John Lewis. The second floor of his general store on the corner of Wisconsin Avenue and Johnson Street hosted over 100 performances in the early 1850s. It seems to have been cramped and dingy, and according to one contemporary writer, the hall had "seats that would not do credit to a cattle show."
14. In an issue of *The Musical Gazette* (Boston, 5/24/1847, p.70), there is an account of his making opening remarks at a meeting in Peoria in which he made a high-minded statement on the value of music in worship.
15. The brief flirtation between Lincoln, by then a successful lawyer and occasionally a circuit court judge *pro tem*, and a teenage Lois Newhall is detailed in several Lincoln biographies: see, for example, Joshua Wolf Shenk, *Lincoln's Melancholy: How Depression Challenged a President and Fueled His Greatness* (New York: Houghton Mifflin Harcourt, 2006): 119–20. The story was recalled over 50 years later by *State Journal* writer William J. Anderson ("A Story About Lincoln," *WSJ* 2/9/1909, 3).
16. J. C. McWilliams, *Were I But His Own Wife* (St. Louis: Balmer & Weber, 1855).
17. Nathaniel Smith Haynes, *History of the Disciples of Christ in Illinois, 1819–1914* (Cincinnati: Standard Publishing Company, 1914): 61.

18   *WSJ* 6/8/1855, 2. Strakosch, in addition to being a composer and an able pianist, was one of the era's leading impresarios, often working with his brothers Max and Ferdinand, and later with his son Robert. At various times he managed the careers of Parodi and the operatic Patti family—Salvatore and his daughters Amalia (whom Strakosch would later marry), Adelina, and Carlotta—and pianist Louis Moreau Gottschalk. He also made tour arrangements for violinist Ole Bull and soprano Christine Nilsson and organized a touring opera company. See William Brooks, "Strakosch, Maurice," *Grove Music Online*, www.oxfordmusiconline, accessed 9/1/2021.

19   Julia J. Chybowski, "Greenfield, Elizabeth Taylor," *Grove Music Online*, www.oxfordmusiconline, accessed 9/1/2021.

20   *WSJ* 5/20/1863, 1. This kind of backhanded reaction to Greenfield's performances was commonplace, and reviews were frequently much uglier than that of the *State Journal*: see Julia J. Chybowski, "Becoming the 'Black Swan' in Mid-Nineteenth Century America: Elizabeth Taylor Greenfield's Early Life and Debut Concert Tour," *Journal of the American Musicological Society* 67 (2014): 147–57.

21   Albert O. Barton, "Ole Bull and his Wisconsin Contacts," *The Wisconsin Magazine of History* 7/4 (June 1924): 425.

22   Einar Haugen and Camilla Cai, *Ole Bull: Norway's Romantic Musician and Cosmopolitan Patriot* (Madison: University of Wisconsin Press, 1993): 161–62.

23   Barton, "Ole Bull," 426.

24   *WSJ* 6/27/1857, 4.

25   *WSJ* 1/25/1868, 4.

26   Barton, "Ole Bull," 429.

27   Quoted in Albert O. Barton, "Ole Bull's Concerts Here Acclaimed By Many Who Still Reside in Madison," *WSJ* 2/10/1924, 7.

28   *WSJ* 11/17/1868, 1. "Miss Barton" was possibly Julia Barton, a singer active in Boston and New York in this period.

29   *WSJ* 3/26/1870, 1.

30   *WSJ* 4/24/1870, 4.

31   There are many published accounts of their courtship and marriage, and Bull's subsequent residence in Madison. Perhaps the best appears in David Mollenoff, *Madison: The Formative Years*, 2nd ed. (Madison: University of Wisconsin Press, 2003): 144–45. There was also an account published by one of the former First Ladies of Wisconsin, Isobel Bacon La Follette (wife of Gov. Philip La Follette), in "Early History of the Wisconsin Executive Residence," *The Wisconsin Magazine of History* 21/2 (December 1937): 143–47. See also Norman Gilliland, "Famed Norwegian Violinist Ole Bull's Madison Years." www.wisconsinlife.org, accessed 10/17/18; and Barton, "Ole Bull," 431–33.

32   *WSJ* 5/23/1876, 1

33   *WSJ* 5/17/1872, 3.

34   Barton, "Ole Bull," 433.

35   At the request of his mother-in-law, Bull offered this concert as a benefit to raise funds for the purchase of a painting by the famous landscape artist Thomas Moran, *Sunrise on Lake Monona*, for the University. Moran exhibited this work and a companion piece, *Sunset on Lake Mendota*, at Madison's Centennial Exhibition in 1876. The Lake Mendota image had already been secured by

a private donation, and Bull's concert raised the $1000 purchase price for the second painting. They were displayed together in the recently completed Science Hall, but both were lost when the building was destroyed by fire in 1884. Local artist Eva Ann Lingenfelter Curtiss (wife of the famous photographer Edwin Curtiss) painted a copy of *Sunrise on Lake Monona* that now hangs in the Wisconsin State Historical Society Museum. (*WSJ* 1/5/1919, 12; "Painting: *Sunrise on Lake Monona*," https://www.wisconsinhistory.org/Records/Image/IM102418, accessed 3/192021.)

36   *WSJ* 1/27/1879, 4.

37   Barton, "Ole Bull," 441–42.

38   *WSJ* 6/26/1855, 2. There was also a New Jersey–based musician, Giovanni Sconcia, who toured under the same name in the 1840s and 1850s. See Charles H. Kaufman, *Music in New Jersey, 1655–1860: A Study of Musical Activity and Musicians in New Jersey from Its First Settlement to the Civil War* (Rutherford, NJ: Fairleigh Dickinson University Press, 1981): 177.

39   Mollenhoff, *Madison*, 220, 241–42, 247.

40   "Storm Bull," *Wikipedia*, https://en.wikipedia.org/wiki/Storm_Bull, accessed 3/12/2019.

41   *WSJ* 11/8/1906, 8.

42   *CT* 5/22/1923, 1.

43   *WSJ* 5/22/1950, 5. From contemporary descriptions provided by Stefanie Walzinger, *King Alfred* was a *pastiche* of music drawn from popular songs, opera, and operetta.

44   Stefanie Walzinger, who has traced the singer's career in painstaking detail, notes that there are simply no significant gaps in Bertha's career in the United States in the late 1890s. (Email correspondence, 1/6/2022.)

45   I am sincerely grateful to Stefanie Walzinger of Freiburg, Germany, for sharing her extensive research on Bertha Waltzinger, who is her distant cousin. Many of the details presented here are drawn, with her kind permission, from our email correspondence (1/5–7/2022). Bertha's burial record confirms that she had planned for a postmortem return to Madison well in advance, making arrangements as early as 1923 to be interred in a plot close to her family. Additional references include: *WSJ* 5/20/1882, 4; *WSJ* 4/6/1895, 1; *WSJ* 7/30/1896, 1; *WSJ* 12/12/1897, 4; "Florodora," *Wikipedia*, https://en.wikipedia.org/wiki/Florodora, accessed 12/9/2021; *WSJ* 2/5/1910, 6; *WSJ* 2/8/1910, 3; obituary, *WSJ* 4/20/1927, 3; and "Stephanie Walzinger Interview," *Sheet Music Singer*, https://www.sheetmusicsinger.com/zz-stefanie-walzinger-interview/, accessed 12/9/2021.

46   *WSJ* 1/7/1923, 17; *WSJ* 12/7/1929, 17; obituary, *WSJ* 5/15/1976, 21.

47   Edward Alsworth Ross was a noted political progressive, but he was also a controversial figure because of his strong advocacy for eugenics, strong immigration restrictions, and American "racial purity." His *The Old World in the New* (1914) was among the leading books laying out the case for eugenics. See "Edward Alsworth Ross," *Wikipedia*, https://en.wikipedia.org/wiki/Edward_Alsworth_Ross, accessed 12/14/2021.

48   Gilbert Ross, "The Auer Mystique," *Michigan Quarterly Review* 14 (1975): 302–22.

49   *CT* 4/10/1924, 1; *WSJ* 4/13/1924, 37. Ross purchased the instrument from Cincinnati Symphony Orchestra concertmaster Emil Heermann, the brother of Walter Heermann, who would become the Madison Civic Symphony's second conductor in 1948.

50   I doubt, however, that Ross served that role during the three months of weekly rehearsals leading up to this concert. Marie Endres seems to have led the section from the very beginning and was listed as concertmaster from the second concert onward.

51 A year later, Ross and Prager published two of their Granados arrangements: Enrique Granados, *Two Transcriptions by Gilbert Ross and Sigfrid Prager: 1. Anoranza (Longing) and 2. La maja y el ruiseñor (The Gallant and the Nightingale), from the Opera "Goyescas"* (New York: G. Schirmer, 1930).

52 William Sidney Mount, *The Cradle of Harmony: William Sidney Mount's Violin & Fiddle Music* (New York City: Folkways Records LP 33379, 1975).

53 "Memoir: Gilbert Ross," University of Michigan Faculty History Project, http://faculty-history.dc.umich.edu/faculty/gilbert-ross/memoir, accessed 12/14/2021.

54 Information on Campbell from an extended blog post by Tim Bennee, in the *Theatre History* group, https://www.facebook.com/theatrehistory/posts/sherwood-abraham-coan-who-performed-under-the-stage-name-sc-campbell-was-concede/2813496985439284/, accessed 8/24/2021; and from my subsequent correspondence with Mr. Bennee.

55 On the phenomenal popularity of *The Bohemian Girl* in the United States from the 1840s onward, see John Dizeckes, *Opera in America: A Cultural History* (New Haven, CT, Yale University Press, 1993): 93–98.

56 The August 20, 1865, issue of the *Wisconsin State Journal*, which would have confirmed the opera performed on that evening, is not contained in any newspaper database, nor is it included in the microfilm copy in the Wisconsin State Historical Society Library. Neither the databases nor the library have any other Madison newspapers for that day. However, in surveying press notices of other stops on the company's tour that summer, they invariably performed *La sonnambula* during their stands.

57 *WSJ* 8/19/1865, 1; 8/22/1865, 1.

58 *WSJ* 12/18/1885, 4.

59 *WSJ* 12/8/1885, 4.

60 *WSJ* 4/25/1866, 1.

61 Paul Essert, Richard Layman, and Eric Walke, *150 Years: Madison Maennerchor* (Madison, WI, Madison Maennerchor, 2002): 4, 19.

62 I suspect that if a score existed, it was lost in a 1940 fire that destroyed Madison's Turner Hall, along with much of the library of the Maennerchor.

63 Details from *WSJ* 12/2/1885, 4; *WSJ* 4/4/1893, 4; *WSJ* 6/5/1895, 1; *WSJ* 12/8/1899, 1; *WSJ* 7/6/1900, 5; *WSJ* 4/17/1902, 5; *WSJ* 11/19/1902, 1; *WSJ* 5/5/1905, 6; *WSJ* 11/5/1909, 5; *WSJ* 5/18/1916, 3; *WSJ* 2/12/1922, 17.

64 Historical Society of Wisconsin, "Historical Essay: Ada Bird (1859–1914)." https://wisconsinhistory.org/Records/Article/CS5461, accessed 9/20/2021.

65 *WSJ* 9/15/1887, 4; 10/31/1890, 3.

66 One testimony to Bird's popularity and importance to Madison's musical community is the creation of a local Ada Bird Society following her death. This group organized recitals of local amateur musicians for several years in the late 1910s.

67 Obituary, WSJ 10/27/1967, 47.

68 Prager's biography is addressed in Chapter 3, and there is a biographical sketch of Endres at the end of Chapter 2.

69 Obituary, *WSJ* 2/15/1929, 1.

70 *WSJ* 9/3/1916, 8

71 Cook, *A Century of Making Music*, 5–11; Barbara K. Gerloff, *Pastiche: A History of Music Hall and the School of Music, University of Wisconsin–Madison* (Madison: University of Wisconsin Board of Regents, 1985): 1–17.

72 The Third Wisconsin Cavalry was organized by Col. William Barstow in Janesville in early 1862, and reported for duty in St. Louis in March 1862. See "Third Wisconsin Cavalry: Regimental History, http://www.secondwi.com/wisconsinregiments/third_wisconsin_cavalry.htm, accessed 8/17/2021. For a brief account of the battle, see "Battle of Baxter Springs," *Wikipedia*, https://en.wikipedia.org/wiki/Battle_of_Baxter_Springs, accessed 8/17/2021.

73 *WSJ* 9/25/1857, 3.

74 *Detroit Free Press* 9/6/1855, 1; *Rock Island Argus* 5/31/1856, 3; *Janesville Daily Gazette* 8/20/1857, 2; *Milwaukee Daily Sentinel* 9/4/1857; *Bangor Daily Whig and Courier* 7/20/1858, 2.

75 *WSJ* 10/13/1857, 3.

76 *WSJ* 4/13/1860, 1; 7/3/1860, 1; 9/12/1860, 1,

77 *WSJ* 7/21/1862, 1.

78 *WSJ* 8/21/1863, 1.

79 *WSJ* 2/26/1864, 1.

80 *WSJ* 3/12/1864, 1; 6/15/1864, 1; 7/6/1864, 1; 7/28/1864, 1.

81 *WSJ* 9/17/1864, 1.

82 *WSJ* 4/8/1865, 9. In a published open letter explaining the delay, Burke noted that the Euterpean Society had disbanded in September (*WSJ* 4/4/1865, 4.).

83 *WSJ* 9/13/1865, 1; 10/3/1865, 1.

84 *WSJ* 7/31/1865, 1. Palmer would lead at least three more summer oratorio performances in the late 1860s.

85 *WSJ* 5/12/1874, 4.

86 Documents accessed on ancestry.com note his marriage there in 1876 and the birth of three sons over the next few years. His work as a musician is well documented in the Oshkosh newspapers.

87 *University of Wisconsin School of Music Bulletin 1903–1904*, 27 (from the William Kerr Collection in the University Archives, accessed through digitalcommons.usu.edu/kerr_applications, 8/2/2021).

88 *WSJ* 10/15/1894, 4; *WSJ* 5/14/1895, 4. Following the departure of Nitschke, the First Regiment Band formally merged with the Lueders Band under the leadership of John Lueders.

89 *WSJ* 8/2/1898, 4; *WSJ* 8/8/1898, 1.

90 *WSJ* 5/1/1900, 6; *WSJ* 5/4/1900, 4.

91 An announcement of a formal opening concert for the school describes Nitschke as a "former member of the instructors' staff of the university school of music, of Madison, Wis." *Oklahoma State Register* 1/3/1907 (Guthrie, OK), 5.

92 Bryan W. James, *One Hundred Years of Orchestra at the University of Wisconsin–Madison* (Madison: University of Wisconsin–Madison School of Music, [1996]): 3–9.

93 *CT* 5/3/1924, 7. If patrons bought a ticket to the concert, they could also stay for the Sunday afternoon feature film, *If Winter Comes*, starring Percy Marmont.

94 Bennett's work in Madison is discussed extensively in Chapter 2.

95 Berigan joined the orchestra of the New Orpheum in November 1927, moving to the Capitol when it opened in January 1928. See Robert Dupuis, *Bunny Berigan: Elusive Legend of Jazz* (Baton Rouge, LA: Louisiana State University Press, 1993): 18–23.

96 Michael M. Katzman, "Louis Katzman: His Musical Life and Times," *Association for Recorded Sound Collections Journal* 24, no. 2 (2014): 179–99.

97 *WSJ* 2/4/1926, 11.

98 *CT* 3/17/1926, 9.

99 "A Daughter of the Gods" *Wikipedia*, https://en.wikipedia.org/wiki/A_Daughter_of_the_Gods, accessed 6/10/2024.

100 *CT* 1/6/1919, 1.

101 "Bach, Christopher (1835–1927)," *Dictionary of Wisconsin History*, https://www.wisconsinhistory.org/Records/Article/CS5082, accessed 11/19/2022.

102 The Turner Society (*Turn-Verein*) was a revolutionary group founded in early 19th-century Germany. Its focus on gymnastics and physical well-being seems to have been a cover for military training. *Turn-Vereine* sprang up across America in the middle of the 19th century, many of them founded by those who had fled after the abortive German revolution of 1848. In the United States, the societies maintained their focus on gymnastics, though they also maintained a progressive political stance. See https://www.milwaukeeturners.org/history, accessed 6/17/2024.

103 Mollenhoff, *Madison*, 147. Christopher Bach also appeared in Madison as a cornet soloist a few years later, at City Hall on November 4, 1870. This was a package program with five other Milwaukee-based soloists.

104 *WSJ* 9/28/1912, 2.

105 *WSJ* 10/19/1912, 5.

106 *WSJ* 10/2/1912, 10.

107 *WSJ* 9/17/1917, 1.

108 *WSJ* 10/4/1918, 6.

109 *WSJ* 11/30/1919, 6.

110 *Cincinnati Enquirer*, 11/2/1921, 14. The University made experimental broadcasts of several concerts in 1920 and 1921 leading up to this. For example, the radio broadcast of a University Glee Club concert on March 11, 1921, was reportedly heard as far away as Missouri (*WSJ* 3/13/1921, 6).

111 *WSJ* 11/19/1922, 10.

112 *WSJ* 2/7/1926, 12.

113 *WSJ* 9/5/1926, 13.

CHAPTER 2

The Madison Civic Music Association and the Founding of the Madison Civic Symphony and Madison Civic Chorus: 1925–1940

"We confidently expect and believe that the orchestra and chorus have come to stay in Madison."

- George P. Hambrecht, MCMA President (1932)

The Madison Civic Symphony, forerunner of today's Madison Symphony Orchestra, was founded in 1926. The Madison Civic Chorus, now Madison Symphony Chorus, followed a year later. From 1926 until 1994, the umbrella organization sponsoring both groups, and eventually the Madison Opera as well, was the Madison Civic Music Association (MCMA).

From the Madison Community Music Committee to the MCMA, 1920–1926

One good way to begin the history of the MCMA is with what the group said about itself. An institutional history titled "History of the Madison Civic Music Association" first appeared in the minutes of the board, but it was later printed in various versions in the program books of the Symphony and chorus from 1926 to 1932. The essential outline of MCMA's early development laid out in this account can be summarized as follows:

> **1920**: The Madison Community Music Committee, a coalition of local groups and University School of Music faculty, was formed to administer Madison's annual Music Memory Contest.
>
> **1925**: Wishing to expand its activities, the committee formally incorporated as the Madison Civic Music Association.
>
> **1926**: The MCMA hired Dr. Sigfrid Prager as its music director and organized the Madison Civic Symphony.
>
> **1927**: The MCMA organized a second community group, the Madison Civic Chorus.
>
> **1928**: The MCMA and the Madison Vocational School began cooperation in creating a music program at the school.

Music Memory Contests were widespread in the United States during the 1920s. The intent, across the country, was to combat what was seen as the pernicious influence of jazz and popular music and to promote "fine" music, particularly among the young. In 1922, Edith Hildebrandt, an Illinois high school music teacher, explained in an article in the educational journal *The School Review*:

> We like the melodies that we can all "join in and sing." This liking of the human heart has been exploited and commercialized by unscrupulous individuals who, particularly since the war, have foisted upon the public such an unlimited quantity of "blues" as fairly to choke out any tendency or desire to hear the better music. The choking process, however, can be practiced only on the immature and uninformed. Fortunately, our country still counts in great numbers its trained leaders who can appreciate fine music and who cannot lend heart or voice to the support of ragtime or jazz.[1]

Of course, for Hildebrandt, "the better music" meant European classical music. The way that Music Memory Contests were conducted varied widely, but in Madison, the contest was a version of that game beloved by music nerds from time immemorial, "Name That Tune." Contestants would be given a list of works to learn. In Madison, the University gave concerts for schoolchildren with the assigned repertoire, and recordings of the works were also available in Madison's public library. Contestants would be played excerpts from works selected from the list and were asked to identify them. Preliminary rounds were held in the schools, culminating in a final citywide round. The first Music Memory Contest in Madison was in 1919 and was sponsored by the University's School of Music; the winner that year was nine-year-old Emma Endres, who would eventually be a touring piano soloist. Hildebrandt singled out Madison's contest of 1922 for special praise, noting that some 3200 contestants entered the contest, with 1200 of them advancing to the finals. (Madison allowed adults to enter the contest alongside schoolchildren.) Since 220 of the finalists scored perfectly, a second and more difficult final round was necessary.[2]

One valuable source of information on the early history of the Madison Community Music Committee is the detailed minutes of their meetings, which are preserved in bound volumes in the MSO archives. The preserved minutes begin with the meeting of December 20, 1922, and for the next few years, the committee's work was entirely taken up by the Music Memory Contest: everything from selection of the assigned excerpts, and the purchase of records, scores, and books for the Madison Free Library, to the replacement of participation pins that had been lost by students. The committee included a few local educators, notably Prof. B. Q. Morgan and Prof. E. B. Gordon of the University School of Music and Elizabeth Buehler, director of the private Wisconsin School of Music. There were also a few local businessmen (e.g., Frank C. Bleid, who ran a successful local printing firm, and who would later sing in the Madison Civic Chorus), and several local women. Perhaps the most significant of them was Susan B. Seastone, an enthusiastic amateur musician who was married to a partner in a Madison civil engineering firm. Though many of the committee's members would later be involved with the activities of the Madison Civic Music Association, Seastone would be a central figure in the MCMA during its formative years, particularly in the creation of the orchestra. Many years later, Sigfrid Prager paid tribute to her roles in organization, publicity, and even settling interpersonal disputes—he noted that, for some years, members of the board referred jokingly to the Madison Civic Symphony as "Susie's Band."[3] Her son, Charles Seastone, recalled in 1972 that

> There seem to be an endless series of crises, usually at the time of concerts, and my mother would be on the telephone for hours. It was necessary to bring in professional musicians, mainly oboe and bass viol, from Milwaukee. On at least one occasion one of them arrived in an advanced state of intoxication.[4]

In late 1924 and early 1925, the committee began discussing an expansion of their role—sponsoring concerts by local ensembles and assisting the work of the Madison Orchestral Association, the local organization that had been sponsoring programs in Madison by the Chicago Symphony Orchestra and other orchestras since 1912.[5] The Committee's first series of sponsored programs was hosted in the State Capitol, beginning with a concert by the University Band and Women's Glee Club on March 8, 1925. A second program on April 5 featured the Woman's Club Chorus, the Mozart Club, and a local piano trio, and the third, on May 3, featured combined choruses, bands, and orchestras from local high schools. Community response was overwhelmingly positive, with audiences of between 1500 and 4000 packing the Capitol for these programs. Encouraged by the success of this first concert series, the committee decided on May 11, 1925, that it would recast itself and incorporate as the Madison Civic Music Association (MCMA). Over the next few months, the MCMA submitted articles of incorporation to the state and formally adopted a set of bylaws, and the board was expanded dramatically in size and makeup. In particular, it began to welcome local musicians, including flutist Florence Bennett, pianist Margaret Otterson, and soprano Helen Supernaw, all of whom would eventually be active in the Civic Symphony and Chorus. At its December meeting, the board discussed eight primary things "we want done":

1. Greater stock of music and records in the library.
2. Aid small music groups with music, etc.
3. Civic auditorium.
4. Civic orchestra.
5. Give musicians opportunity for social and musical intercourse.
6. Monthly dinners with speakers, songs, etc.
7. Continued Sunday concerts.
8. Things needed for enlarged activities: more members, money, willing workers, and the support of all members of the association.[6]

It is fascinating to see that even at this early date, this group was stepping into Madison's decades-long struggle to build a civic auditorium. (Madison's "auditorium wars" will be discussed in Chapter 6.) The Sunday State Capitol concerts were canceled for most of the remainder of 1925, after the state superintendent of public property, John Meeks, insisted on enforcing a 1922 policy that allowed only "organizations of state-wide character" to use the Capitol. However, through the intervention of Gov. Blain, the MCMA was able to sponsor a concert by the Mozart Club there on November 29.[7] The Association also sponsored a successful series of luncheon lectures that year. Its main concern in 1926, however, seems to have been the creation of a civic orchestra, spearheaded by an energetic Orchestra Committee that was chaired by Susan Seastone. Seastone presented a detailed report at the board's annual meeting of May 25, 1926, with four major points:

1. A place and desire for a civic orchestra exists in Madison.
2. A good director is necessary.
3. Between $1200 and $1500 is needed in the first year. Thereafter the financial burden will be carried more and more by the orchestra.
4. Private subscriptions will not be sufficient to carry the financial burden involved.

The MCMA unanimously adopted a resolution to move forward with the creation of the Madison Civic Symphony, and the news was announced publicly in the *Capital Times* the next day.[8]

The Beginnings of the Madison Civic Symphony

With the formal decision to form an orchestra made, the MCMA began to assemble the necessary finances. A leading member of the Association's first board, Dr. Paul Clark, later recalled that:

> ... we had very little money except what we could collect by running around the [businesses on the] square. We ran around the square and everybody gave us something. Mrs. Proudfit, widow of the former president of the First National Bank, gave me one hundred dollars. Well, that was like a thousand dollars [today]. Then we were sure we were going to the top.[9]

By September, the Association could boast of 450 members, all of whom had paid at least the nominal $1.00 annual dues. The MCMA also turned to the critical issue of a music director. Fortunately, an eminently qualified

2.01 Sigfrid Prager in 1931. The inscription reads "To my friends and collaborators Lane Ward, and Cecil Brodt." Ward, a cellist, and Brodt, a trumpeter, both played in the Civic Symphony in the early days. In 1927, they founded the Ward-Brodt Music Company, which remains Madison's leading music store today.

orchestral conductor had just appeared in Madison. Dr. Sigfrid Prager had first worked in Madison in the summer of 1925 as a guest instructor at the Wisconsin School of Music, and he returned in June 1926. Born and trained in Germany, Prager—a conductor, pianist, composer, and musicologist—worked as a conductor in Germany, Italy, Switzerland, and Spain before moving to Argentina in 1919. By 1925–26, he had settled in New York City, where he worked as a conductor, vocal coach, and accompanist. (Prager's full biography appears in the next chapter.) Seastone sat in on a conducting class he taught during the summer of 1926, and it was she who first approached Prager regarding the new Civic Symphony. The MCMA board's minutes of August 4, 1926, reported the recommendation of the Orchestra Committee that Prager be engaged to conduct the orchestra for an annual salary of $1000, with a "gentleman's agreement" that this salary would be increased if possible. There was unanimous agreement.[10] His appointment was announced in both local papers two days later.

The MCMA put out a call for interested players through the University School of Music, Madison Public Schools, and the local newspapers, and the Madison Civic Symphony met for its first rehearsal on September 24, 1926, in the Central High School Auditorium. Writing from retirement in Argentina almost half a century later in March 1972, Prager recalled that first rehearsal in a letter to his longtime Madison friend and collaborator Helen Supernaw, written in his trademark wry style:

> Some 60 young and middle aged people came with instruments to find out what it was all about. Now, an orchestra, as we proudly intended to call our enterprise, is a delicately balanced organization, clearly defined in its composition in order to secure a proper balance of dynamics and colors.
>
> As we said before: quantity there was, but what kind of quantity. There was a whole army of saxophones, little ones, medium sized ones, and big ones. But alas, as almost everyone knows, the saxophone is almost the only instrument on earth which is only very, very rarely employed by composers of symphonic music. So, with tears in my eyes, I had to send away this imposing array of ambitious, but undesirable symphonists…
>
> And there was another army, still more numerous, shinier and noisier: about 15 trumpets. Now the trumpet is a legitimate orchestral instrument, but only in small doses. Our classicists and

even the romanticists were content with two of these glorious noisemakers. Titans of orchestration like Meyerbeer, Richard Strauss, Mahler, and Schoenberg have occasionally used four. But 15? Horrible thought! So again, with tears, we had to send away these proud artists. And trumpeters are a proud race. If we made enemies sending away some mild-mannered saxophones, we made mortal foes out of the arrogant but rejected trumpets.

If there was a surplus of unusable material, there was a lamentable scarcity of other instrumentalists. In fact, there were no oboes or bassoons at all. Kettle drums there were, but there was nobody to play these noble instruments. And a harp? Not a shadow of one. The most important section of any orchestra, the string section, also had its shortcomings. Violins there were quite a few, though of unknown individual capacity. Of violas there were two or three. Of violoncelli there were one and a half. I say one half because the person in question had apparently never learned to read music, because when the rehearsal began, he put the music on his desk upside down, which caused some misunderstandings as to exact text interpretation.

And there was one stringbass player, the stationmaster of the South Madison railway depot. He looked quite impressive in his solitary glory, but I don't remember whether or not he sounded equally impressive. As to the numerous violins: the majority of them crowded together on the second violin side. Quite at random we invited half the violins take seats on the first violin side; a silly shift, since we did not know the qualifications of any of them.

At any rate, somehow the rehearsal started. We began with the relatively innocent second *L'Arlesienne Suite* by Bizet. The first ten minutes of it sounded as if Arnold Schoenberg had written the music when he was in a bad humor. We followed with the *Meistersinger Prelude* which sounded somewhat more human, because part of it is in C Major.[11]

The orchestra clearly was able to fill out most of the parts by the time of the first program in December, however. Some of this recruiting seems to have been by the players themselves. For example, Margaret Rupp Cooper, who was the orchestra's harpist from its second concert through the 1970s—over 50 seasons in all—remembered that she was recruited as an eighth grader by violinist Marie Endres.[12] Recruiting was so successful during that first season, in fact, that by the beginning of the second season, Prager had an orchestra of 90 players and had begun to limit membership in the Madison Civic Symphony to "the best amateur talent in Madison and its vicinity."[13] Prager also recalled that many players at that first concert performed for years afterward, and that they represented a wide variety of professions:

> There was Herman Wittwer, excellent clarinetist, head of a prosperous insurance company, who played every concert from 1926 to 1948. Henry Vogts, trumpet, was the owner of a brass foundry. His son, Harry, University student, played a fine clarinet. Erwin Leonard, viola, was professor of literature at the University of Wisconsin. Erwin Koch, kettledrum virtuoso, owned the print shop that printed our programs for years. Cecil Brodt, brilliant trumpet, and Lane Ward, cello, were owners of the Ward-Brodt Music store. Reverend Norman Kimball, minister, competent violinist ... Max Klieforth, viola, chemist at the French Battery Co. Lawrence Ersland, employee of the Gisholt Machine Co., French horn, who played every rehearsal and concert from 1926 to 1948, was one of the best French horn players I've ever known.[14]

Prager led weekly rehearsals over the next three months, in preparation for the first concert, which was scheduled for December. There was clearly excitement in the community about the new orchestra, and both local newspapers reported on rehearsals in the weeks leading up to the concert. Prager was able to engage a relatively "big name" soloist for this opening program, soprano Esther Dale, who was widely known as a recitalist, and who had appeared with both the New York Philharmonic and Boston Symphony Orchestra. She and Prager had previously worked together at the Yorkville Theater in New York City. (Dale later turned to acting, earning hundreds of movie and television credits from the 1930s through the 1950s.)[15] Dale sang an aria and two sets of art songs with Prager as accompanist between orchestral pieces.

A capacity audience of 1000 heard the first concert in Central High School Auditorium on December 14, 1926:

> Georges Bizet, *L'Arlesienne Suite No. 2*
> Charles Gounod, aria "Plus grand dans don obscurité," from *The Queen of Sheba*
> - Esther Dale, soprano, and Sigfrid Prager, piano

Emile Vuillermoz, *Jardin d'amour*
Peter Ilyich Tchaikovsky, *Serenade*
Tchaikovsky, *Pourquoi*
 - Esther Dale, soprano, and Dr. Prager, piano
Beethoven, *Symphony No. 2*
Tom Dobson, *Yasmin*
Avery Robinson, *Water Boy*
John Alden Carpenter, *Don't Ceäre*
Charles Wakefield Cadman, *Call Me No More*
 - Esther Dale, soprano, and Dr. Prager, piano
Grainger, *Mock Morris*
Berlioz, *Hungarian March from "The Damnation of Faust"*

2.02 The Madison Civic Symphony, inaugural program December 14, 1926. Sigfrid Prager and Esther Dale are standing at center. This remarkable photograph, the only copy in existence as far as I know, came to light in 2018 when John Holmes of Williams Bay, Wisconsin, purchased it at the Goodwill Store in Delavan, Wisconsin, and then donated it to the MSO. The original was badly faded and has been digitally restored.

The community enjoyed themselves, and the musicians enjoyed themselves even more, as reported the next day in the *Capital Times*:

> A thousand persons heard Madison's own first symphony concert last night at the Madison Central high school, and about fifty heard the informal jubilee of the Madison Civic Symphony orchestra about ten minutes after the close of one of the most successful premieres that any Madison organization has experienced. Men and women who, without compensation, have worked unceasingly for the past three and a half months in the ranks of the orchestra, lost the dignity with which they had played Bizet and Beethoven, and the 'S-s-s! B-o-o-m! A-a-a-h!' for their director, Dr. Sigfrid Prager their

soloist, Miss Esther Dale; for Gilbert Ross, their concert master; and for Mrs. C. V. Seastone and Prof. E. B. Gordon rang out with all the enthusiasm of a group of rooters at a Wisconsin football game.[16]

The article included several admiring quotes from MCMA board members and others from the audience. The *Capital Times* that day also included a tribute to Prager by violinist Gilbert Ross, who performed as concertmaster in the concert, and a serious and complimentary concert review by staff writer Adrian Scolten.

The inaugural concert was an amalgam of art songs and orchestral pieces, setting a pattern that would be used many times through Prager's tenure. In part, this was a purely practical move: This amateur orchestra was sometimes unable to put together enough music for a full program, and art songs or chamber pieces could flesh out a concert. For the same reason, it was commonplace to repeat works from concert to concert. Works like the *L'Arlesienne Suite No. 2*, the *Carmen Suite No. 2*, and Brahms's *Hungarian Dance No. 5* might appear on three or four programs within one or two seasons. No one seems to have minded, and it was fairly common for pieces to be repeated "by popular demand." The Madison Civic Symphony's season and programs thus were quite different than those of today's Madison Symphony Orchestra and most modern orchestras. In particular, orchestral concerts in the 1920s and 1930s were longer and more varied in content than today. This was a very different time in American musical life. Today we are surrounded by music—we can listen to any sort we choose for 24 hours a day—and modern audiences seem to have little patience with long programs of live music. An average orchestra concert today might contain up to 70 to 80 minutes of music, enough time for an overture and a concerto before intermission and a symphony afterwards. But 1926 was, literally, a quieter time: audiences expected variety, and they were hungry for live music. Programs that would seem excessive by today's standards were commonplace—many of the concerts put on by Civic Music in the 1920s and 1930s contained nearly two hours of music, not counting intermission and setup changes.

The new orchestra performed three more times that season. Its concert on March 8, 1927, included Gilbert Ross performing the Saint-Saëns *Violin Concerto No. 3* and the *Hornpipe for String Instruments* by Prof. B. Q. Morgan, then vice president of the MCMA board. On April 21, the Madison Civic Symphony performed two works on a lengthy gala concert celebrating the Madison Maennerchor's 75th anniversary. The season closed with a May 21 concert featuring clarinetist Harry Vogts, playing the Weber *Concertino*.

The first season of the Madison Civic Symphony had clearly been a success, with three well-attended subscription concerts sponsored by the MCMA and a surplus in the budget. It is interesting to note, given the later history of the orchestra, a proposal made by Susan Seastone at the board meeting of May 9, 1927, which would have established a core orchestra of about 50 selected players, who would be paid $1.00 per regular rehearsal and 50¢ for sectionals. The proposal was approved, but just a few weeks later the board seems to have reconsidered and unanimously rescinded the plan.[17] It would not be until the 1960s that the MCMA regularly paid all musicians of the orchestra.

The Madison Civic Chorus

Flush with success at the end of the 1926–27 season, the MCMA decided to organize the Madison Civic Chorus. It is not clear who initially made this proposal, but I suspect that it was Prager himself.[18] Calls for interested singers went out through both local newspapers in September, and by late October, Prager could report that the choir included 90 women and 40 men.[19] By the time of its first concert on February 23, 1928, the Civic Chorus was listed at 184 members, though the men's sections had been supplemented by members of the Madison Maennerchor, a group also directed at that time by Prager. This inaugural program, the first of many MCMA concerts in the University Stock Pavilion, included two purely orchestral works, Sibelius's *Finlandia* and Beethoven's *Symphony No. 2*, and two choral works with orchestral accompaniment. The first choral piece was by Charles H. Mills, director of the University School of Music, his cantata on the dramatic Longfellow poem *The Wreck of the Hesperus*. Three local soloists were featured: soprano Evelyn Oldham-Baas (wife of Alexius Baas), tenor Floyd Ferrill, and bass George Miller.

2.03 Madison Civic Chorus, Mozart Club, and Madison Maennerchor at Christ Presbyterian Church, 1/20/1931. Sigfrid Prager and Alexius Baas are standing at the left.

Town and Gown: The University Versus Civic Music

One of MCMA's stated policies in its early years was to perform at least one work by an American composer at each of its concerts, but the programming of Prof. Mills's *The Wreck of the Hesperus* on the inaugural concert of the Madison Civic Chorus may also have been a bit of musical politicking by Prager. Mills had already strongly discouraged music students at the University from joining the Madison Civic Symphony and Chorus. If programming the cantata was intended to soften Mills's resolve, however, it does not seem to have worked. In early 1929, Mills and the University School of Music issued a formal policy that students in the University's band and orchestra were forbidden to play in the Madison Civic Symphony—Mills was quoted as being "violently opposed" to allowing University students to perform in city-sponsored groups. A case in point was Henry "Harry" Vogts, Jr., then a freshman at the University. Vogts played in the orchestra while he was a student at East High School, from the first concert in 1926 onward. He had already been featured as a soloist at age 16, performing the Weber *Clarinet Concertino* in May 1927.[20] The MCMA board issued a resolution expressing their "sympathy and support to the students of the University of Wisconsin, whose membership in the University orchestra and band deprive them of the privilege of playing in the Madison Civic Symphony Orchestra."[21] That spring, Prager and MCMA board President Hambrecht met with Mills, and the University policy may have relaxed slightly, though most faculty continued to discourage School of Music students from performing in MCMA groups well into the 1950s.[22] This was quietly ignored by University students, many of whom did in fact play and sing in Civic Music performances during the 1930s through the 1950s. For his part, Harry Vogts does seem to have stepped away from the Madison Civic Symphony after this policy was instituted in early 1929, but he had rejoined the orchestra by 1931. However, it was not until the 1960s that most School of Music instrumental faculty began to actively encourage their students to join the Madison Symphony Orchestra.

The Madison Civic Chorus closed its inaugural concert with Mendelssohn's cantata *The First Walpurgis Night* (*Die erste Walpurgisnacht*), sung in English. The quality and size of the chorus continued to grow under Prager's leadership, and it regularly performed two or three times each season. Over the next several years, it performed many major works and dozens of smaller pieces. There was clearly an element of working through important repertoire, even if the chorus couldn't always take it all in one bite—between December 1929 and May 1930, for example, the chorus performed the three sections of Handel's *Judas Maccabeus* on three successive programs. Succeeding seasons saw performances of several major works: Massenet's *Eve* (1930), excerpts from Bach's *Christmas Oratorio* (1932), Haydn's *The Creation* (1934), Beethoven's *Symphony No. 9* (1935), a concert version of Saint-Saëns's *Samson and Delila* (1935), Verdi's *Requiem* (twice in 1936), and Mendelssohn's *Elijah* (1939).

The true signature piece of the Madison Civic Chorus, however, was the best-known of Handel's oratorios, *Messiah*. The choir presented four choruses from *Messiah* on its November 1932 program, and its first full *Messiah* was presented on February 11, 1933, in a pair of performances at the Parkway Theatre. Katharine Axley's *Wisconsin State Journal* review was typical of the enthusiastic response:

> ...particularly effective were the opening numbers, including the lovely orchestral overture, the aria "Ev'ry Valley" which was sung by Mr. Kemp with beauty and power, and the exhilirating [sic] chorus "And the Glory of Lord."
>
> Throughout the presentation, the ensemble effects, both vocal and instrumental, seemed particularly effective, reflecting long preparation by all concerned. Sweetness and beauty marked the soloists' performances, although we felt there was some lack of power and volume in the afternoon performance.
>
> As might be expected, the climax of the production came in the "Hallelujah Chorus" which was given with splendor and power. On the whole, the Civic Music Association, the Madison Vocational School and all who participated in this undertaking are to be congratulated on this civic enterprise.[23]

MCMA's *Messiah* performances seem to have been designed as a "tradition" from the very beginning. The February 1933 program included a note that "*The Messiah* is to be presented each year as a festival performance." The next performance took place in December 1933, and the oratorio was staged nearly every December afterward until 1959.[24] The yearly December *Messiah* performances, which Prager referred to as his "annual Christmas gift to Madison," became a beloved part of Madison's holiday season. Prager's *Messiah* concerts were very much in the romantic style—large choruses and full 19th-century orchestration—and were presented with several cuts. Part I (the Christmas section) and Part II each lost a couple of arias, and Part III was truncated even more dramatically—it was represented only by the soprano aria *I Know That My Redeemer Liveth*. Subsequent performances followed this same plan, until Prager's *Messiah* cuts became part of the tradition as well. One of the things that caused the row between Prager and his assistant conductor Kunrad Kvam in 1946 (discussed in Chapter 4) was the fact that Kvam deviated from time-honored cuts, bowings, and tempos. Prager's successor Walter Heermann continued to use the same shortened version until 1956.

MCMA and the Madison Vocational School

By the end of the second season in 1927–28, Sigfrid Prager had built a thriving orchestra and chorus. However, despite healthy ticket sales and solid community support, it was becoming clear that MCMA's programs and Prager's salary could not be sustained without additional outside support. As early as November 1927, the MCMA board was beginning to explore options for outside funding. One initial proposal was to approach Madison's school board about naming him the city's music director.[25] In February 1928, Susan Seastone reported that she had spoken with George Hambrecht, the state director of vocational education, about forging some sort of relationship with the City of Madison Vocational School (later Madison Area Technical College, and now Madison College). Then in March 1928, board president B. Q. Morgan reported that he had been in discussion with Alexander Graham, director of the Madison Vocational School, who was proposing to guarantee a $5000 annual salary for Prager. Prager would in turn become the superintendent of the school's musical activities.[26] Over the next few months the board cemented its relationship with the city by amending its bylaws to ensure that several civic officials would be automatically named to the board. Perhaps the most important of these additions were Alexander Graham, as an *ex officio* member, and George Hambrecht. Hambrecht would become MCMA's longest-serving board president, sharing the position with Prof. B. Q. Morgan in 1928–29, and then serving as president for the next eight seasons. The minutes of the annual meeting of May 1928 note that, while the budget was slightly in the red (income for the year was reported at $4359.25 and expenditures were $4510.80), the actual deficit was much more serious, as they owed Dr. Prager "about $1000.00" in salary.[27] MCMA's most pressing issue was in fact how to keep Prager in Madison. The $1000 annual salary and "gentleman's agreement" agreed upon in 1926 was clearly not enough, even when he supplemented this with work for the Madison Maennerchor and Luther Memorial Church. At its annual meeting in June, the board unanimously adopted a resolution that Prager be given a "guarantee of $4,000.00 for the year [1928–29], with a gentleman's agreement that it will be $5,000.00 if it is possible," though at that time it is not clear that MCMA actually had the funding to make such an offer.[28]

In July 1928, Hambrecht announced to the board that the Vocational School would be requesting an $8000 appropriation in their budget to support a music program, funds which would be used for Prager's salary and to fund MCMA's ensembles.[29] Financial problems continued in the 1928–29 season, despite this ray of hope. The deficit was increased by the fact that the board added several modestly paid positions: a part-time secretary (Florence Anderson, who would eventually be president of the board in the late 1940s), a music librarian, and additional instructors on oboe, bassoon, and bass. Another contributing factor seems to have been MCMA's decision to move its subscription concerts for that season to the newly built 2100-seat Capitol Theater. While this grand movie palace was certainly a much larger and more impressive venue than the Central High School Auditorium, it was also a for-profit enterprise, and rental of the hall and other associated costs proved to be more than the Association could handle. After three programs in the Capitol Theater, the final subscription program of that season was moved to the University Armory. The Capitol Theater, renovated as the Oscar Mayer Theatre, would eventually become the Madison Symphony Orchestra's home in 1980, but in 1928–29, it was beyond the reach of MCMA as a regular venue. MCMA used the equally large Orpheum for a single program in 1935 and staged a few concerts and several operas in the smaller Parkway Theatre (the former Fuller Opera House) during the 1930s. But after the 1928–29 season, the great majority of its programs were in venues that could be used at a lower cost to the MCMA—particularly Central High School and later the Masonic Temple Auditorium, but also at East and West High Schools, local churches, and—for its largest programs—the University Armory and Stock Pavilion.

2.04 George P. Hambrecht and Alexander R. Graham.

On November 27, 1928, Alexander Graham finally presented his formal Vocational School budget proposal for 1929–30 to the Madison City Council, which included $8000 to fund an expansion of music activities. In this ambitious proposal, $5000 would fund an annual salary for Prager, and the remainder would be used to cover the purchase of music, concert hall rentals, and other needs. The programs of MCMA would now come under the auspices of the Vocational School, with ticket revenue being returned to the city. Graham also proposed to form bands and orchestras around the city to train musicians for the Civic Symphony and a yet-to-be-organized Civic Band. (Though these "training groups" never materialized, the Madison Civic Band was in fact organized in 1930, under the direction of John L. Bach. It was also a Vocational School program, but it operated independently of MCMA.) Graham's music proposal met with stiff opposition from a few aldermen, and that part of the budget proposal was tabled.[30] The council finally took up the music proposal on December 21 and December 29, and after a rancorous debate, approved $5000 of Graham's proposed $8000.[31]

Though Prager began work at the Vocational School in 1929, the issue of his salary was not completely resolved for two years, after it became clear that his resignation and a permanent move to Chicago was a serious possibility. The situation was eventually resolved by securing for Prager a guaranteed salary of $4000: $3000 from the Vocational School and $1000 from MCMA. A final proposal was reported to the board in May 1931, whereby Prager would continue to live in Madison, maintaining his positions with MCMA and the Vocational School, and would have "one and one half days per week for Chicago work."[32] As for the musicians, they were expected to enroll as students in an adult education class in orchestra or chorus, costing $1.00 per semester. However, in 1936, Prager argued to the board that the $1.00 fee for players in the orchestra should be covered by the MCMA, noting that instrumentalists were responsible for upkeep of their own instruments and that the investment of time by orchestra members was much higher than that of the chorus. He further suggested that some orchestra members might be unable to pay the fee and would withdraw from the Madison Civic Symphony, and that this would "impair the artistic standard of the group." The board agreed.[33]

The effect of this initiative by Hambrecht and Graham went far beyond guaranteeing a salary for the MCMA's music director, however—quite simply, it *saved* the Madison Civic Music Association. It is unlikely that the Madison Civic Symphony and Madison Civic Chorus would have survived the coming years of the Depression without the stable institutional support offered by the Vocational School. From 1929 through 2007, the Vocational School (later Madison Area Technical College) continued to pay the largest portion of the music director's salary, but it also supported MCMA's work in many other ways. It offered rehearsal and office space, funded and housed the orchestra and chorus library, and provided innumerable types of administrative support. There are a few notes in the MSO archives that attest to a close working relationship and warm friendship between Prager and Graham. For his part, Graham was an unstinting advocate of the ideal of civic music, and he supported the activities of MCMA in countless ways. When Graham died in 1947, the orchestra paid tribute by playing Prager's own arrangement of the Sinfonia to Bach's "actus tragicus," *Cantata No. 106: Gottes Zeit is die allerbeste Zeit.*

Concerts of the 1930s

By the 1930–31 season, Civic Music had a built a firm foundation in the community, and throughout the Great Depression, the Vocational School's invaluable support created a financial safety net. Concerts were well attended, and local sponsorship allowed MCMA to reduce ticket prices several times. By 1940, most Civic Music concerts were free, and they remained free to the public until the middle 1960s. Prager continued to expand the number of orchestra and chorus concerts. The Civic Symphony had performed three concerts in each of its first two seasons, and the chorus performed twice in the second season. In 1930–31, the orchestra performed on four occasions, twice in combination with the chorus, and the chorus sang an additional concert of its own. By the end of the decade, the Civic Symphony and/or Chorus regularly performed six or seven times a season. Popular programs, particularly operas, were often repeated to allow for larger audiences. (MCMA had briefly experimented with routinely repeating *all* of its programs in 1929–30, but was not able to sustain this.)

2.05 Madison Civic Symphony and Chorus at an unidentified program in the Stock Pavilion in the early 1930s. Sigfrid Prager is standing at center in the back.

We really cannot talk about a "typical" Civic Symphony concert of the 1930s, since Prager seems to have aimed for variety. Relatively few of the orchestra's concerts resembled a typical symphony orchestra concert of today. On February 13, 1934, for example, the orchestra performed the following program:

>Mozart, *Overture to "The Marriage of Figaro"*
>Bach, *Concerto for Two Violins and Orchestra*
> (Marie Endres and George Szpinalski, violins)
>Beethoven, *Symphony No. 3, "Eroica"*
>Ferroni, *Spanish Rhapsody*
>Borodin, *In the Steppes of Central Asia*
>Wagner, *Prelude to "Die Meistersinger"*

This program included well over 90 minutes of music, and its first three works would probably satisfy today's audiences. In promoting the concert, local press made much of the fact that three of the works—by Bach, Beethoven, and Ferroni—had never been performed in Madison.[34]

In the early 1930s, the orchestra's repertoire relied heavily on tried and true orchestral warhorses. Works like *In the Steppes of Central Asia* would often appear twice a season, or several times in subsequent seasons.[35] The repertoire champion of these years was Brahms's *Hungarian Dance No. 5*, programmed seven times between 1927 and 1934. Throughout the decade, however, Prager gradually began to add more ambitious and challenging literature: Ravel's *Bolero* and Tchaikovsky's *Symphony No. 5* in 1935, Brahms's *Variations on a Theme by Haydn* in 1936, Rimsky-Korsakov's *Scheherazade* in 1937, and Strauss's *Death and Transfiguration* and Debussy's *Prelude to "The Afternoon of a Faun"* in 1938.

One of MCMA's stated goals at the beginning was that each concert would feature at least one work by an American composer, and its programs largely lived up to that pledge during its first three seasons. Table 2.1 lists works by American and local composers that were performed by the orchestra and chorus during the 1920s and 1930s.

Music by American and local composers featured prominently in the repertoire through about 1935, though the orchestra and chorus turned to more exclusively European repertoire over the course of the 1930s. As shown in Table 2.1, these works were frequently repeated from season to season as well. This list includes works by several of the most prominent American composers of the early 20th century: Charles Wakefield Cadman, John Alden Carpenter, John Knowles Paine, Horatio Parker, and Edward MacDowell. Movements from MacDowell's 1896 suite *Woodland Sketches* in particular were obviously favorites and appeared on several programs.

Table 2.1: Works by American and Local Composers on MCMA Programs, 1926 to 1939

Works (* = premier)	Date	Comments
Tom Dobson, *Yasmin* Avery Robinson, *Water Boy* John Alden Carpenter, *Don't Ceäre* Charles Wakefield Cadman, *Call Me No More*	12/14/1926	Set of American art songs performed at the Civic Orchestra's inaugural program.
B. Q. Morgan, *Hornpipe for String Instruments*	3/8/1927	UW–Madison faculty member.
Edward MacDowell, *"As Told at Sunset" from Woodland Sketches*	3/8/1927 11/11/1929 5/28/1930 4/26/1932 4/25/1933 2/19/1934 6/29/1935	
Henry Hadley, *Silhouettes*	5/31/1927 11/17/1931 12/11/1931	
Cecil Burleigh, *Evangeline**	11/15/1927 5/8/1928	Tone poem by a UW–Madison faculty member.
Charles Mills, *The Wreck of the Hesperus*	2/23/1928	Cantata by a UW–Madison faculty member, performed at the Civic Chorus's inaugural program.
John Knowles Paine, *The Tempest*	5/8/1928	
Horatio Parker, *A Song of Times*	5/22/1928 1/20/1929	
Emerson Whithorne, *"Pell Street" from Chinatown*	10/31/1928	
Edward MacDowell, *"To a Waterlily" from Woodland Sketches*	11/26/1928 4/26/1932 4/25/1933 2/19/1934	
George Gershwin, *Rhapsody in Blue*	2/6/1929 5/28/1929	Featuring Sigfrid Prager as piano soloist.
Sigfrid Prager, *Symphonic Suite, Op. 17**	2/3/1930 4/18/1933 4/25/1933 5/17/1933	MCMA music director. The first two movements were played in 1930, and the complete three-movement suite appeared in 1933.
Alexius Baas, *Flag of Our Fathers (A Tribute to Madison)**	4/14/1931 6/2/1932 5/27/1934	Local composer.

Sybil Hanks, *Decoration Day Hymn**	4/14/1931	Local composer, student of Prager.
Samuel Richard Gaines, *Out Where the West Begins*	4/14/1931 5/27/1934	
Laurence Powell, *Keltic Legend**	5/20/1931	Tone poem by a UW–Madison faculty member, dedicated to Prager.
Sybil Hanks, *Our Washington**	2/22–23/1931 10/16/1932 11/7/1932	Local composer, student of Prager.
Harvey Gaul, *I Hear America Singing*	2/23/1931	
Cecil Burleigh, *Two Sketches from the Orient*	4/8/1932	UW–Madison faculty member.
Alexius Baas, *O How Fair, How Pure Thy World**	5/3/1933	Local composer.
Sigfrid Prager, *The Message of Song**	10/16/1932 11/7/1932 5/17/1933 6/29/1935	MCMA music director.
Sigfrid Prager, *Pale Moon, an Indian Love Song**	4/18/1933	Art song by the MCMA music director.
Sybil Hanks, *Meditation**	5/1/1934	Local composer, student of Prager.
Carl Eppert, *The Argonauts of '49, Symphonic Epic*	4/26/1939	Milwaukee-based composer.
Charles O'Neill, *Romance** and *Suite Symphonique**	5/10/1939	UW–Madison faculty member.

Perhaps the most remarkable appearances of a work by a prominent American composer are Prager's two performances as piano soloist in Gershwin's *Rhapsody in Blue* in the spring of 1929. (Civic Orchestra bassoonist and Prager student Richard Church conducted.) This was less than six years after this groundbreaking work had premiered in New York City. Now it is a century old, and it is hard to conceive of a time when this was a controversial piece, but the *Rhapsody* was clearly enough of a stretch for the usual Madison Civic Symphony audience in 1929 that Prager felt obliged to publish an essay on the work in the *Wisconsin State Journal* two days before the February 6 concert, beginning

> Gershwin's "Rhapsody in Blue!" What a bewildering effect this work has had upon those who have heard it, and still more upon those who have never heard it, and yet give their opinion, mostly condemning. Unquestionably the topic "jazz" has embarrassed

many musicians and amateurs. Magazines and newspapers are full of interviews, discussion, and controversy, [yet] the general conception of jazz is still rather hazy. I have wrestled with the subject for quite a while and have formed some impressions. Take them for what they are worth. They are at least sincere.

Prager goes on to condemn the "vulgarity" of most commercial jazz, but defends the idea of embellishing a melody in a new style, pointing to "Beethoven, Wagner and other masters of the past who did not think it below their dignity to jazz up their tunes in order to tell their audiences something unusual." He then gives a straightforward critique, pointing out both attractive and uninspired features of the *Rhapsody*. Prager ends with a call for hearing the work with an open mind:

> If our public can make up its mind to listen to the Wednesday concert without prejudice I am certain that it will detect plenty of things to enjoy. And if some features produce bewilderment, the public should not forget that all originality is bewildering until we become accustomed to it.[36]

Prager needn't have worried: If the reviews published following the concert by Katharine Hartman Axley of the *Journal* and Lester Velie of the *Capital Times* are any indication, the Madison audience loved the work, and Prager and the orchestra actually repeated part of the *Rhapsody* as an encore. Gershwin's *Rhapsody in Blue* was repeated in full "by popular demand" at a Popular Concert on May 28.

Several local composers also appeared on programs by the orchestra and chorus, including five University faculty members: B. Q. Morgan, Charles Mills, Cecil Burleigh, Laurence Powell, and Charles O'Neill. As noted above, this may in part have been an effort by Prager to maintain good relations with the University School of Music, but there was also a clear civic pride in presenting local compositions. Other local composers included Prager's friend and frequent collaborator Alexius Baas and Prager's composition student Sybil Hanks. (Hanks and her music are discussed in Chapter 3.) Their compositions typically appeared as part of the large-scale

2.06 George Gershwin, 1937.

springtime Civic Music Festivals. The list also includes three works by Prager himself. Prager came to know the Milwaukee-based composer and conductor Carl Eppert through his work directing the WPA-sponsored Wisconsin Symphony Orchestra during the late 1930s. Prager directed the premiere of Eppert's *The Argonauts of '49*, a symphonic poem inspired by the California gold rush, with the Wisconsin Symphony Orchestra in February 1938.[37]

Civic Music Festivals and Other Extravaganzas

Programs performed by the Madison Civic Symphony and Chorus regularly included what might best be described as "extravaganzas"—huge programs that often featured nearly 20 works and included several local groups and soloists. These programs, frequently extending to well over three hours, were often hosted in the largest spaces available in Madison at the time, particularly two University venues: the Stock Pavilion and the newly constructed (1930) Field House. These concerts were generally unlike the programs typically performed by modern symphony orchestras today, though the MSO's current long-standing holiday concert tradition, "A Madison Symphony Christmas," is clearly in the same spirit.

The most prominent tradition of large-scale concerts sponsored by the MCMA were the Civic Music Festivals of the 1930s. The first festival concert was staged on May 28, 1930, in the newly constructed Eastwood Theater on Madison's near east side.[38] By the standards of later festival concerts, this was a relatively modest affair, involving about 170 performers from the Civic Symphony and Chorus, the Grace Presbyterian Boys Choir, and several local soloists. The repertoire for both the orchestra and the chorus was largely recycled from works performed over the course of the 1929–30 season. The orchestra performed works by Boieldieu, Mozart, MacDowell, and Bizet, and the Grace boys sang a folksong arrangement by Kremser. Violinist George Szpinalski, accompanied by Prager at the piano, performed solo works by Massenet and Wieniawski. For its part, the chorus reprised Parts I and III of Handel's *Judas Maccabeus*, the oratorio it had been gradually perfecting over the previous year. The oratorio featured six local soloists, including Prager's wife, soprano Frances Silva.

The Madison Civic Music Festival in April 1931 was staged in the much larger Stock Pavilion, and it was a much more ambitious program, featuring some 16 works. The Civic Symphony and Chorus were joined by the Civic Band, under the direction of John L. Bach, four local choirs—the Madison Maennerchor, the Grieg Male Chorus, the Mozart Club, and the East Side Civic Chorus—

and several local soloists. Each of the guest ensembles performed a feature selection, and several works featured the massed choirs. The program also featured premieres of two works by Madison composers. It opened with a new choral work by Alexius Baas, *Flag of Our Fathers (A Tribute to Madison)*. The other was a choral setting of a Longfellow poem by Prager's composition student Sybil Hanks, her *Decoration Day Hymn*. The program was clearly a spectacular success, with well over 300 musicians performing to an enthusiastic crowd estimated at 3000.[39] The reviews and letters to the editor published in the two local newspapers following the concert testify to a real sense of civic pride in Madison's musical accomplishments.

The April 1931 concert clearly set the pattern for Civic Music Festivals to follow. In May 1932, the concert opened with another newly composed choral work by Baas, *O How Fair, How Pure Thy World*. The finale was the *Polovtsian Dances* from Borodin's *Prince Igor*, performed by the massed choir, accompanying a ballet by the Madison Civic Ballet. This last group, led by local dancer Leonore Johnson, would also appear in some of the early MCMA opera productions. The festival took a different approach in October 1932, recast as the Dane County Music Festival, with the purpose of bringing in singers from around the county. Recruitment began in the late spring of 1932, and in June, Madison funeral director E. N. Gunderson announced that he would award a large silver and gold loving cup to the adult civic chorus that sent the most members.[40] The recruiting efforts were clearly successful, and in October, Prager led a 400-voice choir that included the Madison Civic Chorus, singers from other Madison choirs, and from 17 additional towns from across Dane County. Prager's *The Message of Song* was written specifically for the event and was the opening choral number.

2.07 Madison Civic Music Festival, May 3, 1932.

In May 1933, the concert was staged in the enormous University Field House as the Madison Vocational School Music Festival. As in October 1932, the choir was comprised of the Madison Civic Chorus and guest choirs from Madison and Dane County performing together in a massed 600-voice Festival Choir. This concert was coordinated with the annual Wisconsin school music contest in Madison. The audience, including several hundred public school music students from around the state, was estimated at 7000—by far the largest crowd for any MCMA concert to date.[41] The next concert in the series, now simply called Spring Festival, was staged in the West High School Auditorium in May 1934. This was much more of a patchwork affair, with individual performances by the Civic Choir, Maennerchor, Grieg Chorus, Mozart Club, and East Side Civic Chorus, and just a few massed choir works. The Civic Symphony did not perform on this program, and instrumental accompaniment was provided by the American Legion Band, directed by John Bach. The May 1935 festival at the Stock Pavilion was once again a feature for the "Dane County Civic Chorus," which may have topped 1000 voices for this program.

There was not a festival in 1936—hardly surprising, as Prager and the Civic Symphony and Chorus were involved in Verdi's *Requiem* and a staged production of *Samson and Delilah* in April and May. There also does not seem to have been a festival in 1937, quite possibly because of an ambitious all-Wagner program mounted by the orchestra and chorus on May 4. The last two Civic Music Festivals, in May 1938 and May 1939, were staged in the Masonic Temple Auditorium. The 1938 festival was in the by-then familiar mold, with four guest choruses—the Maennerchor, Grieg Chorus, and Mozart Club, and the newly formed Labor Temple Glee Club—and including a few large works for massed male voices. University professor Charles O'Neill conducted the Civic Symphony in the premier of two of his short orchestral works. Prager led the orchestra in the *Overture to "La dame blanche"* and a rather cheesy novelty piece, *A Hunt in the Black Forest*, and conducted the Madison Civic Chorus in a chorus from Mendelssohn's *Elijah*, which it had performed in full earlier that spring. The large massed choir pieces were led by the Civic Symphony's newly appointed assistant conductor, John L. Bach, and they included Bach's own arrangement of several sentimental "old folks" songs for the chorus and orchestra. The program also included a cornet solo by S. E. Mears, from Whitewater, Wisconsin, accompanied on piano by Prager. The 1939 festival took a somewhat different approach, which represented a step away from the exclusively "civic" nature of earlier programs. While it included a couple of large massed choir works, the real focus of this program was a series of highlights from Bizet's *Carmen* that appeared in the second half, presented by five soloists, with the chorus and orchestra, and ballet scenes designed by local dancer Hazel Conlon. As in the staged opera productions mounted by MCMA in the 1930s, the lead roles were taken by a mixture of Chicago-based professionals (soprano Ruth Heizer, tenor David Johnson, and baritone Edward Stack) and local amateurs (sopranos Viola Wahler and Gertrude Ziebarth).

There was originally a Civic Music Festival scheduled for late May 1940, but on May 16 the Vocational School's Alexander Graham announced that it would be rescheduled to October.[42] The program never happened, however, and after this point, the decade-long tradition of Civic Music Festivals seems quietly to have lapsed, and it never resumed during the wartime years and afterwards.

MCMA briefly sponsored a parallel holiday festival concert series as well. In December 1931, perhaps inspired by the success of the April 1931 Civic Music Festival, MCMA sponsored a Yuletide Music Festival at Christ Presbyterian Church featuring the same four guest choirs as in April—the Maennerchor, the Grieg Chorus, the Mozart Club, and the East Side Civic Chorus—accompanied by a Festival Band comprised of the woodwind, brass, and percussion players from the Civic Symphony. The centerpiece of this program was a series of excerpts from Bach's *Christmas Oratorio* performed by the Civic Chorus and local soloists. A second, very similar Yuletide Music Festival was staged in December 1932, though at this concert, most of the Civic Music contributions were conducted by John L. Bach, with Prager leading only a couple of choruses from *Messiah*, and the final work, an arrangement of *O Come, All Ye Faithful* sung by the massed choirs and four soloists. The Yuletide Music Festival lasted only two years, and from 1933 onward, MCMA began the tradition of annual December performances of *Messiah*.

The extravaganzas discussed so far were all sponsored under the auspices of MCMA and the Vocational School, but the Civic Symphony and Chorus also performed in a few large-scale programs sponsored by other groups. Certainly the largest concerts they were involved in during the 1930s were a pair of gargantuan Norwegian "Sangerfest" programs staged in the University Field House on June 2–3, 1932. Throughout the late 19th and early 20th centuries, amateur choirs were a popular way of expressing ethnic pride and maintaining cultural connections with the old country for many immigrant groups. Madison's Maennerchor, founded in 1852, was among the oldest German singing societies in Wisconsin. The more recent Scandinavian immigrants to Wisconsin also followed the tradition of choral singing, and there were Norwegian, Swedish, and Finnish choirs throughout the state. Madison's Grieg Chorus had been founded in 1925, mostly by first-generation Norwegian immigrants, as the Grieg Mannskor (Grieg Men's Chorus) and was directed by Alexius Baas. In June 1932, the Madison group had the honor of serving as host to the 20th biannual Sangerfest of the Norwegian Singers' Association of

Concerts in the "Red Gym" and the "Cow Barn"

One University building that served as a primary musical venue in early 20th-century Madison is the hulking University Armory—better known today as the Red Gym—that stands next to the Memorial Union. After the destruction of the first University gymnasium by fire in 1891, University President Chamberlin and the Regents agreed on a building that would fulfill a dual purpose as a gymnasium and the university's armory. The Armory (alternatively known as the Men's Gymnasium) formally opened on September 17, 1894. The architecture of this building, with crenellated towers and rounded arches throughout the exterior making it look like a Norman fortress brooding on the shore of Lake Mendota, reflected the political concerns of the age. The 1880s and 1890s saw severe labor unrest in America and episodes of anarchist violence, and one response across the country was to build armories that could serve as headquarters for troops should they be needed to put down uprisings. The University Armory, thankfully, never served this purpose—even during the years of student protests on the campus in the late 1960s and early 1970s—but it did house the University's Military Studies department and Reserve Officer Training Corps (ROTC) programs through the 1960s. (A firebombing aimed at the ROTC Office in January 1970 caused extensive damage.)

2.08 The University Armory (Red Gym) in 1898.

The military purposes of the building also made it suitable as the University's primary assembly and indoor athletic venue, with broad stairways intended to accommodate marching troops also providing easy public access to the second floor. President Chamberlin's successor, Charles K. Adams, insisted upon several design changes before the building was completed, including the creation of a large space on the second floor unbroken by stairways or support columns—the original design had actually sited the building's boilers in this space. The second floor was intended to provide space for military drills, but it also created what was then the largest public venue in Madison, with a seating capacity of over 2200 that was twice as large as both the Fuller Opera House and the Central High School Auditorium. (The gigantic Lakeside Assembly Auditorium was larger still but was usable only during summers.) The Armory hosted intercollegiate basketball games and gymnastics, but it also became a musical venue, particularly for large-scale events—both concerts with a large group of performers and those that were likely to draw large audiences. In the 1890s and 1900s, for example, it hosted several ambitious concerts by the Madison Choral Union, as well as the largest events of the period, such as the gargantuan War Song Jubilee of 1898, the equally large Homecoming Concert of 1907, which featured a 500-voice choir, and the 1913 Yuletide Festival of Song, with a choir of 200 and a 60-piece orchestra. Its size made it a valuable venue for visiting star performers as well. (It was also undoubtedly cheaper to stage large events there than at the much more elegant, but distinctly for-profit Fuller Opera House.) Thus, the Armory was the venue for violin virtuosos Eugène Ysaÿe in 1904 and Mischa Elman and Jascha Heifetz in the 1920s; it also hosted pianists Ossip Gabrilowitsch (1909), Ignacy Paderewski (1912), and Harold Bauer (1914). During the same period, the Armory also played host to some of the era's greatest singers: Lillian Nordica, Ernestine Schumann-Heink, Nellie Melba, Albert Quesnel, Johanna Gadski, Alessandro Bonci, and others. Composer Ruggero Leoncavallo conducted a program by the La Scala Orchestra and several vocal soloists there in 1906, and in 1912 Arthur Nikisch conducted the London Symphony Orchestra at the Armory. During the period 1912 to

1925, the Madison Orchestral Association sponsored concerts there by the Chicago Symphony Orchestra, Minneapolis Symphony Orchestra, Detroit Symphony Orchestra, Cincinnati Symphony Orchestra, and New York Philharmonic. Beginning in 1929, Sigfrid Prager led a few Madison Civic Music concerts at the Armory as well, the last of these a performance of Handel's *Messiah* on December 22, 1940. In the 1920s, the Armory's role as a large music venue was increasingly taken over by an even bigger building, the Stock Pavilion, and in 1930 intercollegiate athletics moved to the newly completed Field House. The University Armory has survived several planned demolitions over the past 70 years and remains a landmark today, but its heyday as a musical venue is long past.[43]

Even in the first couple of decades of the 20th century, when the Armory hosted dozens of musical performances, Madison audiences were well aware of its drawbacks as a music hall. The Armory's second floor was of course designed first and foremost as a gymnasium rather than a performance space, and there were occasionally complaints in the local press about its acoustics. In March 1914, Frederick Stock, conductor of the Chicago Symphony Orchestra, complained after one of their performances in the space, expressing his surprise that a large university town like Madison had no better public space to host large cultural events. He noted that the University's Stock Pavilion was Madison's best large hall, a fact that "showed how much more we valued swine breeding than music."[44] Madison's long, politically tortuous quest for a real public auditorium would in fact last until the opening of the Madison Civic Center in 1980; it would not be satisfactorily resolved until the building of Overture Hall in 2004.

In 1866, the Wisconsin state legislature named the University of Wisconsin the state's land grant college. Under the terms of the Morrill Act of 1862, this brought much-needed federal funding (which seems to have been partly misappropriated by the legislature), but it also entailed the creation of a College of Agriculture, and later a College of Engineering and maintenance of a ROTC program. Several buildings were erected to support the agriculture program, but the grandest of

2.09 The University Stock Pavilion in 1930.

these opened in 1909, the Stock Pavilion. A large and elegant structure in half-timbered Tudor Revival style, the Stock Pavilion was designed to house popular horse and cattle shows in Madison and also to serve the annual Farmer's Course hosted by the University each winter. With a seating capacity of 3500, it was the largest year-round indoor venue of any kind in Madison, and it remained so until the completion of the University Field House in 1930. Most of the Stock Pavilion is taken up by a central dirt arena, 66 by 164 feet, surrounded by cement bleachers. While the space was clearly designed for agriculture, it quickly became apparent that the building's acoustics were marvelous. A large elongated space, with wooden walls and ceiling, a hard-packed dirt floor, and no proscenium arch or large flyspace to absorb sound, its acoustics are magnificently suited to choral and orchestral music. In an interview with Roland Johnson conducted in 2004, as the Madison Symphony Orchestra was preparing to open its new home in Overture Hall, Johnson noted: "Madison will be lucky if the new Overture Hall sounds that good."[45] (Though it has not been used for musical performances for many years, I attended one of the last classical concerts held there, a performance of the Verdi *Requiem* by the University Choral Union in the 1980s, and I can attest to the remarkably clear and warm acoustics of the building.)

2.10 The Madison Symphony Orchestra performing in the Stock Pavilion on October 3, 1969.

Size alone would have made the Stock Pavilion significant in Madison, and it quickly became one of the city's most important venues for its largest events. Both William Jennings Bryan and Theodore Roosevelt gave speeches there in the 1910s, but it became even more important as a musical venue. The first significant musical performance there was on October 3, 1917, at a patriotic event that featured U.S. Secretary of the Treasury James McAdoo, speaking on war plans following America's recent entry into the war in Europe. The "Jackies" band of the U.S. Great Lakes Naval Training Station played a concert before McAdoo's speech. This band had been trained by John Philip Sousa, who, though he was too old for regular military service, had volunteered as an officer in the Naval Reserve at the outbreak of war.[46] (The Jackies would return to the Stock Pavilion six months later for a second concert on April 21, 1918.[47]) Just a few weeks after the McAdoo event, on October 21, 1917, a public sermon by the fiery Chicago preacher Frank Gunsaulus included a "choir of 500."[48] In 1926, the Madison Orchestral Association staged its last two programs there, by the Minneapolis Symphony Orchestra and the Chicago Civic Orchestra. These were only the first of many great touring orchestras that performed in the space; there were later performances by the Chicago Symphony Orchestra, the London Symphony Orchestra, the Cleveland Orchestra, the New

York Philharmonic, and the Philadelphia Orchestra and others.[49] It also hosted solo performances by Ignacy Paderewski, Amelita Galli-Curci, Sergei Rachmaninoff, Marian Anderson, and other classical stars. It would be a particularly important venue in the early history of Madison Civic Music—in the 1930s, Sigfrid Prager annually staged musical extravaganzas at the Stock Pavilion, featuring enormous choirs, orchestra, and dancers. Prager also used the Stock Pavilion for concerts that would draw a large audience, as in 1946, when he was able to engage the soprano Marjorie Lawrence. Prager's farewell concert, a performance of Beethoven's *Missa solemnis* on May 23, 1948, was held in the hall as well. His successor Walter Heermann never staged a concert there, but Roland Johnson led 11 programs at the Stock Pavilion, including concerts featuring soprano Eileen Farrell (1969 and 1975), tenor Richard Tucker (1972), and pianists Van Cliburn (1971) and Claudio Arrau (1979). The final appearance in the Stock Pavilion by the Madison Symphony Orchestra and Chorus was on December 1, 1979, a performance of Mendelssohn's *Elijah*.

While the Stock Pavilion was acoustically suited to classical music, it was not a particularly comfortable place in which to play and listen. Dozens of reviews over the years in the local papers commented with embarrassment over the fact that first-rate concert artists and orchestras were performing in a "cow barn," complaining of the stifling heat in the summer and ineffective and noisy heating in the winter, and of the noise from nearby railroad tracks (and occasionally from livestock housed in the building's basement). George Shook, emeritus professor in the University Animal Sciences Department and a member of the Madison Symphony Chorus since 1966, recalled one performance where the outside noise was more humorous than annoying:

> My wife and I fondly remember a performance by the New York Philharmonic conducted by Seiji Ozawa in the Stock Pavilion [on September 18, 1969]. They were playing a light and lively piece as a train came down the nearby railroad track and did a short, quick "toot toot" in exact tempo with the music. The conductor

> and many musicians could not contain their composure and ultimately interrupted the performance laughing.[50]
>
> Seating on the floor and for musicians was on butt-numbing metal folding chairs, and seating in the cement bleachers was no more comfortable. Betty Bielefeld, who played flute in the Madison Symphony Orchestra for 50 years, recalled one program where bats circled the orchestra for the entire concert. And the ever-present sound and smell of farm animals made it impossible to forget that the Stock Pavilion was not really intended as a concert venue. This was especially apparent during Eileen Farrell's first visit to Madison in October 1969, recalled Johnson. When the orchestra arrived for the dress rehearsal, they found that someone had neglected to move a large wagon filled with ripe manure. (According to Johnson, "stinking to high heaven.") When Farrell arrived, Johnson apologized profusely about the smell. She was a consummate professional about the whole thing until she started to giggle uncontrollably during the first aria, eventually breaking down completely. Her comment: "At least my vocal cords are being well-fertilized."[51]

America, an event that involved some 34 men's choirs from across the Midwest and Canada. The Sangarfest kicked off with a parade around the Capitol square by the uniformed choirs on the morning of Thursday, June 2, and culminated with concerts in the Stock Pavilion on Thursday and Friday evenings, both of them featuring a massed choir of over 1000 voices, including the men of the Madison Civic Chorus.[52] Overall direction of the event was by Frederick Wick, a noted choir director and choral composer and arranger from Minneapolis. The featured soloist both nights was Nora Fauchald, former soprano soloist for the Sousa Band (often billed as the "Norwegian nightingale"), who reportedly charmed the audience by singing some of her numbers in Norwegian traditional costume. The Madison Civic Symphony accompanied the massed choir pieces and played several pieces on its own under Prager's direction: orchestral works by Grieg, Sinding, and Frederick Wick. The repertoire for these two three-hour programs was of course largely Norwegian choral works, though Fauchald also sang operatic arias by Mozart and Wagner, and the Friday program included Baas's *Flag of Our Fathers (A Tribute to Madison)*, which had been written for the April 1931 Madison Civic Music Festival. The Thursday night program was broadcast throughout the United States and Europe over the NBC radio network.[53] Nine years later, on May 31, 1941, the Civic Symphony and Chorus took part in a much smaller Norwegian Sangarfest (this one involving only about 200 singers), which was staged in the Masonic Temple Auditorium.

2.11 Madison Civic Symphony and a massed choir of more than 1000 at a Norwegian concert in the University Field House on June 2, 1932.

MCMA's groups also took part in expressions of German cultural pride. As noted above, one of the concerts performed by the Madison Civic Symphony during its inaugural season was a program celebrating the 75th anniversary of Madison Maennerchor, a group that Prager was also directing at that time. In June 1934 the Madison Maennerchor, now under the direction of Alexius Baas, served as host to the Saengerfest of the Ost-Wisconsin Saengerbund (East Wisconsin Singing Society) for the first time since 1881. While not quite as large as the Norwegian festival of 1932, this was every bit as elaborate a program, featuring a massed choir of about 500 voices. The soloist for the evening was Madison-born Karl Fischer-Niemann, a tenor who had enjoyed a major career with the Vienna State Opera and other European companies. Prager, who spent the summer of 1935 as a guest lecturer at Stanford University, was not involved in this concert (though his *The Message of Song* was on the program). Overall direction was by Alexius Baas, and the Civic Symphony accompanied most of the choral selections. Richard Church conducted the Civic Symphony in its features, works by MacDowell and Wagner. Once again, the program was broadcast nationally over the NBC radio network.[54]

MCMA's tradition of large-scale festival programs seems to have faded away during the first years of World War II, but beginning in 1943, the University began hosting an annual weeklong springtime music festival involving guest artists and orchestras, University groups, and the Madison Civic Symphony and Chorus. Between 1943 and 1950, several of MCMA's May programs—most often involving a large choral work—were presented as part of the festival. The grand Music Festival programs were a major focus for MCMA during the 1930s—a clear expression of the idealistic civic model that guided MCMA during this period, bringing together musicians from several local groups to make music separately and collectively. It is clear from the large audiences that these festivals attracted, and from the reactions of reviewers and local citizens, that they were also sources of great civic pride.

MCMA-Sponsored Opera in the 1930s

Sigfrid Prager came from the world of opera—he worked primarily as an opera and operetta conductor in Europe, Argentina, and New York City before arriving in Madison in 1926—and it is hardly surprising that he arranged opera productions as soon as the MCMA could manage to support them. Among the most ambitious performances sponsored by Civic Music in these years were the fully staged productions of seven operas between 1932 and 1938:

- Gounod, *Faust* (December 9–10, 1932)
- Bizet, *Carmen* (November 10–11, 1933, and January 6, 1934)
- Verdi, *Il Trovatore* (November 9–10, 1934)
- Saint-Saëns, *Samson and Delilah* (three different productions: March 19, 1935 [concert version], November 14–15, 1935, and May 2–3, 1936)
- Verdi, *La Traviata* (November 23–24, 1936)
- Puccini, *Madame Butterfly* (December 1–2, 1937)
- Smetana, *The Bartered Bride* (November 1–2, 1938)

Staged opera and operetta was of course nothing new in Madison in the 1930s: As detailed in Chapter 1, there was a long tradition of traveling professional opera companies, and also local amateur opera, dating back to a production of *Der Peter in der Fremde* in 1866 by Madison's German community. However, these productions by the MCMA represent the first systematic and sustained attempt to produce grand opera locally and regularly. There are, unfortunately, no board minutes surviving from the 1932–33, 1933–34, 1934–35, and 1935–36 seasons, so it is unclear what support MCMA offered at the beginning.

The opening production of the series was *Faust*, in December 1932. Like all of the MCMA productions, this was a collaboration between local musicians and Chicago-based professionals, in this case the Chicago Festival Opera Company, an ensemble that was active throughout the Midwest in the 1930s and early 1940s. As Prager explained when the opera was announced in the *Capital Times* on September 18:

> The Festival Opera Co. is a most unique organization. They specialize in giving the larger grand operas, in English, in conjunction with the choruses, orchestras, and ballets in the various cities where they perform. They bring illustrious cast, complete and beautiful scenery and other equipment, including their own technical staff.[55]

Though it was presented under the auspices of MCMA, and used the Civic Symphony, Civic Chorus, and a newly organized Madison Civic Ballet, *Faust* was designed to be largely self-supporting. Board president George Hambrecht noted in the same article that MCMA would not be approaching local businesses for support, and that the best tickets would be at a premium $1.50. Perhaps with the memory of the financial problems caused by using the Capitol Theater in 1928–29 still fresh, MCMA chose not to stage the opera in the Capitol or the New Orpheum, the two large theaters on State Street. They opted instead for the more modest 1200-seat Parkway Theatre (the former Fuller Opera House), which had an orchestra pit and a stage large enough to accommodate the production. While Prager was the overall director, Alexius Baas assisted with stage direction, and the ballet sequences were directed by Lenore Johnson, a local dancer and dance teacher, who collaborated in several MCMA projects. The lead roles were all sung by members of the Chicago Festival Opera: Lucie Western (Marguerite), Edwin Kemp (Faust), Kai de Vermond (Mephistopheles), William Philips (Valentine), Rex Cushing (Wagner), and Eileen Hutton (Seibel and Martha). In all, between the professional singers, members of the Civic Chorus, the Civic Symphony, and the ballet corps of 11 dancers, nearly 200 people were involved in the production. *Faust* was a rousing success, playing to near-capacity crowds, as reported in glowing reviews in both local papers.

2.12 Scene from the MCMA production of *Faust*, December 1932.

The 1932 *Faust* set the pattern for a successful series of opera productions over the next few years, all staged in the Parkway: From 1933 until 1938, the MCMA mounted a staged opera every year in November or early December.

In November 1933 it was *Carmen*, whose two performances were so successful that it was repeated with the same cast on January 6, 1934, with matinee and evening performances on the same day. In November 1934, MCMA presented *Il Trovatore*.

These first three operas were all very much on the same model, collaborations between the Chicago Festival Opera and Civic Music's chorus, orchestra, and ballet. However in 1935, MCMA's productions began to take on a more local character. The next opera was *Samson and Delilah*, which Prager introduced in a stepwise fashion. In March 1935, the usual spring chorus concert was devoted to a concert version of the opera, presented in a streamlined version, with piano accompaniment by Margaret Otterson. Prager engaged two professionals to sing the title roles: Madison-based tenor Karl Fischer-Niemann and Chicago-based mezzo-soprano Mari Barova, with whom Prager had worked when he directed the Chicago Bach Chorus. (Both of these singers would appear in later opera and oratorio performances in Madison.) The other two roles in this concert were taken by local singers Alexius Baas and Harold Leutscher. This was clearly a warm-up for the staged *Samson and Delilah* in November 1935, when it was produced at the Parkway with full orchestral accompaniment. Barova and Fischer-Niemann returned in the title roles, and Chicago-based baritone Frederick Jencks replaced Baas as the High Priest of Dagon. All of the other roles were sung by local amateurs drawn from the Civic Chorus. During this period, Prager was also directing the Sheboygan Civic Chorus, and in May 1936 he led yet a *third* production of *Samson and Delilah*, again fully staged, using the chorus, and soloists from the Sheboygan group, together with Barova, Fischer-Niemann, and Baas in the leads.

This new model—a few, mostly Chicago-based professional leads with an otherwise local cast and chorus—would continue through the rest of the fall opera productions in the 1930s: *La Traviata* (1936), *Madame Butterfly* (1937), and *The Bartered Bride* (1938). These productions occasionally involved other Madison groups as well, as in the 1936 *La Traviata*, where the offstage *banda* passages were provided by the West High School band.[56] Following *La Traviata*, there seems to have been a suggestion that the operas might carry on entirely with local talent, but Prager stressed to the MCMA board the need to have a few "name" soloists to help with marketing and ticket sales, and the board agreed.[57]

The opera performances of the 1930s were clearly the most elaborate productions sponsored by the MCMA during the 1930s. The series quietly ended after the 1938 *Bartered Bride*, however. This may have been due partly to expense and smaller audiences for some of the later operas, but the primary

> ### The Madison Opera Guild
>
> The cause of staged opera in Madison was taken up briefly at the end of the 1930s by the Madison Opera Guild, a group founded by local soprano and singing teacher Maude DeVoe. The group was initially created in 1937 to assist Prager in training the chorus for MCMA's *Madame Butterfly*,[58] but eventually it sponsored opera and operetta productions of its own, beginning in March 1938 with a double bill of Delibes' *Lakme* and Debussy's cantata *The Prodigal Son* (the latter staged as a one-act opera). This was produced in Turner Hall under the direction of Richard Church, who by this time, was the band director at West High School. The Madison Opera Guild's productions were much more modest than the elaborate stagings of MCMA; they were sung exclusively by local amateurs and University students and were typically accompanied by piano or a small chamber group. In addition to several "opera nights," with collections of arias and short scenes, they staged *Lakme* two more times, Flotow's *Martha*, and Mascagni's *Cavalleria Rusticana*, but the Madison Opera Guild seems to have disbanded after 1940. (Note that it is not to be confused with the later Madison Civic Opera Guild—predecessor of today's Madison Opera—founded in 1962.)

reason was probably Prager's schedule. Always busy, he became increasingly involved in work for the WPA-sponsored Wisconsin Symphony Orchestra in Milwaukee between 1938 and 1941, and he no longer had the time to prepare staged opera. (He also resigned as director of the Sheboygan Civic Chorus in early 1938.) MCMA would not return to staging operas until the early 1960s, after the arrival of Roland and Arline Johnson.

Civic Music and the Local Press

Madison's two daily newspapers may have been political rivals, but they were firmly united in supporting MCMA's activities during the early years. The *Capital Times* and *Wisconsin State Journal* both championed the cause of Civic Music on their editorial pages, and they provided free publicity for concerts.

Prager clearly had a good relationship with longtime reviewers William Doudna and Katharine Hartman Axley of the *State Journal*, and Lester Velie and Sterling Sorenson of the *Capital Times*—they would occasionally comment negatively on works and individual soloists, but in general reviews were quite enthusiastic. Beginning in the 1940s, Alexius Baas also joined the staff of the *Capital Times*, contributing a weekly column and other articles, and he frequently wrote reviews and commentary about Prager and MCMA's current activities.

The press also devoted a great deal of space to concerts *before* they happened. A fairly typical example of local news coverage is what appeared in the *Wisconsin State Journal* for a May 1, 1934, concert. A typical Civic Music extravaganza of the period, this was a program that must have lasted over three and a half hours, featuring a series of three orchestral works and two extended multi-movement ballets performed by the Leonore Johnson Ballet. The orchestral pieces included Smetana's *Bartered Bride Overture*, the premiere of Sybil Hanks's *Meditation*, and Brahms's *Violin Concerto*, with Arthur Kreutz as soloist. The ballets included *Sleeping Beauty Retold*, a 22-scene version of the familiar fairy tale for Johnson's younger dancers, and *Divertissement*, which featured the adult dancers of the company dancing to music by Bizet.[59] The *Journal* began its coverage on Sunday, April 15, some two and a half weeks before the concert, with a two-column piece titled "Concert-Ballet Program to Write New Page in Civic Music History" that briefly described the orchestral pieces and the ballets. A week later, a second article provided a detailed description of the scenario for *Sleeping Beauty Retold* and listed all 75 dancers involved. On Sunday, April 29, the *Journal*'s coverage focused on the orchestral pieces, but it also included a large photo of the principal child dancers. Monday, April 30, saw another small notice in the *Journal*, and on the day of the concert, page 1 of the paper featured the banner headline "Ballet, Symphony Concert in West High Auditorium at 8:15 Tonight" above the paper's masthead. Tuesday's paper also included three more photos (Prager, Hanks, and another one of the lead dancers) and a brief description of the concert, with special attention to the Hanks premiere. Finally, Katharine Hartman Axley published a detailed and complimentary review the next day.

The relationship between the MCMA and the local press went well beyond mere promotion. Concert repertoire would change constantly; the orchestra would program pieces as they were ready, and it was not at all unusual through the early 1940s for programs and even dates to change drastically from what had been announced earlier in the season. Articles in the *State Journal* and *Capital Times* would keep Madisonians abreast of these changes and would even comment on the orchestra's current rehearsals. The Sunday arts pages in the papers also helped promote a more general interest in music and published essays of general interest. While some of these seem a bit mawkish or even racist by today's standards (in August 1926, for example, the *Wisconsin State Journal* published an essay titled "Negro Chants, Spirituals, Melodies show Tragedy, Whimsicality of a Race"[60]), there was a generally high tone to most of the music journalism of the day. Prager himself contributed often to the local papers, writing on the value of civic music and music education in the schools, providing extensive program notes for upcoming concerts, providing more general descriptions of composers and works, and even discussing jazz.

2.13 *Wisconsin State Journal*, May 1, 1934, page 1.

Musicians of the Orchestra and Chorus: Selected Profiles

The next chapter will be devoted to the biography of Sigfrid Prager, first music director of the Madison Civic Music Association. This chapter concludes with brief profiles of a few of the other musicians in the orchestra and chorus during the 1920s and 1930s, and a somewhat more extensive biography of concertmaster Marie Endres.

Marvin Hartman

In November 2020, a pair of artifacts surfaced that turned out to have connections with one of the early members of the Madison Civic Symphony. Nathan Moy, a drummer and drum collector from California, purchased a vintage snare drum on eBay. His primary interest was the drum itself, a Leedy Elite 5" × 14" black nickel-plated and engraved snare drum dating from the early 1930s— according to Moy, "one of the fanciest models that company manufactured."[61] However, the two original calfskin drum heads both had inscriptions that led him to contact the Madison Symphony Orchestra and share photographs. The

J. MICHAEL ALLSEN

2.14-2.17 The Hartman drum heads, with details.

two details above show that the drum belonged to Marvin F. Hartman, and that he was connected to the Madison Civic Symphony. In the detail at the lower left, the venues match up with concerts that the Madison Civic Symphony and Civic Chorus performed that season. The radio towers are probably a reference to the fact that the "International Sangarfest" concert that the orchestra and chorus performed on June 2, 1932, was broadcast throughout the United States and Europe, and that other concerts were occasionally broadcast live on local channels WISJ, WIBA, and WHA. In the other detail, Hartman's drawing of the Greek mask of comedy is surrounded by the words "Opera, Band, Symphony, Dance"—a reference to the various activities that the Madison Civic Music Association and the Vocational School sponsored in 1934.

Of course, the most striking aspect of these drumheads is the signatures. Hartman decided to use his drum has a kind of autograph book, a fact that drew the attention of the *Capital Times*, which reported in October 1932 that:

> Marvin F. Hartman, 602 Spruce St., a member of the Madison Civic Symphony Orchestra, conceived the idea of procuring the signature of men and women who figure prominently in the world today. These signatures are placed upon a snare drum which he plays in the orchestra, and no doubt proves an incentive towards attaining perfection.[62]

There are nearly 200 signatures in all. Hartman started collecting autographs on the bottom (snare) head of the drum, and when that was filled, he began after July 5, 1933, to collect signatures on the top (batter) head, continuing to collect until at least 1941. It is clear that he continued to play the drum after collecting signatures, rendering as many as two dozen of them illegible. Though I have not yet identified all of them, it is clearly an eclectic list of local and national figures. For example, "Roundy" Coughlin (Joseph Leo Coughlin) was a longtime staff writer for the *Wisconsin State Journal*. Grouped around the words "Wisconsin State Senate 1933" are in fact signatures of several Wisconsin State Senators in the early 1930s, as well as other state government officials. There are also several musicians, including both Prager and his wife Frances Silva. Madison-born tenor Lawrence Salerno was a popular radio singer on Chicago's station WGN. On September 12, 1937, he sang a concert in Madison's Vilas Park, accompanied by the WPA-sponsored Madison Concert Orchestra, and was heard by an audience of 4000 to 5000 people—the most likely time for Hartman to collect Salerno's signature. Karl Fischer-Niemann, who lists himself as a member of the Wiener Oper (Vienna State Opera), sang several times with the Civic Symphony in the 1930s and early 1940s. He was a Madison native who seems to have lived partly in Madison from the 1920s onward. Chicago-based soprano Mari Barova appeared with the Civic Symphony in 1935, 1936, 1947, and 1948.

Percussionist Marvin Hartman (1899–1981) was a member of the Madison Civic Symphony for about two years, from late 1931 through at least 1934, and was typical of many of the performers in the orchestra and chorus in this period. He does not seem to have been a professional musician; the 1930 census lists him as a "filling station attendant," and by 1940 he was working as a "construction supervisor" for the state of Wisconsin. At some point later in his life Hartman moved away from Madison to settle in La Crosse, though his obituary notes that he worked for a time for the WPA-sponsored Civilian Conservation Corps at both Devil's Lake State Park and Fort McCoy.[63] This drum was undoubtedly a prized possession, and his own inscriptions on both heads seem to reflect a deep pride in his membership in the orchestra—a pride clearly shared by many of his fellow musicians.

Alexius Baas

One name that has appeared frequently in this chapter is Alexius Baas (1885–1970), a leading figure in Madison's musical life for well over 50 years. Born in Madison, Baas made his public debut as a soloist at age 10, when he sang at a massive temperance rally at the State Capitol. Baas appeared frequently in Madison as a baritone soloist in recitals and choral programs from the time he was a teenager through the 1940s.[64] After initially studying at the University of Wisconsin–Madison, he left for Germany to study voice, returning to Madison to complete a master's degree in music.

2.18 Alexius Baas, ca. 1910.

After touring with a noted Shakespearean company, Baas served on the faculty of Columbia College in Seattle and made further tours as a recitalist and as part of a vaudeville troupe. He returned to Madison in 1912 and joined the faculty of the Wisconsin School of Music, while continuing to tour extensively. He later served on the faculty of Carroll College in Waukesha, Wisconsin. He first worked as a conductor while he was a student at the University, leading the popular University Glee Club. Baas would later lead three of Madison's most prominent amateur choirs: he was the director of the Grieg Chorus in the late 1920s and 1930s, he succeeded Prager as director of the Madison Maennerchor in 1929, directing the group into the 1950s, and he also led the Mozart Club chorus in the 1930s. He was a composer of art songs and choral music—very much in a conservative, romantic style.[65]

In the 1940s Baas became a staff writer for the *Capital Times*, contributing hundreds of concert reviews and a column titled "All Around the Town" that dealt primarily with Madison history. A lifelong environmentalist, Baas participated in one of Madison's first antipollution fights in 1910, when he was part of an effort to stop the city from dumping sewage directly into Lake Monona, and he was among the founders of the Madison Clean Lakes Association in the 1920s. He later wrote extensively on touring Wisconsin's rivers by canoe. Baas and his wife Evelyn Oldham-Baas were particularly devoted to animals, and both were active in the Dane County Humane Society.[66]

Baas was never officially a member of the Madison Civic Chorus, nor did he

2.19 Alexius Baas, pictured with accompanist Grace Snell, February 28, 1952. Published by the *Wisconsin State Journal* as part of its coverage of the Madison Maennerchor's centennial celebration.

ever serve on the MCMA board. However, he played important roles in MCMA's activities from the very beginning. He and Prager met during Prager's first visit to Madison in the summer of 1925, and they remained lifelong friends, continuing to correspond long after Prager retired to Argentina in 1948. As detailed in the next chapter, Baas may also have played a role in attracting Prager to settle in Madison in 1926. Throughout the early years of the Civic Symphony and Chorus, Baas collaborated frequently in MCMA programs as a conductor, directing both the Madison Maennerchor and the Grieg Chorus in many programs. Two of his choral works were premiered at Madison Civic Music Festivals in the early 1930s. Baas was also among the most frequent vocal soloists in early MCMA concerts, appearing as a bass/baritone soloist in nearly 30 programs between 1930 and 1945.[67] He also appears on what is almost certainly the earliest surviving recording of a Madison Civic Music performance: a 78 RPM disc from a live recording of Handel's *Messiah* from December 22, 1941. While the entire program was recorded, the only part that has come to light is Baas singing the aria *Why Do the Nations So Furiously Rage Together?* Baas, at age 56, may have been a bit beyond his prime by this time, notably exhibiting a bit of trouble negotiating the aria's fast triplet passages at the brisk tempo Prager set. However, he clearly had a powerful baritone voice and flawless diction.[68]

Florence Bennett

While the vast majority of players in the Madison Civic Symphony during its earliest days were local amateurs and students, the orchestra also included a few experienced professionals. Flutist Florence Bennett (1876–after 1950) played in the orchestra from 1926 to 1932, and even before the creation of the orchestra, she was one of the local musicians invited to join the MCMA board. She was born Florence Beckett in Portland, Maine, and her father, Edward Parry Beckett, was a professional flutist. The family moved to Massachusetts, and by the time she was a teenager, Florence Beckett was performing in the Marietta Sherman Orchestra, an all-female salon orchestra that performed at Boston society functions. Throughout the 1890s she worked as a touring professional musician, working with other "lady orchestras" and vaudeville troupes, and she was occasionally billed in publicity as "the leading lady flute player of the world." She married Myron Bennett in 1903, but they eventually separated. In 1918, she moved to Madison, where her mother and sister were then living, and joined the faculty of the Wheeler Conservatory.[69] A few years later she moved to Madison's other private conservatory, the Wisconsin School of Music, and she also began to teach flute students at the University, though she clearly continued to tour as well. A *State Journal* article of February 1930, for example, notes that she had just returned from a two-month tour with the Boston Women's Symphony Orchestra.[70] Bennett also led small orchestras that played in Madison's silent movie theaters.[71] She was clearly a respected musician in Madison and in the ranks of the Madison Civic Symphony; she appeared as a soloist on seven different programs between 1929 and 1933.[72] However, in the early 1970s, concertmaster Marie Endres recalled an incident where Bennett butted heads with Prager:

2.20 Florence Bennett in 1930.

> You could wait months for Florence to make one mistake ... which she never did.... One night, the rehearsal hall was cold, and the light was bad. We were doing the Bach *Suite in B minor for Flute and Strings*. Something happened and he stopped and bawled her out. She was the soloist, of course. She walked off the stage. Wham! She would have none of that. He had a student, Doug Seaman take her place. But he made his peace with Florence and she played the concert.[73]

Bennett seems to have left Madison by late 1934 or early 1935,[74] and by June 1935 she was performing again in Boston.[75]

Grace Schumpert

There are many musicians in the history of the orchestra and chorus who had long tenures, and Grace Schumpert (1903–2004) was certainly among the longest-serving members of the Madison Civic Chorus, singing for 49 seasons (1928–1976), most of those years as leader of of the alto section. I met with her in 2000, one of only a few musicians I have spoken to who worked with Prager, and at that time one of the last living links to the very earliest days of the MCMA. She was born Grace Parker in New Haven, Connecticut, and after graduating from Connecticut College in 1926, she married Robert Schumpert. They moved to Madison in 1927, and she joined the Madison Civic Chorus a year later. Schumpert would appear three times as a soloist at chorus concerts in the 1930s.[76] Her long tenure as a singer also bridged two eras of opera productions in Madison: She sang in the chorus in the 1933 *Carmen* production led by Prager ... and was in the chorus again some 37 years later when the Madison Civic Opera Guild staged *Carmen* in 1970.[77] When I met her in 2000—a very dignified and mentally sharp lady at age 97—she remembered Sigfrid Prager respectfully, but recalled that he was quite strict and formal during chorus rehearsals. Schumpert referred to him as "a typical German professor," and she recalled how she was put in a leadership role:

> At a rehearsal—I think that it was a Mozart *Gloria*—I noticed that the woman next to me was singing from a different edition, and trying to sing in a different key. I was sitting back in the fourth row, and I raised my hand and asked whether we should be singing an E or an F-sharp. Dr. Prager said: 'Who's that back there with perfect pitch?' And then he walked right back, took me by the arm, and sat me in the first row. That's where I remained![78]

However, she and Prager were clearly on friendly terms by the 1930s, as revealed in a trio of letters that came to light in 2022. On May 17, 1937, Prager wrote to thank her for helping out with a recently completed concert in Sheboygan—presumably for helping to bolster the alto section of the chorus. At the time, Prager was suffering badly from an arthritic condition in his hip, and he would eventually have surgery that summer. His letter confides that the Sheboygan concert was "the straw that broke the camel's back" and that when he returned to Madison that night he had to seek an injection for the pain. In an outburst unique among all of his writing I have seen, Prager said: "Who invented pain? I would like to meet the man and tell him what I think of him." By 1941, Schumpert was president of the chorus, and on May 27, he wrote to commend her work as "toastmaster" at the recent chorus banquet, an event regularly held at the conclusion of each season. He noted that "I found your

2.21 Grace Schumpert (seated, left) in September 1950, in a photo of singers from the Madison Civic Chorus; also pictured (left to right) are Ralph James, Louise Morrissey, Helen Jansky, and Elizabeth Hunter.

appeal to the chorus to uphold music in the future times of strain and stress very well timed." This was undoubtedly a reference to the war in Europe, and the growing likelihood that the United States would become involved. On December 28, 1941, with America now fully engaged in the war, he wrote to Schumpert again, to thank her for a Christmas gift she had presented on behalf of the chorus. The end of the letter, however, is one of the most revealing and personal surviving statements by Prager:

> Several times, I have been thinking about your prophetic words spoken at the chorus banquet in the spring, about the position of Civic music in a national emergency. Now it is here, with a vengeance. I shall never be able to express convincingly to what an extent I am finding fulfillment of my musical and spiritual ideals in doing civic music in Madison. Nothing could lure me away. Monday night [the Civic Chorus's weekly rehearsal] is the time when I feel happy, useful, creative, engaged in the noblest of all tasks: the promotion of a cause for the benefit of humanity. To you, my loyal and efficient co-worker in the field I extend my profoundest gratitude. With kindest new year wishes to you, your husband, and your family, in which Mrs. Prager joins me, always sincerely, Sigfrid Prager.[79]

Schumpert also remembered her work with Walter Heermann and Roland Johnson with fondness. She died in 2004 at age 100.[80]

Marie Endres: Concertmaster, 1927–1960

One of the most important leaders within the orchestra during its early years—and a powerful force in Madison's musical community—was Marie Endres (1904–1999), who served as concertmaster throughout the tenures of Prager and Heermann. She was born in New Ulm, Minnesota, daughter of a church organist, Mathias Aloisus Endres, and Amelia (Schneyer) Endres, a skilled painter. Mathias had been born in rural Dane, Wisconsin, in 1870 and served as an organist in churches in southern Minnesota, Ohio, and Kentucky before returning to Dane County in 1920. From 1925 until his death in 1933, he was organist at St. Raphael's Catholic Church in Madison. Between 1897 and 1910 the family had seven daughters and one son: Eulalia, Salome, Olive, Flora, Marie, Mildred, Roland, and Emma.[81] Though most of the Endres siblings seem to have been involved with amateur musicmaking in Madison, three of the sisters—Olive, Marie, and Emma—would become particularly important figures in Madison's musical life from the 1920s onward.

Marie Endres trained at both the American Conservatory of Music in Chicago and New York's famed Juilliard School before moving to Madison with her family in 1920, when she began a career as a violinist, string teacher, and conductor that extended over 70 years.[82] She was associated with the Madison Civic Symphony from the beginning, serving as concertmaster almost continuously from the orchestra's second concert in 1927 until 1960. Her role with the orchestra went far beyond serving as concertmaster, however. Throughout much of the 1920s and 1930s, Endres was one of the only regularly paid members of the orchestra, earning a modest stipend for conducting countless string rehearsals and often stepping in to cover rehearsals for the always-overcommitted Prager. Prager and Endres seem to have had a warm, if at first rather formal, relationship, as in a note he mailed to her in April 1930:

> My dear Miss Endres: I wish to thank you heartily for your excellent work as concertmaster in the last concert of the Madison Civic Symphony Orchestra. You were at all times a very reliable and efficient interpreter of my intentions and your solo work in Bach's difficult B minor suite was generally noticed and commented upon with admiration. There is a general feeling that sometime in the future you should appear as soloist. We shall discuss this matter soon. With kindest regards and sincere appreciation, cordially yours, Dr. Sigfrid Prager.[83]

Endres did in fact perform as a soloist in the next season, playing the first movement of Mozart's *Violin Concerto No. 4*, K. 218 with the orchestra on May 20, 1931, the first of 10 appearances as a featured soloist with the Madison Civic Symphony over the next three decades, including

- Vieuxtemps, *Violin Concerto No. 4* (November 17, 1931)
- Bach, *Concerto for Two Violins*, BWV 1043 (May 20, 1933, and February 13, 1934, both with violinist George Szpinalski)
- Beethoven, *Violin Concerto* (February 9, 1937)
- Sibelius, *Violin Concerto* (February 21, 1943)
- Mozart, *Sinfonia Concertante for Violin and Viola*, K. 364 (November 19, 1944—with violist Beatrice Hagen)
- Haydn, *Sinfonia Concertante for Oboe, Bassoon, Violin and Cello* (May 6, 1953—with cellist Mildred Stanke, oboist Leona Patras, and bassoonist Donald Kirkpatrick)
- Saint-Saëns, *Danse Macabre* (April 30, 1960)

Endres and Prager were close musical collaborators throughout his time as music director, and the two frequently performed chamber music together in the early 1930s. In the early 1940s, Prager briefly took beginning viola lessons from her and played a few times under her baton in the Madison String Sinfonia.[84] Endres was also one of many Madison musicians who stayed in contact with Prager in the decades following his retirement and move to Argentina.[85]

When Walter Heermann became the orchestra's music director in 1948, Endres was named assistant conductor of the Madison Civic Symphony. This move seems simply to have been an official acknowledgment by the MCMA of the role she had already been playing for 22 years. Endres would continue to conduct string rehearsals and cover rehearsals that Heermann could not attend, but she also stepped to the podium for the first time at one of the orchestra's regular concerts, conducting Brahms's *Double Concerto* on April 3, 1949. This performance featured Heermann as cello soloist and his brother Emil Heermann on violin. Endres took a leave of absence during the 1950–51 season (when she was replaced temporarily as concertmaster by Shirley Reynolds),[86] but she continued in her dual role through the rest of the 1950s. She eventually stepped away from the Madison Civic Symphony at the end of the 1959–60 season, citing increasingly heavy conducting and teaching commitments outside of the orchestra.[87] Endres's final concert, rounding out nearly 34 seasons as the orchestra's concertmaster, was a pops program at the Loraine Hotel on April 30, 1960, which featured her as soloist in the virtuosic *Danse Macabre* by Saint-Saëns. Her successor as concertmaster was her former student Mary Perssion.

The musical work of Marie Endres went far beyond the orchestra. For most of her career she was the preeminent violin teacher in Madison, doing most of her teaching through the Wisconsin School of Music, whose string department she headed for decades. In 1937, with the encouragement of the school's director, Elizabeth Buehler, Endres founded the Madison String Sinfonia, an amateur string orchestra that she directed for the next 40 years. The Sinfonia's members were primarily her own students and former students, many of whom also performed in the Madison Civic Symphony in the 1940s and 1950s.[88] The group also provided a performance opportunity for local amateur string players in the 1960s and 1970s, when the string section of the Madison Symphony Orchestra was becoming increasingly professionalized. The Madison String Sinfonia gave regular concerts and would combine frequently in performances with one of her other projects, the Madison Baroque Chorus, and with the Milton College Choral Union. Endres was clearly an effective educator and a beloved figure among her former students. Her papers in the Wisconsin Music

Archives include collections of letters and telegrams received on the occasions of the 20th (1957) and 30th (1967) anniversaries of the founding of the Sinfonia, with dozens of letters addressed affectionately to "Teacher" recalling fond memories of studying with her and performing in the Sinfonia. Among the 1967 letters is one from Otto Festge, then Madison's mayor and a former Endres student.[89]

In 1942, Endres joined the faculty of Milton College, where she headed the string department, teaching strings and leading the Milton Civic Orchestra. She began to earn a national reputation as an expert on string pedagogy, presenting at many conferences devoted to string education. In 1965, Milton College recognized her service with an honorary doctorate.[90] Among other honors she received was a 1970 Governor's Award for "distinguished service and performance in the arts."

Also a skilled choral conductor, Endres led the choir of St. James Catholic Church in Madison for 25 years, working alongside her sister Olive, who served as organist. In 1962 she founded the Madison Baroque Chorus, a vocal ensemble that would become one of Madison's leading choral groups over the next two decades, mounting full-scale performances of Bach's *Christmas Oratorio* and Passions, and dozens of other major Baroque works, usually involving the Madison String Sinfonia, and frequently incorporating players from the Madison Civic Symphony. Endres led this choir through 1983.[91]

Any biography of Marie Endres would be incomplete without at least a brief mention of her two musical sisters. Pianist Emma Endres-Kountz (1910–2001), the youngest of the Endres siblings, had the most prominent musical career of the three. She first attracted attention in Madison when, at age nine, she won Madison's first annual Music Memory Contest.[92] That same year she performed as a soloist with the Chicago Symphony Orchestra. Emma frequently played chamber music in Madison before she left for New York in 1932 to study at the Juilliard School. In 1937 she went to Paris on a fellowship that allowed her to study with Nadia Boulanger, Igor Stravinsky, and pianist Richard Casadesus, who called her "one of the finest American pianists of our time." She returned to the United States just ahead of the outbreak of war in 1939 and settled in Toledo, Ohio, after marrying Toledo businessman Frederick Kountz. Emma continued to perform across the United States through the 1940s and

2.22 Olive Endres, Emma Endres-Kountz, and Marie Endres in November 1967.

1950s, performing both solo recitals and chamber music, and appearing as a soloist with several major symphony orchestras. But she was also a mover and shaker in the arts scene in her adopted hometown—among other activities, she is generally acknowledged to have been the founder of the Toledo Symphony Orchestra. The sudden death of the Kountzes' 15-year-old son in 1957 prompted a move to Chicago, where both of them dedicated the next quarter century to service to young people. Emma was one of the founders of an educational docent program for the Chicago Symphony Orchestra, but according to her surviving son Peter, her proudest achievement was MERIT, a music education program serving Chicago's poorest children.[93] During the years when she was actively touring as a soloist, Emma returned to Madison three times to perform with the Madison Civic Symphony:

- Rachmaninoff, *Piano Concerto No. 2* (November 25, 1940)
- Bach, *Keyboard Concerto No. 5*, BWV 1056 and
  Mozart, *Piano Concerto No. 23*, K. 488 (April 6, 1947)
- MacDowell, *Piano Concerto No. 2* (October 25, 1959)

Pianist, organist, and composer Olive Endres (1898–1995) does not seem to have been actively involved with the activities of MCMA, but like her sister Marie, she had a prominent and successful local career. Like Marie, she trained at both the American Conservatory of Music and the Juilliard School, though Olive also studied later at the Manhattan School of Music.[94] She taught alongside Marie at the Wisconsin School of Music and worked for 40 years as organist at St. James Catholic Church, where Marie conducted the choir.[95] She was also the longtime accompanist for the Philharmonic Chorus, an ensemble which had its beginnings in 1946 as a splinter group from the Madison Civic Chorus.[96]

Olive was active as a composer throughout her life—her papers in the Wisconsin Music Archives document a compositional career extending nearly 50 years and producing over 200 compositions, all now preserved there: mostly in manuscript, but including some 33 published works. The majority of her published compositions were short piano pieces intended for children, and sacred choral pieces. She also composed works in many other genres. Olive wrote several complete Latin masses and dozens of other Latin liturgical chant settings and hymns, most of which were composed in the 1940s and 1950s for St. James Catholic Church. She also wrote a wide variety of chamber pieces, including several works for violin and piano for performances with Marie. In 1931, Prager published a detailed review of a recital performed in both Madison and Chicago by the three Endres sisters, singling out her *Violin Sonata in A*—one of the earliest violin/piano works by Olive—for special praise.[97] A few of her choral works include orchestral accompaniment, as in the 1958 *Magnificat* for solo soprano, mixed chorus, trumpet, and strings. This work won first place in the Wisconsin Composers Competition that year. Olive also composed works for full orchestra and string orchestra, many of the latter appearing on programs of Marie's String Sinfonia.

One of the things that comes through in surveying her scores is that she continued to work on the craft of composition and to experiment throughout her career: many of the scores created when she was in her 50s are clearly studies in both orchestration and musical style. Though the majority of her works are in a rather conservative style, particularly her sacred pieces, there are some fascinating experiments as well. Olive spent the winter of 1953 and 1954 in New York City, pursuing additional study in composition and orchestration,[98] and this seems to have sparked some of this experimentation. There are dozens of orchestration exercises from this period, and several short chamber works seem to have been studies in writing for various instrumental combinations. Olive notes that her 1955 cantata *The Canticle of Judith* (for mezzo-soprano solo, women's choir, and piano) is "based upon three of the Hebrew scales in use at the time of the Old Testament (and transpositions thereof)." In at least two other pieces from 1955, she experimented with twelve-tone technique: *Prelude and Fugue for Three Clarinets* and *Divergent Moods* for string orchestra. Olive clearly had a sense of humor as well, and she signed a couple of her more lighthearted pieces with pseudonyms: "Toni Philomena" for a set of women's barbershop quartet songs, and "U. von Flüegge" for a set of German folksong-settings for voice and recorder quartet.[99]

In December 1979, WHA-TV broadcast a special program in its *Over Easy* series, honoring Marie and Olive as Madison's "First Ladies of Music."[100]

2.23 Marie and Olive Endres, 1979 (publicity photo for the WHA-TV Broadcast).

Notes to Chapter 2

1. Edith W. Hildebrandt, "Music Memory Contests," *The School Review* 30/4 (April 1922): 300.
2. Hildebrandt, "Music Memory Contests," 304–5.
3. Madison Civic Music Association, *A History of the Madison Civic Music Association: The First Fifty Years, 1925–1975* (Madison, 1975) [henceforth *MCMA50*], 7.
4. Letter from C. V. Seastone to Roland Johnson, 4/25/1972 (MSO Archives).
5. *Madison Community Music Committee Board Minutes* for 10/3/1924 and 1/12/1925 (MSO Archives). The Madison Orchestral Association's work is discussed at length at the end of Chapter 1.
6. *MCMA Board Minutes* for 12/3/1925 (MSO Archives).
7. *WSJ* 11/28/1925, 7.
8. *MCMA Board Minutes* for 5/25/1926 (MSO Archives); *CT* 5/26/1926, 14.
9. *MCMA50*, 5.
10. *MCMA Board Minutes* for 8/4/1926 (MSO Archives).
11. Letter from Sigfrid Prager to Helen Marting Supernaw, March 1972, printed in *MCMA50*, 7–8.
12. *MCMA50*, 8.
13. *CT* 10/31/1927, 2.
14. Letter from Sigfrid Prager to Helen Marting Supernaw, March 1972.
15. "Esther Dale," *Wikipedia*, https://en.wikipedia.org/wiki/Esther_Dale, accessed 1/16/2020.
16. Review by Ethel M. Max, *CT* 12/15/1926, 1.
17. *MCMA Board Minutes* for 5/9/1927 and 5/21/1927 (MSO Archives).
18. The chorus is first mentioned in *MCMA Board Minutes* for 6/6/1927 (MSO Archives).
19. *CT* 10/31/1927, 2.
20. *CT* 2/15/1929, 10. Vogts's father, Henry Vogts, Sr., who is also quoted in this article, played trumpet in the orchestra.
21. *MCMA Board Minutes* for 2/12/1929 (MSO Archives).
22. Reported by Gerald Borsuk (interview, 7/20/2000). The Prager/Hambrecht/Mills meeting is reported in *MCMA Board Minutes* for 4/24/1929 (MSO Archives).
23. *WSJ* 2/12/1933, 16.
24. The only December Prager seems to have missed programming the work was 1936, when the chorus presented Verdi's *Requiem* instead.
25. *MCMA Board Minutes* for 11/22/1927 (MSO Archives).
26. *MCMA Board Minutes* for 3/13/1928 (MSO Archives).
27. *MCMA Board Minutes* for 5/28/28 (MSO Archives).
28. *MCMA Board Minutes* for 6/7/1928 (MSO Archives).
29. *MCMA Board Minutes* for 7/3/28 (MSO Archives).
30. *WSJ* 11/28/1928, 17.

31 *WSJ* 12/22/1928, 1, 4; *WSJ* 12/29/1928, 1, 5. The City Council meeting is also discussed in *MCMA Board Minutes* for 1/2/1929 (MSO Archives).

32 *MCMA Board Minutes* for 5/22/1930 (MSO Archives).

33 *MCMA Board Minutes* for 11/2/1936 (MSO Archives).

34 *WSJ* 2/11/34.

35 The repertoire champion of these years was Brahms's *Hungarian Dance No. 5*, programmed six times between 1927 and 1934.

36 *WSJ* 2/4/1929, 7.

37 *WSJ* 4/26/1938, 9.

38 The Eastwood, on Atwood Ave., was completed in 1929. It was devoted largely to movies, but it did include a large stage. It changed owners several times over the decades, and despite a few renovations it had declined by the 1980s into a rather seedy theater devoted mostly to porn. In 1987, it was purchased yet again, renovated extensively, and reopened as the Barrymore Theatre. Today, the Barrymore remains one of Madison's most active venues for live music.

39 *CT* 4/15/1930, 7.

40 *WSJ* 6/19/1932, 20.

41 *CT* 5/21/1932, 1.

42 *CT* 5/16/1940, 14.

43 Feldman, *Buildings*, 75–79. Today, the entire second floor of the building is devoted to offices for various student services and student organizations.

44 *WSJ* 1/13/1914, 14.

45 Interview with Roland Johnson, 8/15/2004.

46 *WSJ* 10/2/1917, 6.

47 *CT* 2/20/1918, 1.

48 *WSJ* 1/21/1917, 8.

49 Feldman, *Buildings*, 115–116.

50 George Shook, email to the author, 10/22/2019.

51 Interview with Roland Johnson, 8/15/2004.

52 There was also a smaller concert on Friday afternoon at Christ Presbyterian Church, which did not involve Civic Music's musicians, and which must have involved a smaller group from within the thousand singers attending the Sangarfest.

53 *WSJ* 6/3/1932, 1, 4.

54 *WSJ* 6/28/1935, 16.

55 *CT* 9/18/1932, 11.

56 *CT* 11/23/1936, 2.

57 *MCMA Board Minutes* for 12/7/1936 (MSO Archives).

58 *WSJ* 9/19/1937, 5.

59 At least a few of these numbers were recycled from the season's extremely popular Civic Music production of *Carmen*.

60 *WSJ* 8/1/1926, 22.

61 Email correspondence with Nathan Moy, 11/13/2020.

62 *CT* 10/14/1932, 13.

63 Obituary, *La Crosse Tribune* 12/20/1981, 35.

64 The earliest recital for which I have been able to find documentation was on August 9, 1904, when a 19-year-old Baas shared a Cecelian Society recital with Madison's then-leading violinist Charles Nitschke (*CT* 8/30/1904, 5).

65 Baas's papers, preserved in the Wisconsin State Historical Society archives, include copies of three of his larger choral works, two published settings of the Latin mass, and a manuscript cantata on Henry Wadsworth Longfellow's poem *The Building of the Ship*.

66 Obituary, *CT* 1/30/1970, 1, 4.

67 For a complete listing of his solo appearances, see Allsen, *75 Years of the Madison Symphony Orchestra*, 192.

68 This recording was part of the personal collection of the author. It has been digitized and can be heard at http://www.allsenmusic.com/HISTORY/Recordings. It is now part of the MSO Archives.

69 *WSJ* 7/14/1918, 3.

70 *WSJ* 2/4/1930, 8. Census data was accessed on ancestry.com on 11/16/2020.

71 Much of the information on Bennett's life presented here comes from a 2012 blog essay by her great-nephew Fred Burwell, which is based upon family stories and an unpublished memoir by Bennett herself. Accessed at https://fredburwell.com/2012/05/18/a-writing-family-pt-4-my-great-aunt-florence-beckett-bennett/ 5/8/2020.

72 For a complete listing of her solo appearances, see Allsen, *75 Years of the Madison Symphony Orchestra*, 185.

73 *MCMA50*, 10. This incident probably took place in March or April of 1930.

74 The last mention of her in the local newspapers is in a listing of University School of Music faculty in May 1934 (*WSJ* 5/6/1934, 7).

75 *The Boston Globe*, 6/14/1935, 34.

76 Allsen, *75 Years of the Madison Symphony Orchestra*, 209.

77 Eleanor Anderson, "25 Years—A Silver Jubilee," in *Madison Opera and Guild, 25 Years. 1962–63 - 1987: A Silver Jubilee* (Madison: The Madison Opera, 1987), 10.

78 Interview with Grace Schumpert, 7/20/00. From Mrs. Schumpert's description, this event probably took place in 1929.

79 Letters from Sigfrid Prager to Grace Schumpert, 5/17/1937, 5/27/1941, and 12/28/1941. I found these letters in the portion of Roland Johnson's papers preserved by his daughter Karen. The letters, which were in an envelope marked in Johnson's hand "letters from Dr. Prager–important." I presume that Shumpert passed these letters on to Johnson sometime in the 1960s or 1970s. Copies are now in the MSO Archives as well.

80 *WSJ* 4/4/2004, 39.

81 Death notice, *WSJ* 11/13/1933.
82 Obituary, *WSJ* 9/15/1999.
83 Letter from Sigfrid Prager to Marie Endres, 4/23/1930 (WMA Marie Endres Collection).
84 Prager played in the group in at least two concerts, in April 1943 and April 1945 (programs in the WMA Marie Endres Collection). In a photo of the 1943 concert, Prager—who was always notably modest in the way that he posed in various photos of musical groups—seems to be successfully hiding behind one of the teenage players in the viola section!
85 Noted in Carmen Elsner, "30 Years Boss of Madison's String Sinfonia: Marie Endres," *WSJ* 4/2/1967.
86 *WSJ* 10/5/1950.
87 *WSJ* 10/16/1960.
88 The founding of the Sinfonia is discussed in Carmen Elsner, "30 Years Boss of Madison's String Sinfonia: Marie Endres," *WSJ* 4/2/1967.
89 Letter from Otto Festge to Marie Endres, 2/22/1967 (WMA Marie Endres Collection). Festge also performed on violin in the Madison Civic Symphony as a young man, and he later served as president of MCMA in 1977–80.
90 "Citation to Marie A. Endres at Milton College Commencement, June 6, 1965," WMA Marie Endres Collection.
91 Complete programs included in WMA Marie Endres Collection.
92 *WSJ* 6/13/1920.
93 Obituary, *The Toledo Blade* 10/1/2001; obituary, *Chicago Tribune* 10/3/2001.
94 Obituary, *WSJ* 2/28/1995 31.
95 "Olive Endres Retires as Church Organist," *WSJ* 2/10/1962, 12. Olive eventually assumed both roles, choir director and organist in 1959, until her retirement in 1962
96 The details of this split are discussed in Chapter 4.
97 *WSJ* 6/3/1931, 8; also noted in "Olive Endres Does Violin, Piano Sonata," *WSJ* 5/17/1931, 12.
98 Noted in *WSJ* 3/13/1955, 11.
99 See WMA Olive Endres Collection.
100 Details in *Focus: WHA Television Community Outreach* 12 (December 1979): 4. A copy of this newsletter and a VHS videotape of the program are preserved in the WMA Olive Endres Collection.

CHAPTER 3

Founding Father: Dr. Sigfrid Prager, Music Director 1926–1948

The preceding chapter dealt with the creation and early history of the Madison Civic Music Association. The early success of the orchestra and chorus came from a joint effort by their musicians, board members, and supporters, and from the invaluable assistance of the Vocational School. However, MCMA's first music director, Dr. Sigfrid Prager, seems to have been the single most important factor in this success—his leadership, musical qualifications, and personality were fundamental in creating a lasting musical tradition. Now, over 75 years since his last visit to Madison, virtually all who knew him are gone, but the picture that emerges from his biography is of a remarkable musician and leader: truly the Madison Symphony Orchestra's "founding father."

3.01 Sigfrid Prager in 1929.

Early Life: From Berlin to Service in World War I

According to his official birth record, Prager was born in Berlin on June 12, 1889, as Siegfried Wantzloeben. His father was Philipp Johannes Wantzloeben (d. 1945), and his mother was Minna (Scholz) Wantzloeben (d. 1923). He had two younger siblings, a brother, Ernst, and a sister, Marianne.[1] It is not clear when he adopted the surname Prager and changed the spelling of his given name. His 1911 doctoral dissertation is credited to "Sigfrid Wantzloeben," but his marriage record of 1915 lists him once again as "Siegfried Wantzloeben." He was certainly known professionally as Sigfrid Prager by the time he reached Argentina in 1919 and for the rest of his career, but when he signed a Declaration of Intention to become a United States citizen on April 6, 1925, it was as "Sigfrid Wantzloeben-Prager." The last official appearance of his original surname—though now misspelled—seems to have been on May 19, 1930, when a Certificate of Naturalization filed in Madison's Dane County Circuit Court lists him as "Sigfrid (Wautzloeben) Prager."[2] Exactly when the name change happened is unclear, but why it happened is more intriguing. It was certainly common for emigrants from Europe to adopt new names to go with new lives in an adopted country, and it was also common for musicians to adopt professional stage names. His change in surname most likely occurred around 1918, when he left Germany permanently.

One helpful document that reveals a wealth of details about his early life is a substantial March 1929 article in the *Capital Times*, written by one of the paper's staff writers, Lester Velie. Velie's biographical sketch was clearly based upon an extensive interview with Prager himself, and it is the closest thing we have to a memoir by Prager about his origins. Velie's prose is sometimes flowery, the account a bit romanticized, and there are a few minor errors in chronology, but many of its facts can be verified in other sources. The article makes no reference to the surname Wantzloeben, referring to his family throughout as Prager. There is also a discrepancy between this account and Prager's official birth record with regard to his mother's name: here he says that she was born Mina Ferrara and that she was Spanish. It begins with his early life, when his father, a salesman of school supplies,[3] brought the family with him on travels that included extended stays in Switzerland, Spain, and Italy, allowing young Sigfrid Prager to become fluent in French, Spanish, and Italian by the time he entered gymnasium (high school) in Berlin. While in school he also learned Greek and Latin. His father was an enthusiastic amateur musician, and Prager's earliest musical experiences were musical evenings with his family, where his mother played piano, his father cello, his brother viola, and Prager violin, though he also learned piano. Apparently his only music teacher until he graduated from gymnasium at age 18 was his father.[4]

Prager (still using the surname Wantzloeben) earned his doctorate at the University of Halle in 1911, with a dissertation titled *Das Monochord als Instrument und als System, entwicklungsgeschichtlich dargestellt* (*The Monochord *as an Instrument and as a System, Developmentally and Historically Represented*).[5] The monochord was a musical/scientific instrument dating to classical antiquity, used to explore the connection between mathematical proportions and music. Prager's 1911 dissertation seems to have been the very first important musicological study of the instrument, and it is cited in many later publications on the monochord. The dissertation involved extensive research on manuscripts in the university libraries at Berlin, Lausanne, and Padua, drawing on classical and medieval sources in Greek, Latin, and Aramaic.[6]

According to the Velie article, Prager's introduction to the world of opera came through his younger brother, who worked occasionally as an onstage, non-singing extra for productions at the Royal Opera (Königliches Opernhaus) in Berlin. Shortly after Prager completed his doctorate, his brother invited him to come along one night. Very quickly, Prager was engaged as a *repetiteure* (vocal coach) and accompanist at the Royal Opera and was involved with accompanying the choir and assisting with staging. In an anecdote that clearly shows Prager's wry sense of humor, he also relates that one of his jobs was making sure that the onstage trumpet players in *Lohengrin* did not slip out between acts to get drunk! According to this account, Prager's work at the Royal Opera inspired him to become a conductor, and he took the opportunity to study all aspects of opera, learning "150 operas minutely" in the course of a year.

By 1912, Prager was employed as a chorus conductor at "a civic opera in the Berlin suburbs"—most likely the Deutsches Opernhaus in Charlottenberg, which opened that year. According to the Velie account, his big break came when a drunken orchestra conductor punched the stage director after the first

3.02 Soprano Anna Willner, in the role of Katrinka, in a 1908 production of Smetana's *Die verkaufte Braut* (*The Bartered Bride*) at the Komische Oper of Berlin.

act of an opera performance and left the theater. Prager was suddenly called on to conduct the remainder of the opera, and the next day he signed a contract as assistant conductor. Over the next few years, Prager would conduct in Berlin and at the Stadt-Theatre of Hamburg, in the Sicilian city of Catania (where his symphonic poem *Sicania* was premiered), as well as Lausanne, Turin, and at the Teatro Liceo in Barcelona.

While in Hamburg in early 1915, Prager married his first wife, Anna Luise Bertha Standtke Willner, on February 17, 1915. At age 39, Anna was some 13 years older than him. She was born Anna Standke in Berlin on January 28, 1876, and she had had one previous marriage in 1895.[7] She is almost certainly identifiable with the soprano Anna Willner, who sang various roles at Berlin's Komische Oper in the first decade of the 20th century. During the 1907–8 season, for example, Willner sang lead roles in Smetana's *The Bartered Bride* and Offenbach's *Tales of Hoffmann*.[8] Anna accompanied Prager to Argentina a few years later, but their marriage seems to have ended in 1925.

During the period when he was establishing himself as a conductor, Prager worked on other musical skills as well. He asserted in both the Velie account and in later sources that he had studied piano with one of the leading virtuosos of the age, Ferruccio Busoni (1866–1924). Given Busoni's career, they were probably relatively sporadic lessons between 1911 and 1914. Busoni settled in Berlin in 1894, and he was prominent in the city's musical life through the beginning of the war in 1914. He soon left on an extended American tour, and he spent the rest of the war years in Switzerland, returning to Germany only in 1921.[9] From his later work in the United States it is clear that Prager was a fine pianist, both as an accompanist and as a chamber musician and soloist. Prager also noted that he had studied composition with Max Bruch (1838–1920). Bruch, a leading German romantic composer, was also by the early 20th century one of Germany's most respected composition teachers. Between 1890 and his retirement in 1911, Bruch taught at Berlin's Hochschule für Musik, where his students included both Ottorino Respighi and Ralph Vaughan Williams.[10] He continued to live in Berlin and teach after his retirement, and Prager must have studied privately with him in the years prior to the war. In addition to his piano and composition studies, he also listed organ studies with Walter Fischer (1872–1931); again these lessons probably took place in Berlin before the war. Fischer, one of Germany's great organists, settled in Berlin at the turn of the 20th century, eventually serving as organist in the Kaiser-Wilhem-Gedänkniskirche, and as organ teacher at the Hochschule für Musik. In 1916 he was appointed organist at Berlin's cathedral, a position he held until his retirement.[11]

3.03-3.05 Prager's teachers, prior to World War I: pianist Ferruccio Busoni (ca. 1913), composer Max Bruch (ca. 1920), and organist Walter Fischer (ca. 1919).

The Velie account notes that an "asthmatic complaint" initially prevented Prager from being drafted into the Prussian army when the war broke out. However, he did enlist in the army in 1917, serving through the end of the war at the close of 1918. One of the rare times he commented on the experience in public—though rather facetiously—was a story related in an otherwise serious 1942 guest editorial in the *Wisconsin State Journal* titled "Music at War." Here he recalled conducting amateur opera productions and choral concerts while in the army:

> The writer remembers certain experiences of 1917 and '18 in a garrison north of Hamburg. A whole operatic company was formed out of the ranks, giving "Cavalleria Rusticana," "Pagliacci," "Carmen," "Faust," "Il Trovatore," with guest singers in the female roles. Stage rehearsals were held in the open air in summertime. In the winter, the "cast" practiced in one corner of the drill barn, while in other parts of the hall soldiers marched, jumped, crouched, presented arms, or threw dummy grenades. The shouting of commands mixed with recitatives from opera.
>
> The orchestra was a problem. Concertmaster was a sergeant, the timpanist was a corporal, the first flute was a "Vize-Feldwebel," [a rank equivalent to a junior sergeant], but the conductor was a buck private. While he had the upper hand at rehearsals, they took it out of him on the drill ground the next morning.
>
> The most interested spectator of operatic performances was the commander of the garrison. He liked the singers, the chorus,

the scenery. He also liked the ballet. He liked almost everything excepting the orchestra. At performances he tapped the conductor on the shoulder, inquiring angrily why that so-and-so of a triangle player was not playing all the time. This was bad discipline, and bad for morale; the "fellow" should be reported. The truth was the "fellow" was counting rests....

To keep up the spirit, singing was organized. Four choruses were formed in the garrison, [100] voices apiece. It was hard to find high tenors and low basses. The commander solved the problem. One morning with the whole regiment standing attention, he counted off: "**One, two, three, four … 24, 25, first tenor, left turn, march; one, two, three … 25, second tenor, left turn, march; etc. etc.,**" and the end of the procedure, barked at the unhappy conductor: "**Here is your chorus. And in the future: use your head man, use your head!**"

The band was also quite useful. It traveled across the border of Denmark occasionally and came back with eggs and butter hidden in the roomier instruments such as trombones and tubas. Once it brought back a calf—in the bass drum. Music in wartime![12]

Argentina and New York, 1919-1925

Directly following the war, he received an offer to teach in Argentina.[13] In 1919, Prager was one of thousands of Germans who emigrated there in the early 20th century. The prospect of a Germany that was rapidly being overtaken by postwar economic and political turmoil may also have been a factor in his decision to emigrate.

Buenos Aires, easily the most "European" city in South America, had a large population of European immigrants by the early 20th century. Though Germans and Austrians were actually one of the smaller European immigrant groups, this German-speaking minority had a strong cultural impact, particularly in Buenos Aires.[14] One of Prager's early conducting engagements was with one of the city's leading German institutions, the Singakademie, a group he conducted from 1920 to 1924. Musical singing societies like this sprang up wherever there were concentrations of German immigrants. (Prager would later lead similar groups in both Madison and Chicago, and possibly in New York.) Under Prager's leadership, the group performed many of the great German choral masterworks, including Schumann's *Zigeunerleben*, Haydn's oratorio *Die*

Jahreszeiten, and Brahms's *Schicksalslied*, *Nänie*, and *Liebeslieder-Walzer*.[15]

In the case of the Singakademie, we have an account of Prager's work written by Felix Weingartner (1863–1942), one of the leading conductors of the early 20th century. In 1920, Weingartner and his wife, the singer Lucille Marcel, made an extensive tour of South America, and he published a travel diary the next year. On August 31, 1920, he attended a Singakademie performance in Buenos Aires. His description is complimentary toward Prager and includes a lofty, poetic description of Schubert's great *Wanderer Fantasy*:

3.06 Felix Weingartner and Lucille Marcel, ca. 1915.

> The Singakademie, a German association, invited us to attend their concert. Under the direction of a young conductor, Mr. Prager, it was a competent performance with the limited resources available. We heard the *Schicksalslied* of Brahms and Bruch's *Schön Ellen*, a work completely out of date by now, but still useful for singing clubs. A pianist, Mr. Stephany, played Beethoven's C minor concerto and Schubert's *Wanderer Fantasy*, which Liszt transformed into a piano concerto, in this case particularly well. Has anything better been created than the middle movement of this piece? And the repetition of the main part, which shimmers through all the keys, until it thunders into C Major with a tremendous fugue theme, a boulder that rises to the sky, lifted up by the word of God from the bottom of the ocean.[16]

A month later, on October 1, Weingartner attended a second Singakademie performance, in this case, a program staged in his honor, and devoted entirely to his compositions:

> In the evening, the concert at the Singakademie, which the German ambassador, Mr. von Olshausen, also attended. The conductor, Mr. Prager, brought together a quite strong string orchestra, with which he performed the *Serenade*, now all of 40 years old, which I wrote as a conservatory student in Leipzig. Drangosch repeated my *Phantasiebilder*, my wife sang some older and newer songs by me, and at the end Drangosch and I played two movements from my first

symphony on piano, four hands. A merry, brief supper concluded the successful event, for which the president of the Singakademie, Mr. Wald, rendered outstanding service.[17]

Prager later claimed to have studied conducting with Weingartner, and it was most likely during this brief period when he and Weingartner were both resident in Buenos Aires.

The prominent Argentine musician Ernesto Drangosch (1882–1925) mentioned in this account was a pianist, conductor, teacher, and composer from a German immigrant family, and one of most important figures in Argentina's early classical music tradition at the beginning of the 20th century. Drangosch studied in Berlin in 1897–1900 and again in 1901–5, though it seems unlikely that he and Prager would have crossed paths there. Prager was seven years younger than Drangosch and would only have been 16 years old when Drangosch returned permanently to Argentina in 1905. They were clearly connected to one another after Prager's arrival in Argentina, however.

3.07 Ernesto Drangosch (ca. 1920).

Between 1906 and 1912, Drangosch completed his *Piano Concerto in E Major*—the first piano concerto by an Argentine composer. Drangosch played its premiere in Mar de la Plata on March 13, 1913, and performed it in Buenos Aires on October 27, 1913.[18] According the Argentine conductor Lucio Bruno-Videla of Buenos Aires, director of the Drangosch Group, Drangosch and Prager later performed a two-piano version of the concerto in concert, with Drangosch on the solo part and Prager on the orchestral reduction. They then performed it a second time, and switched roles![19] It must have been after this performance that Drangosch dedicated the published score to Sigfrid Prager.

Prager's most prestigious conducting work in Argentina was as an opera conductor at the Teatro Colón. When it opened in its present building in 1908, it was the finest opera house in Latin America, and it remains one of the world's great concert venues.

His work at the Teatro Colón went beyond

3.08 Performance in the Teatro Colón of Buenos Aires, ca. 1935.

opera: In November 1924, shortly before he left Argentina, Prager conducted a large orchestra accompanying Fritz Lang's silent film *Siegfried* there.[20] *Siegfried* was Part I of Lang's enormous five-hour *Die Nibelungen*, an expressionist version of the same medieval epic that inspired Wagner's "ring cycle." Like many first-rank films of the day, *Siegfried* had an original orchestral score written to be played in conjunction with screenings of the film—in this case composed by Gottfried Huppertz. While there are occasional echoes of Wagnerian style in his *Siegfried* score, it was entirely original and was designed to accompany Lang's storyline and imagery.[21]

It is clear that Prager was also a prominent performer in Buenos Aires. In addition to the recital with Drangosch noted above, he performed dozens of chamber music concerts with the most important Argentine players of the early 1920s. This was a period of burgeoning interest in classical music in Argentina, with performances of both the standard European repertoire and new music by Argentine composers. Prager took part in concert series sponsored by the Argentine Philharmonic Association, the Artistic Concert Group, and the Argentine Society of Chamber and Symphonic Music.[22]

Prager left Argentina in late 1924, arriving in New York City on December 31. According to the Velie account, he did not then speak English, but he mastered the language within a few months of his arrival.[23] I have few specifics on what he was doing in the city in early 1925, but from later references it is possible to infer that he worked as an accompanist and vocal coach. He also seems to have found work as a conductor, probably at the Yorkville Theater. The Yorkville, located in the heart of New York's Upper East Side German immigrant community, was one of a number of theaters that hosted a flourishing German operetta and German-language theater

3.09 The Yorkville Theater, on Manhattan's Upper East Side, ca. 1920.

scene in the late 19th and early 20th centuries. Like many German-American theaters, the Yorkville was obliged to set aside German-language productions in 1918, due to anti-German sentiment during World War I, but by the time Prager arrived in the city, there was again an enormous demand for the latest German and Viennese operettas, both in the original German and in English-language adaptations.[24] One activity that is documented was his work with the baritone Royal Dadmun. Dadmun was among the most popular recording artists of the day, appearing on at least 220 records between 1906 and 1930, primarily for the highly successful Victor label.[25] He also made many stage and concert appearances. In the spring of 1925, Prager was Dadmun's accompanist during an extensive tour of the West Coast. There are a few reviews from this tour that mention Prager, as in a review of Dadmun's recital in Salem, Oregon, on March 19:

> Much of the success of the Dadmun concerts are directly traceable to the artist's accompanist, Sigried [sic] Prager. He is, without a doubt, one of the finest accompanists that a Salem audience has been privileged to hear.[26]

On April 28, 1925, Prager was Dadmun's accompanist for a program at Town Hall in New York City.[27]

At some point when he was in New York in early 1925, Prager met George P. Walker (1874–1964), a Madison native and operatic bass singer, though they may also have known one another previously through Walker's prewar work in Berlin. Walker was born in Fox Lake, some 50 miles north of Madison, but grew up in Madison, son of a local foundry owner and part-time Baptist minister. He studied in Europe in 1900 and had apparently been in Berlin for several years prior to the war. He returned to Berlin in 1916, leaving only in May 1917, a month after the United States declared war on Germany.[28] By 1925, he had an active career in New York City, singing on the radio and in occasional stage roles. On March 20, 1925, for example, he sang the lead role in the premiere of Charles Wakefield Cadman's opera *The Garden of Mystery*, as part of a benefit concert at Carnegie Hall.[29] He also appeared frequently as a soloist in New York City's largest churches, as on Good Friday and Easter Sunday in 1925, when he was a soloist at St. Patrick's Cathedral.[30] Walker would continue to perform until about 1930, after which he spent over two decades as a teacher in Los Angeles and Seattle.[31] It was Walker who was responsible for bringing Sigfrid Prager to Madison.

3.10 George Walker in 1929.

Madison and New York, 1925–1926

The first public mention of Prager in Madison was on May 3, 1925, in a brief *Wisconsin State Journal* article reporting that George Walker would be returning to Madison during the summer to teach at the private Wisconsin School of

Music and that he would be bringing with him the "New York teacher and operatic director, Dr. Siegbried [sic] Prager."[32] A few days later, the *Capital Times* noted that "Siegfried Prager ... has a reputation as an accompanist and inspiring coach."[33] Walker and Prager were in Madison by early June, and though it took a few weeks for the local newspapers consistently to spell his name correctly, it is clear that Prager made an immediate impression on Madison during his two months in the city. He was a guest instructor that summer at the Wisconsin School of Music, and he gave a popular series of public lecture-recitals with Walker titled "Development of the Song from Bach to Richard Strauss." This series would also feature local baritone Alexius Baas and pianist Margaret Otterson, both of whom would become Prager's frequent musical collaborators in coming years. Prager's views on opera and American music were quoted in the papers, and his recitals with Walker were among the musical highlights in Madison that summer, particularly a performance at Music Hall on July 28.[34] On the day after this performance, the *Capital Times* reported that Prager was leaving Madison and would sail briefly to Argentina before returning to New York in the fall to conduct at the Yorkville Theater and to lead the Arion Choral Society. He would also be serving as a lecturer at the New York Institute of Fine Arts and at Harper's Institute.[35]

Though it must remain speculation a century after the fact, I suspect that the primary purpose of Prager's quick trip back to Argentina was to finalize a divorce from his first wife, Anna Willner Wantzloeben. The 1929 Velie article notes that Prager and his second wife, German-Argentine soprano Frances Silva (Franziska Reuttinger), fell in love while she was his student in Argentina.[36] Frances was with Prager when he arrived in New York at the end of 1924, though he was still married to Anna at the time he filled out a citizenship Declaration of Intention on April 6, 1925. This document notes that Anna was at that time still resident in Buenos Aires. In any case, the marriage to Anna had ended by August 28, 1925, when he and Frances were married in New York City.[37] There are a few references to her singing at the Yorkville Theater, where Prager conducted in 1925–26, but Frances Silva Prager (whom Prager affectionately referred to as "Fanny") does not seem to have had much of an independent

3.11 Frances Silva Prager in 1929.

singing career after she came to Madison. However, she frequently appeared as a soloist on programs that her husband conducted in Madison and Chicago through the early 1940s.

While I have not found which specific productions at the Yorkville Theater Prager conducted, there would have been a lot of work available for a skilled conductor that season, particularly given the renewed interest in German operetta. During its 1925–26 season, the Yorkville hosted no fewer than 175 operetta performances.[38] I have likewise been unable to document Prager's connection with the Arion Choral Society, but again he would have been eminently qualified to lead this group, one of New York's oldest and most well-established German singing societies.[39]

Prager's most high-profile appearance in New York City that season was conducting the New Symphony Orchestra in Carnegie Hall. This professional ensemble had first been organized in 1919 by the *avant-garde* composer Edgard Varèse, intended as a more progressive alternative to the major orchestras already existing in the city, the New York Philharmonic and the New York Symphony Society. Varèse conducted its first concert in April 1919, an aggressively modern program beginning with a piece by Bach, but continuing with contemporary works by Debussy, Casella, Bartók, and Dupont.[40] Varèse's vision of a progressive "composer's orchestra" lasted only a few more concerts, however. In the 1920–21 season, the orchestra, now renamed the National Symphony Orchestra and under the direction of Artur Bodanzky of the Metropolitan Opera and Dutch conductor Willem Mengelberg, performed a season of more conventional and conservative orchestral works. In 1922, this orchestra formally merged with the New York Philharmonic. (The merger seems to have been related to an effort to push out the Philharmonic's conductor Josef Stránsky in favor of Mengelberg.[41]) In 1926, the orchestra was reorganized with several of the same musicians as the New Symphony Orchestra of New York, now under the auspices of the American Federation of Musicians.[42] Prager conducted its initial performance in Carnegie Hall on May 1, 1926. This lengthy program—similar to the extravaganzas he would later stage in Madison—included an excerpt from Goldmark's *Die Königen von Saba*, arias by Verdi, Wagner, Flotow, and Boito sung by soprano Dorothy Adrian and tenor Max Bloch, pianist Elsie Kirchgesser playing Liszt's *Fantasy on Hungarian Folk Melodies*, Liszt's *Les Préludes*, Tchaikovsky's *1812 Overture*, the *Intermezzo* from Wolf-Ferrari's *I gioelli della Madonna*, and Wagner's *Tannhaüser Overture*.[43]

In early April 1926, both Madison newspapers announced that Prager and Walker were returning to Madison for the summer, to once again be on the faculty of the Wisconsin School of Music. Prager arrived in late June and began a series of lecture recitals on various topics: "How to Listen to a Symphony Concert," "Three Masters of Song: Brahms, Wolf, and Strauss," "Claude Debussy," and "The History of 'Music Drama.'" This time the lectures included not only Walker and New York–based contralto Viola Ellis, but also Prager's wife Frances Silva.[44] Within a few weeks of his arrival, he had been approached by Susan Seastone on behalf of the Madison Civic Music Association about conducting the soon-to-be-formed Madison Civic Symphony. In early August, he accepted an offer from the MCMA board to conduct the orchestra for an annual salary of $1000, with a promise that this salary would be increased if possible.[45] In 1972, Prager remembered that he been contracted to conduct operettas at the Yorkville Theater for the 1926–27 season, but "felt more attracted by the opportunity to do serious music, renounced my New York contract, and stayed in Madison."[46]

Madison's Maestro: The MCMA, Vocational School, and Other Work in Madison

In October 1941, Alexius Baas published a *Capital Times* article titled "Civic Music in Madison" which in part described Prager's early years in Madison. It is well worth quoting a few extracts from this article here. In his slightly self-aggrandizing account, Baas wrote, in his typically flamboyant style:

> It was the early spring of 1925. My old friend and colleague George Walker, basso, was living in Madison at the time. He had met a musician in New York, he said, a Dr. Sigfrid Prager, formerly of Berlin and Buenos Aires, a man over whose musical knowledge and accomplishments he grew eloquent. I knew Walker to be conservative in his praise as a rule, so when he said that Dr. Prager was planning to spend a summer in Madison, I looked forward to meeting the stranger with great interest. My wife's mother had a spare room and it was arranged that Dr. Prager should stay at her place. One rainy, muggy night he arrived, and I shall never forget my first impression when we clasped hands. A giant of a man with crisp curling hair, fine features, looking like a human dynamo of energy and action. I instinctively felt that Walker's praise had been an understatement.

Baas, who was running a canoe rental operation in Vilas Park that summer, goes on to describe their developing friendship. He implies that Prager was thinking of settling in Madison even during his 1925 visit, and that Baas was already thinking about him as a potential director for a civic music program:

As soon as he was fairly settled in his new quarters, it was to my island that Dr. Prager found his way almost daily with his briefcase of books and papers, and it was here that there was founded an enduring musical and personal friendship. I soon discovered that my own musical knowledge (excepting perhaps the field of song) was a drop in the bucket compared to his. And it came to me with prophetic insight that this was the man Madison needed to unify and coordinate its musical activities ... if such a thing were possible. His questions as to the local situation showed a keen understanding not only of a community's needs in musical fields, but also of human values and equations.

My replies, I confess, were none too encouraging. I had grown up in Madison, and I knew local conditions as well as anyone. I had attempted in my own day to interest certain influential men and women in the forming of something like a coherent musical association. I had failed. [...] The mistake had been made of attempting to combine university and city interests. Every church had a choir. There were half a dozen choral organizations in the city. Attempts had been made at times to organize an orchestra. These had failed. Everything, musically, was at a loose end.

I pointed out these things to him, and emphasized the difficulties confronting any musician who would be rash enough to try to organize these divergent and sometimes conflicting elements into a purposeful and coherent unit. I offered what advice and help I was capable of giving, but told him that any such attempt would be a failure [...] He weighed all that I said and decided to begin the hopeless job. There followed many long talks on the island or floating in a canoe under the stars on the silent lagoon, and always I was more impressed with my companion's vast knowledge of music and his shrewd judgments of the men and women who might help or hinder his plans, and finally realized that, if any man could do this job, it was he. And so he began....

Baas continues, describing both the difficulties ("tedious details of organization," "indifference," and "petty bickering" among musicians) faced by Prager in the early years, and his own doubts about whether the enterprise would survive. He concluded on a high note, however:

But he kept at it. What black hours he went through in those years of grinding effort, he alone knows, and few of us can guess. The result we all know: a civic chorus and orchestra second to none in the United States, even in cities five times our size, and a growing interest in music that will make Madison one of the most music-minded communities in the world.[47]

Prager's work directly for the MCMA is discussed in the previous chapter and the next, so the following section deals with aspects of his life in Madison outside of that work.

The Pragers made Madison their permanent home in 1926 and rented homes in several locations over the next decade, mostly near downtown. By 1936, they had purchased the small house at 637 West Lakeside Street that would be their home until 1948. They lived on the main floor and rented the upper floor to boarders throughout their time in Madison.

Prager had come to Madison initially in the summers of 1925 and 1926 as a guest instructor at the Wisconsin School of Music, and he would continue to teach occasionally there over the next few years, particularly in the summers. By the early 1930s, his work at the Vocational School and his increasingly busy conducting schedule seems to have put an end to this, though he clearly remained on good terms with the school's director, Elizabeth Buehler. When Prager was formally naturalized as a United States citizen at the Dane County courthouse on May 19, 1930, Buehler and her brother Fred stood as official witnesses.

Prager sought conducting activities beyond Civic Music throughout his time in Madison, eventually working extensively in Chicago, Sheboygan, and Milwaukee, but he also worked with other groups in Madison. In September 1926, even before the first rehearsal of the new Madison Civic Symphony, he was named director of the Madison Maennerchor.[48] This venerable Madison chorus, founded in 1852, celebrated its 75th anniversary with a gala concert in the Masonic Temple Auditorium on April 21, 1927, which Prager directed. In addition to the Maennerchor, this extravaganza featured vocal soloists Frances Silva, George Walker, and Alexius Baas, flutist Florence Bennett, and two guest choirs, the Mozart Club and the Carroll College Glee Club. The Civic Symphony appeared at the end of this long program, performing an excerpt from Mendelssohn's music for *A Midsummer Night's Dream*, and accompanying Baas and the massed choirs in Grieg's cantata *Landkjenning* (Land Sighting).

In 1926, Prager also became the music director of Luther Memorial Church, Madison's largest Lutheran congregation, which had recently (1923) completed the large gothic-style church it still occupies on the University campus. Prager held this position for about a year. He resigned from the Maennerchor in February 1929, shortly after he was named director of two choirs in Chicago.[49] Prager was succeeded as director of the Maennerchor by Baas, who would lead the group for over three decades. The Maennerchor would appear many times on MCMA programs over the next 20 years, supplementing the Madison Civic Chorus, which frequently needed additional men's voices.

3.12 Prager and the Luther Memorial Choir, 1927. Paul Jones, the church's organist, is standing next to Prager. Note that the women in the choir are wearing academic robes rather than choir robes, and that they all are wearing mortarboards. This had been part of their uniform since 1915. According to Gary Brown, who has recently published a history celebrating the centennial of the 1923 building, this was popular in church choirs in this period, in part because it allowed women to wear hats in church—de rigueur for the time—but also to maintain a uniform costume for the chorus.

Prager's most extensive work in Madison outside of the MCMA was for the Vocational School, work which began in 1929. The $1000 annual salary and "gentleman's agreement" agreed upon in 1926 was clearly not enough to keep him in Madison, even when he supplemented this with work for the Madison Maennerchor and Luther Memorial Church. The Vocational School's central role in the history of the MCMA—both in securing a stable salary for Prager and in providing an administrative safety net for the orchestra and chorus—was discussed in the previous chapter. In fall of 1929–30—his first full year as a faculty member—Prager taught the first half of a course on music history and appreciation.[50] Beginning in 1932–33, the Madison Civic Symphony and Madison Civic Chorus are listed as classes. While the requirement that symphony players enroll in the class was rather quickly abandoned, chorus members were expected to enroll at least through the late 1940s.[51]

In the summer of 1934, Prager made his first return trip to Germany since leaving in 1918. He visited his father and brother in Berlin and later met Frances Prager in Italy. She had sailed from Argentina, where she had been visiting her family. The Pragers spent a few weeks in Capri before returning to Germany and then home to Wisconsin. Shortly before his return in August, there was a brief flurry of concern in Madison when the *Capital Times*, citing "unconfirmed reports," reported that Prager, then 46 years old, was being detained by Nazi officials. According to unnamed friends in Madison, as a German army veteran, he was now being forced to reenlist. The *Capital Times* reporter did carefully point out that Prager was a naturalized citizen, even confirming his naturalization with the Dane County Circuit Court.[52] When Prager himself arrived in Madison just a few days later, he was completely unaware of the story, and gave a brief interview quashing the rumor:

> I was dumbfounded when I arrived in Madison Saturday night to hear tales of my detention in Germany. Where the story originated, I neither know nor care, but it is utterly false. It would be as impossible for the German government to force citizens of another country to become German soldiers, as it would be for America to draft alien visitors into her army. On the contrary, I was treated with the utmost courtesy, as are all tourists in Germany, for the government needs the results of an influx of foreign currency.[53]

However, the next day the *Capital Times* published a much longer interview, in which Prager was critical of what he had seen in Germany. Rather naïvely, he suggested that "all who went about their private affairs, leaving politics to the government, were unharmed." But he noted that Germany under the Nazis was every bit as tightly controlled and nationalistic as the Imperial Germany he had left in 1918, and that "Germans have never known a democratic government like ours." He lamented the tight Nazi controls over radio and the newspapers, calling German news and entertainment "monotonous" and "stereotyped." He saved his strongest criticism for German music: "Before 1918, there were several national civic symphony orchestras and concerts were numerous. Today, because of the nationalistic trend, there are a few heavy operas, and a series of dull, stale pieces on the government-controlled radio."[54]

Prager initially taught piano, composition, and conducting at the Wisconsin School of Music, and he also taught privately. One of his most successful piano students was Gerald (Jerry) Borsuk (1921–2016). Borsuk, a native of Madison's vibrant Greenbush neighborhood, studied with Prager until he began attending the University as a music student in 1938, where he studied with Gunnar Johansen. He appeared twice as a soloist with the Madison Civic Symphony—

in Beethoven's *Concerto No. 2* in 1935 (at age 14) and Gershwin's *Concerto in F* in 1951. Prager also featured him as a piano soloist with the Wisconsin Symphony Orchestra in 1941. Borsuk played oboe in the orchestra as a teenager and played English horn in the late 1940s and 1950s. At one of Prager's final concerts, in April 1948, he was featured on English horn in Sibelius's *The Swan of Tuonela*. Following military service

3.13 Jerry Borsuk in 2000. (Photo by the author.)

in World War II, Borsuk returned to Madison, where he had a successful 60-year career as a piano teacher and piano tuner and as one of the city's most prominent jazz musicians.[55] In a 2000 interview, Borsuk remembered his studies with Prager with great fondness, noting that "he seemed to know just about everything written for the piano up through Debussy" and crediting him with providing a strong foundation in technique and style. He noted that Prager was always demanding as a teacher, but also warm and friendly.[56]

Sybil Anna Vilas Hanks (1908–1969) was one of Prager's composition students and a member of one of Madison's most powerful and wealthy families. Her father, Lucien (Louis) Mason Hanks, was president of Madison's First National Bank and the son of one of the city's first important bankers, Lucien Stanley Hanks. Her mother, Mary Vilas Hanks, was a member of one of Madison's founding families and daughter of William F. Vilas, a Civil War hero who later served as U.S. Postmaster General, as Secretary of the Interior, and in 1891 to 1897 as one of Wisconsin's United States senators. Their house, built at the top of Wisconsin Avenue, with a large formal garden stretching down to Lake Mendota, was one of the largest homes on Madison's "Mansion Hill."

3.14 Sybil Hanks in the 1950s.

The family was heavily involved with local philanthropy, and they were longtime supporters of the Madison Civic Music Association. Mary Vilas Hanks would eventually serve as president of the MCMA board in 1940–41.

Sybil Hanks initially studied as a teenager with Prager at the Wisconsin School of Music, though he seems to have served as her musical mentor throughout his time in Madison, and the Hanks family was supportive of him in turn. When the Pragers returned to Madison for two extended visits during the 1950s, they stayed at the Hanks home. Hanks died tragically in 1969, during a visit to the Pragers in Argentina. Sybil Hanks never married, and her family was of course wealthy. Hanks herself was heir to part of William F. Vilas's considerable fortune. Her wealth left her free to pursue music throughout her life, and she composed many works between 1930 and 1960. Several of her works were premiered by the Madison Civic Symphony and Chorus, under both Prager and Heermann, including the choral *Decoration Day Hymn* (1931), the cantata *Our Washington* (1932), *Meditation* (1934), the *Concertino for Three Saxophones and Orchestra* (1942), the choral *Quiet My Heart* (1953), and an excerpt from her cantata *The Creation* (1955). Prager also programmed her *Meditation* with the WPA-sponsored Wisconsin Symphony Orchestra, and he conducted performances of the work in Argentina. *The Creation*, with a text by NAACP founder James Weldon Johnson, won first prize in the Wisconsin Centennial Composers Competition in 1948.[57] Both the MSO Archives and the Wisconsin Music Archive hold copies of a recording that preserves what Hanks probably considered to be her finest works: *The Compositions of Sybil Ann Hanks*, a live recording of an MCMA chamber music concert from April 29, 1955. This recording, with members of the Civic Orchestra and Chorus—and undoubtedly financed by Hanks herself—includes the following works:

- *Our Washington* (composed 1929—on a poem by Longfellow)
- *Quiet My Heart* (1951—on a poem by Joseph W. Cochran)
- *Rondo in Old Style for Violin and Piano* (1929—featuring Marie Endres with pianist Margaret Otterson)
- *Three Preludes for Piano* (1940–50—with Margaret Rupp Cooper on piano)
- *Theme with Variations for Winds* (1943)
- *Meditation* (1933—an adaptation of her orchestral piece for cello and piano, featuring Walter Heermann on cello with pianist Margaret Otterson)
- *Concertino for Three Saxophones and Piano* (1942—again an adaptation of the orchestral version)
- finale from *The Creation* (1947—featuring longtime Civic Music bass soloist Henry Peters)[58]

In the 1940s, Prager was officially named a part-time lecturer at the University of Wisconsin–Madison School of Music, teaching conducting and orchestration. During the same period, he gave frequent public lectures through the UW Extension. He also conducted the orchestra at the University's Summer Music Clinic in 1939 and 1946–47.[59] While working at the Music Clinic, Prager met the man who would be his successor, Walter Heermann.

Work in Chicago, Sheboygan, and Beyond the Midwest

Though Prager's dual roles in Madison—as director of the Civic Symphony and Chorus, and as head of the Vocational School's music program—were his primary activities, he also sought additional conducting engagements throughout his tenure, such as the Madison Maennerchor and at Luther Memorial Church in 1926–29. His first major commitments outside of Madison were in Chicago, where he became the music director of two choirs in 1929: the Chicago Bach Chorus and the Chicago Singverein. Both groups had been founded by conductor William [Wilhelm] Boeppler (1863–1928), a German immigrant to Milwaukee in 1894. A strong advocate of German art music, Boeppler founded the Milwaukee A Capella Chorus, and was also among the founders of Milwaukee's Wisconsin Conservatory of Music in 1899. Though he would continue these Milwaukee commitments for the rest of his life, he also began to work extensively in Chicago, moving there in 1903.[60] He founded the Chicago Singverein (Singing Society) in 1910, and the Chicago Bach Chorus in 1925. Boeppler led other amateur choral groups in Chicago as well, and served on several occasions as guest conductor for the Chicago Symphony Orchestra. After Boeppler's death in December 1928, Prager was named as director for both choirs. Programs preserved in the MSO archives and reports in the Chicago newspapers document at least 20 performances between 1929 and 1932 by these choirs which were directed by Prager.

The Chicago Bach Chorus, perhaps the city's finest amateur choir, was closely associated with the Chicago Symphony Orchestra, performing most of its concerts in Orchestra Hall, with accompaniment usually provided by the CSO. For his first program with the group on May 15, 1929, Prager featured his friend George Walker and his wife Frances Silva as vocal soloists. The repertoire

3.15 Prager leading the Chicago Singverein in 1931.

for this program was devoted—as most of the choir's programs were—entirely to works by Johann Sebastian Bach, and included the *Orchestral Suite No. 3*, two complete cantatas (*No. 106* and *No. 11*), two chorales, and two additional choruses from *Cantata No. 76* and *Cantata No. 30*.

The Chicago Singverein, an equally large mixed chorus, sang a more varied repertoire, though heavily weighted towards German works. On April 29, 1931, for example, Prager conducted the ensemble in a concert version of Weber's romantic opera *Der Freischütz* in Orchestra Hall. Their previous program on January 14, 1931, also in Orchestra Hall, was more typical of the Singverein's concerts. Here they performed a program with 42 members of the Chicago Symphony Orchestra that included the following repertoire:

> Weber's *Overture to "Der Freischütz"*
> a multi-movement cantata, *Das Märchen von der schönen Melusina* ("The Tale of the Fair Melusina") by the now-forgotten German romantic composer Heinrich Hofmann
> Nicolai's *Overture to "The Merry Wives of Windsor"*
> Mendelssohn's part-song *Die Primel* ("The Primrose")
> an English madrigal by Thomas Morley, *Now is the Month of Maying*
> Gounod's sacred part-song *Près du fleuve étranger* ("By the Waters of Babylon")—sung in German
> Borodin's *Polovtsian Dances from "Prince Igor"*—with the choral parts in English

Prager stepped away from the podium on at least two of his Chicago programs to perform as a piano soloist. At the Chicago Bach Chorus concert on May 7, 1930, he played the brilliant solo keyboard part of Bach's *Brandenburg Concerto No. 5* with members of the Chicago Symphony Orchestra. Two years later, on April 24, 1932, he performed Franck's *Symphonic Variations* on a Chicago Singverein program in Orchestra Hall, in this case bringing his Madison associate Arthur Kreutz to play a piano reduction of the orchestra part. (Prager had performed the same piece a few weeks earlier with the Madison Civic Symphony.)

Prager found other opportunities in Chicago as well. In October 1930, he conducted the Chicago Civic Opera in their magnificent recently completed opera house (which today houses the Chicago Lyric Opera), in a production of Johann Strauss's *Die Fledermaus*.[61] Reviews of his performances in Chicago were unfailingly positive, and it seems that the membership of both choirs grew significantly under his leadership. In Madison, however, Prager's work in

Chicago presented a serious issue for the Madison Civic Music Association, as laid out in the minutes of the MCMA Board during this period. The combined income from his directorship of the two Chicago choirs was significantly higher than what he was being paid in Madison, and as a much larger musical market, Chicago offered additional professional opportunities that Madison could not. On February 19, 1930, MCMA Board President Otto Hambrecht presented a letter in which Prager announced his intention to resign effective September 1, 1930. As noted in the previous chapter, the issue of his combined salary from the Vocational School and MCMA was finally resolved in 1931. The salary was probably the prime factor in retaining him, but in the end, it also seems to have come down to Prager's personal preference for Madison. At the Board's Annual Meeting on May 25, 1931:

> Dr. Prager explained why he did not prefer Chicago. He stated that there is not the real appreciation of music and artistic beauty among the professional musicians [he worked with there]. Music there is mostly a mere business matter. He welcomes the opportunity to come back to Madison. The work of the orchestra and chorus during the past year was very satisfactory he noted. He expects that season will also be a happy one… he predicts next season will be the best in the Association's history.[62]

Prager continued working in Chicago regularly for another year, but his final performance with the two Chicago groups was a Chicago Bach Chorus concert on May 9, 1932, after which he stepped away from both choirs. I have found no evidence that he worked in Chicago after that. However, his years in Chicago did have a long-term effect on his work in Madison: he seems to have forged a wide network of contacts among Chicago-based musicians, particularly singers, many of whom would appear as soloists in MCMA performances over the next 15 years.

Prager was employed in academia, beyond the Vocational School, at several points in his career, and in the 1940s, he would have an appointment as a lecturer at the University of Wisconsin–Madison. However, a decade earlier, he had a temporary appointment at one of California's most prestigious schools: Prager spent the summer of 1935 as a guest lecturer at Stanford University. While at Stanford, he lectured on musicology and on the psychology and methods of music education. A front-page article in the *Capital Times* that September reported with some civic pride that the Pragers had been entertained by former President Herbert Hoover and his wife at their home in Palo Alto. In the same article, the *Capital Times* reported that Prager had been invited to lecture on ancient Greek music and on the history of chamber music at Oxford University in England during the summer of 1936,[63] but he does not seem to have accepted the invitation.

Sigfrid Prager seems to have possessed almost unlimited energy, but his schedule at the end of the 1930s must have been exhausting even for him. In addition to his direction of the Madison Civic Symphony and Chorus, increasing time commitments conducting the WPA orchestras in Madison and Milwaukee, and his duties at the Vocational School, he was also making weekly trips north to Sheboygan beginning in early 1935, as conductor of the Sheboygan Civic Chorus. This group, sponsored by the Vocational School in Sheboygan, was clearly modeled on elements of the MCMA. Prager led the choir in its first concert on May 15, 1935,[64] and its two annual concerts were every bit as ambitious as programs in Madison. In December 1937, for example, the Sheboygan group performed a staged version of *La Traviata* at the Van Der Vaart Theatre there—a performance that was temporarily halted when a large bar that was supporting lighting equipment collapsed onto the stage. Prager seems to have taken this in stride, and according to a press account the next day:

> Dr. Prager's calm request from the director's stand at the audience remain seated and Nelidoff's prompt announcement from the stage that no one was injured calmed the large crowd, and in an incredibly short time the action was resumed with Violetta and her fellow singers exhibiting a sportsmanship that brought a storm of applause from the other side of the footlights.[65]

In early 1938, after he became heavily involved with the Wisconsin Symphony Orchestra, Prager began delegating some rehearsals to a Sheboygan musician, Adolf J. Wuerl, and he stepped away from the Sheboygan Civic Chorus after its May 1938 performance.

WPA Conductor: The Madison Concert Orchestra and Wisconsin Symphony Orchestra

He would have a much more extensive commitment in Milwaukee beginning in 1937. Prager made his first appearance as a conductor in Milwaukee on November 15, 1931, when he conducted the Milwaukee Philharmonic Orchestra in a performance of two movements from his own *Symphonic Suite*. This group, founded in 1929, was the city's first attempt at creating a fully professional orchestra, though it fell victim to the Depression after just a few seasons.[66] In late 1937, however, Prager was named music director of the WPA-sponsored

Wisconsin Symphony Orchestra.

The Wisconsin Symphony Orchestra—variously known as the Wisconsin WPA Symphony Orchestra and the Wisconsin Federal Symphony Orchestra— was the flagship ensemble of the Federal Music Project (FMP) in Wisconsin. The FMP was part of the Works Progress Administration, the largest and most ambitious of President Roosevelt's Depression-era New Deal initiatives, designed to provide employment for millions of Americans. While the WPA is perhaps best remembered today for thousands of public infrastructure projects completed across the country, it also supported musicians, composers, visual artists, writers, dancers, choreographers, actors, playwrights, and historians. Established in 1935, the WPA's Federal Project One was designed not only to provide employment but also to bring cultural enrichment to the nation. What was commonly known as "Federal One" included the Federal Music Project, the Federal Writers Project, the Federal Theater Project, the Federal Dance Project, and the Historical Records Survey. The Federal Music Project's National Director from 1935–39 was violinist and conductor Nikolai Sokolov, a Russian immigrant who had led the Cleveland Orchestra. Sokolov's thoroughly classical orientation had a strong effect on the FMP. He insisted, for example, that musicians receiving funding met and maintained high professional and technical standards. The FMP sponsored a wide range of musical activities that included concert and dance bands, community choruses, recreational music groups, music copying and research, and (particularly in the west) folk music. However, the most prominent FMP projects across the country were devoted to classical music: chamber groups, opera companies, and orchestras. The repertoire these groups presented was generally conservative and heavily dominated by European works, though the FMP also made a strong effort to promote works by American composers. Some activities of the "Federal One" Theatre, Dance, and Writers Projects would eventually face strong political opposition due to their leftist stance. Though they were not entirely without controversy, the FMP's relatively conservative programs, designed to appeal to the broadest possible audience, remained comparatively free of scandal. The FMP outlived the Federal Dance and Theater Projects (both of which were

3.16 1940 Program cover for the Wisconsin Symphony Orchestra, with a silhouette of Prager.

suspended in 1939), though most of its activities begin to wane after the United States entered World War II in 1941, and it disappeared entirely by 1943.[67]

Wisconsin hosted one of the most active programs of the Federal Music Project, and many of its records are available in the Wisconsin Historical Society Library.[68] They provide a rich source of information, including monthly reports on FMP activities throughout Wisconsin from the state administrators of the program: William V. Arvold, and after 1940, Mark Muth. A document compiled in January 1938—shortly after Prager's official appointment as Director of the Wisconsin Symphony Orchestra—lists 11 FMP projects across the state, which employed 238 musicians: orchestras in Milwaukee, Madison, Superior, Manitowoc, Eau Claire, and Racine; concert bands in Milwaukee, Oshkosh, and Wausau; an African American dance band in Milwaukee; and a Milwaukee-based music arranging and copying unit. (The number of FMP projects in the state had actually been reduced from an original total of 20 in 1936.) The same document reports the following statistics for the period February–December 1937: "the aggregate number of performances is 3,878, with a total audience of 3,221,790; a sufficient proof in itself of the way in which these concerts have been received."[69] A final report on the Wisconsin FMP issued in 1951, years after it suspended activities, estimates that its programs in total presented "nearly 17,000 concerts to approximately 10,000,000 people."[70]

The FMP had, from the beginning, relied heavily on outside support for its programs and had a particularly strong relationship with the American Federation of Musicians, which sponsored union musicians who performed alongside players who were being paid by the FMP. Federal support ended in August 1939, and primary sponsorship of the Wisconsin FMP passed to the Wisconsin Department of Public Instruction, though Arvold and later Muth would continue to report to the national headquarters on FMP activities in the state. With this shift came an increased focus on educational activities in Wisconsin public schools.[71] Arvold noted in October 1939 that some reorganization was in process, particularly in areas outside of Madison and Milwaukee, but the change of sponsorship seems to have had little effect on the number of public performances in Madison and Milwaukee.[72]

In his report to Nikolai Sokoloff for November 1937, Arvold reported on Prager's appointment as conductor of the Milwaukee orchestra:

> Towards the latter part of the month we were assured of getting enough sponsorship to make possible the assignment of Dr. Sigfrid Prager to conduct and train the Wisconsin Symphony. This will be the first time we will have had a major conductor in charge of

the Orchestra. We have also been assured that the Federation of Musicians' Union will augment our orchestra to symphony strength any time we wish it to be made available. We hope to make use of this last sponsorship as soon as Dr. Prager feels he would like to present the orchestra in formal concerts in some downtown theater or auditorium.[73]

Prager had in fact already been heavily involved with the FMP months before his appointment, directing the WPA-sponsored Madison Concert Orchestra. This group had been formed in 1936, and was initially conducted by Prager's frequent collaborator, Arthur Kreutz. In January or February 1937, Prager took over as conductor with Kreutz serving as assistant. The Madison Concert Orchestra had a core of about 20 musicians, regularly supplemented by 20 or more additional musicians funded by the Madison musicians' union, American Federation of Musicians Local 166. The orchestra, one of the most active of the Wisconsin FMP's sponsored ensembles, performed dozens of concerts in schools, in local churches, on the Capitol Square, in Madison parks, and in radio broadcasts on local stations WHA and WIBA. Several players also performed regularly with the Madison Civic Symphony as part of their WPA appointments. Prager seems to have been slowed down briefly by a hospitalization in June, for an operation to relieve a hip joint infection,[74] but by August, he resumed concerts with the Madison Concert Orchestra, and in the fall, direction of the Madison Civic Symphony and Chorus, and his work with the Sheboygan Civic Chorus. The Madison Concert Orchestra's summer concerts on the steps of the Capitol, on the University's Memorial Union terrace, and in various parks were particularly popular. Arvold's reports throughout that summer were enthusiastic about these events, and in October 1937, he reported on a particularly successful closing concert of the summer series in Vilas Park, on September 12:

> On this date, Dr. Sigfrid Prager conducted our Madison Concert Orchestra augmented to 60 musicians before a crowd of four or five thousand people who showed their keen appreciation by their applause. In one sense it marked the close of a successful season of out-of-door presentations, I believe it marked the beginning of an innovation of summer concerts for the future in Madison. From all sides commendation was in order and many proffers of help for coming seasons were existent. Madison, we believe, has been awakened to the need of summer concerts.[75]

The concert featured a nationally known radio star with connections to Madison. Baritone Lawrence Salerno had emigrated from Italy with his parents at age 10. The family settled in Madison's Greenbush neighborhood, and Salerno began his studies at the local Wheeler Conservatory. Local coverage of this concert, was every bit as enthusiastic as the audience, in articles in both newspapers promoting the program, and a glowing review in the *Capital Times* the next day, reporting that

> the crowd applauded loud and long, asking for and receiving a large number of encores. Their applause was their 'thank you' for yesterday's concert and for the series of open-air programs brought to the city during the summer.[76]

While Prager continued to conduct the Madison Concert Orchestra in the fall, he must also have had an eye on Milwaukee's Wisconsin Symphony Orchestra. He had already made a successful appearance as guest conductor with the WSO in Milwaukee on May 27, 1937. Like his Chicago appointments eight years earlier, this must have been a cause for concern for the MCMA, though in this case the minutes of the board are silent on the situation. Prager himself, however, moved quickly to assure Madison in a *Capital Times* interview of December 6, 1937 that the new position would not interfere with his commitments to the MCMA and Vocational School. He noted that he would devote from "8 to 12 hours per week" to the Wisconsin Symphony Orchestra, and would be in Milwaukee Thursday through Saturday for the orchestra's rehearsals. The same article reports that Siegfried Vollstedt would be the new conductor of the Madison Concert Orchestra. Vollstedt had previously been quite successful as the conductor of the FMP's Eau Claire Symphony Orchestra. There is, for example, in the WPA Records a copy of a March 1937 letter from Gov. Philip LaFollette commending Vollstedt on a performance the governor had heard in rural Stanley, WI, and formally inviting the Eau Claire orchestra to perform for the Wisconsin State Legislature.[77] Vollstedt's stay in Madison was relatively brief, however, and by the fall of 1938, local bandleader and assistant conductor of the Madison Civic Chorus John L. Bach was named conductor of the Madison Concert Orchestra. By 1940, the conductor was G. Laurenz (Glenn) White. The Madison Concert Orchestra is last mentioned in the official WPA records in October 1940, but it must have continued in some form for several months afterwards. The last reference to Madison's WPA Orchestra I can find in the local papers is on August 17, 1941, when it performed an outdoor program at Madison's Breese Stevens Field.[78]

While the Milwaukee WPA orchestra would certainly take more time than "8 to 12 hours per week" he promised—particularly during the busy years of 1938, 1939, and 1940—Prager seems to have been as good as his word with regards to the Madison Civic Symphony and Chorus. There was no effect on the quantity, and apparently the quality, of MCMA's orchestral and choral performances in this period, though his new commitment in Milwaukee did seem to have to put an end to both the tradition of MCMA-sponsored staged operas in Madison, and to his work with the Sheboygan Civic Chorus.

Over the next three years, Prager conducted more than 40 formal programs with the Wisconsin Symphony Orchestra.[79] He undoubtedly led many more school and radio performances, though many of these seem to have been delegated to assistants. One of his first programs with the orchestra was in Madison, at the Masonic Temple, on January 24, 1938. This concert, which had a large and appreciative audience despite the "worst blizzard of the year,"[80] included works by Beethoven, Brahms, Vitali, Debussy, and Wagner. Prager brought in a few Madison-based soloists for some of his early programs with the Wisconsin Symphony Orchestra in Milwaukee: tenor Karl Fischer-Niemann appeared on February 20, 1938 at Concordia College, and violinist George Szpinalski, a University faculty member, was featured five days later at the Elks Club Auditorium. Arvold mentioned this February 25 program, Prager's first formal appearance in downtown Milwaukee as the orchestra's conductor, as a particular success in his report for that month, and his hopes that "through a series in this auditorium we can build a permanent support for the Orchestra."[81]

The Wisconsin Symphony Orchestra under Prager did, in fact, institute a regular series in downtown Milwaukee over the next few seasons, the series eventually titled "Music for You." In 1939–40, concerts moved from the Elks Auditorium to the enormous Milwaukee Auditorium. This space was subsequently known as the MECCA (Milwaukee Exposition, Convention Center and Arena) Auditorium, and since 2016 as the Miller High Life Auditorium. The repertoire for the series was generally conservative, standard orchestral literature, and the orchestra's democratic intention to appeal to the widest audience was clear: each printed program included a tear-out page inviting audience members to suggest works. The orchestra occasionally presented new works by Wisconsin composers, however. In February 1939, as part of the FMP's nationwide Festival of American Music, the orchestra played works by Prager himself (probably his *Symphonic Suite*, which appeared on other programs in Milwaukee as well) and by Milwaukee composer Milton Rusch.[82] The opening concert of the 1940–41 season included *Music for Orchestra in Two*

Movements by Arthur Kreutz. (Kreutz, who had been born in La Crosse, WI, was a prominent Madison musician and a frequent Prager collaborator. He had by this time moved to Georgia, for a position at the Georgia State College for Women.[83])

The soloists were most often Milwaukee-based musicians, as on March 4, 1940, when the orchestra's concertmaster Herman Koss performed Mozart's A Major violin concerto, or May 5, 1940, when local pianists Clyde and Cleo Parnell performed solos and works for piano, four hands on the program. Occasionally, however, the "Music for You" series featured nationally and internationally known soloists. On March 24, 1940, Danish piano virtuoso Gunnar Johansen, who had recently settled in Madison to teach at the University, performed a concerto by Finnish composer Selim Palmgren, and several of his own solo piano works. In a few programs during the 1940–41 season Prager also shared conducting duties with guest artists. On December 5, 1940, a joint program with the Milwaukee Lyric Chorus, Prager shared the podium with 20-year-old conducting prodigy Lorin Maazel. Maazel, who was also featured as a violin soloist on this program, would become one of the 20th century's great conductors. On January 19, 1941, Austrian composer Ernst Krenek—one of the many musical emigrés to the United States from Nazi Germany and Austria—conducted two of his own works on a Wisconsin Symphony Orchestra program. Krenek signed Prager's program with a personal note: "With most heartfelt thanks for the splendid preparation of this program and the heart-warming understanding. Cordially, Ernst Krenek."[84] The orchestra's next program on March 9 featured composer Percy Grainger, who conducted two of his works, and was piano soloist for two more of his compositions and the Delius *Piano Concerto*.

By far the most successful concerts performed by the Wisconsin Symphony Orchestra under Prager's direction in terms of reaching a large audience were its outdoor performances in the summers of 1938–1940. This series, largely sponsored by the Milwaukee Parks Commission, was titled "Music Under the Stars." From August 1938 onward, most of these concerts took place at the Temple of Music, known locally as the Blatz Bandshell, in Milwaukee's sprawling Washington Park. This large Art Deco bandshell, set in a surrounding natural amphitheater, was the gift of Emil Blatz, the third generation of the

3.17 Milwaukee's Temple of Music (the Blatz Bandshell), which opened in 1938.

Blatz family to run Milwaukee's Blatz Brewing Company. In comparison to the downtown season in the Milwaukee Auditorium, "Music Under the Stars" programs were more heavily focused on star soloists. Prager led the opening program on August 2, 1938, which featured Metropolitan Opera stars John Carter and Kathryn Meisle. He conducted the formal dedication of the Blatz Temple of Music on August 23, 1938, which showcased a nationally known radio star, Jessica Dragonette, in several light classics and operetta arias.[85] His next program, on August 30, featured the great Wagnerian soprano Lotte Lehmann. The audiences for these performances were enormous: the FMP's director Arvold enthusiastically reported an audience of at least 40,000 for the Dragonette concert, and also noted that the August 23 performance had been broadcast nationwide on the Columbia radio network.[86]

The more ambitious summer 1939 series included 16 programs—both at the Temple of Music and at Milwaukee's Humboldt Park—five of them directed by Prager. It began with a program on June 25, featuring lyric soprano Helen Jepson. The FMP's national director, Nikolai Sokoloff, was guest conductor for the program on July 6, featuring the soprano Lucy Monroe, famed for her rendition of *The Star-Spangled Banner*. Prager again worked with John Carter on July 11, and on August 9 with radio star James Melton (before an audience estimated at 50,000[87]). On August 23, the first anniversary of the Temple of Music's opening, he led a concert with soprano Gladys Swarthout and pianist Frank Glazer. (In this case, the audience was reportedly 55,000.[88]) The final program Prager conducted that season, on August 30, was with movie, radio and Metropolitan Opera star Jean Dickenson. The 1940 series included 10 concerts at the Temple of Music, seven of which were conducted by Prager. During that summer he worked again with Jean Dickenson (July 2) and James Melton (July 30), but also with several other prominent soloists: tenor Richard Crooks (June 25), baritone Donald Dickson (July 9) violinist Albert Spalding and soprano Diana Gaylan (August 6), baritone John Charles Thomas (August 13), and soprano Florence George and tenor Lanny Ross (August 20).

The "Music Under the Stars" series long outlived Prager's tenure in Milwaukee, and the Wisconsin Symphony Orchestra itself. It remained a popular summer attraction, with concerts held at the Temple of Music from the 1940s through 1992. The "Music Under the Stars" orchestra was directed initially by Jerzy Bojanowski (who had been Prager's predecessor as conductor of the Wisconsin Symphony Orchestra), and then for 40 years by John-David Anello.[89]

The Wisconsin FMP also employed Prager to train other conductors within the program. In August 1940, after the conclusion of outdoor concerts for the season, he led "in-service training" for all conductors of Milwaukee-based units. The Wisconsin Symphony Orchestra was used in the training, which was intended to raise conducting standards within the FMP's groups. In September, Prager led a similar session in Madison, this time using the Madison Concert Orchestra, for FMP conductors from throughout the state.[90]

Prager's final performance with the Wisconsin Symphony Orchestra was on April 13, 1941 at the Milwaukee Auditorium, a program featuring the famed Fisk Jubilee Singers and his 19-year-old former student Gerald Borsuk, who played the piano solo part in Gershwin's *Rhapsody in Blue*. The concert also featured movements from Prager's own *Symphonic Suite*, undoubtedly included on this program because of the work's ties to Black spirituals, which were the core of the Fisk Jubilee Singers' repertoire. Beginning in January 1940, most of the orchestra's school performances and an increasing number of its more formal concerts were directed by associate conductor Diego "James" Innes, a young Mexican-American immigrant. Innes would succeed Prager as principal conductor, and led the Wisconsin Symphony Orchestra through September 1942.[91] The orchestra itself quietly disbanded within the next year, in an atmosphere of wartime mobilization. For his part, Prager—after four phenomenally busy years of work for the WPA—seems to have settled gratefully back into his duties in Madison.

Prager as a Performer

Prager was clearly a powerful and skilled pianist—both as a soloist and as an accompanist. His early work in Buenos Aires was noted above, and he continued to perform in Madison. He was a featured soloist with the Madison Civic Symphony on six programs, including a couple of solo (Liszt and Chopin) and chamber (Brahms) works that were included on the orchestra's programs:

- 11/15/1927: Handel, *Organ [Piano] Concerto*, op. 4, no. 4
- 2/6/1929 and 5/28/1929: Gershwin, *Rhapsody in Blue*
- 2/3/1930: Brahms, *Piano Concerto No. 2*, first movement; Wagner/Liszt, "Spinning Song" from *The Flying Dutchman*; Liszt, "Gondoliera" from *Venezia e Napoli*; Chopin, *Polonaise in E-flat Major*
- 1/20/1931: Brahms, *Piano Quintet*, op. 34, first movement
- 4/25/1933: Bach, *Brandenburg Concerto No. 5*

He also appeared as a piano soloist on two of the choral concerts he conducted in Chicago between 1929 and 1931. Much more often, he would serve as an accompanist on MCMA programs. It was common in the early days of the Madison Civic Symphony for concerts to include art songs and instrumental solos, as a way of fleshing out the program. At the orchestra's very first program in December 1926, Prager accompanied soprano Esther Dale in a Gounod aria and five different art songs, and he served as an accompanist on many later programs.

He was also an active chamber musician during his first decade in Madison, appearing on dozens of programs with other local musicians. On New Year's Day of 1929, for example, he performed at Christ Presbyterian Church with violinist Gilbert Ross in a recital that included works by Brahms, Weber, Liszt, Chopin, Boulanger, and Paganini. This program also included a work by local composer Cecil Burleigh, his *Fairy Sailing*, and two transcriptions of songs by Granados that were prepared by Ross and Prager.[92] After the early 1930s, Prager's schedule seems to have prevented preparing concertos, though he continued to appear frequently as an accompanist. He was, however, able to use the piano effectively as a tool in rehearsals and in his many public lectures.

Prager as a Composer and Arranger

Prager, who had studied with Max Bruch in the years before World War I, composed at least a few original works. He seems to have worked very much in the romantic style: Gerald Borsuk remarked that "his interest seemed to go about as far as Debussy." However, Borsuk also noted that he was fascinated by American jazz.[93] His earliest work for which I have evidence is a symphonic poem, *Sicania*, composed in 1912. One work premiered by the Madison Civic Symphony in the early years was his *Symphonic Suite* op. 17, composed in 1929. The orchestra premiered the first two movements in 1930, and the complete three-movement suite on April 25, 1933. Its third movement included an offstage chorus, which was led by Alexius Baas. Though this was clearly an "American" piece in inspiration—each of the movements was based upon a Black spiritual—it was a work very much in a European mold, as Prager says in his program note:

> "No attempt has been made by the composer to present these melodies in their original atmosphere, still less to 'jazz' them. He has rather taken them as Dvorák and others have done before, i.e., as beautiful, expressive tunes, suitable for symphonic elaboration and development. In view of his foreign birth and training, the composer makes raises no claim to have made in this suite a contribution to American music.... "

Prager programmed movements of the *Symphonic Suite* on a few later occasions, and also led movements of the work in Milwaukee.

The orchestra and chorus also premiered his *The Message of Song,* written for the first Dane County Music Festival, and performed at the Stock Pavilion by a mass choir of 400 voices on October 16, 1932. The text for this grand choral anthem was written by a local band director, John Mael:

> Spirited and lofty, soaring to the skies,
> Hear the many voices gleefully arise.
> Hearts are beating fast, thrilled by mighty sounds.
> Strains of glorious rapture bear us on their wings;
> Forth shall go our message, life to man it brings.
> Strains for youth and age, songs of ecstasy,
> Tides of richest music sweep triumphantly,
> Songs that give men courage, heav'nly melody.
> Hail to thee, O song, may thy echoes ring!

A few additional Prager works written during his Madison years include his art song, *Pale Moon, An Indian Love Song*, which was performed at a run-out concert in Prairie du Sac in April 1932. In May 1930 he was reportedly planning to compose a symphonic poem titled *Mendota*, after the largest of Madison's lakes.[94] However if this work was ever finished, it does not seem to been performed by the Madison Civic Symphony.

Prager also orchestrated piano works by Debussy, Albinez, and Granados for the Civic Symphony. Hundreds of pages of his manuscript parts, written in his immaculate hand, still exist in the MSO's music library. In many cases, he

3.18 One of Prager's saxophone parts for Wagner's *Götterdämmerung* finale (1946).

was adapting works to be played by the instrumentation available at the time: some symphonies and operatic excerpts, for example, include newly written saxophone parts. The example pictured here is one of four saxophone parts he created for a February 1946 performance of the finale of Wagner's *Götterdämmerung*, a performance featuring soprano Marjorie Lawrence. Working through this part with a full score in hand, it's possible to reconstruct Prager's thought process: the saxophones occasionally stand in for instruments like Wagner tubas that were simply not available to the orchestra, and at other times they are reinforcing the horns or various woodwind sections. Unfortunately, Prager seems to have taken the manuscript scores for his original works with him to Argentina in 1948, and I have not been able to locate any of his purely orchestral music. Of his original compositions, only *The Message of Song* was published, and that only in a piano vocal score.[95]

Prager as a Writer and Lecturer

Though English seems to have been his seventh language, Prager wrote elegantly and was active as a writer throughout his time in Madison. He seems to have authored the great majority of the unsigned program notes that appeared in MCMA's early program books, and occasional program notes with his byline appeared in the books of the Chicago Bach Chorus, Chicago Singverein, and Wisconsin Symphony Orchestra. He also contributed dozens of essays and guest editorials to both of the local newspapers, on topics ranging from great composers, opera, symphonic works, and chamber music to jazz. His writing is admirably straightforward, free of stilted phrasing, and often tinged with humor.

Prager was an early member of the American Musicological Society (AMS), and in January 1948, read a scholarly paper on the monochord at an AMS meeting in Madison. An abstract of this paper, clearly a version of his 1911 dissertation, appears in the very first volume of the *Journal of the American Musicological Society*—the flagship scholarly journal of the field in the United States.[96]

In the 1940s, Prager planned a series of four "conductor's manuals" for some of the standard works of the orchestral literature:

- Vol. 1 - Dvořák, *New World Symphony*
- Vol. 2 - Franck, *Symphony in D minor*
- Vol. 3 - Mozart, *Symphony in G minor* and Beethoven, *Leonore Overture No.3*
- Vol. 4 - Tchaikovsky, *Romeo and Juliet* and Liszt, *Les Préludes*

While the third and fourth volumes do not seem to been published, I have examined the first two volumes.[97] These are entirely practical measure-by-measure guides to the score written by a deeply experienced conductor, who was also an expert on the pedagogy of conducting. He gives advice on balance issues (e.g., reducing the number of basses in the opening bars the *New World* to correct balance), common rhythmic pitfalls, dynamics, string bowings, and points of interpretation, from minute details to larger sections.

Prager was also effective in talking about music to a general audience. From his earliest days in Madison in 1925, giving lecture-recitals with George Walker, to the series of television broadcasts that were his last appearances in Madison, he was engaged as a lecturer, both in Madison and as part of his engagements in Chicago, Sheboygan, and Milwaukee. It was common practice, for example, for Prager to offer a free lecture-recital a few days prior to each MCMA subscription program, dealing with the upcoming repertoire, and he would often follow this up with remarks from the podium at the concert. He also gave dozens of additional talks each season—always lecturing from the piano bench—that were offered by the Vocational School, or hosted in the homes of MCMA board members.

Prager's Retirement and Final Years

Prager announced his retirement early in the 1947–1948 season. I originally wondered if his retirement might have been in part due to bad feelings between Prager and Civic Music: things like the Kunrad Kvam affair of 1946, and other skirmishes with various musicians and board members, but I found no evidence of this. He seems merely to have wanted to retire to a more relaxed life, and it is also likely that he and Frances wanted to return to Argentina to be close to her family. Prager already held the position of lecturer at the University School of Music, and there were efforts in early 1948 to get him to return to Madison permanently after some time away by offering him a professorship. Though he would eventually return to Madison for two working visits during the 1950s, Prager seems to have been noncommittal.[98] Shortly after he left Madison, it was announced that he would return in 1949 to lecture at the University, but just a few months later he had already changed plans. At his farewell banquet on June 12, 1948 (his 59th birthday), he explained:

3.19 Sigfrid Prager in 1948.

> I have been asked privately why I am retiring. I have no reason to retire—no complaints about work or salary or anything. I am just putting into effect a youthful ambition ... that whenever I am quite happy with my work and with my life, I won't gamble with happiness. Then, if I am financially able to so, I shall refuse to take the chance of destroying that happiness.[99]

The local press was lavish in their praise of the retiring Prager. A *Wisconsin State Journal* editorial early in the year commended him for "... a job splendidly done, not only for Madison, but for others who have envied our lot, and can copy our recipe for its making." On the day of Prager's final concert, William Doudna of the *Journal* wrote:

> Prager's career here has been that of a genius ... in the sense that it is a rare man who can weld amateur, professional, and semi-professional musicians into a homogenous whole. And he has poured love into his work—a love for music, the kind that requires that it be shared with as many as can come within the sound of it.[100]

Prager's farewell concert took place on May 23, 1948, a performance of Beethoven's *Missa Solemnis* given to a crowd of over 2000 at the University Stock Pavilion. (As detailed in the next chapter, a recording of this performance surfaced in 2013.) Prager was reportedly so emotional as he said a few words after the concert that only the first few rows of the audience heard him. The *Wisconsin State Journal* review on the following day includes a photo of a visibly choked-up Prager shaking hands with a chorus member, one of hundreds of musicians and audience members who thanked him after the concert. The local press and community gave the concert and the retiring Prager glowing reviews, and Ellen Hegland, of Hollandale, WI was even inspired to poetry, in her *A Gift from Madison*, published in the *Capital Times* in July:

> In jeweled Madison, upon a brilliant day,
> In 1948 on 23rd of May,
> Forth from her gorgeous auditorium, there rolled
> A glorious intonation, from a door
> No human hand and opened heretofore.
> Beethoven's 'Missa Solemnis,' sad toll
> Sad intimation of a passing soul
> Sad tho its intoned requiem
> Holds clarion prelude of immortal hymn.
> The beauteous clasp of earth is dear to hold
> E'en tho its gleam of restoration to the soul,
> And growth Spiritual, with new life zest,
> Beyond the concept of mere mortal mind,
> Beckons, consoles with silence and deep rest,
> Clearer than sensed on boisterous human stage.
> This prelude of immortal wakening hymn,

> Was heralded by 'Minds' Rosetta Stone,'
> From Beethoven, Sigfrid Prager, and Baas
> And personalities, like to their kind:
> Attuned to chord of the Angelic choirs
> That sang at Bethlehem, 'Good Will to Men.'
> Hail Madison that built, in raging war,
> Your auditorium, acoustically
> Perfect, to amplify the message of these minds...[101]

The poem goes on for some two dozen more lines of increasingly fervent incomprehensibility. (Even the most sympathetic readers must have smiled a bit at her characterization of the University Stock Pavilion as a "gorgeous auditorium"—"acoustically perfect" though it may have been!) Eleven months after Prager's farewell concert, yet another, rather less lofty poem appeared, dedicated to the founding members of the orchestra, *To the Charter Members*, signed "G.Z.":

> Way back when, in nineteen twenty-six,
> A bunch of folks decided to mix
> Their voices,
> Doctor Prager was the gent
> Who started them in this grand event
> Ever since then, it's plain to see
> They have gained in popularity
> And the city of Madison
> Rejoices.
>
> But were it not for the folks of old
> Many of whom have left the fold,
> Who knows?
> We probably wouldn't be here to tell
> The story of success we know so well.
> So here's to the folks were with us tonight.
> Who started us on the road to delight
> To you, dear old-timers, full
> Glory goes.[102]

To be sure, neither of these is exactly an immortal piece of poetry, but both of them were genuine reflections of the kind of universal regard Prager and the orchestra inspired in Madison audiences.

Just a few days later, Prager conducted a "Centennial Band" at a concert on the Capitol Square marking Wisconsin's Statehood Day celebrations on May 29, 1948.[103] He also appears to have conducted a few additional band concerts that summer. The Pragers seem to have delayed their departure to September of 1948, so that he could teach at the University's Summer Music Clinic that summer.

Prager apparently approached retirement with his characteristic energy and humor. He and Frances left for Argentina in September. *State Journal* writer Betty Cass, whose cheerful "Day by Day" column dealt with life in Madison, provided a droll account of the Pragers finishing their packing just a few days before taking the train for New Orleans:

> Mrs. Prager insisted that she had discarded absolutely everything discardable, so they compromised on going through Dr. Prager's personal treasures again to see what else HE could discard, and the first three things that came under scrutiny (by Mrs. Prager) were his two violas and their cases and his beloved pet canary in its cage. Much as she admires his other musical talents, Mrs. Prager doesn't particularly care for Dr. Prager's viola playing, so she didn't see why he couldn't very well leave those two instruments and their bulky cases behind. Dr. Prager, however, is very fond of the violas, which he calls Gorgonzola and Samovarius (which are names of derision which musicians often apply to cheap or "cheesy" violins) and he put in a very fine plea for them.
>
> Mrs. Prager finally relented, then, but she refused to budge an inch from the canary in its cage. 'It's either the canary or me!' she shouted, dramatic-like in her fine soprano. 'you may take one of us to Argentina, but not both. Choose, my Lord!' 'So,' says Dr. Prager sadly, 'I choose her. You see, I've had her longer then I've had the canary, so there was a little priority involved.

Cass goes on to note that one particularly prized possession was a gold-plated lifetime membership card that the local musicians' union had presented to Prager the previous week.[104] The Pragers sailed from New Orleans to Brazil on September 2 aboard the steamer Del Mar. From Rio de Janeiro, they took a train to São Paulo where they met friends. They then traveled to Buenos Aires by way of Uruguay, and stayed with members of Frances Prager's family. Their next stop was in Córdoba, Argentina's second largest city, some 435 miles northwest of Buenos Aires in the Sierras Chicas mountains, where they visited with more of Frances Prager's family members.[105] The Pragers would eventually settle permanently in the nearby town of Villa Carlos Paz—according to his former piano student Gerald Borsuk, the Pragers' home there was named "Villa Madison."

Prager remained in contact with friends in Madison, and after the tradition of the times, some of his letters were published in the local papers. Letters he wrote to Alexius Baas and Betty Cass in the spring of 1949 are filled with details of life in Argentina, appreciative descriptions of local food and wine, plans for further travels in South America and Europe, and wry comments about Argentine culture. Writing to Baas he quipped, "I make plenty of music on my upright piano and my viola. Sometimes we play American tunes as an antidote against the everlasting tangos."[106] In October 1949, the Pragers left for an extended tour of Italy—visiting Genoa, Capri, Pompeii, Naples, Rome, Milan, and Como—before returning to Argentina in April 1950, at which point they settled into their new home in Villa Carlos Paz.

It does not seem to have taken long for Prager to throw himself back into work. As reported by William Doudna of the *Wisconsin State Journal*, in May 1951, Prager became the conductor of the Orquestra Filharmonica de Punilla. (Punilla is the department, or district of which Villa Carlos Paz is the most important town. It lies within the larger north-central, province of Córdoba.) The orchestra was an amateur, "civic" group, built on Madison's model, though its activities were apparently spread throughout several communities in the broad Punilla Valley—Prager reported that he and eight core members of the ensemble traveled together in a station wagon "over tortuous mountain roads" to rehearsals and concerts. Among the pieces that he programmed with the Punilla orchestra was the *Meditation* by his Madison student Sybil Hanks. The orchestra was apparently unique enough in Argentina at the time, that the government planned to make a documentary about it. At the same time, Prager—who was fluent in Spanish—gave lectures on American culture and music, and on music history throughout the district.

The main point of Doudna's article, however, was to announce Prager's return to Madison at the invitation of the University School of Music.[107] Prager was to teach conducting and give a series of public lectures, which began on October 18, 1951, with a talk on "Music Impressions of Italy and Argentina," and several additional talks on the history of opera over the next few months—lectures coordinated with the repertoire of the weekly Metropolitan Opera broadcasts. Prager gave several other informal lectures as well, and performed a few public concerts accompanying sopranos Christine Gunlaugson and Josephine

Raimond. The Pragers left Madison in early February 1952, staying in Florida for several weeks before returning to Argentina.[108] Shortly after his return in March 1952, he conducted the National Radio Orchestra of Argentina get a program of works by North American composers.[109]

The Pragers toured Europe once more in late 1952 and early 1953, but in September 1953, the local papers announced that he would return to Madison to give a series of eight lectures on "Masterworks of Opera" for the University Extension, beginning with a talk on October 19 on *Il trovatore*.

3.20 April 25, 1954 *Wisconsin State Journal* photo of Prager, seated at the piano, with WHA director Ed Sprague and producer William Allen, preparing for a *Looking at Music* broadcast.

While in Madison, Prager also contracted with Wisconsin Public Television station WHA to host a weekly music appreciation program, *Looking at Music*, which began broadcasting on Wednesday, May 5, 1954, and continued for a series of 24 weekly broadcasts.[110] It is unclear when Prager left Madison for the final time, but he had returned to Argentina by November 1954.[111]

Once again, he was deeply involved in musical activities in Argentina, beginning in 1955–56, when he served as director of the Instituto Superior de Música de la Universidad Nacional del Litoral, a music school in the city of Santa Fe. After this, and through at least 1968, Prager taught orchestral conducting and led the chamber orchestra at the Universidad de Córdoba. He also taught piano students privately at his home in Villa Carlos Paz. Prager's former students include several conductors and pianists who had prominent careers in Argentina and beyond.[112]

Prager's letters made a few appearances in the local papers in succeeding years. In August 1960, for example, Alexius Baas published a letter from Prager that described yet another long tour in Europe, this time in Venice, Switzerland, and Germany, where they visited Frances Prager's sisters in Bamberg. He noted that they would soon return to Argentina, and that "we shall be very glad to be again in the idyllic, tranquil environment of our Sierra de Córdoba."[113] In January 1966, Baas again published a letter from Prager—here, Prager discussed his work at the Universidad de Córdoba, and noted that he planned eight concerts there in the coming year. He also described yet another European tour in late 1965, through Spain, Switzerland, Germany, and Austria, with a short stop in New York City as well. Prager expressed his dismay over the United States' increasing involvement in Vietnam, but concluded with lighter notes about their dog and their garden.[114] In 1968, Sam Jones, longtime voice teacher at University, visited the Pragers in Argentina, and reported they were both well and that Sigfrid Prager was still conducting and teaching. Jones noted that he was able to identify their house by the large "Madison" plaque above the door.[115]

The final notices regarding Prager that appeared in the Madison newspapers were more tragic. Sybil Hanks had been one of his composition and piano students throughout his time in Madison, and her family had hosted the Pragers during their two visits to Madison in the 1950s. She traveled to Argentina to visit them in December 1968, but soon became seriously ill, and died in Villa Carlos Paz on February 12, 1969, following surgery.[116] In early 1972, Peter Ersland, who served as principal horn in the Madison Civic Symphony throughout Prager's tenure, reported that he had received a letter from Prager, who was in poor health, suffering from vision and respiratory problems.[117] Then in July 1973 came the news that Frances Prager had died on June 2, 1973.[118]

Sigfrid Prager died at age 85 in April of 1974, news which did not reach Madison for six months. The MCMA had written to see if he would be interested in traveling to Madison to take part in the orchestra's fiftieth anniversary season in 1976–1977, only to find that he had passed away. At a Madison Symphony Orchestra concert on January 31, 1976, Roland Johnson programmed a transcription of Bach's chorale prelude *In Our Hour of Deepest Need* as a tribute to the orchestra's first conductor.[119] Prager's adopted hometown, Villa Carlos Paz, also paid posthumous tribute. In 2013, when the city celebrated its centennial, he was named one of its 100 most prominent personalities by the local historical society. There is also a physical monument: near the Rio San Antonio, which winds through Villa Carlos Paz, is a one-block street named "Sigfrido Prager."[120]

Personality and Legacy

The Madison Symphony Orchestra archives hold a set of bound volumes devoted to printed Madison Civic Music Association programs from the tenures of Sigfrid Prager and Walter Heermann. Though these collections are far from complete—with many programs missing, particularly from the 1930s—they were a primary source of information in my initial reconstruction of the orchestra's repertoire in 2001. However, there is a second set of bound volumes in the archives that contain Prager's own copies of programs he conducted, both in Madison and elsewhere. While these volumes are also incomplete, they provide valuable insight into the work of a phenomenally busy conductor during the period from roughly 1929 through 1941...and perhaps just a bit of insight into Prager's character and reputation among his fellow musicians. He clearly made it a practice in the late 1930s and 1940s to have guest artists and occasionally members of the orchestra sign programs, and the programs included in the book include affectionate and admiring tributes from soloists and musicians that he conducted, in programs from both Madison and Milwaukee. The books include autographs from James Melton, Helen Jepson, Ernst Krenek, Percy Grainger, and many others. The inscriptions often comment on his musicianship and careful preparation, but also on his kindness and humor. Pianist and composer Percy Grainger provided a more effusive tribute in a letter to the Vocational School's Alexander Graham, written the day before Grainger's concert with the Madison Civic Symphony and Chorus on April 29, 1941. Grainger begins by extravagantly praising the Vocational School's support of music in Madison, and the MCMA's free concerts, but then moves on to discuss Prager:

> Yet even all these lofty schemes would fall short without a man of genius at the musical helm. But in Dr. Sigfrid Prager you have a man of outstanding genius, whose rich artistic background and inspiring personality inject the divine spark into the activities of your vocational and adult music groups. The world of music has many conductors of obvious technical skill. But mere technical skill does not lift music above the level of sleight of hand, sleight of mind. If music does not take us farther than 'skill' and 'wizardry,' then in my opinion, the world is wasting too much time and money upon music. It is only when music is a deeply emotional experience, a spiritual life-changer are, that it is worthy of all sacrifice.
>
> Musical genius shows itself in its penetration into the soul-message of the music itself. This penetration, this intuition, this quality of inner revelation, Dr. Prager possesses as do very, very few, even amongst the very greatest musicians. And that is why he is able to evoke a joyous and ecstatic mood in the singers and players he directs... I am proud to have been associated with you, with Dr. Sigfrid Prager, and with your superb chorus and orchestra.[121]

My own impression of Prager's personality comes from his writings, from hundreds of newspaper notices, and most importantly, from a few interviews with surviving members of his orchestra and chorus. He was quite obviously an enormously respected figure, both among his musicians and in the community at large. My first clue regarding his reputation came in the early

1990s, when I was giving a preconcert talk for a MSO program, and made an offhand reference to the orchestra's history, and its first conductor "Mr. *Pray*-ger." (At that point, I knew nothing about him, aside from the name.) After the talk, an elderly couple courteously but quite firmly corrected me: it was "*Dr. Prah*-ger." They talked briefly about what a remarkable conductor he had been.

He seems to have been a very formal personality in the Old World mold. Grace Schumpert, who sang in the Madison Civic Chorus from 1929 through 1978, referred to him as "a typical German professor."[122] Though he wrote eloquently in English, he apparently never shed his German accent. His formality seems to have tempered by friendliness, boundless enthusiasm, and humor, though. This humor comes through in his writing—as in the wry account of the orchestra's first rehearsal quoted in the previous chapter or the account of his army service above, and many of his personal letters—but also in the remembrances of those who knew him. Ted Iltis, who would later become a longtime MSO supporter and board member, played horn under Prager in the 1940s as a student at the University's Summer Music Clinic. Over 40 years later, he recalled one rehearsal when he botched the big horn solo in Liszt's *Les Préludes*: "He stopped the orchestra, stared at me and said: 'Vot ist dis ... *Variations on a Theme by Iltis?*'"[123] Similarly, C. V. Seastone, the son of Susan Seastone, recalled that "in rehearsals after a particularly awful burst of cacophony, he would rap [with his baton] and say, '*Please*, not so *Civic*.'"[124]

The composer and writer Marilyn Ziffrin (1926–2018), who had a long and distinguished career as a college composition teacher, studied conducting with Prager in the 1940s, when she was an undergraduate student at the University of Wisconsin. In 1999, she wrote the following fond remembrance of her former teacher:

> I studied conducting privately with him during my senior year at the University in Madison, and also took a course in conducting from him during my junior year. It was a small class—about six of us, and I was the only woman. Dr. Prager had asked us to study one of the Strauss waltzes. I forget which one, but it was his theory that if we could conduct a Strauss waltz correctly, we could probably handle most of the music we would need to learn. And on the first day in which he introduced the piece, he put the record on the turntable, then stood up and said, 'Come, Miss Ziffrin, we will dance." And we did! I can tell you that he was a superb dancer and we waltzed all around the classroom to the immense amusement of the other students, and to my delight once I got over the shock. By

the way, he smoked cigarettes, and chewed licorice sen-sens so his breath would not offend. And to this day I still associate the smell of sen-sen and the lovely dancing.

My private studies with him took place during my senior year in 1947–48. I remember studying the Strauss *Death and Transfiguration* with him, and a Beethoven symphony. What impressed me enormously was his ability to play the scores at the piano. It seemed to me that he was able to play all of the instruments and do the transposing without any effort. During that same period, I would fill in with the Madison Civic Symphony. For example, one time I played chimes on a Wagner overture, I think. The kind of part where you waited for over one hundred measures or so, and then come in with one or two sounds. After he saw me studiously counting all those measures, he laughed and assured me that he would cue me in, which of course he did. Working with him was a wonderful experience that I remember with great joy. He was so encouraging and supportive.[125]

Sigfrid Prager's 22-year tenure as the MCMA's music director established a solid foundation for a musical tradition that continues almost a century later. His strong leadership, personality, humor, enthusiasm and ability to inspire his musicians and the community were all as important as his eminent musical qualifications in that success. Is also clear that he loved Madison itself. Prager was quite clearly the right conductor at the right time, and the Madison Civic Symphony and Chorus flourished in the late 1920s, 1930s, and 1940s under his leadership.

Notes to Chapter 3

1. "Dr. Prager Learns of Father's Death," *WSJ* 8/2/1946, 1.

2. The dissertation is listed in Michael Bernhard, ed., *Lexicon Musicum Latinum Medii Aevi* [*Dictionary of Medieval Latin Musical Terminology to the End of the 15th Century*] (Munich, Bayerischen Akademie der Wissenschaften, 2006): Bd. 1, lxxxiii. The other documents referenced were accessed through ancestry.com.

3. On Prager's birth certificate, Philipp's occupation is listed as "teacher," so a later move into selling educational materials seems plausible. At the time of his death, Philipp was apparently working as an organist.

4. Lester Velie, "Prager's Life Romantic One, Story Reveals: Civic Music Director Has Lived on Three Continents," *CT* 3/3/1929, 21–22.

5. Bernhard, ed., *Lexicon*, Bd. 1, lxxxiii. The fact that Prager completed a dissertation and could rightfully claim the title *Doktor* at age 21 was not particularly unusual in Germany at the time, when university students could complete a doctorate by writing an *Inauguraldissertation* after their undergraduate studies. Students who wished to teach in the university completed a second dissertation (*Habilitationsschrift*) after five or more years of graduate work. ("Habilitation," *Wikipedia*, https://en.wikipedia.org/wiki/Habilitation, accessed 2/7/2024.) Prager's 1911 thesis was undoubtedly an *Inauguraldissertation*, and he does not seem to have completed further graduate study.

6. Velie, "Prager's Life," 22.

7. Their marriage record in Hamburg, and Anna's birth record in Berlin, were accessed on ancestry.com. Anna's previous husband, whom she married in Berlin on November 4, 1895, was Paul Richard Max Willner.

8. Regarding *The Bartered Bride*, see *Bühne und Welt* 10/1 (1907–8): 185 (illustration included above). "Frau Anna Willner" received a complimentary notice from the British reviewer George Cecil in *The English Illustrated Magazine* (July 1907): 298, for her work in *The Tales of Hoffmann*.

9. Anthony Beaumont, "Busoni, Ferruccio," *Grove Music Online*, www.oxfordmusiconline, accessed 12/31/2019.

10. Christopher Fifield, "Bruch, Max," *Grove Music Online*, www.oxfordmusiconline, accessed 12/31/2019.

11. Fischer's obituary appears in the German music periodical *Die Stimme* (1931): 280.

12. *WSJ* 7/26/1942, 6.

13. Velie, "Prager's Life," 22.

14. The largest spike in European immigration occurred between 1900 and 1910, when some 16,282 Germans arrived in Argentina. By comparison, over 746,000 Italians and 544,000 Spanish immigrated in the same period. See: *Censo general de población, edification, comercio é industrias de la cuidad de Buenos Aires, capital federal de la República conmemorativo del primer centenario de la Revolución de Mayo, 1810–1910* (Buenos Aires, Compañia Sud-Americana de Billets de Banco, 1910): Vol. 2, 51.

15. Silvia Glocer, "Sigfrid Prager," *Proyecto Culturas interiores*, http://culturasinteriores.ffyh.unc.edu.ar/ifi002.jsp?pidf=TT2DDWBBD&po=DB, accessed 7/1/2020. Glocer, professor of music at the University of Buenos Aires, was working on her article—part of a biographical dictionary of cultural figures from the Córdoba region of Argentina—in 2019–2020, at the same time the

present chapter was being written. I benefited enormously from our correspondence at that time, and from her kind willingness to share her research in progress.

16 "Die Singakademie, ein deutscher Verein, lädt uns ein, ihr Konzert zu besuchen. Unter der Leitung eines jungen Kapellmeister, Herrn Prager, wird mit kleinen Mitteln Tüchtiges geleistet. Wir hören das Schicksalslied von Brahms und Bruchs bereits völlig verblaßtes, aber für Gesangverein noch brauchbares 'Schön Ellen.' Ein Pianist, Herr Stephany, spielt Beethovens C-Moll-Konzert und die von Liszt zu einem Klavierkonzert umgewandelte Wanderer-Phantasie von Schubert, diese besonders gut. Ist etwas Schöneres geschaffen worden als der Mittelsatz dieses Stückes? Und die Wiederholung des Hauptteiles, die in allen Tonarten schillert, bis sie mit ungeheuren Fugenthema nach C-Dur hineindonnert, ein zu Himmel ragender Felsblock, den ein Götterwort aus dem Grund des Weltmeeres emporhebt." Felix Weingartner, *Eine Künstlerfart nach Südamerika: Tagebuch Juni-November 1920* (Vienna: Hugo Heller, 1921): 113–14.

17 "Abends das Konzert in der Singakademie, zu dem auch der deutsche Gesandte, Herr von Olshausen erscheint. Der Dirigent, Herr Prager, hat ein ziemlich starkes Streichorchester zusammengestellt, mit dem er meine, jetzt schon vierzig Jahre alte Serenade aufführt, die ich als Konservatorist in Leipzig komponiert habe. Drangosch wiederholt meine 'Phantasiebilder', meine Frau singt älter und neuere Lieder von mir, und am Schluss spiele ich mit Drangosch zwei Sätze meiner ersten Symphonie am Klavier zu vier Händen. Ein fröhliches, kurzes Abendmahl beschließt die gelungene Veranstaltung, um die sich der Präsident der Singakademie, Herr Wald, besonders verdient gemacht hat." Weingartner, *Eine Künstlerfart*, 141.

18 Maria Mondolo, "Ernesto Drangosch: vida y obra," *Musica Classica en la Argentina*, http://www.musicaclasicaargentina.com/drangosch/index.htm, accessed 12/19/2019.

19 I thank Prof. Bruno-Videla of Buenos Aires for his valuable correspondence (email communication, August 2001).

20 Glocer, "Sigfrid Prager."

21 Robert Byrne, review of *Die Nibelungen (1924)* [DVD release], *The Moving Image: The Journal of the Association of Moving Image Archivists* 13, No. 2 (Fall 2013), 120–21. Huppertz, one of the true pioneers of film scoring, is probably best known today for his strikingly modernist score for Lang's 1926 masterpiece *Metropolis*.

22 Glocer, "Sigfrid Prager."

23 Velie, "Prager's Life," 22.

24 Derek B. Scott, *German Operetta on Broadway and in the West End, 1900–1940* (Cambridge: Cambridge University Press, 2019): 171.

25 For a list of recordings, see "Dadmun, Royal (vocalist: baritone vocal)." *Discography of American Historical Recordings*, https://adp.library.ucsb.edu/index.php/talent/detail/28809/Dadmun_Royal_vocalist_baritone_vocal, accessed 12/21/2019.

26 *The Capital Journal* (Salem, OR) 3/20/1925, 5.

27 *New York Times* 4/28/1925, 24.

28 Walker's 1916 passport application, dated April 25, states that he was going to Denmark and Germany for "operatic engagements." (Accessed on ancestry.com.) Regarding his return to United States, see: "American Singers Return from Germany: Food Conditions There Reported by Robert Henry Perkins and George Walker," *Musical America* XXVI, No. 9 (June 30, 1917): 18.

29 *WSJ* 4/12/1925, 37. The full program appears in the Carnegie Hall performance history database: https://www.carnegiehall.org/About/History/Performance-History-Search.

30 *WSJ* 4/19/1925, 12.
31 *CT* 2/27/1964, 38.
32 *WSJ* 5/3/1925, 23.
33 *CT* 5/9/1925, 8.
34 *CT* 9/21/1925, 7.
35 *CT* 7/29/1925, 13.
36 Velie, "Prager's Life," 22.
37 Glocer, "Sigfrid Prager," and *United States of America Declaration of Intention No. 168439*, 4/6/1925 (Accessed on ancestry.com).
38 John Koegel, *Music in German Immigrant Theater: New York, 1840–1940* (Rochester: University of Rochester Press, 2007): 369.
39 On the history of the Arion Choral Society, see *The History of the Liederkranz of the City of New York and of the Arion, New York, 1847 to 1947, Compiled During the Centennial Year of the Liederkranz, 1947, by the History Committee* (New York City: Drechsel Printing Company, 1948). Accessible at https://archive.org/stream/historyofliederk00deut/historyofliederk00deut_djvu.txt.
40 Carol J. Oja, *Making Music Modern: New York in the 1920s* (Oxford: Oxford University Press, 2000): 31–32.
41 Howard Shanet, *Philharmonic: A History of New York's Orchestra* (New York City: Doubleday, 1975): 232–33.
42 *New York Times* 4/25/1926, X7.
43 The full program appears in the Carnegie Hall performance history database. See: https://www.carnegiehall.org/About/History/Performance-History-Search.
44 *CT* 7/2/1926, 7.
45 *MCMA Board Minutes* for 8/4/1926 (MSO Archives).
46 *MCMA50*, 7.
47 *CT* 10/4/1941, 1–2.
48 *WSJ* 9/2/1927, 13.
49 *WSJ* 2/28/1929, 1.
50 Madison Vocational School, *Evening Courses Bulletin*, 1929–1930 (preserved in the Wisconsin State Historical Society Archives).
51 Madison Vocational School, *Evening Courses Bulletin*, 1932–33 (preserved in the Wisconsin State Historical Society Archives). Note that other community choruses were also available as "for credit" classes: the East Side Civic chorus (dir. John L. Bach), the Mozart club (dir. Earle Swinney), the Grieg Chorus (dir. Alexius Baas), and the Madison Maennerchor (dir. Alexius Baas). This continued through the early 1940s, and the all-male Mozart Club continued to be listed as a course until the 1950s.
52 *CT* 4/14/1934, 4.
53 *CT* 4/21/1934, 1.
54 *CT* 4/22/1934, 6.
55 *WSJ* 2/3/2016, 7.

56 Interview with Gerald Borsuk, 7/20/2000.

57 *WSJ* 2/14/1969, 28.

58 Fuller description of the music on this recording, and streaming audio for *Decoration Day Hymn* and *Meditation*, are at http://www.allsenmusic.com/HISTORY/Recordings.html.

59 These dates were provided by Anne Aley, former director of the Summer Music Clinic (email, 4/4/2021).

60 Historical Society of Wisconsin, "Historical Essay: William Boeppler (1863–1928)." https://www.wisconsinhistory.org/Records/Article/CS5591, accessed 12/12/2019.

61 *CT* 10/19/1930, 19.

62 *MCMA Board Minutes* for 2/19/1930, 5/22/1931, and 5/25/1931 (MSO Archives).

63 *CT* 9/6/1935, 1.

64 *The Sheboygan Press*, 5/13/1935, 11.

65 *The Sheboygan Press*, 12/13/1937, 19.

66 Karalee Surface, "The Milwaukee Symphony Orchestra," *Encyclopedia of Milwaukee*, https://emke.uwm.edu/entry/milwaukee-symphony-orchestra/, accessed 11/20/2019.

67 The most important overall survey of the Federal Music Project is Kenneth J. Bindas, *All of This Music Belongs to the Nation: The WPA's Federal Music Project and American Society* (Knoxville, University of Tennessee Press, 1995), though there has been considerable research on the FMP since its publication. See, for example: Peter Gough, *Sounds of the New Deal: The Federal Music Project in the West* (Urbana: University of Illinois Press, 2015).

68 *WPA Federal Music Project (Wisconsin), Records 1936–41* (Wisconsin Historical Society Library microfilm P46092). The most thorough examination of the FMP in Wisconsin is an unpublished paper by my UW–Whitewater colleague Dr. Jane Riegel Ferencz. I thank her for allowing me to consult her work here.

69 William V. Arvold, "Narrative Report for the Month of January" (2/1/1938), *WPA Records 1936–41*.

70 General Services Administration, "Federal Music Project Final State Report, Wisconsin," (Washington: The National Archives and Record Service, 1951), *WPA Records 1936–41*.

71 General Services Administration, "Federal Music Project Final State Report, Wisconsin," *WPA Records 1936–41*.

72 Letter from William V. Arvold to Dr. Earl V. Moore, Special Consultant WPA Music Program (10/4/1939), *WPA Records 1936–41*.

73 Arvold, "Narrative Report for the Month of November" (12/1/1937), *WPA Records 1936–41*.

74 *WSJ* 6/12/1937, 1.

75 Arvold, "Narrative Report for the Month of September" (10/1/1937), *WPA Records 1936–41*.

76 *CT* 9/13/1937, 13.

77 Letter from Philip LaFollette to Siegfried Vollstedt, *WPA Records 1936–41*.

78 *WSJ* 6/12/1937, 1.

79 Most of the printed programs for these concerts are preserved in the MSO Archives.

80 Arvold, "Narrative Report for the Month of January" (2/1/1938), *WPA Records 1936–41*.

81 Arvold, "Narrative Report for the Month of February" (3/1/1938), *WPA Records 1936–41*.

82 *New York Times* 2/19/1939, 38.
83 Wisconsin Symphony Orchestra program book, 10/20/1940. (MSO Archives)
84 Wisconsin Symphony Orchestra program book, 1/19/1941. (MSO Archives)
85 *Milwaukee Journal* 8/24?/1938, [NOTE this is a clipping from the WPA Records, but bibliographic information is pretty much illegible on the film]
86 Arvold, "Narrative Report for the Month of August" (9/1/1938), *WPA Records 1936–41*.
87 Arvold, "Narrative Report for the Month of August" (8/31/1939), *WPA Records 1936–41*.
88 "Notes of Musicians Here and Afield," *New York Times*, 9/3/1939, X6.
89 Wisconsin Music Archives, "Jerzy Bojanowski Collection," https://www.library.wisc.edu/music/home/collections/wisconsin-music-archives/jerzy-bojanowski-collection-c-1932-1960/, accessed 12/18/2019; and Lisa Lamson, "Performance Venues," *Encyclopedia of Milwaukee*, https://emke.uwm.edu/entry/performance-venues/, accessed 12/18/2019.
90 Mark Muth, "Semi-Annual Narrative Report for the Wisconsin Music Project Covering the Period from April to September, 1940, Inclusive," (October, 1940), *WPA Records 1936–41*.
91 On Innes and his work in Milwaukee, see: Charles V. Heath, "Wisconsin's Good Neighbor: Maestro Diego 'Jimmy' Innes and the Wisconsin WPA Symphony Orchestra," *The Wisconsin Magazine of History* ? (Winter 2016–17): 38–49.
92 A year later Ross and Prager later published two of their Granados arrangements: Enrique Granados, *Two Transcriptions by Gilbert Ross and Siegfried Prager: 1. Anoranza (Longing) and 2. La maja y el ruiseñor (The Gallant and the Nightingale), from the Opera "Goyescas"* (New York: G. Schirmer, 1930).
93 Interview with Gerald Borsuk, 7/20/2000.
94 *WSJ* 5/11/1930, 43.
95 Sigfrid Prager, The *Message of Song, for Unison Chorus*, words by John Mael (Chicago: H.T. FitzSimons Company, 1932).
96 Sigfrid Prager. *The Monochord as an Instrument and as a System*. Read in Madison on January 10, 1948, at a meeting of the Western section of the Midwest Chapter." *Journal of the American Musicological Society* I, No. 3 (Autumn, 1948): 52.
97 Sigfrid Prager, *Comments on Anton Dvorák, Symphony No.5 From the New World, Opus 95* (New York: Edwin F. Kalmus, ca.1945); and Sigfrid Prager, *Comments on César Franck, Symphony in D minor* (New York: Edwin F. Kalmus, ca.1945).
98 *WSJ* 2/26/1948, 1.
99 *WSJ* 6/13/1948, 1.
100 *WSJ* 5/23/1948, 32.
101 *CT* 7/24/1948, 10.
102 *CT* 4/23/1949. 16.
103 *CT* 5/28/1948, 4.
104 *CT* 8/26/1948, 17.
105 *CT* 3/22/1948, 8.
106 *CT* 3/4/1949, 7

107 *WSJ* 9/12/1947, 1–2.
108 *WSJ* 1/28/1952, 8.
109 Glocer, "Sigfrid Prager."
110 *CT* 4/13/1954, 9.
111 Glocer, "Sigfrid Prager."
112 Glocer, "Sigfrid Prager."
113 *CT* 4/16/1960, 8.
114 *CT* 1/11/1966, 27.
115 *WSJ* 3/1/1968, 39.
116 *WSJ* 2/14/1969, 28.
117 *WSJ* 1/25/1972, 12.
118 *CT* 7/7/1973, 12.
119 *WSJ* 1/31/1976, 21.
120 Glocer, "Sigfrid Prager."
121 Letter from Percy Grainger to Alexander Graham, 11/28/1941 (MSO Archives).
122 Interview with Grace Schumpert, 7/20/2000.
123 Interview with Ted Iltis, 7/31/2000.
124 Letter from C.V. Seastone to Roland Johnson, 4/25/1972 (MSO Archives).
125 Letter from Marilyn J. Ziffrin to the author, 9/1/1999.

CHAPTER 4

A Tale of Two Maestros:
The Madison Civic Symphony in the 1940s and 1950s

By 1940, the Madison Civic Symphony and Madison Civic Chorus were well-established parts of Madison's cultural life. The cooperative agreement between the Madison Civic Music Association and Madison Vocational School gave these groups a solid financial foundation, including providing most of the salary for music director Sigfrid Prager. During the first decade and a half, these groups, made up almost entirely of volunteer amateur musicians, became a source of tremendous civic pride in Madison, giving concerts that ranged from regular free programs to fully staged operas and large-scale extravaganzas staged in the University Stock Pavilion and Field House.

The War Years

During the years of World War II, Prager reported several times to the MCMA board that the draft was having a severe impact on membership. In the case of the orchestra, a few empty chairs were filled by soldiers stationed at Madison's U.S. Army Air Force base, Truax Field, some of whom had been professional musicians before the war. One particularly notable Truax Field musician was Ashley B. Miller (1918–2006). Trained at the Juilliard School in organ and conducting, Miller directed the 16th Army Band at Truax until he left for combat training as an Army pilot. Prager premiered Miller's *Rhapsody for String Orchestra* on a "Music of the Allied Nations" program in February 1944. By this time, Miller had already been called up for flight training. When he left in November 1943, Miller told *Wisconsin State Journal* reporter William Doudna that he planned to return to Madison following the war,[1] but he instead settled in New York City in 1946. Miller would become one of America's leading organists, and he was particularly prominent as a theater organist, issuing several successful recordings of his performances on the Radio City Music Hall organ.[2] Other Army musicians were welcomed into the orchestra, though Prager apparently had to be quite strict about discipline, particularly given the fact that so many of the community members of the orchestra were teenagers and women. At a board meeting, one of the board members was commended for providing funds for "after-rehearsal entertainment" (presumably beer) for the soldiers. The chorus did not fare so well, and Prager regularly needed to draw men from other area choirs—the Madison Maennerchor, the Mozart Club, and the Milton College Glee Club—to supplement the Civic Chorus in its performances.

During the five seasons that America was involved in the war—1941–42 through 1945–46—MCMA continued the pattern it had established in the late 1930s: five or six free programs each season, though some of the additional programs of the past, like youth concerts, operas, and the grand springtime Music Festivals of the previous decade, disappeared. The Madison Civic Chorus performed on at least two programs each season, the December *Messiah* performance and another large work in the spring. Though the great majority of its soloists were local musicians, MCMA was generally able to engage at least one or two "big-name" artists each season: cellist Ennio Bolognini in February 1942 and May 1945, Chicago-based coloratura soprano Dorothy Cornfield in May 1943, violinist Roman Totenberg in November 1945,[3] and the Australian soprano Marjorie Lawrence in March 1946. One of the greatest Wagnerian sopranos of the 1930s, Lawrence was partially paralyzed by polio in 1941, but she continued to perform for over a decade afterwards, appearing on stage in a wheelchair. An audience of nearly 3500 packed into the University Stock Pavilion on a freezing February evening to hear her perform arias by Wagner, Rimsky-Korsakov, and Bizet, and orchestral songs by Strauss and Huhn. Lawrence also performed two encores: the sentimental *Annie Laurie* and, as a tribute to her homeland, *Waltzing Matilda*.[4]

4.01 Prager with soprano Marjorie Lawrence on March 17, 1946.

4.02 Gunnar Johansen, 1960s.

Two of the big-name soloists who appeared during this period were in fact also "local"— internationally known artists who had settled in Madison as artists-in-residence at the University School of Music. Danish piano virtuoso Gunnar Johansen (1906–1991) came to UW–Madison in 1939 as one of the first musical artists-in-residence appointed at any American university. He was a member of the University faculty until his retirement in 1976, but remained a central figure in Madison's musical life into the late 1980s.[5] Johansen's appearance with the Madison Civic Symphony in February 1945 was only the first of nine solo appearances with the orchestra over more than three decades:

- Beethoven, *Piano Concerto No. 4* (February 25, 1945 and March 21, 1970)
- Saint-Saëns, *Carnival of the Animals* (January 29, 1950)
- Brahms, *Piano Concerto No. 1* (January 31, 1951)
- Brahms, *Piano Concerto No. 2* (October 23, 1955)
- Busoni, *Piano Concerto*, with final chorus for male voices (March 6, 1966)
- Taussig, *Gypsy Fantasy*, orch. Eibenschütz, and Weber *Polacca Brilliante*, orch. Liszt (May 7, 1972)
- Beethoven, *Choral Fantasy* (April 3, 1976)
- Johansen, *Piano Concerto No. 2* (world premiere, May 23, 1981)

Johansen worked with each of the first three conductors of the Madison Civic Symphony but seems to have had a particularly close musical partnership with Roland Johnson. One of Johansen's specialties as a pianist was bringing to light rarely performed and newly discovered repertoire, and he and Johnson collaborated in reviving the rare Busoni concerto, presenting virtually unknown piano transcriptions of violin works by Weber and Taussig, and most significantly, playing the premiere of Johansen's own second piano concerto in 1981.

Also arriving in Madison in 1939 as artists-in-residence at the University were the members of the Pro Arte Quartet. Founded in Belgium in 1912, it was one of the world's finest chamber ensembles. In early 1939, the string quartet was on an extended tour of the United States when they began negotiations with University President Clarence Dykstra and School of Music Director Carl Bricken aimed at bringing them to Madison permanently, negotiations that also involved one of America's most remarkable patrons of music, Elizabeth Sprague Coolidge. The quartet arrived in Madison in May for a series of concerts in the newly completed Memorial Union Theater. At the intermission of their May 10 program, Dykstra came on stage to announce that Germany had invaded Belgium, and publicly offered refuge to the quartet.[6] This was the beginning of a residency that has continued for over eight decades: the Pro Arte Quartet—several generations of players later—remain artists-in-residence at the University today. Pro Arte violist Germain Prévost appeared with the Madison Civic Symphony in May 1944, the first of many solo appearances by members of the quartet with the orchestra. From the 1960s onward, Pro Arte Quartet members also served as concertmaster and principal string players in the Madison Symphony Orchestra.

The biggest events of the early 1940s were two visits by composer and pianist Percy Grainger, in November 1941 and again in November 1942. The Australian-born Grainger was a classical superstar in this period, but was apparently drawn to Madison through a personal connection with Prager.[7] At each visit, the Civic Symphony and Chorus performed a large-scale concert mostly devoted to his works. Grainger shared conducting duties with Prager at

4.03 *Capital Times* photo from November 29, 1942, with Ella Bird Grainger, Sigfrid Prager, Percy Grainger, and Frances Silva Prager. They are posed with specially designed marimba resonators used in one of Grainger's works.

each program and also performed as a piano soloist. The November 29, 1942, program in the Stock Pavilion even included the premiere of a new version of Grainger's *The Lads of Wamphray*.[8]

Events during the course of the war and American wartime patriotism had an impact on several of MCMA's programs. On May 17, 1942, the Madison Civic Symphony played a program of mostly Russian music as a benefit for Russian war relief. The "Music of the Allied Nations" program on February 27, 1944, was more ambitious, bringing together works representing most of the major Allied combatants:

>Ashley B. Miller, *Rhapsody for String Orchestra* (United States)
>Percy Grainger, *Colonial Song* (Australia)
>Ary Barroso, *Aquarela do Brazil* (Brazil)
>Howard Hanson, *Andante* from *Symphony No. 1 "Nordic"* (Scandinavia)
>César Franck, *Symphonic Variations* (France—featuring University student Morton Schoenfeld as piano soloist)
>Stanislav Moniuszko, *Mazurka* from *Halka* (Poland)
>Morton Gould, *New China March* (China)
>Arnold Bax, *Lento* from *Symphony No. 6* (England)
>Peter Ilych Tchaikovsky, *1812 Overture* (Soviet Union)

It was also during this period that Prager began the tradition of beginning many concerts with *The Star-Spangled Banner*, played as an unannounced opening selection.[9] This tradition continues in today's Madison Symphony Orchestra, when the opening concert of each season begins with the national anthem.

During their first two decades, the orchestra and chorus performed and premiered many new works by local composers. This continued in the 1940s: on May 5, 1946, for example, Prager programmed the *Chorale Prelude No. 1* by the University composer Hilmar Luckhardt. One highlight of the war years was the first performance of Oskar Hagen's *Choral Rhapsody in the Romantic Style* on May 7, 1944. Hagen (1888–1957) was born in Wiesbaden and eventually studied musicology at the University of Berlin, while at the same time studying composition with Engelbert Humperdinck. However, he would eventually earn his degree in art history, and in 1918 he took a position as an art historian at the University of Göttingen. While there, he founded the Göttingen Handel Festival. Hagen is credited today as being almost single-handedly responsible for the revival of interest in Handel's operas in early 20th-century Germany. In early 1925, Hagen accepted an offer to chair UW–Madison's newly founded

4.04 Oskar Hagen (with his daughter, actress Uta Hagen), on the University Union Terrace, early 1950s.

Department of the History and Criticism of Art, where he maintained an eminent scholarly reputation as an art historian. He died in Madison in 1957.[10]

Though when he arrived in Madison he was initially dismissive of what he considered to be a relatively provincial music scene, Hagen and his family soon became part of Madison's musical life. He gave public lectures on Handel and other musical subjects. His first wife Thyra sang as a soprano soloist with the Civic Symphony in May 1928, performing arias by Handel and Mozart, and, with Prager at the piano, several art songs. Hagen's second wife, Swiss-born Beatrice Bentz Hagen, was an excellent violinist and violist and had been the founder of the Bentz Quartet in the 1920s—one of Europe's first prominent all-female string quartets.[11] They married in 1940, and soon after her arrival in Madison, she began to perform, appearing first in a violin recital with pianist Samuel Rogers at a private home on May 4, 1940.[12] She performed with the Civic Symphony as a viola soloist in November 1944, playing Mozart's *Sinfonia concertante, K. 364* with the orchestra's concertmaster Marie Endres, and she would later perform as a member of the orchestra through 1971. Hagen also appeared as a second violist with the Pro Arte Quartet several times in the 1940s.[13]

When he began work on the *Choral Rhapsody* in 1943, Oskar Hagen had not written original music since before the First World War, but he was inspired by the March 1943 performance of Honegger's *King David* by the Madison Civic Chorus and Symphony to return to composition. (The *Choral Rhapsody* is dedicated to Dr. Prager.) It is a substantial work, with four vocal soloists, chorus, and full orchestra.[14] In an extended program note, Hagen describes the text as a reinterpretation of Friedrich Schiller's 1782 *Ode to the Sun (An die Sonne)* by Samuel Rogers. Rogers, a UW–Madison professor of French and a successful novelist, was also a fine pianist, performing many times in Madison in the 1940s. The *Choral Rhapsody* was in part a reaction to the war, with its middle section "a mournful dirge referring to the destructions of war" and ending in "a grand fugal development which resolves itself back into the solemn chords which retreat at the rise of the eternal light in the opening passage of the composition." Following the *Choral Rhapsody*, Hagen returned occasionally to composition, turning first to the pseudo-Baroque *Concert Grosso* in 1944. He composed his *Violin Sonata in G Major* in early 1945, completing the work on V-E Day, and it was premiered in February 1946, on a WHA radio program, by Beatrice Hagen and Samuel Rogers.[15] In October 1950, the Madison Civic Symphony would present the first American performance of Hagen's *Concerto Grosso*.[16]

4.05 Madison Civic Chorus and Sigfrid Prager in rehearsal, January 1946. Note that the wartime shortage of male voices was still a factor.

The Kunrad Kvam Affair

Any musical organization larger than an unaccompanied soloist seems to come with its share of politics, jealousies, and interpersonal conflicts. Though most Madison Civic Symphony and Chorus activities seem to have gone relatively smoothly, Prager occasionally had to deal with personal issues. In the fall of 1937, for example, there was a nasty conflict in the cello section. Within a week, Prager received formal letters of resignation from two players who had been offended by a third—in one case, this was a local doctor who reported that the man had "become abusive, and called me a 'dirty loud-mouthed Jew.'"[17] There is no record of Prager's response, but by the next concert, the abusive cellist was not listed in the orchestra, and the two resignees were.

A much more public squabble occurred in the spring of 1946 over control of the Madison Civic Chorus. In the previous fall, the Vocational School had hired Arnold Kunrad Kvam as an assistant to Prager, specifically to conduct chorus rehearsals and concerts. Kvam was a fine cellist and conductor, who had performed before the war in the Munich Philharmonic Orchestra under Richard Strauss. He arrived in Madison in 1943, and he completed a master's degree in music at the University. He was featured as a cello soloist with the Madison Civic Symphony in November 1943, performing the Boccherini *Concerto in B-flat* and, with Civic Symphony cellists John Bach and Elizabeth Statz, in the Popper

Requiem for Three Cellos and Orchestra. In November 1945, Kvam was hired as chorus director by the MCMA and Vocational School.[18] His first—and as it turned out, his only—appearance as conductor was at the December 1945 *Messiah* performance. According to Kvam's later resignation letter, there was an ongoing row between Prager and Kvam that began when Kvam, believing he had authorization, engaged an alto soloist from New York City, only to find that Prager had hired a different soloist. Then there was a dispute over interpretation, with Prager reportedly angrily confronting Kvam before the performance regarding deviations from the usual practices in producing the oratorio, specifically in restoring some material that was usually cut, and changing some of Prager's usual tempos and string bowings.

4.06 Kunrad Kvam in 1946.

Matters again came to a head over the spring performance of *The Creation*. According to Kvam's account, Prager, following the argument in December, told him that the orchestra would not be available to accompany, that he could hire soloists, and that Kvam could "conduct in any manner I saw fit, 'standing on my head' if I cared to." However, on March 2, there was another skirmish, with Prager rejecting the soloists Kvam had engaged and refusing to authorize the New York–based organist Kvam had planned to use for the accompaniment. Later that day Kvam proffered a lengthy letter of resignation to MATC's Alexander Graham and MCMA President Stella Kayser.[19] Graham accepted his resignation a few days later, and news of the resignation was on the front page of the *Capital Times* on March 6. Prager conducted the concert on March 31, 1946, and though the concert went well, the matter was not closed. On May 16, 10 members of the chorus signed a letter to the MATC and MCMA boards protesting Prager's actions, extracts of which appeared in both local newspapers on May 23. The letter reviewed the conflicts between Kvam and Prager but also made claims that Prager and the president of the Madison Civic Chorus had somehow suppressed a letter of appreciation to Kvam from the chorus and were "circulating reports injurious to Mr. Kvam." The signers went on to criticize the subsequent actions of Prager, the MCMA board, and Graham, and called for a thorough investigation, closer supervision of Prager, and a return to exclusively local vocal soloists.[20] On May 24, the editors of the *State Journal* published a "public postcard" asking for peace: "Ladies and gentlemen: For the love of sweet something, with all the scrapping and roaring going on every place else, won't you please do your best to keep the blue notes out of our last refuge, music?"[21] Official action—if not the hard feelings—ended on June 24, when the MATC board indefinitely tabled a response to the petition, and the MCMA board voted its "complete confidence" in Prager.[22]

The end result of the affair was a schism in the chorus, with several singers leaving to form a separate group, the Philharmonic Chorus, which is still active in Madison today.[23] This group was founded in July 1946 as the New Madison Choral Society, initially under Kvam's leadership, and gave its first concert on February 16, 1947. According to the chorus's official history: "Being self-governing was a fundamental issue for the Philharmonic founders; they wanted a chorus that was not 'an extension of a vocational school class.'"[24] For his part, Kvam left Madison soon after the group's founding to take a teaching position at Dartmouth College in the fall of 1946, and he would spend most of his career (1952–1975) at Douglass College in New Jersey.[25]

Prager's leadership role in the orchestra and chorus was almost unfailingly positive and successful over his 22 seasons in Madison. However, it is clear he expected to control all aspects of public MCMA performances. Nearly all of the details on what happened in 1945–46 come from Kvam's resignation letter and the chorus members' May 1946 memo. Prager's side of the story, undoubtedly laid out in conversations with the MATC and MCMA boards, and with Alexander Graham, has not survived. While it is probably unfair to make judgments so long after the facts, the records suggest a degree of authoritarian high-handedness on Prager's part contributed to this conflict.[26]

Civic Music After the War

Correspondence in the fall of 1945 between the Vocational School's Alexander Graham and Carl Bertram, director of the Appleton Vocational School, provides some insight into the state of the Madison Civic Symphony at the end of World War II. Bertram, who wanted to foster an orchestra in his town, was looking for information on Madison's orchestra. Graham's lengthy responses begin by expressing great pride in the Madison Civic Music Association's accomplishments, with special attention to the guest artists (soprano Marjorie Lawrence and violinist Bronislaw Huberman) coming in during the next season. The MCMA's primary expense was Dr. Prager's salary: The MCMA paid $1000 of Prager's $4200 annual salary, with the balance coming from the Vocational School. MCMA also had begun to employ a second conductor (Kunrad Kvam), at $8.00 per service, to direct chorus rehearsals. The only orchestral musicians paid by Civic Music (by way of the Vocational School) were the concertmaster and principal cellist, who were paid $5.00 per service, and the librarian, paid $2.50 per service. Graham's letters conclude with an offer of Prager's services:

"I have talked with Dr. Prager and he will be very happy to go up there and do a good job of selling the idea of civic music to your board."[27]

The Appleton Vocational School did in fact establish an amateur orchestra, the Valley Symphony Orchestra, under the auspices of the Valley Civic Music Association—very much in the mold of the Madison Civic Symphony. It was organized in January 1946, under codirectors E. C. Moore and Michel Gibson, and gave its initial concert on May 28, 1946.[28] Notices in the *Appleton Post-Crescent* document several performances by this group over the next few years, but it seems to have been replaced by a smaller, more professional ensemble, the Fox Valley Symphonette, in early 1950.[29] This orchestra also seems to have disappeared within a year or two, though the Valley Civic Music Association continued to sponsor a concert series featuring local and guest artists through at least 1962. The formation of today's Fox Valley Symphony Orchestra in 1965–66 does not appear to have been directly connected to the previous Association but was a separate, though similar, community effort to create an orchestra.[30] The Fox Valley Symphony Orchestra performed its first program on April 11, 1966, under the direction of UW–Madison professor Karlos Moser, and it continues to perform today.

MCMA's offerings during Prager's last two seasons continued the usual pattern of five free programs each season. MCMA had at least initially planned to offer a production of the Saint-Saëns opera *Samson and Delilah* in the spring of 1948. It is unclear whether this was planned as a staged production or a concert version, but *Samson and Delilah* was scrapped in favor of an April 1948 concert that featured a local male chorus, the Zor Shrine Chanters.[31] Featured soloists were, as usual, mostly local musicians: members of the orchestra (Gerald Borsuk on English horn and harpist Margaret Rupp Cooper) and several members of the chorus, including frequent soloists Josephine Jones-Iltis, Robert Bloodgood, Marshall Straus, and Robert Tottingham. As usual, MCMA was also able to engage a few prominent soloists, with violinist Roman Totenberg returning in November 1946 and Metropolitan Opera soprano Marita Farell appearing in February 1948. Madison-born pianist Emma Endres-Kountz—sister of concertmaster Marie Endres—was at the peak of her international career in the 1940s. She had performed with the orchestra in 1940, playing Rachmaninoff's *Piano Concerto No. 2*, and she returned in April 1947 to play concertos by Bach and Mozart. Endres-Kountz also performed with the orchestra under Prager's successor, Walter Heermann, playing the MacDowell *Piano Concerto No. 2* in October 1959.

One of the great accomplishments of the Madison Civic Chorus during these years was its performance of Beethoven's *Missa Solemnis* in May 1947 in the University Stock Pavilion—a concert that marked the 20th anniversary of its founding. The concert opened with a tribute to five of the charter members of the Madison Civic Chorus who were still in the group 20 years later: Evelyn Baas, Irma Heck, Marie Nelson, Meta Trachte, and Ray Daniels. This program was also the finale of the University's Spring Music Festival, which had opened five days earlier with a performance by the San Francisco Symphony Orchestra in the Stock Pavilion. The chorus combined with the University's A Capella and Women's Choruses. Prager broke with tradition and hired four professional Chicago- and New York–based vocal soloists for the program: soprano Sandra Cortez (a.k.a. Dorothy Cornfield[32]), contralto Mari Barova, tenor Maximilian Schmelter, and bass Harry Swanson. This is certainly among the most challenging works in the choral repertoire, both in terms of range and sheer endurance, and this performance, to an audience of 2500, was obviously a success. The *State Journal*'s reviewer William Doudna called it a "series of triumphs," and Alexius Baas's review in the *Capital Times* was every bit as enthusiastic.[33] Baas continued his discussion of the concert in his "All About the Town" column the next day, noting that when he spoke to Prager afterward, Prager's comment was, "We shall never forget this day."[34]

Another thoroughly successful concert of the postwar years was the appearance of African American contralto Carol Brice, on February 23, 1947, the first Black artist to appear with the Madison Civic Symphony. Brice's fame was rising in the 1940s, beginning with an appearance at the third inauguration of Franklin Delano Roosevelt in 1941. She would later have a successful career on Broadway and in opera. Brice would be one of several Black singers to integrate the Metropolitan Opera in 1954. The Madison Civic Symphony took

4.07 Carol Brice in about 1947.

the then-unusual step of presenting her program twice on one day, in the Masonic Temple Auditorium. Brice performed arias by Handel and Verdi and sang a series of solo songs, accompanied by Prager at the piano, ending with the spiritual *Witness*. It was a rousing success, with a capacity crowd of 1350 packing the hall for the afternoon concert, and 950 attending in the evening.[35] Though Brice never appeared again with the Madison Civic Symphony, she did work with one of its future conductors many years later. In 1976, she played the role of Maria in the Houston Grand Opera revival of *Porgy & Bess*, a production conducted by John DeMain. The recording of this production won a Grammy Award that year for Best Opera Recording.

The End of the Beginning: The Retirement of Sigfrid Prager

Prager publicly announced his retirement early in the 1947–48 season, stating that "the responsibility of directing Civic Music would be placed on younger shoulders." (The orchestra's second music director, Walter Heermann, who seems to have been Prager's handpicked successor, did not in fact possess "younger shoulders"—he was only a year younger than Prager.) His letter of resignation concluded on a high note:

> I wish you personally and all board members continued success in promoting the noble cause of civic music. In view of the ideally balanced coordination of the Civic Music Association and the Vocational and Adult Education School, the cooperation of Madison's schools, the University of Wisconsin, the Musicians' Union, the press, numerous organizations and individuals, backed by the enthusiastic support of Madison's citizens, this success seems to need to be firmly guaranteed.[36]

4.08 Prager's farewell program, May 23, 1948, in the University Stock Pavilion. Note the microphone above the orchestra.

The organization he had led for 22 years in Madison was a thriving one, based on ideas of civic service and outreach; Prager later referred to it as "a fine democratic effort."[37] It is clear that Prager, Graham, and the leaders of the MCMA board believed that they were doing something important, and it is equally clear that Civic Music was a source of great community pride, and its concerts were nearly always well-attended.

Prager's retirement, and the outpouring of compliments and honors that surrounded it, are discussed in the previous chapter. However, it is worth discussing his farewell concert here. At the invitation of the organizers of the University's Spring Music Festival, Prager chose for his final program as music director to reprise the Beethoven *Missa Solemnis*, which the chorus and orchestra had performed so successfully in May 1947. As in 1947, the Madison Civic Chorus combined with groups from the University, and Prager engaged the same quartet of professional soloists who sang the 1947 performance. Though the reviews of the concert were mainly concerned with praising Prager's leadership of the orchestra during his years in Madison, it is clear that this was also a fine performance by the chorus and orchestra.

One detail in the photo of this event shown here that had always intrigued me was the microphone hung above the orchestra. Clearly the program had either been broadcast on radio or recorded—but no recording existed in the archives, nor was there any mention of a recording in the Madison Symphony Orchestra archives. However, in July 2013, I was contacted by Roger and Marie Futterer of Iron Ridge, Wisconsin, a small town 60 miles north of Madison. Marie's mother had recently passed away, and in clearing out her house they found a box with eight 10-inch 78 rpm aluminum records. There was enough information written on the recordings to lead the Futterers to material I had posted online about the history of the orchestra. From Roger's description of what was written on the discs, I knew immediately what they had found: a recording of the 1948 *Missa Solemnis*! The Futterers came to my home in Madison the next day and graciously donated the recordings to the Madison Symphony Orchestra. Just how these recordings made it into the home of a woman with no connection to the orchestra or chorus, some 50 miles from Madison, remains an unsolved mystery, however.

The technology of recording on aluminum discs was frequently used in the 1930s and 1940s, most often as an efficient way to archive live radio broadcasts or concerts. The discs themselves are quite delicate and can be ruined if played on a standard turntable. The MSO underwrote the cost of having the original recordings transferred to digital format. The final result, a series of 16 digital audio tracks, is a nearly complete live recording of the 1948 *Missa Solemnis*, and apparently the only surviving recording of a full concert by the Madison Civic Symphony and Chorus under Sigfrid Prager. Like most 78 rpm discs, these are limited to about five minutes per side, so the recordings often have gaps of several seconds in the middle of movements as the recording engineer turned over the disc as quickly as possible to resume the recording. The audio quality is generally quite clear, though there are occasional skips and passages of distortion. Most frustrating of all, the engineer apparently ran out of blank discs at the end and was not able to record the concluding few minutes of the *Agnus Dei*! Despite these flaws, this remains a truly remarkable recording of these groups performing in one of the most significant concerts of the 1940s.

How good were the orchestra and the chorus in the 1940s? Making an objective judgment on the quality of performances from this long ago is difficult; both reminiscences and contemporary reviews of MCMA concerts are perhaps a little rosy. However, there are two surviving audio recordings from concerts that Prager directed during the 1940s: a single aria from the *Messiah* performance of 1941 (discussed at the end of Chapter 2 in connection with Alexius Baas), and the 1948 *Missa Solemnis*. Though this is a vanishingly small sample of the more than 140 concerts led by Prager, it enables us to make a few observations. The orchestral background in the *Messiah* performance is quite muted in the recording, but what can be heard of the orchestral playing is quite good, with excellent intonation in the strings and tight ensemble playing, even at Prager's brisk tempo. There is of course much more to judge in the *Missa Solemnis* recording. The quality of the orchestral playing is uneven. Though overall intonation and ensemble playing are generally very good, there are many times when it is quite apparent that this was an orchestra of enthusiastic amateur players. However, there are also some particularly fine instrumental moments, most notably the lyrical reading of the extended violin solo in the *Sanctus* by concertmaster Marie Endres. The four professional soloists are, unsurprisingly, excellent. But the real highlight of this recording is the singing of the Madison Civic Chorus and the guest choral ensembles from the University. Their performance of this difficult choral work is tightly controlled and precise, with flawless diction and phrasing. Most importantly, what comes through in the *Missa Solemnis* recording is the *spirit* of this performance: despite the flaws in the recording itself, this is a thoroughly satisfying and exciting performance of this work.[38]

A New Music Director: Walter Heermann

The first official mention of a search for Prager's replacement in the discussions of the MCMA board was in December 1947, when President

Florence Anderson shared that there were several applicants. The final decision was to be made by the Vocational School, with input from MCMA.[39] In February, the board made its recommendation in support of Walter Heermann, a distinguished German immigrant who was already relatively well known in Madison's musical community.[40] Heermann, principal cello and longtime member of the Cincinnati Symphony Orchestra, had been part of the faculty of the University's Summer Music Clinic since 1936 and had performed public recitals with other faculty each summer. He arrived in Madison on March 12, 1948, for talks with the Vocational School and MCMA board, and his acceptance was announced publicly the next day.[41] (Chapter 5 is devoted to Heermann's full biography.)

4.09 Walter Heermann in 1948.

Heermann seems to have been the only candidate considered for the position, and it is almost certain that Prager, with whom he had worked at the Summer Music Clinic, was a primary advocate for hiring him as the second music director of the Madison Civic Symphony and Chorus. Though Heermann had spent most of his 40 years in Cincinnati performing with and conducting musicians of the highest professional caliber, he also had a background that made him thoroughly qualified for the dual roles he would take on in Madison: MCMA music director and supervisor of the music program at the Vocational School. He had taught at the College of Music of Cincinnati for nearly 30 years, and he directed the college orchestra for the last 20 of those years. He had also spent many of his summers teaching at the Interlochen Arts Camp and later at the Summer Music Clinic in Madison. Heermann's résumé also included experience that was directly parallel to his eventual work with the Madison Civic Symphony and Chorus: He had organized and directed an amateur orchestra and chorus during the 1930s for the May Festival in Charleston, West Virginia. In 1946–48, he also served as the music director of the Springfield (Ohio) Symphony Orchestra, then a civic/community group closely similar to the Madison Civic Symphony.

Heermann made a trip to Madison in May 1948 to attend Prager's farewell concert, and he settled permanently in Madison in June. In September, MCMA announced its 1948–49 season, which expanded the number of concerts from five to six. Heermann's inaugural season with the Madison Civic Symphony and Chorus was successful, with six well-attended concerts in the Masonic

Temple Auditorium. His debut was an all-orchestral program on November 16, 1948, that included two of his own orchestrations of works by Bach:

> Beethoven, *Leonore Overture No. 3*
> J. S. Bach, Chorale *Komm, süsser Tod ("Come, Sweet Death")*, BWV 478
> J. S. Bach, *Fugue from "The Musical Offering,"* BWV 1079
> Griffes, *The Pleasure-Dome of Kubla Khan*
> Sibelius, *Symphony No. 2*

The next program was his debut with the Madison Civic Chorus, the annual December *Messiah* performance. Heermann continued to present the oratorio with Prager's time-honored cuts from this concert through 1955, though one change he instituted was to divide the recitatives and arias among an ever-increasing number of soloists from the Madison Civic Chorus—by December 1955, *Messiah* included 11 vocal soloists. Beginning in December 1956, however, Heermann abandoned the usual cuts: That year he presented uncut versions of Parts I and II. In December 1957, the chorus presented what was billed as its first "complete" *Messiah*, with all three parts presented over two concerts on the same day. In 1958, Heermann returned to the traditional cuts to accommodate a statewide radio broadcast of the concert over station WHA.[42] Finally, in December 1959, Heermann broke with tradition for the first time since 1933, devoting most of the December concert to the chorus's first-ever performances of the Bach *Magnificat* and Haydn's *"Timpani" Mass*. Heermann returned to *Messiah* during his last season as music director, however, and December *Messiah* performances continued—though generally only once every two or three years—into the 1990s.

The Madison Civic Chorus followed the December *Messiah* with a varied choral program. An audience of over 500 braved subzero temperatures on February 2, 1949, to hear a concert that ranged from a 16th-century French song to Randall Thompson's 1940 *Alleluia*. The program, with nearly 20 pieces, was accompanied by longtime MCMA pianist Margaret Otterson and included selections by harpist Margaret Rupp Cooper. It included two relatively substantial pieces: a complete performance of Bach's *Cantata No. 104* and Brahms's *Nänie*. The orchestral concert a few weeks later on February 19 featured four of the orchestra's principal players—oboist Leon Kiley, clarinetist Robert Woollen, bassoonist Don Kirkpatrick, and hornist Bob Williams—in the *Sinfonia Concertante, K. A9*, attributed to Mozart.[43] This program also featured pianist Peter Paul Loyanich playing the Tchaikovsky *Piano Concerto No. 1*. (Loyanich was then a student at the Cincinnati College of Music, where

J. MICHAEL ALLSEN

4.10 Madison Civic Symphony and Chorus, directed by Walter Heermann, in the Masonic Temple Auditorium on May 8, 1949. The soloist is Nan Merriman, singing Brahms's *Alto Rhapsody*. In this program, the chorus was supplemented by singers from the Mozart Club and the Zor Shrine Chanters.

Heermann had taught until moving to Madison, and had performed the concerto there under Heermann's direction a year earlier.[44]). In April, Heermann himself performed as a soloist, playing the Brahms *Double Concerto* with his brother, Emil Heermann, on violin. Chicago-based Rosetta Matrose was also featured on the program, singing the soprano part for the *Prelude und Liebesbestod* from Wagner's *Tristan und Isolde*.

Heermann's first season closed with a concert in May 1949 that was associated with the University's Spring Music Festival. During his 12 seasons, Heermann seldom brought in extra voices to supplement the Madison Civic Chorus, but for this concert, the chorus's small numbers seem to have obliged him to incorporate singers from two local all-male choirs: the Mozart Club and the Zor Shrine Chanters. The featured soloist—the biggest "name" of the season—was star mezzo-soprano Nan Merriman, who sang the arias in Bach's *Cantata No. 34*, Brahms's *Alto Rhapsody*, and an aria by Tchaikovsky. Alexius Baas reviewed the program the next day and noted that the performance of the Bach cantata was flawed: Reading between the lines of Baas's flowery prose, it seems that the chorus or the trumpets—or possibly both—got badly lost in the final movement and the performance "was saved from absolute disaster only by the superhuman efforts of the conductor." Other than this shaky moment, the program went well, and Baas concluded: "So ends Walter Heermann's first year as leader of Madison's Civic Music forces. His intelligence, musicianship, and other sterling qualities have earned for him a well-deserved place in the esteem of Madison's music loving public."[45]

In June 1949, after the close of his first season, Heermann presented an enthusiastic report to the MCMA's annual meeting of the membership:

> Quite often in these past months, people have asked me: "Well, have you found enough to do in Madison to keep you busy?" My answer is: "enough to fill up an entire scrapbook with one season's activities, which never happened before!" Indeed, it was fortunate that my added classes at the University of Wisconsin did not start until February, so that there was time to get used to my new work as Supervisor at our Vocational School as well as directing our Civic Music forces....
>
> Dr. Prager's final and friendly counsel was: "Now don't change anything!" And generally, we did adhere to the well-established routine of the Civic schedule. Quite naturally, when a man of his caliber's achievements leaves for good, you will find that a number of members leave with him, and so with us—a somewhat smaller orchestra and a quite diminished chorus reported last fall—so one thing we almost had to change was the choral repertoire, substituting, not lighter perhaps, but shorter *a cappella* choruses, cantatas, etc., for the usual and annual big oratorio or opera. In the long run, this procedure, including an added solo concert for the Chorus, actually gave them a wider range of activities, fitting with their size and capabilities. We did keep up the annual *Messiah* performance just before Christmas and again, this concert drew a capacity crowd. I am quite aware that some of our older Chorus members have missed the glamour of *King David* and *Samson and Delilah* gala nights, and it is also obvious that they don't recall one feature of those past glories. The *Missa Solemnis* and like performances were made possible through Dr. Prager drafting as "guests" almost every good voice from other choral organizations all over town and University, a process I have no access to nor inclination for—I can only tell this to our ambitious souls: Give us time and a better Chorus, and you shall have Beethoven's Ninth or Bruckner's Mass in no time!

Heermann continued, noting his plans for the next season (adding a Young People's Matinee), and praising "our best friend," the Vocational School and its director, Dr. Bardwell (successor to Alexander Graham). He also outlined several goals for the long term:

> **Programs**: We will continue to present the best there is in orchestral and choral repertoire. **Soloists**: We are going to feature young American artists of proven worth, but just before they rate a New York manager and a large fee. **Attendance**: We played to about 6500 people last year, which is not impressive. We hope to improve this record by advertising more than we have been.... **Finances**: Our big wish came true—we finished in the black—in fact, we don't recognize red as a financial color any more, but we do hope to finish next season with enough surplus to for a reserve fund or to spend same in a way where it will be a real help for Civic Music.[46]

4.11 Madison Civic Symphony and Chorus in rehearsal under Walter Heermann in the Vocational School's Scanlan Hall, October 1953. Note: The grinning violist is Margaret Pickart, who played in the orchestra for 46 seasons (1944–1989).

Concerts of the 1950s

It is clear that, despite his predecessor's friendly (and perhaps a bit meddlesome) advice about changing things, Heermann clearly had his own ideas about programming: During Heermann's first season in 1948–49, there was an immediate and notable change in the character of the orchestra's repertoire. Heermann had come to Madison after 40 years in one of America's leading professional orchestras, and the Civic Symphony's programming began more closely to resemble that of a big-city orchestra. Where Prager had favored large extravaganzas with a dozen or more varied works, Heermann's orchestra concerts seldom featured more than three or four pieces, most often in a format that is now more or less standard: an opening overture, followed by a concerto, with a larger symphonic piece after intermission.

Not surprisingly, given Heermann's background, the orchestra's repertoire also took on a distinctly German-Austrian character, and the works of Brahms were given pride of place. All four of Brahms's symphonies were performed during his tenure, as well as the two piano concertos, the "double" concerto, and vocal works like the *Alto Rhapsody*, *Nänie*, and the *German Requiem*. Beethoven, Schubert, Haydn, Mozart, Handel, and Bach were also heavily featured in these years. This is not to say that Heermann neglected non-German repertoire, however. The orchestra's programming included works by composers as wide-ranging as William Schuman, Barber, Milhaud, Sibelius, Kodály, and even Monteverdi.

During the 1930s and 1940s, the Madison Civic Symphony and Chorus had frequently performed music by local composers. Heermann seems generally to have been less interested in local compositions, but he did program works by four composers who were all familiar names in Madison:

- Alexius Baas, *Nature Hymn* (May 7, 1950).
- Raymond Dvorak, *The Cataract of Lodore* and *Canto Buffo: Singer's March* (May 7, 1950).[47]
- Oskar Hagen, *Concerto Grosso* (October 31, 1950—first American performance). A recording of this work is discussed below.
- Sybil Anne Hanks, *Decoration Day Hymn* (April 11, 1951—this work had been premiered by the chorus and orchestra in 1931).
- Alexius Baas, *Recessional* (April 11, 1951).
- Sybil Anne Hanks, *Quiet My Heart* (March 11, 1953—premiere).

On April 29, 1955, MCMA musicians performed in a choral/chamber music program devoted to eight works by Sybil Anne Hanks. A recording of this repertoire is discussed below.

As usual, the majority of the soloists on MCMA's programs were drawn from the ranks of the orchestra and chorus, though one or two programs each season would feature guest artists. These were primarily Chicago-based soloists. A few of the major artists who appeared during these years were mezzo-soprano Nan Merriman (1949), violinist André de Ribaupierre (1951),[48] cellist Madeline Foley

(1952), and violinist Henri Aubert (1953). The University's artists-in-residence and faculty also made solo appearances during the 1950s. Gunnar Johansen performed both Brahms piano concertos with the orchestra under Heermann. German-born soprano Bettina Bjorksten arrived in Madison in 1948 and joined the University faculty in the 1950s, becoming a legendary voice teacher there for over a quarter century until her retirement in 1978. Heermann wasted no time in engaging her as a soloist: she sang in the Madison Civic Symphony performance of Beethoven's complete incidental music to *Egmont* in November 1949. Bjorksten became a frequent soloist, appearing in 17 MCMA programs between 1949 and 1980.[49] Her vocal colleague bass Dale Gilbert joined the faculty in 1955. He would eventually serve for 16 years as the director of the University School of Music, including overseeing the School of Music's consolidation from several annexes widely dispersed across campus into the newly completed Humanities building in 1969.[50] Gilbert first appeared with the Civic Symphony and chorus in April 1958, singing Giannini's *Canticle of the Martyrs*, and would sing as a soloist eight more times through 1975. He would also appear several times in productions of the Madison Civic Opera Guild during the 1960s and 1970s.[51]

4.12 Heermann with Joan Taliaferro, November 1951. Taliaferro, a 16-year-old student at Central High School, played the opening movement of Beethoven's *Piano Concerto No. 1* at the orchestra's Young People's Matinee.

Youth concerts had been part of the orchestra's programming in the early years, but during the late 1930s, these programs were largely taken over by the WPA-funded Madison Concert Orchestra. This group disappeared in the early 1940s, but Prager did not reinstitute youth concerts in his final few seasons. Heermann established an annual November "Young People's Matinee" in the 1949–50 season. Heermann's youth concerts, modeled upon concerts he had conducted in Cincinnati, were aimed at education and featured pieces that were designed to be entertaining and engaging to a very young audience. Innovation was very much a part of these concerts, as in the first program, when a local art teacher, David Carman, sketched a series of abstract images on an overhead projector as the orchestra played a Weber overture. MCMA worked closely with local teachers to run an essay contest in connection with these programs. Most importantly, they also featured children themselves: small ensembles from various studios and soloists selected through an MCMA-sponsored "talent contest." These matinees were successful, and the orchestra performed them annually through the 1955–56 season.

Another innovation introduced by Heermann in his last years was an annual pops concert. Prager had occasionally programmed "popular concerts" in his earliest seasons, but these consisted of little more than a collection of movements from works done in the season, repeated "by popular demand." Heermann was working from a very different model. The famous Boston Pops had established a distinctly American style of concert with light classics and orchestral arrangements of works in popular styles, and Heermann had been involved with many pops concerts in Cincinnati. The first pops program, or "Orchestra Gala," on April 30, 1960, at the Loraine Hotel was very much in this mold, presenting a series of light and entertaining works in a socially informal setting. The first program drew on works by Johann Strauss, Suppé, and the most well-known of American pops composers, Leroy Anderson. This program was also the final Madison Civic Symphony performance by its assistant conductor and longtime concertmaster, Marie Endres. Endres, who had been concertmaster since the orchestra's second program in 1927, was a featured soloist, playing the Saint-Saëns *Danse Macabre*. This program was run as a benefit by the Women's Committee and was a great financial and social success, though some community members were upset that the Madison Civic Orchestra broke with long-standing tradition by charging for tickets.[52] Heermann's final concert as the orchestra's music director was the second pops program on April 29, 1961.

Heermann was obliged to spend some years rebuilding the Madison Civic Chorus. Many longtime members had retired with Prager, and there had also been a loss of membership a few years earlier when several singers from the Civic Chorus left to form the Philharmonic Chorus.[53] The chorus had regularly included as many as 150 singers in the 1930s and 1940s, though its ranks were sometimes supplemented by singers from the University and from the Madison Maennerchor, Mozart Club, Zor Shrine Chanters, and other local choirs. Hermann reported that he had 46 singers at his first rehearsal with the chorus in September 1948: 25 sopranos, 16 altos, 4 tenors, and 7 basses.[54] By the later 1950s, Heermann was able to recruit a larger and somewhat better-balanced choir, but it remained a smaller group than under Prager, with a core of about 60 members, sometimes swelling to 90 for the annual *Messiah* performance.

As noted already, Heermann continued the annual December *Messiah* tradition, though he gradually instituted changes. He featured the Civic

Chorus every spring in a choral concert. For the first few years, these programs contained a variety of works, usually with piano accompaniment. Increasingly, though, Heermann used the spring choral concert for larger, more ambitious works—a return to "the usual and annual big oratorio" of the Prager years. Larger works performed during these years include Mendelssohn's *Elijah* (1951), Brahms's *German Requiem* (1952), Verdi's *Requiem* (1954), Rossini's *Stabat Mater* (1955), Orff's *Carmina Burana* (1956), Beethoven's *Mass in C Major* (1957), and Kodály's *Te Deum* (1961).

While Prager had been able to mount staged productions of several operas in the 1930s, MCMA did not sponsor any fully staged operas during the 1940s and 1950s. (Staged opera performances would return in the 1960s with the arrival of Roland and Arline Johnson and the creation of the Madison Civic Opera Guild.) However, MCMA did present several concert versions of operas under Heermann's direction. These performances, which sometimes took the place of the spring choral program, featured the chorus and local singers in the solo roles. MCMA presented four of these concert operas in the late 1950s: Mozart's *Cosi fan tutte* (1956), Act III of Wagner's *Die Meistersinger* (1957), Strauss's *Ariadne auf Naxos* (1958), and Mascagni's *Cavalleria rusticana* (1959). *Ariadne auf Naxos* seems to have been a late substitution. Heermann originally planned to program the American premiere of Carl Orff's 1943 opera *Die Kluge* (*The Wise Girl*) in 1958, but MCMA was unable to secure performance rights.[55]

Another change in approach instituted by Heermann was in the matter of performance venues. MCMA's primary performance space in its earliest years had been the Central High School Auditorium, centrally located downtown and next door to the Vocational School, where most orchestra and chorus rehearsals were held. Then, from 1937 to 1953, the majority of MCMA concerts were held at the Masonic Temple Auditorium, located across Wisconsin Avenue from Central High School. However, throughout his tenure, Prager also staged concerts in virtually every other large performance space in town, with the biggest programs appearing in three University venues (the Stock Pavilion, Armory, and Field House), and with many other programs in Madison's three other high schools (East and West High Schools and the Edgewood Academy), several theaters (the Capitol, Orpheum, Parkway, and Eastwood), the Hotel Loraine, Christ Presbyterian Church, and the Capitol rotunda. Heermann, however, only made one major move of the orchestra's concerts. All of the programs in his first five seasons remained in the Masonic Temple Auditorium. Though the details are unclear, there seems to have been some kind of rift between MCMA and the Masonic Lodge in early 1953 that brought 18 years of concerts there to an end.[56] From the 1953–54 season onward, concerts moved back to the Central High School Auditorium. Despite its convenience, the stage was cramped, even for the much smaller Madison Civic Symphony of the 1950s, and the auditorium, by then 45 years old, was beginning to show its age. Heermann seems to have worked with the high school to make minor improvements to the stage, lighting, and acoustics throughout the 1950s.[57] The Central High School Auditorium would remain MCMA's primary performance venue (later renovated slightly as the MATC Auditorium) until the opening of the Madison Civic Center in 1980. Aside from a 1952 concert for the state conference on vocational education, and the Orchestral Galas (pops concerts) in 1960 and 1961, all three of which were staged in the Hotel Loraine, all of Heermann's programs were staged in either the Masonic Temple Auditorium (1948–1953) or the Central High School Auditorium (1953–1961). Despite the problems with these two spaces—acoustics in the Masonic Temple and stage space in Central High School—performing consistently in the same space probably had a positive impact on the musical performances of the orchestra and chorus.

In the background of the issue of performing venues was one of Madison's most rancorous political issues in the 1950s and 1960s: the ultimately unsuccessful attempt to build a Frank Lloyd Wright–designed community center on Lake Monona. The original design included a civic auditorium, and as early as 1947, local alders had approached MCMA for support in pushing the project through. Heermann and other Civic Music representatives were active throughout the late 1950s on city committees devoted to the Civic Center issue. (I will return to this issue in Chapter 6.)

Publicity and Program Books

As the programming of the orchestra was changing to reflect a more big-city orientation, MCMA's printed publications were also acquiring a degree of polish and consistency. During Prager's years as music director, the announcement of a coming season and even printed season brochures often seem to have been merely a working outline of what an audience could expect to hear, with repertoire, soloists, and even concert dates frequently changing from what had been announced initially. While there were a few unavoidable last-minute changes in soloists during Heermann's tenure, the repertoire and soloists for each MCMA season were clearly planned and confirmed carefully in advance, allowing for more consistent marketing of its concerts.

There was similarly a change in program books. In its earliest years, MCMA's printed programs were fairly elaborate, including photos and biographies for soloists, and program notes (all unsigned, but probably by Prager). By the late

1930s and 1940s, however, most programs had shrunk to a single bifold, or even a single page, simply listing the repertoire and soloists. Most frustrating—at least to me—is the fact that, by the later 1930s, few programs included the roster for the orchestra and chorus; in some cases, MCMA would go through an entire season or two without printing a roster of the musicians. This changed in the 1948–49 season at Heermann's insistence. Programs expanded back to 8 to 16 pages with a standardized cover design for each season. They took on a consistent format that again included soloist biographies, program notes (authored by MCMA volunteer Helen Marting Supernaw), a listing of the board members, and full rosters for the chorus and orchestra. For the first time in its history, the Madison Civic Symphony's rosters, which had previously been democratically alphabetical, began to list principal players and to reflect seating within sections. The expanded format also allowed for the promotion of upcoming concerts and for a small additional revenue stream from selling advertising in program books.

Much of the improvement in programs—and countless other administrative details—was due to the work of Helen Marting Supernaw (1897–1973), who served on the MCMA board throughout the 1950s. Supernaw trained as a singer at the Detroit Institute of Musical Art. She arrived in Madison in 1923 and taught voice and speech lessons for several years, both privately and at the University.[58] Though she does not seem to have sung regularly as a member of the Madison Civic Chorus, Supernaw appeared five times with the chorus as an alto soloist in the early 1930s.[59] She would later become phenomenally important to the MCMA as a volunteer. With an annual budget that seldom exceeded $6000 during the 1950s, MCMA's volunteers, primarily local women, were essential in running the day-to-day operations of the orchestra and chorus. Supernaw, however, seems to have been ubiquitous—in essence, she served as the administrative staff of MCMA, running the office, answering the phone, overseeing printed material,[60] and taking care of countless details, all as an unpaid volunteer.[61] Supernaw also established and wrote most of MCMA's first regularly published newsletter, *Civic Music Notes*, which began publication in 1949. Following her death in September 1973, Roland Johnson dedicated the first concert of the 1973–74 season to her memory.

4.13 MCMA board members Helen Marting Supernaw, Florence Anderson (president), and Beatrice Goldberg in 1950. [WHS 67421]

From the Women's Committee to the Madison Symphony Orchestra League, 1956–1980

The Madison Symphony Orchestra League (MSOL) was formally founded as the Women's Committee of the Madison Civic Music Association on June 7, 1956. The idea to create a formal auxiliary group to support the activities of MCMA came from two well-established volunteers who were deeply committed to the association, Helen Supernaw and Viola Ward. Supernaw had been involved with MCMA since the 1930s, and she was among the association's most active volunteers in the 1950s, essentially serving as MCMA's administrative manager. Ward would become the first president of the newly formed Women's Committee and would later (1959–61) serve as president of the MCMA board. They accompanied Walter Heermann to a meeting of the American Symphony Orchestra League in the summer of 1954, where they attended sessions on auxiliary groups, and they returned determined to create one for the MCMA. The MCMA's board president, Eugenie Mayer Bolz, hosted the first meeting of the Women's Committee at her home, where 85 local women met with Mona Falletti, an ASOL board member from Evansville, Indiana.[62] The group worked as the Women's Committee for over 20 years. In the beginning, the committee limited its membership to 100 local women, by invitation only, and it had a distinctly "society" orientation.

4.14 ASOL board member Mona Falletti (left) and MCMA board president Eugenie Mayer Bolz, at the initial meeting of the Women's Committee, June 7, 1956.

The Women's Committee began offering invaluable volunteer support and financial assistance to MCMA almost immediately. Members took care of a host of concert details: serving as greeters and ushers, purchasing flowers for soloists, and selling refreshments at intermission. Members also began to pitch in with office duties, and when ticket sales became an issue in the late 1960s, they made innumerable phone calls, sorted tickets, and mailed them to subscribers.

One of the first large-scale Women's Committee projects was the Orchestra Gala in May 1960 at the Hotel Loraine. As described in Chapter 6, this was the beginning of a series of successful pops benefit concerts sponsored by the committee that lasted into the 1990s. The first Orchestra Gala raised some $2400—a considerable contribution for MCMA, whose annual budget at the time was under $6000. The group also held a series of varied and creative fundraising campaigns in this period, beginning with a popular cookbook, *Compositions for Cooking* (1967), which Marian Bolz noted was singled out for an award by *Good Housekeeping* magazine. The group followed this with a sequel, *Compositions for Cooking II*, in 1979. That year, the group also produced a jigsaw puzzle picturing the MSO in the MATC Auditorium. (Copies of the puzzle regularly surface in Madison attics today and are often donated back to the MSO!)

4.15 MSO jigsaw puzzle.

> In 1977, after it had existed for over 20 years as the Women's Committee, the group's president, Marian Bolz (daughter-in-law of Eugenie Mayer Bolz, and later, in 1989–94, a highly impactful president of the MCMA board) decided that it had been an "exclusive sorority" for too long. She pressed for a rule change that would open membership to anyone who wished to support the MSO, including men. The group formally changed its name at that time to the Madison Symphony Orchestra League, and by 1980, the membership had grown to over 500.[63]

MCMA and the Vocational School did hire a part-time business manager, Marvin Foster, in 1954. Foster, who also worked for the University Extension, was primarily responsible for paying bills and maintaining the budget, but he also worked extensively with the board to organize meetings, take minutes, and perform other duties. Foster was succeeded by Berniece Traver in late 1955; she would remain in the position through December 1962. (It is interesting to note, and perhaps typical for the time, that while they had the same duties and same pay, Foster was consistently referred to as the MCMA "business manager" in public documents, board minutes, etc., while Traver was instead a "business secretary.")

The Orchestra and the Community

In reading between the lines of board minutes during the Prager years, it seems obvious that while the MCMA board was nominally in charge of the Association's activities, Prager and the Vocational School's Alexander Graham made most of the real decisions. The board, which expanded from 20 members in the early 1940s to 30 members in the 1948–49 season, began to take a much stronger hand in running the affairs of the MCMA during the 1950s, with particularly active programming and marketing committees. The MCMA board was led by a series of formidable local women from the community all through Heermann's tenure: Florence Anderson (1946–49), Stella Kayser (1949–51), Eleanor Carter (1951–53), Eugenie Mayer Bolz (1953–59), and Viola Ward (1959–61). Theirs was very much a working board; its membership was largely made up of women who volunteered to run the support activities of the orchestra, from marketing and fundraising to answering phones and stuffing envelopes.

The Association's budget was never large in the 1950s, but through the board's efforts, MCMA was able to maintain the tradition of free concerts throughout the decade. With well-attended concerts and outreach programs like the annual Young People's Matinee, the orchestra and chorus were very much a part of Madison's cultural life, and they were frequently mentioned with pride in Chamber of Commerce pamphlets and other literature promoting the city.

Heermann was a strong believer in the American Symphony Orchestra League, and MCMA joined the ASOL in his first season as music director. He would attend the annual convention each year or would arrange for one or two board members to attend. Viola Ward and Helen Supernaw attended one such meeting in 1954 and returned convinced that some sort of auxiliary organization could be useful to the MCMA. The Women's Committee organized in 1956 proved to be a success, running social events to benefit the orchestra and beginning a series of educational efforts. Later reorganized as the Madison Symphony Orchestra League, this vital organization continues to provide invaluable volunteer and financial support today. Beginning in 1949, again at Heermann's insistence, the MCMA also became a member of American Society of Composers, Authors, and Producers (ASCAP).

Toward a Professional Ensemble

One of the more significant moves during Heermann's tenure had little to do with the music itself but had an enormous long-term impact on the orchestra's evolution. Since the beginning, the Madison Civic Symphony and Chorus had been largely volunteer organizations. A few musicians were paid by the Vocational School: concertmaster Marie Endres was paid a modest sum per service, which included her supervision of hundreds of string rehearsals over the years, and the principal cellist and librarian also received small honoraria. Prager occasionally brought in professionals for performances through the 1930s and 1940s—largely professional players from Milwaukee—to bolster the string section. They were clearly paid in some way, though no information exists in the MCMA financial records. (There had undoubtedly been some sort of private arrangement.) Between 1937 and 1940, performers from the WPA's Madison Concert Orchestra occasionally sat in on Civic Symphony concerts as part of their federally funded activities. However, the vast majority of players in the early 1950s were still rehearsing and performing as volunteers.

The issue of paying the regular members of the orchestra has its roots in the 1949–50 and 1950–51 seasons. At this point, the only pay available to most players was babysitting money arranged by the MCMA; it was available to those members, mostly women and the several husband-wife pairs who played in the orchestra, who could not otherwise play for performances. In March 1950, Heermann reported to the board regarding the Music Performance Trust Fund (MPTF), which had recently been established by the national musicians' union, the American Federation of Musicians. The MPTF, a fund created from recording royalties paid to the national union, was used (and is still used) to support live performances. Heermann noted that accessing this fund would allow union members who played in the orchestra to receive a modest fee for performances, and the board strongly approved.[64] In February 1951, Heermann reported that the draft, by then in full force during the Korean War, was beginning to have an impact on the membership of the orchestra, and he asked the board for permission to hire substitute players. After some discussion, the board tabled the matter of establishing a regular fund to pay substitutes, but it did allow Heermann some discretionary funds.[65] The matter remained officially tabled for the next several years, but Heermann apparently used rather wide discretion in bringing in players, particularly in the string section, the Madison Civic Symphony's weak link during this period. It also became traditional for a few of the prominent players in the orchestra—the principal strings and the principal trumpet—to receive a bonus check from the MCMA at Christmas.

By the end of the 1950s, many orchestra members were in fact being paid for performances. Players who were in the union, most of them members of the American Federation of Musicians, Madison Local 166, received a performance fee of about $7.00 funded by the MPTF. Even this relatively small amount caused some controversy within the orchestra and among its supporters. Memories of the Prager years were still fresh in the minds of many longtime orchestra members and patrons, who held to his ideal of Civic Music as a noble effort, created for the sheer love of music. Two people who were members of the orchestra during that period commented on this issue in interviews with me: James Crow noted that there were several vocal opponents to allowing pay of any kind to the members of the orchestra, and Gerald Borsuk related that there was occasionally friction between those orchestra members who were being paid and those who were not.[66] It was not until years after Heermann retired that the orchestra concluded its first Master Agreement with the MCMA, but the 1950s saw the first steps toward putting the Madison Symphony Orchestra on a fully professional footing.

Performances and Recordings of the 1950s

To reframe a question I asked earlier in the chapter: How good were the orchestra and the chorus in the 1950s? There was clearly a contrast between

Prager and Heermann in their approaches to conducting the orchestra and chorus. It is clear that, while he was generally friendly and much admired, Prager ran tightly disciplined rehearsals and earned a reputation as a perfectionist. Though some former players noted that Heermann's knowledge of the orchestral repertoire was much deeper than Prager's and that he was every bit as good a conductor as his predecessor, Heermann's general approach to leading the Madison Civic Symphony and Chorus was much more easygoing. Violist James Crow, who joined the orchestra in 1949, noted that Heermann (whom he characterized as "pretty laid-back") was very relaxed about attendance at rehearsals and that the musical quality occasionally suffered.[67] This is occasionally borne out in concert reviews, as in Alexius Baas's description of a near-catastrophe in the performance of a Bach cantata. Betty Bielefeld, who was the orchestra's principal flutist in the late 1950s, "liked Heermann very much" but recalled that the orchestra's weekly Monday rehearsals seldom started and ended on time and that the preconcert Friday night dress rehearsals often turned into marathons: "He would rehearse us until it couldn't get any better or until we couldn't play any more." She enjoyed playing in the orchestra, characterizing it as "very cordial ... like playing with friends," but noted that "you knew it was never going to get any better under Heermann, because it was really just a community orchestra in those days."[68]

Of course, responsibility for many flaws in any performance lies with individual players. Gerald Borsuk—for many years an English hornist in the Madison Civic Symphony, and a piano soloist on two occasions—recalled an incident in his 1951 performance of the Gershwin *Concerto in F*. One of the most dramatic moments in the concerto is punctuated by a loud crash on the gong. Heermann borrowed a gong from Chicago especially for this performance, and when the climactic moment came, gave a large and dramatic cue ... to absolute silence, as the percussionist had failed to count.[69] This and other anecdotes, and occasional newspaper reviews, leave the impression that MCMA performances in the 1950s often had rough patches. Roland Johnson, Heermann's onetime protégé in Cincinnati and his successor as music director, remembered it differently. Though he acknowledged that the string section had weaknesses and that Heermann was never able to recruit enough string players to balance the brass and woodwinds adequately, he also said that he was "really pleased with the orchestra I inherited from Walter."[70]

There are a few surviving recordings from the 1950s, preserved in the Wisconsin Music Archives and MSO. The first is a 33 rpm 12-inch disc containing Oskar Hagen's *Concerto Grosso*. Hagen composed this work in Madison in 1944, and it was premiered in Germany in 1946, in Frankfurt-am-Main. The Madison

Civic Symphony performed its American premiere in 1950. Though there is no indication on the label which orchestra is playing, there is other evidence that shows that this is almost certainly the Madison Civic Symphony.[71] It is a well-executed performance of Hagen's composition, which is pseudo-Baroque in form but thoroughly Romantic in musical style. The playing and intonation of the surprisingly large string section (possibly including some additional professionals) are well-disciplined, and the playing of the woodwinds and brass is generally quite fine.

Another recording is a better document of a single composer than of normal MCMA performances: a 33 rpm double disc titled *The Compositions of Sybil Anne Hanks*. Hanks, whose career and long association with Sigfrid Prager were discussed in Chapter 3, was a local composer, and by the 1950s she was a significant patron of the MCMA and a member of the Association's board. Throughout the 1950s, MCMA sponsored occasional chamber music concerts, and on April 29, 1955, several musicians from the orchestra and selected members of the chorus performed a program devoted entirely to her works. The recording seems to be a collection of live recordings from this concert. This was undoubtedly a project financed by Hanks herself; at this time she was among Madison's wealthiest women. Though most of the works are chamber pieces, nearly all of the musicians involved were Madison Civic Symphony or Chorus members. Eight pieces are included in the recording:

- *Decoration Day Hymn* (1929)—Madison Civic Chorus, Margaret Otterson, piano, conducted by Walter Heermann. Hanks described *Decoration Day Hymn* as "my very first composition." It was premiered by the Civic Chorus in 1931. *Decoration Day Hymn* is a setting, in a romantic style, of a short poem by Longfellow.

- *Quiet My Heart* (1951)—Madison Civic Chorus, Margaret Otterson, piano, conducted by Walter Heermann. Premiered by the chorus in 1953, it is a rather somber setting of an original text.

- *Rondo in Old Style for Violin and Piano* (1932) features Marie Endres, violin, and Margaret Otterson, piano. By this time, both performers had been involved with the Madison Civic Music Association for nearly 30 years, Endres as the Symphony's concertmaster and Otterson as the primary accompanist for the chorus.

- *Three Preludes for Piano* (1940–1950)—Margaret Rupp Cooper, piano. Cooper was for many years the Symphony's harpist. These are some of the more harmonically adventurous works on the recording. The first two preludes took first prize in the 1940 Wisconsin Centennial Composer's Competition, and the third was composed 10 years later.

- *Theme with Variations for Winds* (1943)—Robert Messner, flute, Leona Patras, oboe, John Varsik and Robert Kirkpatrick, clarinets, Donald Liebenberg and Charles Faulhaber, bassoons, Ruth Zerler and William Wahlin, horns, conducted by William Druckenmiller. This is a craftsmanlike, though not very interesting, work for wind octet.

- *Meditation for Cello and Piano* (1933)—Walter Heermann, cello, Margaret Otterson, piano. This is a chamber version of an orchestral piece premiered by the Civic Symphony in 1934. The music is lyrical, melancholy, and a bit dull, but the recording is remarkable in documenting the playing of Walter Heermann.

- *Concertino for Three Saxophones and Piano* (1942)—Margaret Phelps, Josephine Petratta, and Ann Hansen, saxophones, and Margaret Otterson, piano. An orchestral version of this work had been premiered by the Civic Symphony in 1943 (with three different soloists). This is the liveliest and perhaps the most engaging Hanks composition in the collection.

- The last work on the recording is the finale from Hanks's cantata *The Creation* (1947)—Henry Peters, bass soloist, Madison Civic Chorus, Margaret Otterson, piano, conducted by Walter Heermann. This cantata, which won the first prize in the 1948 Wisconsin Centennial Composer's Competition, is based upon a poem by NAACP leader James Weldon Johnson. This work is in much the same very solemn style as the two other choral works on the recording.

There are no full orchestra performances on the recording, and the chorus of about two dozen voices is obviously a fraction of the full Madison Civic Chorus. The choral performances are weak, with the vibrato of individual singers sometimes threatening to overwhelm the group, and almost constant *portamento*—sliding from pitch to pitch. The other choral recordings preserved in the MSO archive include much larger and better-sounding choruses, though these performances from the 1950s fall well short of the level reached in the 1948 *Missa Solemnis* recording. However, the playing of the individual members of the orchestra on the Hanks recording is uniformly excellent. Perhaps the real prize here is the recording of Walter Heermann himself, who contributes a passionate and powerful performance of Hanks's otherwise rather dreary *Meditation*. One player who knew him described Heermann's cello sound as "big as a house,"[72] and this is clearly heard here.

Musicians of the Orchestra and Chorus: Selected Profiles

The Kirkpatricks

Performing in MCMA's groups was often a family affair: down to the present day, there have been many husband-wife or parent-child pairs, or siblings who performed together in the orchestra and chorus, but no family was as well represented during this period as the Kirkpatricks. All five brothers of this musical Madison family were playing in the Madison Civic Symphony in 1941: Donald, bassoon; Neal, flute; Vernon, oboe; Wendell, violin; and Robert, clarinet. The four oldest brothers also performed frequently together in Madison as a woodwind quartet in the early 1940s.[73] All five of them attended the University and performed in musical groups there (Vernon and Donald attending on Summer Music Clinic scholarships), but only Vernon seems to have pursued a career as a professional musician: He performed briefly with the Cleveland Orchestra and served as second oboe in the National Symphony Orchestra of Washington, DC, from 1944 to 1989.[74] Their father, R. Bruce Kirkpatrick, was also involved, singing in the Madison Civic Chorus during the 1950s.

4.16 The five Kirkpatrick brothers, pictured in 1941: Donald, bassoon; Neal, flute; Vernon, oboe; Wendell, violin; and Robert, clarinet.

Robert Kirkpatrick would return to the Madison Civic Symphony, playing in the clarinet section in the early 1950s, but his brother Donald (1922–2014) would have a particularly long association with the orchestra. He returned to Madison after World War II service in the U.S. Army and rejoined the orchestra in 1946, serving as principal bassoon from 1948 to 1959. He appeared twice as a soloist with the orchestra. As noted earlier, he was one of four soloists in Mozart's *Sinfonia Concertante, K. A9* in February 1949. In May 1953, Kirkpatrick, together with violinist Marie Endres, cellist Mildred Stanke, and oboist Leona Patras, performed Haydn's *Sinfonia Concertante in B-flat Major*. Though his undergraduate degree was in music, Donald Kirkpatrick earned graduate degrees in management from the University of Wisconsin–Madison and spent most of his career as a professor in the University's Management Institute. In 1950, he married another University music graduate, Fern Abraham (1924–2014), who was then teaching band in Cudahy, Wisconsin. She joined the Madison Civic Symphony in 1951, initially sharing principal trumpet duties with Robert

4.17 Fern Kirkpatrick, principal trumpet, in 1952.

Tottingham, and then continuing as sole principal trumpet from 1952 to 1959. Fern and Donald both seem to have stepped away from the orchestra during the 1959–60 season. (Fern was replaced as principal trumpet by University trumpet professor Donald Whitaker, who occupied the chair until 1976.) Fern Kirkpatrick appeared as a soloist three times in the 1950s, performing the Haydn *Trumpet Concerto* in two concerts in the spring of 1952, and in May 1956—with James Kowalski—playing one of the Vivaldi concertos for two trumpets. Following their retirement from the orchestra, Donald and Fern Kirkpatrick remained devoted audience members until they moved away from Madison. When Fern and Donald died within a few months of one another in 2014, their children set up a memorial fund with the Madison Symphony Orchestra. The Kirkpatricks were honored as sponsors of the appearance of the Empire Brass Quintet as part of the MSO's Overture Hall Organ series on May 12, 2015.[75]

James and Ann Crow

Another husband and wife who performed together in the orchestra in this period were violist James Crow (1916–2012) and clarinetist Ann Crow (1922–2001). Born in Pennsylvania and educated at the University of Texas (where he met his future wife Ann playing in the student orchestra), James F. Crow arrived in Madison in 1948 to join the University faculty. A world-renowned researcher in the field of genetics, Crow pioneered the application of genetics to the study of evolution, and he was later an influential figure in studying the application of DNA tracing in criminal cases. Among his many honors, he was a Fellow of the Royal Society of London, and he was elected to the National Academy of Sciences, the American Academy of Arts and Sciences, the American

Philosophical Society, and others. In 2010, the University of Wisconsin–Madison also named its J. F. Crow Institute for the Study of Evolution in his honor.[76] He and Ann joined the Madison Civic Symphony at the beginning of the 1949–50 season, and he would remain in the viola section until 1994, a total of 45 seasons. (Along with a few other longtime performers, he stepped away from the Madison Symphony Orchestra when Roland Johnson retired at the end of the 1993–94 season.) He would spend several years as a member of the MCMA board as well and served as president in 1973–74—the only active orchestra musician to preside over the board in the Association's history.

4.18 James and Ann Crow in 2000. (Photo by the author.)

Jim was a fine violist, skilled enough to sit in with the Pro Arte Quartet at a November 1997 program given in his honor, playing the second viola part in the Bruckner *Intermezzo for String Quintet*.[77] After retiring from the orchestra, he continued to play chamber music until shortly before his death. When I interviewed Jim and Ann Crow in 2000, he recalled his earliest days with the Madison Civic Symphony, saying "It was really a lot of fun to play in the orchestra under Walter Heermann," and he had nothing but praise for Heermann's musicianship, both as a conductor and as a cellist.[78]

Violist Katrin Talbot, a current member of the orchestra who spent several years as Crow's stand partner, remembered him with fondness:

> In the years sitting next to James Crow in the symphony, I had the privilege of getting to know the man, the violist, and the scientist. What a kind and delightful stand partner he was! Not only did he

show me the ropes of playing in a *grownup* orchestra, but he shared so many wonderful stories of past musical experiences and instilled in me a feeling of gratitude for the privilege of playing the luscious inner voices in a symphony. We had almost too much fun talking about music, science, violas and were not above a little gossip now and then. When I think of Jim, I think of his humble demeanor, kindness, and that contagious delight in the world he lived in.[79]

I also remember him warmly from our time together in the orchestra in the early 1990s: a dignified but friendly colleague who would frequently talk to me after concerts, with thoughtful comments—and sometimes pointed questions—about what I had written in the program notes.

Ann Crockett Crow, also from Pennsylvania, joined the clarinet section in 1949. When we talked in 2000, she echoed Jim's comments about the character of the orchestra under Heermann and recalled one near-disastrous 1950 performance of Tchaikovsky's *Nutcracker:*

> They didn't have anybody who was actually a bass clarinetist to play the *Nutcracker*—you know the part [in the *Dance of the Sugar Plum Fairies*] "ta-da-da-da-dah." So they asked me if I could play the bass clarinet. I said that I didn't know, I'd never tried, but that if they gave me the instrument for a couple of weeks, I could probably play that short little solo. Anyhow, Walter was conducting, and we had a pair of very excellent dancers from New York who were to do the *Dance of the Sugar Plum Fairies*. They came on stage, and I played my solo—"ta-da-da-da-dah" and then nothing happened. There was a pianist who was playing the celeste part, and she was looking off to the stage at the dancers. So Walter started whistling her part....[80]

She only played in the clarinet section for a few seasons, but she would later sing for several years during the 1960s and 1970s in both the Madison Civic Chorus and the Philharmonic Chorus. Some of Ann's most significant work for the MCMA, however, was as a volunteer, and she clearly took special pride in this when we spoke in 2000. During the 1960s, she and Helen Hay took over the role filled earlier by Helen Supernaw, serving as the Association's administrative staff for several years before these duties were taken over by hired full-time staff members. Ann died on August 11, 2001, two days after she and Jim celebrated their 60th wedding anniversary.[81]

Robert Tottingham

Another prominent member of both the orchestra and chorus during these years was Robert Tottingham (1919–2012). Born in Madison, Tottingham was playing trumpet in the Madison Civic Symphony by 1937, a year after his graduation from West High School. Following service as a U.S. Army bandsman in World War II, he returned to Madison for graduate work in English at the University. Tottingham taught English for several years at Central High School before joining the journalism faculty of the UW Extension.[82] He rejoined both the Madison Civic Symphony and the Civic Chorus in the late 1940s, eventually doing double duty as principal trumpet and leader of the chorus's bass section. Tottingham stepped away from the orchestra after 1952, but he was a member of the Madison Civic Chorus through 1989. His most important musical work in Madison was as a bass singer, and between 1946 and 1980 he appeared as a soloist nearly 30 times with the Madison Civic Chorus, singing repertoire that ranged from Schütz, Bach, Haydn, and Mozart to Romantic and 20th-century works by Mussorgsky, Verdi, Fauré, and Honegger. He was also a soloist in 10 *Messiah* performances between 1946 and 1961. Tottingham was devoted to opera, and he sang the role of Don Alfonso in the concert version of Mozart's *Cosi fan tutte* that Heermann programmed in February 1956. Four years later, he appeared as Mephistopheles in the grandiose "Prologue in Heaven" from Boito's *Mefistofele*.[83] Tottingham was a founding member of the Madison Civic Opera Guild in the 1960s, singing the role of Frank in the inaugural "semi-staged" performance of Strauss's *Die Fledermaus* in May 1962. Over the next two decades he had roles in Civic Opera Guild productions of Puccini's *La bohème* (1963), Verdi's *Falstaff* (1965), Puccini's *Tosca* (1966), Foss's *The Jumping Frog of Calaveras County* (1968), Moore's *The Ballad of Baby Doe* (1969), Bizet's *Carmen* (1970), Mozart's *Le nozze di Figaro* (1972) Puccini's *Madama Butterfly* (1974), Verdi's *La traviata* (1975), and Verdi's *Aïda* (1980).

4.19 Robert Tottingham (with padded belly) in the title role of the Madison Civic Opera Guild production of Verdi's *Falstaff* in February 1965. Arcenia Moser was in the role of Mistress Ford.

4.20 Madison Civic Symphony principal woodwind players, pictured in Scanlan Hall in October 1957: Donald Kirkpatrick, bassoon, Frank Bencriscutto, clarinet, Leona Patras, oboe, Betty Bielefeld and Shirley Dominik, flutes.

Betty Bielefeld

The final musician profiled in this chapter is flutist Betty Bielefeld (b. 1929), who performed in the orchestra for nearly 50 years, working with music directors Heermann, Johnson, and DeMain. Born Betty Gyspers in Fond du Lac, Wisconsin, she studied violin and flute at Northwestern University and then spent three years in Atlanta, teaching full time and performing in the Atlanta Symphony Orchestra. She moved back to Wisconsin, taking a public school music teaching job in Madison, and joining the Madison Civic Symphony for the 1955–56 season. After spending a year in Philadelphia studying with flutist William Kincaid, she returned to Wisconsin and married George Bielefeld, who was then working as a banker in Beloit. They settled initially in Edgerton (halfway between Beloit and Madison), and Betty rejoined the orchestra as principal flute in the fall of 1957. She was featured as a soloist the next year, playing the Ibert *Flute Concerto* in October 1958. Betty took a part-time job teaching in the Madison public schools, and in 1962 the Bielefelds settled permanently in Madison. (George Bielefeld turned down a job offer that would have taken them to Wausau in northern Wisconsin because there were no musical opportunities for Betty, and he eventually found work in Madison.)

Her work with the Madison Symphony Orchestra during a very long tenure is characteristic of the traditionally friendly and cooperative culture of this orchestra. In the 1960s and 1970s, she shared the principal flute chair with the University's flute teacher, Robert Cole. (Before coming to Madison, Cole played in the Philadelphia Orchestra with Bielefeld's teacher William Kincaid.) Bielefeld became the sole principal again upon Cole's retirement in 1983, and she was again featured as a soloist, performing Bach's *Brandenburg Concertos No. 2* and *No. 5* in February 1985. When Cole's eventual successor at the University, Stephanie Jutt, joined the orchestra in the 1991–92 season, she and Bielefeld were co-principals for three seasons, though after the arrival of John DeMain, Bielefeld was "happy to work as second flute," the position she retained until her retirement. Bielefeld retired from the Madison Symphony Orchestra at the end of the 2004–5 season after playing a total of 48 years—she noted that she timed her retirement so that she could play her final season in Overture Hall. When I interviewed her in 2019, Betty was, at age 90, retired from public performances and private teaching, but still practicing every day and regularly playing duets with her former students.[84]

4.21 Betty Bielefeld in 2004, shortly before her retirement from the MSO.

Notes to Chapter 4

1. *WSJ* 11/19/1943, 5.
2. Garden State Theatre Organ Society, "Ashley B. Miller," https://gstos.org/artists/ashley-miller/, accessed 9/23/2020.
3. Totenberg was in fact a last-minute substitution for Bronislaw Huberman, who had originally been engaged for the concert. His performance of the Beethoven violin concerto was so exciting that he was invited back the following season to play the Brahms concerto.
4. *CT* 2/16/1946, 2.
5. Obituary, *WSJ* 6/2/1991, 27.
6. John W. Barker, *The Pro Arte Quartet: A Century of Musical Adventure on Two Continents* (Rochester, NY, University of Rochester Press, 2017): 55–62.
7. The details of their friendship are not clear. Interestingly, Grainger also had similar ties to the second conductor of the orchestra, Walter Heermann. A Grainger photo in the MSOA is autographed to Heermann and refers to "happier times in Frankfurt." A letter from Grainger to Alexander Graham (11/28/1941) following the first visit is effusive in its praise of the Vocational School's role in supporting Civic Music, and of Dr. Prager. A copy of the letter survives in the MSO Archives, and part of it is quoted in Chapter 4.
8. *The Lads of Wamphray*, one of the famous "Child Ballads," was the inspiration for Grainger's well-known *The Lads of Wamphray March* for wind band. However, *The Lads of Wamphray* performed at this program was a much less frequently performed work for large chorus, vocal soloists, and wind band that sets the ballad's Scots text. Grainger often produced multiple versions of his compositions, and the version performed in Madison apparently substituted a full orchestra for the original wind band.
9. See for example *CT* 2/25/1942, 17.
10. Abbey E. Thompson, *Revival, Revision, Rebirth: Handel Opera in Germany, 1920–1930* (master's thesis, University of North Carolina at Chapel Hill, 2006): 6–10.
11. Howard Hibberd, *Caravaggio* (New York City, Taylor & Francis, 1983): xii.
12. *WSJ* 5/19/1940, 12.
13. Obituary, *WSJ* 7/12/1976, 4. It is worth noting that both of Oskar Hagen's children from his first marriage became prominent actors. His son Holger earned dozens of film and television credits, both in the United States and Germany. His daughter Uta had an even more prominent career, beginning on Broadway in the late 1930s, and eventually winning Tony Awards for best actress in 1951 and 1963, and a special Lifetime Achievement Tony in 1999 that recognized both her acting and her work as a teacher. Uta Hagen also appeared in film and television; perhaps her most famous film appearance was a brief but chilling turn as a former concentration camp guard in the 1978 thriller *The Boys from Brazil*.
14. The soprano soloist was Prager's wife, Frances Silva Prager. This would be the last of her performances, at least 15 in all, as a soloist in MCMA concerts. See Allsen, *75 Years of the Madison Symphony Orchestra*, 209.
15. *CT* 2/17/1946, 14.
16. This pseudo-Baroque work, clearly inspired by Hagen's fascination with Handel, had been premiered in Frankfurt, Germany, in 1946.

17 Letters from Leon Perssion (10/23/37) and Eugene M. Juster (10/25/37) to Sigfrid Prager, MSOA.

18 *WSJ* 11/2/1945, 1.

19 Letter from A. Kunrad Kvam to Alexander R. Graham and Stella Kayser, 3/2/1946, MSOA.

20 Letter addressed to "the members of the Board of Vocational and Adult Education, and the Board of Directors, Madison Civic Music Association," 5/16/1946.

21 *WSJ* 5/24/1946, 6.

22 *WSJ* 6/25/1946, 1.

23 Interview with James and Ann Crow, 9/19/2000.

24 "Philharmonic Chorus of Madison: History of the Chorus," www.philharmonicchorusofmadison.org/history, accessed 10/22/2020. Both of Prager's successors, Walter Heermann and Roland Johnson, made efforts to repair this breach. Heermann actually performed as a cello soloist at one of the Philharmonic Chorus concerts during his first season in Madison, and incorporated the chorus into a few MCMA concerts. Johnson also maintained good relations with the Philharmonic. Some 20 years after its founding, the Philharmonic board asked about the possibility of joining MCMA as an independent group, much like the opera (*MCMA Board Minutes* for 4/20/1967). Nothing seems to have come of this request, however.

25 Obituary, *The Central New Jersey Home News* (New Brunswick, NJ), 10/29/1981, 47.

26 There are a few additional events that show that Prager could react strongly when his authority was challenged. In 1972, in a letter regarding his mother Susan Seastone's early work with the orchestra, Charles V. Seastone recalled a row between Prager and Oskar Hagen. (This was almost certainly in connection with a concert on May 8, 1928, where Hagen's wife Thyra sang an aria from Handel's *Julius Caesar*.) "Dr. Oskar Hagen, art historian and musicologist at the University, had translated all of these operas from Italian to German.... As a result, Dr. Hagen came to feel that although he had perhaps not really composed these operas, he nevertheless had a firm copyright on the music; he refused to permit the performance. [Apparently because Prager planned to have the work sung in the original Italian.] The ensuing uproar can be imagined. Prager threatened to go to the sources and copy the parts himself. At one point, the two titans were cut off during a telephone conversation. Each thought the other had hung up." Seastone implies that his mother was able to patch things up between the "titans." (Charles V. Seastone letter to Roland Johnson, 4/25/1972 [MSO Archives].) In any case, the concert did in fact occur, and Hagen and Prager were clearly on good terms in the 1940s, as evidenced by Hagen's *Choral Rhapsody*, which is discussed elsewhere in this chapter.

27 Letters in the MSO Archives.

28 *Appleton Post-Crescent*, 5/11/1946, 8. Gerald Borsuk (interview, 7/20/2000) suggested that Prager directed this orchestra over the next few seasons, but I have found no evidence to substantiate this.

29 *Appleton Post-Crescent*, 2/16/1950, 27.

30 In particular, see "Fox Valley Symphony Sounds First Note of Organization," *Appleton Post-Crescent*, 10/13/1965, 18; and "5 Subcommittees Formed for Fox Valley Symphony Orchestra," *Appleton Post-Crescent*, 11/23/1965, 16.

31 *MCMA Board Minutes* for 1/13/1947 (MSO Archives). This change was due to the decision to perform Beethoven's *Missa Solemnis* in May, on the date originally planned for the program with the Zor Shrine Chanters.

32 Dorothy Cornfield had appeared twice previously with the Madison Civic Symphony, but both in this performance and the 1948 *Missa Solemnis*, she was billed as "Sandra Cortez." See *WSJ* 4/24/1947, 13.
33 *WSJ* 5/5/1947, 1 and *CT* 5/5/1947, 3.
34 *CT* 5/6/1947, 14.
35 *WSJ* 11/24/1947, 3.
36 Letter from Sigfrid Prager to Florence Anderson, 9/28/1947. The letter is preserved in *MCMA Board Minutes* for 10/14/1947 (MSO Archives).
37 *CT* 2/27/1947, 20 and *CT* 2/28/1947, 6.
38 Steaming versions of the *Messiah* recording and three tracks from the 1948 *Missa Solemnis* are available at: http://www.allsenmusic.com/HISTORY/Recordings.html.
39 *MCMA Board Minutes* for 12/9/1947 (MSO Archives).
40 *MCMA Board Minutes* for 2/18/1948 (MSO Archives).
41 *WSJ* 3/13/1948, 1.
42 *MCMA50*, 20.
43 The attribution of this work to Mozart is today considered to be doubtful.
44 *Cincinnati Enquirer* 2/1/1948, 67.
45 *CT* 5/9/1949.
46 Included in *MCMA Board Minutes* for 6/21/1949 (MSO Archives).
47 Raymond Dvorak was director of bands at the University from 1934 to 1968. These works, among his only known choral compositions, were written while he was convalescing from a terrible train accident in 1948 that cost him his right arm. According to the *Wisconsin State Journal*: "'The Cataract of Lodore' is based on a poem that appeared in the *McGuffey Reader* in 1836. 'Canto Buffo' is a marching song whose text consists of Italian musical terms which describe the way in which it is to be sung." (*WSJ* 4/30/1950, 21)
48 Ribaupierre and Heermann had been colleagues in the Cincinnati Symphony Orchestra and had frequently performed chamber music together in the early 1920s.
49 Allsen, *75 Years of the Madison Symphony Orchestra*, 193.
50 Gilbert died tragically, a suicide, in May 1984 (*WSJ* 5/20/1984, 1–2). He is still warmly remembered some four decades later by his former students and colleagues.
51 For a listing of his nonoperatic solo repertoire, see Allsen, *75 Years of the Madison Symphony Orchestra*, 199.
52 Interview with James and Ann Crow, 7/21/2000.
53 Heermann seems to have achieved a reconciliation with the members of the Philharmonic Chorus by inviting them to take part in the December 1951 *Messiah* performance.
54 *MCMA Board Minutes* for 10/19/1948 (MSO Archives).
55 *WSJ* 12/29/1957, 21. Heermann is quoted as saying that "we hope to present the opera in 1959." This did not come to pass, however.
56 In their February 1953 meeting, the board addressed a request by the Zor Shrine Chanters to appear on a program in the upcoming season. The minutes note that "There seems no reason

to do favors for either the Masonic Lodge or Mr. Fred Hilary, director of the Zor Chanters." *MCMA Board Minutes* for 2/18/1953 (MSO Archives). Heermann's successor, Roland Johnson, did, however, stage a few performances in the Masonic Temple Auditorium several years later.

57 For example, in May 1953, he reported to the board on the progress of a project to rebuild the stage. *MCMA Board Minutes* for 5/20/1953 (MSO Archives).

58 *CT* 10/4/1924, 7; Obituary, *WSJ* 9/7/1973, 12.

59 Allsen, *75 Years of the Madison Symphony Orchestra*, 210.

60 Speaking for myself, as a longtime program annotator for the Madison Symphony Orchestra and other ensembles, I very much admire the program notes she wrote for the orchestra in the 1950s.

61 MCMA board records for 1958 record that she was paid a small stipend as "publicity director," but this does not seem to have been a lasting policy.

62 *WSJ* 6/10/1956, 39.

63 Interview with Marian Bolz, 6/22/2018.

64 *MCMA Board Minutes* for 3/21/1950 (MSO Archives).

65 *MCMA Board Minutes* for 2/23/1951 (MSO Archives).

66 Interviews 7/20/2000 (Borsuk) and 9/19/2000 (Crow).

67 Interview with Gerald Borsuk, 7/21/2000.

68 Interview with Betty Bielefeld, 5/1/2019.

69 Interview with James and Ann Crow, 7/21/2000.

70 Interview with Roland Johnson, 8/10/2000.

71 The Hagen LP in the Wisconsin Music Archives is made of translucent red vinyl. Precisely the same material is used in three undoubtedly authentic recordings preserved in the MSO archives, all of which preserve recordings of choral/orchestral concerts from the 1950s: the Verdi *Requiem* (March 1950), Vaughan Williams's *Dona nobis pacem* (March 1955), and Vivaldi's *Gloria* (March 1956).

72 Interview with James and Ann Crow, 7/21/2000. Streaming versions of the *Concerto Grosso* and three tracks from the Hanks recording are available at: http://www.allsenmusic.com/HISTORY/Recordings.html.

73 For example, they were featured performers at a concert at West High School on May 18, 1941 (*WSJ* 5/18/1941, 12).

74 "A Listing of All the Musicians of the Cleveland Symphony Orchestra," www.stokowski.org/Cleveland_Orchestra_Musicians_List.htm, accessed 11/5/2020.

75 Details confirmed with MSO Director of Development Casey Oelkers, 11/5/2020.

76 Obituary, *WSJ* 1/8/2012.

77 Barker, *The Pro Arte Quartet*, 220. Crow studied for several years in the 1950s and 1960s with Pro Arte violist Bernard Milofsky, and he was a patron of the quartet throughout his time in Madison. Two weeks after his death in January 2012, the Pro Arte Quartet performed a special concert as a memorial to Crow (Barker, 228).

78 Interview with James and Ann Crow, 7/21/2000.

79 Email correspondence with Katrin Talbot, 2/3/2021.

80 Interview with James and Ann Crow, 7/21/2000.
81 Obituary, *WSJ* 8/12/2001, 16.
82 Obituary, *WSJ* 6/10/2012, 18.
83 For a listing of his MCMA solo repertoire, excluding staged opera performances, see Allsen, *75 Years of the Madison Symphony Orchestra*, 210.
84 Interview with Betty Bielefeld, 5/1/2019.

CHAPTER 5

Walter Heermann, Music Director 1948–1961

The previous chapter showed that the Madison Civic Music Association's second music director, Walter Heermann, inherited a thriving orchestra and chorus from his predecessor, Sigfrid Prager. Heermann also inherited Prager's positions at the Vocational School and University. There were obvious parallels between the two: Both were German immigrants, and they were close contemporaries, born less than a year apart. The contrasts between the two were more striking, and each put a personal stamp on the Madison Civic Symphony and Chorus with clear differences in style and musical vision. Both of them came to Madison with eminent qualifications, but again there are marked differences in their backgrounds. As detailed in this chapter, Heermann came from a prominent musical family, the son of a celebrated 19th-century German musician, and one of several siblings with successful musical careers of their own. Heermann also came to Madison after a 40-year career performing with and eventually conducting one of America's great orchestras.

One invaluable source of information on Walter Heermann's biography is a set of comprehensive scrapbooks he kept that document nearly 60 years of his career. I had already been in contact with his daughter, Paulita Heermann Neal, for several months when she invited me to visit her summer home in Interlochen, Michigan, in July 2021, where I was able to spend three days with the scrapbooks. That information is cited frequently here.

Hugo Heermann

Before turning directly to the life of Walter Heermann, I need to discuss his family and particularly his father, Hugo Heermann (1844–1935)—undoubtedly the prime influence on his early life and career. The elder Heermann was one of the preeminent German violin virtuosos and pedagogues of the late 19th and early 20th centuries. At age 21 he was appointed concertmaster of the Museum Concerts Orchestra in Frankfurt-am-Main. Two years later he became leader of the Frankfurt Quartet, thereafter known as the Heermann Quartet. It was at about this time that he met Clara Schumann, widow of the composer Robert Schumann, an excellent composer in her own right and one of the leading piano virtuosos of the day, forging a friendship that would last until her death in 1896.

5.01 The Heermann Quartet in the 1890s: Hugo Becker (cello), Fritz Bassermann (second violin), Johann Naret-König (viola), and Hugo Heermann (first violin).

In 1878, Heermann joined the faculty of the newly established Hoch Conservatory in Frankfurt, and though he continued to tour extensively, Heermann remained on the faculty until 1904, when he made a brief attempt to establish his own violin school and then had a four-year sojourn in the United States beginning in 1906. While in America he taught at the Chicago College of Music (1906–9) and then spent most of a season as concertmaster in the Cincinnati Symphony Orchestra in 1909 and 1910. After returning briefly to Berlin, Heermann spent the next 10 years teaching in Geneva. Shortly before his death in 1935, Heermann completed a memoir titled *Meine Lebenserinnerungen* (*Memories of My Life*).[1]

It was through Clara Schumann that Heermann met Johannes Brahms in 1863, and he would remain a close associate of the composer for over 30 years. The Heermann Quartet, together with other Frankfurt musicians, including Schumann—and frequently Brahms himself—introduced most of Brahms's chamber works in Frankfurt in the 1870s and 1880s. The Heermann Quartet also performed Brahms's works frequently on their tours through Germany.[2] However, the Brahms work with which Heermann was most closely associated was the *Violin Concerto*. Brahms composed this work in 1878 for his longtime friend Joseph Joachim, and the concerto, particularly the difficult solo part, was the result of close collaboration between them. Joachim played the concerto's premiere in Leipzig on January 1, 1879, and also played successful performances in England that February. However, the process of revising the score for publication went on through much of that year, with letters from Brahms pressing Joachim ever more insistently to provide his edits. Brahms seems to have sought out opinions from other violinists as well, and in March 1879, Heermann played through the concerto in Frankfurt, with Clara Schumann playing a piano reduction of the orchestral accompaniment.[3] It is not known whether Heermann provided any input, but three months later he and Schumann were the first players to try out another brand-new work by Brahms, the *Violin Sonata No. 1 in D Major, Op. 78*.[4] Heermann was among the first violinists after Joachim to take up the formidable challenge of the *Violin Concerto*, and he made it one of the cornerstones of his solo repertoire, helping to popularize it throughout Europe and later America.

Brahms and Hugo Heermann seem to have had a public and rather spectacular falling-out in early 1895, as reported in the diary of Ferdinand Schumann, the grandson of Robert and Clara, who was living with her in Frankfurt at the time. He reports that Brahms played piano in a program that included his two recently completed clarinet sonatas and the 1861 *Piano Quartet in G minor*, with members of the Heermann Quartet. Brahms, wearing a tight suit "which emphasized his corpulence," was red-faced and sweating profusely, appearing "out of sorts" throughout the concert. During the performance of the *Piano Quartet*, Brahms stood up after each movement and angrily pointed a finger at Heermann. At the end, the composer stalked off the stage followed by the other musicians, and it was only after several minutes that he returned for a bow, accompanied only by the quartet's cellist Hugo Becker. Whatever the reason for Brahms's anger on stage, Heermann apparently refused to appear with him for a curtain call. According to Ferdinand Schumann, the furious composer vowed never again to play with Heermann and said that he did not want to see him again.[5] It is not clear whether or not Brahms—notoriously irascible in his later years—and Heermann ever reconciled, but it seems unlikely; Brahms died two years later, in 1897. However, for his part, Hugo Heermann continued to make Brahms's music a main feature of his chamber music repertoire, and he also continued to champion the *Violin Concerto*. In his posthumously published memoir, he comments with great pride on being able to give the first performances of the concerto in Paris, New York and other American cities, and Australia.[6] He clearly passed his reverence for Brahms on to his sons Emil and Walter.

5.02 Hugo Heermann and his children, ca. 1893. L to R: Emil, Victor Hugo, Bella, Hugo, Norbert, Maja, and Walter. Norbert and Walter are wearing dresses according to 19th-century tradition in which young boys were generally not "breeched" until the age of four or later.

Hugo Heermann was relatively late to marry and have children. In 1881, the 37-year-old violinist married 24-year-old Chilean-born Maria Isabella Moeller Garcia Huerta (1857–1939), known as Isabella. According to a much later report, Isabella was gracious, high-spirited, and "party-mad," and their home became one of the social hubs of Frankfurt. At various times, the Heermanns played host to Emperor Wilhelm I and his chancellor Otto von Bismarck, writer Ivan Tugenev, artist Gustav Doré, and many of the great musicians and composers of the day: Clara Schumann, Brahms, Camille Saint-Saëns, Richard Wagner, Edvard Grieg, Fritz Kreisler, Georges Bizet, Charles Gounod, and many others.[7]

They had seven children, and five of the six who lived to adulthood would follow musical careers:

- Maria Karoline Paulita Heermann (1882–1886).

- **Victor** Hugo Heermann (1884–1933): pianist, actor, opera and church musician, and, possibly, composer. I have found few specific details regarding his career, aside from the fact that he worked at Vienna's Volksoper during the early 1920s, though I am unsure in what capacity. Paulita Heermann Neal described him as "multitalented." Günther Ewig notes that he worked as a church musician and cites a small collection of songs, *Drei Lieder*, by him. However, it should be noted that this collection was published sometime prior to 1896, so if the "V. H. Heermann" credited as author was indeed Victor Hugo, he composed these songs by the age of 14. I have found no other references to compositions by Victor Heermann, however.

- **Emil** Theodor Ferdinand Heermann (1885–1954): violinist and teacher. Emil toured with his father as a young man and later emigrated to the United States. He was a member of the Cincinnati Symphony Orchestra from 1909 until his death, performing in the orchestra and playing chamber music alongside his brother Walter. Emil's career is discussed in this chapter.

- Enrichetta Victoria Elisabeth Maria ("**Maja**") Heermann Korst (1889–1991): cellist. Maja Heermann accompanied her father, mother, and two youngest siblings to the United States in 1906 and returned in 1909 (unaccompanied). Following the war, she toured Europe as a cellist before returning to the United States in 1922, where she toured and eventually took a teaching position in Indianapolis in 1923. She continued to tour in America through at least 1925. At some point prior to 1932, she returned to Germany and became the second wife of the Austrian baritone, singing teacher, and opera director Robert Korst. They left Germany in 1932 and settled in Cincinnati in 1933. He took a position at the College of Music, where his colleagues included her brothers Emil and Walter. They eventually settled in Woodstock, New York, near her brother Norbert. While there in 1956, Maja and Robert Korst collaborated on the libretto to an opera, *Don Juan's Strangest Adventure*. She died in 1991, just 10 days before her 102nd birthday.

- Heinrich **Walter** Heermann (1890–1969): cellist, teacher, and conductor. He is, of course, the subject of this chapter. After emigrating to the United States, he generally went by the name Walter Henry Heermann.

- Leo **Norbert** Heermann (1891–1966): artist and art critic. The only one of the Heermann siblings not to follow a musical career, Norbert trained in Chicago, Paris, Berlin, and Cincinnati and had a successful career as a painter and later as a photographer, primarily working in portraiture. He lived in Cincinnati for several years before moving to Woodstock, New York, in the mid-1930s.

- Henriette Isabell ("**Bella**" or "**Belli**") Heermann Kambert (1892–1996): soprano. According to Ewig, she appeared with the Berlin Staatsoper in the 1920s and 1930s and married a Berlin banker, who died in about 1927, the first of four times she was married and widowed. She seems to have been with her father in Italy when he died, and she may have assisted him in preparing his memoir for publication. Following his death, she brought her mother to Berlin, and then in 1937 the two of them traveled to Cincinnati, where Bella performed with her brothers Emil and Walter and also appeared with the Cincinnati Symphony Orchestra. Their mother remained in Cincinnati, dying there in 1939 at age 82. Bella returned to Germany but was banned from performing when she refused to join the Nazi Party. She escaped Germany in 1938. She settled in New York City, where she traded singing for fashion design, working successfully for many years as "Madame Isabel." Late in life, she also settled near Woodstock, New York, and like her sister Maja, Bella was remarkably long-lived, dying at age 103.[8]

5.03 The Heermann siblings: Victor (ca. 1905), Maja (1941), Emil (ca. 1940), Norbert and Walter (early 1920s), and Bella (early 1920s).

Hugo Heermann's residence in America in from 1906 to 1910 seems to have had a long-lasting effect on his family. Maja, Norbert, and Bella traveled with him to Chicago in 1906, and all three would eventually return to settle permanently in the United States. Emil and Walter arrived shortly afterward, clearly with the intention of staying permanently. Emil and Walter would work side-by-side in the Cincinnati Symphony Orchestra and as chamber musicians for four decades. Above and beyond their musical collaboration, Walter's daughter notes that they were also "lifelong best friends."[9]

Hugo Heermann first traveled to the United States to perform in 1904, and he returned in late 1905 on a tour that went as far west as San Francisco, from where he traveled on to play concerts in Australia and New Zealand before returning to America. Emil Heermann accompanied his father on this tour and took part in several concerts. One German correspondent, reporting on a program in San Francisco, was sharply critical of the younger Heermann for what the reviewer considered to be an over-flashy performance:

> Hugo Heermann opened our winter season with three concerts in which he performed music by Brahms, Beethoven, Spohr, Joachim, etc. His mature, dignified art found the rich recognition it deserved in halls that were, unfortunately, sparsely occupied. His son, Emil Heermann, who, in addition to duets with his father, also played music by Paganini, Tchaikovsky, the Chaconne, etc., still needs some thorough study, however. This very talented young violinist follows the lamentable modern Sevčik school in his style of playing rather than following his father as a teacher. I mean to say that, with the violin, one should first strive to express everything that is inherent in the instrument, and not put all one's emphasis on visible frippery. The purpose of playing an instrument is to make music, and not to be like an athlete who shows the astonished crowd how fast he can move his fingers.[10]

Hugo Heermann returned to Germany but was enticed to return to America for a longer stay by Florenz Ziegfeld, who offered him a teaching position at the Chicago Musical College.[11] The terms offered by Ziegfeld were generous and allowed him ample time to tour the United States. Hugo Heermann returned to America in August 1906, with his wife and three of his children, and settled in Chicago. His sons Emil and Walter arrived together in the United States a few months later, in January 1907.

While he was teaching in Chicago, Hugo Heermann appeared in Madison at least three times, and he seems to have had friends in the city. He played two formal recitals. The first, sponsored by the Madison Women's Club, was in a private home on October 6, 1907, with baritone Hans Schroeder and an unknown pianist. He appeared again at the University's Library Hall on February 4, 1909, with local pianist Alice Regan in a concert sponsored by the University School of Music. However, he and his wife also traveled to Madison in April 1908 to spend the Easter holiday with their friend Hedwig Presber, a recent German immigrant whose home was one of the centers of German cultural life in the city. While there, Heermann volunteered to perform at one of the Easter services at the First Congregational Church.[12]

He moved to Cincinnati in 1909. The recently reorganized Cincinnati Symphony Orchestra had just hired the young Leopold Stokowski as music director. Stokowski aggressively rebuilt the orchestra, enlarging it to 77 players and bringing in carefully selected, primarily European leaders for most sections. Among them, Stokowski engaged Hugo Heermann as concertmaster for the reorganized orchestra's first season in 1909–10. Heermann also appeared as a soloist that season, and it is no surprise that he chose to play the Brahms *Violin Concerto* in March 1910.[13] Heermann would ultimately serve as concertmaster for less than a season before returning to Germany. For his part, Hugo Heermann wrote relatively little about his sojourn in America in his autobiography, where he disposes of four years of his career rather laconically (following a much longer and more enthusiastic description of the short tour in Australia and New Zealand), saying only that:

> After a quiet three-week return trip to San Francisco, I gave two sonata evenings there with Harold Bauer. A Beethoven celebration followed in Chicago, where I spent three years at the Musical College led by Dr. Ziegfeld. Then I worked in Cincinnati for another year and then finally returned to Europe.[14]

However, he did reminisce enthusiastically about some of the American orchestras he had performed with, and he also commented briefly on his sons:

> What a joy it was for me to play with the wonderful American orchestras, for concert audiences in New York, Boston, Chicago, San Francisco, who are largely of a high cultural level, the concertos of Brahms, Joachim ([*Violin Concerto No. 2*] in the Hungarian style), and also Richard Strauss, [and] to be able to introduce most of them for the first time [in America], or to perform the more well-known [concertos] by Beethoven, Mendelssohn and Bruch among the great conductors: Theodore Thomas, Gericke, Safonoff, Wetzler,

Damrosch and in Boston under the concertmaster Willy Hess. My sons Emil (violinist) and Walter (cellist) were able to find respectable positions in America in a short time, which they would not have been able to do in Germany, given the poor economic situation. And our youngest son Norbert also later succeeded in establishing himself as a painter in New York and gaining recognition and a reputation.[15]

His list of outstanding orchestras and conductors does not include the Cincinnati Symphony Orchestra and Stokowski. In fact, Heermann seems to have been unhappy there and announced in March 1910, well before the end of the season, that he was leaving for Germany—a resignation that turned acrimonious.[16] However, part of Hugo's agreement in coming to the orchestra was clearly securing steady positions for his sons Emil and Walter (then age 19), who also joined the Cincinnati Symphony Orchestra for its 1909–10 season.[17] Emil served as assistant concertmaster for the remainder of the season and formally succeeded his father as concertmaster in 1910–11. Walter was listed at the end of the cello section in the initial season, though he gradually worked his way up in the section until he was named principal in 1937–38, a fact he wryly noted years later: "I'm the only cellist who occupied all of the chairs, from sixth to first."[18] The brothers would remain in the orchestra for decades— Walter until 1948 and Emil through late 1953, shortly before his death—during a period when the Cincinnati Symphony Orchestra became one of the world's premier musical ensembles. Though there was clearly little love lost between the elder Heermann and the people of Cincinnati, the city became home to his two sons for the next four decades. Three of his other children and his widow would eventually live there at various times as well.

Walter Heermann: Early Life and Emigration to America

Walter Heermann was born in Frankfurt-am-Main on February 6, 1890, into the highly social and intensely musical household of Hugo and Isabella Heermann. There was a constant stream of first-rank musicians coming to the house, both his father's Frankfurt colleagues and many of the great musicians who visited the city. It seems that the Heermann children were occasionally part of the entertainment at family parties: the following photo shows the five eldest children dressed as clowns for a musical routine that they performed at a party in the Heermann home.[19]

The tradition of staged family entertainments clearly continued as the children grew older. The oldest document relating to Walter in the Heermann scrapbooks is a typewritten program dated January 30, 1904, for the "Only guest appearance of the Pfeil-geschw ("Quick as an arrow") - Heermann - Gudden - Lichtenstein Troupe" at the "Westend-Theater." I suspect that the Westend-Theater was, in fact, the parlor of the Heermann home in Frankfurt. The show began with a duo for cello and violin by [Sebastian] Lee played by Walter and W. Lichtenstein. The troupe then performed [Theodore] Körner's *Die Sühne* (*The Atonement*), a tragedy published about a century earlier ... though the fact that a 13-year-old Walter was playing the only female role may have lent this performance a slightly less than tragic tone! The second half began with a "singing recitation" by 11-year-old Bella, and then the troupe, now including 12-year-old Norbert, performed Carl Görlitz's 1890 comedy *Vergesslichkeit* (*Forgetfulness*), with Walter taking the role of Frau Roll.

5.04 Five of the Heermann children dressed as clowns for a family party, ca. 1895: Maja, Walter, Emil, Norbert, and Victor.

Walter Heermann almost certainly attended the Hoch Conservatory where his father taught. One of Germany's leading conservatories in the late 19th century, it was founded in 1878 under the patronage of the wealthy Frankfurt lawyer Joseph Hoch. One piece of indirect evidence for his training there is held today in the Madison Symphony Orchestra archives: an autographed photo of the Australian pianist/composer Percy Grainger inscribed to Walter Heermann with a reference to "happier times in Frankfurt." Grainger had moved to Frankfurt with his mother at age 13 to attend the Hoch Conservatory and studied there between 1895 and 1901. His daughter also noted that Walter studied cello with his father's string quartet and Hoch Conservatory colleague, Hugo Becker.[20] One story that Walter related at several points was that he made his formal debut in a concert with his father, which also included performances by Richard Strauss. This program is in fact preserved in the Heermann scrapbooks. It was a concert on July 26, 1906, in the Bavarian town of Garmisch, the favorite summer retreat of Richard Strauss, where he would eventually build a villa in 1908. The program opened with the Beethoven *Piano Trio* op. 70, no. 1, played by Walter, then age 16, with his father on violin and another Frankfurt musician, Hugo Reichenberger, on piano. Strauss then accompanied a performance of selections from Schumann's song cycle

Liederkreis, and—with Hugo Heermann on violin—his own *Violin Sonata in E-flat Major*, op. 18.[21]

Walter emigrated to the United States in 1907. Emil had toured with his father there in early 1906, and both he and his brother Walter arrived together in America just a year later to become permanent residents. Hugo Heermann's new position in Chicago, together with the fact that their mother and three of their siblings had moved there with him, must have been one factor in their decision to emigrate. However, poor economic prospects at home also seem to have encouraged them to leave Germany. In his memoir, Hugo Heermann noted that there were few playing opportunities in Germany at that time, and this was also mentioned by Walter's daughter as a prime reason for coming to America.[22] Emil (age 22) and Walter (age 17) sailed from Naples and arrived in New York City on January 20, 1907. They seem to have stopped first in Philadelphia, where both of them completed Declaration of Intention forms on February 6 asserting that they intended to seek citizenship.[23] Emil, at least, was in Chicago by early May, documented by a review of a joint recital by Hugo and Emil on May 4.[24]

Over the next two years, there are scattered notices of performances in Illinois, Indiana, and Ohio by Emil Heermann, occasionally playing in a quartet led by his father and also in his own solo recitals. In 1908, Emil joined the orchestra of the Metropolitan Opera at the invitation of Gustav Mahler.[25] Paulita Heermann Neal notes that Walter earned his living during this period playing in theater orchestras in New York City. She also recalled that her father, who had studied English while still in Germany, did not speak it well when he arrived in 1907, and he really learned the language by following the dialogue on stage every night.[26]

The Cincinnati Symphony Orchestra and Military Service

Hugo, Emil, and Walter Heermann arrived in Cincinnati in October 1909 to take up their positions in the Cincinnati Symphony Orchestra, which during the long tenures of Emil and Walter would become one of the world's finest musical ensembles. There had been professional orchestras in the city since the 1850s, but in 1873 Cincinnati also held its first May Festival, a large-scale choral festival that built upon a well-established *Sängerfest* tradition among the city's German immigrant population. Chicago conductor Theodore Thomas was the festival's initial music director, and after its founding in 1895, the Cincinnati Symphony Orchestra was employed as the festival orchestra.[27] The orchestra and the festival would continue to exist side-by-side as two of the city's most important musical institutions. The orchestra was successful for 13 seasons, but financial and labor issues forced it to shut down in early 1907. In 1909, a board of directors under the leadership of Anna Sinton Taft (sister-in-law of soon-to-be President and later Supreme Court Chief Justice William Howard Taft) reorganized the Cincinnati Symphony Orchestra, hiring the 27-year-old English-born Leopold Stokowski as music director. His tenure with the Cincinnati Symphony Orchestra was successful, if brief.[28] In 1912, he left for the Philadelphia Orchestra, where he built his reputation as one of the 20th century's leading conductors, a sometimes idiosyncratic interpreter of the classics, and a champion of the *avant-garde*.

Following Stokowski, the brothers worked under a series of distinguished music directors, beginning with Austrian Ernst Kunwald, whose tenure (1912–1917) included the American premieres of Mahler's *Symphony No. 3* and Richard Strauss's *Alpine Symphony*. However, anti-German war hysteria put an end to his directorship. Cincinnati had a large German-American population, but it was thoroughly caught up in the sentiment that raged across the country before and after the United States declared war on the German Empire on April 6, 1917. As an Austrian, Kunwald was immediately under suspicion by some of Cincinnati's more hysterical citizens, and after an embarrassing debacle over a concert in Pittsburgh, he proffered his resignation in mid-November. The board refused his resignation, but after two weeks of relative calm, the United States declared war on Austria-Hungary and other German allies on December 4. Three days later, U.S. Marshal Michael Devanny received orders from Washington to arrest Kunwald, and he was taken to the federal jail in Dayton. Though he was released on parole the next day, the Cincinnati Symphony Orchestra board now felt that it had no choice but to accept his resignation. The government continued to build a case against Kunwald, based upon supposedly seditious statements that violated the terms of President Wilson's "Alien Enemy" proclamation. Kunwald was arrested again on January 2 and was interned for the rest of the war at Fort Ogelthorpe in Georgia.[29]

Three months later, federal authorities arrested concertmaster Emil Heermann. Emil had recently returned from a Cincinnati Symphony Orchestra tour directed by Victor Herbert, one of the guest conductors hired to complete the season after Kunwald's arrest. Emil had not completed his naturalization, and in going on tour, he had—apparently unwittingly—violated the restrictions placed on "enemy aliens" by the Wilson Administration: that they must seek formal permission before leaving their town of residence. Marshal Devanny arrested him on March 9, though he was promptly released into the custody of members of the College of Music administration, pending a ruling from Washington. On March 12, Devanny arrested Emil a second time, now taking him to the federal jail in Dayton. It was widely reported that his wife Dorothy and Walter Heermann visited him the next day. His brother brought his violin, but Emil refused to keep it, saying that he was too depressed to play. Emil's public comments during what must have been a thoroughly humiliating experience were remarkably humble and conciliatory. On March 14, the *Cincinnati Enquirer* published an interview in which he acknowledged that he had "unintentionally" violated the law and said:

> I realize that these are war times and the Government has done nothing it had not a perfect right to do under the circumstances. The people of this country have accepted me wherever I have gone. They have made me successful and I thank them all. Regardless of what action is taken now it is my intention to become an American citizen as soon as the war is over. I would rather die than have anyone believe that I would have violated intentionally this country's decrees.

News coverage of his arrest invariably mentioned that he was held in the relatively "comfortable" second-floor "banker's row" of the Dayton jail, in the same cell that had been occupied briefly by Kunwald. Emil Heermann was released on March 23, 1918, and the terms of his parole included checking in weekly with Marshal Devanny and with officials from the College of Music. He was also strictly restricted to travel between his home, the College, and the orchestra's hall, with any out-of-town travel contingent upon a special permit. Emil, in a clear attempt to clear his name with the public, pledged to spend three-quarters of his income purchasing Liberty Bonds.[30]

Walter Heermann was already a naturalized citizen by 1918, and he does not seem to have been harassed by government officials.[31] Within a few months of his brother's release, he followed the course of hundreds of thousands of German-Americans by volunteering for service in the U.S. Army. According to his daughter, he

5.05 Sgt. Walter Heermann and unidentified soldier at Fort Sheridan, 1918 or 1919.

quickly learned saxophone in order to be assigned to an Army band.[32] He formally enlisted on June 13, 1918, and within a few days he was attached to the base hospital at Camp Sheridan, near Montgomery, Alabama, assigned to the 9th Infantry Division. It is unclear whether he actually had a chance to play saxophone, however, as he seems immediately to have been put to work conducting and playing cello in a small orchestra attached to the base's hospital. The *Montgomery Advertiser* proudly boasted that this group was the "only camp symphony orchestra in the country."[33] A program of one of the orchestra's concerts on November 19, 1918, preserved in the scrapbooks shows that it was a group of over 30 players, with a string section of 15. (Nearly half a century later, Heermann would quip, "I owe my conducting career to Uncle Sam."[34]) His service in the Army lasted slightly over eight months, and all of it was spent at Camp Sheridan. Despite the fact that he spent his entire service on an Army base, some 4500 miles from the battlefields in France, there must have been some harrowing moments for a musician associated with an Army hospital. This was during the great influenza pandemic, and crowded military bases across the country were particularly hard-hit. In the fall of 1918, there was a serious outbreak at Camp Sheridan, with hundreds of soldiers falling ill. It is possible that Walter was one of them; his military record notes that he was discharged by the Medical Department on October 1, 1918. He was certainly back on duty as director of the camp orchestra by November. On January 25, 1919, the Cincinnati Symphony Orchestra visited Montgomery during a tour of the South. The orchestra was now conducted by Eugène Ysaÿe, and the program included a solo performance by Emil. While in Montgomery, the orchestra gave a special performance at the Camp Sheridan hospital.[35] Walter Heermann was honorably discharged with the rank of sergeant on February 15, 1919, when his entire unit was decommissioned.[36] A letter of commendation from his commanding officer, Col. L. A. Fuller, praised Sgt. Heermann's work in glowing terms:

1. Upon your discharge from the Army and your return to civil life I wish to take the opportunity to express the appreciation of myself and of the entire Hospital personnel of the splendid work which you have done at this Hospital in [conducting] the Orchestra, training the musicians of the Hospital, arranging for concerts at the hospital by the Orchestra, and, in every way possible, exerting yourself to give much needed entertainment to the patients and personnel of the hospital, the sick and giving much-needed entertainment of the highest class to the well.

2. The Orchestra, under your management, has acquired a reputation not merely local to the hospital or to the City of Montgomery, but extending far beyond this. The Orchestra and their enthusiasm to perform splendid work, not only in the Orchestra but in their medical department duties, must have been, at least in part, inspired by your example.

3. On your return to civil life you were accompanied by the gratitude and heartfelt best wishes of every member of the Base Hospital.[37]

By March 1919, he had returned to Cincinnati.

The Cincinnati Symphony Orchestra's next music director was Belgian violin virtuoso, composer, and conductor Eugène Ysaÿe (1918–1922), who first conducted the orchestra during the early 1919 tour as one of a series of substitutes for the interned Kunwald. He led several nationwide tours. In the course of these tours, Ysaÿe led a concert in Madison, at the University Armory, in November 1921, which as noted in Chapter 1 was also a pioneering radio broadcast and Walter Heermann's first visit to his eventual hometown.[38]

Following Ysaÿe's departure in 1922, the board approached four prominent European candidates: Wilhelm Furtwängler, Felix Weingartner, Serge Koussevitsky, and Fritz Reiner. Though Koussevitsky expressed some interest, his salary demand was too high. (He would eventually come to America to direct the Boston Symphony Orchestra in 1924.) Reiner, who had just resigned as the director of Dresden's Hofoper, accepted and would serve as music director of the Cincinnati Symphony Orchestra from 1922 to 1931. The 34-year-old Hungarian was already recognized as one of Europe's great conductors, and Hugo Heermann, then living in Geneva, wrote to his son Emil about Reiner's growing fame.[39] In contrast to Ysaÿe's relatively relaxed approach, Reiner already had a reputation as an exacting perfectionist and a sometimes fearsome presence on the podium. Uncompromising in his desire for the highest musical quality, he had replaced over half of the orchestra by the end of his first season, including all of the principal players except concertmaster Emil Heermann and the principal cellist and clarinetist. Within a few years, Reiner's Cincinnati Symphony Orchestra was widely recognized

5.06 Cincinnati Symphony Orchestra cello section clowning around, early 1920s.

as one of the finest orchestras in the world. The players came to respect him deeply, and one indication of the respect and trust he had toward them was when he sprang a "little surprise" in an all-Schubert program in October 1928. The concluding work on the program was the *"Unfinished" Symphony*, and after intermission the orchestra returned to a stage that had been reset with chairs in a large semicircle. Reiner appeared in the box of Charles and Anna Taft, and Emil Heermann led a "conductorless" performance of the symphony, demonstrating the orchestra's now-flawless ensemble playing. Reiner was also an uncompromising advocate for contemporary music, introducing the often-resistant Cincinnati audience to works by Stravinsky, Bartók, Kodály, Honegger, Hindemith, Scriabin, Respighi, Weill, and many modernist works by American composers. When Reiner led the orchestra in a return visit to Madison on November 28, 1922, preconcert publicity played up this part of his character, with the headline "Reiner Is Radical In Music."[40] (The program he led was hardly radical, however. It did include a work by American composer Henry Hadley, and the thoroughly romantic third symphony of Glazunov, which Reiner had only recently introduced to American audiences. The other two pieces on the program, however, were familiar and popular works by Richard Strauss and Wagner.) After a thoroughly successful nine seasons, Reiner left the Cincinnati Symphony Orchestra in 1931. Reiner would go first to Philadelphia to teach at the Curtis Institute, and he would later have impressive tenures with the Pittsburgh and Chicago Symphony Orchestras.[41]

The Cincinnati Symphony Orchestra board had, it seems, already chosen Reiner's successor before his formal resignation: Eugene Goossens.[42] Born in England, Goossens (music director 1931–1947) was a member of a distinguished Belgian musical family. His 16-year tenure in Cincinnati would be particularly important in the career of Walter Heermann, whom Goossens engaged to conduct the orchestra on several occasions, initially as an emergency substitute, but eventually as a regular conductor of youth and tour programs and as a guest conductor for a few of the orchestra's regular subscription concerts. Goossens left Cincinnati in 1947 to take up a post in Australia and was eventually knighted for his service to Australian music.[43]

5.07 Walter and Emil Heermann in the early 1940s.

The final conductor for whom the Heermann brothers played was Thor Johnson. Born in Wisconsin Rapids, Wisconsin, Johnson served as the Cincinnati Symphony Orchestra's music director from 1947 to 1958. Johnson was particularly interested in outreach and took a very active hand in the orchestra's youth programming. He also began a series of Neighborhood Family Concerts that took the orchestra to various venues around the city and suburbs. (This may have been Roland Johnson's inspiration for instituting the same sort of concert in Madison in the late 1960s.) Thor Johnson was a particular champion of American music, commissioning some 60 works by American composers.[44]

Conducting the Cincinnati Symphony Orchestra and Solo Appearances

Walter Heermann's debut as a conductor in Cincinnati was on August 28, 1919, conducting the "Cincinnati Summer Orchestra" (40 players from the Cincinnati Symphony Orchestra) at the Cincinnati Zoo. Apparently, conductor Theodore Beresina, who normally led the zoo programs, had heard of Heermann's work with the Camp Sheridan orchestra and invited him to conduct. Heermann led two programs that day, both featuring vocal soloist Billie Huber. Heermann received a glowing review the next day, noting that the "soldier-musician ... acquitted himself in brilliant style" and that his audience "demanded encore after encore and evinced heartiest approval and appreciation of his high musical attainments."[45]

Conductor Ralph Lyford founded the Cincinnati Opera in 1920, and that same year he established a summer series of outdoor opera performances at the zoo, which were accompanied by the Cincinnati Summer Orchestra. Between opera performances, the orchestra performed concerts, often featuring vocal soloists and multiple conductors. It is unclear whether or not Heermann appeared again as a conductor in 1920 or 1921, but in 1922 he led five concerts at the zoo. On July 4, 1922, he led the program's "all-American" second half, opening with Sousa's *U.S. Artillery March*, Lucius Hosmer's *Northern Rhapsody*, Charles Sanford Skilton's *Two Indian Songs*, and closing with a medley of familiar American tunes by Victor Herbert, the *American Rhapsody*.[46] Heermann conducted parts of four more concerts on July 17, July 22, August 5, and October 1.[47]

Though he did not apparently conduct the Cincinnati Symphony Orchestra over the next two decades, Heermann built a strong reputation as a conductor in Cincinnati and beyond during this period. In the late 1920s, he served as musical director for the Stuart Walker Company, one of Cincinnati's leading professional theatrical troupes. In 1929, Heermann founded the Cincinnati Little Symphony, a professional chamber group that included many of his colleagues from the Cincinnati Symphony. He had joined the faculty of the College of Music as a cello teacher in 1918, but in 1930 he became the director of the College Orchestra as well. This group was particularly active in the 1930s, presenting concerts in the city and making extensive tours across the country. He was also director of the Charleston, West Virginia, Music Festival from 1934 to 1940.

A story that is almost a cliché in discussing the lives of great conductors is that of the "big break"—of a conductor called in at the last minute to substitute for the ailing Maestro and succeeding brilliantly. Probably the most famous of these stories is Leonard Bernstein's last-minute substitution for guest conductor Bruno Walter at a New York Philharmonic concert in 1943. Maestro Walter came down with the flu, and Bernstein stepped in with no rehearsal to conduct the orchestra, a triumph that jump-started Bernstein's career as a conductor. In the case of Walter Heermann, there is a similar story, which, as it happens, also involved the flu. In January 1941, a nasty strain of influenza was raging through the city, and it also affected several members of the Cincinnati Symphony Orchestra. Among those laid low by the flu that month was Emil Heermann, who had originally been scheduled to perform the Brahms *Double Concerto* with Walter on January 31; a performance was eventually rescheduled to the orchestra's closing concert of that season in April. Conductor Eugene Goossens also came down with the flu, shortly before the concerts of January 17 and 18, and Heermann was asked to substitute. This program, one of the orchestra's regular subscription concerts, was a large and challenging one: Weber's *Overture to "Der Freischütz,"* Tchaikovsky's *Piano Concerto No. 1* (featuring pianist Arthur Rubinstein), and *A London Symphony* by Vaughan Williams. Heermann seems to have handled this unexpected challenge ably. A brief, unsigned review of the concert on January 18 noted that:

> It was a matter of deep concern to yesterday's audience that Mr. Eugene Goossens, who is confined to his bed with influenza, was unable to conduct. In his place, Mr. Walter Heermann, violoncellist of the Cincinnati Symphony Orchestra, brilliantly presented yesterday's program. Mr. Heermann, together with the orchestra, receiving an enthusiastic ovation from this large throng of music lovers.[48]

Three months later, the *Cincinnati Enquirer*'s regular reviewer Frederick Yeiser, in a retrospective article surveying the orchestra season just past, recalled this program with admiration:

Shortly after mid-season the grippe played havoc with the personnel, and two of the soloists. On cruelly short notice, Walter Heermann, the first cellist, became a sort of minute man by conducting a tough program in the absence of Mr. Goossens, who was confined to his bed.[49]

This success, and Heermann's by then well-established reputation as a conductor, seem to have led to more opportunities to conduct the Cincinnati Symphony Orchestra. In the 1943–44 season, Goossens's schedule would not allow him to conduct some of the orchestra's youth programs, and he delegated them to Heermann. Over the next three seasons, Heermann would lead at least eight of these programs, an experience that clearly affected his later creation of youth programming for the Madison Civic Symphony. In February 1945, Heermann conducted two more subscription programs, again substituting for an ailing Goossens. On February 10 and 11, it was a mostly Spanish program featuring famed flamenco dancers Argentinita, Pilar Lopez, and José Greco. Two weeks later, on February 23 and 24, Heermann conducted a program that included Beethoven's *Symphony No. 1* and Ravel's *Bolero*. The soloist was Spanish pianist José Iturbi playing Mozart's *Piano Concerto No. 22* and his own *Fantasy for Piano and Orchestra*.[50]

Heermann led the orchestra in several programs during a tour through New England in November 1945 and in a subscription program in Cincinnati that December. This concert, on December 7 and 8, 1945, was an impressive one, an all-Wagner program featuring Cincinnati-based bass Hubert Kockritz and one of the 20th century's great Heldentenors, Lauritz Melchior.[51] Though the soloists apparently arrived in Cincinnati too late to rehearse with the orchestra, Heermann once again seems to have led a thoroughly successful program. Reviewer Mary Leighton did note "some pretty cautious going in spots" in the first concert due to the lack of rehearsal with the singers, but she gave a mostly enthusiastic review of the concert and Heermann's leadership: that "... despite the lack of preparation, Walter Heermann, assistant conductor, proved to himself as much of a helden conductor as Melchior is a helden tenor." She concluded with a slightly more mixed review of his work:

> In these [interpretations], Mr. Heermann proved his conductorial mettle. He is a very painstaking conductor whose perception of propriety in sectional insets, well-gauged climaxes economically projected to hold interest through to a peak, commend him highly. Though he doesn't hit the dynamic jack pot, he's an expert

conductorial craftsman, a sound musician who knows his way around Wagnerian tradition.[52]

Heermann, Melchior, Kockritz, and the orchestra traveled to Louisville, Kentucky, two days later to repeat the program there.[53] Heermann conducted three more programs during a midwestern tour in December 1946, once again substituting for Goossens, who once again came down with the flu and had to be hospitalized in Dubuque, Iowa.[54]

Eugene Goossens left the Cincinnati Symphony Orchestra for Australia at the end of the 1946–47 season and was succeeded as music director by Thor Johnson. Under Goossens, Heermann had conducted regularly throughout the early 1940s, serving as a last-minute substitute on a few occasions, but also leading many youth and tour programs. He had clearly been the orchestra's assistant conductor in all but title for several years when he was named "permanent assistant conductor" in June 1947. His duties seem mostly to have been tied to the Cincinnati Chamber Orchestra, a group that grew out of the Cincinnati Little Symphony that Heermann had founded in 1929.[55] When Johnson became music director, he seems to have taken a much more active hand in directing youth concerts than had Goossens, so Heermann did not conduct any more of these programs, nor did he lead any other Cincinnati Symphony Orchestra concerts during his final season with the orchestra.

5.08 Undated charcoal sketch of Walter Heermann (ca. 1940) by Nikolas Boris.

He did, however, return to the Cincinnati Symphony Orchestra's podium one last time, for subscription concerts on January 21 and 22, 1949, seven months after he moved to Madison. According to newspaper notices that week, it was a warm reunion between Heermann and his colleagues, both in the orchestra and at the College of Music. The program he led was a varied one:

> Weber, *Overture to "Euryanthe"*
> J. S. Bach, Chorale *Komm, süsser Tod ("Come, Sweet Death")*, BWV 478
> J. S. Bach, *Fugue from "The Musical Offering,"* BWV 1079
> Haydn, *Symphony No. 31*
> Saint-Saëns, *Violin Concerto No. 3* (with Zino Franchescatti, violin)

Griffes, *The Pleasure-Dome of Kubla Khan*
Tchaikovsky, *Capriccio Italien*

The two Bach works were Heermann's own arrangements for string orchestra; two months earlier they had appeared on his opening program with the Madison Civic Symphony. Though *Cincinnati Enquirer* reviewer John P. Rhodes was critical of what he criticized as an overlong and poorly matched selection of repertoire, he clearly admired Heermann's conducting and was particularly complimentary toward the Bach transcriptions.[56]

Both Heermann brothers appeared as soloists with the orchestra on multiple occasions. As concertmaster, Emil Heermann was a frequent soloist and made his debut during his initial season as concertmaster, playing the Tchaikovsky *Violin Concerto* in January 1911. He would appear as a soloist over 60 times with the orchestra, in varied repertoire ranging from Bach, Handel, and Mozart to Respighi and Weill. Like his father, he particularly favored Brahms, performing the *Violin Concerto* in 1914 and 1922, and the *Double Concerto* in 1924, 1935, and 1941—the first two performances with Walter Heermann's predecessor as principal cello, Karl Kirksmith, and the third with Walter himself. Emil Heermann's final appearance as a soloist was at a January 1946 program led by guest conductor Leonard Bernstein, where he was one of the soloists in the Bach *Brandenburg Concerto No. 5*.

Walter Heermann, a section player for most of his career in Cincinnati, appeared as featured soloist on just three occasions, including one appearance playing the Baroque viola da gamba:

- Bach, April 18–19 *Brandenburg Concerto No. 6* (February 21–22, 1931; he was one of two viola da gamba players featured in the second movement)
- Brahms, *Double Concerto* (April 18–19, 1941; with Emil Heermann)
- Weber, *Invitation to the Dance*, arranged for solo cello and orchestra by Felix Weingartner (November 28–29, 1947)[57]

The Brahms *Double Concerto* performance with his brother in 1941 must have been among the most important playing moments of his 40 seasons with the Cincinnati Symphony Orchestra. The *Double Concerto*, Brahms's final large orchestral piece, is a dense and challenging work that calls for sensitive balance and collaboration between the two soloists. It was seemingly tailor-made for two brothers who had spent decades playing chamber music together and honing their communication skills. This is borne out in Frederick Yeiser's review of the concert in the *Cincinnati Enquirer*. Yeiser, who called the brothers "two of the community's best-liked musicians," noted that:

> The brothers Heermann handled their assignment in the solo roles with fluency and understanding—not only of Brahms, but of one another. So it was a happy collaboration on the whole and one which was abetted by the generous support given them by their colleagues in the orchestra. Their performance met with a genuine warm response on all sides.[58]

Emil and Walter Heermann would reprise the *Double Concerto* with the Memphis Symphony Orchestra on May 5, 1942.[59] The brothers also performed the concerto with two of the orchestras that Walter would later conduct, first with the Springfield Symphony Orchestra in February 1948, and then in Madison in April 1949, near the end of his first season as music director of the Madison Civic Symphony.

I suspect that his final solo appearance with the Cincinnati Symphony Orchestra, playing the much lighter Weber *Invitation to the Dance* at the end of 1947, may have been more bittersweet, a kind of solo swan song at a time when the Heermanns were clearly coming to the end of their time with the orchestra. At the end of the 1945–46 season, Emil Heermann had been pushed out of the concertmaster position, switching roles with associate concertmaster Sigmund Effron. The demotion was apparently requested by Goossens and was front page news in the *Cincinnati Enquirer* on May 19, 1946. Though he later asserted that he been treated fairly, Emil seems to have been particularly irked by the fact that this news was leaked to the public just a few weeks later, rather than being announced at the beginning of the next season, as he had agreed upon with orchestra management.[60] Emil would remain in the associate position until shortly before his death on January 13, 1954. According to both Paulita Heermann Neal and Roland Johnson, Walter Heermann was disillusioned by this move, and Johnson noted that "Walter saw the writing on the wall with regards to his own status as principal cello. He jumped at the chance when the orchestra in Madison became a possibility."[61] This disillusionment was probably compounded by a very public flap over Emil's position at the College of Music just a few weeks after his demotion in the orchestra. In March 1948, near the end of his 40th season with the Cincinnati Symphony Orchestra, Walter Heermann announced his resignation and his forthcoming move to Madison.[62]

Other Musical Work in Cincinnati: Chamber Music, Conducting, and Teaching

During Walter Heermann's long tenure, performing in the Cincinnati Symphony Orchestra became a sought-after position among musicians nationwide and internationally. By the 1920s, the orchestra's wages were competitive with orchestras in the larger cities of New York, Chicago, Boston, and Philadelphia, and the city offered many chances for supplemental work and year-round employment for the orchestra's musicians. Most principal players and many section players (including Walter) taught at one of the city's two conservatories. Many players were able to earn significant income playing in theater orchestras and movie theaters, though these opportunities became scarcer with the advent of "talkies" in the 1930s. There was also a constant demand for live music on the radio. Playing in the Cincinnati Summer Symphony at the zoo was also a welcome source of income during the lean summer months.[63] For Walter and Emil Heermann, however, their primary "side gig" was performing chamber music.

From the years before World War I through at least 1927, Walter played in a string quartet led by Siegmund Culp, with Ernst Pach and Carl Wunderle—all of them his orchestra colleagues. Walter's scrapbooks document dozens of performances in and around Cincinnati with this quartet between 1915 and 1927, including regular radio performances between 1921 and 1925. Walter also performed regularly with a quartet led by André de Ribaupierre. Emil played in a quartet with his father during Hugo Heermann's brief tenure in Cincinnati and then led a quartet of his own for the next two decades. His brother Walter became the quartet's regular cellist by 1925.

However, the brothers' most enduring joint musical project was the Heermann Trio, with Emil and Walter and a series of several pianists over the years. This trio, initially with pianist Romeo Gorno from the College of Music, seems to have given its debut performance on April 18, 1918, shortly after Walter's return from military service. This group became particularly active by the mid-1920s with pianist Thomie Prewett

5.09 The Heermann Quartet, ca. 1925: Emil Heermann, first violin, Ernst Pach, second violin, Herman Goerlich, viola, Walter Heermann, cello.

Williams, who was part of the faculty of the Cincinnati Conservatory of Music. They were, of course, most active in Cincinnati, giving hundreds of local performances in the 1920s, 1930s, and 1940s. The Heermann Trio's local and regional fame grew even more when they began a weekly broadcast program on radio station WLW in 1926, broadcasts that continued until 1930.[64] According to Walter's daughter, radio stations in the beginning were desperate to fill broadcasting hours with live content, and many of the trio's broadcasts were not carefully planned programs but simply broadcasts of their rehearsals.[65] In 1929, the trio also made at least three records, issued on the Brunswick label, with the six sides including a trio arrangement of Debussy's *Deux arabesques*, and four lighter selections.[66] They also played dozens of concerts in the region around Cincinnati; there are newspaper notices and reviews for performances throughout Ohio, Kentucky, Tennessee, Indiana, and West Virginia. On April 9, 1933, the Heermann Trio—now with pianist John Quincy Bass—performed at the auditorium of the Library of Congress in Washington, DC.[67] Though the frequency of their performances seems to have dropped significantly during the 1940s, the Heermann Trio played concerts as far afield as Tennessee and Wyoming during the war years and continued to play together until Walter left for Madison in 1948.

The scrapbooks detail dozens of other chamber programs and church services Heermann performed in and around Cincinnati in the 1920s, 1930s, and 1940s. One notable program was in March or April 1921 at the Cincinnati Art Museum: a "concert of music for old instruments," on which Walter performed on viola da gamba, together with his Cincinnati Symphony colleague Carl Wunderle on treble viola and viola d'amore.[68] Typically for early music concerts of the day, the performers appeared in full costume. Walter would perform on viola da gamba on at least two other programs. In 1925, he played on a similar early music program at the Art Museum, and in 1931, he played the instrument as part of the Cincinnati Symphony Orchestra performance of Bach's *Brandenburg Concerto No. 6*.

5.10 Carl Wunderle on viola d'amore and Walter Heermann on viola da gamba in costume for a concert at the Cincinnati Art Museum in early 1921.

I have already discussed Walter Heermann's experience conducting the Cincinnati Symphony Orchestra; his conducting skills also allowed for many other "moonlighting" opportunities. Stuart Walker led one of Cincinnati's best theatrical companies in the 1920s, and Heermann later described himself as the company's musical director.[69] This does not seem to have been a conventional pit orchestra, as the Stuart Walker Company performed almost exclusively nonmusical dramas and comedies. The ensemble Heermann led seems to have been employed primarily for entr'acte and incidental music.[70] He also directed occasional live radio broadcasts; for example, on February 10, 1946, he conducted an unnamed ensemble in a Wintertime Concert on station WLW.[71]

5.11 The Cincinnati Little Symphony, ca. 1930.

In 1929, Heermann organized a chamber orchestra, the Cincinnati Little Symphony. This ensemble, which was initially known alternatively in the press as the "Cincinnati Chamber Orchestra," usually performed with 12 to 15 players drawn from the Cincinnati Symphony Orchestra, eventually including Emil Heermann as concertmaster. After performing several concerts in the South in 1929 and 1930, the orchestra finally made its Cincinnati debut in a concert celebrating Armistice Day on November 11, 1930.[72] It was particularly busy in the first half of the 1930s, performing several more concerts in Cincinnati, including radio broadcasts over WLW. However, it appeared more frequently as a touring group: Between 1929 and early 1934, the Cincinnati Little Symphony performed concerts in Raleigh, North Carolina, Wilmore, Kentucky, Louisville, Kentucky, Richmond, Kentucky, Dayton, Ohio, Indianapolis, Indiana, and Montevallo, Alabama. Their most extensive tour was in October 1934, when the Cincinnati Little Symphony played concerts across Alabama, Mississippi, Louisiana, and Texas.[73] There was enough of a market for the group that in 1932, Heermann engaged a business manager, his friend and colleague Burnet Tuthill, to oversee bookings.[74] However, touring by the ensemble seems to have been abandoned in the late 1930s—probably due to the ongoing Depression—and there were relatively few performances by the group in Cincinnati. Heermann seems to have stepped away from the Cincinnati Little Symphony by 1940. Eugene Goossens conducted programs in 1940 and 1941, and in April 1941, Sherwood Kains, a local choral conductor, became its director.[75] The Cincinnati Little Symphony was eventually absorbed by the Cincinnati Symphony Orchestra in June 1947, shortly after Thor Johnson was hired as music director. Walter Heermann was again named director of the ensemble, now reconstituted as the Cincinnati Chamber Orchestra.[76] However, this new group does not ever seem to have performed under his direction, and I have found no evidence that it survived after Heermann left for Madison. The Cincinnati Little Symphony did re-form briefly under that name and under the direction of William C. Byrd as a summer orchestra in the mid-1950s. There is no historical connection between these groups and today's Cincinnati Chamber Orchestra, which was established in the 1970s.[77]

During Heermann's tenure in Cincinnati, the city had two competing music schools, both of which employed musicians from the Cincinnati Symphony Orchestra. The Cincinnati Conservatory of Music had been founded in 1867 and had its campus in the suburb of Auburn Hills. The College of Music of Cincinnati, founded in 1878, was located in the same block as the orchestra's performance hall. In 1955 the two schools merged to form today's Cincinnati College-Conservatory of Music, which became part of the University of Cincinnati.[78] Heermann seems to have joined the faculty of the Cincinnati Conservatory as a cello instructor in 1910, and programs and clippings in his scrapbooks document several chamber music performances with other Conservatory faculty over the next several years, until he moved to the College of Music in early 1918. The College of Music would employ both Heermann brothers for decades: Emil was hired as a violin instructor in 1915 and Walter as a cello instructor briefly in 1918;[79] he presumably rejoined the faculty soon after returning from his military service in 1919. Both of them performed frequently at the College, both in individual recitals and with the Heermann Trio. In 1930, Walter also became the director of the College Orchestra, a full orchestra that gave five concerts a year. Heermann was apparently a particularly well-liked and respected instructor, and he returned his students' affection, saying in 1946 that "I have always received a bigger thrill from conducting the College of Music Orchestra than from conducting a [professional] symphony. The students' hearts are always in it."[80] One of his students in the 1940s was a young Tennesseean, violinist and conductor Roland Johnson. Johnson started his work at the College of Music in 1939 and returned in 1946 after wartime service in the U.S. Navy. He became a protégé of Walter Heermann, particularly in the years after the war. Johnson would eventually become his successor as conductor of the Madison Civic Symphony. (Their relationship is discussed extensively in Chapters 6 and 7.)

5.12 Walter Heermann and the College Orchestra of the College of Music of Cincinnati, early 1930s.

Near the end of his tenure at the College of Music, there was a troubling incident that had to do with the status of Walter's brother Emil. On May 31, 1946, just six weeks after his demotion in the orchestra, the College of Music asked for Emil Heermann's resignation. The Cincinnati Symphony Orchestra's new concertmaster, Sigmund Effron, who was also on the faculty, was to take over as primary violin teacher. Emil Heermann had been teaching at the College since 1915, and no reasons were apparently offered in public for his termination. Just a few hours after the College communicated to Emil, Walter Heermann proffered his own resignation from the College in solidarity. When the brothers were interviewed by the *Cincinnati Enquirer*'s James Golden, Emil seems to have been relatively untroubled by the changes, saying that he felt he had been treated fairly by the orchestra and that, with regard to teaching, he would simply start taking on private students in the fall. He concluded with: "My wish is that the whole affair should blow over and I continue to enjoy my musical career and associations." His brother Walter was a bit more combative:

> The whole action of the college coming so soon after the demotion in the orchestra, is very distasteful. I can see no reason why Emil should have been asked to resign from the faculty, and even if there had been, the request still would have been in poor taste—you don't kick a man when he's down, do you?

Continuing on to comment on the change in the orchestra, Walter hinted that there had been a "two-year campaign" to replace Emil with a younger player and argued that:

> Of course, Emil doesn't play the solo works and takes the concertos he did in earlier years. After all, at 60, one can't be expected to. But artistically he is at the top of his powers, still a good teacher. The teacher improves from year to year; he learns a lot from his pupils, you know.

Walter concluded by saying that he regretted the fact that he would miss the friendship of his students, but that "I cannot work for them after what they have done to [Emil], and I do not think that they expect me to."[81]

Though it is clear that Walter Heermann made his decision to resign from the College of Music because he was outraged over the school's treatment of his brother, it was also an opportune time to resign. As the *Enquirer*'s Golden notes later in the article quoted above, Heermann was already in negotiations for another conducting position. In fact, just a few days later, on June 4, he announced that he had accepted a position as the music director of the Springfield (Ohio) Symphony Orchestra. Heermann would conduct this group for two seasons before accepting the position in Madison.

In the end, the dispute between the Heermanns and the College of Music was resolved—and very quickly. Following Walter's precipitous and very public resignation, other faculty members began to threaten resignation as well, and there were apparently several communications to the College from donors and members of the community. On June 6, 1946, College of Music students and parents showed their support of Walter Heermann with loud and sustained applause when he appeared with the College Orchestra at that year's commencement ceremony.[82] On June 8, it was announced publicly that the matter had been settled, and that both Heermanns would be returning as faculty for the 1946–47 school year. In an attempt to explain their request for Emil's resignation, and probably to put an end to what had become a very public and increasingly embarrassing flap, the College administration noted that the problem had been that Emil had not signed a formal contract, asking instead for a verbal agreement.[83] Whatever the case, both brothers returned to teaching, and Walter would continue to conduct the College Orchestra for two more years while also retaining the position in Springfield. Though this brief kerfuffle was eventually resolved satisfactorily on his part, it seems to have been one more cloud that hung over his last few years in Cincinnati. His final concert with the College Orchestra, the last of more than 100 programs he conducted, was at the College's commencement on June 3, 1948, just a few weeks before he left for Madison. A clipping in his scrapbooks notes that the commencement service was delayed for nearly 15 minutes by a sustained standing ovation for Walter by the students and families present.[84] For his part, Emil taught one more year at the College before resigning permanently, though in the fall of 1948 he began teaching at the Cincinnati Conservatory.[85]

Life in Cincinnati

In 1922, Walter Heermann married Louisiana-born Martha Amelia Sheila Bodebender (1905–1993—known as Sheila, and occasionally in the press as Marguerite). According to their daughter Paulita, Sheila, some 15 years younger than Walter, was a professional dancer, who worked under the stage name Sheila O'Day. I have found relatively little regarding her dance career, though she was a member of a "Russian Ballet Company" that visited Cincinnati in 1920. She also toured South America with a theater company in late 1921.[86] According to a clipping in Heermann's scrapbooks, they first met in 1920, when the Russian Ballet Company performed at the Cincinnati Zoo summer concerts, where Walter was playing in the orchestra. A colleague in the orchestra reportedly pointed her out to Walter as the "prettiest girl in the ballet," and he met her after the concert. He apparently made several trips to visit her in Chicago, and they were married there on November 13, 1922.[87] They had two daughters, Eileen (1923–1994) and Paulita (b. 1927). According to Paulita, Walter and Sheila divorced in about 1935. Sheila later remarried and eventually relocated to southern California.[88]

Cincinnati would also become home to the extended Heermann family. Emil also married there and had two sons. With the exception of the eldest brother Victor, who died in Germany in 1933, all of the Heermann siblings would join Walter and Emil in Cincinnati at various points in the 1920s and 1930s. Norbert spent several years there as a successful artist and art critic; he studied the work of the Cincinnati artist Frank Duveneck (1848–1919) and later published a monograph on him. He seems to have been a favorite of Cincinnati's high society. In May 1934, for example, Norbert Heermann had a high-profile exhibition at the Cincinnati Town Club, with the Heermann Trio providing entertainment.[89] Norbert moved to Woodstock, New York, in the later 1930s.

Paulita Heermann Neal noted that sisters Maja and Bella left Germany permanently after the Nazis took power. They would be part of a wave of European artistic emigrés—composers, conductors, musicians, artists, dancers, writers, and others—who fled an increasingly dangerous Europe for the United States in the 1930s, to the immeasurable benefit of American cultural life. When Maja Heermann returned to the United States in 1922, she came first to Cincinnati, before setting off on at least two or three years of touring and a teaching position in Indianapolis. She seems to have returned to Germany by the early 1930s. Maja returned to Cincinnati with her husband Robert Korst by 1933. Korst, who had had a prominent operatic career in Germany, took a position at the College of Music, directing its opera productions. It is not clear whether his brothers-in-law Walter and Emil had a hand in his hiring, but it seems highly likely. Maja continued to perform while in Cincinnati, and she and Robert were there until the late 1940s. They eventually settled near Norbert in Woodstock.

The last of the siblings to arrive was Bella. She had built a career as an opera singer in Berlin. Following the death of Hugo Heermann in Italy in 1935, she brought their mother Isabella to live with her in Berlin, but by 1937, Bella and Isabella were both in Cincinnati as well. She made her musical debut in Cincinnati on April 8 at the Town Club, singing with the Heermann Trio. The event was a family affair, with Bella, Emil, and Walter performing, and Norbert, Maja, and their mother in attendance.[90] Isabella stayed in Cincinnati, but Bella apparently returned to Germany relatively soon after the Town Club performance, only to find herself banned from performing after she refused to join the Nazi Party. She escaped Germany in 1938, with her life savings in 10,000-mark banknotes that she had hidden in liverwurst sandwiches. In a story that she often repeated, German border guards flirtatiously asked the glamorous Bella for one of the sandwiches, but they apparently stopped bothering her when she told them, "Oh, no, you don't want those—they're kosher." She settled in New York City and initially tried to restart her operatic career in the United States. In May 1939, for example, Bella appeared with the Cincinnati Symphony Orchestra, singing as one of the "flower maidens" in a concert version of Act II of Wagner's *Parsifal*. However, she found much greater success in New York City as a fashion designer, working as "Madame Isabell."[91] Late in life, she also settled near Woodstock, New York, near her sister. Their mother, Isabella Heermann, stayed in Cincinnati in 1937 and died there on November 7, 1939.[92]

Summer Performances and Teaching in Interlochen and Madison

Walter Heermann certainly found off-season work as a cellist and conductor in and around Cincinnati, performing at the zoo concerts in the early 1920s and performing with the Heermann Trio and other chamber ensembles. One of his most high-profile early appearances as a soloist in Cincinnati was on May 24, 1918, just a week before he left for military service, where he was featured with violinists Eugene Ysaÿe, Mischa Elman, and Gabriel Ysaÿe (Eugene's son) at a grand Red Cross benefit concert. However, he also sought out opportunities much farther afield. He apparently made connections in Colorado Springs while on tour there in 1914 with other faculty from the Cincinnati Conservatory, and he performed concerts there as a soloist in the summers of 1914, 1915, and 1916.[93] From the late 1920s through the 1950s, however, he spent most of his summers as a teacher at music camps in Interlochen and Madison.

5.13 Cincinnati Symphony Orchestra musicians at Interlochen in the summer of 1929. Walter Heermann is seated at far right.

The Interlochen National Music Camp in Michigan was founded as a summer program in 1928 by Joseph Maddy and Thaddeus Giddings. It is now known as the Interlochen Center for the Arts, which includes the Interlochen Arts Camp, the summer program, and the Interlochen Arts Academy, a boarding high school. In 1929, a large cohort of musicians from the Cincinnati Symphony Orchestra, including Walter Heermann, joined its faculty. This was the beginning of a long-standing connection between the camp and the orchestra, with more Cincinnati Symphony Orchestra members joining its faculty over

5.14a-5.14b The Heermann Cottage in Interlochen: (1) Summer 1958, with Walter Heermann, Cora Hardy, with unidentified woman and boy; (2) July 2021, with Peter Neal, Paulita Heermann Neal, and the author.

the next few years, including Emil Heermann, who taught violin from 1932 to 1938. Music director Thor Johnson also worked at Interlochen during the war years and then served as its director during parts of the 1960s and 1970s.[94]

Heermann taught at Interlochen for six years (1929 to 1934), but his connection to this scenic part of Michigan would last the rest of his life. The benefactors of the camp made sure that faculty had the opportunity to build summer cottages near the camp. Walter's daughter notes that he built a cottage on Duck Lake in the early 1930s, which he sold in the early 1940s. At about the same time he bought a smaller cottage and three lots on Duck Lake for $500 from pianist Miriam Otto, wife of Cincinnati-based singer Hubert Kockritz.[95] These lots were in a small area that came to be known as the Orchestra Camp Colony that originally housed exclusively faculty from the camp. One of the adjacent properties, for example, had a cottage built by famed conductor Frederick Fennell. The roads in this subdivision are named after Interlochen faculty: there is, in fact, a Heermann Road, though Walter's property is on Tuthill Lane, named for his friend Burnet Tuthill. This second Heermann cottage would be expanded many times by the family and is now owned by his daughter Paulita, who resides there for about half of each year. Another cottage was built on an adjacent lot by his daughter Eileen and passed to her children. Paulita recently completed a third structure, this one a fully modern year-round house, on another adjacent lot; this is where I stayed during my 2021 visit. Interlochen would become a beloved summer retreat for Heermann and his extended family from the 1930s to the present. His grandson Peter Neal remembers spending summers there in the 1950s and 1960s, describing it as "a magical place for us kids." The property remains in the family today and

5.15 Walter Heermann (left) with cello students at the Summer Music Clinic in Madison in 1939.

remains a summer retreat.[96] Heermann clearly retained his affection for the Interlochen organization as well. In 1967, he donated a valuable autographed letter from Johannes Brahms to Clara Schumann to the camp.[97]

In the summer of 1936, Heermann came to Madison to teach cello at the University's Summer Music Clinic, a large summer camp that had been founded in 1929. His daughter credits Richard Church with recruiting him for this position. Church (1908–1976) was an important figure in Madison's musical life, serving as band director at West High School from 1930 to 1944. By 1936, he was also conducting the University Orchestra, and he formally joined the faculty of the University in 1944 as a professor. He was also a prominent figure in the Madison Civic Symphony, playing principal bassoon in the 1930s and serving as an assistant conductor to Sigfrid Prager. Like many local music educators, Church was involved with the Summer Music Clinic. It is unclear how he knew Walter Heermann, though it seems likely that he knew of Heermann's work at Interlochen. Heermann would teach at the Summer Music Clinic for several years: 1936–40, 1945, 1947–48, and 1950–55. Emil Heermann also joined the faculty in 1950–53.[98] This introduced Madison audiences to Walter Heermann; as a faculty member he would give public recitals every summer. It also introduced Heermann to life in Madison. Paulita Heermann Neal recalled spending time with her father there in the summers, and she said that he very much enjoyed his time in the city. Heermann also would have come to know about the Madison Civic Symphony both from Church and from Sigfrid Prager, who taught with him at the Summer Music Clinic in

1939 and 1945. As discussed in the previous chapter, this personal connection with Prager was probably an important factor in Heermann being hired as his successor in 1948.

Conducting in Charleston and Springfield

The elaborate May Festival in Cincinnati was an annual event that focused on large choral works and involved musicians of the Cincinnati Symphony Orchestra and at least some of its music directors. It seems to have inspired festivals in other cities in the region, including Charleston, West Virginia. That city held its first May Festival in 1933, a one-day event directed by Harry Mueller from nearby Marshall University. Walter Heermann was hired as music director for the 1934 festival, now expanded to three concerts. He made an initial trip to Charleston in April 1934 to rehearse the chorus and the newly formed Charleston Little Symphony, returning in May to conduct final rehearsals and two of the three concerts.[99] Heermann had appeared multiple times in Charleston in the years leading up to 1934 with the Heermann Trio. For example, the trio—the Heermann brothers and pianist Thomie Prewett Williams—performed there with local soprano Esther Davis in May 1931.[100] It was probably a combination of his local performances and his burgeoning reputation as a conductor in Cincinnati that led to Heermann's engagement as music director. He returned as director in 1935 and 1936. Following the 1936 festival, it became a biannual event, and Heermann directed the 1938 and 1940 festivals as well. Before each of these festivals, he would make multiple trips to Charleston to discuss plans and direct rehearsals during the winter and spring leading up to the festival itself.

The 1936 May Festival was typical of these events. Heermann conducted three concerts bringing together well over 200 local musicians: several soloists, the Festival Chorus of more than 100 singers, the Junior Chorus (a large children's choir), and the two dozen players of the Little Symphony. The May 4 program included the Bach cantata *Gottes Zeit ist die allerbeste Zeit* BWV 106, Beethoven's *Symphony No. 8*, the opening movement of the Grieg *Piano Concerto*, and Grieg's cantata *Olaf Trygvason*. On May 6, the orchestra opened with four pieces: Bizet's

5.16 Advertisement for the 1936 Charleston May Festival.

L'Arlesienne Suite No. 1, Borodin's *In the Steppes of Central Asia*, and two works by Rimsky-Korsakov, *Flight of the Bumblebee* and *Dance of the Tumblers*. Heermann did not direct the second half, which was devoted to the cantata *Evangeline* by Chicago-based composer Noble Cain, sung by the Junior Choir and local soloists. The final concert on May 8 was dominated by American composers: the *Missa latreutrica* by Heermann's College of Music colleague Martin Dumler, a set of Black spirituals arranged by African-American composer Clarence Cameron White, John Powell's *Natchez on the Hill*, and *The Chambered Nautilus* by Deems Taylor. It should be no surprise that Heermann also included a work by Brahms in this otherwise all-American program, the *Schicksalslied*. A review of the program in the *Charleston Daily Mail* the next day commended Heermann, "who has endeared himself with musicians and audiences alike for his skill, his personality, and in his faith in the progress of Charleston's music."[101] Clearly, Heermann was able to work well with this large group of mostly amateur musicians, a skill that would be fundamental to his later success in Madison.

During his last two years in Cincinnati, Walter Heermann took on another position that had even closer parallels to his eventual work with the Madison Civic Symphony. The Springfield (Ohio) Symphony Orchestra was founded in 1943. Very much like the contemporaneous Madison Civic Symphony, it was initially a civic/community group with a mixture of local professionals and amateurs. William Fiedler from nearby Antioch College conducted its first three seasons.[102] In June 1946, Heermann became the second conductor of the orchestra, by that time a group of nearly 70 players, and led six concerts over the next two seasons. His first concert, on November 10, 1946, included his own transcription of the Bach chorale *Komm, süsser Tod ("Come, Sweet Death")*, BWV 478, for harp and strings, a work he would later reprise in Madison and Cincinnati. The program also included another Bach transcription, *Jesu, Joy of Man's Desiring*, BWV 147, Mendelssohn's *Symphony No. 4 (Italian)*, Liszt's *Les préludes*, and arias by Mozart and Wagner sung by the fine American baritone Paul Matthen.

5.17 Emil and Walter Heermann rehearsing the Brahms *Double Concerto* with the Springfield Symphony Orchestra, Roland Johnson conducting, February 1948.

Though members of the orchestra occasionally appeared as soloists, each of the Springfield Symphony Orchestra's programs under Heermann featured prominent professional soloists, including violinist Frances Magnes (February 1947), pianist Barbara Holmquest (May 1947), tenor William Hess (November 1947), and pianist Vivien Harvey (April 1948).

For the program on February 15, 1948, Emil and Walter Heermann appeared together as soloists in the Brahms *Double Concerto*, reprising the work they had performed so successfully in Cincinnati in 1941 and in Memphis in 1942. Heermann brought in his College of Music protégé Roland Johnson to conduct the concert opener, Mozart's *Overture to "Don Giovanni,"* and the Brahms. Johnson is also listed as assistant conductor for the April 1948 program, Heermann's final concert with the Springfield Symphony Orchestra, though it is unclear which pieces he conducted.[103] By this time, Heermann had publicly accepted the position in Madison and had submitted his resignation to the Cincinnati Symphony Orchestra, and presumably to Springfield as well. It is possible that he was trying to open the way for Roland Johnson to take over in Springfield—the same move Heermann made successfully in Madison when Johnson became his successor in 1961. However, the next conductor of the Springfield Symphony Orchestra would be Guy Taylor, who led the orchestra for three seasons and would later have a successful career leading the orchestras of Nashville, Phoenix, and Fresno.[104]

Work in Madison

Walter Heermann clearly settled comfortably into his new hometown; his daughter recalled that "my dad was completely happy in Madison."[105] His work with the Madison Civic Symphony was discussed in the previous chapter. His other main position in Madison—and indeed, the one that paid most of his wages—was supervisor of music at the Vocational School. This was the same position that Sigfrid Prager had held since the late 1920s.

One result of his work at the Vocational School had nothing to do with music or coursework: his relationship with Cora Hardy (1898–1986). Hardy spent much of her career as an English teacher at the Vocational School, but by 1948, she was supervisor of the Executive Department there, which included Music, a position she held until her retirement in 1964.[106] As described by his daughter, their relationship began almost immediately when he moved to Madison in 1948. She reached out to Walter to help him get settled in town and at the Vocational School. This developed into a close, affectionate partnership that would last until Walter's death, and according to Paulita Heermann Neal, "They were mutually devoted to one another."[107] Clearly, she was quickly accepted as part of Walter's family, and they would spend summers together at the cottage in Interlochen. Walter's grandson Peter Neal describes her as "very much like a grandmother to us." Peter's mother Paulita recalled that she spent a lot of time with Walter and Cora in Madison, and she described Cora as "the best stepmother anyone could want." Roland Johnson's son Carl, whom she frequently cared for when Roland and Arline Johnson were busy with the Madison Opera Guild in the 1960s, referred to her affectionately as "kind of an aunt." Paulita completed her doctoral work in Los Angeles in clinical psychology when she was in her early 50s, and would dedicate her dissertation to Walter and Cora. Though the two of them maintained separate living arrangements through most of their relationship, in 1966 they purchased a house together on Hintze Road, near Madison's Warner Park.[108] Cora continued to live in the house after Walter's death in 1969, until her own death in 1986.

Heermann also inherited Prager's teaching duties at the University, beginning in 1949. He taught conducting and also taught a music appreciation course which he had initially developed for the College of Music of Cincinnati, "What to Listen For in Music," which became very popular with University undergraduates.

After more than 40 years of earning most of his living as a cellist, Walter seems to have turned more or less exclusively to conducting and teaching after he moved to Madison. His appearance with Emil Heermann in the Brahms *Double Concerto* at the end of his first season in Madison seems to have been his final appearance as an orchestral soloist. He did continue to perform chamber music, however, and continued to perform at a very high level, as evidenced in the 1955 recording of the Hanks *Meditation* described in Chapter 4. He did not teach at the Summer Music Clinic for his first two years in Madison, but he rejoined the faculty in the summers of 1950 through 1955, and he performed a faculty recital during each of those summers. Hermann seems to have forged a particularly close musical friendship with pianist Leo Steffens, a member of the University faculty. On August 5, 1949, Emil Heermann visited Madison and performed a recital with Walter and Steffens at the University's Music Hall. The same trio performed recitals on July 26, 1950, and July 25, 1951. The 1951 recital was entirely devoted to *Enoch Arden*, a melodrama composed in 1897 by Richard Strauss, based upon a poem by Tennyson. Richard Church joined the trio as narrator. This work was performed in a version arranged for piano trio by Walter Heermann from the original piano part. Over the next few summers, Heermann and Steffens appeared again in chamber recitals with musicians from the University and the Madison Civic Symphony.[109]

Retirement

In 1960, the Vocational School caused a flap locally when it announced that Heermann had to leave his post—in early 1960 he would reach the mandatory retirement age of 70. There was an outcry among musicians and community members, with petitions and open letters protesting the Vocational School's policy. In March 1960, the Vocational School and MCMA reached a cordial agreement that allowed Heermann to stay on for one additional year, through the end of the 1960–61 season.[110] This would allow the MCMA and the Vocational School some 14 months to conduct a search for Heermann's successor. However, once again, the orchestra's music director seems to have chosen his own successor, in this case Heermann's onetime College of Music protégé Roland Johnson. According to James Crow, "Walter stayed on that extra year to allow Roland time to get here," a story confirmed by Johnson himself.

5.18 Walter Heermann at his cottage in Interlochen during the mid-1960s.

At his final MCMA board meeting, Heermann humorously misappropriated a famous quote, remarking that "old conductors never die; they just quietly leave town."[111] Despite this, Heermann settled down to a quiet retirement in Madison. He continued to play chamber music with friends and to teach private cello students in Madison and at Milwaukee's Wisconsin Conservatory of Music throughout the 1960s. His grandson Peter Neal notes that he remained physically fit by religiously doing a set of exercises and walking every day, and that he also continued to practice every day—often, during the summers, playing in the woods outside the cottage in Interlochen. The last documents included in his scrapbooks are a pair of programs from "cello musicales" he hosted at his home in Madison on June 13, 1965, and June 11, 1966. These were clearly private gatherings with a potluck supper and performances by Heermann, a few of his students,

5.19 Dr. Peter Neal, far right, and his grandfather's Haenel cello, with the Lakeside Quartet, in February 2020.

and musical friends from Madison, including several members of the Madison Civic Symphony.[112]

Walter Heermann died in Madison on June 10, 1969, at age 79. Roland Johnson programmed a special work in memory of his predecessor and former mentor at a Madison Symphony Orchestra concert in October 1969, Barber's *Adagio for Strings*. Heermann's estate was divided between his daughters, Eileen and Paulita, though he also made provisions for Cora Hardy: both a trust and a provision granting her free use of the cottage in Interlochen for the rest of her life. At the time of his death, Heermann owned two fine cellos, an instrument by Frederick Haenel and a Belgian cello by DuCombles. These were passed on to two of his grandsons: the Haenel to Peter Neal, and the DuCombles to Peter's younger brother William. Peter Neal, a physician in Rice Lake, Wisconsin, still plays the instrument today, performing with the amateur Red Cedar Orchestra and a string quartet. The DuCombles cello also remains in the family.[113]

Legacy

Walter Heermann's musical abilities and his vast knowledge of the orchestral repertoire—gained from a musical career that lasted well over half a century—were central to his success in both Cincinnati and Madison. However, in tracing his career, it seems that his personality was just as important to this success. Chapter 4 included testimony on how he was viewed by the musicians he led; he was popular in the city and respected as a person and as leader of the orchestra and chorus. He clearly worked well with this group of largely amateur musicians. He was also able to work well with the board and community—according to his daughter, "my father had a wonderful ability to schmooze and charm." She notes that the board "absolutely adored" him and that at his retirement they gave him a silver platter inscribed "To Walter Heermann with love from the Madison Civic Music Board."[114]

There are similar tributes from his time in Cincinnati; in the hundreds of newspaper references to Heermann detailing his work there, he is often described as "well-liked," "genial," and "friendly." Many of his colleagues in the orchestra and College of Music paid affectionate tributes as well. Heermann's grandson Peter Neal shared a wonderful caricature, titled "General Bernstein at the Battle of Parkersburg" by Cincinnati Symphony Orchestra violist Siegfried "Sigi" Humphreys, whose witty drawings, poking affectionate fun at his colleagues and documenting the backstage life of the orchestra, occasionally appeared in local newspapers.[115] This caricature was inspired by the first appearance of Leonard Bernstein in Cincinnati on November 3 and 4,

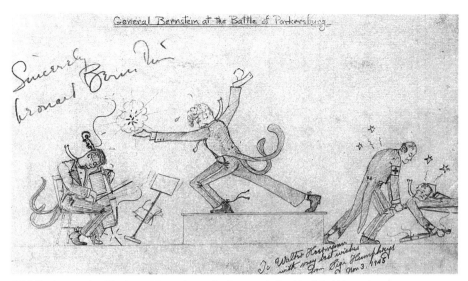

5.20 Caricature by Cincinnati Symphony Orchestra violist Siegfried Humphreys, November 3, 1945.

1945, when he both conducted a program of Mozart's *Symphony No. 39*, Ravel's *Piano Concerto in G Major*, and Brahms's *Symphony No. 1* and appeared as piano soloist in the Ravel. Bernstein clearly made an impression with his passionate interpretations, particularly in the Brahms: one concert review characterized his conducting as having "something near a cataclysmic effect."[116] It must have been tumultuous on stage as well; Humphreys has Heermann playing furiously with a broken string, under the wild gestures of a ferocious Bernstein, as a violinist (almost certainly Emil) is taken away wounded. For his part, Bernstein must have accepted this in the good humor in which it was intended, and autographed the caricature as well, probably at the concert on the next day.[117]

In 1946, College of Music composition teacher Dale Dykins had recently returned from four years of wartime service as part of a bomber crew. He would channel this experience into his first major postwar composition, the *Symphonic Suite*. In describing its composition. Dykins remembered returning from war traumatized and exhausted,

> but the only person who saw this was my best friend, Walter Heermann, first cellist of the Cincinnati Symphony. He insisted that I spend the summer at his cabin in Michigan and I used that time for hiking, swimming and rowing a boat I rented. It was a reviving and wholesome experience and that is what the first movement is about.[118]

At least two compositions were dedicated to Walter Heermann by his colleagues during his time in Cincinnati. In 1928, Louise Harrison Snodgrass, recently hired to teach piano in composition at the College of Music, wrote a piece for solo cello titled *Fair Sailing*, for him. Heermann premiered the work in a recital that fall.[119] Another more substantial work was inspired by Heermann's friendship with a very young Gunther Schuller. The multitalented Schuller joined the Cincinnati Symphony Orchestra as principal horn in 1943 at age 17. In 1945 he wrote his *Cello Concerto*, one of his earliest large orchestral works, for Heermann, though Heermann would never perform it. As Schuller explained decades later:

> I wrote the work for a dear friend, Walter Heermann, first cellist of the Cincinnati Symphony for nearly forty years, under Stokowski, Ysaÿe, Reiner and Goossens. When I came to the Cincinnati Symphony in 1943, I immediately fell in love with Walter's luscious cello tone, his impeccable taste and style, his consummate musicianship. In 1948 Walter retired from the Cincinnati Symphony, but after a 40-year orchestral career gave up cello playing—just my luck—within a few years after I finished my *Cello Concerto*. He was also a fine conductor and became, for the next fifteen [sic] years, conductor of the Madison Civic Symphony in Wisconsin.

Schuller eventually shelved the concerto for nearly half a century. It was finally premiered in a revised version in 1995.[120]

As significant as Walter Heermann's work in Cincinnati was, he probably had a much larger and longer-lasting impact on the musical life of Madison. Though his predecessor Sigfrid Prager can clearly be credited as the founding father of the Madison Symphony Orchestra, Heermann established a different and distinctively big-city approach during his 14 years as music director—in repertoire and programming, in the relationship between the board and the organization as a whole, and in taking the first steps toward a professional orchestra. All of these initial moves would be taken much further during the 33-year tenure of his chosen successor, Roland Johnson.

Notes to Chapter 5

1. W. W. Cobbett and John Moran, "Heermann, Hugo," *Grove Music Online*, www.oxfordmusiconline, accessed 2/15/2021; Peter Clive, *Brahms and His World: A Biographical Dictionary* (Lanham, MD: Scarecrow, 2006): 203. Note that both sources incorrectly give the date of his move to Chicago as 1907.

2. Clive, *Brahms and His World*, 203.

3. The most comprehensive description of the work's composition is Boris Schwarz, "Joseph Joachim and the Genesis of Brahms's Violin Concerto," *The Musical Quarterly* 69 (1983): 503–26. See p. 508 regarding Heermann's involvement.

4. Paul Berry, *Brahms Among Friends: Listening, Performance, and the Rhetoric of Allusion* (New York: Oxford University Press, 2014): 240.

5. Ferdinand Schumann, "Brahms and Clara Schumann," *The Musical Quarterly* 2 (1916): 512–13.

6. Hugo Heermann, *Meine Lebenserinnerungen*, ed. Günther Ewig (Heilbronn: Stadtbücherei Heilbronn, 1994), accessed as a Kindle e-book. The first edition was published in Leipzig in 1935.

7. *Cincinnati Enquirer* 4/4/1937, 81.

8. This listing of Hugo Heermann's children is drawn from Hugo Heermann, *Meine Lebenserinnerungen* (specifically, a *Nachwort* added by editor Günther Ewig in his 1994 edition), my interview with Paulita Heermann Neal and Peter Neal, 10/16/2020, and information posted on ancestry.com by Heermann family members, particularly Oliver Thompson. Additional references include (on Victor) Alfred Metzger, "Giacomo Minkowski Returned from Europe," *Pacific Coast Musical Review* 41/19 (2/4/1922): 4; (on Maja and Robert Korst) *Indianapolis Star* 10/19/1923, 18; Karl-Josef Kutsch and Leo Riemens, *Großes Sängerlexikon*, 4th edition (Munich: Saur, 2003): Vol. 4, 2466; *Kingston Daily News* (Kingston, NY) 8/8/1956, 17; (on Norbert) *Kingston Daily Freeman* (Kingston, NY) 12/15/1966, 20; (on Isabell) Enid Nemy, Obituary: "Isabel Kambert, 103, Opera Singer and Creator of Sweater Designs," *New York Times* 2/9/1996, B6.

9. Interview with Paulita Heermann Neal and Peter Neal, 10/16/2020.

10. "Unsere dieswinterliche Saison eröffnete Hugo Heermann mit drei Konzerten, in denen er Konzerte von Brahms, Beethoven, Spohr, Joachim etc. zum Vortrag brachte. Seine reife gediegene Kunst fand in den leider nur spärlich besetzten Sälen die verdiente reiche Anerkennung. Sein Sohn, Emil Heermann, der ausser Duetten mit seinem Vater auch Konzerte von Paganini, Tschaikowsky, die Chaconne etc. spielte, bedarf dagegen noch sehr tüchtigen Studiums. Der sehr beanlagte junge Geiger folgt in seiner Vortragsart mehr der leider eben modernen Sevčik-Schule, statt seinen Vater als Lehrmeister anzuerkennen. Ich meine, beim Geigen soll man zunächst sich bestreben, alles das herauszuholen, was in der Geige ist, und nicht seine ganze Schwerkraft auf äusserlichen Firlefanz legen. Der Zweck des Spielens eines Instrumentes ist doch der, Musik zu machen, und nicht als Sportsmann aufzutreten, der der staunenden Menge zeigt, wie schnell er die Finger bewegen kann." A Wilhelmi, "Kritik: Konzert," *Die Musik* 5, No. 9, (February 1906): 209. From babel.hathitrust.org, accessed 1/15/2021.

11. Ziegfeld's son, Florenz Ziegfield, Jr. (who changed the spelling of the family name), producer of the famous *Ziegfield Follies* on Broadway, would be one of the most successful theatrical entrepreneurs of the early 20th century.

12. *WSJ* 4/18/1908. Hedwig Presber's relationship with the Heermanns is unknown, but it is likely that they knew one another in Germany. Tragically, Presber was in the news again just a month

later when she was confined to the Mendota asylum after suffering a mental breakdown and threatening the life of her daughter (*WSJ* 5/27/1908, 1).

13 Information from the Cincinnati Symphony Orchestra repertoire database, provided by Christina Eaton, 1/16/2021.

14 "Nach einer ruhigen Rückfahrt von drei Wochen nach San Francisco gab ich dort noch zwei Sonatenabende mit Harold Bauer. Es folgte eine Beethovenfeier in Chicago, wo ich dann drei Jahre am Musical College des Dr. Ziegfeld unterrichtet habe. Dann war ich noch ein Jahr in Cincinnati tätig, um dann endgültig wieder nach Europa zurückzukehren." Heermann, Hugo. *Meine Lebenserinnerungen.*

15 "Welche Freude bedeutete es nun für mich, mit den herrlichen amerikanischen Orchestern dem großenteils auf hoher Kulturstufe stehenden Konzertpublikum in New York, Boston, Chicago, San Francisco die Konzerte von Brahms, Joachim (in ungarischer Weise), Richard Strauss ebenfalls zum großen Teil erstmals bringen zu können oder ihnen die bekannteren von Beethoven, Mendelssohn und Bruch vorzutragen unter den großen Dirigenten: Th. Thomas, Gericke, Safonoff, Wetzler, Damrosch und in Boston unter dem Konzertmeister Willy Heß. Meine Söhne Emil (Geiger) und Walter (Cellist) konnten sich in kurzer Zeit in Amerika ansehnliche Stellungen machen, was ihnen in Deutschland angesichts der schlechteren wirtschaftlichen Lage nicht möglich gewesen wäre. Und auch unserem jüngsten Sohn Norbert glückte es später, sich in New York als Maler durchzusetzen und zu Anerkennung und Namen zu gelangen." Heermann, Hugo. *Meine Lebenserinnerungen.*

16 Venting to a reporter for the *Cincinnati Post*, Hugo complained of inadequate pay and the community's lack of interest in chamber music, saying that "Cincinnati is barbaric in its musical taste." He did suggest that, while the women of Cincinnati might have had some interest in music, the men "are so busy that they don't care about music at all." Stokowski responded publicly a week later with a defense, if a rather patronizing one: "This is a young country, and men are too busy building it up, building railroads and cities, to take time for the enjoyment of art and music… In my association with businessmen of Cincinnati, I have found that although they might not know much about music, they are interested." (Louis Russell Thomas, *A History of the Cincinnati Symphony Orchestra to 1931* [Ph.D. dissertation: University of Cincinnati, 1972]: 333–334.) Though he struck a slightly more conciliatory tone in a subsequent interview, Hugo Heermann quickly left Cincinnati, embarking for Germany on March 12, 1910. (Undated clipping from a Cincinnati newspaper, probably *The Cincinnati Times-Star*, from *Heermann Scrapbook: 1910–1923 (1904)*.)

17 Interview with Paulita Heermann Neal and Peter Neal, 10/16/2020.

18 Walter Heermann, biographical note in the MSO Archives.

19 There is a similar, closely contemporary photo of the five children dressed as "cooks" and a brief reference to musical routines that they performed published in *The Cincinnati Enquirer*, 2/8/1937, 5.

20 Interview with Paulita Heermann Neal and Peter Neal, 10/16/2020. Peter Neal has shared a scan of an autographed photo of the great Spanish cellist Pablo Casals. The inscription reads "A Walter Heermann mon colleague - con [admiration?] de Pablo Casals. ("To Walter Heermann my colleague - with [admiration?] from Pablo Casals / Frankfurt 1906."). Though the seventh word in this inscription is only partially legible, the fact that Casals referred to the 16-year-old Heermann as a "colleague" is certainly intriguing.

21 Preserved in *Heermann Scrapbook: 1910–1923 (1904)*.

22 Interview with Paulita Heermann Neal and Peter Neal, 10/16/2020.

23 Document accessed on ancestry.com, 2/19/2021.

24 *Musical Courier* 1415 (5/8/1907): 26.

25 This is noted both in an article describing new members of the Cincinnati Symphony Orchestra in 1909 (*Cincinnati Enquirer* 11/21/1909, 45) and in his obituary (*Cincinnati Enquirer* 1/14/1954).

26 Interview with Paulita Heermann Neal and Peter Neal, 10/16/2020.

27 Robert Copeland, "May Festival (Cincinnati)," *Grove Music Online*, www.oxfordmusiconline, accessed 3/5/2021.

28 This was Stokowski's first major orchestral post; he actually had little formal training and experience in orchestral conducting, and relatively little knowledge of the orchestral repertoire. There were several other more experienced candidates, but Stokowski aggressively campaigned for the job despite his relative inexperience, traveling to Cincinnati in April 1909 to mount a kind of charm offensive with members of the board. Following positive reviews of a concert he directed in Paris in May, the board offered him the job (Thomas, *A History*, 160–293).

29 Prior to his arrest, the orchestra's board and its mild-mannered conductor made immediate public relations moves: playing *The Star-Spangled Banner* at the end of each program and inviting troops from nearby military bases to attend concerts. Matters first reached a head in mid-November 1917, when the Cincinnati Symphony Orchestra was scheduled to perform a concert in Pittsburgh that was to have concluded with Beethoven's *Symphony No. 5*. On the eve of the program, Pittsburgh's public safety director, responding to protests by the local Daughters of the American Revolution chapter, refused to let the program go on, implying that not at all "enemy aliens" are spies, but "most of them are." The orchestra and the city reached an agreement the next day to let the concert go on, provided that no German music was played, but then, just a few hours before the concert, Pittsburgh officials again denied permission unless Kunwald was also replaced as conductor. Anna and Charles Taft promptly moved to cancel the concert, and Kunwald, wanting no more trouble, attempted to submit his resignation (Thomas, *A History*, 428–437). Also interned at Fort Ogelthorpe was conductor Karl Muck, who had similarly been ousted from the Boston Symphony Orchestra.

30 The arrest was widely reported in Cincinnati and across the country. This account of the incident has been drawn from *Cincinnati Enquirer* 3/13/1918, 8; 3/14/1918, 11; 3/28/1918, 3; *Evening Star* (Washington, DC), 3/9/1918, 2; *Dayton Daily News*, 3/13/1918, 20; 3/23/1918, 2; and *Tagliches Cincinnatier Volksblatt* (Cincinnati, OH), 3/28/1918. 7. German-Americans in Cincinnati were widely pressured to buy Liberty Bonds as a sign of patriotism (Thomas, *A History*, 429).

31 A clipping dated October 2, 1915, from a Cincinnati newspaper notes that he had completed the naturalization process on October 1, and that "his petition had been pending in the court for some months, owing to the fact that his absence from the city with the orchestra made continuances of the hearing necessary." *Heermann Scrapbook: 1910–1923 (1904)*.

32 Interview with Paulita Heermann Neal and Peter Neal, 10/16/2020.

33 *Montgomery Advertiser*, 6/16/1918, 17.

34 *Traverse City Record Eagle* (Traverse City, MI) 10/28/1967, 7.

35 *Montgomery Advertiser*, 1/26/1919, 9.

36 Details of his military service are drawn from *Ohio, Roster of Soldiers, Sailors, and Marines in World War I*, p. 7268, accessed on ancestry.com, 2/21/2021. Additional information drawn from "Camp Sheridan," *Encyclopedia of Alabama*, accessed at http://www.encyclopediaofalabama.org/article/h-3733, 2/21/2021.

37 Letter dated 2/17/1919; *Heermann Scrapbook: 1910–1923 (1904)*.

38 The orchestra's board offered Ysaÿe the directorship soon afterwards. At this point in his career, Ysaÿe was beginning to have physical problems that interfered with his playing, and he was turning increasingly to conducting. Not surprisingly, given his nationality and the wartime political atmosphere, the orchestra's repertoire took on a much more Belgian and French character. Though German repertoire became acceptable again after 1919, Ysaÿe continued to favor French music, often relatively modern works. Ysaÿe was a fantastic musician, but he seems to have had little interest in small details, whether administrative or musical. His approach to rehearsal was also relatively relaxed, and it seems that the quality of the orchestra's performances may have declined under his directorship. Though he remained very popular with the Cincinnati audience, and was well-respected by his musicians, there was increasing tension between Ysaÿe and the orchestra board, and he left at the end of the 1921–22 season. (Thomas, *A History*, 425–497; Michel Stockhem, "Ysaÿe, Eugène(-Auguste)," *Grove Music Online*, www.oxfordmusiconline, accessed 2/27/2021.)

39 Kenneth Morgan, *Fritz Reiner: Maestro and Martinet* (Urbana, IL: University of Chicago Press, 2010): 44.

40 *Capital Times* 11/25/1922, 5.

41 Thomas, *A History*, 498–602; Morgan, *Fritz Reiner*, 44–65; Philip Hart, "Reiner, Fritz," *Grove Music Online*, www.oxfordmusiconline, accessed 2/27/2021.

42 Thomas, *A History*, 634–645.

43 After establishing a career in England, first as a violinist and composer, and increasingly as a conductor, Goossens came to New York in 1923 to conduct the newly created Rochester Philharmonic Orchestra. In the years leading up to his recruitment by Cincinnati, Goossens built an impressive orchestra in Rochester, and a fine nationwide reputation as a guest conductor. Unlike Reiner, Goossens was also hired as the director of the annual May Festival. (Carole Rosen, "Goossens family; (3) Sir (Aynsley) Eugene Goossens," *Grove Music Online*, www.oxfordmusiconline, accessed 2/27/2021.)

44 Richard Bernas, "Johnson, Thor," *Grove Music Online*, www.oxfordmusiconline, accessed 2/27/2021; *Cincinnati Symphony Orchestra: A Tribute to Max Rudolf and Highlights of its History* (Cincinnati: Women's Committee of the Cincinnati Symphony Orchestra, 1967).

45 Unidentified and undated clipping in *Heermann Scrapbook: 1910–1923 (1904)*. The review has the headline "Walter Heermann's Debut As Conductor Was Auspicious: Musician Received Encore After Encore During Masterly Concert By the Summer Orchestra of Symphony Players at Zoo."

46 *Cincinnati Enquirer* 7/4/1921,13.

47 *Cincinnati Enquirer* 7/17/1921, 5; 7/22/1922, 7; and 8/3/1922, 5. The October program is documented by a program in *Heermann Scrapbook: 1910–1923 (1904)*.

48 *Cincinnati Enquirer* 1/18/1941, 13.

49 *Cincinnati Enquirer* 4/20/1941, 45.

50 Programs and clippings in *Heermann Scrapbook: 1942–1948 (1909–1910)*. Heermann was not actually credited as conductor on February 10–11, 1945—Goossens apparently took ill after program books had already been printed.

51 The Heldentenor, or "heroic tenor," is the particularly powerful voice-type needed for Wagner's operatic tenor roles

52 *Cincinnati Enquirer* 12/8/1945, 20.

53 *The Courier-Journal* (Louisville, KY) 12/9/1945, 34.
54 *Cincinnati Enquirer* 12/9/1946, 3.
55 *Cincinnati Enquirer* 6/11/1947, 13. In the orchestra's program book listings for that season, he is listed as "First Assistant Conductor."
56 *Cincinnati Enquirer* 1/22/1949, 9.
57 The information on solo performances by both Walter and Emil is from the Cincinnati Symphony Orchestra repertoire database, provided by Christina Eaton, 1/16/2021.
58 *Cincinnati Enquirer* 4/19/1941, 13.
59 Review from an unidentified Memphis newspaper, 5/6/1942, *Heermann Scrapbook: 1942–1948 (1909–1910)*.
60 *Cincinnati Enquirer* 5/19/1946, 1.
61 Interview with Paulita Heermann Neal and Peter Neal, 10/16/2020; interview with Roland Johnson, 7/31/2000.
62 *Cincinnati Enquirer* 3/14/1948, 1. He was succeeded as principal cello by Arthur Bowen, a 15-year veteran of the orchestra's cello section (*Cincinnati Enquirer* 4/11/1948, 3).
63 Thomas, *A History*, 541–549.
64 *Hamilton Daily News* (Hamilton, OH), 6/1/1928, 9. Newspaper radio schedules document that their programs were heard as far afield as Delaware, Florida, Louisiana, and Wisconsin.
65 Phone conversation with Paulita Heermann Neal, 3/27/2021.
66 Brunswick 4229—*Arabesque in E Major / Arabesque in G Major*; Brunswick 4153—*An Old Italian Love Song / Andalusian Caprice*; Brunswick 4228; *Dalvisa (Song of The Dale) / Pierrette (Air De Ballet)*. From www.discogs.com/artist/6926406-Heermann-Trio, accessed 3/6/2021.
67 *Evening Star* (Washington, DC) 4/10/1933, 16.
68 Program in *Heermann Scrapbook: 1910–1923 (1904)*.
69 *Cincinnati Enquirer* 3/14/1948, 1.
70 *Cincinnati Enquirer* 7/22/1928, 64.
71 *Cincinnati Enquirer* 2/10/1946, 76.
72 Program and reviews in *Heermann Scrapbook: 1933–34 / 1930*.
73 *Cincinnati Enquirer* 10/21/1934, 48.
74 *Cincinnati Enquirer* 10/7/1934, 54.
75 *Cincinnati Enquirer* 4/6/41, 14.
76 *Cincinnati Enquirer* 6/7/1947, 13.
77 Phone conversation with LeAnne Anklan, executive director of the Cincinnati Chamber Orchestra, 1/25/2021.
78 "College-Conservatory of Music: History," https://ccm.uc.edu/overview/history.html, accessed 3/7/2021.
79 Orlando, Vincent A., *An Historical Study of the Origins and Development of the College of Music of Cincinnati* (D.E. dissertation: Teachers College of the University of Cincinnati,1946): 194.
80 *Cincinnati Enquirer* 6/7/1946, 13.

81 This account of the affair has been summarized from James T. Golden, "Walter Heermann May Seek New Post; Defends Brother In Musical Tempest; Soft Pedal Provides a Loud Overtone," *Cincinnati Enquirer* 6/2/1946, 20. Golden does cite an unnamed "person close to the affair not authorized to comment on it" who implied that the College's decision was due to the fact that Emil "refused to cooperate or conform to rules, and would become ill-tempered." The explanation eventually offered by the College within a week of this report—that he had refused to sign a formal contract—does not fully contradict this.

82 *Cincinnati Enquirer* 6/7/1946,13.

83 *Cincinnati Enquirer* 6/8/1946, 22.

84 Undated (though certainly mid- early June 1948) and unidentified clipping in *Heermann Scrapbook: 1942–48 (1909–10)* 1.

85 *Cincinnati Enquirer* 9/9/1948, 14.

86 Interview with Paulita Heermann Neal and Peter Neal, 10/16/2020. Her passport application, completed in New York City in September 1921, confirms that she was "professionally known as "Sheila O'Day" (accessed on ancestry.com, 3/5/2021).

87 Undated (though certainly mid-1922) and unidentified clipping in *Heermann Scrapbook: 1910–1923 (1904)*. The date of their marriage is confirmed in *Cook County Illinois Marriage Index, 1912–1942*, accessed on ancestry.com, 7/25/2021.

88 Interviews with Paulita Heermann Neal and Peter Neal, 10/16/2020 and 7/21/2021; email note from Peter Neal, 3/12/2021.

89 *Cincinnati Enquirer* 5/22/1934, 7.

90 *Cincinnati Enquirer* 4/4/1937, 81.

91 *New York Times* 2/9/1996, B6.

92 *Cincinnati Enquirer* 11/27/1939, 81.

93 Documents in *Heermann Scrapbook: 1910–1923 (1904)*.

94 "From the Archives: Queen City Connections," *Crescendo*, https://crescendo.interlochen.org/story/archives-queen-city-connection, accessed 3/10/2021.

95 Phone conversation with Paulita Heermann Neal, 3/27/2021.

96 Interview with Paulita Heermann Neal and Peter Neal, 10/16/2020.**[AU: Date or text missing?]**

97 *Traverse City Record Eagle* (Traverse City, MI) 10/28/1967, 7.

98 These dates have been supplied by Anne Aley, former director of the Summer Music Clinic (email note, 4/4/2021). I have, however, with caution, made one change to the dates she supplied, which have him joining the faculty in 1938. Both Heermann's own recollections and those of his daughter are that he first taught at the Summer Music Clinic in 1936.

99 The amateur Charleston Little Symphony was a predecessor to the Charleston Symphony Orchestra (today's West Virginia Symphony Orchestra), which was founded in late 1939. ("West Virginia Symphony Orchestra: Mission and History," https://wvsymphony.org/missionhistory, accessed 2/28/2021). One of the local musical deputies who led rehearsals in Heermann's absence was clarinetist George Crumb, Sr., father of the noted American composer George Crumb.

100 *Charleston Daily Mail* 5/24/1931, 5.

J. MICHAEL ALLSEN 243

101 This account of the May Festival has drawn primarily on local newspaper accounts: *Charleston Daily Mail* 5/7/1933, 13; 6/23/1935, 13; 5/3/1936, 73; 5/6/1936, 16; 5/9/1936, 19; 3/26/1938, 7; 10/10/1939, 2; 2/11/40, 2; *Charleston Gazette* 4/22/1934, 3; 5/6/1934, 16; 5/21/1939, 28. I thank Patricia McClure, volunteer historian, West Virginia Symphony Orchestra, for providing me with several of these clippings.

102 Springfield Symphony Orchestra, "About the SSO," www.springfieldsym.org/about-the-sso/, accessed 3/2/2021; Tom Stafford, "As the Springfield Symphony Orchestra Celebrates Its 75th Season, Let's Look Back at Its History," *Springfield News-Sun* 9/29/2018, www.springfieldnewssun.com/news/local/stafford-the-springfield-symphony-orchestra-celebrates-its-75th-season-let-look-back-its-history/H45GaBF9rQF4WpNAH2y6LK/, accessed 3/2/2021.

103 I thank Nuggie Libecap of the Springfield Symphony Orchestra for providing scans of all of Heermann's programs with the orchestra.

104 "Guy Watson Taylor," prabook.com/web/guy.watson.taylor/466659, accessed 3/2/2021.

105 Interview with Paulita Heermann Neal and Peter Neal, 10/16/2020.

106 *CT* 6/10/1986, 24.

107 Phone conversation with Paulita Heermann Neal, 3/27/2021.

108 Interview with Paulita Heermann Neal and Peter Neal, 10/16/2020.

109 Programs in *Heermann Scrapbook: 1949–1950*, *Heermann Scrapbook: 1951–1953*, *Heermann Scrapbook: 1954*, and *Heermann Scrapbook: 1955–1956*.

110 *WSJ* 3/15/1960, 1.

111 *MCMA Board Minutes* 6/21/1957 (MSO Archives).

112 Programs in *Heermann Scrapbook 1956–1959*.

113 *CT*, 6/18/1969, 37. Peter and William are the two oldest sons of Paulita Heermann Neal; email note from Peter Neal, 3/12/2021.

114 Phone conversations with Paulita Heermann Neal, 3/27/2021 and 10/20/2021.

115 Cincinnati Symphony Orchestra, *Cincinnati Symphony Orchestra: Centennial Portraits* (Cincinnati: Cincinnati Symphony Orchestra, 1994): 96.

116 *Cincinnati Enquirer* 11/3/1945, 7.

117 There is at least one other Humphreys caricature of Walter Heermann from the 1940s, which was published in one of the newspapers in Cincinnati. This one was inspired by a program directed by French conductor Charles Munch. Munch's explosive comments from the podium apparently came with so much spittle that Walter jokingly threatened to bring protection to the next rehearsal. The caricature has Hermann doggedly playing cello under a large umbrella, under a rain of droplets coming from the podium. A copy of this caricature currently hangs on the wall of the cottage in Interlochen.

118 Dale Dynkins, "Program Note, *Symphonic Suite*," http://www.orchestralist.net/olist/registry/ol/Dale_Dykins.php, accessed 3/10/2021.

119 *Cincinnati Enquirer* 11/27/1928, 81. Snodgrass, daughter of two wealthy Cincinnati families, would later move to New York, and she had a successful career as a soloist and composer of songs. (See her obituary, *Cincinnati Enquirer* 5/27/1945.)

120 Gunther Schuller, "Program Note: Cello Concerto," https://www.wisemusicclassical.com/

work/32626/Concerto-for-Cello-and-Orchestra--Gunther-Schuller/, accessed 3/10/2021; Norbert Carnovale and Richard Dyer, "Schuller, Gunther," *Grove Music Online*, www.oxfordmusiconline, accessed 3/11/2021; David Griesinger, "Brilliant Resurrection of Schuller Piece," *The Boston Musical Intelligencer* 3/27/2011, https://www.classical-scene.com/2011/03/27/schuller-piece/, accessed 3/11/2021. A few years before Schuller's death in 2015, Heermann's grandson Peter Neal wrote to the composer about the concerto, and Schuller sent an inscribed copy of the score.

CHAPTER 6

A Time of Changes:
The Orchestra, Chorus, and Opera in the 1960s and 1970s

The decades of the 1960s and 1970s were turbulent and eventful in Madison itself, but they were also a period of tremendous change in the Madison Symphony Orchestra. At the opening of the 1960s, the Madison Civic Symphony was still the largely volunteer community group it had been since 1926, though under Walter Heermann, there had been a few small steps toward professionalizing the orchestra. By 1980, the orchestra had transformed into a fully professional ensemble, known since 1966 as the Madison Symphony Orchestra. The Madison Civic Music Association, which had been the umbrella organization for the orchestra and the Madison Civic Chorus since 1926, had a third, relatively independent component beginning early in the 1960s, the Madison Civic Opera Guild. MCMA's annual budget, never more than $6000 before the 1960s, had expanded to over $500,000 in the 1979–80 season. The 1960s and 1970s also saw the growth of a professional administrative staff. In 1980, the orchestra moved into a large new venue, the refurbished 1928 Capitol Theater (renamed the Oscar Mayer Theatre), which would remain its primary performance space for the next quarter century. This period of change and growth began with the arrival of a new music director, Roland Johnson, in the 1961–62 season.

A New Music Director: Roland Johnson

In February 1960, the Vocational School board announced that Walter Heermann, who turned 70 on February 9, had reached the school's mandatory retirement age and would need to step down at the end of that school year. Heermann's appointment, of course, was not a typical faculty position, but also included the directorship of the Madison Civic Symphony and Chorus. The announcement caused a panic among MCMA's musicians and patrons and particularly in the board, which was unprepared to mount a search for his replacement. At the orchestra's concert on February 21, the board circulated a petition asking for Heermann to be retained in the position. By mid-March, the MCMA board was able to conclude a cordial agreement with the Vocational School that allowed Heermann to retain both positions through the end of the 1960–61 season/academic year, allowing time for a proper search.[1]

There were apparently several applicants for the position, and one early applicant mentioned in the board minutes was Vernon Westlund, who was at that time director of Madison's Philharmonic Chorus and on the faculty of Milton College. Heermann and board member Charles Faulhauber attended the American Symphony Orchestra League (ASOL) convention in the spring of 1960, where they met with several possible conductors and recommended three of them to the board: Erik Kahlson (Cincinnati, Ohio), Harry Levenson (Worcester, Massachusetts), and Laurent Torno (St. Louis, Missouri).[2] However, it is clear that Heermann, who had a strong hand in the search, already had a chosen successor in mind: Roland Johnson, who had been Heermann's protégé at the College of Music in Cincinnati in the 1940s.

Though Johnson had some initial hesitation about leaving his academic position in Alabama, he was also intrigued by the possibility of moving to Madison. This was the very time when *Life* and other national magazines began to praise Madison as one of America's most "livable" cities. Heermann seems to have stayed on during the 1960–61 season at least partly to allow Johnson to take the job—this was later confirmed by both James Crow and Johnson himself. Heermann was persistent in recruiting Johnson as a candidate, praising the city, the

6.01 Roland Johnson in 1961.

professional prospects for Johnson and his wife Arline, and the possibilities for growth of the orchestra. In a 2000 interview, Johnson recalled that "Walter kept after me ... he had to work hard to talk me into it."[3] The Johnsons visited Madison over Thanksgiving weekend in 1960 to meet with the MCMA and Vocational School boards, and he was offered the position a few weeks later. In fact, he seems to have been the only candidate formally interviewed by the Vocational School and the MCMA. Heermann continued to apply gentle pressure after the interview. In an informal letter addressed to Roland and Arline Johnson on December 7 (a week *before* the board met for an official decision), Heermann privately assured Johnson that an offer was forthcoming and went on to stress a few additional things to consider: the possibility of teaching at the Vocational School for Arline, and his assurance that "with outside work bound to come your way, you'd be in the ten thousand [dollar] bracket before very long—I know how these things work out!" He further suggested that "as to keeping you busy, as Cora [Hardy] says: 'a man makes his job!' I don't think that you'd be bored. and the fact that you create your own hours & have more sleep & time with your family would probably add many years to your career." He notes that "in the event that your Dean [at the University of Alabama] should make a 'last-ditch effort' to keep you with them, your possible refusal would be perfectly understood." But Heermann concludes, "Personally, I am hoping that you will be with us of course!"[4] Johnson formally accepted the position in early January and became the orchestra's third music director in 1961–62, the first of 33 seasons. (Chapter 7 is devoted to his full biography.)

I was able to interview Johnson on a few occasions, and in 2000, he recalled his move to Madison in 1961, saying, "I had no idea then what a wonderful thing I was moving into." As Johnson described it, his predecessor had left him a competent semiprofessional orchestra and an accomplished chorus.[5] Heermann was a well-respected musical figure and was well-liked by members of the orchestra, board, and community. However, the difference in energy level between the 71-year-old Heermann and his 41-year-old successor was palpable, and within just the first five seasons of his leadership, there were dramatic transformations in several areas of MCMA's activities:

- Expansion of the orchestra/chorus season, and addition of new types of programming.
- Reinstitution of youth programming and expansion of the educational mission of MCMA.
- Establishment of a third group, devoted to fully staged operas, under the auspices of the MCMA.

- Institution of pay for performances and rehearsals for all orchestra members.
- Moves toward ticketing most of MCMA's programs, which had been free to the public since 1940.

While Johnson certainly deserves some of the credit for these innovations—particularly the first four items—implementing them was also accomplished by an active and effective MCMA board.

It was clear from the outset that with a new conductor at its helm, this was a different Madison Civic Orchestra. According to James Crow, a longtime member of the viola section, and eventually president of the MCMA board, "There was a sort of quantum leap right after Roland came, just as there was later when John DeMain took over."[6] The discipline of both orchestra and chorus had been rather relaxed under Heermann, but Johnson instituted much higher standards of attendance and musicianship in both groups.

Johnson's first program, on October 22, 1961, included four works: Gluck, *Overture to "Alceste,"* Brahms, *Symphony No. 1*, Riegger, *Dance Rhythms*, and Tchaikovsky, *Romeo and Juliet*. The concert in the Central High School Auditorium played to a near-capacity crowd, and both newspapers included admiring reviews. Carmen Elsner in the *Wisconsin State Journal* wrote, "All the reports filtering out of the music groups at Madison vocational and adult school definitely are true. The new music director is dynamic and then some." Alexius Baas, in the *Capital Times*, also complimented Johnson, saying, "He has direct and accurate, intuitive feeling for his music. He is at once dynamic and tender. He has quick command over his forces—the kind of a command which inspires leadership."[7] This first concert reflected a pattern Johnson would repeat many times over the course of over 375 concerts, mixing well-known orchestral standards like the Brahms and Tchaikovsky works with lesser-known repertoire like the relatively obscure Gluck overture. His inclusion of the mildly modernist *Dance Rhythms* (1954) by American composer Wallingford Riegger also signaled an interest in contemporary music, with much more adventurous repertoire to come in the next few decades.

MCMA clearly saw the arrival of a new conductor as an opportune moment to expand its season. By the end of Heermann's tenure, the annual routine of MCMA programs was well established: a yearly series of four free concerts, two of which would include the chorus, and a spring pops program. In Johnson's first season, the MCMA's series expanded to five regular concerts—three orchestral and two choral/orchestral programs—and an additional pops concert. The number and types of programs performed each season steadily expanded over the next 20 years.

The first season of concerts under Johnson went well, and he closed the regular season with an impressive performance of Honegger's 1921 "symphonic psalm" *King David* on March 21, 1962. Though Heermann had rebuilt the Madison Civic Chorus into an effective ensemble by the turn of the 1960s, it grew by some 30% during Johnson's first year, and this program featured a chorus of over 100 voices. This performance of *King David* could have been heard—whether intentionally or not on Johnson's part—as an emblem of the new conductor's place in the history of the Civic Chorus. The performance of *King David* under Sigfrid Prager in 1943 seems to have been remembered, along with the two performances of the Beethoven *Missa Solemnis* in 1947 and 1948, as one of the most glorious moments in the Civic Chorus's history.[8] While only a few of the members of the 1943 chorus were still there in 1962, this performance must have reclaimed the "glory days" for many in the audience.

6.02 The Madison Civic Symphony and Roland Johnson at the Dane County Youth Building, May 6, 1962.

The season closed on May 6 with the orchestra's third annual pops concert, a program titled "Vienna, City of Music." The second section of the program included something entirely new in these programs: a staged version of Act II of Johann Strauss's *Die Fledermaus*, sung in English. The cast—Lois Dick (Rosalinda), Alice Schacht (Adele), Margaret Pickart (Orlofsky), Warren Crandall (Eisenstein), Robert Tottingham (Frank), and Henry Peters (Falke)— and the small chorus were mostly Madison Civic Chorus stalwarts. They had been organized by Arline Johnson, a veteran stage director, as the Madison Civic Opera Workshop. This performance, the first staged opera performance under the auspices of MCMA since the 1930s, marked the beginnings of what would become the Madison Opera.

Concerts of the 1960s and 1970s

Johnson's programming in the orchestra's regular free concerts took a step away from the rather conservative repertoire of his predecessors. He had been deeply involved with contemporary music in the 1950s, and he continued this advocacy after he moved to Madison. While standard orchestral repertoire still accounted for the bulk of what was heard at MCMA programs, the orchestra and chorus began to perform many more 20th-century works: these decades saw the orchestra's first performances of works like Bartók's *Concerto for Orchestra* (1965) and *Piano Concerto No. 3* (1967), Berg's *Lulu Suite* (1973), Holst's *The Planets* (1972), Prokofiev's *Piano Concerto No. 3* (1968) and *Violin Concerto No. 1* (1979), Ravel's *La valse* (1963), *Daphnis et Chlöe, Suite No. 2* (1965), *Alborada del gracioso* (1968), and *Piano Concerto for the Left Hand* (1977), Scriabin's *Poem of Ecstasy* (1972), Shostakovich's *Concerto for Piano, Trumpet, and Strings* (1968) and *Festive Overture* (1978), and Stravinsky's suites from *Pulcinella* (1967), *Le chant de rossignol* (1968), and *Petrouchka* (1971). The orchestra and chorus also gave early performances to works by established composers, in some cases the first midwestern performances of works that have since become standard repertoire: Barber's 1960 *Die Natali* (1961), Poulenc's 1960 *Gloria* (1963), and Britten's 1962 *War Requiem* (1966). In 1973, an ensemble of 16 singers from the Madison Civic Chorus gave what was billed as the "first American performance" of Vaughan Williams's 1938 *Serenade to Music*.

Johnson was particularly interested in promoting contemporary American composers. A work by Wallingford Riegger appeared on his first concert, and the next two decades saw pieces by familiar names like Aaron Copland, Samuel Barber, Charles Ives, Leonard Bernstein, and George Gershwin. However, the orchestra and chorus also performed music by William Schuman, Felix Labunski,[9] Lukas Foss, Wayne Barlow, Roy Harris, Richard Bales, Ray Luke, Hial Bancroft King,[10] and Morton Gould. One composer heavily represented during Johnson's tenure was Gunther Schuller; seven of his works appeared between 1962 and 1993, four of them premiered by the MSO. This was the result of a close friendship between Johnson and Schuller that extended back to the 1940s.

Johnson was also active in commissioning and premiering new music, particularly from local composers or composers with Madison connections. The orchestra and chorus premiered 10 works during this period:

- Gunther Schuller, *Fanfare for Brass Instruments* (2/27/1962).
- Gunther Schuller, *Vertige d'Eros* (10/14/1967). This was a relatively early work by Schuller, written nearly 20 years earlier, which had

never been performed.
- Robert Crane, *Exsequiarum Ordo: In Memoriam Berlioz* (3/22/1969). This is the first of three works that Crane, a professor of music theory and composition at the University, wrote for the MSO in the 1960s and 1970s.
- Lee Hoiby, *The Tides of Sleep* (11/22/1969 with baritone John Reardon). This Wisconsin-born composer had studied earlier at the University. This is the first of two Hoiby works premiered by the MSO.
- Alec Wilder, *Concerto for Clarinet and Chamber Orchestra* (1/26/1974 with Glenn Bowen, clarinet).
- Robert Crane, *Cino* (5/20/1975 with the Madison Civic Chorus).
- Lee Hoiby, *Music for a Celebration* (9/27/1975).
- Stephen Chatman, *3 A.M. on Capitol Square* (10/18/1975). Chatman's connection to the orchestra is discussed later in this chapter.
- Robert Crane, *Fanfare for Christmas* (12/13/1975 with David Hottmann, narrator, the Madison Civic Chorus, and Madison Boychoir).
- Stephen Chatman, *Occasions* (11/18/1978).

Johnson also programmed a few truly *avant-garde* works. On October 17, 1965, the opening concert of the orchestra's 40th season, the program included the *Concerted Piece for Tape Recorder and Orchestra* by Wisconsin-born composer Otto Luening and his collaborator Vladimir Ussachevsky. This nine-minute 1960 work was a pioneering experiment in combining synthesized and electronically manipulated sound on a tape with a live orchestra. It is a challenging work, alternating and combining taped sounds with atonal orchestral passages.

6.03 Otto Luening and Vladimir Ussachevsky at the Columbia-Princeton Electronic Music Center, New York City, late 1950s.

Luening was in the audience for this performance. While reviews in both newspapers were generally supportive of this work, and the board sent a letter of thanks to Luening,[11] one must wonder what the musically conservative Madison audience's reaction was to this work. The orchestra played the piece again at a pair of youth concerts a month later. In March 1971, the orchestra performed the equally challenging *Atmosphères* (1961) by György Ligeti. This work, with its constantly evolving texture of tone clusters, was probably familiar to many in the audience from its appearance in the 1969 film *2001: A Space Odyssey*. In December 1974, the string section of the orchestra performed Krzysztof Penderecki's *Threnody for the Victims of Hiroshima*. This 1961 work, replete with quarter-tones, tone clusters, and a host of extended string techniques, may have been just a bit too much for some of the audience. Johnson was careful to introduce the work from the stage, but reviewer Barry Chudakov noted that "[t]he audience muttered and became restless, yet applauded the piece with appreciation."[12]

6.04 Roland Johnson and MSO Manager Winifred Cook accepting the ASCAP Award for Service to Contemporary Music from ASCAP representative Morton Gould (Washington, DC, June 15, 1973).

The MSO's performance of contemporary music and of music by American composers in particular was recognized four times in the 1970s by the American Society of Composers, Authors and Publishers (ASCAP). ASCAP's Symphony and Concert Committee, chaired in the 1970s by composer Morton Gould, annually presented cash awards to orchestras whose commitment to performing 20th-century music was exemplary. (Each year, the MSO competed with orchestras of similar budget size across the country.) In 1976, ASCAP President Stanley Adams, in his letter of congratulations to the MSO, wrote: "The creative conductors and orchestras whom we honor with these words are making a significant contribution to the health and vitality of our musical life. Their performances of contemporary music are attracting ever-increasing audiences for both American musicians and composers."[13]

A hallmark of Johnson's tenure was his constant willingness to experiment with new kinds of programming and program venues. The expansion of youth and family programs and pops concerts is discussed below, as is the evolution of the Madison Opera. There had been many live radio broadcasts in the orchestra's history, but the MSO appeared on television a few times in the 1970s, playing two live television concerts from the studio of WHA-TV (Wisconsin Public Television) in January 1974 and September 1975. A few years later, two productions of the Madison Civic Opera were also broadcast live from the Wisconsin Union

6.05 Performance on WHA-TV, January 8, 1974.

Theater on WHA-TV, with simultaneous radio broadcasts on Wisconsin Public Radio: Massenet's *Manon* (February 1977) and Strauss's *Die Fledermaus* (February 1978).[14] Outdoor programs had been rare in the orchestra's history, but in the summers of 1974 and 1975, Johnson programmed a series of informal noontime "Brown Bag Concerts" on the capitol square. There were also a few innovative one-off programs. On March 3, 1967, for example, a chamber orchestra from the MSO played Stravinsky's *Pulcinella Suite* at the Madison Art Center as part of a Marc Chagall exhibition in the gallery. On July 4, 1976, the orchestra played a "Bicentennial All-American Concert" at the Wisconsin Union Theater.

6.06 MSO in rehearsal with pianist William Doppmann (playing Rachmaninoff's *Rhapsody on a Theme of Paganini*) in Central High School Auditorium, December 1961. Note the stage extension for the piano, harp, and several string players.

Walter Heermann staged nearly all of MCMA's concerts from 1953 onward in the Central High School Auditorium (later renovated as the MATC Auditorium), and this remained the orchestra's primary venue until the opening of the Madison Civic Center in 1980. Its small stage could barely contain the orchestra: several orchestra players who performed at Central High School have recalled cramped, uncomfortable conditions. The orchestra often had to add a large extension to the stage. Even as the orchestra was increasingly being packed together on stage, by the late 1960s the audience had outgrown Central High School Auditorium, with its seating capacity of 1046. Subscription concerts were regularly doubled, with Saturday evening and Sunday matinee performances. The opportunity to perform each program twice actually had great musical benefits for the orchestra and chorus, and it also represented a financial benefit for orchestra players who were, by then, being paid on a "per-service" basis.

After the first few seasons, Johnson began to move concerts into many other venues around town. He staged 11 programs in the University Stock Pavilion between 1964 and 1979. Despite its fine acoustical properties, the drawbacks of the University's "cow barn" were well known. However, it remained one of the largest venues in Madison, and like Prager, Johnson used it for programs with large choral groups, or for concerts with star performers likely to draw particularly large audiences: Eileen Farrell (1969 and 1975), tenor Richard Tucker (1972), and pianists Van Cliburn (1971) and Claudio Arrau (1979). From the late 1960s onward, Johnson mounted most choral concerts away from Central High School, using both East and West High Schools, the Stock Pavilion, the Masonic Temple Auditorium, St. Bernard's Catholic Church, and First Congregational Church. This was partly a practical matter: By the late 1960s, the large Madison Civic Chorus could no longer fit on the stage of Central High School, even with the orchestra seated on the floor. The Madison Civic Opera Guild used Madison's high school auditoriums and the Masonic Temple for most of its performances before moving to the Wisconsin Union Theater in the late 1970s. The first few pops programs under Heermann had been held at the Loraine Hotel, but under Johnson these programs were held in the much larger venues of the Dane County Youth Building at the fairgrounds, and eventually in the massive Dane County Coliseum.

6.07 MSO "Brown Bag" Concert on the capitol square, August 21, 1974. [MSO Archives]

Madison and the MSO had an impressive number of fine instrumental and vocal soloists who appeared on MCMA concerts. Many of the orchestra's principal players—most of them University faculty—performed as soloists in this period. Johnson also drew upon other University faculty as soloists. Gunnar Johansen performed eight times with the orchestra during Johnson's tenure, and other University pianists performed as well: Leo Steffens, Arthur Becknell, Howard Karp, and Paul Badura-Skoda. The Madison Civic Chorus maintained its long-standing tradition of featuring chorus members in solo roles, but University vocal faculty Bettina Bjorksten, Lois Fischer, Ilona Kombrink, Samuel Jones, and David Hottmann were also frequent soloists.

In the early 1960s, the orchestra would routinely bring in at least one star performer each season, but hiring internationally known soloists for the orchestra's regular subscription programs was relatively rare until the later 1960s, when a larger budget, buoyed by ticket sales and increased community and business support, made it possible. Beginning in this period, each season would typically feature at least a couple of stars. Johnson seems to have been particularly interested in vocal soloists, and soprano Eileen Farrell, mezzo-soprano Shirley Verrett, alto Maureen Forrester, tenor Richard Tucker, and baritone John Reardon were all featured in orchestra concerts of the 1960s and 1970s. Orchestra concerts featuring pianists are always popular, and MCMA was able to bring in some of the greatest virtuosos of the day: William Doppmann, Van Cliburn, Mischa Dichter, John Browning, Earl Wild, James Tocco, Claudio Arrau, Lorin Hollander, Cristina Ortiz, and Alicia de Larrocha all appeared with the MSO during these years, as did violinists Sidney Harth, Pinchas Zukerman, Kyung-Wha Chung, and Ruggiero Ricci and cellists Raya Garbousova and Zara Nelsova.

6.08 Pianist Van Cliburn, one of the star performers who appeared with the MSO in this period.

Youth and Neighborhood Family Concerts

Youth programs had been a sporadic part of the orchestra's offerings since its very earliest years. Sigfrid Prager had staged the first Youth Concert in March 1929, and there were two more in the 1931–32 season. The WPA-sponsored Madison Concert Orchestra performed several school concerts in the late 1930s, and when this group disbanded in the early 1940s, Prager scheduled two Youth Concerts by the Madison Civic Symphony during the

1941–42 season. The tradition lapsed during the war years, and MCMA did not stage another youth program until November 1949, when Walter Heermann led a Young People's Matinee. Heermann came to Madison with a great deal of experience in youth programming; he had conducted many of the Cincinnati Symphony Orchestra's Young People's Concerts in the early 1940s. Unlike Prager's youth concerts, which were mostly collections of short classical works and movements, Heermann's programs included a wide variety of music designed to appeal to children, and they also featured young performers. The Madison Civic Symphony presented Young People's Matinees in each of the next three seasons, but after 1953, youth programs were quietly abandoned once again.

On October 27, 1962, Johnson and the Civic Symphony reinstituted youth programming with a tremendously successful concert featuring beloved TV personality Captain Kangaroo (Bob Keeshan), which played to an audience of 7500 at the Dane County Fairgrounds arena. This was a ticketed event and was quite profitable. Though this initial program had been sponsored by MCMA and the Madison Jaycettes, funding and promoting youth programming increasingly became one of the primary missions of the Women's Committee. In November 1964, the orchestra performed its first free Youth Concert, bussing hundreds of local schoolchildren to Central High School for this specially designed program. These programs, held at Central, East, or West High Schools, were often performed twice to accommodate more children. There

6.09 Captain Kangaroo (Bob Keeshan) in 1961.

were two pairs of concerts in the 1965–66 season, in November 1965 and April 1966. (The November concerts included performances of a challenging *avant-garde* work, the Luening/Ussachevsky *Concerted Piece for Tape Recorder and Orchestra* played a few weeks earlier at the orchestra's regular program.) The 1966–67 season included two more youth programs, in November 1966 and March 1967. The MSO's youth programs usually included young performers. For example, the March 1967 program at East High School featured East High School student Stephen Chatman as a piano soloist, playing two movements from the Mozart *Piano Concerto No. 23*. Like many of the MSO's youth soloists, he later had a successful career in music: Chatman became a composer and eventually joined the faculty of the University of British Columbia, Vancouver, in 1976.

Johnson and the MSO later commissioned and premiered two of his works: *3 A.M. on Capitol Square* (1975) and *Occasions* (1978). These are programmatic pieces, based on Chatman's memories of Madison. The MSO also played his *Crimson Dream* in 1988. Chatman, whose father played harpsichord with the orchestra in the 1960s and who, while still in high school, played in the MSO percussion section himself in 1968, remembered:

> Playing the Mozart concerto was a once in a lifetime experience; it was a real pleasure to work with a wonderful conductor, Roland Johnson. I am grateful for the MSO commissioning opportunities and for programming my *Crimson Dream,* an award-winning early work.[15]

There was another Youth Concert in April 1969, but this was followed by a five-year period without specifically designated youth programming.

In addition to youth programming, Johnson instituted a series of "Neighborhood Family Concerts" in the late 1960s. At a time when the MSO was beginning to charge for all of its regular concerts, these were free programs, designed to appeal to families with children. They were also intended as outreach to the community: to get the orchestra out of downtown and into Madison's neighborhoods.[16] The orchestra eventually performed four of these programs, at LaFollette High School on Madison's far east side (March 1967 and December 1970) and at Memorial High School on the far west side (November 1968 and December 1969).

In 1974, Evelyn Steenbock, a great supporter of both the orchestra's youth programs and the Wisconsin Youth Symphony Orchestra, established an endowment to support an annual competition and scholarship award for promising young instrumentalists. The first Steenbock Awards Program in April 1974 featured three young soloists—pianists David Askins and Tania Heiberg, and violinist Sharan Leventhal—and dozens of young musicians were featured at these springtime concerts in succeeding seasons. The concerts were presented free to an audience of students from Madison and surrounding communities. This marked the beginning of an unbroken annual series of youth concerts that continues to the present day. In the 1982–83 season, the MSO instituted a second annual youth program, the Fall Youth Concerts (eventually with three performances on a single day). These concerts were aimed at two different audiences, with the fall program intended for elementary school students, and the spring Steenbock program for middle school and high school students.

Pops Concerts

The pops tradition that began in Heermann's last years as the Orchestra Gala continued under Johnson, run as a benefit concert by the Women's Committee. In 1962, the venue moved to the Dane County Youth Building, where it would be staged almost exclusively until 1976. The concert continued as a large-scale fundraising event for the Women's Committee, with a concert in late April or May, typically following the season's final regular programs. Like the first pops program conducted by Johnson in 1962, "Vienna, City of Music," pops concerts were usually created around a unifying theme: "Moods in Blue" (1963), "Symphony to Spring" (1964), "Americana" (1965), and "The Grand Tour" (1966). Like the 1962 program, a few of these included selections performed by members of the Madison Civic Opera Guild, with selections from *La Traviata* in 1964 and Act I of *The Merry Widow* in 1966.

There was a distinct change in 1968, when the focus of pops shows shifted from a theme to star performers. In May 1968, the pops concert was conducted by Mitch Miller, a well-known television personality at the time. His variety show *Sing Along with Mitch*—based upon a popular series of LP record albums he produced beginning in the 1950s—had been a television hit in the early 1960s. Virtually every pops concert through the 1970s featured star performers, including conductors Skitch Henderson (1970) and Leroy Anderson (1971), pianists Victor Borge (1972), Peter Nero (1976), and Steve Allen (1977), classical/Broadway singers Marguerite Piazza (1969), William Walker (1973), and John Gary (1975), jazz stars Benny Goodman (1978) and Sarah Vaughan (1979), and Los Indios Tabajaras, a popular guitar duo of two Brazilian brothers (1974). After 14 years in the Dane County Youth Building, pops concerts moved to the even larger Dane County Coliseum in 1976. Marian Bolz described producing concerts in the Coliseum as a "tremendous bunch of work, involving about 150 volunteers," but also remarked that "we had such fun doing it." Pops programs remained in the Coliseum for the next three seasons before moving to the Oscar Mayer Theatre in 1980.

6.10 Mitch Miller, with dancers from his television program, in 1961.

Opera Returns to Madison

MCMA had sponsored a successful series of staged opera performances during the 1930s under Sigfrid Prager. This series ended in 1938, at least partly due to Prager's increasingly busy schedule as a WPA conductor, and it was not revived during or after the austere war years. It would be 24 years before the MCMA sponsored staged opera again, but Walter Heermann did program several concert versions of operas in the late 1950s. There was clearly an appetite for producing opera in Madison, and almost immediately on their arrival in Madison, Roland and Arline Johnson were approached by a group of local singers—most of them members of the Madison Civic Chorus—about producing opera performances. The Johnsons were well equipped to take on this challenge. Roland had a great deal of experience working with voices and had conducted several stage productions. Arline was a singer, vocal teacher, and seasoned stage director. The two had collaborated on several staged operas when they were faculty members at the University of Alabama.

Beginning in the fall of 1961, the Johnsons began working with a group of two dozen local singers in what was known initially as the Madison Civic Opera Workshop. Their work culminated in a staged performance of Act II of *Die Fledermaus* at the pops concert in May. Buoyed by the audience reaction and the enthusiasm of the singers, Johnson approached the MCMA board with a proposal for the formation of a third group under the auspices of the Association, a group devoted to the production of staged operas. After a lengthy discussion in November 1962, the board approved the establishment of the Madison Civic Opera Guild. Though the opera

6.11 Arline Johnson directing members of the Madison Civic Opera Workshop (clearly rehearsing a drinking song!), spring 1962.

remained under the umbrella of the MCMA, it would eventually be governed by its own board and would maintain a separate budget.[17] By the late 1970s and 1980s, this would occasionally be a source of tension between groups that were sometimes working at cross-purposes; Robert Palmer later remarked wryly that "you could write an entire book on the relationship between the Madison Civic Opera Guild and Civic Music boards." Palmer noted that in the late 1970s, he was still responsible for signing contracts for the Opera's guest soloists, rental agreements, contracts with music publishers, and other "legal" details, but the opera began to hire its own administrators in the 1980s.[18] The Madison Civic Opera Guild, later known as the Madison Civic Opera (1977), and eventually renamed the Madison Opera in 1984, would become entirely independent of the Madison Symphony Orchestra during the sweeping reorganization of 1994 (discussed in Chapter 8). However, the Madison Opera and the orchestra still share their director (John DeMain) today, and the MSO remains the exclusive pit orchestra for Madison Opera's productions. Just as the MCMA was starting the Opera Guild, the University School of Music organized the University Opera, under the directorship of Prof. Karlos Moser. The two companies maintained a friendly rivalry throughout this period.[19]

The Opera Guild's first full-scale production was Puccini's *La Bohème*, sung in English, which had three performances in the Madison East High School Auditorium on January 11 and 12, 1963. All were nearly sold out, despite subzero temperatures and blizzard conditions. The leads were sung by several local singers. Marion Paton and Lois Dick shared the role of Mimi (Paton in Friday and Saturday evenings, Dick in a Saturday matinee); Arcenia Moser and Joanna Overn similarly split the role of Musetta. The male leads were also mostly shared: John Paton and Warren Crandall as Rodolfo, Henry Peters and Robert Towner as Colline, and Arthur Becknell and Don Roebuck as Schaunard. Robert Tottingham sang Marcello at all three performances. Another local figure who would remain a fixture of the Opera for over four decades was Ann Stanke, who served as rehearsal pianist and as prompter during performances. The dress rehearsal was broadcast live over WHA-TV on January 9, the very first appearance of the Opera Guild and the Madison Civic Symphony on television. Carmen Elsner, who wrote reviews of both casts for the *Wisconsin State Journal*, did remark on a few flaws, due to "lack of experience"—revealed in "voices suddenly fading into the footlights and stiff acting by singers whose performances otherwise would be great." She celebrated the company's decision to perform in English, noting that "Madison's interpretation of *La Bohème* showed a quality [that] leading opera houses can't seem to match— clearly understood opera in English." Elsner hailed the production overall with: "The bright light of opera is casting a warm glow over Madison with the healthy acceptance over the weekend of Madison Civic Opera [Guild's] *La Bohème*."[20]

The successful 1963 *La Bohème* set the pattern for Civic Opera Guild productions over the next dozen years, with leads taken mostly by local singers, though University vocal faculty John and Marion Paton, Karl Brock,

Lois Fischer, Samuel Jones, and David Hottmann frequently appeared as leads as well. Like *La Bohème*, productions were often double-cast, allowing more singers to sing lead roles, and most productions continued to be in English through the 1960s. Like Johnson's programming for the orchestra and chorus, Roland and Arline Johnson mixed standard operatic repertoire with less conventional works, including several works by contemporary American composers. The 1963–64 season, for example, followed the familiar *La Bohème* with two unorthodox pieces, beginning in November 1963 with Benjamin Britten's *Noye's Fludde*, a 1958 "children's opera" based upon a 15th-century mystery play. Then on February 29, 1964, the opera presented the midwestern premiere of another 1958 work, Francis Poulenc's *La voix humaine* (sung in English as *The Human Voice*). This one-movement work for a single performer was based on a stage play by Jean Cocteau. This production, which was held at the Park Motor Inn as part of a gala fundraiser for the Opera Guild, featured noted soprano Marjorie Madey, the Guild's first hired professional soloist. There was only a single production in 1964–65, Verdi's *Falstaff* in February with local bass Robert Tottingham in the title role. It was planned that he would split the role with Platteville-based singer Paul Balshaw, but Balshaw contracted a virus and lost his voice days before the performance. In the end,

6.12 La Bohème, January 12, 1963. L–R: Robert Tottingham (Marcello), Joanna Overn (Musetta), Lois Dick (Mimi), Don Roebuck (Schaunard), Warren Crandall (Rodolfo), and Robert Towner (Colline). [MSO Archives]

Balshaw played the part on stage, while Tottingham, stationed in the orchestra pit, sang as Falstaff![21] In January 1966, the Opera Guild and MSO presented a concert version of Puccini's *Tosca*, with three Metropolitan Opera stars— soprano Eleanor Steber, baritone John Reardon, and tenor Jon Crain—and local singers Robert Tottingham, Bert Adams, Lois Dick, and Carroll Gonzo. They returned to staged opera in February 1967 with a full version of *Die Fledermaus*, a production that also toured to Portage, Spring Green, and Waupun.

Over the next few seasons, the Opera Guild mounted a fully staged production every February. Standard repertoire performed during this period included Humperdinck's *Hansel and Gretel* (1968), Bizet's *Carmen* (1970), Mozart's *The Marriage of Figaro* (1972), and a double bill of Puccini's *Gianni Scicchi* and Mascagni's *Cavalleria rusticana* (1973). Again, the Johnsons alternated standard repertoire with newer works, including *The Jumping Frog of Calaveras County* by Roland Johnson's longtime friend Lukas Foss, presented on a double bill with *Hansel and Gretel* in February 1968. This 1950 opera was based on a short story by Mark Twain.[22] In 1969 they staged Douglas Moore's *The Ballad of Baby Doe* (composed in 1956). In 1971 the Opera Guild presented an even more recent opera, *Help, Help, the Globolinks!* written by Gian Carlo Menotti in 1968, which was presented on a double bill with a ballet, *Creation of the Sun*, choreographed by Marsha Leonard from the University and performed by students from the University's Dance Division. This ballet was danced to Darius Milhaud's jazz-inspired 1923 score *La Création du monde*. *Globolinks!* has a science fiction plot (invading aliens who capture a busload of children, and who can only be defeated by music) and is written partly for children: the primary lead, Emily, is a 14-year-old girl, and the cast includes a children's chorus of at least a dozen voices. In this production, both of the Johnsons' children, Carl and Karen, were part of the chorus. In 2022 Karen Kretschmann recalled that, at age five, she was the youngest on the stage, and as the youngest, she got to sit on the bus driver's lap onstage, "which of course I thought was very cool." However, she caught tonsillitis prior to the show and could not do the performances. She remembers being very disappointed that Ann Stanke's daughter Kristin, who was the next youngest, got to sit in the driver's lap, but also that the young singer who played Emily gave her a rose to cheer her up.[23] On June 5, 1971, the Opera Guild celebrated its tenth anniversary with an "Opera Fest" program in the Central High School Auditorium, featuring excerpts from several of the operas it had produced in its early years.

In her account of the Madison Opera's history, written for its 25th anniversary in 1987, Eleanor Anderson referred to the 1974–75 season as the beginning of a "second phase." Up to this point, productions were staged in the auditoriums of Madison's high schools: Central (later MATC Auditorium), East, West, and Memorial. Beginning with the March 1974 production of Puccini's *Madame Butterfly*, the Guild moved most of its productions into the University's Wisconsin Union Theater, a decidedly more "professional" space, though its tiny orchestra pit often presented a space problem for the orchestras of grand operas.[24] Moving to the Memorial Union also came with higher production costs, reportedly some $3000 more per production than in previous years. Anderson relates that there was a rancorous debate in the MCMA board meeting about this increase, which finally ended when Louise Brown, a board member and opera supporter, simply offered to write a check to cover the $3000 increase.

6.13 Daniel Nelson in the 1970s.

Also remarkable about the 1974 *Madame Butterfly* was that, for the first time, the Opera Guild hired a professional singer to sing a role in one of its regular staged productions. Milwaukee-based tenor Daniel Nelson was brought in for the role of Pinkerton. (He had just sung the role with Milwaukee's Florentine Opera.)[25] The trend toward hiring lead performers continued through the 1970s and 1980s, and for his part, Nelson would return several more times over the next decade, singing with both the opera and at concerts of the orchestra and chorus. The Opera Guild's productions during the remainder of the decade continued to mix standard and newer repertoire. The more standard works were Mozart's *Cosi fan tutte* (September 1974), Verdi's *La Traviata* (February 1974), Massenet's *Manon* (February 1977), a revival of *Die Fledermaus* (February 1978), and Mozart's *The Impresario* (June 1979). Newer works included a revival of *The Ballad of Baby Doe* (February 1976) and Menotti's *Amelia Goes to the Ball* (a double bill with *The Impresario* in 1979). The Opera's productions often included amusing "local references." Joel Skornicka, MCMA board president from 1974 to 1977, was elected mayor of Madison in 1979, and in 1981 he had a brief walk-on (and, he was careful to note, non-singing) appearance in *Carmen* as the mayor of Seville.[26]

In 1977, the Madison Civic Opera Guild shortened its name to Madison Civic Opera, in part as a reflection of the increasing professionalism of its stage productions. This would change again to Madison Opera in 1984. As discussed in Chapter 8, it would open MCMA's new performance space, the Oscar Mayer Theatre, with its most ambitious performance to that time, Verdi's monumental *Aïda*.

The Quest for a Civic Auditorium and the "Auditorium Wars"

When it was first incorporated in 1925, one of the Madison Civic Music Association's stated goals had been to build an adequate civic auditorium in Madison. Over the years, various proposals arose, auditoriums variously set in Olin Park, on the west shore of Lake Monona (where the enormous dirt-floor Olin Park Auditorium—an unheated, and, by the 1930s, increasingly decrepit structure—was discussed, not too seriously, it is hoped, as a possibility), Conklin/ James Madison Park on the south shore of Lake Mendota, Law Park on the north shore of Lake Monona, and Olbrich Park on the east shore of Lake Monona. Architect Frank Lloyd Wright stepped into the fray in 1938 with a proposal for a "Dream Civic Center," initially called the Olin Terraces. Wright's plans, which extended out over Lake Monona, were sited in Law Park, at the end of Monona Avenue (now Martin Luther King Blvd.). His plan called for a centerpiece 5600-seat Civic Auditorium, but also a railroad depot and provision for county courts and a jail! This proposal was narrowly defeated by the Dane County Board of Supervisors, though Wright seems to have taken heart when Madison voters approved $750,000 to build a Civic Auditorium in April 1941. The onset of the war in December 1941 brought this project to a halt, but up to and after the war, Wright campaigned actively for the project, submitting several emended plans.

In 1954, Madison voters strongly approved a $4 million bond issue to fund a civic auditorium that largely conformed to Wright's plan and preferred location. In a second referendum, voters—by a much closer margin—approved Wright as the architect. Wright signed a contract with the city in 1956, and amid reports that the project's eventual cost would be far in excess of $4 million, the Wisconsin state legislature effectively killed the project in 1957, with a law specifically limiting any structure on the site to 20 feet in height. This law was repealed two years later, and Wright finished one last drawing of the Monona Terrace, just seven weeks before his death in 1959.[27]

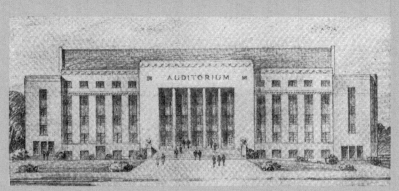

6.14 1941 preliminary sketch of a 5000-seat civic auditorium by Madison architect Ferdinand Y. Kronenberg, published on the front page of the *Wisconsin State Journal* on March 30, 1941, ahead of the referendum on funding an auditorium. It appeared above the absurdly hopeful headline "40 Years of Auditorium Agitation May End at the Polls Tuesday." This was planned for the east end of Law Park, possibly in combination with a boathouse on Lake Monona.

In 1962, after Madison voters passed a somewhat slyly worded referendum that effectively allowed Mayor Henry Roberts to kill the project, the Monona Terrace project was once again defunct. The city began planning for an auditorium on the west end of James Madison Park ... that is, until a judge ruled that the city's contract with the Wright Foundation was "valid and enforceable." Attempts to negotiate a mediated settlement in 1964 failed, and the matter was still unresolved two years later when yet another site, this one on Wilson Street, was proposed by Mayor Otto Festge and rejected by a deeply divided city council. For a time, there was interest in siting an auditorium in Olin Park, near the just-completed Dane County Coliseum. In 1966, the city hired Wright Foundation architect William Wesley Peters, who shared yet another revised plan for Law Park—now as part of a grand "Monona Basin Project"—encompassing plans for the entire swath of shoreline from Law Park to Olin Park, centered on a large, circular 2360-seat auditorium. This plan, which would start with construction of the auditorium, was passed by the city council, despite the fact that its price tag was more than twice what the city had in hand and that there was still debate over whether this would be built in Law Park, as Wright had proposed, or in Olin Park. Given this, Peters gutted as much as possible from the auditorium: for example, there were no elevators planned in this seven-story structure! The two bids received from contractors in 1968 came in well above budget, and when the council refused to agree to increase the budget, the project was again dead.[28]

After the failure in 1972 of yet another downtown site for an auditorium/convention center designated the "Metro Square Project," a group of local businesses, calling themselves the Central Madison Committee, announced plans to buy the Capitol Theater and the vacant Montgomery Ward store next door as the center of a civic cultural complex. This project was eventually supported by Mayor Paul Soglin, who openly preferred the Wright design but pragmatically said that he would support the CMC's alternative should the Wright proposal be impossible. In the background was a ticking fiscal time bomb: the $4 million in bonds issued in 1954 would mature in 1974, and the provision

6.15 Madison Civic Center exterior, ca. 1997. The distinctive tower of the 1928 Capitol Theater was retained as the main entrance to the Madison Civic Center in 1980. It also remains as part of the Overture Center's State Street façade.

that this money be used for an auditorium would no longer be valid. Early that year, voters roundly rejected a referendum increasing the original $4 million to $8.5 million, the projected cost of the Monona Basin auditorium. However, the wording of this referendum allowed for the original $4 million to be used for the Capitol Theater option. Soglin flew to New York City and purchased the Capitol Theater from the RKO Corporation—who had built the theater in 1927–28 and still operated it—for $650,000.[29]

How was the MSO involved? Scanning through the board minutes, it seems that while the MCMA had consistently supported various auditorium proposals from the 1930s onward, that support had largely come in the form of rather toothless resolutions and speeches by music directors. In the building of what came to be known as the Madison Civic Center, MCMA joined forces with four other arts organizations[30] as the Civic Center Residents Alliance in order to have a stronger voice in planning. As early as 1975, Joel Skornicka, then president of the MCMA board (and later Madison's mayor from 1979 to 1983), expressed concerns regarding the acoustical properties of the Capitol Theater.[31] While Skornicka remembered in 2019 that Johnson and Robert Palmer had been involved in the planning process, by 1979, when he had succeeded Soglin as mayor, his main concern had been simply "getting the place open." In the end, it seems that little or nothing was done to address acoustical issues. Skornicka noted that he realized, even at the time, that the Capitol was only "a temporary fix."[32]

Madison now had a civic auditorium, and the Madison Symphony Orchestra had a new home venue: the Capitol Theater, now renamed the Oscar Mayer Theatre, in honor of local philanthropist Oscar G. Mayer, who had made a major donation to the Civic Center project. Wright's "Dream Civic Center" seemed completely dead. In June 1990, however, Mayor Paul Soglin, recently reelected after a decade practicing law privately, announced that he felt that Wright's design, repurposed as a convention center, should be built. A former Wright associate, Anthony Putnam, shared plans that retained the essential

6.16 The Monona Terrace in 2000.

outer shell of Wright's 1959 final design. This was in the wake of five other convention center designs, including one for Law Park, the Nolan Terrace, which was roundly rejected by voters in a 1989 referendum. The resurgence of interest in the Wright design had been fueled in part by a major Wright exhibition at the University's Elvejhem Museum of Art that included a sizable 1955 model of Monona Terrace produced by Wright's apprentices. In a pair of 1992 referenda, Madison voters narrowly approved the project and a $12 million bond issue. (Much of the over $70 million cost of the building was raised through private and business donations.)[33] Work began in 1995, and in July 1997, the Monona Terrace Convention Center formally opened with a public gala. The MSO, together with the Madison Opera Chorus and local mezzo Kitt Reuter-Foss, performed an all-American rooftop concert there on July 17. Former MCMA board president Terry Haller notes that there was some discussion of an elaborate outdoor performance facility on the Monona Terrace roof in the late 1990s, but that "it became clear as we pursued this possibility that there is simply not enough rooftop space to accommodate the size of audience the MSO would require for an outdoor concert to make economic sense."[34]

The MCMA Board Evolves

The makeup and mission of the Madison Civic Music Association board also changed in the 1960s. During Prager's tenure, it is clear that he took a strong hand in the day-to-day operations of MCMA, and that nearly all decisions of any consequence were made by him in consultation with the Vocational School's Alexander Graham. (After studying him for many years, I've concluded that Prager was a consummate musician and a fine leader, but also a bit of a control freak!) The board took a much stronger leadership role during the directorship of Walter Heermann. Heermann came to Madison after nearly 50 years playing in the Cincinnati Symphony Orchestra, an organization run from its earliest days by a very strong board.[35] He remained firmly in control of artistic decisions and clearly influenced the way that the orchestra represented itself to the public in its programming and in programs and other printed material. However, Heermann also seems to have been much more willing than his predecessor to let the board run the operations of the orchestra. In the 1950s the board was dominated by local women, and in addition to overseeing fundraising, marketing, and operations, the board also provided a corps of volunteers who did most of the behind-the-scenes work.

In the 1960s and 1970s, the MCMA board was gradually transformed from a volunteer-oriented group to a governing group that more closely resembles today's Madison Symphony Orchestra board: a large group of individuals from the community with a wide range of backgrounds and skills, united by an interest in assisting the orchestra and by a devotion to public service. The board's focus gradually shifted from volunteering to oversight, particularly through committees devoted to various aspects of what needed to happen in the background to put the orchestra, chorus, and opera on stage: marketing, fundraising, and other committees. These committees increasingly included members who could bring professional, business, and legal experience to bear on these issues. There are at least three factors in the background of the board's transformation in the 1960s and 1970s: (1) The kind of volunteer work needed by the organization—envelope-stuffing, phone-answering, ushering, etc.—was increasingly taken over by the active Women's Committee (later Madison Symphony Orchestra League), which had been founded in 1956. (2) A second factor was the ever-increasing size of MCMA's budget and the increasing complexity of its operations—simply put, the activities of MCMA became too big to be run by enthusiastic amateurs. (3) Closely intertwined with this growth in size and complexity was the gradual growth of a staff of professionals like Robert Palmer who were trained in arts administration and who were responsible to the board.

In the spring of 1961, directly on the heels of hiring Roland Johnson, the board adopted a revised set of bylaws, overseen by local attorney and board member Earl Cooper.[36] Among its provisions were the establishment of several standing committees and the expansion of the board itself by an increase in the number of nonvoting advisors. In 1960, the board had a total of 22 directors and advisors. By 1963 it had grown to a total of 29 members, and in 1979 it was 32.

Professionalizing the Orchestra

There were a few steps toward putting the orchestra on a professional basis in the 1950s under Walter Heermann. The only pay available to most members of the orchestra during the 1950s was a modest fund of "babysitting money," designed to help mothers and couples who played in the orchestra, who might otherwise be unable to attend rehearsals and performances. However, by the end of the decade, a few players within the orchestra (concertmaster and principal cello) were being paid by MCMA, and players who were members of the American Federation of Musicians union were paid a small performance stipend through the Music Performance Trust Fund (MPTF). Heermann also used discretionary funds from the board to hire additional players, in particular to bolster the string section. He summed up the situation at a board meeting in June 1960 when he discussed the coming period of transition to a time when "the orchestra is no longer made up of people who play for enjoyment, but rather for compensation." Heermann suggested that the orchestra stood to lose some of its leading instrumentalists if it did not go on a professional footing. He proposed an interim solution of offering bonuses "to various groups within the orchestra which would be paid at the end of the season if they participate in all rehearsals and concerts."[37] Bonus payments to at least some principal players were instituted by the end of the 1960–61 season.

The issue of paying orchestra musicians was a recurring topic at board meetings over the next few years. Roland Johnson later noted that one of the first "courtesy calls" he made after arriving in Madison was to the secretary of Madison's AFM Local 166. He then reported to the board in October 1961 that due to a downturn in record sales nationwide, MPTF (funded by recording royalties) would soon be unable to fully fund payments to union members in the orchestra. After discussion at two more meetings, the board authorized payments to union members to make up for the reduced MPTF funds. In March 1962, the board authorized a payment of $10 to all orchestra members (union and nonunion) who would be playing the March 21 concert (Honegger's *King David*, the final concert of the regular season).[38] This seems to have been a one-time payment, but it clearly signaled the direction the board intended to move. On May 19, 1962, the board's Long-Range Planning Committee presented a "Three-Year Plan" that would establish a set of pay scales for players in the orchestra based on rank and experience. At the same meeting, Johnson noted that MPTF funding would be even more sharply cut in the future. By union policy, these funds were designated for free concerts, and when the orchestra began charging admission a few years later, these funds would have been unavailable in any case. The orchestra did, however, continue to use MPTF to pay union musicians for its free youth programs into the 1980s.

By 1963, many of the principal chairs, particularly in the winds, were occupied by University faculty, professionals of the highest caliber, and in March of that year, the board approved payment of additional seasonal bonuses to all principal players.[39] By April 1964, the board, with encouragement from board member and orchestra musician James Crow, had begun to discuss an agreement with the musicians that might cover conditions in addition to pay: auditions, seating within sections, etc.[40] Beginning with the 1964–65 season, all orchestra members were being paid on a rather complex sliding scale based on experience, from principal players to less skilled community musicians, and a few high school and college students. MCMA continued to depend in part on MPTF funding, but musicians were paid regardless of union status, receiving an average of about $20 per concert. The pay was funded in part by a successful chair sponsorship drive. Later that season, Donald Whitaker and Helen Hay, in consultation with Johnson, provided a detailed "Five Year Plan for compensation of orchestra personnel." Among their recommendations was a significant raise in pay, roughly 50% across the board, with higher raises for players at the high end of the scale, to bring payment in line with union scale. They also proposed a "per-service" system, where musicians were compensated at a lower rate for rehearsals (from $2 up to $10) and a higher rate for concerts ($5 to $20).[41]

The End of Free Concerts and a New Name: The Madison Symphony Orchestra

The orchestra gradually began to professionalize during the early 1960s, and the quality of its musical product increased. This came with costs, and though community fundraising and donor programs were successful, it became increasingly clear that the MCMA would eventually need to sell tickets.

Since the 1940s, the regular programs by the Madison Civic Symphony and Chorus had been offered free to the public under the sponsorship of MCMA and the Vocational School. When the Women's Committee sponsored its first pops program, the Orchestra Gala of April 30, 1960, it was billed as a benefit concert for the orchestra, and tickets to the event were sold for $5. The Hotel Loraine ballroom was filled to capacity for the event, and it was a success, raising $2400. However, there were some negative reactions from community members, both to the idea of charging for a Civic Symphony performance and to the perceived "high society" nature of the event.[42] There was also pushback from some members of the Vocational School board, as reported in the MCMA board minutes.[43] The annual pops concert continued to be a ticketed event in the early 1960s, however, and when the Madison Civic Opera Guild began independent performances in 1963, those were ticketed as well.

The issue of ticketing the orchestra's regular programs seems to have been raised—or at least documented—for the first time at a board meeting in May 1965, during discussion of a proposed recital and chamber music series. Board member Viola Fenske wondered openly if the time was approaching when MCMA would need to begin charging for all concerts; she noted that there were only two other orchestras of comparable size in the country that were offering free programs. It came up once more in February 1966, during discussion of a few recent programs where the audience was disappointingly small, and the board discussed the possibility that free admission might be the reason.[44] The issue was finally raised formally at the next meeting by James Crow, who, together with the Vocational School's Norman Mitby, raised several practical issues that needed to be considered in the decision.

In May 1966, the board received a detailed plan for creating a 1966–67 subscription series of five MCMA programs, setting season ticket prices at $7.50 ($1.50 per concert) and $5.00 ($1.00 per concert) according to seating in Central High School Auditorium, with student tickets at $2.50 ($.50 per concert). Rates were higher for single tickets purchased during the season: $2.00, $1.50, and $1.00.[45] While there is no record of the board's discussion, it is clear from the 1966–67 season brochure that they decided to start with a partial measure: The three symphony concerts in Central High School Auditorium remained free, as did the fall and spring youth concerts and a March Neighborhood Family Concert. The opera, pops, and chamber programs were ticketed as they had been previously, but the two large choral/orchestral programs were also ticketed: a performance of the Vivaldi *Gloria* and Honegger *Christmas Cantata* in the University Stock Pavilion (December 15, 1966) and the Bach *Mass in B minor* at First Congregational Church (April 12, 1967).

6.17 The MSO performing in the University Stock Pavilion, ca. 1972.

While the issue of ticketing concerts does not show up in the board minutes for 1966–67, two things are clear from the 1967–68 season brochure: (1) Ticketing of additional concerts does not seem to have driven away the audience. In fact, attendance at concerts had risen to the point that four of the five regular symphony and choral/orchestral programs—all of them in the 1000-seat Central High School Auditorium—were repeated, as was a special Bach Festival performance in May 1968, with Saturday evening and Sunday matinee performances, to accommodate a larger audience. The December *Messiah* program was held in the newly completed Dane County Coliseum, with a seating capacity of some 10,000, more than large enough to hold the audience. (2) MCMA actually raised the season ticket prices, to $10.00, $7.50, or $5.00 for the five subscription programs. From that point onward, only youth and family concerts and outdoor performances were free to the public.

As this fundamental change was beginning to work its way through the board in the spring of 1966, another fundamental change was initiated by the orchestra itself. At a meeting of orchestra players on April 2, 1966, the orchestra voted to change its name from the Madison Civic Symphony to the Madison Symphony Orchestra. Orchestra members felt that this name change reflected the evolution of the orchestra in the early 1960s from an almost purely amateur group to a professional ensemble. The board formally ratified the change on April 21, and beginning with 1966–67—its 40th anniversary season—the orchestra formally became the Madison Symphony Orchestra. The name change was made public in June, just ahead of the announcement of paid tickets.[46] The Madison Civic Chorus retained its original name until 1983, when it formally became the Madison Symphony Chorus.

The Madison Symphony Orchestra in the 1960s and 1970s

Who were the musicians playing in the orchestra at this time? One useful snapshot of the orchestra's membership in the middle of this period appeared in the pages of the *Capital Times*. Between October 1969 and January 1970, the paper ran a nine-part series titled "Know Your Symphony Orchestra." This was a section-by-section introduction to the membership of the orchestra that season, with photos of sections and a short profile of each player, 74 musicians in all.[47] A few statistics can be gleaned from these profiles:

6.18 An installment in the *Capital Times* "Know Your Symphony Orchestra" series from 1969–70.

- University music faculty were heavily represented, mostly in principal chairs: 10 players.
- There were also many public school music teachers, including the orchestra directors of all three Madison high schools, and string, band, and general music teachers from Madison and several surrounding communities: 16 players.
- While many players gave private lessons, a few seem to have worked primarily as private music teachers: 9 players.
- There were several students in the orchestra, including 4 graduate students in music, 3 graduate students in nonmusical fields, 3 undergraduate/adult students, and 2 high school students.
- 6 players were otherwise employed in music or were semiretired professional musicians.
- 15 women identified themselves as homemakers.
- There were also a wide range of nonmusical day jobs represented: University professors of philosophy and genetics, the director of the State Laboratory of Hygiene, a realtor, a social worker, and a professional portrait painter.

- The orchestra was relatively equally divided by gender, with 41 women and 33 men, but the string section was dominated by women: 32 of 49 players, including an all-female first violin section.

Though a majority of the orchestra was in fact employed full- or part-time in music outside of their work in the MSO in 1969–70 (most of them as University or public school teachers), and all players were being paid by this point, it is clear that the orchestra still retained some of the "community" feeling it had had since 1926. This was still true in the early 1980s when I joined the orchestra. Though professional standards were certainly higher than they had been in the early 1960s, nearly all of the orchestra's players were from Madison or nearby, and there were still many players, particularly in the string section, who were skilled amateurs. A few veteran players—notably flutist Betty Bielefeld and bassoonist Richard Lottridge—have suggested that, despite the fact that the quality of the MSO's performance had improved tremendously by the 1990s, it continued to feel like a "community orchestra" until the arrival of John DeMain in 1994.

Johnson arrived at an opportune time in the musical history of Madison: a period of dramatic expansion in the University's School of Music. The influx of artist-level faculty had begun in the 1940s and 1950s with the residency of the Pro Arte Quartet and the hiring of pianist Gunnar Johansen. During the 1960s and 1970s, many of the instrumental studio positions at the University were filled with musicians who were nationally known soloists or who had played with America's major orchestras. By the 1970s, most of the principals of the orchestra—hired directly by Johnson—were University faculty. In the 1970–71 season, a year after the "Know Your Orchestra" profile, University faculty occupied the concertmaster's chair (Thomas Moore) and principal chairs in several other sections: viola (Martha Blum), cello (Lowell Creitz), flute (Robert Cole), oboe (Henry Peters), clarinet (Glenn Bowen), bassoon (Richard Lottridge), horn (Nancy Becknell), trumpet (Donald Whitaker), trombone (Allen Chase) and timpani (James Latimer). These faculty also brought their students into the orchestra, a trend that increased in the 1970s and 1980s—ending four decades during which University faculty often discouraged music majors from playing in the orchestra. The presence of University music students continues in the orchestra today with students who perform with the orchestra—most often at the back of the string sections, or as extra players in the winds—for a few years while they are in Madison.

Concertmasters of the 1960s and 1970s

For the orchestra's first 35 seasons, the position of concertmaster was held by Marie Endres, who also served (unofficially under Prager and officially under Heermann) as assistant conductor of the Madison Civic Symphony. During her long tenure, Endres provided solid leadership to the string section, in addition to conducting countless string rehearsals. As Madison's most prominent string teacher, she was also able to recruit many of her more advanced students into the orchestra. Endres resigned at the close of the 1959–60 season, citing an increasingly busy teaching and conducting schedule.[48] Her successor as concertmaster was another local violinist, Mary Perssion, who had served as assistant concertmaster for 20 years. Perssion took the position at the beginning of the 1960–61 season. Beatrice Hagen, wife of Oskar Hagen and another longtime member of the orchestra, became assistant concertmaster. Perssion, a faculty member at the Wisconsin School of Music, studied in the 1930s and 1940s both with George Szpinalski at the University and with Endres. She was the orchestra's concertmaster for three years, but she moved away from Madison at the end of the 1962–63 season to work in a series of orchestral positions, including 19 seasons with the Denver Symphony Orchestra.[49]

6.19 MSO concertmaster Mary Perssion (right) and assistant concertmaster Beatrice Hagen in October 1960.

Two more women, both of whom were longtime players, served as concertmaster through most of the remainder of the 1960s. Annetta Rosser moved to Madison from Princeton, New Jersey, in 1961 with her husband, a professor of mathematics at the University. Rosser had played professionally before coming to Madison, and she had also played in a string quartet with Albert Einstein when she lived in Princeton![50] She served as concertmaster in the 1963–64 and 1965–66 seasons and continued to perform in the violin section through 1981. She served on both the MCMA and Madison Opera boards well into the 1980s and was president of the MSOL from 1982 to 1984. Rosser was also a composer, and she published a collection of her art songs in 1977.[51] I remember her fondly as a warm and friendly presence at many preconcert talks and as someone who would often seek me out after concerts or by phone to comment on program notes.

Miriam Schneider was born in Germany in 1925. In 1939, with war imminent in Europe, her parents were able to get her on one of the last *Kindertransport* trains out of Germany—a last-ditch effort to get children of Jewish families

6.20a/6.20b Madison Civic Symphony in the Wisconsin Union Theater, January 22, 1964, and detail. Concertmaster Annetta Rosser is at front, center in the detail, and Miriam Schneider, who was seated as principal second that season, is behind Johnson.

out of Germany. The most important possession she brought with her was her violin, a valuable early 19th-century French instrument by Nicolas Lupot. Her mother, who was Jewish, later managed to escape to Canada, and her father, who was not Jewish, and her brother managed to survive the war in Germany.[52] Miriam spent the war years in a boarding school in Scotland. She performed professionally in Britain after the war, including a position in Manchester's famed Halle Orchestra. Schneider and her husband Hans (another *Kindertransport* refugee) moved to Madison in the late 1950s, and she joined the Madison Civic Symphony in 1959.[53] She served as concertmaster for three seasons, 1966–67, 1967–68, and 1968–69. Like Rosser, Schneider had a long tenure in the orchestra following her work as concertmaster: she was assistant concertmaster from 1970–71 through 1993–94, and she continued to perform with the MSO through May 1996—a total of 37 seasons. Schneider also appeared twice as a soloist: in Bach's *Brandenburg Concerto No. 5* (1968) and *Brandenburg Concerto No. 1* (1974). Schneider died in 2018, but there is a moving postscript, related by her daughter Barbara, a professor at the University of Calgary in Canada. Violins of Hope is a traveling collection of violins that emerged from the Holocaust. Part of this exhibition is to have the instruments played by musicians in the towns it comes to. In 2024 Barbara had Miriam's violin included in a Violins of Hope performance by the Calgary Philharmonic. As a result of this, Barbara has an invitation to go to the Jewish Museum in Berlin and speak about the violin and her family's history.[54]

The tradition of promoting concertmasters from within the ranks of the orchestra was set aside once in the 1960s when Roland Johnson invited the Korean-American violinist Won-Mo Kim to serve as concertmaster for the 1964–65 season. Kim arrived at the University as a visiting lecturer in early

1964 from the Eastman School of Music in Rochester, New York, and was an artist-in-residence, playing in the faculty piano quartet.[55] That season began with a program on October 14, 1964, that also featured Kim as soloist in the Tchaikovsky *Violin Concerto*. Though he remained on faculty at the University through 1970, when he left for a teaching position in Illinois, Kim played only a single season with the Madison Civic Symphony.

In the 1969–70 season, Johnson promoted Martha Blum to the concertmaster's chair. She had arrived in Madison in 1957 with her husband, violist Richard Blum, when he joined the University faculty and the resident Pro Arte Quartet. The Blums had performed together in the Dallas and San Antonio orchestras before coming to Madison, and Martha Blum maintained an active professional career after 1957, performing with the Chicago Lyric Opera and Grant Park Orchestra, and as concertmaster of the Kenosha Symphony Orchestra.[56] She also performed on an occasional basis with the Madison Civic Symphony—playing either violin or viola—from 1963 onward. She served as concertmaster for only a single season but continued to serve in leadership roles: as principal viola in 1970–71 and as principal second violin in 1977–78, 1983–84, and then for 17 seasons from 1989–90 through 2006–7. Martha Blum eventually joined the Pro Arte Quartet as second violin in 1974. For his part, Richard Blum joined the MSO as principal viola in 1979, serving in that role for 27 seasons, from 1979–80 through 2006–7. Both Blums appeared as soloists with the orchestra, Martha in the Corelli *"Christmas" Concerto*, op. 8, no. 6 (1977), and Richard in Berlioz, *Harold in Italy* (1980), Vaughan Williams, *Flos campi* (1992), and Strauss, *Don Quixote* (1999).

The next two concertmasters were members of the Pro Arte Quartet. As described by John Barker in his history of the ensemble, the quartet was essentially nonexistent for a few years after 1962, when first violinist Rudolf Kolisch stepped away. The remaining members of the Pro Arte, violinist Robert Basso, violist Richard Blum, and cellist Lowell Creitz performed with faculty pianist Leo Steffens for the next five years as the UW–Madison Piano Quartet. (Basso resigned in 1963 and was replaced as artist-in-residence by Won-Mo Kim.) However, in 1967, the University School of Music resurrected

6.21 Thomas Moore (foreground) in September 1970; also pictured are Lowell Creitz, newly hired principal cello, and new business manager Winifred Cook (standing). Miriam Schneider (associate principal violin) is seated.

the Pro Arte Quartet by hiring two new violinists for the 1967–68 academic year—Norman Paulu as the quartet's first violin and Thomas Moore as second violin—both of whom would also serve as concertmasters of the MSO. This was, incidentally, the first time in the history of the venerable Pro Arte that all four members were Americans.[57] Johnson hired Moore as concertmaster for the 1970–71 season. (His Pro Arte colleague Lowell Creitz joined the MSO as principal cellist that same year and remained in the position for three seasons.) A native of North Carolina, Moore had performed in the Rochester (NY) Philharmonic Orchestra, Columbus Symphony Orchestra, and the Hughes String Quartet before joining the Pro Arte. Though he resigned from the Pro Arte Quartet in May 1972, he remained on faculty at the University for several more years.[58] Moore would serve as concertmaster for seven seasons: from 1970–71 through 1975–76 and then again in 1977–78. (He was replaced in 1976–77 by Norman Paulu.) Moore would also appear as a soloist with the orchestra five times between 1970 and 1978.[59]

Norman Paulu was born in Cedar Rapids, Iowa, and was a student of the great Hungarian virtuoso Joseph Szigeti. He came to Madison from Oklahoma, where he was concertmaster of the Oklahoma City Symphony and a member of the Lyric Quartet. His wife, Catherine Paulu, joined the MSO as principal oboe in 1970–71 and remained in that position into the 1987–88 season. After serving as concertmaster in 1977–78, Norman Paulu returned in 1979–80 and served for 10 successive seasons, until 1988–89. Also a frequent soloist, Paulu was featured on 11 different works before and during his tenure as concertmaster.[60] A few of these appearances were with his wife. The Paulus first appeared together with the orchestra as soloists on May 24, 1968, playing Bach *Concerto for Oboe and Violin in C minor*, BWV 1060r. On October 28, 1973, they played the *Dialogues for Violin, Oboe, and Orchestra* by Oklahoma City University composer

6.22a/6.22b Norman and Catherine Paulu, late 1970s. [MSO Archives]

Ray Luke. This work had been written for and premiered by the Paulus in 1965, a commission by the Oklahoma City Symphony.[61] Together, Moore and Paulu inaugurated a long period of stability in the concertmaster's chair that continues to the present day: Moore's seven seasons as concertmaster and Paulu's 11 seasons were followed by the 20-year tenure of Tyrone Greive. Naha Greenholtz succeeded Greive in 2011–12 and remains in the position today.

The Madison Civic Chorus in the 1960s and 1970s

Johnson worked much more actively with the Madison Civic Chorus than his predecessor, and he expanded its role. He had worked for several years as a choral conductor in Alabama and was obviously comfortable in this medium. The chorus also grew in size and quality in Johnson's first few years, both by word-of-mouth recruitment among local singers and through active recruitment by Johnson. In 1963, for example, Johnson instituted a series of informal "Summer Sings"—open rehearsals popular among regular Civic Chorus members during the summer months, but also a way of attracting new singers. By the middle 1960s, the chorus had doubled in size and would no longer fit on the stage of Central High School Auditorium. Choral concerts were regularly scheduled in larger venues: the University Stock Pavilion, the Dane County Coliseum, and the First Congregational United Church of Christ.

During a period when the orchestra was an increasingly professional ensemble, the chorus remained (and remains today) an all-volunteer group, and Johnson's genial personality and his skill as a choral conductor made him an inspiring leader for the group. In a letter to the Johnson family following Johnson's death in 2012, longtime chorus member George Shook (who joined the chorus in 1966 and who is profiled at the end of this chapter) paid affectionate tribute to Johnson's work with the Madison Civic Chorus:

6.23 The Madison Civic Chorus in December 1962, just barely fitting onto an expanded Central High School Auditorium stage. The orchestra for this concert (Bach's *Christmas Oratorio*) was seated on the floor.

Mr. Johnson was a masterful chorus leader. He, unlike many orchestra conductors, directed the chorus rehearsals himself; he did not turn that task over to another director. He was always positive and constructive in his instruction of the chorus. We always felt well prepared for our performances. In the final moments before every performance Mr. Johnson appeared at the Chorus warm-up room and delivered a heartfelt, inspirational message. He had equal respect for the chorus and orchestra.... Mr. Johnson taught us a lot of music and a lot about music, for which we are always grateful.... When I began singing in the Chorus, I did not "get" the music of J. S. Bach with all its counterpoint and style. Over time I have learned a great appreciation for the Bach compositions. Four performances we remember very fondly are the *Christmas Oratorio*, *St. Mathew Passion*, and two performances of the *B Minor Mass*, all under Mr. Johnson's direction. Many other highlights with Mr. Johnson include our first performances of the Verdi *Requiem*, Mozart *Requiem*, Brahms *German Requiem*, Handel's *Messiah*, Haydn's *Creation*, Mendelssohn's *Elijah*, Bernstein's *Chichester Psalms*, and many more. One of the most euphoric experiences of my life was our first performance of the Beethoven *Ninth Symphony*. We have deep gratitude to Mr. Johnson for being the person, the musician, and the teacher that he was as director of the Madison Symphony and Chorus.[62]

University pianist Arthur Becknell was engaged as accompanist in 1971–72, remaining in that role for 11 seasons.

From the chorus's earliest days in the 1920s, there had been a strong tradition of selecting soloists from within the group. This continued under Johnson, and there were several chorus members who performed multiple times as soloists in the 1960s and 1970s. However, by the end of the 1970s, vocal solos were increasingly being taken by University faculty and professional singers.

By tradition begun in the 1930s, Handel's *Messiah* was an annual December event, but Johnson broke with this tradition early in the 1960s to explore other great choral works in the December concerts. *Messiah* was still heard once every two or three seasons, but December chorus and orchestra concerts began to feature a much broader repertoire: 17th-, 18th-, and 19th-century works by Bach (*Christmas Oratorio* in 1962 and 1968, and *Magnificat* in 1965), Schütz (*Historia von der Geburt Jesu Christ* in 1963), Vivaldi (*Gloria* in 1967), Mozart (*"Great" Mass in C minor* in 1977), and Mendelssohn (*Elijah* in 1979), as well as 20th-century works by Britten (*St. Nicholas* in 1963), Respighi (*Lauda per la Nativita del Signore* in 1965), Honegger (*Christmas Cantata* in 1966), and Vaughan Williams (*Hodie* in 1975).

Johnson also began to program a major choral work near the end of every season, and occasionally in November if the chorus was not doing a major work in December. The repertoire reflected the same approach seen in his programming for the orchestra, a mixture of standard repertoire and lesser-known works from before 1900 with a relatively equal number of 20th-century works. This began in his first season with a fine performance of Honegger's *King David*. The pre-1900 repertoire sung by the chorus in these concerts included works by Mozart (*Requiem* in 1963, *Coronation Mass* in 1972), Bach (*St. Matthew Passion* in 1963 and 1977, *Mass in B minor* in 1967 and 1968, *Motet No. 1: Singet des Herrn* in 1972), Brahms (*German Requiem* in 1964 and 1974, *Alto Rhapsody* in 1975, *Liebeslieder Waltzes* in 1975), Verdi (*Requiem* in 1965 and 1978), Mendelssohn (*Elijah* in 1969), Handel (*Israel in Egypt* in 1970), Haydn (*The Creation* in 1974 and *"Timpani" Mass* in 1979), Bruckner (*Te Deum* in 1975), and Beethoven (*Symphony No. 9* in 1976 and 1980). Major 20th-century works performed by the chorus outside of December included works by Poulenc (*Gloria* in 1963 and 1973), Britten (*War Requiem* in 1966, and *Festival Te Deum* and *Rejoice in the Lamb* in 1979), Orff (*Carmina Burana* in 1968, and *Die Sänger der Vorwelt* and *Catulli Carmina* in 1969),⁶³ Bernstein (*Chichester Psalms* in 1971), Vaughan Williams (*Five Mystical Songs* in 1971, *Serenade to Music* in 1973), Walton (*Belshazzar's Feast* in 1971), Copland (*In the Beginning* in 1972), Honegger (*Jeanne d'Arc au bûcher* in 1973), Elgar (*The Music Makers* in 1973), and Fauré (*Requiem* in 1980). By the late 1970s and 1980s, the chorus usually appeared in three programs each season, twice on the subscription series and in a special choral concert presented in the late spring, typically a program dedicated to the works of a single composer.

6.24 Dress rehearsal, Britten, *War Requiem*, May 17, 1966, in First Congregational United Church of Christ (first midwestern performance of the work).

Celebrating a Half Century

The Madison Symphony Orchestra celebrated its 50th season in 1975–76. Coinciding with the American bicentennial celebration, this was in many ways the most elaborate season sponsored by MCMA to that time, including an ambitious all-Wagner program in the University Stock Pavilion in October 1975, featuring soprano Eileen Farrell and Heldentenor Jon Andrew. The season wrapped up with an enormous "Star-Spangled Pops" program staged in the Dane County Coliseum and a special bicentennial program by the orchestra in the Wisconsin Union Theater on July 4, 1976. The Opera Guild staged a successful performance of an American opera, Douglas Moore's *The Ballad of Baby Doe*, in that season as well. The orchestra's anniversary was marked by a banquet in April 1976.

Part of the celebration was the publication of a short history of the MCMA: *A History of the Madison Civic Music Association: The First Fifty Years, 1925–1975*, written by volunteer Eleanor Anderson. This 38-page illustrated booklet was the first published history of MCMA, the orchestra, chorus, and opera. A well-written and useful account, it included several quotations from Prager's letters (some of them republished at various points here) and anecdotes from many figures from the early history of the orchestra still living in Madison at that time.[64]

The 50th anniversary celebrations did include one bit of sadness. The orchestra's second conductor, Walter Heermann, had died in Madison in 1969. However, the first conductor, Sigfrid Prager, was—as far as anyone in Madison knew—still living in retirement in Argentina. Johnson wrote to him in early 1975 to invite him to be part of the celebration, only to find that Prager had passed away in April 1974.

Toward a Professional Staff

No thriving orchestra can make music on stage without a support staff: those who raise funds, pay bills, oversee budgets, write contracts with musicians and soloists, arrange for the rental of music and halls, set up chairs, stands, and equipment for rehearsals and performances, sell tickets, answer phones, stuff envelopes, produce program books and season brochures, write press releases, and perform all of the innumerable other tasks that go on in the background of live performances. From the beginning through the late 1950s, the administrative work for MCMA's groups was supported to a small degree by the staff of the Vocational School, but otherwise, it was mostly done by community and board volunteers. In the 1950s and early 1960s, day-to-day operations of the orchestra and chorus were still run by volunteers, particularly Helen Supernaw, who effectively served as the manager through the 1950s. As discussed in Chapter 4, the MCMA did employ a part-time business manager/secretary (Marvin Foster and then Berniece Traver) beginning in 1954, though most of the orchestra's day-to-day administrative work continued to be done by volunteers.

Supernaw continued to play a leading role in administering MCMA's activities in the early 1960s, together with other volunteers, notably Ann Crow and Helen Hay. Berniece Traver, who had joined the MCMA as business secretary in late 1955, remained in the position through December 1962. In September 1961, the board authorized the hiring of another part-time staffer, Daniel Andresen, to work in public relations: writing press releases, overseeing brochure and program printing, and selling advertising. When Traver resigned at the end of 1962, Helen Hay—who had arrived in Madison at the same time as the Johnsons—was named MCMA's business and public relations manager in 1963. She was still a part-time employee, but Hay clearly approached the position with great professionalism, and the duties she took on expanded far beyond the original position. In February 1964, for example, the board sent her to New York City, where she attended an ASOL-sponsored Orchestra Management course, designed to train managers of smaller civic and community orchestras like Madison's. Her 64 pages of typed notes from the course are preserved in the MSO Archives, and in March 1964, she wrote an extensive report on the course to the board. In it, Hay made several perceptive suggestions regarding the makeup and responsibilities of the board, publicity, fundraising, and the activities of the women's auxiliary organization; many of these were implemented over the next couple of years.[65] Hay seems to have been an effective administrator, and she worked well with a large group of devoted volunteers during these years of explosive growth and change in the scope of MCMA's activities. It was becoming increasingly apparent to the board, however, that with a now-professional orchestra, ticket and subscription sales, and a much larger budget, a full-time professional manager was going to be a priority. In a 2000 interview, Hay noted that, in anticipation of this, her position and pay were expanded in 1966, though she had been "perfectly happy" working as a volunteer. She stepped aside in 1968 when the MCMA finally hired a full-time manager, but she continued to do volunteer work for the orchestra for decades afterward.[66] Also joining the staff on a part-time basis in the early 1960s was Donald Whitaker, the orchestra's principal trumpet and trumpet professor at the University, who served as personnel manager. Among other activities on behalf of the orchestra, Whitaker would lead the effort to put the orchestra on a paid, professional footing.

In June 1968, MCMA hired its first full-time manager, John R. Reel. Reel brought significant arts administration experience to Madison. He had worked as an intern with both the Cleveland Orchestra and the Kansas City Philharmonic on a fellowship from the Ford Foundation. He came to Madison from positions with the Washington (DC) Performing Arts Society and the Westchester (NY) Symphony Orchestra. Helen Hay commented on the transition:

> We've been working toward the point for the past four or five years when Civic Music can function like the kind of professional organization it has become. We've grown from a budget of $5000 to $70,000 in the past five or six years, exclusive of the support we receive from the Madison Area Technical College.[67]

In January 1969, at the request of the board, Reel presented a report of his activities over the previous seven months, dryly noting that "it might be easier to say what a manager does not do in his job rather than what he does." He then laid out a wide range of duties: overseeing and writing copy for publicity and the newsletter, a page-long list of duties relating to ticket sales, working with the board on corporate and individual donations, maintenance of mailing lists, overseeing MCMA's finances, and a host of duties in the office and in operations of the orchestra. He pointed to several accomplishments: organization of board committees (Public Relations, Future Planning and Development, and Friends of Civic Music), several changes and efficiencies to ticketing and budget practices, and actively representing the orchestra to the community.[68]

Reel would stay in the position for two years, leaving in June 1970 to return to school as a graduate student at the University's newly established arts administration program. He was succeeded as business manager by Winifred Cook in September 1970. Cook came to Madison with a background in education and nonprofit management as well as a musical background gained from years of piano study and singing with the Cincinnati Symphony Chorus. She remained in the position for five years before leaving to take a position at the Wisconsin State Legislative Audit Bureau.[69]

In 1972, the full-time staff grew to two with the hiring of Jean Feige as secretary. She would remain in the position for over 20 years. The relationship between MCMA and Madison's Vocational School (MATC), which had been forged in the 1920s, continued in the 1960s. Like his predecessors, MCMA music director Roland Johnson served as supervisor of music at MATC and received most of his salary from the school. However, MATC also provided MCMA with office, library, and rehearsal space. From the 1920s through the late 1990s, the organization's offices were in the basement of MATC's Carroll Street building. There was a large common space occupied by Feige, with workspace for volunteers. There were also offices for the manager and music director, and a large storage space for files and the music library.

In 1975, Cook was succeeded as manager by Robert Palmer. Palmer, born in Chicago, studied music at Augustana College before coming to Madison to pursue a master's degree in the newly established program in arts administration. He was one of the very first class of students in this program, and one of his junior classmates was Richard Mackie, who would become the MSO's executive director in 1999. In a 2022 interview, Palmer expressed special pride in his working relationship with Roland Johnson. He noted that while "the business end was mine and the music end was clearly his," over time they developed a close working relationship, and Johnson came to respect his musical judgments. Palmer had developed a network of relationships with agents, and he was primarily responsible for finding soloists, which had a strong impact on the repertoire. He noted that:

6.25 Robert Palmer in 1975.

> We would sit down together to talk programs, and between the two of us tried to come up with a sense of what hadn't been represented yet [in the MSO's repertoire], and what might sell tickets. But we weren't afraid to play something by Webern. He wasn't afraid to do an obnoxious piece by a contemporary American composer.[70]

Palmer was a relatively relaxed administrator, and he had good relations with the orchestra musicians, who generally liked and respected him.

Musicians of the Orchestra and Chorus: Selected Profiles

Richard (Dick) Lottridge

Bassoonist Dick Lottridge joined the MSO in 1965 as part of the wave of University faculty who took leadership roles in the orchestra during this period. He was born in Schenectady, New York, and studied initially at Philadelphia's Curtis Institute. During the Korean War, Lottridge played in the U.S. Army Field Band for three years before returning to Curtis and then taking a position with the New Orleans Symphony Orchestra for a season. He completed his formal musical training at Yale University, graduating with a bachelor's degree in music. Lottridge auditioned into the Chicago Symphony Orchestra in 1958, spending seven seasons as the orchestra's contrabassoonist. In a 2019 interview, he laughingly remembered that playing the contrabassoon "was one of the reasons I left.... In seven seasons with an orchestra, you can play nearly all of its literature."[71] Though he certainly had had occasional opportunities to play bassoon in Chicago, he wanted to do more of it.

Lottridge was one of the artist-level faculty recruited by the University School of Music in the 1960s, and he was hired in 1965 to teach bassoon and perform with the resident Wingra Wind Quintet. He remembered that he knew hornist John Barrows and flutist Robert Cole, who were already teaching at the University, and when the bassoon position opened, he applied and got the position. Lottridge noted that he wanted to keep his "hand in orchestra playing and literature," and joined the Madison Civic Symphony, which he described as "a good community orchestra at that time, but one with a lot of potential." It would also allow him to play more of the major orchestral literature. He noted that the experience of playing in the orchestra in 1965 was far different than it is today. When he started with the orchestra in 1965–66, it was still meeting once a week for rehearsals as it had done since the 1920s, meaning that concert preparation was often spread over several weeks. Lottridge, as one of the "rabble rousers on the orchestra committee," was able to effect a change in the schedule: to a single reading rehearsal two weeks prior to the concert, with multiple rehearsals during the concert week, which was much more productive. He also noted that "a few of us who had played in professional orchestras and knew how they worked" began to advocate for changes in the rather informal letter of agreement between the board and musicians regarding pay. By the early 1970s, what came to be known as the master agreement also began to specify working conditions, and in particular the

6.26 Richard (Dick) Lottridge, 2004.

length of rehearsals and overtime, with the benefit that it forced both the players and the conductor to come in prepared, limiting wasted time. Lottridge felt that this was a major factor in improving the quality of the orchestra's performances. He also noted that another major factor in this improvement was the orchestra's move into the Oscar Mayer Theatre in 1980, a space that allowed the orchestra to hear one another.[72]

Like many musicians who performed in the orchestra prior to 1994, when John DeMain became music director, Lottridge had ambivalent memories of Johnson, expressing respect for his legacy, and noting the quality of soloists and repertoire played by the orchestra. However, he also remarked that "while Mr. Johnson clearly valued musicality, he didn't always know how to get it out of the orchestra." He contrasted this with the experience of working with Gunther Schuller, who was one of relatively few guest conductors during Johnson's tenure. Schuller conducted a concert in February 1988, which included the world premiere of his *Concerto for String Quartet and Orchestra*, written for the Pro Arte Quartet and the MSO. The concert also included two more standard pieces of literature, *The Walk to the Paradise Garden* by Delius and Rimsky-Korsakov's *Scheherazade*. He noted that Schuller was demanding, and that "when he really got the strings to play together, it was like, wow! This really shows the potential of the orchestra. [laughs] The sun came up!" Regarding DeMain, he noted: "He knew exactly what he wanted and exactly how to get it. He made the orchestra sound wonderful."[73]

Lottridge retired from the University in 1999, but he remained in the MSO through 2004–5, wanting to play a season in Overture Hall. In the course of 40 seasons, he appeared as soloist nine times:

- Mozart, *Sinfonia Concertante for Oboe, Clarinet, Bassoon, and Horn*, K. C14.01 (3/18/1967).
- Martin, *Concerto for Seven Winds, Timpani, Percussion, and Strings* (3/22/1967 and 1/31/1976).
- Vivaldi, *Concerto in E minor for Bassoon and Cello*, RV 409 (11/29/70)
- Mozart, *Bassoon Concerto*, K. 191 (1/26/1974).
- Bach, *Brandenburg Concerto No. 1*, BWV 1046 (11/17/1974 and 2/9/1985).
- Haydn, *Sinfonia Concertante for Oboe, Bassoon, Violin, and Cello in B-flat Major*, H.I:105 (11/18/1978).
- Weber, *Bassoon Concerto* (1/29/1989).

In his final seasons, Lottridge was able to get an agreement from the orchestra to allow him to play second bassoon and have Cynthia Cameron, one of his former students and the orchestra's longtime second bassoon, play as principal. She would formally succeed him as principal bassoon in 2004–5 and remains in the position today.[74] Lottridge continues to attend most of the MSO's concerts, and he concluded our interview by saying, "I don't think there's an orchestra that has a better spirit than this one. They all want to dig in and do a good job and they're proud to be there."[75]

George and Nancy Shook

The longest-serving current members of the Madison Symphony Chorus, as of early 2024, are baritone George Shook, who joined in the fall of 1966, and alto Nancy Shook, who joined in the fall of 1967—59 and 58 seasons respectively! I interviewed them in January 2023. Like the vast majority of chorus members from 1927 to the present, the Shooks are amateur musicians. Born in Pennsylvania, George came to Madison as a graduate student in 1963 and joined the University faculty as professor of dairy science in 1967. He taught until 2006, when he became an emeritus professor. He remembers hearing his first Madison Civic Orchestra and Chorus concerts as soon as he moved to town. At the time he was dating a flute student at the University, and it was her teacher, Robert Cole (then a member of the orchestra), who encouraged him to join the chorus. Nancy was also born in Pennsylvania, but her family moved to Madison when she was in middle school, and she graduated from West High School. She would earn degrees in nursing and social work, and she had a long career as a nurse in several units at UW Hospital and in community health before retiring in 2009. She also recalled attending Madison Civic Symphony and Chorus concerts on dates (in her case, it was a bassoon player) before she met George in the spring of 1966. She remembered with a chuckle that "our first date was the Britten *War Requiem*."[76] George joined the chorus in the fall of 1966, and Nancy joined a year later. Both of them would eventually perform with the Madison Opera chorus as well.

6.29 Nancy and George Shook, 2023. (Photo by the author.)

The Shooks have a uniquely long view of the development of the Madison Symphony Chorus. Both of them clearly remember Roland Johnson and his work with the chorus with warmth and fondness, and a written tribute by George was quoted earlier in this chapter. Nancy also paid tribute to Arthur Becknell, who served as accompanist in the 1970s, calling him "amazing" and "astonishing." She remembered that Johnson would occasionally decide that a work was too high or too low for the chorus, and would ask for it to be sung in a different key. Becknell was able to transpose choral parts and accompaniments on the spot ... and flawlessly. Both Shooks remembered Ann Stanke with great affection both as an excellent accompanist and as a great chorus manager, who took care of endless details effectively and with humor. (Stanke is profiled below.) Regarding Alan Rieck, who directed the chorus for two seasons following Johnson's retirement, Nancy noted that "it was certainly hard to follow Roland, but he did a very good job with the chorus."

Both of them were enthusiastic about Beverly Taylor, who has directed the chorus since 1996, particularly that her focus was not simply on preparing the music, but also on making them better singers: working on vocal quality, range, and diction. They were thankful for her role in arranging the chorus's 2017 tour to Germany, and both of them were particularly grateful for the efforts of Taylor and Daniel Lyons (Stanke's successor as accompanist/chorus manager) to keep the chorus rehearsing remotely during the Covid pandemic. Regarding DeMain, Nancy said that "we simply love singing under John DeMain," with George adding that the excitement level jumps immediately (and that tempos often get faster) when the chorus combines for rehearsals with DeMain and the orchestra. The one concern expressed by the Shooks—shared by other chorus members I have spoken to—is that over the last 20 years, the Madison Symphony Chorus has often performed just twice each season, as part of the holiday program and on a large choral work near the end of each season.[77] Through the 1990s, the chorus usually performed two substantial choral/orchestral concerts each season, with a third concert featuring the chorus, which was accompanied by piano or organ or by a small group from the MSO.

Ann Stanke

One of the most significant figures in the history of the orchestra, chorus, and opera—from the 1950s through the 2000s—was Ann Stanke (1935–2011). She was born Ann Calhoun in Madison and graduated from West High School in 1952. It was there that she met Ernest Stanke (1912–1986), who was the band and orchestra director at West for 21 years (1945–1965). Ernest played in the Madison Civic Symphony for 40 seasons, as principal viola from 1945 to 1974, and afterward playing as assistant principal viola (1974–1976) and in the first violin section (1976–1984). He was also one of Madison's most prominent church musicians, directing music at Luther Memorial Church and later at First Congregational Church.[78] Ann Calhoun first joined the Madison Civic Symphony as a violist in the 1951–52 season, her senior year of high school. After graduation from high school, she became a student at the University School of Music, where she auditioned on piano, viola, voice, and horn, and won a four-year scholarship. Her studies at the University were cut short when she married and moved to Kansas for a few years. However, she returned to Madison with her young son when this marriage ended in divorce. She rejoined the Madison Civic Symphony's viola section in 1959–60, and in 1961, she married Ernest, her former high school director, who had been widowed in 1960. (His first wife, Mildred Stanke, had been a cellist in the orchestra in the 1950s.) Their marriage would last until his death in 1986, and they raised a blended family, with his son and daughter, her son, and their daughter.[79]

6.30 Ann Stanke, ca. 2000.

In total, Ann Stanke was a member of the MSO for some 49 seasons. She performed as a violist in 1951–52, and then from 1959 to 1987. Her increasingly busy schedule as director of Madison Opera in the late 1980s seems to have obliged her to set aside the viola (though she posed with it in the 2000 photo printed here). However, her most significant performing role with the MSO was as a pianist: Beginning in the early 1960s, she also served as orchestral keyboard player throughout these years, stepping away from the viola section whenever a score called for piano, celeste, or organ. Though her work as orchestra pianist was usually as an ensemble player, Stanke was featured as a soloist, together with Arthur Becknell, in the prominent piano duo part of Saint-Saëns's *Carnival of the Animals* at a subscription program on February 2, 1986. She was later featured as a soloist in two of the orchestra's family concerts, playing excerpts from Beethoven's first and fifth concertos for *Beethoven Lives Upstairs*™ in April 1997, and then playing part of the Tchaikovsky *Piano Concerto No. 1* for *Tchaikovsky Discovers America*™ in April 1998. She would remain the orchestra's pianist through the 2006–7 season.

Stanke also served as rehearsal pianist and manager for the Madison Civic Chorus from 1982 to 2007. Many singers and instrumentalists who performed with her as an accompanist over the years have commented on her powerful and accomplished technique and her sensitivity as an accompanist. Her role with the chorus went well beyond that: As manager, she represented the chorus's interests to the MCMA, but she also took care of innumerable details, overseeing wardrobe, stage presence, and generally organizing the chorus so that Johnson could simply conduct.[80]

Ann was also the rehearsal pianist for the Madison Civic Opera Workshop in its very first performance, *Die Fledermaus*, in 1962, and she was the prompter during the performance. She continued in this dual role for over 40 years, through over 70 productions. However, her most important role with the Madison Opera would eventually be administrative. Stanke became Madison Opera's manager in 1984, first as a volunteer, though she was eventually hired as the company's full-time general manager in 1988. She would remain in this position through 2005, overseeing Madison Opera's transformation into a professional opera company with a national reputation. (She would eventually serve for 10 years on the board of Opera America.) Notably, her tenure included the commission and premiere of a new grand opera, *Shining Brow*, in 1993, Madison Opera's formal separation from MCMA in 1994, and the company's transition into the Overture Center in 2004. She was also a writer, contributing several articles to the *Capital Times* and to Madison's *Brava* magazine over the years.

Ann could be formidable and was clearly unafraid of conflict—even with music directors—when she saw something wrong. I remember, for example, a dress rehearsal for *Aïda* in 1994, the last Madison Opera production Roland Johnson directed as the Opera's music director. Of course, the most spectacular scene in this opera is the great triumphal march in Act II, which includes a fanfare played on "herald" trumpets. The onstage trumpet players—all University students who were unfamiliar with these treacherous instruments—botched the fanfare badly. When Johnson seemed inclined to move on with the rehearsal following this scene, Stanke brought things to a halt, demanding to know what Johnson and the MSO's personnel manager were going to do to remedy the situation. (I'm not sure what happened behind the scenes, but the fanfares during the two performances went relatively well.)

Nor was she afraid of John DeMain, who was capable of losing his temper during his early years in Madison. In December 1995, I was at a rehearsal for a performance of *Messiah* by the Madison Symphony Chorus. A previous rehearsal that week had been canceled due to snow, and many singers who had previous church choir commitments were missing at this hastily scheduled makeup rehearsal. DeMain, frustrated by the missing singers and the chorus's failure to keep up with his tempo, angrily chewed them out. The orchestra—all professional players by this time—had experienced a few outbursts already over the previous few months, and we generally took them in stride, but the all-volunteer chorus had not, and I remember that Ann was clearly furious. In this case, she waited until after the rehearsal to talk to the maestro ... and DeMain made a point to shake every chorus member's hand and thank them after the performance.

Lest these anecdotes give the wrong impression, her reputation among her colleagues was as someone who was thoroughly competent in many ways, friendly, very funny (Nancy Shook called her "droll") and deeply generous.[81] At her retirement as Madison Opera's general manager in 2005, some 500 people gathered in the Overture Center lobby for a celebration in her honor.[82] Ann continued to play keyboard in the MSO and serve as the opera's accompanist for a few years after this until she was stricken with ALS and was unable to play. She died on May 18, 2011, at age 76.[83]

Notes to Chapter 6

1. *WSJ* 2/22/1960, 1; *MCMA Board Minutes* for 3/16/1960 (MSO Archives).
2. *MCMA Board Minutes* for 5/18/1960 and 6/26/1960 (MSO Archives).
3. Interview with Roland Johnson, 8/10/2000.
4. Letter from Walter Heermann to Roland and Arline Johnson, 12/7/1961 (Johnson Papers). Additional letters from Heermann in the Johnson papers written in the first half of 1961 show that Heermann worked actively to make the transition a smooth one: helping to arrange the purchase and rental of music, hiring soloists, overseeing publicity, answering questions from Johnson about venues, and even privately sharing some internal politics and gossipy observations about local musicians.
5. Interview with Roland Johnson, 8/10/2000.
6. Interview with James and Ann Crow, 7/21/2000.
7. *WSJ* 11/23/1961, 37; *CT* 11/23/1961, 34.
8. This was still certainly the case in 1949, as witnessed in Heermann's remarks to the board at the end of his first season, which I quoted in the Chapter 4.
9. The Polish-American Labunski had been one of Johnson's teachers at the Cincinnati College of Music in the 1940s. The orchestra played his *Canto di aspirazione* in October 1963 and his ballet suite *Salut à Paris* in January 1972.
10. In February 1974, the orchestra played King's 1971 *Future Shock*, a fusion of jazz-rock and traditional orchestral music. The performance featured a six-piece electric "jazz-fusion" ensemble.
11. *MCMA Board Minutes* for 10/10/1965 (MSO Archives).
12. *WSJ* 12/16/1974, 21.
13. Robert Palmer, press release, 5/2/1976 (MSO Archives).
14. *Die Fledermaus* was conducted by David Lewis Crosby, conductor of the Wisconsin Chamber Orchestra. He was one of several guest conductors engaged that season as Roland Johnson was recovering from a heart attack.
15. Email note from Stephen Chatman to the author, 10/6/2022.
16. The concept and name for these concerts may have originated with the Cincinnati Symphony Orchestra, which held a very similar series of outreach concerts in the 1940s, when Johnson was a student in Cincinnati, and probably played some of these programs as a substitute member of the orchestra.
17. *MCMA Board Minutes* for 11/23/1962 (MSO Archives).
18. Interview with Robert Palmer, 3/22/2022.
19. Eleanor Anderson, "25 Years—A Silver Jubilee," in *Madison Opera and Guild, 25 Years. 1962-63–1987: A Silver Jubiliee* (Madison: The Madison Opera, 1987), 3–4.
20. *WSJ* 1/14/1963, 23.
21. Anderson, "25 Years," 8.
22. Johnson had actually conducted a very early performance of the opera—less than eight months after its premiere—at the Cincinnati College of Music on February 13, 1951 (*Cincinnati Enquirer* 1/1/ 1951, 15).

23   Interview with Karen and David Kretschmann 10/22/2022.

24   Robert Palmer notes that this move was partly at the invitation of the Union Theater itself, which had previously hosted the productions of the University's Theater Department. Vilas Hall, completed in 1972, included dedicated theaters for the University program, thus leaving much more space in the Union Theater's schedule. (Interview with Robert Palmer, 3/22/2022.)

25   Anderson, "25 Years," 5, 11.

26   Interview with Joel Skornicka, 5/8/2019.

27   See David V. Mollenhoff and Mary Jane Hamilton, *Frank Lloyd Wright's Monona Terrace: The Enduring Power of a Civic Vision* (Madison: University of Wisconsin Press, 1999) for a definitive account covering Wright's life, his connections to Madison, and the building of the Monona Terrace.

28   The most exhaustive account of the local struggles surrounding the Monona Terrace in this period is in Stuart D. Levitan, *Madison in the Sixties* (Madison: Wisconsin Historical Society Press, 2018), where the author treats the cultural and political debates over the auditorium as one of several historical threads he traces throughout the decade.

29   Mollenhoff and Hamilton, *Frank Lloyd Wright's Monona Terrace*, 184–91.

30   The other organizations involved were the Madison Children's Museum, the Madison Art Center, the Madison Civic Repertory theater, and the Wisconsin Chamber Orchestra [MSO Archives].

31   Letter from Joel Skornicka to John Urich, Madison City Planning Department, 10/27/1975 [MSO Archives].

32   Interview with Joel Skornicka, 5/8/2019.

33   Mollenhoff and Hamilton, *Frank Lloyd Wright's Monona Terrace*, 194–234. The opposition to this project over the course of nearly 60 years was driven by many things: fiscal conservatism, genuine aesthetic and environmental concerns, and political and personal enmity toward Wright himself. Indeed, one local joke current in the 1990s was that Monona Terrace could never be built until every Madisonian to whom Wright owed money had died.

34   Email from Terry Haller, 6/12/2024.

35   See Louis Russell Thomas, *A History of the Cincinnati Symphony Orchestra to 1931* (Ph.D. dissertation: University of Cincinnati, 1972).

36   *MCMA Board Minutes* for 4/19/1961 and 5/17/1961 (MSO Archives).

37   *MCMA Board Minutes* for 6/26/1960 (MSO Archives).

38   Interview with Roland Johnson, 8/10/2000; *MCMA Board Minutes* for 10/18/1961, 11/15/1961, and 1/17/1961 (MSO Archives).

39   *MCMA Board Minutes* for 6/26/1963 (MSO Archives).

40   *MCMA Board Minutes* for 4/15/1964 (MSO Archives).

41   Memorandum: Donald Whitaker and Helen Hay to the MCMA board, 3/10/1964 (MSO Archives).

42   Interview with James and Ann Crow, 7/21/2000.

43   *MCMA Board Minutes* for 5/18/1960 (MSO Archives).

44   *MCMA Board Minutes* for 5/19/1965 and 2/17/1966 (MSO Archives).

45   Memorandum: Finance and Ticket Sales Committee, Donald Whitaker, Chair, to the MCMA board, 5/13/1966, in *MCMA Board Minutes* (MSO Archives).

46 *WSJ* 6/19/1966, 42.

47 *CT* 10/24/1969, 37 (first violins); *CT* 11/10/1969, 17 (second violins); *CT* 11/22/1969, 23 (violas); *CT* 12/6/1969, 25 (cellos); *CT* 1/3/1970, 22 (basses and harps); *CT* 1/10/1970, 21 (flutes, oboes, English horn and clarinets); *CT* 1/10/1970, 21 (bassoons and horns); *CT* 1/24/1970, 21 (timpani: James Latimer); and *CT* 1/31/70 (trumpets, trombones, and tuba).

48 Endres's life and work with the Madison Civic Symphony are discussed at the close of Chapter 2. She took a leave of absence during the 1950–51 season, when she was replaced by Shirley Reynolds, but otherwise Endres served as concertmaster from the orchestra's second concert (March 1927) through the May 1960 Orchestra Gala, where she was also a featured soloist, playing the Saint-Saëns *Danse Macabre*.

49 *WSJ* 10/23/1960, 55; obituary, *WSJ* 10/24/2004, 39.

50 Obituary, http://funeralinnovations.com/obituaries/view/31720/2/, accessed 11/15/2022.

51 Annetta Rosser, *An Offering of Song: 48 Songs in English for Medium to High Voice* (Madison: Gilbert Publications, 1977). Rosser's manuscripts, papers, programs, and recordings of her compositions are now held in the Wisconsin Music Archives.

52 Jacob Stockinger, "One of the Lucky ones: Madison musician was one of 10,000 children who escaped the Nazis," *CT* 12/6/2000, A1, A3.

53 Obituary, *WSJ* 6/12/2018, A6.

54 Email correspondence with Barbara Schneider, 6/17/2024. Regarding the Violins of Hope project, see James A. Grymes, *Violins of Hope: Instruments of Hope and Liberation in Mankind's Darkest Hour* (New York: Harper Perennial, 2014). This project was also the subject of a 2016 PBS documentary *Violins of Hope: Instruments of the Holocaust*.

55 *CT* 2/3/1964, 7.

56 Barker, *The Pro Arte Quartet*, 174.

57 Barker, *The Pro Arte Quartet*, 142–54, 166–67.

58 Barker, *The Pro Arte Quartet*, 167; *MSO Program Book* 10/18/1975, 6; Ann Stanke, "Symphony Has New Business Manager, 2 Pro Arte Members," *CT* 9/30/1970, 49.

59 See Allsen, *75 Years of the Madison Symphony Orchestra*, 182.

60 See Allsen, *75 Years of the Madison Symphony Orchestra*, 182.

61 The Paulus performed the work in Oklahoma at least three times between 1965 and 1967. Phone conversation with Joel Levine, former conductor and current archivist of the Oklahoma City Philharmonic (successor to the Oklahoma City Symphony), 11/21/2022.

62 Letter from George Shook to the family of Roland Johnson, 6/7/2012. (Shared with the author by Dr. Shook.)

63 While the Madison Symphony Chorus had already sung Orff's well-known *Carmina Burana* twice prior to 1969, this performance of *Catulli Carmina* must have been one of the first handful of performances of this rarely performed work in the United States. This setting of Latin texts by the Roman poet Catullus was part of a trilogy of large-scale choral works by Orff that included *Carmina Burana* (1936) and *Trionfo de Afrodite* (1951).

64 Cited here as *MCMA50*. There is an unsigned typescript history of the orchestra that had been prepared in 1966 for the 40th anniversary in 1966, which is preserved in the MSO Archives. Ten years later, Anderson wrote an equally useful brief history of the Madison Opera for that group's 25th anniversary in 1986 (Anderson, "25 Years—A Silver Jubilee").

65 Memorandum: Helen Hay to the MCMA board, 3/10/1964 (MSO Archives).

66 Interview with Helen Hay, 6/17/2000.

67 *MCMA Board Minutes* for 4/19/1966 (MSO Archives); *WSJ* 6/9/1968, 70.

68 Memorandum: John Reel to the MCMA board, 1/27/1969 (MSO Archives).

69 In 1987, Cook married long-time MSO principal clarinetist Glenn Bowen, and the two of them retired to Tucson, Arizona, in about 2003. According to a death notice sent by a friend of Cook's, she died in Tucson on February 15, 2024, a few years after Bowen.

70 Interview with Robert Palmer, 3/22/2022. The MSO did in fact program a work by Anton Webern in 1981, his *Passacaglia, Op. 1*. While this early 1908 work by Webern is mostly in a lush late romantic style, rather than the more austere serial style of his later works, Palmer was undoubtedly correct in implying that Webern's name alone was probably enough to scare many audience members!

71 Interview with Richard Lottridge, 6/3/2019.

72 Interview with Richard Lottridge, 6/3/2019.

73 Interview with Richard Lottridge, 6/3/2019.

74 Cameron had been Lottridge's student as an undergraduate at the University and later studied at the Manhattan School of Music. Regarding his successor, Lottridge said, "You know, Cindy is really marvelous.... She could play principal in any orchestra in the country and sound as good as anyone that's there, and that's saying a lot." (Interview with Richard Lottridge, 6/3/2019)

75 Interview with Richard Lottridge, 6/3/2019.

76 Interview with George and Nancy Shook, 1/17/2023. The Britten performance was on May 18, 1966.

77 Interview with George and Nancy Shook, 1/17/2023.

78 Obituary, *WSJ* 7/6/1986, 47.

79 Obituary, *WSJ* 5/22/2011, 20.

80 Interview with George and Nancy Shook, 1/17/2023.

81 I benefited personally from her generosity. Among other things, Ann gave me the unique *Messiah* recording from 1941 that is discussed in Chapters 2 and 4—the earliest surviving recording of the Madison Civic Symphony. I have since donated this disc to the MSO Archives.

82 Jake Stockinger, "Artful Exit," *CT* 6/1/2005, 11, 13; Gayle Worland, "Gala Honors Opera's Star," *WSJ* 6/11/2005, 45, 48.

83 Obituary, *WSJ* 5/22/2011, 20.

CHAPTER 7

Roland Johnson, Music Director 1961–1994

As described in the previous chapter, the Madison Symphony Orchestra's third music director, Roland Johnson, led the orchestra through an unprecedented time of change and transformation in the 1960s and 1970s. Chapter 8 will describe his later years with the MSO and Madison Opera, including what he clearly considered to be one of his greatest accomplishments, the commission and premiere of the opera *Shining Brow*. I played in the orchestra and wrote its program notes for much of his last 11 years, and I was a regular member of the orchestra for his last five seasons. However, it was not until after he retired that I really came to know Roland: through interviews we did for the 75th anniversary chapters and work we did together on the chronicle I wrote in 2001 (a work that I dedicated to him).[1] I have benefited tremendously in this chapter from interviews with his children, Carl Johnson and Karen Kretschmann, and their spouses, Barbara Westfall and David Kretschmann. Karen and David, both singers, were also longtime members of the Madison Civic Chorus and Madison Opera Chorus. The family has kindly granted me full access to his papers, particularly to a collection of memoirs that Roland wrote following his retirement.[2]

Early Life: Johnson City

Roland Albert Johnson was born in Johnson City, Tennessee, in his grandmother's house, on September 14, 1920. His parents, Carl Albert Johnson

(1888–1971) and Anna Laura Christine Dahl Johnson (1891–1982) were both children of parents who had immigrated from Sweden to western Pennsylvania in the early 1880s. The Johnson and Dahl families worked together for a lumber company, and the families moved together to the tiny town of Konnarock, in the Blue Ridge Mountains of southwestern Virginia, near the turn of the century. Johnson's parents were married in nearby Abingdon, Virginia. Carl Johnson moved to Johnson City in about 1910, eventually joined by Anna and his parents; Anna's mother would eventually move to Johnson City as well, purchasing a house a block away. Their three children were widely spaced: Roland's sister Violet Helen was born in 1914 and sister Carolyn in 1935. Johnson was clearly aware of his Swedish heritage. He heard the language spoken at home, and in his memoirs, he refers to his paternal grandfather and grandmother by the Swedish *farfor* and *farmor*, and to his maternal grandparents as *morfor* and *mormor*.[3]

Johnson City at the time of Roland Johnson's birth was a busy and prosperous small city of 12,422, and its population had doubled by 1930. Set in a hilly area west of the Blue Ridge Mountains, it had been founded as a railroad depot in 1856 by merchant Henry Johnson, and the city became an important railroad hub in the late 19th century. Though there had been hard times in Johnson City following the panic of 1893, prosperity returned after the turn of the century, spurred in part by the opening of new rail lines and a major highway connecting to the rest of the state. The East

7.01 Roland Johnson, age 6.

Tennessee Normal School (now East Tennessee State University)—which Johnson would attend in the 1930s—opened in 1911. During Prohibition, Johnson City, with its close proximity to Appalachian moonshine production and multiple transportation connections, was notorious as a "wide open city" where alcohol use was rampant and as a center of bootlegging operations. It was sometimes referred to as "Little Chicago," and Chicago gangster Al Capone reputedly maintained a suite at the local Montrose Hotel.[4] (None of this seems to have affected Johnson, who described his family as churchgoing "teetotalers!")

In scanning local newspapers of the 1930s, it is clear that Johnson City, a relatively prosperous small city, had a relatively active classical music scene, primarily local performers playing in church and school concerts but also featuring occasional touring artists. Nearby Bristol, Tennessee, also had an active Community Concert Association that sponsored concerts by major touring artists. Among the concerts that Johnson recalled hearing in Bristol in the 1930s were programs by flutist Georges Barrère and his chamber orchestra (March 20, 1936), violinist Albert Spalding (December 10, 1936), and Metropolitan Opera tenor Richard Crooks (April 23, 1937).[5] He also described hearing great music on the radio, particularly the Sunday night Ford Music Hour.[6] Johnson does not mention it in his memoirs, but Johnson City was also an important center of what is now broadly known as "American Roots Music." The famous blues guitarist Blind Lemon Jefferson lived there briefly in the early 1920s, playing for tips on the street. Fiddler Charlie Bowman, a major figure in early country music, was born in the hills nearby and performed frequently in and around Johnson City before forming his own string band and touring the country in the 1930s and 1940s. One of the landmark events in the early history of country music was a series of recording sessions conducted in Johnson City in 1928 and 1929 on behalf of Columbia Records' newly formed "hillbilly" division. Several local singers and bands cut records during the sessions, and one of the hits was *Johnson City Blues* by Clarence Greene, a local guitarist who had learned to play the blues by watching Blind Lemon Jefferson.[7]

Johnson's family was comfortably middle class, even during the Depression, and beginning in 1928, his father Carl ran a successful auto dealership, selling Plymouths and DeSotos. A profile of Carl Johnson published in the *Johnson City Press* in October 1935 celebrates his "25 years in the auto business," noting that he had opened the first garage in Johnson City.[8] Roland Johnson mentioned this in his memoirs as well; he noted that his father had the second automobile in town and that the first gas pump in Johnson City still belonged to his niece. Carl Johnson would eventually serve a term as Johnson City's mayor from 1957 to 1959.[9] Johnson noted that his mother Anna played piano and was interested in "bettering" herself and her family by exposing them to education and good music.

7.02 Carl and Anna Johnson, ca. 1938.

Both of his parents supported his later decision to become a musician.

Johnson remembered that he had had some piano lessons when he was in kindergarten, but that they "didn't take." However, at age 10, he was given a violin to start group lessons at school, which he described as "the seminal event in my life," "an explosion," and the beginning of "the first great love affair of my life." His daughter Karen asserted that "as soon as he had that violin in his hand, he really knew who he was."[10] He apparently decided early on that music would be his career. His parents soon arranged for him to take private lessons with a local teacher, Elsie Artz, a Johnson City native who had studied piano and violin at the Cincinnati Conservatory before returning home to start a private music studio. He noted that he was soon playing frequently in recitals and in church: "I had a good vibrato and tone [and] was able to play simple melodious phrases almost immediately."[11] The very first public mention of a Roland Johnson performance was a studio recital at Elsie Artz's home on April 4, 1931, where he played *Little Rose Bud* by William Berold.[12] This was the first of dozens of notices over the next eight years tracing his performances in and beyond Johnson City: playing recitals and school concerts, performing in churches and private homes, and competing in music contests. In April 1934, he played in Knoxville and Chattanooga as part of the statewide Tennessee Federation of Music Clubs contest and won second prize in his division.[13] Two years later, he took first prize in the same competition, and in 1937 he was named concertmaster of the All–East Tennessee Orchestra, as part of the annual state music teachers' convention in Knoxville.[14] By the time he left Johnson City to become a full-time student in Cincinnati in September 1939, Johnson was clearly a local star. For his part, he noted:

> I got a lot of local playing experience, [though] in a bigger city with more competition and better teaching, I would have developed technically much more quickly. I didn't practice much—didn't have to—because not enough was demanded of me and everybody thought I was wonderful. I eventually changed to a different teacher, Margaret Wright [director of the local junior high school orchestra], and I was challenged and began to work more effectively.[15]

Cincinnati

Johnson was able to graduate from Johnson City's Science High School almost two years early, in January 1938. He spent the next year and a half taking courses at East Tennessee Normal School and performing locally. He does not note in his memoirs how he made contact with Emil Heermann,[16] but in 1936 or 1937, Johnson began traveling to Cincinnati for regular lessons with him. (The career of Emil Heermann, then concertmaster of the Cincinnati Symphony Orchestra, was discussed in Chapter 5.) In what was obviously a beloved family story, both of his children related that, although his father took him to Cincinnati for the first few trips, after he had his driver's license at age 16, Johnson drove himself the 325 miles to Cincinnati. To pay for lessons, he would regularly tow a second car back to Johnson City from Cincinnati for his father's auto dealership. It sounds like this trip—while towing another car on partly unpaved roads through mountainous and very remote Kentucky—was sometimes harrowing.[17]

7.03 Roland Johnson, ca. 1937.

In September 1939, Roland Johnson left Johnson City to begin school at the College of Music of Cincinnati on a scholarship. Emil Heermann, with whom he had been studying over the previous two years, was the primary violin teacher there, and this is clearly what drew Johnson to the school. However, he also met another teacher at the College of Music who would have an even more important impact on his later career. Walter Heermann—Emil's brother, and principal cellist of the Cincinnati Symphony Orchestra—was director of the College Orchestra. During Johnson's undergraduate years and later master's study, Walter Heermann would become his primary mentor, particularly after the war, when Johnson returned to school focused on conducting. [Note: In newspaper and other accounts of Johnson's life, there is occasional confusion about which school he attended. In the 1930s and 1940s, there were two separate music schools in Cincinnati: the College of Music of Cincinnati—where the Heermann brothers taught and where Johnson was a student and later a faculty member—and the Cincinnati Conservatory of Music. The two merged in the 1950s to create the present-day Cincinnati College-Conservatory of Music.] He was clearly eager to hear great music, taking every opportunity to observe rehearsals of the Cincinnati Symphony Orchestra—the building that housed the College of Music was adjacent to the orchestra's concert hall—and working frequently as an usher for its programs. (His son Carl has several programs that Johnson saved from this period, including one autographed by Igor Stravinsky.) He also seems to have relished the atmosphere there, where, for the first time in his life, he was surrounded by musicians as good as he was and every bit as passionate about music. In 2002, Johnson returned to Cincinnati for a reunion and made some sketchy notes for some remarks that are preserved in his memoirs. They include fond memories of the music he heard and of his studies with the Heermanns and other faculty. It is also clear from his later letters and memoirs that he forged several deep and lifelong friendships among his fellow College of Music students.

In the summer of 1941, Johnson attended the Juilliard School of Music in New York City, where he studied with violinist Édouard Dethier, whom he credited with "rebuilding my bow arm completely." Though Dethier suggested that he audition for Juilliard for the fall, Johnson decided to finish his senior year in Cincinnati.[18] Newspaper notices in Cincinnati in 1941 and 1942 show Johnson performing frequently outside of the College as a soloist or leading a quartet of his fellow students, performing at the Taft Art Museum, in local churches, and on radio programs. In early 1942, he played the Sibelius *Violin Concerto* with the College Orchestra. He graduated in June 1942 with a bachelor of music degree in violin performance "with highest distinction."[19] In his memoirs, Johnson remembered that he was able to spend the summer after graduation living at the mansion of Helene Wurlitzer, one of Cincinnati's leading patrons of the arts. Wurlitzer, whose fortune came from her husband's musical instrument business, was a trustee of the College of Music and frequently hosted its students at her home.[20] He initially returned to start a master's degree in September, and on November 3, 1942, was soloist in the Saint-Saëns *Introduction and Rondo Capriccioso* with the College of Music Orchestra, directed by Walter Heermann.

Navy Service and a New Career Path

By November 1942, nearly a year into the United States' involvement in World War II, 22-year-old Roland Johnson was eminently draftable. In his memoirs, he wrote that Cincinnati Symphony Orchestra conductor Eugene Goossens offered him a position in the violin section, and even wrote to his draft board on his behalf, though this was not successful. Instead, Johnson volunteered for the U.S. Navy. There was initially a promise from the Navy that he could perform in the Navy's Great Lakes Naval Training Station Orchestra, but after he enlisted, there were no slots left in the orchestra. Given his musical talents, Johnson was sent to the Fleet Sonar School in Key West, Florida. He was quickly given a position as a trainer, and he would spend the rest of the war in Key West. Clearly one of his favorite stories—related to me in 2000 and by both of his children—concerned what he wryly called "my great contribution to the war effort." At the time, German U-boats were having a devastating

7.04 Johnson in Key West, ca. 1943.

effect on shipping off the American East Coast, and sonar was becoming a major factor in successfully detecting and destroying enemy submarines. However, the crude sonar of the time used a set of half and whole tones to signal whether a target was approaching or receding and its relative speed. Johnson began training sonar operators to sing the opening few notes of Irving Berlin's 1942 hit *White Christmas* as a way to distinguish half and whole tones.

His daughter Karen notes that her father and his Navy buddies bought a 21-foot sailboat that they would use to get into town, and Johnson recalled that they also used it to fish for plentiful snapper and grouper "that practically jumped onto the hook" (undoubtedly a welcome addition to Navy rations). Johnson seems to have wasted little time finding opportunities to play, and in 1943 there are several notices in the *Key West Citizen* of occasions when he played for Sunday services and concerts at the Congregational Church and St. Paul's Episcopal Church. Carl Johnson notes that he also performed frequently at the homes of "ladies of means" throughout his time in Key West.

In December 1943, Johnson organized a chorus and orchestra made up of about 100 Navy personnel and civilians from Key West to mount a performance of Handel's *Messiah*. He worked with Stanley Plummer, who seems to have been in charge of the base choir, though Johnson conducted the performance. It took place on December 26, 1943, at the Episcopal Church.[21] Johnson remembered that it was a huge success in the community: the church was already packed an hour before the performance, and many more people sat outside the open windows to hear it. Both Johnson's memoirs and his children assert that this conducting debut put him on a new path. He would become a conductor. It also left him with a lifelong fondness for *Messiah*. He later programmed the oratorio at both the Cincinnati College of Music and the University of Alabama.[22] When he arrived in Madison in 1961, the Madison Civic Symphony and Chorus already had a long-established association with *Messiah*, and Johnson would conduct 14 complete performances of the work during his 33-year tenure there.

Johnson also seems to have put his leaves to good musical use. In the summer of 1944, he briefly attended the Summer Musical Institute at Black Mountain College, the famous experimental and progressive liberal arts school in North Carolina. During the war years, musicologist Heinrich Jalowitz organized free-form summer sessions that included performances, lectures, and discussions between students and a revolving faculty that included prominent performers and composers. The summer session in 1944 included violinist Rudolf Kolisch (of the Pro Arte Quartet), harpsichordist Yella Pesel, composers Aaron Copland, Ernst Krenek, Virgil Thomson, and Mark Brunswick, dancers Agnes de Mille and Doris Humphrey, and others. Johnson referred to this as a "fascinating look into another musical world."[23]

On an earlier leave in 1943, Johnson returned to Cincinnati and met Gunther Schuller (1925–2015), who would become a close friend and one of Johnson's most important musical colleagues. Schuller, a horn prodigy, joined the Cincinnati Symphony as principal horn in 1943 at age 17 and remained there until 1945, when he moved on to the Metropolitan Opera Orchestra. While in Cincinnati, he taught horn at the College of Music, and he came to deeply admire Walter Heermann, who was also, of course, his colleague in the orchestra. (As noted in Chapter 5, one of Schuller's first large compositions was a cello concerto written for Heermann in 1945.) In his 2011 autobiography, Schuller remembered that Johnson "not only became one of my best friends and colleagues but also played a significant role in my young life as a composer by commissioning and premiering one of my earliest orchestral works" and that "within hours of getting to know Roland I knew that he was a musical soul mate, and particularly one whose interest in music and the other arts were almost as wide-ranging as mine. We knew instantly that we were destined to be close, long-time friends." Schuller would later emerge as one of America's leading composers, experimenting with crossovers between jazz and contemporary classical form (what he labeled "Third Stream" music), and as an advocate for ragtime and other American styles. The two renewed their friendship in 1946, shortly after Johnson was discharged and had returned to Cincinnati for graduate school, when Schuller returned to Cincinnati for a short visit.[24] It is clear that Johnson returned Schuller's friendship and respect, both in letters preserved in his papers and in his later programming of many of Schuller's works.

7.05 Gunther Schuller, 1943.

Graduate Study and Teaching at the Cincinnati College of Music

Like millions of newly demobilized World War II veterans, Johnson used the G.I. Bill to fund college. Shortly after his discharge from the Navy in February

1946, he was back in Cincinnati, picking up the graduate study that had been cut short in 1942. His earlier work at the College of Music had been focused primarily on the violin; Johnson seems initially to have been destined for a career as a performer. As a master's student, he continued to study violin with Emil Heermann, and soon after he returned to Cincinnati, he was featured as soloist in the Chausson *Poéme* with the College Orchestra (January 24, 1947).[25] However, his focus was now on conducting, and his relationship with Walter Heermann became particularly important. Johnson remembered him fondly a half century later as "my most important mentor in Cincinnati," while Heermann's daughter Paulita Heermann Neal noted in 2020 that "my dad had a lot of protégés at the College, but Roland was clearly his favorite."[26] From 1946 through 1948, Johnson frequently appeared as an assistant conductor in concerts of the College Orchestra. In a 1947 interview, Heermann wryly referred to him as Cincinnati's "Lesser Johnson" (the "Greater Johnson" being the Cincinnati Symphony Orchestra's recently hired music director Thor Johnson). In discussing Johnson's role as assistant conductor, Heermann said that "I realized that the hardest thing for the young American conductor, in spite of the excellent technical training in our schools, is lack of technique and the opportunity to develop it."[27]

This would in fact be one of the most important relationships in Johnson's later career. When Heermann left the College of Music in 1948 to move to Madison, Johnson became his handpicked successor as conductor of the College Orchestra. (Johnson recalled that he not only inherited Heermann's job, he also occupied Heermann's apartment in Cincinnati.) As discussed in Chapter 5, Heermann also seems to have groomed Johnson to succeed him as director of the Springfield Symphony Orchestra, an amateur orchestra in nearby Springfield, Ohio, that Heermann had conducted in 1946–47 and 1947–48. Johnson was listed as assistant conductor and

7.06 Walter Heermann and Roland Johnson, January 1947.

directed several pieces on the orchestra's concerts in 1947–48, but if having Johnson succeed him in that post was Heermann's intent, this did not happen. However, Heermann would be successful in recruiting Johnson to succeed him as music director of the Madison Civic Symphony and Chorus in 1961.

While he was a graduate student in Cincinnati, Johnson spent the summers of 1946 and 1947 at the Tanglewood Festival, enrolling in 1947 as a conducting student. The festival had been founded in the 1930s as the summer home of the Boston Symphony Orchestra, and by the postwar years its Berkshire Music Center hosted one of the nation's largest summer festivals.[28] Johnson remembered that he had to audition for Leonard Bernstein and that in 1946 he heard the first American performance of Benjamin Britten's opera *Peter Grimes*. In 1947, he studied choral conducting with Robert Shaw and Hugh Ross. That summer he sang with a festival chorus that performed and recorded Beethoven's *Symphony No. 9* with Serge Koussevitsky and the Boston Symphony Orchestra. He recalled that "the whole Tanglewood experience was a great one for me—it expanded my horizons."[29]

He made his first trip to Europe in the summer of 1950, and it seems to have been a pilgrimage to hear as much opera as possible. In his memoirs, he recounts seeing Wilhelm Furtwängler conduct *Fidelio* in Salzburg, with Kirsten Flagstad as Leonora and Elisabeth Schwarzkopf as Marzelline, and also hearing Hans Hotter as Wotan in Bayreuth, among many other opera performances.

Johnson was part of the faculty at the Cincinnati College of Music for four years, from 1948–49 through 1951–52. (He officially received his master's degree in 1950.) His primary duty was conducting the College Orchestra, though he notes in his memoirs that he also conducted the chorus and opera productions at the school[30] and taught conducting. Johnson also appeared as a guest conductor on several occasions with Cincinnati's Orpheus Club, a long-established community chorus. It was a perfect training ground for a young conductor: the College Orchestra traditionally gave four concerts each year and also played for opera productions and other performances, allowing him to work through a great deal of repertoire. Johnson's programming for the orchestra was progressive and reflected his interest in contemporary music. Contemporary pieces he led in this period included Stravinsky, *Symphony of Psalms*, Vaughan Williams, *Serenade to Music*, Diamond, *Young Joseph*, Khachaturian, *Piano Concerto*, Vaughan Williams, *Oboe Concerto*, Milhaud, *Protée*, Poulenc, *Concerto for Organ, Strings, and Timpani*, Britten, *Festival Te Deum*, Villa-Lobos, *Bachianas Brasileiras No. 5*, Barber, *Knoxville: Summer of 1915*, and Prokofiev, *Piano Concerto No. 3*.[31] As a conductor, Johnson was also deeply involved with the annual Contemporary Music Symposiums sponsored by the College of Music each spring from 1949 onward. These events included lectures and performances focusing on the work of contemporary American composers. On April 14, 1949, for example, he conducted the following program, all of them works written within the previous seven years:

- Peter Mennin, *Folk Overture* (1945)
- Walter Piston, *Prelude and Allegro for Organ and Strings* (1944)
- William Schuman, *A Free Song* (1942)
- Virgil Thomson, *The Seine at Night* (1947)
- Aaron Copland, *Four Dance Episodes from "Rodeo"* (1942/43)[32]

During his first year as conductor of the College Orchestra, Johnson commissioned a work by Gunther Schuller—something he remembers "with lifelong pride" in his memoirs. Johnson conducted the premiere of *Symphonic Study* on May 31, 1949. (Schuller would restore its previous title, *Meditation*, when he recorded the work in the 1990s.) Schuller recalled that the "unorthodox instrumentation," which included unusually large woodwind and brass sections (including six flutes, five oboes, six horns, and four trombones) was that, following the war years,

> his [1948–49] student orchestra still had a rather unbalanced woodwind section. There was still a serious shortage of male students, many having acquired other skills in the army during the war that took them away from music; in some cases, they were still finishing their tours of duty. As a result, he had in his woodwind section six female flutists, five oboists, a mere two clarinets and one bass clarinet and only two bassoons (no contrabassoon). On the other hand, he had six horns in the brass section.... That's why my *Adagio for Orchestra* (soon renamed *Meditation*, but eventually ending up with a more prosaic title *Symphonic Study*) sports such an oddly balanced wind section. In effect, I simply accepted the odd instrumentation of Roland's orchestra. I could have settled for a typical Mozartean orchestra of winds and horns in [pairs], but I became fascinated with the idea of having the luxury of six flutes, five oboes, and six horns, never mind that this produced a strangely unbalanced wind and brass section. This has been, of course, a serious impediment to further performances, since orchestra managers, always mindful of the financial bottom line, are rather reluctant to hire three extra flutists, two extra oboists, and two extra horns, while one of the orchestra's clarinetists, and one bassoonist sit idle and receive their usual salary.[33]

This work can be heard today in Schuller's 1998 recording. It is very much a piece of the postwar *avant-garde*: an uncompromising essay in serial (twelve-tone) writing.³⁴

Johnson's conducting in Cincinnati attracted a few admiring reviews. For example, on April 4, 1949, he conducted the Cincinnati Little Symphony (a chamber orchestra made up of players from the Cincinnati Symphony Orchestra) and students from the dance department of the College of Music in Samuel Barber's 1947 ballet *Medea*. John Rhodes of *The Cincinnati Enquirer* wrote:

> The talented young conductor obviously had studied the score with sympathetic care and perception. His beat was precise, though not inflexible. The orchestra responded with great assurance and found its way through the intricate rhythms with considerable finesse.³⁵

On March 13, 1950, he led a College of Music opera double bill of Pergolesi's *The Music Master* and Puccini's *Suor Angelica*. Eleanor Bell of *The Cincinnati Post* noted that "Roland Johnson coordinated the efforts on both sides of the footlights with skill and assurance."³⁶ Johnson was succeeded as director of the College Orchestra by William C. Byrd.³⁷

Johnson as a Composer

An important part of Johnson's graduate study was the composition class of Felix Labunski (1892–1979), which expanded his knowledge of contemporary styles. Labunski was part of the wave of composers who emigrated to the United States from Europe in the years before World War II. Labunski came to the United States from Poland in 1936 and became an American citizen in 1941. Like many of his fellow émigrés, he found security in teaching, and he taught at several American universities before arriving at the Cincinnati College of Music in 1945. He would remain at the College (later College-Conservatory) until his retirement in 1964. While Labunski's style is occasionally described as "romantic," his music was in fact based upon a large range of techniques and a creative conception of harmony.³⁸ For Johnson's part, he clearly admired Labunski and his engagement with contemporary styles:

7.07 Felix Labunski, ca. 1951.

> I have always been an advocate of new music—therefore on my

return to the College from the Navy in 1946 it was a breath of fresh air to find a new faculty member in Felix Labunski. Felix, who was Polish, studied in the 1920s in Paris as a pupil of Paul Dukas and Nadia Boulanger. He was friends with Arthur Honegger and Francis Poulenc ... and for a short time was secretary to Prokofiev prior to his return to Russia. Felix quickly developed a circle of young composers.[39]

Johnson was clearly part of that circle. He mentions that, when Poulenc came to perform his *Piano Concerto in G Major* with the Cincinnati Symphony Orchestra, Labunski brought the French composer into their composition class, and that he was able to show Poulenc his woodwind quartet.

Johnson's papers preserve dozens of pages of compositional sketches and eight compositions from this period and earlier:

- *One Perfect Love*—art song, for medium voice and piano, setting a poem by Dorothy Parker. What appears to be a later note on one of two copies of this song notes that it was written in "Key West, ca. 1943, for Emily."

- *Prelude for Flute and Piano*—cover page of the autograph is inscribed "To Petunia" (dated Oct. 1946).

- *Trio for Flute, Viola, and Cello*—probably survives incomplete: the surviving piece, a 90-measure work in sonata form, is labeled "1st Mvt."

- *Stopping by a Woods on a Snowy Evening*—art song for medium voice and piano, setting the well-known Robert Frost poem. (undated).

- *It Was a Lover and His Lass*—eight-voice madrigal, setting a text by Shakespeare (undated).

- *Have Mercy on Me, O Lord*—SATB motet, setting of Psalm 56 (undated).

- *Quartet for Flute, Oboe, Clarinet, and Bassoon*—two surviving movements of a planned three-movement work (dated April 1947).

- *Song for Orchestra with Mezzo-soprano*—identified in autograph as "Opus 1" (dated "Oct. 12, 1947"). This art song, accompanied by full orchestra, sets part of the Goethe poem *An die Entfernte*, in an English lyric translation: *For the Parted One*.

J. MICHAEL ALLSEN

7.08 Roland Johnson, *It Was a Lover and His Lass* (ca. 1947, ed. J. M. Allsen), mm. 1–11.

These are clearly the works of a talented student, and I would like to discuss a few of them here. I found his madrigal *It Was a Lover and His Lass* to be particularly engaging. This is a well-known text by Shakespeare, included in the comedy *As You Like It*. It was famously set as a madrigal and as a lute song by Shakespeare's contemporary Thomas Morley, but it was also set to music by 20th-century composers: Frederic Delius, Gerald Finzi, Arthur Foote, Roger Quilter, and several others. Johnson's response is a setting of the text filled with madrigalesque word-painting, and which makes particularly witty use of Shakespeare's nonsense refrains ("hey nonino," etc.). The texture is mostly SATB, but all four lines include multiple *divisi* passages, so a performance of this challenging *a capella* work would require eight singers.[40] It is clear that this was the work of a young composer who was showing off his familiarity with a whole host of modernist idioms: modal writing, octatonic scales, free dissonance, quartal and quintal harmonies (harmonies based upon stacked fourths and fifths), and freely shifting meters. All of these idioms are in fact typical of music by his teacher, Labunski.[41] He also uses melodic inversion (as in the soprano and bass in mm. 4–8 in the example above), possibly as a nod to Labunski's interest in serial (twelve-tone) writing. It is amusing that this piece, which includes only a few recognizable triadic harmonies in its 75 measures, ends with a *fortissimo* D Major chord! In contrast, Johnson's much less cheerful choral motet *Have Mercy on Me, O Lord* is an exercise in serial writing, its opening point of imitation presenting four transpositions of a twelve-tone row.

The two largest, and possibly latest, works listed here may have been the capstones of his study with Labunski. The *Quartet for Flute, Oboe, Clarinet, and Bassoon* seems to have been planned as a substantial chamber work in three movements, but only two movements survive in Johnson's papers. The opening *Passacaglia*, written in what is clearly a "fair copy," is an intensely chromatic and rather academic piece in F minor, with a dissonant introduction and 18 statements of an 8-measure *passacaglia* theme that modulates to several different keys, and which is occasionally absorbed completely into the texture. While the title page indicates three movements—*I. Passacaglia, II. Aria,* and *III. Rondo*—I found no trace of the *Aria* in his papers. The *Rondo*—also in F minor—survives in two versions: what is clearly a preliminary score, with several sections crossed out and reworked, and a fair copy. Johnson apparently changed his mind regarding the title, crossing out *Rondo* on the fair copy in favor of *Finale*. The piece, however, does have the essentials of classically structured rondo: versions of the lively, syncopated opening music appear five times in the course of the movement's 204 measures to tie the piece together. The final contrasting episode is an extended and intense fugato. Johnson's memoirs note that this work won a composition prize in 1947.

Johnson's *Song for Orchestra with Mezzo-soprano*, his only surviving work for orchestra, is a setting of a wistful poem by Goethe, in a lyrical translation (a rhymed translation intended for singing) by 19th-century American poet Christopher Pearse Cranch.

> *To the Parted One*
>
> And thou art now no longer near!
> From me, O fairest, thou hast flown!
> Nor rings in my accustomed ear
> A single word — a single tone.
>
> As when, at morn, the wanderer's eye
> Pierces the air in vain to see
> Where, hidden in the deep-blue sky,
> High up the lark goes singing free —
>
> So wanders anxiously my gaze
> Piercing the field, the bush, the grove;
> On thee still call my frequent lays:
> O, come to me again, dear love.

This expressionistic and rather haunting setting is carefully bound together by a duplet motive (in 6/8 meter) that appears several times in the work and is heard at the beginning of the orchestral introduction. The voice enters with a lyrical melody for the opening stanza above a dense, chromatic accompaniment. The texture changes for the more pastoral second verse, with pianissimo string tremolos, and a prominent set of harp solos. The third verse hints occasionally at the opening rhythmic texture, though it heightens the tension with switches to 5/8. At the very end there is a reprise of the introduction in muted strings before the singer's final line, "come to me, dear love," and a quiet conclusion in E minor.

Studies with Hermann Scherchen

In 1952, Johnson received one of the first fellowships from the recently established Fleischmann Foundation, which funded a year's study in Europe with conductor Hermann Scherchen (1891–1966).[42] Johnson expressed special pride—both to me and in his memoirs—in having studied with one of the 20th century's great conductors, and his daughter Karen called it a "life-changing experience."[43] Scherchen, born in Berlin, became one of Europe's leading conductors and was associated throughout his life with contemporary music. He had a particularly close relationship with the composers of the "Second Vienna School" (Arnold Schoenberg, Alban Berg, and Anton Webern), conducting performances and premieres of works by all of them, beginning with his preparation of Schoenberg's *Pierrot lunaire* in 1912. (Schoenberg conducted the premiere, but Scherchen directed rehearsals and later performances that year while it was on tour.) As a violinist, he led a quartet that specialized in contemporary works during the 1920s, and he also founded the contemporary music journal *MELOS* in 1919. Scherchen continued to champion contemporary works after the Second World War, when he was associated with the influential Darmstadt International Summer Course for New Music, and he conducted works by many of the younger generation of composers leading the European postwar *avant-garde*: Bruno Maderna, Luigi Dallapiccola, Pierre Boulez, Karlheinz Stockhausen, Luigi Nono, Hans Werner Henze, Iannis Xenakis, and others.[44] He was also a respected pedagogue of conducting: His 1929 *Lehrbuch des Dirigierens* (translated in 1933 as *Handbook of Conducting*) was a standard text.[45]

7.09 Johnson and Hermann Scherchen in Naples, 1952.

Johnson arrived in London in September 1952, and he began his studies with Scherchen in October in Rapallo, Italy. He recalled that they began with an in-depth study of Bach's *Cantata No. 1* (*Wie schön leuchtet der Morgenstern*, BWV 1). According to Johnson, this experience "opened me to the remarkable order and power of his music" and began a lifelong fascination with Bach. Scherchen at the time was active as a guest conductor and conducting at festivals. Over the next six months, Johnson and a German student, Hilmar Schatz, accompanied Scherchen on his travels to Naples, Zürich, Vienna, Paris, London, and back to Italy. (Schatz would later become a successful conductor and writer in Germany.) His son Carl notes that Johnson and Schatz would alternate in leading rehearsals, and choral preparation when necessary.[46] This work, together with Scherchen's critiques, was undoubtedly invaluable experience for Johnson. However, Johnson also seems to have relished the opportunity to hear performances all through Europe, remembering that he heard the reigning Italian *prima donna assoluta* of the age, Renata Tebaldi, sing Desdemona in Verdi's *Otello* while they were in Naples in late 1952. He also heard Maria Callas in Florence in May 1953. On the other end of the stylistic scale, he reports that, while he was in London, he heard some early performances of *musique concrète* (*avant-garde* works created on magnetic tape) by Pierre Schaeffer. Traveling with the well-connected and widely respected Scherchen also gave Johnson an *entrée* to a wide range of European musicians, including established figures like composers Ralph Vaughan Williams and Humphrey Searle, and musicologist Egon Wellesz, all of whom he met while in England. Given Scherchen's work in contemporary music, Johnson also met many of the leading figures of the postwar *avant-garde*. His memoirs mention meeting Luigi Nono in Rapallo, meeting Pierre Boulez and Karlheinz Stockhausen on the Left Bank in Paris, a memorable night out in Munich with Hans Werner Henze, and a party at Hilmar Schatz's home in Böblingen, where Johnson played four-hand Schubert piano pieces with composer Bruno Maderna. His daughter Karen notes that in 1991, she accompanied him on a tour through Germany and Italy that retraced part of his travels with Scherchen.[47] He returned to the United States in June 1953, staying with his parents in Johnson City while he began a job search. In August, he interviewed for and was offered a position at the University of Alabama in Tuscaloosa.

Alabama

Johnson was initially hired by the University of Alabama to conduct choirs and teach elective voice lessons, though he almost immediately began guest conducting with the University Symphony Orchestra, and by 1954, he was officially listed as conductor of the orchestra as well. He made his debut as a conductor in Alabama on November 8, 1953, at a Festival of French Music with Honegger's *King David*.[48] Johnson's eight years at Alabama were intensely busy, as he prepared multiple orchestral, choral, and opera performances each school year. He was also engaged as a performer throughout his tenure in Alabama. Johnson had been involved with the Contemporary Music Symposium while he was at the Cincinnati College of Music. Beginning in the spring of 1954, he was deeply involved with a similar annual program at Alabama, the Southeastern Composers Forum, which had been established about five years earlier. He recalled:

> Professional composers submitted works that were read and recorded (symphonic works, concerti, or works with chorus). Each year [featured] a famous composer and one of his works.... The University Orchestra prepared about 20 works submitted for the weekend of the forum. A number of professional players from area symphonies and teachers at southeastern schools were invited to perform and guest conduct. After the reading, the guest composer selected about three works to be repeated for the Sunday afternoon concert as the first half of the concert. For the second half I conducted a selected piece from the guest composer. For instance: Lukas Foss, *Parable of Death for Chorus, Orchestra, and Narrator* (with Arline), Vincent Persichetti, *Symphony No. 3*, Wallingford Riegger, *Symphony No. 3*, Norman Dello Joio, *Song of Affirmation, for Four Soloists, Chorus, Orchestra, and Narrator* (Dello Joio himself) on a text by Stephen Vincent Benét, [and] Ernst Krenek, *Eleven Transparencies*.[49]

Johnson received a bit of national attention in March 1957 when he was selected to conduct the National Civic Orchestra at the Interlochen National Music Camp in the summer of 1957.[50]

Johnson continued to perform as a violinist throughout his time in Alabama. The first notice I have found was during his first year there, in March 1954, when he was one of four string players joining the resident Čadek Quartet to play the Mendelssohn *Octet*.[51] The primary violin teacher when Johnson arrived in Tuscaloosa was Ottokar Čadek, who had been a member of the renowned New York Quartet in the 1920s and 1930s. Čadek tragically died on stage while performing in July 1956 at the Interlochen National Music Camp.[52] Johnson joined two remaining members of the Čadek Quartet—violist Henry Barnett and cellist Margaret Christy—and pianist Roy McAllister at a memorial concert for Čadek on November 10, 1956.[53] This ensemble performed as the Alabama

7.10 The Alabama Quartet in the late 1950s: Emil Raab, violin, Henry Barnett, viola, Margaret Christy, cello, and Roland Johnson, violin.

Quartet throughout the 1956–57 school year, and Johnson also seems to have taken over temporarily as violin teacher. When violinist Emil Raab was hired in the fall of 1957 to replace Čadek, the Alabama Quartet was reconstituted as a string quartet with Raab, Johnson, Barnett, and Christy. Over the next four years, the quartet performed frequently in Tuscaloosa and also toured widely around the state. The quartet was also involved in the Composers Forum, and together with many contemporary works, they presented the premieres of Vincent Persichetti's *String Quartet No. 3* and Ross Lee Finney's *String Quartet No. 8* during Johnson's tenure.

Johnson first met Arline Hanke—his "second great passion"—during his job interview at Alabama in 1953. She had joined the voice faculty at Alabama in 1943 and was also director of the University's Opera Workshop. (She is profiled later in this chapter.) In his memoirs, Johnson recalled that his interview with the voice faculty took place at her apartment, and that "before they came, I sat down at the piano. There was a book of contemporary songs which I knew. I started playing a beautiful Debussy song and Arline came into the room singing it—such a beautiful voice!" They began collaborating almost immediately when Johnson arrived in Tuscaloosa. He relates how Arline introduced him to Howard Goodson, a friend of hers in the art department, and the three of them designed some unique lighting effects for his innovative "semi-staged" version of *King David* that November. Johnson also seems to have helped Hanke in a production of the musical *Carousel* that spring. Over the next six years, they collaborated on several opera productions, beginning in November 1954 when he directed her and members of the Opera Workshop in a brief one-act opera, *Riders to the Sea* by Vaughan Williams. They followed this in February with a double bill: Pergolesi, *La serva padrona* and Foss, *The Jumping Frog of Calaveras County*.[54] He notes that she made it clear from the start that it was to be an equal partnership: she as stage director and he as music director, setting the pattern they would later follow in Madison. Their first full-scale opera together was Puccini's *La Bohème* on November 18–19, 1955, with Johnson leading the full University Symphony Orchestra in the pit. This was a lavish production, featuring the reigning Miss Alabama, Patricia Huddleston (then a music student at the University), as Mimi, and a mixture of University students, faculty, and professional singers in the other roles.[55]

At the end of the 1955–56 academic year, Roland and Arline added a new element to their partnership. They were married in Tuscaloosa, at the University of Alabama's Canterbury Chapel, on May 19, 1956.[56] They left for an extended honeymoon: four months in Europe. Johnson reports that they bought a new Ford Anglia on arriving in London and put on "several thousand miles." Not surprisingly, much of this trip was devoted to opera— Arline later recalled that they "attended 35 different operas, seeing what innovative things others were doing." They spent a week at Bayreuth and a week at the Salzburg Festival (where they saw four different Mozart works), and he also recalled seeing *Aïda* and *Mosè in Egitto* in Rome, *Pelléas et Mélisande* (with the original 1902 sets) in Paris, and *Samson et Dalilah* in London, before returning to Alabama in time to start the school year.[57] Their son Carl was born in January 1958.

7.11 Johnson and Arline Hanke, ca. 1956.

The Johnsons would partner on four more productions before they left the University of Alabama:

- Mozart, *Così fan tutte* in November 1956. This was performed twice, and then again 10 days later for a live television broadcast.
- Single acts from Verdi, *Aïda* and Wagner, *Die Meistersinger* in November 1957.
- Menotti, *The Consul* in November 1958.
- Handel, *Acis and Galatea* in November 1959.[58]

They were also frequently involved in the late 1950s with the nearby Birmingham Civic Opera, particularly in helping with auditions.[59]

Johnson left Alabama in 1961 to take the position in Madison. As described in the previous chapter, this job offer was partly engineered by Johnson's old mentor from the Cincinnati College of Music, Walter Heermann, who also actively lobbied with Johnson to take the job. However, one factor that led the Johnsons to leave Tuscaloosa came from the University of Alabama itself. In 1960, Roland Johnson was offered tenure by the University, but Arline, who was equally qualified, and who in fact had been at the University for 10 years longer than her husband, was not. Their children feel that both of their parents saw this as an injustice, making the decision to leave Alabama easier.[60]

Arline Hanke Johnson

Roland Johnson's wife and his most important artistic partner, Arline Hanke, was born in Chicago on April 18, 1919, to Julius and Dorothy Hanke. Both parents were amateur musicians and sang in church choirs. According to a 1975 profile published in Madison, Arline made her public singing debut at age three, singing *Away in a Manger* with her father at Chicago's Pilgrim Lutheran Church. Her son Carl said that she graduated from high school in Chicago, but at roughly that time, her father lost his job at a Chrysler dealership during the economic downturn of 1936–1937. He was offered a job at a dealership in Montgomery, Alabama, and Arline

7.12 Arline Hanke and her parents, ca. 1925.

moved to Alabama after graduation, joining her father and sister Dolores. (Her mother had died in 1927, just a few months after giving birth to Dolores.) Julius Hanke had already started singing in a church choir, and she accompanied him one night to rehearsal. The director also directed the choir at Montgomery's Huntington College—a small Methodist liberal arts college, at that time exclusively for women—and immediately offered her a scholarship as a voice major.[61] She graduated from Huntington in 1941 with a bachelor's degree in voice and public school music. Hanke then took a four-month tour of Europe, "visiting opera houses in eight countries."[62] She then moved on to the Eastman School of Music in Rochester, New York, where she earned a master's degree and a performer's certificate in voice in 1942. In March of that year, she was a soloist with the Rochester Civic Orchestra, conducted by Howard Hanson, singing *Pace, pace, mio Dio* from Verdi's *La forza del destino*.[63] She would later study at the Juilliard School of Music, Columbia University, the University of Syracuse, and the Cincinnati Conservatory of Music.[64]

In 1943, Hanke moved to Tuscaloosa to join the faculty of the University of Alabama. Programs preserved by her family show that she was an active recitalist at Alabama, performing frequently with pianists Roy McAllister and Margaret Rodgers, violinist Ottokar Čadek, and cellist Margaret Christy (who was her roommate in Tuscaloosa for several years, and who would later move to Madison). She would regularly produce operas at the University of Alabama as a stage director, for example, leading a production of *Carmen* in August 1948. Hanke would also appear throughout the region as a soloist, singing the Verdi *Requiem* with the Birmingham Symphony Orchestra in March 1953, and Honegger's *King David* with the Chattanooga Symphony Orchestra in March 1954. She apparently shared some of the lighting effects developed for the "semi-staged" *King David* production that she, Johnson, and Howard Goodson had arranged earlier in Tuscaloosa. A letter written to Johnson while she was on this visit provides a taste of her humor, and their shared (and sometimes snarky) passion for opera:

7.13 Arline Hanke in 1941.

> Dear Roland - Have charmingly oozed my way through the first day of this gathering of resonators—met Mr. Duke tonight & we're going to practice at 1:30 tomorrow.... Saw the most awful "Cavalleria" tonight that you could possibly imagine. [Tenor] Ralph Erolle is worse than I remembered. (He's the one who told me that I was in the change of larynx!)[65]

She also moonlighted as a soloist at Tuscaloosa's First Presbyterian Church and at Temple Beth-Or, a synagogue in nearby Birmingham. Arline Johnson left the faculty of the University of Alabama at the end of the 1959–60 academic year, a year before her husband; presumably the result of the tenure decision discussed above.

According to Arline, she arrived in Madison prepared to abandon her career. However, on October 22, 1961—the day that Roland Johnson made his debut with the Madison Civic Symphony—*Wisconsin State Journal* staff writer Carmen Elsner published a feature story titled "Johnson and Johnson: They're a Team," that highlighted their partnership in Alabama and hinted that Arline was not quite ready to give up on opera.[66] By this time, the Johnsons had in fact already been approached by a group of about two dozen singers about starting an opera company in Madison, the beginnings of what would become the Madison Civic Opera Guild and eventually the Madison Opera. The history of this group prior to its final organizational split from the Madison Symphony Orchestra in 1994 is discussed in Chapters 6 and 8. Like her husband, Arline was wholeheartedly interested in introducing contemporary works and incorporating innovative staging in Madison Opera's productions. Between 1961 and 1987, she would serve as stage director and/or producer for nearly 40 productions in Madison. She would also collaborate with the MSO and other local groups as producer of some of the grand Festival of the Lakes concerts in the 1980s.[67]

7.14 The Johnsons in 1986.

> In late 1986, in the lead-up to Madison Opera's 25th anniversary celebration and an upcoming production of *Fidelio*, Arline revealed publicly that she was "battling cancer for the third time in 23 years," telling Jacob Stockinger of the *Capital Times* that "I don't know how long I'll be able to continue doing opera, but as long as I feel I have something to contribute, I will. It's been one of the great happinesses of my life."[68] Her final Madison Opera work as producer was *Tosca* in April 1987, and that same month, Arline and Roland Johnson were named Fellows of the Wisconsin Academy of Sciences, Arts, and Letters.[69]
>
> Arline died on November 22, 1988. Johnson dedicated the performance of *Messiah* on December 11 to her. Their daughter Karen remembers that her father, who would invariably address the chorus with a few words before each performance, was too emotional to do it, and delegated her to read a short statement that he had written. Among the published tributes to Arline was one by *Capital Times* associate editor (and local opera lover) John Patrick Hunter, who wrote: "The Madison area is peopled by Arline Johnson fans. Many of them got their first taste of opera from her productions." He continued: "Few will forget a memorable night in 1963 when we sat in the East High School auditorium to hear 'La Boheme' ... it was Arline Johnson's first big triumph here and many more were to follow."

Madison

Roland Johnson's work for the Madison Civic Music Association—including *Shining Brow* and his retirement—and Arline's work with the Madison Civic Opera Guild (later Madison Opera) are discussed in Chapters 6 and 8. The following concentrates on his life and work in Madison outside of his MCMA activities.

Like his predecessors, Sigfrid Prager and Walter Heermann, Johnson was hired into a dual role in Madison: as music director of the Madison Civic Symphony and Chorus (and later Opera) and as supervisor of the music program at the Madison Vocational School. [Note: The school officially changed its name to Madison Area Technical College (MATC) in January 1968. Since 2010, it has more generally been known as Madison College.⁷⁰] Like his predecessors, Johnson devoted a great deal of time to the job: hiring faculty, occasionally teaching courses himself, and dealing with the innumerable details and general "herding of cats" that go into administering an academic department. Throughout his tenure, Johnson maintained a particularly good working relationship with Norman Mitby, who served as MATC's director from 1960 to 1988, and on many occasions in board meetings, interviews, and other statements, paid tribute to Mitby's strong support of MCMA. MATC paid the bulk of Johnson's salary, and he was part of its benefits system. However, his salary from MCMA was apparently negotiated annually. Walter Douma, who would eventually serve as MCMA board president from 1983 to 1985, served as the board's negotiator and recalled that he and Johnson met each year at Madison's Cuba Club for a friendly lunch to discuss the issue.⁷¹

7.15 Roland Johnson in 1962.

The Johnsons' second child, daughter Karen, was born in Madison in 1962. The family initially rented a house on Tokay Blvd. on Madison's near west side. Karen Kretschmann noted that the "symphony ladies" clearly expected that the Johnsons would eventually move into Maple Bluff (the wealthy Madison suburb where many of the MCMA board and Women's Committee members lived) and "even had a house picked out for them." However, Arline "put her foot down" and insisted that the family would remain more grounded in the middle-class neighborhood they already lived in. This was also close to their friends Ann and Ernest Stanke. They purchased a home at 3823 Birch Ave.

Unlike his predecessors, Johnson was never associated with the UW–Madison Summer Music Clinic. However, he did return to Tennessee each summer from 1963 to 1968 to serve as principal conductor of the Sewaunee Summer Music Center (now the Sewaunee Summer Music Festival). The festival, still an annual event today, takes place on the campus of the University of the South in Sewaunee. This is an Episcopal liberal arts college which has a particularly beautiful setting, on top of "the Mountain"—the Cumberland Plateau. The festival was founded in 1957 by the University's vice chancellor, Edward McCrady, and its principal conductor for the first six summers was Julius Hegyi, then conductor of the Chattanooga Symphony.⁷² He was succeeded

7.16 Johnson conducting the student orchestra at the Sewaunee Summer Music Center, 1963.

by Johnson, who remembered that he was "conductor of the very fine student orchestra made up of mostly the best student players in nearby cities like Nashville and Chattanooga." Though he valued this experience, he noted that "with my busy Madison year it finally got to be too much." Johnson noted that he did return to Sewaunee on a few later occasions to guest conduct.[73]

Johnson's genial personality made him an excellent representative to the community for MCMA at a time when its activities were expanding tremendously. He was an accomplished public speaker, and he spoke frequently at meetings of the Rotary, Kiwanis, and other community organizations. He also seems to have worked well with the increasingly powerful MCMA board, and where possible, played a role in balancing the sometimes competing interests of the MCMA and the Madison Civic Opera Guild. Johnson and his family clearly became Madisonians and developed a large circle of friends, primarily among their musical associates. His daughter Karen noted that Ernie and Ann Stanke and Jim and Ann Crow remained particularly close.

After moving to Madison in 1961, Johnson devoted nearly all of this time to his work for MCMA and the Vocational School. He did occasionally guest conduct elsewhere, though it does not seem ever to have conflicted with his work in Madison. In November 1977, however, he was obliged to step away from several concerts. Johnson had a heart attack, and he eventually had bypass surgery in early 1978.[74] As he recuperated, he stepped away from conducting MCMA programs from December 1977 through May 1978—the only time in his 33-year tenure that Johnson missed more than a single concert in a season, aside from the 1993–94 season when each finalist for the MSO artistic director position led a program. To cover in his absence, Robert Palmer engaged several guest conductors, beginning in December, when two University faculty led the MSO and Civic Chorus: Marvin Rabin conducting the Corelli *Christmas Concerto*, and Arthur Becknell leading the Poulenc *Concert Champetre* and *Mozart's "Great" Mass in C minor*. (Becknell was also the harpsichord soloist on the Poulenc and conducted from the keyboard.) The director of the University Symphony Orchestra, Phillip Lehmann, conducted in January, and the opera in February, *Die Fledermaus*, was led by David Lewis Crosby, director of the

7.17 James Latimer, MSO timpanist and guest conductor, ca. 1975.

Wisconsin Symphony Orchestra. Four orchestra members led the Steenbock Awards concert in March: bassist Walter Fandrich, violinist Ernest Stanke, hornist Douglas Hill, and cellist Thomas Buchhauser. For the Verdi *Requiem* in April, MCMA hired Margaret Hillis, longtime conductor of the Chicago Symphony Chorus; many veteran chorus and orchestra members recall this as one of the most outstanding concerts of the 1970s.[75] Milwaukee Symphony Orchestra associate conductor James Paul conducted the final subscription program in April. James Latimer, University percussion professor and MSO timpanist, conducted the pops program in May, which featured clarinetist Benny Goodman.

Johnson was music director of the MCMA for 33 seasons. Both of his children have mentioned that he had opportunities to move on at several points during his career, and in his memoirs, Johnson himself refers to an offer in 1963 to become associate conductor of the Minneapolis Symphony. However, he clearly valued the challenge of building programs in Madison over the long term. He also—and perhaps foremost—had his family in mind, valuing Madison as a fine place for his children to grow up, and as a community where his family was among a large circle of friends. Looking back from the vantage point of retirement, Johnson wrote, "If I had remained single, I surely would have moved on to more places—but, how much better to have the balance of a loving wife and family."

Retirement

Johnson retired as music director of the Madison Symphony Orchestra in May 1994, at age 73. His retirement and the search for his successor are discussed in Chapter 8. I asked both of his children about his feelings toward retiring, and son Carl said, "I think he really felt that it was time for new blood.... I think it was a little harder for him after he left than when it was happening. He was ready to stop all of the preparation, but my dad also talked about missing the applause." Both children agreed that having had the opportunity to commission and premiere *Shining Brow* as a kind of capstone to his long career made retirement a bit easier. Johnson also became a grandfather rather late in life, after Arline's death; his children and their spouses all noted that being part of his grandchildren's lives was clearly important to him.[76]

Johnson, in fact, continued to conduct into his early 80s. On June 17, 1994, just a month after his final program as MSO music director, he conducted a pair of Mozart concertos as part of the First Unitarian Society's concert series: the *Flute Concerto No. 1 in G Major*, K. 313 featuring flutist Thomas Boehm, and the *Piano Concerto No. 27 in B-flat major*, K. 595, featuring pianist Ellsworth Snyder.[77] The chamber orchestra assembled for this program included many MSO players. As the MSO's "Music Director Laureate," he also led the orchestra on two later occasions. On September 23–24, 2000—the opening programs of the MSO's 75th season—Johnson conducted the world premiere of *Jubilare!* by University composer John Stevens, written in honor of the orchestra's 75th anniversary. Recalling this a few years later, Johnson remarked on what an honor it had been and noted "John [DeMain]'s incredible generosity in inviting me to conduct a premiere."[78] Johnson's final appearance on the MSO's podium was at the New Year's Eve Gala in 2002 where, according to his memoirs, "John [DeMain] wanted to have a chance to dance with [his wife] Barbara, so he asked me to conduct the *Blue Danube Waltz*."

A more regular conducting commitment was directing the Madison Opera Chorus. At the invitation of Ann Stanke and John DeMain, Johnson continued to direct the chorus and assisted in the preparation of nearly 20 productions between 1994 and 2000. His final staged production as chorusmaster was Madison Opera's November 2000 *La Bohème*. According to his daughter, he found special significance in ending with this work: It had been the first full-scale opera that he and Arline had collaborated on at the University of Alabama in 1955, and it was also the first work that the Madison Civic Opera Guild had staged in 1963. However, two years later, he stepped in for Ann Stanke, who was recovering from surgery, to prepare the chorus for Madison Opera's first Opera in the Park concert in July 2002.

Johnson traveled extensively during his last years as music director and in retirement, with frequent vacations in Door County and Florida. He made at least eight trips to Europe between 1988 and 1998, often with his children and their spouses, and on his final European trip in 1998, traveling with his sister Carolyn and her husband to Sweden, where they met relatives. In July 1994, he celebrated retirement with a trip to Australia with Karen and David Kretschmann and two of his grandchildren. His final foreign trip, however, was a remarkable conducting opportunity. In 2001, Johnson traveled to Japan at age 81 to conduct concerts in Tokyo and Osaka. This trip was arranged by a local Madison patron, Inez Baskerville, on behalf of the Japan International Volunteer Center, an agency supporting "rural development, vocational

7.18 Johnson conducting *Messiah* in Tokyo, Japan, December 1, 2001. His daughter Karen is singing at the far left side of the chorus.

training and education in Thailand, Cambodia, Laos, Vietnam, South Africa, and among the Palestinians."[79] Baskerville, who had been secretary of this agency, sponsored the trip, and both concerts were benefits for this group. Karen Kretschmann accompanied her father to Japan and ended up singing in the chorus in both programs. On December 1, he conducted Handel's *Messiah* in Tokyo with the Tokyo Oratorio Society and the New Japan Philharmonic, with four American soloists: soprano Margaret O'Keefe, mezzo Mary Westbrook-Geha, tenor Frederick Urrey, and baritone Robert Honeysucker. On December 8, he led the Bach *Christmas Oratorio* in Osaka, with the Quodlibet Choir, the Telemann Chamber Orchestra, and the same four soloists. In his memoirs, he recalled "beautiful halls—splendid concerts—what a fantastic bonus for a long career!"[80]

His daughter notes that Johnson also returned eagerly to the violin following his retirement. He often played chamber music with friends like Ann Stanke and James Crow, occasionally including his son Carl on violin. He also performed on many occasions at Midvale Lutheran Church in Madison, both with Karen and with Tyrone and Janet Greive. In his final years, when he was in an assisted living facility, Karen remembered that she, David, and their children would perform programs with him that he had organized. He would also play for hours on a piano that was just outside of his room.

Johnson died in Madison on May 30, 2012, at age 91. His memorial service included music selected by his children. Former MSO concertmaster Tyrone

Greive performed the Bach-Gounod *Ave Maria*, a Johnson favorite and a piece that he played frequently in his later years. Madison-based mezzo-soprano Kitt Reuter-Foss—a veteran of many Madison Opera and MSO performances and one of many singers whose careers Johnson had helped to foster—sang an art song he had composed some 65 years earlier, a setting of the Robert Frost poem *Stopping by a Woods on a Snowy Evening*.

7.19 Johnson in his home in 2000. (Photo by the author.)

Legacy

Each of the four music directors of the Madison Symphony Orchestra had a profound influence on the MSO's history. Johnson's 33-year tenure was transformative in many ways. In 1962, the Madison Civic Symphony was still a largely amateur ensemble, as it had been since 1926. In 1994, the Madison Symphony Orchestra was a fully professional and well-regarded regional orchestra. Johnson deserves much of the credit for this. In the 1960s he was an active advocate for the gradual professionalization of the orchestra begun by his predecessor, Walter Heermann. In the 1960s and 1970s, he worked to bring in fine professional performers to provide leadership across the orchestra's sections, in particular members of the Pro Arte Quartet and other University faculty. However, the orchestra as a whole began to include a higher proportion of professional musicians and local music teachers. While soloists drawn from the orchestra and chorus remained relatively common throughout his tenure, Johnson, working with executive directors Robert Palmer and Sandra Madden, was increasingly able to work with first-rank instrumentalists and vocalists to perform in MCMA's programs. "Big-name" performers were still a relative rarity when Johnson arrived in 1961, but by the early 1990s, the majority of the orchestra subscription programs featured star soloists. Johnson's programming was remarkably progressive, particularly in the 1960s and 1970s, but he also seems to have been willing to experiment endlessly with different types of programs, and he staged concerts at venues across Madison. The sheer number of performances staged by MCMA each season also expanded dramatically, effectively quadrupling by the end of his tenure. In 1980, he led the orchestra through its transition into a new performance space, the Madison Civic Center's Oscar Mayer Theatre. Johnson had in fact worked behind the scenes during the previous decade as part of the effort to make the Madison Civic Center—including Madison's long-awaited civic auditorium—a success.

He certainly improved the musical quality of the orchestra and chorus. By the 1990s, however, there was a general feeling among the orchestra's musicians that the Madison Symphony Orchestra was as good as it was ever going to get under Johnson's leadership. However, those same musicians also acknowledge his role in reaching that level. Members of the chorus, however, seem to have revered Johnson, who worked intensely with the chorus and expanded its role and repertoire throughout his tenure.

While Johnson was justifiably proud of the transformations in the orchestra and chorus, it is clear that his proudest achievement was the creation of the Madison Opera. This began as a pure labor of love as soon as the Johnsons arrived in Madison in 1961: a collaboration between Roland and Arline Johnson, their close friend Ann Stanke, and an enthusiastic group of Madison opera lovers. Like the orchestra, the Madison Civic Opera Guild was gradually transformed from a purely amateur effort to a much more professional company. From the 1980s to the present, Madison Opera has been one of America's leading regional opera companies. Johnson's triumphant, valedictory accomplishment was the Madison Opera's premiere of the opera *Shining Brow* in 1993.

7.20 At the end of his final MSO program in May 1994, Johnson memorably laid his baton on the podium, after a thunderous ovation and two curtain calls. The MSO later presented the baton to Johnson, mounted on wood from his podium.

J. MICHAEL ALLSEN   329

Notes to Chapter 7

1 Allsen, *75 Years of the Madison Symphony Orchestra*.

2 I have referred to these documents collectively here as the "Johnson Papers." The memoirs are a collection of over a dozen documents, both manuscripts and typescripts compiled by Johnson, mostly between 1994 and 2003. These various accounts frequently overlap; his various descriptions of events within his life often include different details. Wherever possible, I have tried to verify dates and other things from his memoirs with other sources. For the sake of simplicity, I will cite information from this collection as *Johnson Memoirs*.

3 *Johnson Memoirs*.

4 Jean Haskell, "Johnson City," *Tennessee Encyclopedia* https://tennesseeencyclopedia.net/entries/johnson-city/, accessed 1/10/2023; "Johnson City, Tennessee, *Wikipedia*, https://en.wikipedia.org/wiki/Johnson_City,_Tennessee, accessed 1/10/2023.

5 *The Bristol Herald-Courier* 3/19/1936, 3; 12/10/1936, 7; 4/22/1937, 7.

6 *Johnson Memoirs*.

7 Becky Campbell, "Fiddlin' Charlie Bowman," *Johnson City Press* 6/8/2019; "Johnson City Sessions," *Wikipedia*, https://en.wikipedia.org/wiki/Johnson_City_sessions, accessed 1/10/2023; "Johnson City Blues," http://www.stateoffranklin.net/johnsons/oldtime/jcblues/jcblues.htm, accessed 1/11/2023.

8 *Johnson City Press* 10/25/1935, 28. This article and Carl Johnson's 1971 obituary both give 1910 as the date of his arrival in town, which conflicts with the date of 1913 given in the *Johnson Memoirs*. 1913 appears to be incorrect: There is a legal notice from Johnson City in August 1912 noting the dissolution of a partnership between C. A. Johnson and E. F. M. Dahl (his father-in-law?) and the creation of a new company, Johnson Auto (*The Comet* [Johnson City, TN], 8/29/1912, 3). However, Roland Johnson's date of 1912 for his parents' marriage is confirmed by the 1920 census (accessed on ancestry.com, 1/11/2023).

9 Obituary, *Johnson City Press* 5/13/1971, 1, 14.

10 Interview with Karen and David Kretschmann, 10/24/2022.

11 *Johnson Memoirs*. There are several notices of recitals by Artz's large studio in the *Johnson City Press* in the early 1930s.

12 *Johnson City Press* 4/7/1931, 3.

13 *Johnson City Press and Staff-News* 4/6/1934, 5.

14 *Johnson City Press and Staff-News* 6/8/1936, 5; *Johnson City Press* 11/7/1937, 11. Among his performances during this time were many at First Christian Church, which his family attended. He was frequently accompanied by the daughter of the church's pastor, Dorothy Wright, whom Johnson identifies in his memoirs as his "first girlfriend."

15 *Johnson Memoirs*.

16 I suspect it was through Elsie Artz.

17 Interview with Carl Johnson and Barbara Westfahl, 10/14/2022; interview with Karen and David Kretschmann, 10/24/2022. Both Carl and Karen noted that, for some reason, the car that their father drove had a governor that limited it to 35 mph. Apparently, a feature of every trip was a stop at the roadside diner of Harland Sanders in North Corbin, Kentucky. This was long before Sanders began to franchise his recipe and cooking process as Kentucky Fried Chicken, but according to Roland, the attraction was not the chicken but the pie!

18 *Johnson Memoirs.*

19 *Cincinnati Post* 6/15/1942, 14; *Johnson Memoirs.*

20 "Helene Billing Wurlitzer," *Wikipedia,* https://en.wikipedia.org/wiki/Helene_Billing_Wurlitzer, accessed 1/16/2023.

21 Unfortunately, there is a gap in the newspapers.com database in the coverage of Key West newspapers that starts in August 1943 and continues for a few years. The same gap appears in the microfilms held by the Key West Public Library and Florida State University, so I have been unable to find any record of community reaction. However, the date of the concert and Johnson's participation are confirmed in Kevin M. McCarthy, *Christmas in Florida* (Sarasota, FL: Pineapple Press, 2000) and in the base newspaper, *The Key Outpost* 12/24/1943, 2. I thank Breana Sowers of the Key West Public Library for her assistance with newspapers.

22 Johnson led his first *Messiah* in Cincinnati while he was still a student, on December 16, 1947, when he directed a performance with a chorus of 150 and a 30-piece orchestra at the College of Music. In an interview with the College newspaper, he noted that "we are attempting to restore *The Messiah* in its baroque style, not from the purist approach (or that of the musicologist) but from the standpoint of live performance values." This seems to have been an attempt to restore the original contents of the oratorio, which Johnson referred to as "our endeavor to approach the true spirit of this great piece," *The College of Music Clarion* VII/4 (December 1947): 1 [in Johnson Papers].

23 *Johnson Memoirs; Black Mountain College Bulletin/Bulletin-Newsletter,* Vol. II, No. 7 (April 1944), accessed 1/18/2023 at https://digital.ncdcr.gov/digital/collection/p249901coll44/id/735.

24 Gunther Schuller, *A Life in Pursuit of Music and Beauty* (Rochester, NY: University of Rochester Press, 2011): 117, 241. Johnson does not record how they first met in his memoirs, and Schuller's accounts are actually conflicting, implying that he met Johnson for the first time in *both* 1943 and 1946. In describing the 1943 meeting, he notes that Johnson was "visiting Cincinnati on a week's leave from the navy," (p.117): a telling detail I think, and I have reconstructed their first meeting as written above.

25 *Cincinnati Post* 1/23/1947, 13. The photograph of Johnson and Walter Heermann reproduced here originally appeared with this article.

26 Interview with Roland Johnson, 8/10/2000; interview with Paulita Heermann Neal and Peter Neal, 10/16/2020.

27 *Cincinnati Enquirer* 10/19/1947, 64.

28 On the history of the Tanglewood Festival through the 1980s see Andrew Pincus, *Scenes from Tanglewood* (Boston: Northeastern University Press, 1989).

29 *Johnson Memoirs.*

30 Operas he conducted for the Cincinnati College of Music included Smetana, *The Bartered Bride* (May 1949—*Cincinnati Enquirer* 4/5/1949, 98); Pergolesi, *The Music Master* and Puccini, *Suor Angelica* (March 1950—*Cincinnati Post* 3/14/1950, 20; Vaughan Williams, *Riders to the Sea* and Foss, *The Jumping Frog of Calaveras County* (January 1951—*Cincinnati Enquirer* 1/16/1951, 15); William Byrd, *The Music Master of 1952,* Hindemith, *There and Back,* and Purcell, *Dido and Aeneas* (February 1952 - *Cincinnati Enquirer* 1/16/1951, 82.).

31 *Cincinnati Enquirer* 2/13/1949, 76; 3/20/1949, 81; 4/12/1949, 18; *Cincinnati Post* 5/9/1948, 9; 10/24/1949, 11; *Cincinnati Enquirer* 1/29/1950, 90; *Cincinnati Post* 2/27/1950, 10; *Cincinnati Enquirer* 11/19/1950, 110; 1021/1951, 106.

32 *Cincinnati Enquirer* 4/18/1949, 15.

33 Schuller, *A Life*, 328. Once again, Schuller's chronology in this memoir seems to be off, as he infers that the commission and performance took place a year earlier, when Johnson was still a student at the College of Music. The premiere date is confirmed in the local newspaper (*Cincinnati Enquirer* 4/29/1949, 49).

34 Gunther Schuller, *Orchestral Works*, Radio Philharmonic of Hannover, conducted by Gunther Schuller (GM Recordings, GM2059CD, 1998. See also Schuller, *A Life*, 386–87.

35 *Cincinnati Enquirer* 4/5/1949, 15.

36 *Cincinnati Post* 3/14/1950, 20.

37 *Cincinnati Post* 9/4/1952, 34.

38 The most extensive study of Labunski's life and work is James Wierzbicki, "Traditional Values in a Century of Flux: The Music of Feliks Łabuński (1892–1979)," *Polish Music Journal* IV/1 (Summer 2001), accessed at https://polishmusic.usc.edu/research/publications/polish-music-journal/#vol4no1, 11/3/2022.

39 *Johnson Memoirs*.

40 Like most of these compositions, there is some evidence that *It Was a Lover and His Lass* was performed, or at least rehearsed, at some point. The madrigal, the motet, the flute *Prelude*, and the two art songs for piano all survive with multiple manuscript copies of the score. However, if Johnson copied performance parts for the *Quartet* or the *Song for Orchestra*, they have not survived in his papers.

41 Wierzbecki, "Traditional Values."

42 The Fleischmann Foundation was established after the death of Max C. Fleischmann (1877–1951), one of the heirs to the Cincinnati-based Fleischmann's Yeast Co. fortune. (Hattie Beresford, "Moguls and Mansions: Max C. Fleischmann," *Montecito Journal*, accessed 1/21/2023 at http://www.digitaleditiononline.com/publication/?i=26368&article_id=263857). His brother Julius and nephew Julius Jr. were also noted philanthropists.

43 Interview with Roland Johnson, 8/10/2000; interview with Karen and David Kretschmann 10/24/2022.

44 Thomas Schippers, "Scherchen Familie: 1. Hermann," *Die Music in Geschichte und Gegenwart, Personenteil* (Kassel: Bahrenreiter-Verlag, 1999): Bd.c14, cols. 1301–1304; Gerhard Brunner, "Scherchen, Hermann," *Grove Music Online*, www.oxfordmusiconline, accessed 1/21/2023.

45 Hermann Scherchen, *Lehrbuch des Dirigierens* (Leipzig: J. J. Weber, 1929); Hermann Scherchen, *Handbook of Conducting*, translated by M. D. Calvocoressi (Oxford: Oxford University Press, 1933).

46 Interview with Carl Johnson and Barbara Westfahl, 10/14/2022.

47 *Johnson Memoirs*; interview with Karen and David Kretschmann, 10/24/2022.

48 *Birmingham News* 11/15/1953, 83.

49 *Johnson Memoirs*.

50 *Birmingham News* 3/3/1957, 82.

51 *Birmingham News* 2/28/1954, 82.

52 Caroline, Cepin Benser, "Ottokar Čadek," *The Encyclopedia of Alabama*, http://encyclopediaofalabama.org/article/h-3022, accessed 1/23/2023.

53 *Birmingham News* 10/19/1956, 40.

54 *Birmingham News* 11/14/1954, 84; *Birmingham Post-Herald* 1/27/1955, 4.

55 *Birmingham News* 10/23/1955, 90

56 *Birmingham News* 5/25/1956, 30.

57 *Johnson Memoirs*; Marion Mills, "Select Salutes Arline Johnson, Woman of the Month," *Madison Select* (May 1975): 5.

58 *Birmingham Post-Herald* 10/27/1956, 27; 11/24/1956, 27; 11/23/1957, 24; 11/3/1958, 13; *Birmingham News* 11/22/1959, 41.

59 *Birmingham News* 5/3/1959, 95

60 Interview with Carl Johnson and Barbara Westfahl, 10/14/2022; interview with Karen and David Kretschmann, 10/24/2022.

61 Mills, "Select Salutes Arline Johnson," 4–5; interview with Carl Johnson and Barbara Westfahl, 10/14/2022.

62 Obituary, *CT* 11/24/1988, 44. I have not found dates for her first trip to Europe, but it must have been prior to the United States' entry into the war in December 1941. It was most likely during the summer of that year.

63 Program (3/19/1942) preserved in the Johnson Papers.

64 Obituary, *CT* 11/24/1988, 44.

65 The letter and Birmingham Symphony Orchestra program are in the Johnson Papers. Details on the Chattanooga program come from the *Chattanooga Daily Times* 3/14/1962.

66 *WSJ* 10/22/1961, 3.

67 *CT* 9/22/1986, 32.

68 *CT* 11/3/1986, 34.

69 *CT* 4/5/1987, 39

70 *CT* 12/22/1967, 8; "Madison Area Technical College," *Wikipedia*, https://en.wikipedia.org/wiki/Madison_Area_Technical_College, accessed 1/31/2023.

71 Interview with Walter Douma, 5/23/2019.

72 "History of the Sewaunee Summer Music Festival," *Sewaunee Summer Music Festival*, https://ssmf.sewanee.edu/about-us/, accessed 1/31/2023.

73 *Johnson Memoirs*.

74 *CT* 1/25/1978, 9.

75 George Shook, for example, remembered that "it was really memorable—clearly one of our top ten performances." Interview with George and Nancy Shook, 1/17/2023.

76 Interview with Carl Johnson and Barbara Westfahl, 10/14/2022; interview with Karen and David Kretschmann, 10/24/2022.

77 *CT* 6/15/1994, 43. Snyder later issued the piano concerto, together with three earlier solo piano recordings, on a CD: *Haydn Mozart Schubert* (Madison: ca. 2001). Snyder had twice been a soloist with the Madison Symphony Orchestra.

78 Interview with Roland Johnson, 8/15/2004.

79 *CT* 11/22/2001, 106.

80 *Johnson Memoirs*; interview with Karen and David Kretschmann, 10/24/2022.

CHAPTER 8

Passing the Baton:
The Orchestra, Chorus, and Opera in the 1980s and 1990s

By 1980, the Madison Symphony Orchestra had gone through two decades of transformation under the leadership of Roland Johnson and an active Madison Civic Music Association board. The MSO was by then a fully professional orchestra, and the quality of its performances had risen tremendously; it was a well-regarded regional orchestra with a reputation for progressive programming. Beginning in the 1960s, Johnson had recruited a cadre of musical leaders within the orchestra, with principal chairs dominated by performance faculty from the University. The orchestra was also playing four times as many performances each season as it had in 1960, including well-established annual youth and pops programming, and constant experimentation with other types of concerts. The size and quality of the Madison Civic Chorus also increased during Johnson's first 20 years, and it regularly performed three concerts each year. After decades of free concerts, MCMA had begun charging for tickets and had built a large base of season subscribers. The MCMA had added a third performing ensemble, the Madison Civic Opera (Madison Opera after 1983), which had grown from a group of amateur enthusiasts to an increasingly professional company. MCMA's annual budget had increased from $6000 in 1960–61 to nearly $550,000 in 1980–81, and this much larger organization was now administered by a pair of professional full-time staffers, Robert Palmer and Jean Feige.

The next two decades, covered by this chapter, would also be transformative. The 1980s began with the opening of a new performance space, the Oscar Mayer Theatre. The programming of the orchestra, chorus, and opera continued to expand, culminating in one of Madison Opera's finest moments: the commissioning and premiere of a new grand opera, *Shining Brow*, in 1993. This period also saw the retirement of Roland Johnson and the hiring of the MSO's fourth artistic director, John DeMain, in 1994. DeMain's arrival also coincided with a profound administrative change: the dissolution of MCMA, which had been the umbrella organization over the orchestra, chorus, and, eventually, the opera for 68 years. The Madison Symphony Orchestra and Chorus formally separated from the Madison Opera, though connections between these two groups continue today.

Opening the Oscar Mayer Theatre

Madison's decades-long, highly political, and sometimes tortuous quest for a civic auditorium finally ended in 1980 with the opening of the Madison Civic Center, a large multipurpose space occupying most of the 200 block on State Street. It served several of Madison's performing arts companies and included an art museum, a theater, and other performance spaces surrounding a large central "crossroads" space. The largest venue was the 2100-seat Oscar Mayer Theatre, a renovation of the Capitol Theater, a grand movie palace that had originally opened in 1928. This would be the primary performance venue for the orchestra, chorus, and opera for the next quarter century. On February 23, 1980, the orchestra and chorus were part of a grand opening celebration for the Madison Civic Center. This program opened with *The Star-Spangled Banner* and Copland's *Preamble to a Solemn Event*, narrated by Gerald Bartell, a local broadcasting executive who had done much to foster the Civic Center project. The star soprano Martina Arroyo sang arias by Verdi and Puccini. The Madison Symphony Orchestra and Madison Civic Chorus then closed the program with Beethoven's *Symphony No. 9*, joined by vocal soloists Arroyo, Ilona Kombrink, Daniel Nelson, and Samuel Jones.

A month later, on March 28, the Madison Civic Opera performed for the first time in the Oscar Mayer Theatre, presenting Verdi's monumental *Aïda*. This was the company's most ambitious production to that time, featuring several professional leads and spectacular sets and staging that made the most of the theater's large stage. It was accompanied by the full MSO, performing in a true opera pit for the first time since the long-ago performances of the 1930s in the Parkway Theatre. In an enthusiastic review the next day in the *Capital Times*, Mark Morris wrote: "Civic Opera took a giant step towards the big leagues

Friday night."[1] In fact, this production marked the beginning of Madison Opera's national reputation, including a favorable notice in *Opera News*.

8.01 The orchestra on stage in Oscar Mayer Theatre in 1982.

After decades playing on the cramped stage of the MATC (formerly Central High School) Auditorium, the orchestra now had a large stage in a much larger space, which could accommodate twice as many people in the audience. This actually caused a financial issue for members of the orchestra: Since the 1968–69 season, the MSO had regularly doubled its subscription programs to accommodate an audience of up to 2000 people in the MATC Auditorium, with Saturday evening and Sunday matinee performances. Since players were paid on a per-service basis, going back to single Saturday programs in the much larger Oscar Mayer Theatre was effectively a cut in pay for the players. Robert Palmer noted that it took a few years of adjustments worked out in negotiations with the players to make up for this loss.[2] There were immediate musical impacts on MSO programming as well: the vastly larger stage could now accommodate both the full orchestra and the Madison Civic Chorus, ending the need to stage large choral concerts in the Stock Pavilion, First Congregational Church, and other venues.[3] It also accommodated programs with expanded orchestras, as in the ambitious all-Wagner concert of October 1983 and the cycle of Mahler symphonies that John DeMain began in 1994. Bassoonist Richard Lottridge noted that "for the first time we could actually hear one another." He also remarked that, at MATC Auditorium, the orchestra almost always played too loudly for the hall, but that in the vastly larger Oscar Mayer Theatre, "the sound had someplace to go."[4] Several players who went through this transition—James Crow, Betty Bielefeld, Marc Fink, and others—have remarked on a more intangible benefit of the new space: the pride that members of the orchestra felt in playing in a much larger and more "professional" venue.

Concerts of the 1980s and Early 1990s

In 1980, the orchestra's regular subscription series included five Saturday concerts. This expanded to six in 1983–84, with the addition of a Sunday afternoon program in January, a "Midwinter Matinee of Light Classics." This program, intended to bring in families and new listeners, continued through the early 1990s. The Midwinter Matinees included lighter symphonic repertoire and typically featured a member of the orchestra as soloist. Though the Sunday matinee was moved to Saturday night in 1992–93, the tradition of a lighter January program, including Broadway and pops-style concerts, continued into the late 1990s.

The series expanded to seven classical concerts in 1984–85, and in 1988–89 to eight, plus an additional fall pops program. Unlike the spring pops programs, which were run as benefit concerts by the Madison Symphony Orchestra League, the Fall Pops programs were administered as part of the regular season—as an addition to the classical concerts of the subscription series—and appeared on the season brochure. The first Fall Pops in October 1988 featured conductor Keith Brion, in the role of John Philip Sousa, leading *Sousa at the Symphony*, a program that recreated a typical Sousa concert of the early 20th century. (Brion returned in March 1992.)

The MSOL continued to sponsor an annual springtime benefit pops concert at the end of each season, initially remaining in the Dane County Coliseum, though from 1982 onward moving into the Oscar Mayer Theatre. As in the previous decades, these programs featured a variety of popular stars, instrumentalists, and composers—to name a few, Diahann Carroll (1981), Henry Mancini (1983), Doc Severinsen (1984), the Canadian Brass (1989), Chet Atkins (1991), and Judy Collins (1992). This annual event, which had been established in 1959, retired alongside Roland Johnson: the final MSOL pops program was in May 1993. However, in 1995, the newly created Concert on the Green effectively replaced the Spring Pops as a lucrative benefit concert run by the MSOL.

In general, as the number of concerts increased in the 1980s and 1990s, the orchestra's programming became slightly less progressive than it had been in the 1960s and 1970s. A smaller proportion of its repertoire was contemporary, and there were no works that could be classed as even remotely *avant-garde*. However, the MSO continued regularly to program works by late-20th-century American composers. Gunther Schuller, Lukas Foss, John Corigliano, Jan Bach, Christopher Rouse, Daron Hagen, John Adams, Joan Tower, David Ott, and Lowell Liebermann all had works programmed in these years. There were also a few relatively challenging 20th-century works: Bartók, *Bluebeard's Castle*

(1981) and *Concerto for Orchestra* (October 1986), Berg, *Wozzeck: Three Excerpts, Op. 7* (1985), Ives, *The Unanswered Question* (October 1989), and Pärt, *Cantus in Memory of Benjamin Britten* (1990). The MSO continued to play commissions and premieres as well, including:

- Gunnar Johansen, *Piano Concerto No. 2* (May 1981). Pianist Gunnar Johansen had appeared many times with the orchestra since arriving in Madison in 1945. This was his first appearance as a composer and his final appearance as a soloist.
- John Harbison, *Overture: Michael Kohlhaas* (October 1982). His *Violin Concerto* appeared on the program as well.
- Crawford Gates, *Lake Songs* (September 1986). Commissioned for the first Festival of the Lakes.
- Michael Torke, *Verdant Music* (February 1987). Joint commission with the Milwaukee Symphony Orchestra.
- Gunther Schuller, *Concerto for String Quartet and Orchestra* (February 1988). With the Pro Arte Quartet, the composer conducting.
- Daron Hagen, *Joyful Music* (December 1993). With mezzo-soprano Kitt Reuter-Foss and the Madison Symphony Chorus.

MSO principal players, University faculty, and local professional singers still appeared frequently as soloists in the 1980s and 1990s. One favorite, for example, was Madison-based mezzo-soprano Kitt Reuter-Foss, who appeared dozens of times in orchestra and chorus programs and Madison Opera productions, and who would eventually sing at the Metropolitan Opera.[5] By the 1980s, however, the majority of the MSO's concerts featured national and international guest artists, and these star performers became a focus of the MCMA's marketing and publicity. Robert Palmer seems to have been particularly successful in bringing in many of the finest pianists of the day, including Emanuel Ax (who appeared with the MSO five times over the course of 30 seasons, beginning in September 1979), Earl Wild, Lorin Hollander, Alicia de Larrocha, Horacio Gutiérrez (who was also featured five times, beginning in 1982), Ruth Laredo, Garrick Ohlsson (seven times, beginning in 1984), Misha Dichter, Jorge Bolet, Cristina Ortiz, Grant Johannesen, Vladimir Feltsman, and Santiago Rodriguez. Other star soloists included violinists Ruggiero Ricci, Elmar Oliveira, Miriam Fried, Joshua Bell (as a 21-year-old in 1989), cellists Lynn Harrell (five appearances beginning in 1987) and Nathaniel Rosen, guitarist Angel Romero, clarinetist David Shifrin, flutists Ransom Wilson, Eugenia Zukerman, and James Galway, and singers Martina Arroyo, Maureen Forrester, and Lorna Haywood. One particularly memorable soloist was Itzhak Perlman, who played the Brahms *Violin Concerto* in October 1991. His performance was, of course, stunning, but I particularly remember getting to meet him backstage. There were three or four of us who played in the first half of the program but who were not involved in the Brahms, and we gathered offstage during intermission so we could listen to his performance. Perlman showed up about five minutes early, and we all stepped back to give him some space. Clearly a lot more relaxed than we were, he walked over to where my friends and I were standing, and politely asked us about ourselves and the orchestra ... and then, until a few seconds before he had to go on stage, entertained us with a couple of outrageous rabbi jokes!

8.02 Itzhak Perlman, ca. 1990.

There were several noteworthy programs during these years. In October 1983, the orchestra opened its season with an all-Wagner program that presented excerpts from all four of the operas in the Ring Cycle. Headlining the program were a pair of Wagner specialists: dramatic soprano Linda Kelm, and Heldentenor Gary Lakes, both of whom would later be Metropolitan Opera stars.[6] The orchestra was expanded for this program, including four Wagner tubas borrowed for the concert. The MSO returned to Wagner in December 1987, presenting a concert version of Act III of *Die Meistersinger von Nürnburg*.

8.03 Madison Festival of the Lakes brochure, 1986.

In January 1987, the orchestra accompanied a ballet program led by ballet superstar Rudolf Nureyev, which included two rather challenging works by Stravinsky, *Apollon Musagéte* and the *Concertino for Twelve Instruments*.

In September 1986, the MSO was a prominent part of the large-scale Festival of the Lakes. Preparations for this complex event began several years earlier, and the original plan was to bring together a wide range of national and local performing groups and artists in performances and exhibitions in venues and parks around the city.[7] (The festival's slogan was "When a City Becomes a Stage.") By the spring of 1986 this ambitious plan was scaled back to focus on local artists, and some logistical problems were coming to light. In late June, for example, the opening concert (September 18), featuring the MSO and followed by an elaborate fireworks display, had to be moved from Olbrich Park on the east side to Warner Park on the city's north side.[8] The final lineup for the four-day festival included a few national groups (the Chicago Symphony Orchestra and a ballet company led by Edward Villella), but otherwise it was almost exclusively local artists with a huge variety of musical styles (classical, jazz, rock, folk, gospel, world, hip-hop, and more), ballet, modern dance and folk dance, several theatrical events (including a Madison Opera production of Britten's *Noyes Fludde*), visual art exhibitions, and much more. For its concert, the MSO played in combination with the University Symphony as a single 160-piece orchestra. The centerpiece of the concert was a newly composed work by Wisconsin composer Crawford Gates, *Lake Songs*, with movements inspired by each of Madison's four lakes. The crowd, estimated at 30,000, was by far the largest audience the MSO had ever played for to that date.[9] Beginning with a disagreement over dates and a large budget deficit, the troubled second festival was eventually postponed until September 1988, though there was a small "Minifestival" in 1987.[10] The second Festival of the Lakes in 1988 was slightly smaller than the first, and cold, wet weather put a damper on many of the outdoor events. This time, the MSO simply coordinated its first regular subscription program of the season with the festival. Once again, the Festival ended with a significant deficit, though donors stepped in to cover it.[11] The Festival of the Lakes was brought back in July 1989 and August 1990, but the MSO did not participate in either of these. Though these festivals ran on a different financial basis, this time ending with balanced books, it was clear that public interest was waning, and in September the organizers announced that there were no plans to revive the Festival of the Lakes in the future.[12]

MSO players were of course also accompanying Madison Opera productions throughout this period. By the 1980s and early 1990s, the opera usually mounted two productions each season. The fall production was typically a somewhat lighter work, often an operetta or a Broadway musical, staged in a smaller venue (most often the Memorial Union Theater), and typically featuring local singers in some lead roles. The spring production was always grand opera, staged in the Oscar Mayer Theatre, and tended to be increasingly dominated by out-of-town professionals.[13]

Changing Course

In 1989, Marian Bolz was elected president of the MCMA board, and she would serve for five seasons: she was the first president since the 1950s to serve more than two or three years (her mother-in-law, Eugenie Mayer Bolz, had served a five-year term in 1953–58), and she would be one of the most impactful leaders of the MCMA board in the 70 years of its existence. Bolz had already been involved with the orchestra as a volunteer for more than 30 years, initially as part of the Women's Committee, an auxiliary group that she eventually led through its transition to the much broader-based Madison Symphony Orchestra League in the 1970s. On her term as MCMA president, she recalled, with typical forthrightness in a 2019 interview, that:

8.04 Marian Bolz, MCMA board president, ca. 1992.

> I came into the job with the idea that we needed five things to happen. First, it was time for a new conductor. Second, we needed a new manager. Third, we needed to separate from the opera. Fourth, we needed a new legal counsel. Fifth, we needed to start a foundation.[14]

In fact, all five of these things had happened by 1995 ... though not in that order.

In 1991, local attorney Robert Horowitz joined the board as MCMA's legal counsel, a position he maintained for decades. He would also serve as board president from 1998 to 2001. Staffing changes occurred incrementally. MCMA had had a professional staff of two full-time employees since the 1970s: general manager Robert Palmer and secretary Jeanne Feige. By the beginning of the 1985–86 season, the staff had expanded to three with the hiring of Ria Michaels as director of development and marketing, and the following season saw the addition of a part-time administrative assistant position as well. In 1988, the orchestra hired its first full-time development director, Robert Lange, with the marketing area covered by a part-time person. In 1992, MCMA expanded the marketing director position to full-time as well, hiring Tom Robbins. Robert Palmer submitted his resignation in May 1992, though his departure was not without controversy. Palmer was particularly well liked and respected by the members of the orchestra. The fact that he had been pushed out by Bolz and the MCMA board was a very open secret, and many players viewed his departure with suspicion and anger.

Palmer was succeeded as executive director[15] by Sandra K. Madden. Madden, a Wisconsin native, had served in administrative posts for the Rockford (Illinois)

8.05 Sandra Madden in 1992.

Symphony Orchestra, the Denver Chamber Orchestra, and the Colorado Children's Chorale before coming to Madison in September 1992. She would head the administrative staff of the orchestra until early 1999—a momentous period that saw the production of *Shining Brow*, Roland Johnson's retirement, the arrival of John DeMain, the dissolution of MCMA, and the beginnings of the Overture Hall project. Looking back some 30 years in a 2023 interview, Madden clearly remembered her time in Madison with great pride and affection. She was very complimentary about the organization she inherited, praising Johnson, Palmer, and Bolz, and recalled that "there was nothing that really needed to be fixed—all I really needed to do in that first few years was not screw up!"[16] Madden left in the spring of 1999 for a position with the Colorado Symphony Orchestra. The work of her long-serving successor, Richard Mackie, will be discussed in Chapter 10.

The most sweeping organizational change of the 1990s was the dissolution of the Madison Civic Music Association and the separation of the chorus and orchestra from the opera. The MCMA had administered the orchestra and chorus since their founding in the 1920s, and beginning in the 1960s, the Madison Opera also operated under MCMA's umbrella. However, since its official founding in 1962, the opera had operated with a great deal of autonomy, with its own board and budget, and by the late 1980s, its own professional staff. As its productions evolved from all-amateur, do-it-yourself affairs in the early 1960s to the much more professional and elaborately staged operas of the 1980s and 1990s, there was increasing tension between the boards, volunteers, and staffs of MCMA and the Madison Opera. Terry Haller, who succeeded Bolz as board president in 1994, noted that there was an ineffectual Opera Integration Committee, one of several efforts beginning in the 1970s to try to balance the competing interests. The most divisive issue was, of course, money. (The French playwright Moliere famously quipped, "Of all the noises known to man, opera is the most expensive.") The Madison Opera's productions had in fact often run into deficit, which was necessarily covered by MCMA, at a time when MCMA's own finances were precarious. Both Madden and Haller noted that the *Shining Brow* project, starting in 1991—the Madison Opera's biggest (and most expensive) project ever—marked a turning point. In 1992, Bolz created an Organizational Structure Committee to study the issue. As Haller remembered, the committee presented three options: (1) merging the boards and bringing the orchestra, chorus, and opera together under the control of a single board; (2) a formal split, with the opera becoming an independent entity; or (3) some modification of the status quo. With a search underway for a new music director who would take up the baton for the beginning of the 1994–95 season, some on the board favored deferring any action until the new music director was in place. However, the majority agreed on solving the issue and allowing the new director to start with a clean slate. The group's final report, issued October 4, 1993, supported a formal split between the orchestra and chorus on one hand and the opera on the other, and this was ratified by both boards.[17] A month later, the details were announced to the public:

- The Madison Civic Music Association, which had existed since 1925, would be formally dissolved, to be replaced by two new separate nonprofit entities: Madison Symphony Orchestra Inc. and Madison Opera Inc.
- The Madison Symphony Orchestra would administer the orchestra and chorus and would continue the long-standing formal relationship with Madison Area Technical College, which would continue to pay most of the music director's salary.
- Pending the outcome of the conductor search, it seemed likely that the MSO and Madison Opera would share a music director and that the MSO would remain the exclusive pit orchestra for Madison Opera productions.
- The split would be effective for the 1994–95 season.[18]

Countless issues remained to be worked out—particularly the division of money and other resources between the MSO and Madison Opera—but the split did take place in 1994, and the two separate organizations continue to flourish 30 years later. Haller, who became president of the MSO board in 1994–95, notes that other administrative changes included expansion of the board and a much more "serious" approach to fundraising: for example, promoting concert sponsorships.[19]

An important factor in the orchestra's success and financial stability over the last few decades has been the growth of a revenue-generating endowment. Madden noted that, when she arrived, MCMA had a $250,000 "reserve fund" that served as the seed of an endowment fund. This had grown to $1.5 million by 1999.[20] Growing the endowment became an important priority for the board and administration over the next few decades. The Madison Symphony Orchestra Foundation was formally incorporated in 1995 in the wake of the 1994 reorganization. The Foundation proved to be an important factor in the orchestra's continuing success and financial stability over the next 30 years. As of 2023, with assets of more than $30 million, the Madison Symphony Orchestra's endowment is by far the largest of any orchestra of comparable budget in the United States.[21]

Shining Brow

The search for a new music director would be the MCMA's primary concern in the 1993–94 season, but first came one of Madison Opera's proudest achievements. According to Terry Haller, who served on the Madison Opera[22] board in the late 1980s, the initial idea for what would become *Shining Brow* came at a meeting of the Madison Opera's opera selection committee in early 1989.[23] Haller had just been reading a recently published "warts and all" biography of Wisconsin-born architect Frank Lloyd Wright and suggested him as a subject for an opera, and even suggested the name *Shining Brow*.[24] Haller noted that board member Marvin Woerpel took charge of shepherding this idea, and later chaired the *Shining Brow* steering committee. It was also supported by the Opera board president, Ted Iltis.

8.06 Scene from *Shining Brow*, Act I: Bradley Garvin (as Edwin Cheney), Michael Sokol (as Frank Lloyd Wright), and Carolann Page (as Mamah Cheney).

By the end of 1989, *Shining Brow* had evolved from a discussion topic to a *project* ... at least as far as Madison Opera was concerned. A pair of longtime Opera supporters, Joanna Overn and Margaret Winston, had already pledged to cover the commissioning fee if the project could clear the next few hurdles. Roland Johnson had a young composer in mind, Daron Hagen, whose music he had judged at a composition contest. In those pre-internet days, however, Johnson had no idea how to contact him, until he had a chance meeting with Hagen's brother at the American Symphony Orchestra League meeting that summer.[25] Hagen was then resident at the famed MacDowell Colony, and he later recalled:

> I received a call on one of the payphones in Colony Hall from conductor Roland Johnson asking whether I might consider

composing an opera about the American architect Frank Lloyd Wright for Madison Opera. He even had a title: *Shining Brow*. It might be a year or so before the company would be in a position to offer a commissioning agreement—let alone an advance—so saying yes in a way didn't mean anything in practical terms. Paul [Muldoon] was reading the newspaper a few feet away. Without thinking, I leaned out of the booth and quipped "Say, Paul, do you want to write an opera?" I'm not sure how serious I was. A beat later, he replied, "Sure, why not?"[26]

The poet Paul Muldoon, who would eventually write *Shining Brow*'s libretto, and Hagen had in fact already discussed the possibility of writing an opera together.

This would be the first opera for both Hagen and Muldoon. Daron Hagen (b. 1961) was born in Milwaukee and trained at the University of Wisconsin–Madison, Philadelphia's Curtis Institute (with Ned Rorem), and the Juilliard School in New York City (with David Diamond, Bernard Rands, and Joseph Schwantner). By the time he was offered *Shining Brow*, Hagen already had a burgeoning national reputation as a composer, attracting commissions from the New York Philharmonic, Milwaukee Symphony Orchestra, the Denver Chamber Orchestra, and other prominent orchestras and chamber ensembles. Johnson programmed Hagen's *Heliotrope* on the MSO's April 1991 concert, partly as a way to introduce him to Madison.[27]

8.07 Paul Muldoon and Daron Hagen, 1993.

In 1989, Paul Muldoon (b. 1951) was already recognized as one of Ireland's leading poets. He had emigrated to the United States in 1987 and was then teaching at Princeton University.

One hurdle was to secure the approval of the Frank Lloyd Wright Foundation, stewards of Wright's legacy. This came in April 1990. A higher hurdle was the approval of the MCMA board. The MCMA was in financial distress at the time, and there was understandable reluctance to take on such an enormous project. Haller noted that he and others "sold" *Shining Brow* as an opportunity "to raise the visibility of the opera company and the arts in general," while also stressing that:

> we could do it in a financially responsible way, because all of the sudden we had something new and exciting to attract money. We

could do it in incremental stages ... we could raise money for the music, raise money for the libretto ... and do it gradually, in such a way that we were only spending money when we had it. That was the theory, anyway.[28]

In the end, the MCMA board approved the *Shining Brow* project by the margin of a single vote. Financing the opera continued to be the primary behind-the-scenes drama. The premiere was originally scheduled for performance in the spring of 1992, but it was later moved to May 1993 to provide more time for fundraising. Haller notes that at one point it became apparent that they were going to be about $100,000 short, but then "like a *deus ex machina*" came word that *Shining Brow* had received a grant from the National Endowment for the Arts that nearly covered this deficit. In the end, the opera cost nearly $450,000.[29]

Hagen and Muldoon began work on the opera in 1990, before they had a contract in hand, researching Wright and deciding on the events from his life that they would use. They finished a full treatment of the two-act opera in fairly short order, and then worked mostly separately, though in "constant communication."[30] Hagen remembered that one seminal moment was sharing extracts from *Shining Brow* with Leonard Bernstein during a visit to Bernstein's New York City apartment in The Dakota. Bernstein gave feedback on the music, and Hagen revealed that some aspects of Wright's character were in fact based upon Bernstein. It was also Bernstein who suggested Stephen Wadsworth to Hagen as a stage director for *Shining Brow*.[31]

Act I was presented in Madison on January 16, 1991, to backers, board members, and representatives of the Wright Foundation. Just as people were assembling in MATC's rehearsal room, the news broke that an American-led coalition had begun the bombardment of Iraq: the opening of the Gulf War. After a pause to watch President Bush's address, the presentation continued, and Hagen was given the "green light" to move on to Act II.[32] This was presented in Madison that July.

The opera deals with events in Wright's life between 1903 and 1914, focusing on Wright's relationship with Mamah Cheney, wife of his client Edwin Cheney. It is also framed by scenes that deal with Wright's relationship with his mentor Louis Sullivan. The climax of the drama in Act II is the horrendous mass murder of seven people, including Mamah and her two children, at Taliesin, Wright's home and studio. The murderer, Wright's chef Julian Carlton, kills himself after he sets fires that destroy Taliesin. The murders and fire are represented by a fierce orchestral interlude.

Before *Shining Brow* went into production in Madison, there was a workshop performance for donors and press in New York City, held in Leonard Bernstein's apartment.[33] The premier performance, in the Oscar Mayer Theatre on April 21, 1993, was a triumph, and a triumph that was noticed well beyond Madison. Haller remembered that there were over 50 critics in attendance from across the United States and representing a few international publications. In the reviews, Muldoon's libretto came in for occasional criticism for being overly dense and "literary," but the constants in the reviews were enthusiastic approval of Hagen's music as effective and full of witty musical allusions, and praise for the "plucky little company"[34] that had successfully premiered and staged an important new American grand opera. John von Rhein, writing for the *Chicago Tribune*, was typical:

> *Shining Brow* gave further evidence that the salvation of new American opera will come not necessarily from the big East Coast companies but from enterprising regional theaters like Madison's.... This is modern music theater any major opera company could present with pride.[35]

Unlike many newly composed operas, *Shining Brow*'s life has extended well beyond its premiere. It has been revived successfully multiple times, and it was also recorded in 2009.[36] Hagen has composed nine new operas since 1993, as well as several additional works of musical theater. He and Muldoon would collaborate on three more stage works: the "nightmare in one act" *Vera of Las Vegas* (1996), the opera *Bandanna* (1999), and the "dramatic recital for four singers" *The Antient Concert* (2005). Its legacy was important in Madison as well. As advocates for launching the project had argued, the opera certainly did bring national recognition for Madison Opera. *Shining Brow* was also a factor in the fundamental changes that would affect the orchestra, chorus, and opera over the next few years: the retirement of Roland Johnson, the hiring of John DeMain, and the dissolution of MCMA.

The Retirement of Roland Johnson and the Search for a Successor

By the 1990s, Roland Johnson had overseen three decades of momentous change in MCMA's orchestra, chorus, and opera. The MSO had reached a relatively high level in the quality of its performances, but there was a general sense among the players of orchestra that we had in fact, reached a plateau: that the MSO needed new musical leadership if it was going to improve further. This conviction was increasingly shared by the MCMA board and—

from the evidence of my interviews with his children—by Johnson himself. One indication of the orchestra's potential was a few performances with first-rank guest conductors.

It was commonplace by the early 1990s for guest conductors to lead youth, pops, and other special programs, particularly David Becker (conductor of the University Orchestra) and Eric Townell (conductor of the Central Wisconsin Symphony Orchestra and the Madison Festival Choir). However, guest conductors for subscription concerts were exceedingly rare during Johnson's tenure. He had been obliged to step away for several concerts due to illness in 1977–78, and he had been replaced by a series of mostly local conductors. However, for the May 1978 Verdi *Requiem*, the MCMA brought in Margaret Hillis, longtime chorusmaster of the Chicago Symphony Orchestra. Veteran chorus and orchestra members remember the program as one of the most exciting choral concerts of the 1970s.[37] It would be another decade before another prominent "out of town" guest conductor led the MSO in a subscription program. In February 1988, Johnson's old friend Gunther Schuller conducted a program that included the premiere of his *Concerto for String Quartet and Orchestra* (with the Pro Arte Quartet) and two orchestral standards, the Delius *Walk to the Paradise Garden* and Rimsky-Korsakov's *Scheherazade*. Schuller, used to leading first-rank orchestras around the world, was demanding in rehearsals, and the results were clear, particularly in the familiar "warhorse" *Scheherazade*. Richard Lottridge and others who were in the orchestra in 1988 remember this concert as a clear indication of the MSO's potential.

8.08 Guest conductor Catherine Comet in 1992 (MSO program book cover).

Another pivotal moment was in February 1992, when the orchestra brought in Catherine Comet to lead a subscription concert. Comet was already a familiar name in Madison; the French-born conductor had been director of the University Orchestra from 1979 to 1981. However, by 1992 she had earned a national reputation with the orchestras of St. Louis, Baltimore, and Grand Rapids, and she was by that time music director of the American Symphony Orchestra in New York City. Comet's program was a pair of standard works: the Franck *Symphony in D minor* and the Mussorgsky/Ravel *Pictures at an Exhibition*. My colleagues in the MSO and I remember her fiercely concentrated rehearsals, and the excitement of the concert, in which the orchestra gave one of its finest performances to date. (I remember my friend, tubist Paul Haugan, putting it most succinctly: "She kicked our butts for a week, and the orchestra ended up sounding great.") The audience and local reviewers clearly noticed as well. In the *Capital Times*, Jay Rath's review began: "The city owes a debt to guest conductor Catherine Comet for finding the unrealized talent of the Madison Symphony Orchestra."[38]

A month later, on March 18, 1992, the MSO formally announced Roland Johnson's retirement to the public: he would step down as music director at the close of the 1993–94 season. His children note that Johnson, who was 71 years old by this time, had been thinking about retirement for some time and felt that it was time for "younger blood." Clearly, the prospect of capping his tenure with an accomplishment like *Shining Brow* was also attractive. The timing of his announcement also gave MCMA two full years to search for his successor.

A formal search for a music director was in fact something entirely new in the history of the orchestra. In the summer of 1926, Sigfrid Prager was an eminently qualified conductor who happened to be in Madison at the very time that the MCMA was creating the Madison Civic Symphony. His hiring as music director was quite informal, based upon a "gentleman's agreement" with regard to pay. By the time of his retirement in 1948, most of his annual salary came from the Madison Vocational School, where he served as supervisor of music. Despite the now more formal, partially academic position, there seems to have been very little in the way of a formal search for his successor. Prager and his longtime associate Richard Church, by then director of the University Orchestra, recruited Walter Heermann, a cellist and conductor with whom they had worked at the University Summer Music Clinic. Heermann was the only candidate interviewed, and it is likely that Prager, who took a strong hand in nearly every part of the MCMA's activities, and who had a close partnership with the Vocational School's president, Alexander Graham, essentially chose Heermann as his successor. When Heermann retired in 1961, once again the MSO's outgoing music director effectively chose his own successor: his former Cincinnati College of Music protégé Roland Johnson. In 1992, it was clear that the now-professional orchestra would go through a rigorous and formal search process.

The search committee included eight people, divided between MCMA and MATC. Representing MCMA were board members Bolz, Haller, and Iltis, and oboist Marc Fink, then president of the MSO player's committee, on behalf of the orchestra. Representing MATC were the school's president, Beverly Simone, and three administrators: Augusta Julian, Rosie Findlan, and Ken Niemeyer. There were 159 applicants from across the United States, and a few international conductors as well. The plan was to have three finalists, each of them conducting a subscription program in the 1993–94 season. According to Haller and Fink, the committee eventually pared the list down to eight conductors, each of whom had a phone interview. They settled on three finalists in the spring of 1993, though the identity of the finalists was not announced publicly until shortly before the beginning of the season. Though soloists and their repertoire for these programs were set well before the finalists were determined, the candidates themselves would select the rest of the repertoire for their concerts, in consultation with Sandra Madden.

8.09 a–c The finalists: John DeMain, Joseph Giunta, and George Hanson.

On August 28, 1993, MCMA announced its finalists to the public and listed the repertoire that they would be conducting.[39] John DeMain, certainly the biggest "name" of the three, had been artistic director of the Houston Grand Opera for 18 years, with extensive guest conducting in opera houses around the world. The MCMA cited his "international renown." Known at the time primarily as an opera conductor, DeMain also had extensive credits as an orchestral conductor, with the Los Angeles Chamber Orchestra, Seattle Symphony Orchestra, Pittsburgh Symphony Orchestra, St. Paul Chamber Orchestra, Houston Symphony Orchestra, and others. Joseph Giunta, then and (as of 2024) still conductor of the Des Moines Symphony Orchestra, also had notable guest conducting credits: with the Chicago Symphony Orchestra, London Philharmonic Orchestra, Philharmonia Orchestra, and others. The MCMA praised Giunta for his "reputation for being able to build programs." George Hanson, whom the MCMA described as a "dynamic, rising young star," was the youngest of the three, and was then resident conductor of the Atlanta Symphony Orchestra. Though he had yet to assume a full-time conducting position, Hanson had already built an impressive resumé as a guest conductor and had served as an assistant to Leonard Bernstein at the Vienna State Opera and as assistant to Giuseppe Patene at La Scala, Covent Garden, and Munich's Bavarian State Opera.

DeMain was the first to perform, on October 16. He had, in fact, already heard the orchestra perform: In April 1993, shortly after he knew he was a finalist, DeMain had flown to Madison to attend the premiere of *Shining Brow*. He was, of course, interested in the opera itself, but he related to me in a 2000 interview that he was also there to "check you guys out."[40] Fink recalled that DeMain sought him out at the reception afterward and "talked my ear off" about the orchestra.[41] The opening work of DeMain's program, Wagner's *Tannhaüser Overture*, was plagued by poor intonation in the strings.[42] But the remainder of the program was stunning, with an exciting performance of a virtuoso showpiece, the Vieuxtemps *Violin Concerto No. 5* by soloist Alyssa Park, that showed DeMain to be a sensitive accompanist. He closed with a powerful and passionate reading of Shostakovich's fifth symphony. This is a work that includes a vast range of emotions, and DeMain drew all of them from the MSO, from the bitter sarcasm of the second movement, and the heartbreak of the third, to the noisy bombast of the finale. Giunta was next, leading an all-romantic program on November 8: the Tchaikovsky *Serenade*, the Liszt *Piano Concerto No. 1*, in a brilliant performance by José Feghali, and Rachmaninoff's second symphony. Though this concert was well received by the audience, Giunta withdrew his application soon afterward. Hanson was the final candidate, appearing on January 15, 1994. His program included Mozart's *Magic Flute Overture*, Bernstein's *Prelude from "A Quiet Place,"* Elgar's *Cello Concerto*, and the Dvořák *Symphony No. 9 (From the New World)*. Again, the program was a success, with an expressive performance of the somber Elgar concerto by Shauna Rolston and a surprising version of the familiar orchestral "warhorse" by Dvořák. Hanson's choice of the challenging Bernstein *Prelude* was intended as a tribute to his mentor, but it also was a (probably unintentional) bit of one-upmanship: DeMain, who also counted Bernstein as a mentor, had actually directed the 1983 premiere of *A Quiet Place*, Bernstein's last opera, in Houston.

The members of the orchestra anxiously waited for a decision from the committee in the weeks following Hanson's appearance. Fink noted that a formal poll of the MSO after Hanson's concert had a majority of players in favor of DeMain. Those of us who had expressed a preference for DeMain appreciated how hard he had worked us during his visit and how exciting the Shostakovich had been. At the same time, many were doubtful that he would take what seemed like, at best, a sideways step from his position in Houston to come to Madison. The vast majority of us, however, felt that either of the two remaining candidates, DeMain or Hanson, would be an effective leader. There was also hot speculation in the community at large: a phone poll conducted by the *Wisconsin State Journal* showed a strong preference for Hanson.[43] From later statements by Haller, Madden, and Fink, it seems that, for the search committee, DeMain had been the frontrunner from the start.

The news that DeMain had accepted the position broke on February 5, and DeMain himself flew to Madison to appear at a press conference. Bringing him to Madison was widely viewed as a coup for the MSO, but as for its being a "sideways move," one person not surprised by DeMain's acceptance was DeMain himself. Reflecting on the move in 2000, he noted that he had been looking for a few years for an opportunity to move back into orchestral conducting, and to find an orchestra with potential for development like Madison's, noting that: "In this country, you get tracked as either an opera conductor or orchestra conductor, and I wasn't ready to be pigeonholed."[44] To be sure, DeMain continued to work internationally in opera as a guest conductor, and the fact that he also became the artistic director of the Madison Opera—like the MSO, a successful regional company—clearly made Madison attractive as well. There were also personal factors: John and his wife Barbara had a daughter, Jennifer, then just a toddler, and Madison seemed to them to be a fine place to raise a child.

Passing the Baton

For his part, Johnson finished strong. There was *Shining Brow*, of course, but in the closing two and a half seasons of his tenure, he led several particularly fine programs with the orchestra and chorus: Bach's *Mass in B minor* (March 1992), Mendelssohn's *Elijah* (March 1993), and the opening program of the 1993–94 season, featuring flutist James Galway and a performance of the Stravinsky *Firebird Suite* stand out in my memory. On February 12, 1994, a week after John DeMain was announced as his successor, Johnson conducted one of the most memorable concerts of the 1990s: a performance of Prokofiev's

8.10 *Wisconsin State Journal*, front page, May 15, 1994.

original score for the film *Alexander Nevsky*, played with the film itself. For his farewell appearance as music director of the Madison Opera in April 1994, Johnson chose Verdi's *Aïda*, the same opera used 15 years earlier to open the Madison Civic Center's Oscar Mayer Theater. With the exception of *Shining Brow*, the 1994 *Aïda* was the Madison Opera's most lavish production to that time. His farewell to the MSO and the Madison Symphony Chorus was an all-Brahms program on May 14, 1994: the *German Requiem* and the *Symphony No. 1*. Johnson's choice of the Brahms symphony was doubly symbolic, as explained in the program notes for the concert:

> Mr. Johnson views the symphony's long path from C minor towards a resolution in C Major as symbolic of his 33 seasons as the MSO's director. Equally significant is the fact that this work brings his career in Madison full circle—the *Symphony No.1* was included on the very first MSO program Mr. Johnson conducted, in October of 1961.[45]

The program book included tributes from state and local politicians, MCMA board members, and local and nationally known musicians, soloists, and composers with whom Johnson had worked. The concert itself featured excellent performances by the chorus and orchestra, but of course the main point of the evening was honoring Johnson. A thunderous standing ovation from a near-capacity crowd in the Oscar Mayer Theatre, and from the orchestra, brought Johnson back to the stage three times at the conclusion of the concert. On his second bow, Johnson—in a memorable and moving gesture—laid his baton on the podium.[46] A review by Jess Anderson in *Isthmus* was typical of the praise Johnson received for this concert but also paid tribute to the orchestra he had built over his 33 seasons as music director:

> There was no great drama and no empty hype of the occasion, as one might have expected. Rather, they just played their hearts out, as they should for any concert, for every concert. If there was anything out of the ordinary, it would be that Johnson leaves the podium and delivers up to his successor, John DeMain, the best orchestra the town has ever had. That should make anyone proud.[47]

John DeMain and the MSO

The orchestra's new music director began rehearsals in September 1994, but several important changes for both orchestra and chorus were already in place before he stepped onto the podium. DeMain asked that all string players—on a purely voluntary basis—play individually for him prior to the season, and he noted that he planned to reseat the sections based on what he heard from veteran players and from auditions for new players in all string sections that were also held prior to the season. This of course caused consternation, though it was clearly DeMain's prerogative as music director. He made it clear that he had no intention of depriving anyone of their seat in the orchestra, but several players decided to retire rather than go through what felt very much like an audition. In auditions for new players, DeMain also instituted blind auditions for the first time in the orchestra's history, ensuring a more objective approach to hiring new players. This move, which brought the MSO in line with most other professional orchestras across the country, would have important consequences for the MSO over the next three decades, as the orchestra began to attract and hire players from well beyond the Madison area.

8.11 Roland Johnson and John DeMain in 1994. The MSO's incoming music director, DeMain, and the newly named music director laureate, Johnson, maintained a friendly, mutually respectful relationship.

A comparison of the orchestra rosters for Johnson's final concert in May 1994 and DeMain's inaugural program in September 1994 is revealing. The two string sections are nearly identical in size, but 11 players, many of them longtime members, from the May string section do not appear in the September roster, and there are some 15 new names in September, mostly younger players. The sections had also been reorganized, with several players who had been at the back of sections moved forward significantly, and a few who had been in front stands moved back[48] Thus, when the orchestra began rehearsals in September, it was with a thoroughly reseated string section, roughly a third of them new members of the orchestra. The result was dramatic and immediate: many veteran woodwind and brass players remember being astonished at that first rehearsal by the quality and power of what truly sounded like a *new* MSO string section. Over the next few years, DeMain consistently advocated for incrementally enlarging the strings. The string section in September 1994 included 44 players, slightly larger than it had been during the last several years of Johnson's tenure. However, by the 2000–2001 season, the orchestra's regular string section totaled 61 players, roughly the size it has maintained since then. These changes not only addressed long-standing problems of balance between the strings and the rest of the orchestra, but a more powerful and flexible string section also opened up a much wider range of repertoire that the MSO could tackle. The resonant sound of over 60 string players has become a standard part of the MSO's sound.

A second change was in the rehearsal schedule. Though the days of once-a-week orchestra rehearsals were long gone by 1994, rehearsals for the MSO's subscription concerts were still a rather leisurely affair, with five rehearsals (typically including an initial strings-only rehearsal) spread over the two weeks prior to the concert. It was clear that DeMain was going to maintain a busy schedule of conducting commitments outside of Madison, and the two-week schedule would simply not work. A one-week schedule of rehearsals was going to be needed—and was in fact relatively standard in American orchestras—and the long-standing tradition of strings-only rehearsals was abandoned as well. For the first few years, dress rehearsals for the Saturday evening subscription programs were held on Saturday mornings, but most MSO players were relieved when they later moved back to Friday nights. The new schedule, with five two-and-a-half- to three-hour rehearsals on successive nights, occasionally starting on Sunday to allow for a night off, could be exhausting during symphony weeks, particularly for the many players who had full-time "day jobs" (university and public school teachers and other professions). However, this new, much more concentrated schedule clearly paid off in the increasing quality and intensity of the orchestra's performances.

Another important change that came with DeMain was in his approach to rehearsing the orchestra. Our previous rehearsals had focused on the pieces as a whole, familiarizing the players with the music, but Johnson often let smaller details and intonation problems slip by without correction. DeMain, used to working with first-rank, fully professional orchestras, had clear ideas about what he wanted on both the large and small scale and demanded that even small problems be fixed. We would usually begin with a complete read-through of the repertoire for the week, but most of our rehearsal time was spent working out details. He was businesslike and efficient and seldom failed to put every minute of our contracted time to productive use. Though players had always prepared parts in advance, it was now clear that the first rehearsal was not a time to learn the music: we needed to come in with parts thoroughly mastered and with a clear idea of how those parts fit into the whole. I know him well enough to say that he has mellowed considerably in three decades, but in the early years, DeMain could be fierce, particularly when a player or section managed to make the same mistake more than once. (I speak from personal experience.) This was rare, however, and we as an orchestra generally felt respected as fellow professionals doing our job. Indeed, when I interviewed him a few years later, DeMain described his job as tapping into the "collective intelligence" of 90 highly trained players.[49]

Since the founding of the Madison Civic Chorus in 1927, the music director had also rehearsed the chorus and led all of its performances. While the MCMA had occasionally engaged assistants to cover some choral rehearsals (e.g., Kunrad Kvam in the 1940s, Ralph James in the 1950s, and Arthur Becknell in the 1970s and 1980s), Prager, Heermann, and Johnson had all maintained a dual role conducting both orchestra and chorus. DeMain had a dual role as music director of the MSO and as artistic director of the now-separate Madison Opera, but he would not be able to conduct the regular weekly rehearsals of the Madison Symphony Chorus. Beginning in 1994, the MSO hired a separate chorus director, Alan Rieck, at that time a doctoral student at the University. Rieck, in consultation with DeMain, took over all regular weekly rehearsals, preparing the chorus for its performances with the orchestra. He worked very well with the chorus for two seasons, preparing several fine performances; the season finales of May 1995 (Beethoven, *Symphony No. 9*) and May 1996 (Mahler, *Symphony No. 2*) remain in my mind as truly excellent choral performances. In February 1996, Rieck also reinstituted the long-standing tradition of a separate choral concert, leading performances of the Fauré and Rutter *Requiems* at the First Congregational Church. At the end of the 1995–96 season, Rieck left to take an academic job at the University of Northern Arizona.[50]

8.12 The Madison Symphony Chorus in late 1994. Seated: Alan Rieck (chorus director) and Ann Stanke (accompanist and chorus manager).

Rieck's successor as chorus director was Beverly Taylor, who remains in that position today. Born in Philadelphia in 1951, she studied vocal music at the University of Delaware. Her first choice for graduate school in choral conducting was actually UW–Madison, where she hoped to study with Robert Fountain. However, finding that Fountain was scheduled for a sabbatical that year, Taylor went instead to Boston University. This led to a teaching

8.13 Beverly Taylor, 1997.

position at the summer Tanglewood Institute, where she also studied orchestral conducting. Following her graduate work, Taylor remained in the Boston area, teaching at a private girls' school and freelancing as a conductor. (One fond memory was directing the Boston Bar Association Orchestra for several years, an amateur group made up entirely of lawyers.) She eventually joined the faculty of Harvard University, where she directed the Radcliffe Women's Chorus and the Harvard/Radcliffe Chorus. Taylor joined the University School of Music in 1995, succeeding Fountain as the director of the University Concert Choir and the UW Choral Union. She also served as director of the University's graduate choral conducting program. She approached the MSO relatively soon after arriving in Madison, and in the summer of 1996, Taylor was named assistant conductor. Her duties included not only rehearsing the chorus, but also serving as the MSO's cover conductor, learning scores for each subscription program to be ready if DeMain or a guest conductor were unable to lead a concert. She would usually attend the last couple of rehearsals before the concert, and she frequently offered notes on balance and other issues. Looking back from 2024 on this hire, DeMain remembers that Ann Stanke, whom he said had an "outdated town versus gown mindset," was initially resistant to hiring a University-based conductor for the chorus. However, he insisted, and he notes that Ann "immediately fell in love with Beverly" the moment she stood in front of the chorus.[51]

Thinking back to her early years with the Madison Symphony Chorus, Taylor describes a situation very much like what DeMain faced with the MSO strings. She insisted upon hearing all members individually so that she had a clear idea of the voices she was working with. The chorus, an all-volunteer group, had never had formal auditions, and her expectation to hear individual singers— including sight-reading—caused "some feathers to fly." Over the next few years, Taylor instituted formal auditions for new members and much higher musical standards overall.[52] The results are clearly heard in today's Madison Symphony Chorus, which is, quite simply, a much better chorus than it was in the early 1990s, with regard to intonation, ensemble, and a standard tone quality. Taylor describes her collaboration with DeMain as "trust built up over many years." In the early years, DeMain frequently attended chorus rehearsals, but they are now much more likely to communicate by phone regarding tempos and other details.

DeMain's touring schedule also meant that he would not conduct all of the regular subscription performances during the season and that he would also delegate many of the MSO's youth, choral, and other non-subscription programs.[53] During his first season in 1994–95, three of the eight subscription programs were led by guest conductors, and for the next several years, most seasons featured at least two guests leading subscription concerts. From the standpoint of the orchestra, this was nearly always a good thing. While members of the MSO appreciated working with DeMain, working intensively for a week under a guest conductor was usually a positive experience. The guests, all of them established conductors with national or international reputations, brought their own interpretations of the works and ways of working with the orchestra, and the resulting concerts were often memorable. A few guest conductors of the late 1990s who led particularly fine programs and who are remembered with fondness by veteran players include JoAnn Falletta (October 1995), Murry Sidlin (November 1996), Janna Hymes-Bianci (March 1998 and February 2000), Harvey Felder (April 1999), and Leslie Dunner (November 1999).

DeMain's Inaugural Season and the Close of the 1990s

DeMain's first program as music director, performed to a sold-out Oscar Mayer Theater on September 17, 1994, was a challenging one. After opening the season with the *Star-Spangled Banner*—a tradition going back to the Prager years—the first two works featured the Madison Symphony Chorus: Mozart's brief *a capella* motet *Ave verum corpus*, and Bernstein's difficult *Chichester Psalms*, included as a tribute to Bernstein, with whom DeMain had collaborated. The chorus, prepared for the first time by newly hired chorus director Alan Rieck, did a fine job with the work's Hebrew text and sometimes treacherous rhythms. The second movement includes a pair of extended solos for boy soprano, and the young soloist Andrew Morgan struggled with them. After intermission, the focus shifted to the orchestra, which played Mahler's weighty first symphony, the beginning of a complete cycle of Mahler symphonies promised by DeMain. The orchestra's performance was not perfect, but DeMain led an exciting and emotional reading of the score that marked a promising beginning of his tenure as music director.

Over the remainder of the 1994–95 season, the orchestra tackled a series of challenging works under DeMain: Kodály's *"Háry János" Suite*, Britten's *Sea*

Interludes from "Peter Grimes," and to close the season, a program with Beethoven's first and ninth symphonies. The subscription series also included concerts led by guest conductors Richard Buckley (November 1994) and Elizabeth Schulze (March 1995). As in Johnson's final years, the midwinter concert was a lighter pops-style program, and in January 1995, it was film and television music led by Broadway/Hollywood composer Bill Conti. The MSO and the chorus also continued the tradition of a holiday variety program that had evolved in the early 1990s. DeMain's program in December 1994, now rebranded as the "Holiday Spectacular," was particularly ambitious, including short semi-staged versions of both Humperdinck's *Hansel and Gretel* and Herbert's *Babes in Toyland*, as well as a variety of choral, orchestral, and solo selections. Many of the orchestra's youth programs were delegated to Erik Townell and other guest conductors over the next few years, but DeMain—who had led many youth programs during his time with the St. Paul Chamber Orchestra—conducted the February Young People's Concert, and he continued to be involved with youth programming throughout his tenure.

Though the Madison Opera was now a separate entity, the MSO continued to be its exclusive pit orchestra, and opera performances remain an important part of the orchestra's work today. Roland Johnson directed the first two productions of the 1994–95 opera season, a Broadway show in November (Lerner and Loewe's *Brigadoon*) and a children's opera in March (Franklin's *The Very Last Green Thing*). DeMain's debut as artistic director of the Madison Opera was an unforgettable production of Mozart's *Die Zauberflöte* in April 1995. For those of us in the orchestra, it was our first chance to work with him as an opera conductor—which of course had been his primary gig over the previous 18 years in Houston. His ability to exercise thorough command over both the stage and the pit, while allowing space for artistic expression by the cast and orchestral soloists, was truly impressive.

There was also a new MSO tradition that began just before the opening of the 1995–96 season. The Concert on the Green was largely the brainchild of DeMain and Candy Gialamas, a member of the MSO board and the MSOL. This benefit event combined afternoon golfing at Bishop's Bay, a golf club on the north shore of Lake Mendota, and an evening concert and dinner staged in an enormous tent on the club's south lawn, overlooking the lake. The first Concert on the Green, on September 21, 1995, was an unqualified success, both as an event and as a fundraiser. The second was staged in June 1996, and it has remained an annual June event since then; it also remains one of the MSOL's most lucrative fundraisers. The Concert on the Green was held at Bishop's Bay

8.14 Concert on the Green, 2018.

through June 2023. Of course, outdoor concerts, even when held under a tent, are at the mercy of Wisconsin weather, and the second Concert on the Green, on June 17, 1996, was memorable for reasons having nothing to do with music. Shortly after the orchestra's program began, a severe thunderstorm blew in over Lake Mendota, and the sound of torrential rain on the tent completely drowned out the orchestra. When streams of mucky water began flowing among the tables, the power was shut off for safety, and the event was canceled. MSO players later referred to the event jokingly as the "Concert in the Mud."

Innovative Auxiliary: The Madison Symphony Orchestra League, 1980 to present

In Chapter 6, I discussed the early history of the MSOL. By 1980, this auxiliary group had shed its roots as a rather exclusive "society"-oriented women's organization to become a much broader-based group supporting the orchestra in many ways. Today, the MSOL is actually one of the orchestra's largest single annual donors. According to Robert Reed, "the amount varies but the MSOL makes a six-figure donation every year."[54] As noted already, the MSOL's major fundraiser in the 1960s and 1970s was the annual benefit pops concert. This continued into the 1990s, though its place as an MSOL fundraising event was largely taken over by the Concert on the Green from 1995 onward. To survey merely one busy season, in 2001–02, the group organized the Symphony Showhouse, the Arts Ball, a benefit fashion show, a bridge (the card game) marathon, and a presence at the Hilldale Holiday Tree Walk, and it sponsored several special parties, Magic of Music luncheons, and informal concert previews.[55]

MSOL continues a tradition from its earliest days of creative fundraising and advocacy for the orchestra. In 1979, inspired by a group they had seen at the American Symphony Orchestra League conference, MSOL organized the Symphony Singers, led by Evelyn Jennings. The group's main repertoire was parody songs written by Jennings: Broadway or popular songs with witty new lyrics promoting the MSO. The group performed about 15 times a year at meetings of community groups and clubs, with each performance followed by a pitch for the upcoming concerts. For over 40 years, through 2017, the MSOL partnered with the Madison Art Center to stage the annual Arts Ball as a benefit for both groups. One effort in the 1990s and early 2000s was the Symphony Showhouse. This involved selecting a home in Madison, which was then remodeled completely by a group of local contractors. MSOL then sold tickets to tour the home. The group has long held the orchestra's education and outreach programs as a special concern, and the Concert on the Green provides the largest annual donation to those programs. In the days before MSO had a professional director of education (pre-1999), MSOL actually developed curricular materials and distributed them to schools. (These education brochures were largely the work of Nan Becknell, an active MSOL member and a former hornist in the MSO and University.) To this day, the group continues to provide docents who visit the local schools to give preparatory talks for the fall youth concerts.[56]

The essential outlines of the season remained fairly similar to what it had been in the last few years of Johnson's tenure: eight Saturday night subscription programs, including a holiday concert and a midwinter pops-style program, fall and spring youth concerts, a special chorus concert, and two or three opera performances. However, in DeMain's first season, the MSO began to double subscription programs, starting with the popular Christmas concert and the final May program featuring the Beethoven ninth symphony, in each case adding a Sunday matinee to the Saturday night performance. After the first Concert on the Green, the MSO also began adding programs to the season, beginning with springtime concerts aimed at very young children and families. At first, the MSO played a series of prepackaged programs for young audiences: *Symphonosaurus™*, *Beethoven Lives Upstairs™*, and others. In 1999, the MSO hired its first director of education, Hope Horton, and in May 2000 the orchestra instituted its own annual program for young children, "Symphony Soup."

8.15 Terry Haller, 1997. Haller succeeded Marian Bolz as president of the MSO board, serving for four years (1994–98) and overseeing momentous changes in the organization.

There seems to have been continuing excitement in Madison about DeMain and the ever-improving MSO. (Sandra Madden referred to these years as "like lightning in a bottle.") Subscriptions and single ticket sales kept rising in the late 1990s, and the MSO began to work toward expanding the subscription season, moving to paired concerts with performances on Saturday night and Sunday afternoon to accommodate a larger audience. In DeMain's second season, 1995–96, four of the eight programs were doubled. This expanded to six in the next season, and finally to all eight programs in 1997–98. For the orchestra, this was of course a welcome raise in pay, but the opportunity to perform a carefully prepared program twice on successive days also improved the quality of our performances overall.

One overarching theme in these years was the Mahler cycle that began in DeMain's first concert. The idea of a Mahler cycle—working through his nine completed symphonies—may have been inspired in part by DeMain's mentor Leonard Bernstein. Bernstein, as conductor of the New York Philharmonic in the 1950s and 1960s, played a leading role in the popularization of Mahler's music in the United States. However, these works also played a role in the musical growth of the MSO. Playing the first symphony in September 1994 had been an exciting beginning, and over the next four seasons, the MSO worked its way through his second, third, fourth, and fifth symphonies, with the chorus joining on the second and third.[57] Not every orchestra musician is a Mahler fan, but for many of us, the prospect of being able to play all nine of his completed symphonies in order was a kind of "bucket list" dream come true. Gustav Mahler's symphonies present a series of formidable challenges to any orchestra, including sheer endurance: with the exception of the first and fourth, all of them last well over an hour, with the sprawling third topping out at nearly 100 minutes. Mahler calls for a wide range of techniques from instruments across the orchestra. The symphonies also call for a huge breadth of expression, from truly enormous moments for an enlarged orchestra to transparent chamber music and extended solo passages. I believe that meeting these challenges on a yearly basis over the first few years of DeMain's tenure was a factor in the growing quality of the MSO's performances overall.

8.16 Gustav Mahler in 1907.

The MSO was also "stretched" by other challenging repertoire under both DeMain and guest conductors—to name just a few highlights: Bartók's *Dance Suite* (October 1995), Ives's *Symphony No. 2* (November 1996, with Murry Sidlin), Stravinsky, *Petrouchka* (November 1998, with David Lockington), and Hindemith, *Symphony "Mathis der Maler"* (March 1999). Under DeMain, the MSO also continued a tradition of commissioning new works. World premieres in this period included

- Daron Hagen, *Taliesin: Choruses from "Shining Brow"* (September 1995: an adaptation of four extracts from the opera, for chorus and orchestra)
- Stewart Wallace, *Kaddish from "Harvey Milk"* (February 1997: adapted from the closing scene of Stewart's critically acclaimed 2013 opera; with mezzo-soprano Jill Grove, countertenor Randall Wong, baritone Kurt Ollmann, and the Madison Symphony Chorus)
- David DiChiera, *Four Sonnets of Edna St. Vincent Millay for Soprano and Orchestra* (January, 1998: with soprano Helen Donath)
- Daron Hagen, *Forward!* (May 1998: short fanfare, played by the MSO brass and percussion at the ceremonial unveiling of Wisconsin sesquicentennial postage stamp)

- Michael Torke, *Jasper* (September 1998: joint commission with the Milwaukee Symphony Orchestra, in honor of the Wisconsin sesquicentennial)
- Taras Nahirniak, *Hodie Christus* (December 1998: joint commission with the Madison Boychoir by a local composer)
- Arthur Weisberg, *Concerto for Oboe, Bassoon, and Strings* (August 1999: presented at the conference of the International Double Reed Society in Madison, with oboist John Dee and the composer on bassoon)

The MSO continued to feature its own players as soloists; it became standard, for example, to feature at least one or two principal players on the annual Holiday Spectacular program. However, the great majority of its subscription programs were headlined by internationally known soloists. Among those appearing in these years were pianists Ignat Solzhenitzen, Jon Kimura Parker, John Browning, and Horacio Gutiérrez, violinists Benny Kim, Hilary Hahn (as a 16-year-old prodigy in 1996), Elmar Olivera, and Robert McDuffie, cellist Desmond Hoebig, guitarist Christopher Parkening, hornist Gail Williams, trumpeter Arturo Sandoval, and the percussion ensemble NEXUS.

Musicians of the Orchestra: Selected Profiles

Tyrone and Janet Greive

Tyrone and Janet Greive were in the MSO string section for 30 years: Tyrone as a member of the first violin section, as associate concertmaster, and (for 20 seasons) as concertmaster, and Janet on cello.[58] I interviewed them in November 2022. Tyrone was born in 1943 in Sioux City, Iowa. His working-class parents were supportive, but neither was particularly musical, although his great-grandfather had been a professional violinist before he emigrated from Germany, and both of his grandfathers played violin as amateurs. He started violin in the Sioux City public school program and began studying at age 13 with members of the Sioux City Symphony Orchestra, and then in his last two years of high school, with the orchestra's director, Polish-born violinist and conductor Leo Kucinski. Tyrone was already playing professionally when he entered Morningside College in Sioux City, where he continued his studies with Kucinski. He secured his first college teaching job, at Augustana University, a year before earning a bachelor's degree from Morningside.[59]

Janet was born Janet Rayburn in 1940 in Vermillion, South Dakota, and initially studied cello with a teacher from the University of South Dakota. Vermillion did not have a public school string program, but by middle school,

8.17a/8.17b Tyrone and Janet Greive, 2004.

she was playing with the local university/community orchestra, and in high school she performed with the Sioux City Symphony Orchestra, while also spending summers at the Interlochen Music Camp. Janet won a scholarship on cello that funded her bachelor's and master's degrees at the Peabody Conservatory in Baltimore, Maryland. While at Peabody, she frequently played outside performances, including with a string quartet of Baltimore Symphony players, and she also spent summers at the Aspen Music Festival. Janet proudly notes that she was able to study with several of the world's finest cellists during her time at Peabody and in succeeding years: Richard Kay, Zara Nelsova, Raya Garbousova, Janos Starker, Lazlo Varga, and others. After completing her master's and teaching certification coursework in 1963, she taught in the Sioux Falls, South Dakota, public schools, while also playing principal cello in the Sioux Falls Symphony. In 1964 she met Tyrone, the orchestra's new concertmaster who had just joined the faculty of Augustana College (now Augustana University). After a highly successful performance of the Beethoven *Triple Concerto*, they played together in a piano trio in residence at Augustana, where Janet became a faculty member in 1966. Over the next 46 years they played together in various orchestras at the Aspen and Shreveport Summer Festivals, the Black Hills Chamber Orchestra, the Longview Symphony Orchestra, and others, culminating with their three decades in the MSO. They also jointly performed in a host of chamber ensembles, primarily piano trios, as well as appearing as soloists. (For example, they performed the Brahms *Double Concerto* on multiple occasions.)

The Greives married in 1968, and shortly after their honeymoon, Tyrone's draft notice appeared. After successfully auditioning into the Army orchestra at Fort Myer, Virginia, and three weeks of basic training, he failed to pass an eye exam—laughing, he described his lenses as "like the bottom of a coke bottle." He left the Army with an honorable discharge, and as he was already on leave from Augustana, he took the opportunity to study with Sidney Harth and complete a master's degree at Carnegie Mellon University. The Greives returned to Sioux Falls and Augustana in the fall of 1971. In early 1975, they left Sioux Falls, and over the next two years Tyrone finished a doctorate at the University of Michigan. After two years (1977–79) teaching at Stephen F. Austin State University in east Texas, the Greives moved to Madison in the fall of 1979, where he joined the University faculty as a violin teacher and director of the University's Pre-College Institute.[60] Janet joined the Institute faculty as well, and both of them joined the Madison Symphony Orchestra. After a year as a section violinist, Tyrone became associate concertmaster, and in 1980 he succeeded Norman Paulu as the MSO's concertmaster. Tyrone appeared as a soloist on 12 different works on 12 MSO programs:

- Tippett, *Fantasia Concertante on a Theme of Corelli* (2/11/1984)
- Mendelssohn, *Violin Concerto* (12/11/1984; third movement, 6/19/2000, at Concert on the Green)
- Handel, *Concerto Grosso*, op. 6, no. 12 (2/9/1985)
- Bach, *Brandenburg Concerto No. 5* (2/9/1985 and 12/4/1999)
- Bach, *Brandenburg Concerto No. 2* (2/9/1985)
- Mozart, *Violin Concerto No. 5*, K. 219 (5/16/1991)
- Bach, *Brandenburg Concerto No. 1* (1/18/1992)
- Beethoven, *Triple Concerto* (3/26/1994)
- Bach, *Brandenburg Concerto No. 4* (9/24/1995)
- Strauss, *Don Quixote* (11/6/1999)
- Kroll, *Banjo and Fiddle* (6/18/2001 at Concert on the Green)
- Vivaldi, *Winter* from *The Four Seasons* (11/25/2003)

He also played the opening movement of Vivaldi's *Spring* concerto on several youth and Symphony Soup programs between 2000 and 2010.

Tyrone noted that "I've done a lot of concertmastering over the years," and he commented extensively on what he sees as the multiple responsibilities of the position, summing it up by saying, "you just have to be ready to lead when it's needed."[61] Regarding the transition from Roland Johnson to John DeMain, Tyrone called it an "evolution" and asserted that "John DeMain could not have done what he did with the Madison Symphony if Johnson hadn't prepared the way." Both Greives cited the "positive attitude" of MSO players as an important factor in its success. Tyrone said that "an orchestra is more than a collection of good players," stressing that good orchestras develop traditions that are maintained by the veteran players. The Greives also noted that the long-term stability of the orchestra's artistic leadership in Johnson and DeMain has been fundamental in maintaining the creative and constructive "orchestral culture" of the MSO.

Today the Greives live in retirement in Madison. Tyrone still performs occasionally and serves as a member of the MSO board. Janet has been suffering from a degenerative condition that left her unable to play. (She donated her 18th-century cello to the Peabody Conservatory.) They clearly enjoy one another's company and remain passionate about music; Janet noted that, during the Covid lockdown, they made it a point to listen together to *all* of the hundreds of recordings they had accumulated over the years.[62]

Marc Fink

Oboist Marc Fink had a 49-year career in the MSO, beginning shortly after his arrival in Madison in the fall of 1973. Born in Waukegan, Illinois, he studied initially with Robert Mayer, formerly of the Chicago Symphony Orchestra, and Ray Still, then the CSO's principal oboe. He did his undergraduate work at Indiana University, studying with yet another former member of the CSO,

8.18 Marc Fink, 2009.

Jerry Sirucek. Shortly after beginning graduate studies, Fink joined the Air Force, as an alternative to being drafted into the Army for likely service in Vietnam. He served for three and a half years before returning to Indiana University to complete a master's degree. He came to Madison in 1973 for a one-year position at the University, teaching oboe and playing in the Wingra Woodwind Quintet. The next year he received a permanent appointment, and he remained on the faculty of the University School of Music until his retirement in 2013. He joined the MSO in 1973 on English horn, playing for 15 seasons in the section led by oboist Catherine Paulu. He became principal oboe unexpectedly in February 1988, during rehearsals for the Gunther Schuller program discussed above. Just before the second rehearsal, he received a call from Robert Palmer informing him that Catherine Paulu was ill and unable to play the rest of the rehearsals and the concert. (As it turned out, she had terminal-stage cancer and died at age 52 just a few weeks later.[63]) Fink would continue as principal oboe until his official retirement from the orchestra at the end of 2019–20, after 48 seasons— though he played principal for the first half of the 2021–22 season as well.

Looking back during an interview in late 2022, he noted that "the Madison Symphony was always my first priority," and that he did not take on playing commitments that would conflict with MSO services. However, Fink expressed special pride in his work with the University of Chicago Contemporary Ensemble, directed by composer Ralph Shapey. He also fondly remembered performances in Fairbanks, Alaska, as a soloist with the Fairbanks Symphony Orchestra, led by former Madison musician Gordon Wright,[64] and as part of a summer arts festival there for several years. He recalled traveling with a chamber orchestra by plane to remote Alaskan towns "where they had probably never seen a violin." Fink appeared as a soloist with the MSO 12 times:

- Bach, *Brandenburg Concerto No. 1*, BWV 1046 (11/17/1974, 2/9/1985, and 1/18/1992)
- Martin, *Concerto for Seven Winds, Timpani, Percussion, and Strings* (1/31/1976 and 9/19–21/2014)
- Cimarosa/Benjamin, *Oboe Concerto* (1/26/1991)
- R. Strauss, *Oboe Concerto* (2/22/1997)
- Marcello, *Oboe Concerto in C minor*, second movement (12/5–6/1998)
- Handel, *Entrance of the Queen of Sheba from "Solomon"* (7/15–17/1999)
- Bach, *Brandenburg Concerto No. 2*, BWV 1046 (12/4–5/2000)
- Vivaldi, *Oboe Concerto in C Major*, RV 447 (6/14/2004)
- Mozart, *Oboe Concerto*, K. 314 (9/23–24–25/2022)

The final performance listed here was remarkable for a couple of reasons ... including the fact that it took three attempts to actually get it done. DeMain wanted to celebrate Fink's long tenure with the orchestra by featuring him as a soloist in the opening program of the 2020–21 season, and Fink chose the Mozart concerto, "a work I'd always wanted to play with the orchestra." It would be paired with Beethoven's ninth symphony, as the beginning of a planned season-long celebration of Beethoven. However, in the spring of 2020, shortly after the season was announced, the MSO went into pandemic lockdown, and the entire 2020–21 season was eventually canceled. Performances resumed in 2021–22 and the Mozart/Beethoven program was scheduled for September 2021, but once again Covid stood in the way: amid a surge of cases in August and September, the MSO wisely decided it was not yet time to put some 250 instrumentalists and singers on stage at the same time for the ninth symphony. The orchestra instead performed a program of works for string orchestra, which could be performed with a safe spacing of players, and the Mozart/Beethoven program was postponed again. Fink finally had his chance to play the concerto in September 2022. (He wryly noted that "[My wife] Marcia had to listen to that piece every day for two years.") Not only was it a fine performance of the concerto, it also included a memorable bit of humor: Fink's original cadenza for the final movement included—very much in the spirit of Mozart—a rousing version of *On Wisconsin!* Fink recalled, chuckling, that the MSO's newly hired executive director, Robert Reed, who was completely new to Wisconsin and attending his very first MSO concert, was apparently bewildered when the audience started laughing and clapping along with an oboe cadenza.[65]

Paul Haugan

Tubist Paul Haugan (1955–2012) was an unforgettable presence at the back of the orchestra for 40 years. Not only was he the powerful bottom end of the MSO brass section, he was *literally* a large presence: Paul was a big man, at nearly 6' 8" towering over all members of the orchestra. He was also my friend and musical partner: As the MSO's bass trombonist, I sat next to Paul for 22 seasons.[66]

8.19 Paul Haugan, 2006.

Paul was born in Madison, graduating from West High School. One of his first professional engagements was playing in the Clyde Beatty Cole Brothers Circus Band at age 15. The circus wanted to hire him on the spot as part of its traveling band, but his parents refused. Nevertheless, he did perform frequently with circus bands while still in high school, and he also made his first appearances with the MSO. At age 18, he traveled to Switzerland to study at the Institute for Advanced Musical Study, but what was supposed to be a "practice audition" with the Nuremberg Opera Orchestra turned into a job offer. Paul accepted and spent the next five years in Germany. Returning to the United States, he spent the next few years working primarily in Chicago as a freelance and recording musician, substituting frequently with both the Chicago Symphony Orchestra and the Chicago Lyric Opera, and performing with the Chicago Brass Ensemble.[67] While in Chicago, he studied with CSO principal tubist Arnold Jacobs, one of the 20th century's great tuba pedagogues. He became a regular member of the MSO in 1982 and joined what musicians refer to as the "Freeway Philharmonic." Over the next few years, he also became principal tuba in the Green Bay Symphony Orchestra (now defunct), the Rockford Symphony Orchestra, and Milwaukee's Festival City Symphony, while also performing with the Capitol City Band, and freelancing in situations ranging from recording sessions to polka bands. (The sight of Paul in *Lederhosen* was memorable!)

One of the prime concerns of an orchestral low brass section is intonation, and Paul served as our anchor. Constantly experimenting in search of the perfect sound, he would sometimes—to the consternation of his sectionmates—bring in two or three different instruments and up to a dozen different mouthpieces during the course of a week's rehearsals.[68] I teased him for years about his search for "tuba nirvana." He would also occasionally play *cimbasso*, the now-rare valve contrabass trombone that Verdi and other 19th-century Italian composers called for in their opera scores, parts that are now usually played on tuba. In search of an authentic sound, Paul would borrow *cimbassi* from friends in Chicago and Milwaukee when the program included 19th-century Italian repertoire. However, I remember one time he brought in a *cimbasso* that he had assembled himself from trombone and tuba parts he happened to have around his house. (It was not a successful experiment.) Paul was a powerful player, perfectly capable of overbalancing a 90-piece orchestra singlehandedly, but he also played the rare solo passages for tuba with great sensitivity. I remember his performances of music by Mahler, Prokofiev, and Shostakovich with particular fondness.

Music was far from Paul's only passion. He was deeply devoted to environmentalism, and he loved the outdoors. I remember that one of his pastimes was to hike the hills and bluffs near the Mississippi, capturing rattlesnakes that he then provided to a laboratory that "milked" them to produce antivenom. Paul had a collection of reptiles at home, including a large albino boa constrictor named—of course—Fafnir, whom he brought to visit schools and community centers on many occasions. Orchestral brass players tend to have a lot of downtime during rehearsals, and Paul was an interesting guy to sit by. We had wide-ranging conversations on and off stage over the years, talking about music—instrument construction, and music from orchestral works to the late medieval styles I was studying in my musicological work—but also science, the environment, history, politics, and swapping jokes.

Paul made no secret of his struggle with mental illness. At several points over the years, his medications became unbalanced, and he would sometimes go off medication, often triggering a manic episode and sometimes bizarre behavior. As a side effect of his medications, he put on a tremendous amount of weight, and eventually just getting up the few steps to the stage became

8.20 MSO low brass with Samuel Ramey, backstage at the Oscar Mayer Theatre. This was during a May 2001 concert featuring the Metropolitan Opera's star bass, where we brought in additional players for Boito's "Prologue in Heaven" from *Mefistofele*. **L–R**: Katie Kretschman (MSO second trombone), Rick Seybold, Joyce Messer (MSO principal trombone), Brian Whitty, Samuel Ramey, Mike Allsen (MSO bass trombone), Bill Irving, Terry Sliester, Paul Haugan (MSO tuba, with cimbasso).

exhausting for him. Despite his mental and physical challenges, the quality of his playing never suffered. Paul's ending was tragic. His final performance was at the annual Opera in the Park concert in July 2012, when he was in the midst of a particularly serious episode. Shortly after this, he entered the Milwaukee County Mental Complex, where he died on July 28 at age 57, a victim of obesity and sleep apnea.[69] At the opening concert of the 2012–13 season, DeMain programmed the *Adagio for Strings* by John Stevens, as a dual tribute to Paul and Roland Johnson, who had died a few months before Paul. His ending was not how he should be remembered, however. Paul was an amazing musician, a person of wide interests, and a joyful man. I miss him.

Notes to Chapter 8

1. *CT* 3/29/1980, 10.
2. Interview with Robert Palmer, 3/22/2022. The orchestra would eventually double its programs in the Oscar Mayer Theatre, but this was not until the late 1990s. The MSO began tripling its subscription programs after the move to Overture Hall in 2004.
3. Some choral concerts were still staged in the First Congregational United Church of Christ and other venues, but the MSO ended its long association with the Stock Pavilion. Its final concert there was a performance of Mendelssohn's *Elijah* in December 1979.
4. Interview with Richard Lottridge, 6/3/2019.
5. For a complete list of her appearances with the orchestra and chorus, see Allsen, *75 Years of the Madison Symphony Orchestra*, 207–8.
6. Dramatic soprano and Heldentenor (heroic tenor) are specialized voice-types, developed to meet the challenges of Wagner's music dramas. These singers are noted for their power, enabling them to balance with Wagner's dense orchestral accompaniments.
7. The Festival of the Lakes was initially conceived in 1979, and documents in the MSO archives show that Robert Palmer and other MSO representatives were involved in the planning as early as 1983.
8. See Barbara Mulhern, "Lakes festival faces logistical woes," *CT* 5/8/1986, 27, 32; and *CT* 6/24/1986.
9. Kris Kodrich, "Festival of Lakes has bangup start," *WSJ* 9/19/1986, 1.
10. Jacob Stockinger, "Festival of Lakes planners squabble over dates," *CT* 11/7/1986, 1, 7; Jacob Stockinger, "Festival of Lakes wound up with deficit, official says," *CT* 11/20/1986, 28; Genie Campbell, "Festival of Lakes off till '88," *WSJ* 12/4/1988, 1.
11. Jacob Stockinger, "Lakes festival owes workers, closes office," *CT* 9/20/1988; David Callendar and Mike Hill, "Donors will erase Lakes fest debt, *CT* 9/23/1988, 1.
12. Kevin Lynch, "Troubles finally swamp Festival of the Lakes," *CT* 9/19/1990, 3A.
13. For a complete list of Madison opera productions from 1963 to the present, see "Madison Opera: History," https://www.madisonopera.org/history/.
14. Interview with Marian Bolz, 6/3/2019.
15. The title "executive director" for the chief administrator replaced "general manager" when Madden was hired. Today, the MSO has both an executive director (Robert Reed) and a general manager (Ann Bowen, who oversees operations and budget).
16. Interview with Sandra Madden, 4/11/2023.
17. Interview with Terry Haller, 5/24/2019.
18. Madison Symphony Orchestra Press Release, November 10, 1993. (MSO Archives)
19. Interview with Terry Haller, 5/24/2019.
20. Interview with Sandra Madden, 4/11/2023.
21. As of January 2024, the Madison Symphony Orchestra Foundation had approximately $23,000,000 in assets, with a further $7,000,000 administered for the MSO by the Madison Community Foundation.

22 The organization had been known publicly as the Madison Opera since 1983, but in the early 1990s, its board still operated under the older name Madison Opera Guild. To avoid confusion, I will use "Madison Opera" in this account.

23 The following brief account of *Shining Brow*'s creation and premiere is based largely upon the much more extensive coverage of the opera in Daron Hagen, *Duet with the Past: A Composer's Memoir* (Jefferson, NC: McFarland & Company, 2019), and an interview with Terry Haller (5/24/2019), as well as an unsigned article in the program book for the premiere, "The Making of *Shining Brow*," *Madison Opera Program Book: Shining Brow World Premiere* [4/21/1993], 4–5.

24 Interview with Terry Haller, 5/24/2019. The biography was Bernhard Gill, *Many Masks* (New York: Random House, Inc., 1987). The opera's title derives from the name of Wright's famous home and studio in Spring Green, Wisconsin: Taliesin. Taliesin was the name of a legendary Welsh bard, but the name translates from Welsh as "shining brow." I will add that some of my colleagues in the orchestra referred to the opera jokingly as *Sweaty Forehead*, a nickname that was clearly appreciated by the composer! (Daron Hagen, Facebook message with the author, 8/10/2022.)

25 "The Making of *Shining Brow*," 5.

26 Hagen, *Duet with the Past*, 109.

27 This exuberant work, channeling tango, ragtime, and jazz, was written in 1989 for a commission celebrating the 75th anniversary of ASCAP. It was premiered in October 1989 by the Brooklyn Philharmonic under Lukas Foss.

28 Interview with Terry Haller, 5/24/2019.

29 Interview with Terry Haller, 5/24/2019.

30 "The Making of *Shining Brow*," 5.

31 Hagen, *Duet with the Past*, 122–25. Wadsworth had written the libretto for and stage-directed Bernstein's final opera, *A Quiet Place* (1983).

32 Hagen, *Duet with the Past*, 127.

33 Leonard Bernstein died in October 1990. This performance was arranged by permission of Bernstein's daughter Jamie. (Hagen, *Duet with the Past*, 135.)

34 James R. Oestereich, "Shining Brow: Frank Lloyd Wright Joins Opera's Pantheon," *New York Times*, 4/28/1993, C13.

35 John von Rhein, "Work peers past Wright façade, *Chicago Tribune*, 4/23/1993, 8.

36 Daron Hagen, *Shining Brow*, libretto by Paul Muldoon; Buffalo Philharmonic and Chorus/JoAnn Falletta, (Naxos Digital Stereo 8.669020–21, 2009).

37 For example, George Shook noted that "this was so memorable—and easily one of my top ten favorite performances." (Interview with George and Nancy Shook, 1/17/2023).

38 *CT* 2/4/1992, 3.

39 *WSJ* 8/28/1993, 17.

40 Interview with John DeMain, 6/5/2000.

41 Interview with Marc Fink, 11/29/2022.

42 DeMain was, in fact, already familiar with some of the issues with the MSO string section, from his April 1993 visit to hear *Shining Brow*. As described later in the chapter, he would take relatively dramatic steps to address these issues when he was named music director.

43 *WSJ* 1/22/1994, 17.
44 Interview with John DeMain, 6/5/2000.
45 J. Michael Allsen, "Program Notes," *Madison Symphony Orchestra Program Book, May 14, 1994*, p.14.
46 DeMain answered Johnson's gesture at his first program as music director in September 1994 by picking up his baton from the podium before the first work.
47 Review in *Isthmus*, 5/18/1994.
48 I know that that being demoted back into the section occasioned at least two resignations by longtime string players. In fact, the May 1994 string section also included three members of the Pro Arte Quartet (including former concertmaster Norman Paulu) who were not then regular members of the MSO, but who had joined for this concert to honor Johnson. I have not included them in my count of players (11) who were gone in September.
49 Interview with John DeMain, 6/5/2000.
50 Longtime member William Frost, the chorus's librarian for decades, also played a role, assisting chorus manager Ann Stanke and directors Johnson, Rieck, and later, Beverly Taylor in organizing rehearsals.
51 Interview with John DeMain, 6/14/2024.
52 Several chorus members have noted that Taylor not only prepares repertoire effectively, she also works to make them better singers.
53 It was in fact fairly common in the last few years of Roland Johnson's tenure for guest conductors to lead youth and pops programs. The most frequent guest conductors for these programs during the 1990s were Eric Townell (conductor of the Central Wisconsin Symphony Orchestra) and David Becker (conductor of the University of Wisconsin–Madison Symphony Orchestra).
54 Interview with Robert Reed, 6/11/2024.
55 The MSOL has extensive archives in the MSO office, including comprehensive scrapbooks for each season.
56 I thank the following MSOL members for their assistance with this section: Valerie Kazamias, Emy Andrew, and Carolyn White. I also thank Evelyn Jennings for sharing her typescript history of the Symphony Singers.
57 When it became clear that the MSO would be moving into Overture Hall in the near future, the intervals between Mahler symphonies slowed so that the titanic eighth was performed in our first season there.
58 Both Greives retired from the orchestra at the close of the 2009–10 season. However, Tyrone returned as a guest concertmaster for several additional programs in 2010–11, as the orchestra brought in three finalists for the concertmaster position. This search is discussed in Chapter 10.
59 Tyrone Greive, approved professional narrative pages for *Marquis Who's Who*, dated 2/22/2019.
60 He retired in 2013, after 34 years at the University
61 Interview with Tyrone and Janet Greive, 11/29/2022. Tyrone also shared a document supporting the Bartell Award for Outreach in the Arts he won in 2013, after his retirement from the MSO. In addition to detailing his history with the MSO, it summarizes all of the various musical duties that come with the position while also commenting on some of the more intangible parts of the job.

62 Interview with Tyrone and Janet Greive, 11/29/2022.
63 Carmen Elsner, "Celebrated Oboe Soloist Loses Battle with Cancer," *WSJ* 3/2/1988, 2.
64 In 1960, Wright founded the Madison Summer Symphony, predecessor of today's Wisconsin Chamber Orchestra. He left for Fairbanks in 1969. ("Wisconsin Chamber Orchestra: History," https://wcoconcerts.org/meet-the-wco/history, accessed 12/10/2023.)
65 Interview with Marc Fink, 11/29/2022. The next weekend, one of the board members took Reed to a UW–Madison football game, where he heard *On Wisconsin!* in its more usual setting.
66 I thank Paul's sister, Judith Ryan, for her comments on this section. Judi also shared a short biography that the family assembled after Paul's death, which has provided background for this account.
67 Obituary, *WSJ* 8/5/2012, 16–17.
68 Paul owned what certainly must have been one of the largest private collections of tubas in the country, eventually nearly 90 instruments, many of them appearing in MSO rehearsals and performances over the years.
69 He died while sleeping, when a nurse at the facility did not reattach an oxygen mask Paul had apparently removed. ("Milwaukee Co. Mental Health Complex patient died of complications of obesity, sleep apnea," *Milwaukee Journal Sentinel* 11/1/2012, A4.)

CHAPTER 9

John DeMain, Music Director 1994 to Present

It should be clear from the preceding chapter that John DeMain was already responsible for consequential changes in the orchestra during his first six years as music director. His leadership has continued to be impactful during the period covered by Chapter 10, during which the orchestra moved into its stunning new home, Overture Hall, and continued to improve musically.

In the context of this book, however, John presents a bit of a problem. In the cases of his three predecessors, I have presented relatively detailed biographies, in part because no extended biographies existed for any of them. In the case of Sigfrid Prager, I had to rely on a vast range of primary and secondary documentary evidence: I largely constructed Dr. Prager's life from documents; nearly everyone who actually knew him is now gone. For Walter Heermann and Roland Johnson, however, I certainly relied on documents, but I also had many living contacts who could fill in the more personal details. In particular, I had the enthusiastic assistance of their families: their children and grandchildren, descendants who clearly revered their memory, and who in each case gave me virtually unlimited access to their private papers. Of course, I could also rely on my own memories of and conversations with Maestro Johnson. However, DeMain is in the process of publishing a memoir of his own: *An American Conductor: Working with My Heros—The Life and Music of John DeMain* (to be published by the University of Wisconsin Press in at some point in 2025), which he very kindly allowed me to see in draft form. It is a fascinating double narrative with a biographical sketch by Greg Hettmannsberger alternating with John's own memories and reflections. Hettmannsberger died tragically in an automobile accident in December 2020 with the book nearly finished, and the project has been shepherded to completion by Gayle Worland, a writer for the *Wisconsin State Journal*. So, knowing that readers will have access to the memoir, how have I decided to deal with John's career outside of his work for the MSO here? First of all, this chapter will be shorter and less detail-filled than the chapters for his three predecessors. John has told his own story very well, and I don't see any need to walk the same ground. Secondly, while I will of course refer to the memoir here, I have tried to write a fairly concise and complementary story of DeMain's life.

Early Life in Youngstown

John Lee DeMain was born on January 11, 1944, in Youngstown, Ohio, to parents who were the children of Italian immigrants: Dominic and Nancy DeMain. Youngstown at the time was a thriving city of over 160,000 that was an important center of the steel industry. Dominic worked in a steel mill, and Nancy was a travel agent. John's only sibling, his brother Dominic, was born in 1949. According to Hettmannsberger's account, John was quite talented at a very young age, singing along perfectly with the women's choir at the family church when he was still a toddler. His parents purchased a piano and, when he was still in first grade, enrolled him in piano lessons with Ruth Berkey, a local pianist. A few years later he began taking lessons from Hermann and Blanche Grüss. That same year, in third grade, he transferred to Saint Charles Borromeo Catholic School and met an early mentor, Michael Ficcocelli, music teacher for the parish schools and also the founder of the Youngstown Symphony Orchestra, then conducted by John Krueger. Ficcocelli taught young John to conduct, and he was soon filling in for his teacher in leading classes when Ficcocelli was away. John made his operatic debut at age nine, singing the title role in a Youngstown Playhouse production of Giancarlo Menotti's opera *Amahl and the Night Visitors*, the first of many appearances on stage at the Playhouse. By the time he was in high school, DeMain was serving regularly as the musical director for the

9.01 Nancy and John DeMain in 1948.

Playhouse, directing *Brigadoon, The Most Happy Fella*, Menotti's operas *The Medium* and *The Telephone*, and *The Fantasticks*—in which he had not only served as musical director but also played one of the lead roles.[1]

DeMain continued to improve as a pianist as well: at age 12, he won a gold medal at the International Recording Festival in Houston, Texas, and a year later he was the winner of the Philharmonic Piano Competition. He capped off his busy high school years by winning a concerto competition held by the Youngstown Symphony Orchestra, and he played the Beethoven *Piano Concerto No. 1* with the orchestra in 1962.[2] He then decided to attend the Juilliard School in New York City.

9.02 A teenage John DeMain (center left) as musical director for a Youngstown Playhouse production in the 1950s (probably *Brigadoon*).

Though DeMain never returned to live in Youngstown, his home town continued to keep tabs on him long after he left, with extended articles in the *Youngstown Vindicator* marking all of his major accomplishments over the years: the Julius Rudel Award, his position with the St. Paul Chamber Orchestra, his Grammy Award and appointment as director of Houston Grand Opera, conducting the premiere of Leonard Bernstein's *A Quiet Place*, and his move to Madison. In 1987, when he was 10 years into his work in Houston, DeMain did an extended interview with the *Vindicator*'s entertainment editor Tom Williams. Looking back more than three decades, DeMain noted that:

> I think that what we have to remember was that Youngstown was not just a steel town in the '50s and early '60s. Youngstown was in its heyday, meaning that it was economically successful. All the extracurricular activities in the city—the Playhouse, the Symphony—were very well established. It was a time when the high schools put on musicals so if someone with my talent came along there was an outlet for it. I was very enterprising and advanced for my age and I took advantage of the opportunities available.

Remembering his introduction to conducting and his decision to follow music as a career:

> When I was in fourth grade, the director was not present for rehearsal for one day so they let me conduct. I had a special affinity for it. Between the time I was 9 and 18, I was very much involved with musical comedy but I was always privately studying the piano. I won the symphony [concerto] competition at age 18 and, in March of my senior year, I was trying to decide whether to go to law school, medical school, or drama school. Finally I decided that I owed it to myself to get formal training in music because I spent so much time with music when I wasn't studying.

When asked about what he considered to be his major accomplishments, DeMain answered:

> I've had the privilege of collaborating with all of the people that I regarded as my heroes while growing up. I am very proud of my relationship with, among others, Leonard Bernstein, Harold Prince, and Stephen Sondheim. Even though I deal with a lot of dead composers, I have an ongoing relationship with some of the leading creators of our time. I'm very proud that I am able to contribute new works as well as deal with the classics.[3]

Juilliard and the Kenley Players

DeMain entered the Juilliard School in New York City in the fall of 1962. He was accepted (rather grudgingly) into the piano studio of Adele Marcus, who had taught great players such as Horacio Gutiérrez, Stephen Hough, Byron Janis, and many others. As he describes it, he was never going to be a concert pianist; he had simply not started the kind of obsessive practice that it takes early enough. Though by his junior year—after "practicing my ass off for two years"[4]—he had won a full scholarship. DeMain goes on to describe the hypercompetitive atmosphere at Juilliard, but he clearly found close friends as well, particularly pianist Larry Graham and his roommates, scenic designer Ken Lewis (another Youngstown native), clarinetist and saxophonist Dave Tofani, conductor Dennis Russell Davies, violinist Broderick Olsen, and later, clarinetist Edwin Riley. He also describes hearing a great deal of great music: the New York Philharmonic under Leonard Bernstein, concerts in Carnegie Hall (including the famous 1965 comeback concert of Vladimir Horowitz), and operas at the Metropolitan and the New York City Opera in Lincoln Center.

While most of his attention as an undergrad at Juilliard had been focused on piano, he also took conducting classes from Jorge Mester. Following his freshman year—at least partly because of connections he had made in Youngstown—he landed a job at the South Shore Music Circus, a successful summer stock company in Cohasset, Massachusetts, where he found himself conducting by the end of the summer. He conducted again for the company in the summer after his sophomore year, and then in the summer of 1965, he attended the Aspen Festival.[5]

During DeMain's senior year at Juilliard (1966), famed producer John Kenley came to New York to audition actors and singers for his summer stock company, the Kenley Players, based in Ohio in Warren (near Youngstown), Columbus, and Dayton. This regular circuit of performances had started in 1961 and was phenomenally successful for over 30 years.[6] Kenley hired his headliners from the most prominent of Broadway, Hollywood, and television stars and was unafraid to tamper with existing Broadway shows to accommodate his stars.[7] DeMain would eventually work for the Kenley Players for the next 10 summers, though it was not until 1967 that he had the opportunity to serve as a musical director for an entire production, the Rodgers/Laurents musical *Do I Hear a Waltz?* On the strength of this performance, which starred television and recording star Anita Bryant, Kenley hired him as a full-time musical director for the next eight years. In his memoir, DeMain talks about the challenges of adapting songs for stars who were not necessarily singers, and he shares a series of wonderful anecdotes about working with the flamboyant Kenley himself and a series of star performers: Arthur Godfrey, Ethel Merman, Metropolitan Opera star Giorgio Tozzi, Jack Jones, Tommy Tune, Joey Heatherton, and others. Published reviews of shows DeMain directed often singled him out for praise, as in a *Cleveland Plain Dealer* review of *Can-Can* (1968), which starred Heatherton: "A first-rate chorus of singing dancers and John DeMain's expert musical direction are also responsible for making this 'Can-Can' enjoyable."[8] In an overly cutesy review of *Camelot* (1969), starring Broadway singer John Raitt, a *Dayton Daily News* writer noted that "the 'Camelot' vocal chorus is the best of the Kenley coterie, and the musical director John DeMain lords it over them—and the augmented pit orchestra—with a royal baton. Long may he reign."[9] DeMain's work with the Kenley Players continued until the summer of 1975, by

9.03 Producer John Kenley in the 1960s.

which time he was already engaged by the Houston Grand Opera. He clearly views working for Kenley—with the almost constant need to adapt and "fix" shows on very short notice—to have been an invaluable experience.

DeMain graduated from Juilliard with a master's degree in 1968. Prior to and following his graduation, DeMain continued to work widely as a pianist and as a conductor in jobs as varied as playing solo recitals at the Toledo Museum of Art (1964),[10] serving as musical director for the actress/singer Arlene Fontanna (1969),[11] accompanying French violinist Romuald Tecco (then concertmaster of the Juilliard orchestra, and later concertmaster of the St. Paul Chamber Orchestra while John was there) in educational concerts sponsored by Lincoln Center (1969) that went as far afield as Raleigh, North Carolina,[12] accompanying his former Juilliard roommate, clarinetist Edwin Riley, and his wife, Marcia Riley, in a recital in Bridgeport, Connecticut (1970),[13] and playing the Gershwin *Rhapsody in Blue* with the Youngstown Symphony Orchestra (1971).[14] In the summers of 1971 and 1972, he studied conducting at the Tanglewood Festival.

Despite years of experience directing mostly Broadway-style musicals, DeMain really wanted to conduct opera ... and in 1969, Rhoda Levine, with the National Educational Television (NET) network's Opera Project, invited him to apply to be assistant director to the Opera Project's conductor Peter Herman Adler. In his previous work for NBC in the 1950s, Adler had been responsible for commissioning *Amahl and the Night Visitors* and other television operas.[15] As DeMain relates it in his memoir, he initially frittered away much of the unstructured time that came with this job, but after a serious discussion with Adler, he began to use the time to study scores. Adler eventually noticed and began giving DeMain more responsibility.[16]

9.04 Conductor Peter Herman Adler, 1951.

Julius Rudel and Exxon/Affiliated Artists Awards: From New York City to St. Paul

Conductor Julius Rudel immigrated to the United States in 1938 from Austria, part of the wave of artists who came to America fleeing from Nazi oppression. After studies at the Mannes School of Music in New York, he joined the New York City Opera when it was created in 1944, founded as a "people's opera" (in comparison to the more elitist Metropolitan Opera). After Rudel became the NYCO's principal conductor and general director in 1957, he forged a reputation for innovative programming, and he oversaw the move to its home in Lincoln Center in 1969. In 1971, Rudel was also named Music Director of the Kennedy Center in Washington, DC.[17] Rudel established a fellowship for promising young opera conductors that would involve working as his assistant at the NYCO. It was awarded to DeMain in early 1972, actually causing a bit of a dilemma for DeMain, who had made plans to fly to Germany for study in Frankfurt, and possibly a European career.

DeMain decided to accept the Rudel Award and spent the next year working productively under Julius Rudel's mentorship. At the same time, he also had his first job with an orchestra, the Norwalk (Connecticut) Symphony Orchestra. At first this just meant taking over some rehearsals for his old Juilliard roommate Dennis Russell Davies, who directed the orchestra, but who had just accepted directorship of the St. Paul Chamber Orchestra. However, in 1973–74, DeMain prepared and led a concert of his own with Norwalk.

9.05 John DeMain, 1972.

In 1973, DeMain received another fellowship, this one from the Exxon/NEA/Affiliate Artists Conductors Program, administered by Affiliate Artists, a large nonprofit arts agency based in New York City and funded by grants from the National Endowment for the Arts and oil giant Exxon. The idea behind this grant was to put five promising young conductors into full-time residencies.[18] According to DeMain, this was to "shine a light" on young American conductors, who at that time were largely being ignored when it came to decisions about who was to lead American orchestras. As one of the first class of five winners, he already had a contact from one of the program's target orchestras: Davies had asked him to come to Minnesota to audition for assistant conductor of the St. Paul Chamber Orchestra. DeMain is careful to point out that Davies, in view of their previous friendship, recused himself from his audition—according to John, "I was picked entirely by the orchestra."[19] He won the job, though he confesses to having a bit of trepidation about breaking the news to Julius Rudel. Rudel was supportive, however.[20]

Shortly after he arrived in St. Paul, DeMain led his debut concert in August 1973, part of the SPCO's summer "Gettogether" series. In the words of one reviewer, "DeMain proved to be not only a personable host, in his introductory remarks, but, as well, a young conductor of considerable taste and intelligence."[21] DeMain found himself immediately busy, conducting programs as varied as children's concerts, a runout program staged in an airplane hangar, and in November, a concert in the SPCO's Perspectives series featuring several works by the notoriously gnarly contemporary composer Elliot Carter.[22] His debut on the mainline Capital series was scheduled for January—a relatively tame program featuring the Bach *Brandenburg Concerto No. 1*, a Chopin concerto with Grant Johannesen as soloist, a fairly conservative work by American composer Eric Stokes, and a closing orchestral piece by Ginastera.[23] However, in December, Davies was unable to conduct the Capital series program, and DeMain's formal debut was a much more challenging program, a double bill of two theatrical works in *very* different styles: Monteverdi's concerted madrigal *Il combattimento di Tancredi e Clorinda* from the early 17th century, and a brand new work commissioned by the SPCO and Minnesota Opera, *Vox Populous* by Canadian composer Sydney Hodkinson. Billed as an "active oratorio for male and female actors, electronics technician, 4 vocal soloists, mixed chorus, jazz ensemble, and chamber orchestra" this *avant-garde* piece involved a whole range of techniques and styles, from jazz and pop to aleatoric/chance music: Reviewer Roy Close called it "musical theater of the absurd," and "musical comedy of no manners whatsoever, but witty, hugely entertaining, and unique."[24] Looking back, DeMain clearly saw his successful performance of this very eclectic piece as a vindication of his choices over the years of his career: that he was not simply a conductor of classical music but rather an *American* conductor, with the "chops" needed to tackle just about any sort of American music.[25]

In 1974, he made a couple of trips back to Youngstown, first to conduct a revue celebrating the 50th anniversary of the Youngstown Playhouse, and then on tour with the SPCO, a concert in which he performed as soloist in the Beethoven *Piano Concerto No. 2*, directing from the keyboard. In June 1975, at the end of his second year in St. Paul, DeMain was one of three Exxon/NEA / Affiliate Artist fellows called to conduct the Pittsburgh Symphony Orchestra; he led a triumphantly successful program of Mozart and the Schumann *Symphony No. 1*.

Houston and *Porgy and Bess*

After two very successful years in St. Paul, DeMain's thoughts turned to opera again. The Houston Grand Opera had just started a traveling company called the Texas Opera Theater. When he met the HGO's general director, David

9.06 John DeMain and David Gockley, early 1980s.

Gockley, in New York City to talk about the Texas Opera Theater job, the two 31-year-old men were clearly on the same page from the start, particularly their shared progressive approach to repertoire and mutual feeling that opera companies should occasionally present the best of Broadway musicals. Gockley had been hired as a business manager by the HGO in 1970, and by 1972 he had been promoted to general manager. He led the HGO until 2006, when he moved to the San Francisco Opera, which he led until his retirement in 2018. DeMain accepted the Texas Opera Theater job with the implied promise from Gockley that it would lead to an opportunity to conduct one of HGO's main productions. As he was in the process of putting on sometimes rough-and-ready productions of opera across Texas, DeMain also found himself an increasingly frequent guest conductor of the Houston Symphony Orchestra. The transition to the HGO's main stage took only a year. By the beginning of the 1975–76 season, he was at work on a production that would be one of the great triumphs of a long career: *Porgy and Bess*.

The beginnings of *Porgy and Bess* date to 1926, when Gershwin read DuBose Heyward's *Porgy*—a novel inspired by characters and situations Heyward observed in the black community of his hometown, Charleston, South Carolina. It would be nearly six years before Gershwin would return to the work. In the meantime, in 1927, Heyward and his wife Dorothy produced a successful stage version of *Porgy* that ran for some 369 performances in New York. Their play included several spirituals and other musical material, but Gershwin had something much more elaborate in mind. Work finally began at the end of 1933. Eventually, Ira Gershwin was brought into the project.

9.07 The main doors into the Houston Grand Opera's David Gockley Rehearsal Hall are emblazoned with the names of the operas that HGO produced during his 33-year tenure there.

By the end of 1934, Gershwin was looking for a producer and beginning to cast the production. Both Gershwin and Heyward agreed that *Porgy and*

9.08 DuBose Heyward's 1925 novel *Porgy*.

Bess was to be a serious work, produced with an all-black cast, dealing in a sympathetic and realistic way with its characters. At the time, African American singers were excluded from the operatic stage: Marian Anderson, possibly the finest alto of the day, would not appear on the stage of the Metropolitan Opera until the 1950s. Black characters were also largely absent from Broadway, and when they were there, it was still routine for these characters to be played in blackface, the ugly legacy of the old minstrel show tradition.

Porgy and Bess was given a tryout performance in Boston before settling in on Broadway, and Gershwin found it necessary to cut several numbers. There had been some rumors of a place for *Porgy and Bess* at the Met, but when it was produced in New York it was on Broadway, at the Alvin Theater, where it opened on October 10. The New York audience was just as enthusiastic as the Boston audience had been, but the reviews ran from lukewarm to savage—the kiss of death for a Broadway production. *Porgy and Bess* closed after a respectable but hardly profitable run of 124 performances. Though several of the individual songs quickly became well known, Gershwin did not live long enough to see his proudest creation acclaimed as one of the masterworks of American music.[26]

Despite its status as Gershwin's masterpiece, the production of *Porgy and Bess* on stage, on film, and on record was problematic. The opera had simply never been heard before in its complete form. At the end of 1975, Lorin Maazel and the Cleveland Orchestra issued a nearly complete concert version of the opera that won a Grammy award. However, DeMain and his collaborators, producer Sherwin Goldman, Gockley, and stage director Jack O'Brien, had something different in mind: a performance that attempted to reflect authentic black musical style, with references to gospel, traditional spirituals, 1930s jazz, and the blues ... in the words of O'Brien, to "give it back to the people it was written for." In the memoir, Hettmannsberger and DeMain provide an extended section on how this production came together, and they note that referring to the play and the original novel were key elements in constructing a more genuine *Porgy and Bess*. The HGO production, which debuted in June 1976, was a triumph, putting the HGO on the map internationally as an opera company, and it was a great personal success for DeMain.[27] The recording, which was a complete version of all of the music heard in the Boston tryouts in 1935, won a Grammy

Award for Best Opera Recording in 1977. Since that time, *Porgy and Bess* has become a true signature piece for DeMain: he estimates that he's conducted it over 400 times since 1976.[28]

In 1977, DeMain was named the HGO's music director. Surveying nearly 80 works[29] that he conducted while there reveals a fascinating mix: only about half of the productions were from the operatic standard repertoire. The remainder includes carefully crafted revivals of neglected American operas and operettas like Sousa's *El Capitan*, Joplin's *Treemonisha*, Herbert's *Babes in Toyland*, Blitzstein's *Regina*, and Friml's *The Vagabond King*. There were also revivals of Broadway shows: Herman's *Hello, Dolly!* (featuring Broadway legend Carol Channing, who had originated the title role in 1964[30]), a meticulously restored version of Kern and Hammerstein's *Show Boat*,[31] Sondheim's *Sweeney Todd*, Rodgers and Hammerstein's *Carousel*, Lerner and Loewe's *My Fair Lady*, and Berlin's *Annie Get Your Gun*. DeMain also led recently composed operas, including Piazzolla's 1968 "tango opera" *María de Buenos Aires*. But one part of Gockley and DeMain's vision was also to commission and premiere new works. (The HGO website currently includes the proud boast "90 premieres and counting."[32]) DeMain led premieres of 10 high-profile new works over the course of 18 seasons:

9.09 DeMain and composer Carlisle Floyd (to his left), preparing the premiere of Floyd's *Willie Stark* in 1981.

- Carlisle Floyd, *Willie Stark* (1981)
- Henry Mollicone, *Starbird*
- Leonard Bernstein, *A Quiet Place* (1983)
- Philip Glass, *Akhnaten* (1984—American premiere)
- John Adams, *Nixon in China* (1987)
- Philip Glass, *The Making of the Representative for Planet 8* (1988)
- Stewart Wallace, *Where's Dick?* (1989)
- Michael Tippett, New Year (1989)
- Carlisle Floyd, *The Passion of Jonathan Wade*[33] (1991)
- Robert Moran, *Desert of Roses* (1992)

The first premiere DeMain directed at Houston was Carlisle Floyd's *Willie Stark*, an operatic version of *All the King's Men*, the 1946 Robert Penn Warren novel based loosely upon the life of Louisiana's senator Huey P. Long. As his

2012 "authorized" biography makes clear, Floyd really valued working with DeMain, which led to opportunities to conduct other works by the composer, including his durable *Susannah* and a revised version of his *The Passion of Jonathan Wade*.[34]

In one of the longest passages on any one work in the memoir, DeMain discusses the HGO's premiere of Leonard Bernstein's final opera, *A Quiet Place*, in 1983. It was designed as a sequel to his first opera, *Trouble in Tahiti* (1951), revisiting the same characters some 30 years later. The libretto was written by Stephen Wadsworth, who would later serve as *Shining Brow*'s stage director. DeMain had first worked with Bernstein briefly at Tanglewood in 1971, and he had worked with him extensively on *West Side Story* in 1980 (described below). He seems to have been somewhat wary of dealing with the temperamental genius composer/conductor. As he describes it, getting the opera on stage and working successfully with Bernstein came down to dealing with him in a rather businesslike way: as Leonard Bernstein, just another composer, rather than as "Lenny" the outsize personality. In the end, *A Quiet Place*, which opened in Houston on June 17, 1983, on a double bill with *Trouble in Tahiti*, was successful with the audience, but it was largely savaged by the critics. Bernstein revised the score extensively twice prior to his death in 1990—among other changes, incorporating the scenes of *Trouble in Tahiti* as extended "flashback" episodes within *A Quiet Place*.

9.10 DeMain and Leonard Bernstein, during the 1983 rehearsals for *A Quiet Place*.

Perhaps the most important HGO premiere DeMain conducted was *Nixon in China* (1987) by American composer John Adams. Richard Nixon's 1972 trip to China was the greatest diplomatic coup of his presidency. The staunchly anti-communist Nixon surprised the world by visiting a then-closed and isolated China and meeting with both Premier Zhou Enlai and Chairman Mao. Though the actual results of the visit were limited, it was a powerfully symbolic opening in what had been a thoroughly hostile relationship. Some 15 years later, John Adams wrote *Nixon in China*—his first full-length opera—on the events of the three-day presidential visit to Peking.[35] Again, the opera opened to mixed reviews, though DeMain's direction was universally praised. In March 1988, it played at the Kennedy Center in Washington, DC, again under DeMain's direction. Critic Tom Page, writing for *Newsday*, wrote:

"John DeMain's conducting was skilled and purposeful."[36] Despite the critical response, however, *Nixon in China* has proved to be a very durable work, revived many times, and receiving no fewer than five different recordings.[37]

Moonlighting and Marriage: Work in Omaha and Elsewhere

Though he was busy in Houston, conducting up to six productions each season, DeMain maintained a busy schedule of national and eventually international guest conducting. In 1980, he led a major Broadway revival of *West Side Story*, which was to involve all four of the original collaborators: composer Leonard Bernstein, lyricist Stephen Sondheim, choreographer Jerome Robbins, and Arthur Lawrence, who wrote the show's book. Bernstein, who had been thrilled by DeMain's direction of *Porgy and Bess*, recommended him for the job. In the memoir, DeMain gives an entertaining account of balancing the titanic egos involved, particularly Bernstein and Robbins.[38] In the end, the production was relatively successful, and DeMain conducted over 80 performances.

In 1992, an even larger opportunity came DeMain's way. He capped a short world tour with superstar tenor Placido Domingo—with stops in Hong Kong, Adelaide, Australia, and Auckland, New Zealand—with a huge gala concert at the close of the World Climate Summit in Rio de Janeiro: the Concert for Planet Earth. This was an all-star affair headlined by Domingo, actor Jeremy Irons, jazz trumpeter Wynton Marsalis, piano virtuoso Sarah Chang, and Brazilian star Antonio Carlos Jobim. It was also, according to the account in DeMain's memoir, a poorly planned event that nearly turned into a debacle!

In 1980, DeMain was named music director of Opera Omaha, a relatively small but clearly ambitious company that had been formed in 1958. For the next 10 seasons, he led a very successful company there in addition to his work in Houston. As at the HGO, DeMain worked with a forward-looking general manager, Mary Roberts, who shared his views on repertoire and outreach. He looks back with particular pride to a fall festival that he and Roberts staged each year, devoted to new and neglected repertoire.[39] As in Houston, Opera Omaha aimed at accessibility—for example, frequently performing with projected surtitles, when this was still unusual in American opera—and presenting a mix of repertoire, including Broadway shows.

John met his wife, Barbara Dittman DeMain, in 1991. Born in Germany, and a dozen years younger than DeMain, Barbara was at the time running a cultural agency of her own. In 1991 she traveled to Houston to assist Gockley with securing the rights to perform Astor Piazzolla's *María de Buenos Aires*. In the memoir, it is Barbara who somewhat wryly tells the story of their whirlwind courtship. She returned to Germany but came to Colorado in the summer of

1991, where DeMain was conducting Britten's opera *Owen Wingrave* at the Aspen Music Festival. He proposed marriage, and they eloped; they were married by a justice of the peace in Jackson Hole, Wyoming, on August 23, 1991.[40] Barbara once again returned to Germany, but she was back in Houston in September for a concert featuring Placido Domingo. Back in Germany once more, she found out she was pregnant. Their previous plans of maintaining lives on two continents had ended, and Barbara moved to Houston, in time for a proper "church wedding" with both families in attendance, in November.[41] Their daughter Jennifer was born in Houston in 1992.

9.11 John, Jennifer, and Barbara DeMain in 1998.

The DeMains' 28-year marriage came to a tragic end on Friday, February 7, 2020, with Barbara's unexpected death. That night was the first of two scheduled performances of Madison Opera's production of the 2016 Gregory Spears opera *Fellow Travellers*. In a seemingly unbelievable display of self-possession, John conducted both the Friday night and Sunday matinee performances. The next week was an MSO subscription program, which he also conducted. However, in a show of sympathy for their bereaved maestro, the entire orchestra stayed after the Monday night rehearsal had ended, and assistant conductor Kyle Knox led them in a performance of the gentle, stirring *Nimrod* movement of Elgar's *Enigma Variations*—a gesture organized by orchestra librarian Kathy Taylor.[42] John remembers Barbara with love, calling her "a great wife, a great mother, and a great first lady for the symphony."[43]

Madison and Beyond

Maestro DeMain's work for the Madison Symphony Orchestra is discussed at length in the previous and succeeding chapters. However, he has continued to work as a guest conductor widely since 1994. Indeed, in the early years at Madison, it seemed that he was heading to the airport after the conclusion of nearly every Sunday MSO matinee.

Just as he had split his time between Houston and Omaha during the 1980s and early 1990s, another outside offer came from Opera Pacific, a company located in wealthy Orange County, south of Los Angeles. Opera Pacific had been founded in 1985, and in 1998 DeMain, who had been active as a guest conductor since the company's beginnings, was offered its artistic directorship. By 1996, Opera Pacific was running a large deficit. The deficit disappeared over the next few years due in part to the fine productions directed by DeMain, but also because of a few donors with very deep pockets, some of them cultivated by DeMain himself. Unfortunately, the economic downturn of 2008 was the last straw; deficits had once again begun to grow, and despite efforts to expand its base of donors, Opera Pacific declared bankruptcy on November 4, 2008, dismissing nearly 20 employees, including John DeMain.[44]

9.12 John Demain, at the February 1994 press conference announcing his appointment as MSO music director.

DeMain worked frequently as a guest conductor from the 1990s through the 2010s beyond Madison and Opera Pacific, beginning with a world tour of *Porgy and Bess* in 1995 that took him to La Scala in Milan, the Paris Opéra, and Tokyo. On the strength of his 1992 tour with Domingo, DeMain was invited back to Adelaide to conduct opera four more times in Australia in the 1990s and 2000s, including the Australian premiere of Jake Heggie's *Dead Man Walking*. This period saw him conducting both *Porgy and Bess* and *Show Boat* at both the Chicago Lyric Opera and the San Francisco Opera, and engagements at the Glimmerglass Festival (Cooperstown, New York) and the Aspen Festival. He was also

9.13 John DeMain, 2000.

principal conductor of the Chautauqua Opera Company in upstate New York. In January 2023, DeMain was awarded a Lifetime Achievement Award from the National Opera Association.

Retirement and Legacy

DeMain has announced his retirement from the MSO at the end of its 100th season in May 2026, stepping down after 32 seasons as the orchestra's music director. He will, however, remain artistic director for the Madison Opera, and as of 2024 has announced no plans to retire from that post. The orchestra is currently in the midst of a search for his successor.

Looking back in 2024 over his 30 seasons as music director, DeMain recalls that Roland Johnson asked just two things of him in 1994: "Make it better. Make the audience bigger." DeMain has certainly done both. Regarding his legacy in Madison, he says,

> when I came to Madison and evaluated the orchestra—where it was in relation to other orchestras around the country, I saw a real window of opportunity to kick over the last vestiges of "Ma and Pa" [-style management of the orchestra].... Not having blind auditions was clearly "Ma and Pa," as was the notion of University faculty setting up "fiefdoms"—determining which students would play extra parts in the orchestra. I remember telling the orchestra after that first round of auditions that "if you want your students to play in the orchestra, they need to know their excerpts." I had heard many young players who might have been able to play their concerto beautifully, but were terrible on the excerpts. That's all fine if you want to go out and be the next Heifetz, but if you want to be an orchestra player, you need to know your part! And at the next year's auditions, they did. I also think that it made a real difference to put all of the rehearsals into a single week, as most American orchestras do. It allowed our players to play in more than one orchestra.

He also points with pride to the upbeat culture of the MSO:

> They call the MSO the "happy orchestra," and I'm really proud of the orchestra's *esprit*. I was doing an evaluation of Emma [Potter], our new principal horn, last week, and she said "Oh, this is the happiest orchestra I've ever played in: everyone is so friendly and warm." I don't think it has anything to do with whether or not they

like me as a conductor, but I think everybody knows that I respect them. We work in a positive atmosphere ... I love the fact that we work together in a quiet, purposeful way.

Regarding the orchestra's administration—particularly his 22-year partnership with Rick Mackie—DeMain notes:

> I'm also very proud of the administration I've worked with. Rick was an incredible partner—he kept me honest.... I think that he genuinely liked me and liked what I was doing. So, when he said "no" to me, I always felt that it was to keep us healthy, to keep us solvent.... Mutual respect is what made this relationship work.

Regarding repertoire:

> Just before the pandemic, I was on a committee talking about diversity, equity, and inclusion (DEI), and during the shutdown, I had time to do a lot of soul-searching. I had never really paid much attention to William Grant Still or other black composers, like Florence Price—composers whose work was pretty much unknown due to institutional racism. So having a chance to program some of their music over the last couple of seasons has been really wonderful, as well as works by younger black composers and women.... And over 30 years, I'm also proud that we've managed to cover an awful lot of the standard repertoire as well as lots of new music.

And finally, DeMain expresses justifiable pride in the many significant changes that have been wrought under his leadership:

> In programming, we've gone to triples for our subscription programs, and so far we've managed to keep triples. The community Christmas program, bringing in the Mt. Zion choir and the Madison Youth Choirs, has become very successful. We've also added some really wonderful annual programs: Concert on the Green, Opera in the Park, and Final Forte. I'll say that I am particularly proud of the Final Forte. Having a chance to work with those phenomenally talented young players is amazing, and something that I'm looking forward to in my last few seasons. We've also expanded our other youth concert offerings as well. And to be able to open Overture Hall was really a dream come true.[45]

Like each of his predecessors, DeMain has put his personal stamp on the history of the Madison Symphony Orchestra. Sigfrid Prager created both a thriving community orchestra and chorus, and a loyal and enthusiastic audience for their music. Walter Heermann, coming to Madison from the Cincinnati Symphony Orchestra, brought a level of big-city polish and organization and began the professionalization of the group. Roland Johnson was responsible for a whole range of changes: creating a professional regional orchestra and vastly expanding the number and types of concerts played by the orchestra. Beginning with his very first concert in 1994, DeMain has consistently challenged the orchestra to move to the next level, and in Chapter 10, I will also discuss his fundamentally important role in moving the orchestra to its magnificent new home, Overture Hall, in 2004.

9.14 John DeMain on the podium, 2023.

J. MICHAEL ALLSEN

Notes to Chapter 9

1. Most of this paragraph on his early life was summarized from an unpublished draft of John DeMain and Greg Hettsmannberger, *An American Conductor: Working with My Heros—The Life and Music of John DeMain* (Madison: University of Wisconsin Press, 2025).
2. "Talented John DeMain to play with Symphony, *Youngstown Vindicator* 1/15/1987, B11.
3. "Local opportunities gave DeMain solid start," *Youngstown Vindicator* 5/5/1987, B1, B6.
4. Interview with John DeMain, 6/14/2024.
5. DeMain/Hettmannsberger, *An American Conductor*.
6. "Kenley Players History: Timeline" http://www.kenleyplayershistory.com/timeline.htm, accessed 6/15/2024.
7. "Kenley Players," *Wikipedia*, https://en.wikipedia.org/wiki/Kenley_Players, accessed 5/30/2024; "Producer John Kenley dies at 103," *Variety*, 11/1/2009, https://variety.com/2009/legit/markets-festivals/producer-john-kenley-dies-at-103-1118010715/ , accessed 5/30/2024.
8. "Cole Porter's 'Can-Can' Is a Winner at Kenley," *Cleveland Plain Dealer*, 7/18/1968, 50.
9. "'Camelot' Makes Women Cry a Lot...And Men a Little," *Dayton Daily News*, 8/20/1969, 11.
10. *Port Clinton Daily News*, 11/6/64, 2.
11. *New York Daily News*, 1/21/1969, 51.
12. *The Raleigh News and Observer*, 2/15/1969, 8.
13. *The Bridgeport Post*, 4/23/1970, 48.
14. *Youngstown Vindicator*, 1/7/1971, 21.
15. "Peter Herman Adler," Wikipedia, https://en.wikipedia.org/wiki/Peter_Herman_Adler, accessed 5/31/2024.
16. DeMain/Hettmannsberger, *An American Conductor*.
17. Robert D McFadden, "Julius Rudel, Longtime Impresario and Conductor of City Opera, Dies at 93," *New York Times*, 6/26/2014. After years of financial difficulties, New York City Opera declared bankruptcy in 2013. In 2016, the company was revived ("New York City Opera," Wikipedia, https://en.wikipedia.org/wiki/New_York_City_Opera, accessed 6/15/2025. However, DeMain notes that it is on a much smaller scale than the former NYCO.
18. "Affiliate Artists," *Wikipedia*, https://en.wikipedia.org/wiki/Affiliate_Artists, accessed 6/1/2024.
19. Interview with John DeMain, 6/14/2024.
20. DeMain/Hettmannsberger, *An American Conductor*.
21. Michael Anthony, "Music Review," *Minneapolis Tribune*, 8/4/1973, 11.
22. *Minneapolis Tribune*, 11/11/1973, 53
23. "St. Paul Chamber Orchestra to stress Bach, Stravinsky," *Minneapolis Star*, 7/3/1973, 11.
24. Roy M. Close, "'Vox Populous' satire slashes social values," *Minneapolis Star*, 12/3/1973, 18.
25. DeMain/Hettmannsberger, *An American Conductor*.
26. This summary of the opera's history is largely drawn from my Madison Symphony Orchestra program notes for May 9–11, 2025.
27. DeMain/Hettmannsberger, *An American Conductor*.

28 Interview with John DeMain, 6/14/2024.
29 I thank Beverly Vich of the HGO for providing me with this list. I also thank HGO Archivist Brian Mitchell for his kind assistance with photographs.
30 Once again, I will leave the juicy details to Maestro DeMain! See DeMain/Hettsmannberger, *An American Conductor*.
31 DeMain/Hettmannsberger, *An American Conductor*.
32 https://www.houstongrandopera.org/about, accessed 6/3/204.
33 This work had originally been written and premiered in 1962. The version played in 1991 was a substantially revised version of the score Floyd prepared in 1989.
34 See Thomas Holliday, *Falling Up: The Days and Nights of Carlisle Floyd: the Authorized Biography* (Syracuse, NY: Syracuse University Press, 2012).
35 This summary was largely drawn from my Madison Symphony Orchestra program notes for September 22–24, 2023.
36 Tom Page, review of Nixon in China, *Newsday* 3/28/1988; quoted in Thomas May, *The John Adams Reader: Essential Writings on an American Composer* (Prompton Plains, NJ, Amadeus Press, 2006): 295.
37 "Nixon In China," Wikipedia, https://en.wikipedia.org/wiki/Nixon_in_China, accessed 6/4/2024.
38 DeMain/Hettmannsberger, *An American Conductor*.
39 Interview with John DeMain, 6/14/2024.
40 Barbara DeMain obituary, *WSJ* 2/23/2020, C6.
41 DeMain/Hettmannsberger, *An American Conductor*.
42 Interview with Kyle Knox, 4/25/2024.
43 Interview with John DeMain, 6/14/2024.
44 "Opera Pacific donors 'exhausted'," *Los Angeles Times*, 11/6/2008, E11; see also DeMain/Hettmannsberger, *An American Conductor*.
45 Interview with John DeMain, 6/14/2024.

CHAPTER 10

The Madison Symphony Orchestra in a New Millennium

This chapter deals with the history of the Madison Symphony Orchestra from circa 2000 up to the present day. In general, this is a relatively upbeat story of continued success and improvement in quality, notwithstanding a few real challenges (most notably the 2008 recession and the Covid pandemic). However, it does include one more epochal event in the history of the MSO—the opening of Overture Hall in 2004—as well as the MSO's responses to greater world events like the 9/11 attacks and the Covid pandemic.

Marking a New Millennium and Celebrating 75 Seasons

One innovative set of programs created by the orchestra, in cooperation with the Madison Art Center (now the Madison Museum of Contemporary Art) was designed to focus on the artistic trends of the century just passed. The "Decade by Decade" series brought together lectures on artworks from the Art Center's permanent collection with chamber music performances of works from that same decade, largely performed by MSO players. DeMain and the Center's director, Stephen Fleischmann, introduced each program, and Prof. Jo Ortel of Beloit College gave lectures on the visual works. The first event, for example, on October 1, 1998, was devoted to the decade 1900 to 1910 and juxtaposed visual works by Paul Gaugin, Paul Cezanne, Wassily Kandinsky, Kathe Kollwitz, and Max Klinger with music by Arnold Schoenberg, Ralph Vaughan Williams, Maurice Ravel, and Charles Ives.[1] DeMain's programming for the orchestra followed the same pattern, presenting works from each decade of the 20th century during the course of the 1998–99 and 1999–2000 seasons:

- 1900s: Gustav Mahler, *Symphony No. 5* (1901–2): October 1998
- 1910s: Igor Stravinsky, *Petrushka* (1911–12): November 1998
- 1920s: William Walton, *Viola Concerto* (1928–29) and Ottorino Respighi, *The Pines of Rome* (1923–24): February 1999
- 1930s: Paul Hindemith, *Symphony "Mathis der Maler"* (1934) and Sergey Prokofiev, *Selections from "Romeo and Juliet"* (1934–35): March 1999
- 1940s: Aaron Copland, *Appalachian String Suite* (1944) and Francis Poulenc, *Stabat Mater* (1950): April 1999
- 1950s: Dmitri Shostakovich, *Symphony No. 10* (1953): September 1999
- 1960s: Samuel Barber, *Piano Concerto* (1961–62): October 1999
- 1970s: John Corigiano, *Gazebo Dances* (1974) and Benjamin Lees, *Passacaglia for Orchestra* (1976): November 1999
- 1980s: Ellen Taaffe Zwillich, *Celebration for Orchestra* (1984): February 2000.
- 1990s: John Adams, *Violin Concerto* (1993): March 2000

The 2000–2001 season was the orchestra's 75th. As noted in the Preface, I was commissioned to write four historical chapters that were published in the four program books that season, and I also completed a chronicle of performances and lists of repertoire and soloists for the first 75 years. Though that research was really quite preliminary, in many ways it represented a start toward the book now in your hands.

10.01 Composer John Stevens.

Also part of the 75th anniversary was the commission of a new work, *Jubilare!*, written by University composer and tuba professor John Stevens, who provided the following note:

> The title, which translates as "to shout for joy," reflects the generally celebratory mood of this short, season-opening "mini-overture." Although the piece celebrates the anniversary milestone and bright future of the Madison Symphony Orchestra, I chose to title it in

Latin as a small way to honor the past as well. The music itself also honors all those who have contributed to the success of the orchestra over its first 75 years by opening with a solemn "fanfare" by the solo trumpet. This theme, based on a tune appropriate to the occasion, is then taken up by the horns and the rest of the orchestra in a fanfare of celebration. This gives way to jubilant new musical material, joyfully announcing a new era, as the Madison Symphony Orchestra sails into the new century. I want to congratulate current and former members of the Madison Symphony Orchestra, its Board of Directors, its staff, Music Director John DeMain, Music Director Laureate Roland Johnson, and all of the members of the MSO family on this historic occasion, and to express my thanks for the opportunity to contribute to the celebration with new music."

DeMain invited the MSO's Music Director Laureate, Roland Johnson, to conduct this work, a gesture that Johnson found to be "incredibly generous," and the concerts of the premiere, September 23–24, 2000, also marked Johnson's last formal appearance on the MSO's podium.

Of course, the dominant event of that period was the terrorist attacks of September 11, 2001. The orchestra's 76th season was set to begin on September 22, 2001. DeMain had a few weeks' grace period to consider a response, and he chose a dignified memorial: Barber's *Adagio for Strings*, played as an unannounced prelude. This work has come to have an association with tragedy—particularly with great public events of death and mourning—that Barber never really intended. It was played directly after the radio announcement of President Roosevelt's death in 1945, and similarly after the Kennedy assassination in 1963. The work had a devastating effect: by the end, there were few dry eyes in the Oscar Mayer Theatre, in the hall or on stage. DeMain then began the season in a more traditional manner: with the singing of the *Star-Spangled Banner*.[2] The concert was slated to begin with the Beethoven *Triple Concerto*, featuring the Eroica Trio, a New York City–based ensemble widely acclaimed for their interpretations of this work and chamber music by Beethoven, Mozart, and more. However, the trio did not immediately

10.02 Roland Johnson in 2000: publicity photo for his appearance at the MSO program in September, directing the premiere of *Jubilare!*

appear on stage, and the expectant silence extended for what seemed like a long time (though in reality, probably no more than a minute or two) before they finally appeared on stage to take their bows and begin the piece. We later found out that the members of the trio had been totally unprepared for the Barber and needed the extra time to regain their composure. The trio's pianist, Erika Nikrenz, recalled in 2024:

> It remains so vivid in our memory. While many were not sure it was a good idea for us to travel in the days following the attack on our beloved home of NYC, we threw any fear aside and traveled when the airports were virtually empty. We made it to Madison and will never forget our performance that September, playing for the audience with the wonderful Madison Symphony Orchestra, in their beautiful hall—it was extremely moving for us and indeed cathartic ... and I am not surprised to hear that we may have delayed our appearance a few minutes to help us compose ourselves before performing Beethoven's epic *Triple Concerto*. We are very grateful to be a part of that performance and hoped from the bottom of our hearts that it helped to heal some of those in attendance.[3]

Musical responses to the 9/11 attacks and their aftermath were immediate and powerful—ranging from sad elegies, angry country songs, Mexican-American *corridos*, and rock concept albums to classical works, and dance and theater pieces. Ten years after the attacks, in September 2011, DeMain programmed a memorable work written expressly as a memorial for the attacks, *On the Transmigration of Souls* by John Adams. Adams composed this work, for orchestra, chorus, and prerecorded sound and voices for the New York Philharmonic, to be played on the first anniversary, in September 2002. At DeMain's request, the audience marked the end of this work not with applause, but with contemplative silence.

10.03 John DeMain, 2002.

From the Oscar Mayer Theatre to Overture Hall

The Oscar Mayer Theatre had been the orchestra's primary venue since 1980. It was an only slightly modified version of the Capitol Theater, a grand movie palace that had been built in 1928. The Capitol had been completed prior to the overwhelming popularity of "talkies" (movies with a coordinated soundtrack).

It had a large orchestra pit and served occasionally as a musical theater and vaudeville house in its early years. However, it was always clear that live music was not its primary purpose. It featured a single wide, sweeping balcony, where the sound of the orchestra mixed well, particularly in the front half. However, the drawbacks of the hall for live music became apparent almost immediately. Particularly notorious were the seats under the balcony—well over half of the hall's 2200-seat capacity—where sound was piped in from the projection booth and stage through speakers in the ceiling. While this may have been adequate for movie dialogue and prerecorded soundtracks, it was not satisfactory for live music. DeMain speaks in his memoir about discovering this early in his tenure when listening to a rehearsal for a youth concert directed by Beverly Taylor. As he walked around the hall to get a sense of the orchestra's blend and balance, and he was utterly flabbergasted by the fact that the orchestra "sounded like a bad high school orchestra" in the seats under the balcony—where the richness of sound and most overtones were swallowed by the hall—but it sounded "like Carnegie Hall" when he went up into the balcony.[4] Another issue was the proscenium arch, which captured much of the orchestra's sound. The MSO addressed these issues in the next few years by moving the orchestra forward into the hall and by constant experimentation with placement of the thin, largely useless, sound-reflective panels surrounding the orchestra.[5] There were also judicious warnings about the "dead seats." But these were clearly mere band-aid solutions.

The Orpheum Theater, directly across State Street from the Madison Civic Center, was briefly, in 1996, under consideration as a rehearsal/performance/office space for the MSO. The Orpheum opened in 1927, just a few months before the Capitol/Oscar Mayer. It was an equally ornate space, and despite a few later modifications, like walling off part of the main stage to create a second, small movie venue, it was virtually a twin of the Capitol. By February 1996, the board had secured copies of the original blueprints of the Orpheum, and a month later had appointed a task force of board members, civic officials, and orchestra members Tyrone Greive and Cynthia Cameron-Fix to oversee the project. Ultimately, the effort seems to have gone only as far as commissioning an acoustical study of the space. The preliminary review, delivered on July 2, 1996, contained the following wonderful bit of understatement:

> However, specific architectural attributes will remain within the Orpheum which will limit the achievable improvement in sound quality for musical performance. These attributes, together with room width and depth of under-balcony seating will result in the

Orpheum not having a sound equal to that of the world's great concert halls.

And also that:

> As the seating of the Orpheum Theatre is almost identical in size and shape to the Oscar Mayer Theatre, the acoustical signatures of the two rooms are likely to be more similar than different.[6]

Though the report did conclude that the theater could "no doubt be developed into a performance space with acoustics significantly better than the Oscar Mayer Theatre," the Orpheum project was quickly abandoned. The next step was to organize with other arts organizations in Madison. Together a consortium of some 15 arts organizations commissioned a study through the Wisconsin Foundation for the Arts. In October 1996, Joseph Golden, a consultant based in Charlotte, North Carolina, issued a report titled *Hunger Amid Plenty: The Quest for Cultural Space in Madison, Wisconsin*.[7] After brief introductions of the MSO, Madison Opera, Wisconsin Chamber Orchestra, Madison Children's Museum, Madison Art Center, Madison Theatre Guild, and others, Golden surveyed the various venues in Madison, including the spaces in the Madison Civic Center. The study concluded with a series of recommendations that were realistic within the financial and other restrictions of the various groups. However, another, unexpected solution was on the horizon.

Terry Haller, then president of the MSO board, notes that the next few years were a time of almost constant discussion of the facility issue, together with much work with other arts organizations. He notes that they examined every large-scale venue in town, including churches. The orchestra certainly had the largest problem. As Haller put it, "We were an organization with a very

10.04 a-c Jerry Frautschi, Pleasant Rowland Frautschi, and Cesar Pelli, 2004.

10/05a/10.05b Demolition, 2001. **Left**: View from State Street, showing the Yost's storefront that was maintained as part of the final design. **Right**: View from Fairchild Street. The structure on the far side of the block is the Capitol/Oscar Mayer Theatre, the only portion of the old Madison Civic Center that was not razed.

large audience, who had *sound* as our main product, and a clearly inadequate facility."[8] Gradually, this consortium of local arts organizations came to the conclusion that what was needed was to purchase the entire 200 block of State Street for a downtown arts district.

On July 27, 1998, news broke that W. Jerome (Jerry) Frautschi had pledged $50 million toward the development of a downtown arts district, named initially the Overture Project.[9] To head the Overture Foundation, Frautschi named George Austin, a civic official, who had been responsible for shepherding the Monona Terrace project in the 1990s. In the background of this gift was generations of history in Madison, and a doll. Frautschi was a sixth-generation Madisonian whose family had a long history of supporting the arts: They had been among the earliest members of the Madison Civic Music Association, and, through his business foundation, he had already donated thousands of dollars to the MSO. His wife, Pleasant Rowland Frautschi, was a primary supporter of the Wisconsin Chamber Orchestra and its annual Concerts on the Square series. As founder of the Pleasant Company, she had created American Girl, a phenomenally successful line of dolls and accessories that had backstories drawn from American history. In 1998, American Girl was acquired by toymaking giant Mattel, earning Pleasant and Jerry Frautschi some $700 million. Haller, Madden, and others close to this story have all noted that the sudden quantum leap in quality and potential of the MSO under John DeMain, and John's advocacy, were dominant factors in this gift and in the eventual construction of the hall. By the project's completion, the Frautschis had donated $205 million, the largest single donation to the arts in history.

The Overture Foundation and its representatives surveyed performing arts centers around the country and selected architect Cesar Pelli (1926–2019). Pelli was world famous for designing enormously tall buildings, like the 1483-foot Petronas Towers in Kuala Lumpur, but he also had a reputation for building sensitive urban spaces. Demolition work began in earnest in March, and Pelli's exterior design was approved by the City Council and Planning commission in May 2001.[10]

10.06 Cover of Pelli's "schematic design" booklet, 2000.

DeMain and others have noted that, while Overture Hall was always going to be a multiuse space, able to accommodate touring Broadway companies and a huge range of other performances, the hall was first and foremost designed as a venue for the Madison Symphony Orchestra. This extends to features that are invisible in the structure, including a nearly two-foot-thick double wall that surrounds the entire backstage stage and the hall itself, effectively sealing the hall off from outside noise. The orchestra plays on a set of semicircular risers that fill the entire stage, and which accommodate hearing one another. When the Madison Symphony Chorus is involved, they are accommodated by similar risers behind the orchestra. There is also a substantial orchestra shell that makes sure that every bit of the sound goes into the audience: massive panels over a foot thick that completely seal off the backstage, the sides, and the flyspace above. Even the case of the organ behind the orchestra is part of this design. There is no proscenium arch, and the flyspace above is effectively sealed off by the shell. DeMain quotes an old maxim about concert halls: that the best of them are where the orchestra and the audience are "in the same room." This is clearly the case in Overture Hall when it is configured for an orchestra concert. Many who are close to this issue point to DeMain as one of the most important motivators for the new hall. According to Rick Mackie, MSO executive director during the construction and opening of Overture,

> John said what, to many people, seemed unthinkable: that the Oscar Mayer Theatre was inadequate; that we needed a hall.... John was the voice; John DeMain came from a bigger place, a bigger picture, a different tier in the classical Music industry—from Houston, Texas, where money is no object [chuckles], and his expansive thinking—

let's do this right, let's do it *big*.... Well, he deserves all the credit, in my view, because he brought his credibility and his was the voice—the new voice and a big voice in Madison that got the attention of everyone, including Jerry and Pleasant. It was his credibility as an artist on a much bigger stage than Madison. So John DeMain gets 100 percent of the credit from me for sparking the discussion.[11]

One addition to the new hall was a new piano for the orchestra. First-time donors Peter Livingston and Sharon Stark agreed to underwrite the cost of a new nine-foot Steinway concert grand, to be selected and shipped from the Steinway factory in Hamburg, Germany. The piano was given in memory of Peter's mother, Magdalena Friedman.[12] John and Barbara DeMain, along with the donors, traveled to Hamburg in March 2004 to personally select an instrument from the Steinway factory there. In his memoir, DeMain talks about the process of playing nine different instruments in the showroom—working with Hamburg-based pianist Matthias Kirschnereit before selecting the wonderful instrument that audiences have been hearing in Overture Hall for the past 20 years.

10.07 Peter Livingston, Sharon Stark, Matthias Kirschnereit, John and Barbara DeMain at the Steinway plant in Hamburg, posed with *the* Hamburg Steinway, March 2004.

The Grand Opening occurred in September 2004. That week, I published a feature article in the *Wisconsin State Journal*, dealing with some of the venues in which the MSO had performed in its past history—Central High School/MATC Auditorium, the Stock Pavilion, and the Oscar Mayer Theatre—and gushing about the new hall from the perspective of an orchestra member:

> It's often said that a symphony orchestra works collectively as an "instrument" under the baton of a good conductor. In the same sense, a good orchestra "plays" its hall. Every performance venue has its acoustical peculiarities and learning a new hall is just as much a process of experimentation and practice as taking a new instrument out of the case. The world's great orchestra halls are those that allow the audience to hear music just as it comes from the players with the added dimension of mixing and balancing sounds between sections. On Friday the Madison Symphony Orchestra

picks up its deluxe new instrument, Overture Hall, to begin its 79th season. This is an important turning point....

The move to Overture Hall is as much a quantum leap forward as the 1980 move to the Oscar Mayer Theatre. The sound is *great*. In Overture Hall, by necessity another multipurpose space, there is no real proscenium arch, and the orchestra is surrounded by a shell that completely insulates the stage from the wings and flyspace. The dramatic curves of the Overture Concert Organ provide a backdrop, but the organ's sound box is an integral part of the hall's acoustic design. The stage itself is far roomier than that of Oscar Mayer, with a substantial and dramatically swept series of orchestra risers that concentrate the sound and make it much easier for us to hear one another. The spacious backstage area, with several dressing rooms, a large "green room," and ample restrooms seems like a luxury [compared to the spartan backstage area of the Oscar Mayer].

Playing in Overture Hall during the Grand Opening has, quite simply, made us proud to be members of this orchestra and this community. This was never more apparent than at a special invitation-only concert on September 10 [2004], hosted by Jerry Frautschi for the men and women who built Overture and their families. We are used to applause, but the most emotional moment in the program was when we had a chance to applaud the people who had built our brand-new instrument.

At some point—not soon—playing in Overture will become as much a routine pleasure as taking a well-worn and familiar horn or violin out of the case. But for the time being, we can all relish the honeymoon period.[13]

The formal opening of the season, on September 19, 2004, explored all of the hall's new possibilities. After a couple of patriotic openers, the Madison Symphony Chorus sang an *a cappella* performance of Randall Thompson's *Alleluia*, and then Handel's *Coronation Anthem No. 1 (Zadok the Priest)*. The orchestra was then joined by a favorite star pianist, André Watts, to play the Beethoven *"Emperor" Concerto*.[14] This also marked the orchestral debut of the orchestra's new nine-foot Hamburg Steinway concert grand piano. The final work on the program was perhaps inevitable: the most popular of all works for full symphony orchestra and organ, the Saint-Saëns *Symphony No. 3*, with Samuel Hutchison at the Overture Concert Organ. A few days later, the opening festivities closed with a "Resident Companies Gala," in which the MSO, performing in Overture's relatively spacious orchestra pit, played with the Madison Ballet and Madison Opera. This program opened with three ballets, choreographed to excerpts from Mendelssohn's *A Midsummer Night's Dream*, Stravinsky's *Capriccio*, and a new work by Madison composer Taras Nahirniak, *Night Dances*. The Madison Opera did the second half, a semi-staged version of Act II of Bizet's *Carmen*.

Community reaction to the new hall was enthusiastic, even exuberant, as was the critical response. And there were notices from well beyond Madison. In November, *New York Times* critic James R. Oestreich attended two of the November concerts, billed as the formal dedication of the Overture Concert Organ. This program, opening with the Vaughan Williams *Wasps Overture* and the Mendelssohn *"Scottish" Symphony*, included guest organist Thomas Trotter, playing a virtuoso showpiece, Joseph Jongen's *Symphonie concertante*. Oestreich, who had grown up in Wisconsin and attended the University in the early 1960s, had heard "the plucky but sorely challenged Madison Civic Symphony labor in a high school auditorium" during his student days. He had also been among the out-of-town critics who reviewed *Shining Brow* in 1993. His review, extolling both the organ and Overture Hall itself, was also complimentary toward the MSO, noting that, a few quibbles aside, this group "could have passed for a full-time orchestra."[15]

Overture Hall has been a major factor in the orchestra's evolution over the last 20 years. Not only is the venue itself an attraction for audiences, but

10.08 The MSO in Overture Hall, 2023.

playing in a hall where players can actually hear one another, and where the audience can hear what they play, has a tremendous positive impact on the quality of the musical product. It has also allowed for adventurous repertoire. For example, when it became clear that Overture was in the future, DeMain slowed down the Mahler cycle so that the monumental *Symphony No. 8* could be performed in Overture during the first season there. This is an enormous work that would have been a true challenge—if not indeed impossible—to mount effectively in the Oscar Mayer Theatre. Overture also allows for the kind of innovative multimedia programming that will be important to the orchestra going forward, with programs like the February 2024 *Pixar at the Movies*™. For my part, I will note that, despite what I said in 2004 about playing in Overture Hall becoming a "routine pleasure," I played in that space for 14 seasons, and I never stopped mentally pinching myself each time I walked on stage—it was hard to believe that a midsized orchestra, in a relatively small midwestern city, was able to work in a truly world-class hall.

The original plan called for the Oscar Mayer Theatre to be razed completely to provide space for the Madison Children's Museum, but after an outcry from local preservationists, it was instead converted into an 850-seat hall. The stage, pit, and backstage areas were left untouched, but a new wall was erected to convert the former seating under the balcony to a large lobby space. Thus, the acoustically decent seating was preserved, as was the ornate interior of the building. Reopened and renamed as part of the Overture Center in 2005, the new Capitol Theater has become an active live music venue, hosting programs by the MSO, Wisconsin Chamber Orchestra, and—with its functioning orchestra pit—some of Madison Opera's productions as well.

The Overture Concert Organ

There are very few, if any, newly built multipurpose halls in the country that feature a built-in organ. To be sure, many older halls, converted from silent movie theaters, did include large theater organs, like the "mighty Barton" organ in the Capitol/Oscar Mayer Theatre, though these are seldom usable for symphonic or serious solo organ repertoire. As described by Haller, the "odyssey" of building the Overture Concert Organ began in June 2000, when he and Marian Bolz attended a concert of the Chicago Symphony Orchestra for the premiere of John Stevens's tuba concerto. The Overture project was by this time well underway, and noting the organ built into the CSO's Orchestra Hall, Bolz mused, "Why can't we have an organ in Overture Hall?" Haller, Bolz, MSO executive director Rick Mackie, and Sam Hutchison—a fine local organist, who was at that time working as part of the MSO staff—began to explore the

10.09 The Overture Concert Organ under construction, April 2004.

possibility. They initially worked as well with Margaret Chen, a Chicago-based organ consultant. Though the Overture Foundation was not opposed to building in an organ, Jerry Frautschi and George Austin did not feel that the purchase of an organ was part of their purview.[16] In the end, as the estimated cost ballooned to over $1 million, together with $300,000 needed to create the movable case, it was Pleasant Rowland Frautschi who stepped forward with over $1 million; anonymous gifts from two other donors completed the funding. After considering organ-building firms in San Francisco, Montreal, and Germany, the committee decided on the German firm Orgelbau Klais, a multigenerational family firm based in Bonn.[17] DeMain later recalled that the organ did face concern from Ann Stanke, on behalf of the Madison Opera. She felt that it would not be conducive to set storage backstage and opera productions. He said that the solution was to store scenery on Overture's spacious loading dock; a pair of enormous, 30-foot-tall doors in the left stage wall allowed access to the loading dock.[18]

Organ builder Philipp Klais is the fourth-generation head of a firm founded by his great-grandfather Johannes in 1882. He took on the substantial challenge of creating the Overture Concert Organ. Not only did it need to be done by the planned opening in 2004, it had to be able to *move*. For an organ in a church or a dedicated concert hall, the organ pipes, console, and mechanism can be permanently installed parts of the structure. However, in multipurpose Overture Hall, the organ needed the ability to be moved forward on the stage for orchestral and solo repertoire, and then to be completely off stage for operas, musicals, ballet, and the like. The solution was to put the entire chamber of the organ on 16 boxcar wheels on four train tracks in the stage floor. The entire assembly, weighing some 174 tons, is widely reported to be the heaviest permanently installed movable object on any stage in the world. It doesn't move quickly, taking about a half hour to travel the 21 feet from midstage to its backstage parking area. For choral programs, the organ comes forward only about eight feet, in order to leave space for the choir risers between the orchestra and the organ. The sizeable organ console is also movable: It can be rolled from its storage area on stage left to center stage. It is certainly technically ingenious, but the Overture Concert Organ is also beautiful: its sweeping curves have variously been described as emblematic of sound waves, of waves on Madison's four lakes, or of the rolling hills surrounding the city. It provides a dramatic backdrop to the orchestra that accords perfectly with the rolling curves Pelli designed in the ceiling and in the hall itself. As organs go, the Overture Concert Organ, with 72 ranks and over 4000 pipes, is a large but not enormous instrument; Samuel Hutchison notes that there are actually church organs in Madison that are technically larger. However, the *sound* in Overture Hall is enormous. Hutchison points out that this was partly a function of its careful registration to the hall (a process that took months in the spring and summer of 2004, but which has continued since then) but also because of the particularly beefy pedal ranks. Hutchison notes that there are three 32-foot pipes (low C—one of them weighs 1200 pounds).[19]

10.10 Philipp Klais.

10.11 Samuel Hutchison, 2010.

The organ project soon generated interest among lovers of organ music and led to the formation of the Friends of the Overture Concert Organ (FOCO). As noted above, the organ was purchased entirely with private donations, and FOCO members have stepped forward to fund sizeable endowments: one of them to support organ programming and education/outreach efforts (by Diane Endres Ballweg), and another to endow the curator position that Hutchison filled for 13 years and which is currently held by Greg Zelek (by Nicholas and Elaine Mischler). Individual FOCO members have also served as concert sponsors. The MSO pays the sometimes high cost of ongoing maintenance on the instrument. The organ was showcased in the summer of 2005 in a series of free Saturday concerts associated with Madison's famous Farmer's Market, concerts that featured several local and guest organists. Then in autumn 2005, a formal concert series opened with a concert featuring the Los Angeles Master Chorale. This group had recently issued an acclaimed recording of the works of Morten Lauridsen, and the composer accompanied them to Madison to conduct his works. Since then, the Overture Concert Organ Series has grown into a phenomenally successful part of the MSO's annual offerings, with four programs, now featuring MSO organist Greg Zelek and guest organists from around the world.

Hutchison retired in 2017, and it was he who suggested that the MSO take a look at the organist Greg Zelek, a young Juilliard-trained organist whom a longtime patron of the MSO had heard play in Florida. After playing at one of the concert series programs to great acclaim, Zelek was named curator of the Overture Concert Organ and principal organist of the MSO. He is profiled at the end of this chapter.

10.12 Greg Zelek at the console of the Overture Concert Organ, 2023.

The Musicians of the Madison Symphony Orchestra

Surveying the evolution of the orchestra's membership over the course of nearly 100 years is fascinating. There are three points at which a clear snapshot of the membership is available. The earliest of these is an undated directory of orchestra members (probably from 1936 or 1937) in the MSO Archives, listing some 57 members of the Madison Civic Symphony, together with their occupations and employers. There are only four members of the orchestra who are listed as professional music teachers, and the list also includes 10 professional musicians who worked for the WPA: musicians, primarily string players, who performed in the orchestra as part of their WPA appointments. There were 15 University and Vocational School students and seven high school students. As for the rest, the Madison Civic Symphony included a cross-section of Madison: a post office clerk, a laborer for the University Forest Products Laboratory, salesmen, a dentist, a lawyer, engineers, and clerical workers for the state government. It seems that every person included in this list was a resident of Madison.

A little over 30 years later, during the winter of 1969–70, the *Capital Times* ran a series of section-by-section profiles of the orchestra titled "Know Your Symphony Orchestra." Though I have discussed this already in Chapter 6, it is worth noting that this particular moment shows an orchestra that is much more heavily populated by music teachers, with University studio faculty in most of the principal chairs, and nearly half of the orchestra membership made up of private and public school music teachers. The remaining orchestra membership was divided among housewives and a variety of other day jobs. While the profile was not specific with regard to where people lived, contemporary personnel records confirm that almost all of the membership of the orchestra lived in Madison or nearby.

10.13a-d A Madison Symphony Christmas, December 2023. One tradition that has arisen over the last several years is to do section costumes, or at least to coordinate sectional headgear for the lighter second half of the holiday concert:

In the spring of 2024, with the help of MSO general manager Ann Bowen, I put out a survey to the current membership of the MSO. Response was quite good, with nearly 70 of the orchestra's 91 players responding. First of all, I was surprised by the wide range of terms of service in the orchestra. When you look at the MSO on stage, you are seeing over 1300 seasons' worth of collective experience playing in the orchestra. The average length of service among current MSO players is about 18 years, though there is a somewhat lower average in the string section. I was particularly impressed by the length of service of some of my veteran colleagues. The MSO's current "elders" are Joyce Messer (principal trombone, 50 seasons), Wendy Buehl (section violin, 49 seasons), and Greg Smith (bass clarinet, clarinet, saxophone, 48 seasons), though there are also a few other players with over 40 seasons in the orchestra: Rick Morgan, (percussion, 45 seasons), John Aley (principal trumpet, 42 seasons) and Rolf Wulfsberg (section violin, 41 seasons). It is also a well-educated group, with well over half of the membership reporting a master's degree or equivalent.

10.14 Joyce Messer, 1999.

Perhaps the most dramatic change from 1969 is the nature of who is playing in the group. There are certainly university and local public school music faculty involved, including those who have since retired from teaching, but the numbers are not nearly what they were previously, when university faculty were routinely hired as principals. There are also players with nonmusical day jobs, but not very many (about 10). While the majority of players teach privately, the fact is that in 2024, the great majority of players in the MSO are in the business of playing music for a living. This includes many variants of what is wryly known as the "Freeway Philharmonic"—that is, making one's living by stringing together performance in several orchestras. Players report work in some of this country's "tier 1" orchestras—Chicago and the Chicago Lyric Opera, Milwaukee, St. Louis, Minnesota, and Louisville—as well as many of Madison's regional peers—Chicago Civic, Kalamazoo, Elgin, Fort Wayne, Grant Park, Quad City (Davenport, Iowa), Orchestra Iowa (Cedar Rapids, Iowa), and the Wisconsin Chamber Orchestra. Players also report performances in many of the small orchestras in the area as well, including Racine, Kenosha, La Crosse, Rockford, Fox Valley, Dubuque, Oshkosh, Beloit-Janesville, and Green Bay (now defunct). MSO players also report a great deal of chamber music work. Players like these tend to be less sanguine about working conditions and pay, and, understandably—given the fact that they are making a living playing—they tend to be just a bit more demanding in their approach to dealing with the orchestra's management.

One gradual change that I noted during my years as an orchestra member, which has come up in both formal interviews and informal conversations with veteran players, is the fact that Madison Symphony Orchestra no longer identifies as a "community" group. In part, this is the result of 30 years of blind auditions, instituted by DeMain in 1994. Orchestra membership is now largely determined by the quality of a player's performance. While some veteran players have expressed a bit of reservation at the loss of local character, this approach has clearly been a very fine thing with regard to the overall quality of the orchestra's performance. Responses to one question on the survey indicate that over half of the orchestra still defines themselves as long-term residents of the Madison area, living within 30 miles of Overture Hall. Another question revealed that, in fact, employment in the MSO was responsible for *creating* Madison-area residents: 15 respondents noted that "I relocated to the Madison area within the past 10 years at least partly because of my position in the MSO." (This was actually more than the 13 respondents who reported commuting from more than 30 miles away.) This certainly accords with my impression in talking to former colleagues. I note that my former section-mates, second trombone Benjamin Skroch and tuba Josh Biere, both of whom maintain freelance careers around the region, have both relocated with their families to the Madison area, coming from Minneapolis and Chicago respectively. Madison remains a nice place to be, and even players who are dedicated Freeway Philharmonic members seem to see the benefit of living here, even if it means taking on nonmusical part-time work to do so. With regard to compensation and long-term planning in the orchestra, there were more open-ended questions at the end of the survey. I will deal with responses to those questions in the next chapter.

In Chapter 6, I discussed the history of the concertmasters of the MSO in the late 20th century. After many changes in the 1960s, there was a long period of relative stability in the concertmaster's chair: Thomas Moore served through most of the 1970s, Norman Paulu through the 1980s, and Tyrone Greive (profiled at the end of Chapter 8) through the 1990s and 2000s. All three were University faculty and/or members of the Pro Arte Quartet, and all had been appointed directly to the position by music director Roland Johnson. When Greive announced his retirement at the end of the 2009–10 season, the now more professional orchestra decided on a much more rigorous audition process for his replacement. During the 2010–11 season, the orchestra brought in three finalists for the position, each of whom took the concertmaster chair for two subscription programs. The first candidate was a familiar face: Suzanne Beia, who had joined the MSO as associate concertmaster in 1995, shortly after arriving in Madison to take a position with the Pro Arte Quartet. By 2010, she was listed as "co-concertmaster" with Greive. Beia was by then concertmaster of the Wisconsin Chamber Orchestra and had also played leadership roles in the New World Symphony, Wichita Symphony Orchestra, and Spoleto Festival Orchestra. The second candidate, Isabella Lippi, was at that time (and as of 2024, still is) concertmaster of the Elgin Symphony Orchestra. Lippi had a growing reputation as a soloist and recording artist. The final candidate was Canadian violinist Naha Greenholtz, who was then playing with the Milwaukee Symphony Orchestra. She also had a burgeoning reputation as a soloist and had served as concertmaster for both the Vancouver Symphony Orchestra and the Reno Philharmonic. She was also at the time studying at the Concertmaster Academy of the Cleveland Institute of Music. In the end, the orchestra and DeMain chose Greenholtz, though Beia remains co-concertmaster. At age 26, Greenholtz became the orchestra's tenth concertmaster, and the second youngest player to hold that chair.[20] She clearly had the training and inclination to take on this specialized role, and she has provided consistently strong leadership to the MSO for 13 years since taking the concertmaster position in 2011–12. She has also performed as a soloist during most seasons. (She is profiled at the end of this chapter.)

The orchestra's approach to dealing with management changed in 2009. Since the late 1960s, negotiations on what came to be known as the "master agreement"—the agreement regarding pay and working conditions for the orchestra—had been worked out directly in biannual or triannual negotiations between the elected orchestra players' committee and management. The local union, the American Federation of Musicians, Local 166, was only nominally involved in these negotiations. As Bob Palmer told me when I joined the orchestra in 1983, membership in the union was "strongly encouraged but not required" for members of the MSO; this was primarily because throughout the 1980s the MSO still relied on Music Performance Trust Fund (MPTF) money to fund part of the payroll for its free youth programming, not because the union was in any way involved in representing the musicians of the orchestra. However, beginning in 2007, several orchestra players—most of whom had been involved in contract negotiations—began to advocate for a stronger union presence in collective bargaining. This effort was largely endorsed by members of the players' committee, and on February 2, 2009, in a process overseen by the National Labor Relations Board, the entire orchestra voted on whether or not to have AFM representation in collective bargaining in contract negotiations. It was a relatively close vote (43 to 36), but the "Yes" votes won, and since that time, triannual contract negotiations have been between representatives of the management and board on one side and the orchestra committee, with representation from Local 166 of the American Federation of Musicians, and AFM Symphonic Services on the other. Though negotiations have sometimes been intense, they have always been successful. Wisconsin is a "right to work" state, meaning that union representation cannot in any way be mandated, even when the union is part of collective bargaining for all employees, but a large majority of MSO members today are in fact members of AFM Local 166 or other AFM locals.

Of course, like all performing artists, the musicians of the MSO were severely affected by the Covid lockdown of 2020–21. Following its March 2020 program (which included a fine performance of Strauss's *Ein Heldenleben*), the orchestra suspended all concerts for the rest of the season and eventually canceled the entire 2020–21 season as well. Even the first concert of 2021–22 was affected: it included a planned performance of the Beethoven ninth symphony, but in the midst of a Covid flare-up, the orchestra wisely decided to do a smaller program that could be performed with proper distance between players. The MSO, almost uniquely among part-time orchestras in the country, decided that not only would the administrative staff continue on salary as before, but also that all of the musicians in the MSO would be paid at a rate that approximated what they would have made in a normal season. Executive director Rick Mackie, obviously moved at the memory, called this "the thing I'm proudest of in my career."[21] It was accomplished with a combination of reserve funds, various federal relief programs, and an extraordinary response by MSO patrons to a fundraising appeal on behalf of the players.

Administrative Changes

Richard (Rick) Mackie, who became executive director in April 1999, is the longest-serving administrator in that position to date. A native of New Orleans, Mackie grew up in a very musical family, with close ties to the traditional jazz scene in New Orleans. His father Dick and uncle "Red" had been well-known musicians in New Orleans, playing in the New Orleans Owls and other traditional jazz bands and dance orchestras in the 1920s and 1930s, and his older brother Hank is a first-rank studio guitarist and teacher. Mackie remembers playing drums at age 13 with a college-age traditional jazz band, the St. Charles Avenue Stompers, a group that was featured on the Ted Mack Amateur Hour in the 1960s. In 1972, after graduation from Tulane University, he decided to forgo a planned MBA in international business; on the advice of his younger brother, Mackie contacted Prof. Arthur Priebe at the still very new arts administration program at the University of Wisconsin. He decided to pursue a master's degree in Madison, though it meant waiting an entire year to start. That year in New Orleans was filled with music: in particular, he was the leader and drummer and primary promoter of the New Leviathan Oriental Fox-Trot Orchestra, a group dedicated to reviving dance music of the 1920s.[22] He arrived in Madison in 1973 and earned a master's degree in arts administration. His first job, in 1977, was managing the Baton Rouge Symphony Orchestra, where, according to Mackie, "I basically did everything!"—an experience that served him well later. He then returned to Madison in 1985 for a 15-month stint working with WHA-TV. He returned to symphony administration in 1986, when he began four years as executive director of the Memphis Symphony Orchestra. However, it seems that a return to the Madison area was inevitable: Mackie and his wife Diane had already purchased the property in Cooksville where they live today, and rented it out for the four years they spent in Memphis, clearly intending to return. They did return in 1990 when he took a job as director of development for Edgewood College. In April 1999, he succeeded Sandra Madden as executive director of the Madison Symphony Orchestra.[23]

10.15 Rick Mackie, 2018.

Mackie's 22 seasons as executive director were very successful. Under his leadership, the orchestra gained a firm financial footing, moved into Overture Hall, and weathered the storms of the 2008 recession and the 2020 Covid lockdown. A strong advocate of fiscal responsibility and development of the donor base, Mackie successfully led efforts to increase the orchestra's endowment, to the point that it is now, at over $30 million, the largest endowment by far of any orchestra in the country of similar budget size. He also led in the creation of a sizeable reserve "rainy day" fund, which paid off well during the recession of 2008 and the Covid crisis. Regarding his work with DeMain, Mackie called it

> a fantastic working relationship that developed into a really close friendship ... we never had a problem with his role versus my role ... first of all, I always took a step back anytime there was something on

the artistic side... In fact, the relationships between managers and conductors are famously fraught in the symphony business, and having gone through some of that in my previous jobs I just thought that, wow, this makes my job is so much easier that I'm not in a struggle, though there's certainly some give and take. I'm certainly willing to give however. Why? Because he is the conductor he is. He's not some wannabe, up there flailing around trying to prove something and making life difficult for everybody. John didn't come here to prove something, he came here to *do* something.[24]

Mackie was also responsible for expanding the administrative side of the orchestra, and he made a couple of very fine, long-lasting hires: marketing director Peter Rodgers and development director Casey Oelkers. The longevity of Rodgers and Oelkers, and of other MSO staff in their positions—in a profession that is notoriously a revolving door of short-term hires—contributes to the stability and success of the orchestra. I will profile Mackie's successor, Robert Reed, who took over in 2022, in the next chapter.

The longest-serving member of the MSO's leadership team is general manager Ann Bowen. A native of Olympia Fields, Illinois, a southern suburb of Chicago, she played trumpet all the way from fifth grade to grad school, when she played in the non-music major band at the University. Bowen has a master's degree in arts administration from the program at the University's Bolz Center and was first employed by the MSO as an operations intern during the 1992–93 season, with the production of *Shining Brow* presenting an exciting challenge. She spent the next season with an orchestra in Jackson, Mississippi, and three years with the Honolulu Symphony Orchestra. Sandra Madden then hired Bowen as operations manager in the fall of 1997. She actually wears a couple of hats for the orchestra, taking care of finances as well as operations. As Bowen explains, Madden was in charge of maintaining the MSO's finances, and when she left, Bowen took over that duty on an interim basis. When Rick Mackie was hired, he had no interest in keeping the books, and since Bowen "likes numbers," she took this on permanently. She explains the operations side of her job as taking responsibility

10.16 Ann Bowen, 2011.

for everything that happens on stage—except for the quality of the performance, which is all on the musicians and John DeMain—making sure that, with the help of the personnel manager [Alexis Carreon], that all of the right musicians are on stage, and the librarian [Jennifer Goldberg], that everyone has the correct music, and that the stage is set up correctly. Basically, it's making sure that the musicians have everything they need in order to do their job.

For MSO musicians, Ann Bowen is the friendly, compassionate, seemingly unflappable face of the orchestra's management—I have heard her described as the "heart of the Madison Symphony Orchestra." She attributes part of this rapport to the fact that

> I think that my background as a musician—though not to the quality that I would hire to put on stage. (I have this recurring nightmare of hiring myself to sit next to [MSO principal trumpet] John Aley [laughs].)—gives me an understanding of the musicians' needs and concerns in getting their job done. It gets a little frustrating, because there's 91 individual personalities, some of them harder to deal with than others. I guess I try to make the most people happy that I can.[25]

Bowen manages all of this with admirable grace. One particularly trying period during her tenure was the interregnum between Rick Mackie's retirement in June 2021 and the arrival of Robert Reed in July 2022, a period of over a year during which she shouldered the duties of "interim executive director," in addition to her own job. This period included the depths of the pandemic shutdown, the search for Mackie's successor, and the MSO's attempts to get the 2022–23 season off the ground. Associate conductor Kyle Knox, who is profiled at the end of this chapter, has called the MSO one of the most "immaculately well-managed orchestras in the country." Surely much of the credit for that goes to Ann Bowen.

In 2002, a growing staff had in fact outgrown the former office space at MATC, and—possibly with an eye toward the eventual separation from MATC—Mackie moved the MSO offices and library to an office suite on Odana Road, on Madison's far west side. Reorganizing the orchestra's library, previously held in a large, flood-prone storage room in the basement of the MATC downtown building, was a particular need, and as part of the new offices, the orchestra purchased a large specialized compact shelving unit. The Odana Road offices were much more professional in nature, but they were also remote (over four miles) from where the orchestra did most of its work. In 2005, the orchestra offices moved to their present location, a suite occupying half of the fourth floor of 222 West Washington Avenue, just a block away from Overture Hall. According to former librarian Kathryn Taylor, one challenging aspect of the move concerned the compact shelving. There was no way to get the shelving into the space designated for the library, so the movers had to temporarily remove a wall in order to get the shelving unit in place.

2007 marked the end of the orchestra's relationship with Madison Area Technical College. Since its 1928 agreement with the Madison Vocational School, MATC's predecessor, the orchestra's music director had also been an employee of MATC, with the title supervisor of music. MATC, in fact, paid most of the wages for this dual position. Prager, Heermann, and Johnson had all worked diligently at supervisory duties: overseeing staff and course offerings, reporting on budgets, and even teaching classes. In the beginning, the orchestra and chorus were actually Vocational School courses that members could sign up for. (This was still the case for the Madison Civic Chorus into the 1960s.) Perhaps the writing had been on the wall for a long time, but by the early 2000s, there was increasing pressure from some members of the MATC board to sever financial ties with the MSO.[26] Though he was not particularly active as an administrator, DeMain notes that he did propose "a really fun adult music appreciation course" to MATC. The MSO, of course, remained a potent

10.17 MSO Administrative staff, May 2024.
Seated L–R: Meranda Dooley, Chris Fiol, Robert Reed, Yumian Cui, Peter Rodgers. **Standing**: Casey Oelkers, Ann Bowen, Lindsey Meekhof, Alexis Carreon, Amanda Dill, Lisa Kjentvet, Katelyn Hanvey, Emmett Sauchuck, David Gordon, Jennifer Goldberg.

arts outreach for the school. In 2007, the MSO and MATC formally severed their ties. However, this historical relationship was fundamentally important to the orchestra and chorus for nearly 80 years, providing rehearsal, office, and library space, and most importantly, an administrative and financial safety net that allowed the orchestra to survive and thrive for much of its history.

As the budget and outreach of the MSO have expanded, so has the size of the administrative staff. When I was employed by the MSO in 1995–96, the annual budget was roughly $955,000, and the administrative staff was four full-time people: executive director (Sandra Madden), director of marketing (Craig Robida), director of development (Lisa Fusaro), and office manager (me). Nearly 30 years later, with an annual budget of nearly $6 million, the staff has expanded to 14 specialists, with an executive team, and directors of marketing, development, and education, each with their own small staff:

- Robert Reed, executive director
  - Alexis Carreon, office and personnel manager
  - David Gordon, executive assistant and board liaison
- Ann Bowen, general manager
- Peter Rodgers, director of marketing
  - Amanda Dill, marketing communications manager
  - Lindsey Meekhof, audience experience manager
  - Chris Fiol, marketing and volunteer coordinator
  - Yumian Cui, data analytics manager (also serves the development area)
- Casey Oelkers, director of development
  - Meranda Dooley, manager of individual giving
  - Emmett Sauchuck, manager of grants and sponsorships
- Lisa Kjentvet, director of education and community engagement
  - Katelyn Hanvey, manager of education and community engagement

The orchestra also employs specialized librarians: orchestra librarian Jennifer Goldberg and Madison Symphony Chorus manager and librarian Dan Lyons.

The Madison Symphony Chorus

For the past 25 years, the chorus has had one director, Beverly Taylor. In Chapter 8, I noted Taylor's initial struggles with the social inertia of a group that was rather set in its ways by the time she took over in 1996. Her efforts to raise standards, institute auditions, and promote the basics of vocal technique have paid off in constant, incremental improvements in the chorus's performances over the long term. Though it was no longer an annual event as it had been under Johnson, the chorus sporadically did independent concerts throughout Taylor's tenure in addition to the holiday program, and the usual large choral/orchestral piece at the end of each season. One particularly beloved tradition has been to sing traditional carols *a capella* in the resonant atrium of the Overture Center lobby prior to the Madison Symphony Christmas program. In 2010, the MSO issued a CD of the chorus's 2009 performance, titled *Hear the Angel Voices*.[27]

In May 2017, Taylor led the chorus on a memorable tour of Germany, performing the Brahms *German Requiem* in several German cities, including at the famed Thomaskirche in Leipzig, where J. S. Bach spent the last quarter century of his career. In-person rehearsals, of course, stopped during the pandemic, but many chorus members have expressed their sincere gratitude to Taylor and chorus manager/librarian Dan Lyons for their efforts to make sure that the chorus could continue to meet "virtually" during the lockdown.

In my opinion, the chorus's performances over the last few years have been the best I've heard in my over 40 years with the orchestra, most notably in the Beethoven *Missa Solemnis* (2022)—among the most challenging works in the choral repertoire—Orff *Carmina Burana*, (2023), and Verdi *Requiem* (2024). Rose Heckenkamp-Busch, currently vice president of the chorus, credits this to Taylor's consistent attention to vocal production, but also to an influx of younger singers in recent years, many of whom are traveling significant distances to sing in this chorus. She has also noted a shift in approach in recent years: from singers coming in cold "to learn the notes" to singers who take responsibility for learning parts on their own so that Taylor is freed up to rehearse the music itself.[28]

MSO Concerts of the Past Quarter Century

By the time of the move into Overture Hall in 2004, the MSO was routinely doubling all of its subscription concerts, with Saturday evening and Sunday matinee performances of eight programs. With the tremendous interest in the new hall, administration took a bold step: adding a Friday night performance to each subscription concert, and adding a ninth tripled subscription program. This gamble paid off, financially and artistically. By the end of its first three years in Overture, the MSO had nearly 5000 subscribers. (5000 subscriptions for 6300 seats over three programs is a rate that would be the envy of any comparable orchestra in the world.) On the artistic side, just as going to double concerts in the late 1990s had led to an increase in the quality and assurance of the orchestra's playing: a third performance was an additional enhancement. Adding a ninth program and nine additional performance services was also a financial boon to MSO players. The financial crisis of 2008 eventually put an end to the ninth subscription program, though the MSO has steadfastly maintained eight triple programs since then.[29]

The cycle of Mahler symphonies that began with DeMain's first program concluded in Overture Hall with the eighth (2004) and ninth (2007), and since then, the orchestra has repeated the first (2009), second (2011), fourth (2016 and 2023), eighth (2019), and fifth (2024). In January 2024, I heard the orchestra play the fifth symphony. I clearly remember performing this work in 1998, when it was exciting but still seemed to be at the very limit of what the MSO could effectively do. The orchestra's excellent and thoroughly assured 2024 performance was a telling reminder of how much the MSO has *continued* to grow in the last quarter century. DeMain has, with much less fanfare, also programmed other "cycles" during his tenure: The MSO has played all nine Beethoven symphonies and all four of Brahms's symphonies. The orchestra has also performed nearly all of Richard Strauss's symphonic poems over the last 25 years, including the titanic, seldom-played *Alpensinfonie* in 2017 (an extraordinary concert under one of the MSO's favorite guest conductors, Carl St. Clair), as well as the "big three" Stravinsky ballet scores: *Firebird* (2006 and 2012), *Petrushka* (1998), and *Rite of Spring* (2007 and 2023).

Overall, the repertoire of the orchestra has remained relatively conservative, concentrating on classical standard repertoire, but there were many notable exceptions. There were four premieres in the early 2000s:

- John Stevens, *Jubilare!* (2000)
- Daniel Catán, *Suite from "Florencia en el Amazonas"* (2003)
- Ned Rorem, *Mallet Concerto* (2004, with percussionist Evelyn Glennie)
- Taras Nahirniak, *Night Dances* (2004, with the Madison Ballet)

Notable contemporary works performed since 2000 include music by John Adams (four works[30]), John Harbison (three works[31]), Jennifer Higdon (three works), Astor Piazzolla (three works), John Corigliano (two works), Christopher Rouse, Joan Tower, Osvaldo Golijov, Kevin Puts, Aaron Jay Kernis, Steven Stucky, and Chris Brubeck. In the past few years, the MSO has begun to program works by neglected 20th-century composers of color: Florence Price, George Walker, William Levi Dawson, and Silvestre Revueltas have all had their works performed in the last few seasons. The MSO has also begun to showcase works by contemporary composers of color and women. The past few seasons have included music by Jessie Montgomery and Wynton Marsalis (his virtuosic and eclectic *Violin Concerto*, in a stunning performance by violinist Kelly Hall-Tompkins), and the 2024–25 season includes works by Valerie Coleman and Anna Clyne. The same season also includes contemporary works by Jonathan Lesnoff and Kevin Puts.

As always, the MSO has continued to feature its own performers as soloists, most often on the holiday program, though concertmaster Naha Greenholtz performs frequently on subscription programs as well. Most instrumental soloists who have played with the MSO since 2000 have been national names, some of whom have returned several times. I will not attempt to give a complete list, but some highlights include pianists Philippe Bianconi (a particular favorite of DeMain and the orchestra), Emanuel Ax, André Watts, Yefim Bronfman, Peter Serkin, Vladimir Feltsman, Horacio Gutiérrez, Garrick Ohlsson, Michelle and Christina Naughton,[32] Marc-Andre Hamelin, Christopher O'Riley, Christopher Taylor, Joyce Yang, and Olga Kern. Violinists have included Shlomo Mintz, Vladimir Spivakov,[33] bluegrass sensation Mark O'Connor, Sarah Chang, Robert McDuffie, Nadja Salerno-Sonnenberg, Hilary Hahn, Joshua Bell, Midori, Augustin Hadelich, Pinchas Zukerman, James Ehnes, Henning Kraggerud, Gil Shahan, Rachel Barton Pine, Blake Pouliot, and Kelly Hall Tompkins. Cellists have included Janos Starker, Carter Brey, Steven Isserlis, Alban Gerhardt, Alisa Wellerstein, Linda Harrell, Sara Sant'Ambrosio, Zuill Bailey, and Thomas Mesa. Though the MSO has only rarely played with other star instrumentalists, Norwegian trumpeter Tine Thing Helseth was sensational in her two appearances.

10.18 Cellist Steven Isserlis clowning with MSO cellist Lisa Bressler, March 2024.

The Overture Concert Organ has been played most frequently on symphonic programs by the MSO's own principal organists, Sam Hutchison and Greg Zelek, but the MSO has also hosted noted organ virtuosos Thomas Trotter and Nathan Laube. There have been too many vocal soloists to name, but I must mention the *prime donne assolute* Denyce Graves and Dawn Upshaw.

Formal pops programs, often held outside of the regular season, had been a feature of the MSO's programming since the 1960s. Under DeMain and Mackie, pops programs gradually disappeared. The tradition of a lighter pops-style program in January continued for a few seasons into the 2000s, with appearances by Bravo Broadway, Arlo Guthrie,[34] and Peter Shickele/P.D.Q. Bach. Mackie notes that this decision was made after a survey of subscribers regarding what they would like to see in an expanded season, and that overwhelmingly what they wanted was more classical programming.[35] While the orchestra certainly continues to play lighter repertoire, the old "pops" label was gone, and the place of the pops concert as a revenue-generating event for the MSOL was largely taken by the Concert on the Green going forward through June 2023. (In June 2024, the event was rebranded as Symphony at Sunset and moved to a new home, Madison's Burrows Park.) Another lighter program was the annual holiday concert, the Christmas Spectacular (rebranded as A Madison Symphony Christmas in 2014.). These complex programs typically begin with more serious repertoire and then move to lighter, popular holiday music after intermission. If there is anything that the Madison Symphony Orchestra does today that hearkens back in a clear way to its earliest days, it is this program, which is very much in the spirit of the great Civic Music Festivals of the 1930s: a long program, involving guest vocalists, guest choirs from the community (the various groups of the Madison Children's Choir, and the Mt. Zion Gospel choir), with a grand massed choral finale and audience sing-along. The Madison Symphony Chorus actually does a preconcert concert, singing traditional carols from the galleries around the central atrium of Overture Hall. A Madison Symphony Christmas is also *very* popular: In the past several years, the MSO has routinely sold out or nearly sold out all 6300 seats for the three concerts.

10.19 Soloists from the Mt. Zion Gospel Choir (Rene Robinson, Tamera Stanley, and Latanya Taylor) at A Madison Symphony Christmas, December 2023.

One popular feature over the past few seasons has been presentations in the Beyond the Score™ series developed by the Chicago Symphony Orchestra. These innovative programs combine live actors (drawn from American Players Theatre), multimedia, and the orchestra to present deep background on a featured work in an entertaining way—followed by a performance of the full work. Between 2014 and 2023, the MSO presented Beyond the Score™ programs on Dvořák's *Symphony No. 9 (From the New World)*, Rimsky-Korsakov's *Scheherazade*, Elgar's *Enigma Variations*, Mendelssohn's *Symphony No. 4 (Italian)*, Prokofiev's *Symphony No. 5*, Stravinsky's *Rite of Spring*, and Mahler's *Symphony*

No. 4. In the 2023–24 season, the MSO instead did *Pixar in Concert*™, an appealing set of excerpts from several Pixar films, with scores by Randy and Thomas Newman, and Michael Giacchino played live by the orchestra. Given the response to this program, the MSO is presenting two "movie shows" in 2024–25: Pixar's *Coco* and *Star Wars, Episode IV: A New Hope*.

Youth programming has continued to expand since 2000, and the MSO currently employs two full-time staffers devoted to educational programming and outreach, Lisa Kjentvet and Katelyn Hanvey. There are the usual Fall Youth Concerts in November, typically for elementary and middle school children, and the Spring Young People's Concert in March, largely for middle and high school students. Both concerts have traditionally included young soloists, the November concerts featuring winners of the Fall Youth Concerto Competition and the March program featuring winners of the Bolz Young Artist Competition, who win either the Bolz Award or the Steenbock Award,[36] and a scholarship. In 2007, the orchestra launched a new program in cooperation with WHA-TV, known as "The Final Forte." This was a live television broadcast across the state of the actual competition on the eve of the Young People's Concert. The four finalists each play their selection with the orchestra (after a pretaped feature profile/interview with each one), and winners are announced at the conclusion of the broadcast. This program is well-produced and widely watched. In 2000, the MSO launched a third annual program, Symphony Soup, this one aimed at younger children (kindergarten to third grade), designed as the culminating concert experience for the MSO's Up Close and Musical® program The most recent addition is Link Up, designed for grades three through five, and involving a year-long curriculum in which students learn about music and also learn to play soprano recorder.[37]

The MSO's educational outreach extends beyond the concert hall, however. Its guest artists are frequently engaged to give master classes to local students. The Up Close and Musical® program brings MSO musicians into local Dane County elementary school classrooms to introduce musical instruments and the fundamental concepts of music. The Hunt Quartet, the resident ensemble of the program, was originally established in 1999 as a group of University graduate student musicians who were also members of the MSO, and until 2020 it was jointly funded by the UW and MSO. The Hunt Quartet now functions exclusively under the auspices of the MSO. The other resident quartet is the Rhapsodie Quartet, founded in 2006: MSO co-concertmaster Suzanne Beia and longtime section violinist Laura Burns, principal violist Christopher Dozoryst, and principal cellist Karl Lavine. In addition to giving annual recitals, they are the resident ensemble of the MSO's internationally recognized HeartStrings® program. This is a unique music therapy–informed program, piloted in 2005 by former MSO director of education and violinist Michelle Kaebisch, that partners with retirement communities, residential facilities, and schools to present a directed music therapy program: over 90 events per year in the few seasons. This model has been adapted widely.[38]

10.20 The MSO and Madison Opera Chorus at Opera in the Park, early 2000s.

Performances with the Madison Opera continue to be an important part of the orchestra's work. In a 2024 interview, DeMain talked about wanting the Opera's 2004 debut in Overture to be something that simply could not have been done in the Oscar Mayer Theatre. That turned out to be a stunning production of Puccini's *Turandot* (with sets by the English artist David Hockney, created for the Lyric Opera of Chicago in 1992).[39] Over the past 20 seasons, the Madison Opera has continued its commitment to combining works in the standard repertoire with 20th-century works by American composers and musical theater, and challenging new works: notably two operas by Jake Heggie, *The End of the Affair* (2005) and the deeply moving *Dead Man Walking* (2014), *Galileo Galilei* by Philip Glass (2012), *Little Women* by Mark Adamo (2016), *Charlie Parker's Yardbird* by Daniel Schnyder (2017), *Florencia en el Amazonas* by

Daniel Catán (2018), and *Fellow Travelers* by Gregory Spears (2021). I know that many orchestra members remember the November 2022 production of Richard Strauss's *Salome* with particular pride. In 2002, the Opera started Opera in the Park—a free midsummer program that brings thousands of people to a natural amphitheater in Madison's Garner Park for an evening of opera excerpts accompanied by the full MSO. As DeMain recalls it, the initial idea came from Marian Bolz, who

> came back from Palm Springs one summer all excited about an outdoor opera performance she had seen in a park, with a couple of singers and a five- or six-piece chamber group. She wondered if we could do something like that in Madison, and I said "Marian, we have a very big opera company that does very big productions. Palm Springs has no opera company so that [little park concert] is all they get. If we're going to do it, we need to do it *big*...." Ann Stanke loved the idea and we scouted around town until we found Garner Park, which has this great hill with seating for thousands.[40]

The MSO also played at one of Madison's largest summer events during the 2000s. On June 29, 2002, the orchestra played a program at Warner Park, with country artist Lee Greenwood, as part of the city's grand fireworks display Rhythm and Booms. The audience for this patriotic event (still very much in the wake of 9/11) was estimated at 300,000—by far the largest live audience to which the MSO has ever played. Following the program, the orchestra played a series of classical excerpts broadcast by radio and coordinated with a huge fireworks display ... that was set off directly behind the stage, from a raft in the Warner Park lagoon. For the orchestra, it was a surreal experience: we played in headphones throughout, without really being able to hear one another— or ourselves, for that matter—over the tremendous noise of the fireworks. I gather that it sounded fine over the radio. The MSO, together with the Madison Symphony Chorus, played a second Rhythm and Booms program, this one featuring Christian music sensation Sandy Patti, in 2005.

The reputation and quality of the orchestra are such that the MSO has occasionally been hired to perform independently to back classical and popular artists. The orchestra has played with prog rock pioneers The Moody Blues (1993 and 1998), country singer Vince Gill (1996), pianist Jeffrey Siegel as part of his well-known "Keyboard Conversations" series (1994 and 1998), soprano Sarah Brightman (2001), as part of a Led Zeppelin tribute show (2003), and others. Beginning in 2017, the MSO has also been featured in an annual series of presentations of the *Harry Potter* films at Overture Hall.

Musicians of the Orchestra and Chorus: Selected Profiles

Greg Zelek

For this final set of profiles, I have chosen four relatively young musicians—all currently in their 30s—who will provide leadership to the MSO in the coming years. The first of them, principal organist and curator of the Overture Concert Organ Greg Zelek, was hired by the orchestra in 2017. A native of Miami and part of the Cuban-American community there, he initially studied piano, but his interest in the organ was sparked early when the family's church installed a large and particularly fine Italian instrument. Beginning as a teenager, he began to study piano and organ with the church organist. Zelek notes that

10.21 Greg Zelek, 2023.

> the organ was perfect for me in some ways. As a teenager I was looking for motivation; I wasn't one of those kids who wanted to come home and practice. But when you have the opportunity to work as a church organist at age 15, there's always the opportunity to perform preludes and postludes every Sunday.

He began to focus on the possibility of doing undergraduate study in organ at age 16 and met Paul Jacobs, who would be his teacher at the Juilliard School. He admired Jacobs's vision of the organ as a virtuoso instrument in its own right that could flourish in the concert setting. Zelek notes that his father sent him a clipping of an article that said that 99% of all organists are church musicians, saying that "you want to try to be part of the 1%." Regarding the job in Madison, Zelek is full of praise for his predecessor, Sam Hutchison, for his "tremendous integrity and his willingness to do whatever is best to promote and maintain this unique art form." Zelek notes that the organ has some problems in building an audience, that "in comparison to the orchestra, very few people know much about the organ: how it works, what its repertoire is … in an organ concert, just about any piece you're going to play is going to be unfamiliar to a large proportion of the audience." However, he points with justifiable pride to the ever-expanding audience for the Overture Concert Organ series. These programs, particularly the ones that he performs in, are a blend of standard organ repertoire and arrangements and works for organ, often featuring a wide range of guest players. Zelek typically speaks before each piece, introducing the music with a thoroughly approachable combination of personal reflections and humor. The 2023–24 season, for example, opened with a concert that celebrated his own Cuban heritage by bringing in musicians from Miami on guitar (his childhood guitar teacher Alvaro Bermudez), flute, bass, and percussion, for a program that combined repertoire by Bach, Piazzolla, and Lecuona with adaptations of Cuban popular standards. After two somewhat more conventional performances by solo guest organists Ken Cowan and Chelsea Chen, Zelek closed the season with another innovative program, played in combination with the UW–Madison Wind Ensemble. One particularly memorable concert was in February 2022, when a planned guest artist had to back out of a performance with less than two weeks to go before the scheduled program. Rather than cancel, Zelek put together a concert with UW–Madison trombonist Mark Hetzler. I remember it not only as a success in its own right as an attractive and eclectic program, but also for the fact that it introduced some really formidable *avant-garde* repertoire in a thoroughly audience-friendly and accessible way. For his part, Zelek notes that while trust might have been hard to come by when he first arrived at "age 25 and looking 17," he's now been in Madison long enough to have earned the trust of both the audience and the MSO administration. He enthusiastically praises the Friends of the Overture Concert Organ for their consistent and growing support and closed our interview by saying that "the future is bright for the instrument and the program."

Though the recently married Zelek lives in Madison, he still maintains a national career. He curates an organ series similar to that in Madison for the Jacksonville Symphony Orchestra and is the regular guest organist at St. John's Abbey in Minnesota. He also performs frequently as an organ soloist around the country.[41]

Rose Heckenkamp-Busch

In 2024–25, Rose Heckenkamp-Busch will become president of the Madison Symphony Chorus, certainly one of the youngest chorus members to hold that office in recent decades. She grew up near Sussex, Wisconsin, and "figured out I could sing when I got into high school." She sang in Wisconsin School Music Association (WSMA) state honors choirs, and then for three years was part of the Kids from Wisconsin, the well-known musical revue group. It was while in KFW that she met her husband, Luke Busch. Heckenkamp-Busch graduated from St. Norbert College with a minor in vocal performance. She then did a master's degree in speech language pathology, with an emphasis on

10.22 Rose Heckenkamp-Busch, 2024.

voice disorders, at UW–Madison. After several years working in skilled nursing facilities with medically complex patients, she decided "to shift gears completely," and now works for Communication Innovation, doing therapy primarily for children. While voice disorders are a smaller subset of what she does now, she clearly sees connections between her musical training and her therapeutic work.

Heckenkamp-Busch has had many earlier connections with Beverly Taylor, whom she describes as a "close friend," beginning at age 16 when she sang in a WSMA honors choir that Taylor directed. When she was in graduate school at the University, she sang for two years under Taylor in the Concert Choir. After taking several years off from choral singing due to time constraints, she joined the Symphony Chorus.

Heckenkamp-Busch expresses a bit of surprise that she will be president of the chorus, "since I really haven't been in the chorus for that long." But she expresses an active agenda as president: qualifying a mission statement and a set of musical standards for chorus members, and better defining the roles of the officers. She also wants to clarify the relationship between the chorus and the MSO, particularly as the chorus will celebrate its centennial season in 2026–27. Heckenkamp-Busch notes that there is a "real hunger to do more than we've been doing"—that is, singing on the holiday concert and doing one large choral/orchestra piece each season. She notes that the chorus last did an independent concert in February 2018, and they have not been able to organize one since Covid. Heckenkamp-Busch envisions the Madison Symphony Chorus becoming the "best in the state." She would also like to find ways for the chorus to be involved in the kinds of civic outreach that the orchestra does.

In addition to her work with the Madison Symphony Chorus, Heckenkamp-Busch enjoys collaborating with a wide variety of local musicians in the greater Madison area. She also does voiceover work, is a regular guest vocalist with the Ben Ferris Octet, a Madison-based jazz ensemble, and has recently started Luminaria, a voice/harp duo, for "weddings and elegant events."[42]

Naha Greenholtz and Kyle Knox

If the Madison Symphony Orchestra has a "power couple," it is concertmaster Naha Greenholtz and associate conductor Kyle Knox, who are married and have two small children together. Greenholtz was born in Japan to a Japanese mother and a Canadian father, and she lived there until she was five, speaking mostly Japanese. (Although she now acknowledges that "I've let my Japanese slide a bit," she has been speaking exclusively Japanese to the couple's three-year-old daughter Miki, in hopes that she will remain bilingual.) Like many Japanese children, Naha started as a Suzuki student, and though she has little memory of her earliest days on violin, it quickly became her "main extracurricular activity." The family moved to Ottawa for a couple of years as her father trained as a diplomat, and they then returned to Tokyo for his first posting. By the time she was in high school, they were living in Vancouver, and Greenholtz began to "audition for all of the big conservatories." She chose Juilliard after attending its New York String Seminar. (She also attended the Encore School for Strings associated with the Cleveland Institute of Music.) During her last semester at Juilliard, she successfully auditioned for a "second chair job" in the Louisiana Philharmonic and soon found herself "playing a lot of concertmaster" after the previous concertmaster left suddenly. She describes her season in New Orleans as difficult. This was after the devastation of Hurricane Katrina; infrastructure in the town was still a disaster, and the orchestra had no hall. However, she also describes a special feeling of community among the players and a sense that "we were punching above our weight class that season."

10.23 Naha Greenholtz and Kyle Knox, 2023.

She next had a series of one-year positions in the Milwaukee Symphony Orchestra, followed by a year in Cleveland, studying at the Cleveland Institute of Music's Concertmaster Academy with William Preucil. She then won the job in Madison, and after spending the first half of the season being put up at the Concourse Hotel by the orchestra, she and Kyle moved to Madison permanently in January 2012.[43]

Greenholtz feels particularly proud of the progress of the violin section, and talks about how lucky she is "to be surrounded by Suzanne [Beia], Leanne [Kelso], and Huy [Lui], who are all such lovely people and lovely musicians.... I always enjoy what I hear around me." To date, Greenholtz has appeared six times as a soloist:

- Mendelssohn *Violin Concerto* (2013)
- Bernstein, *Serenade (after Plato's Symposium)* (2015)
- Corigliano, *Chaconne from "The Red Violin"* (2016)
- Prokofiev, *Violin Concerto No. 2* (2019)
- Haydn, *Violin Concerto No. 4* (2022)
- Shostakovich, *Violin Concerto No. 1* (2023)

When asked what solo repertoire she would like to do in the future, she notes that she would love to do more collaborations with other players in the orchestra, like the Bach *Concerto for Violin and Oboe*, or the Haydn *Sinfonia Concertante* for violin, cello, oboe, and bassoon. Greenholtz notes that "I think that I've been able to check off all of my dream concertmaster solos with the Madison Symphony, the last being the [Beethoven] *Missa solemnis* [in April 2022]." She retains her position as concertmaster with the Quad City Symphony in Davenport, Iowa, and will perform as a soloist with them (the "Winter" movements of Vivaldi's *The Four Seasons* and Piazzolla's *The Four Seasons of Buenos Aires*) next [2024–25] season. Regarding other engagements, she says, "You know, since I've had kids, I've sort of shed all of the driving and travel for work." Looking back over her time with the MSO, Greenholtz calls it "a real learning experience. I feel really lucky to work with such a nice group of people, and to call that hall our home. Being in Madison is the longest I've ever lived in one place, and it really feels like it's home."[44]

Kyle Knox was born in New Jersey. He talks about being last chair clarinet in his middle school band and wanting to quit. Apparently, what stopped him was the fact that he was playing a clarinet that his uncle had played in the 1960s and which his grandma had had refurbished for him; he would have felt guilty about giving up. As he remembers it, what saved his eventual career was switching to bass clarinet for a year. Knox remembers that it felt very cool to be the only one playing his part in the band. By 9th grade, he was sitting first chair clarinet in the top middle school band and taking some lessons. It was at this point that he found that he really loved classical music. In 10th grade, he auditioned into the New Jersey Youth Symphony and struck up a friendship with another clarinetist, through whom he met his teacher Andy Lamy. Lamy provided introductions to two important figures, "the best clarinetist in the world," Ricardo Morales (then playing in the Metropolitan Opera Orchestra and now with the Philadelphia Orchestra) and Yehuda Gilad, whom Knox describes as "the best clarinet teacher in America, if not the world." Gilad moonlighted as a conductor and led the Colonial Symphony, near where Knox lived, and with nothing to do for four days in his hotel room, he invited Kyle to come in for clarinet lessons. Knox describes himself as anything but the typical overachieving, well-rounded young virtuoso player: he apparently devoted all of his attention in high school to classical music, to the detriment of other classes. During his senior year, he attended the Juilliard pre-college program, and he later earned an undergraduate degree from the Juilliard School.

After graduation in 2004, Knox had what he described as "my time in the wild," working in a bookstore in Los Angeles, taking lessons with Gilad, and flying around the country taking auditions. At age 23, he won a chair in the Milwaukee Symphony Orchestra as associate principal clarinet and E-flat clarinet. He also began teaching clarinet at UW–Milwaukee and performing in the Santa Fe Opera during summer breaks. However, at age 28, he began to have trouble with his hands, eventually diagnosed as task-specific focal dystonia, a neurological condition that disproportionately affects musicians and others who perform repetitive fine motor tasks. Fortunately, the union contract included health benefits that had a robust long-term disability provision that allowed him to retrain and paid a significant part of his salary for the next five years. Though he had "never held a stick before," he began working as a conductor. Chuckling, he recalled that "conducting and being a clarinet repairman were my two options, and they are kind of at the opposite ends of the glory scale." Since he knew many students at UW–Milwaukee, he began putting together pickup orchestras to perform works under his direction. He briefly attended graduate school at Northwestern University before moving to Madison with Naha in 2012. Here he began working with the University's James Smith, who had a similar background, having been a professional clarinetist before turning to conducting. Knox continued the practice of putting together orchestras he could conduct, including a performance of Mahler's *Symphony No. 4* at the Capital Lakes retirement community, that was attended by John DeMain. In 2014, Smith invited Knox to be his assistant, which involved a lot of podium time, conducting operas and orchestral repertoire with the UW–Madison Symphony Orchestra. He also began to conduct other Madison-area groups: the Middleton Community Orchestra, the Madison Savoyards, and the Middleton Players Theater. "Literally, any time I could get in front of a group I did it," he noted, "and, little by little, I really got to know how to do it well."[45]

In 2018, Knox was appointed associate conductor of the MSO. That same year, he also assumed the role of music director of the Wisconsin Youth Symphony Orchestras and conductor of the Youth Symphony, WYSO's top orchestra. He also oversees the WYSO artistic staff and the Music Makers music education program. As MSO associate conductor, he serves as the orchestra's "cover conductor," learning all of the scores of the orchestra's repertoire and being ready to step in if need be. Knox's first opportunity to conduct the MSO was in February 2016, when he directed the Madison Opera production of Mark Adamo's *Little Women*. He conducts the MSO regularly on stage, including nearly all of their education series concerts, Community Concerts, Concert on the Green/Symphony at Sunset, and the MSO's new movie series (including *Pixar in Concert*™ in February 2024).

He notes that he and Naha met for the first time when he was a sophomore at Juilliard, and she was a high school senior in Vancouver. They both played in the New York String Seminar, a program directed by Jamie Laredo, primarily made up of young conservatory students and a few select high school players. The next year, she came to Juilliard, but according to Knox, they really didn't get to know each other until the summer of his senior year, when the Juilliard orchestra was resident for six weeks at the Spoleto Festival in Italy … just as he was leaving New York City. At the urging of his roommate in Los Angeles, Kyle began to write to Naha, and the two struck up a long-distance romance. He got the job in Milwaukee, while she took a position in New Orleans, "so we were both at least in the same time zone." And then finally she got a job in Milwaukee as well, "so it was a long process of getting closer and closer to one another and finally being together." Naha had joint Canadian/Japanese citizenship at the time, and her visa was expiring. Kyle notes wryly that "we shotgunned it at the Milwaukee County Courthouse," partly to secure a green card, though Naha has since become a United States citizen.[46]

Regarding the quality of the MSO, Knox feels that "on a good day, playing in that hall, there's really not much difference between the Madison Symphony and just about any full-time professional orchestra in the country." And regarding the orchestra's culture, he notes that the MSO has been able to strike a balance between being a "well-managed group who plays at a high level and musicians who are actually having fun doing it."[47]

A Katrin Talbot Gallery

One of the many pleasures of working on this project has been collaborating with my friend Katrin Talbot, MSO violist, photographer, and poet. She has generously looked up and scanned over 80 photos from the 1990s and 2000s—many of which have appeared in this book already—and granted me permission to use them here. Her portraits of orchestra members are wonderfully evocative, conveying the personality of the players and, I think, the positive spirit of the orchestra itself. I'll conclude this chapter with a selection of some of our favorites. And I give the final word to Katrin: her 2024 poem "The *A* that Lasts a Hundred Years."

10.24 Katrin Talbot, viola, playing Dvořák (*col legno*), 2010. One of many humorous self-portraits Katrin has done over the years.

10.25 Dueling Maestros: Roland Johnson and John DeMain, 1994. This publicity photo, though clearly staged, also reflects the friendly, mutually respectful relationship between the two MSO music directors.

10.26a/10.26b Richard and Martha Blum, 2005. The Blums' long careers in the MSO (Rich as principal viola and Martha as concertmaster and longtime principal second violin) and the Pro Arte Quartet are discussed in Chapter 6.

10.27 John Aley, principal trumpet, 2010. Aley, who joined the University faculty and the orchestra in 1982, is among its longest-serving principals.

10.28 Eden Kainer, violin, 1999. Kainer played in the first violin section during the 1990s.

10.29 Hiram Pearcy, associate concertmaster, 1998. Hiram (1929–2023) was the longtime orchestra director at West High School. He played in the orchestra for 35 seasons until his retirement in 2000. He was also well known locally as a gardener, at one point maintaining some 700 varieties of daylilies in his garden in Verona!

10.30 Linda Bartley, principal clarinet, 2010. A member of the University faculty, Bartley was in the orchestra from 1992 to 2013.

10.31 John Jutsum, principal timpani, 2007. The Oberlin- and Juilliard-trained timpanist joined the MSO in 2001 and for many years commuted from Minneapolis. John now commutes from New York State!

10.32 Karl Lavine, principal cello, 2003. Karl, who remains principal today, is pictured here shortly after he won the chair.

10.33 Cynthia Cameron-Fix, principal bassoon, 2004. Cindy joined the orchestra as second bassoon in 1981–82, but then studied in New York City for two years, returning to the MSO in 1985. In 2003–4, she switched places with her former teacher Dick Lottridge to serve as interim principal. Dick, who wanted to play his final season in Overture Hall, continued for another season as second. Cindy won the principal chair in 2004.

10.34 Warren Downs, principal cello, 1999. Warren (1925–2020), a former member of the Cleveland Orchestra, came to Madison in 1971 to study journalism at the University and had a long career as an environmental writer for the University's Sea Grant Institute. He led the cello section from 1976 to 2000.

10.35 Greg Smith, bass clarinet, 2018. In his 48th season with the MSO in 2023–24, Greg is among the longest-serving members of the orchestra. He also plays clarinet and saxophone as needed. He gigs regularly with the *klezmer* band Yid Vicious and other local groups,

10.36 Patrick Nowlin, cello, 1999. Nowlin was one of several MSO youth soloists who later played with the orchestra. He won the Steenbock Award and played the Kabalevsky *Cello Concerto No. 1* in 1993, and then played in the cello section from 1998 to 2000.

10.37 Marika Fischer Hoyt, viola, 2004. Marika (1962–2023), in addition to her work with the MSO for over 20 seasons, was known regionally as a performer of early music. She died—far too young—of cancer in 2023.

10.38 Kathryn Taylor, violin, 2010. Kathy joined the first violin section in 1994 as one of a dozen new string players who auditioned into the MSO that year. She also served ably as orchestra librarian from 1995 to 2022.

10.39 Rick Morgan, percussion, 2014. Rick, a member of the MSO since 1979, managed a successful public relations firm for many years. He now chairs the MSO board's marketing committee.

10.40 Rolf Wulfsberg, violin, 2002. Rolf, who has been in the first violin section since 1984, is a second-generation MSO player: his mother, violinist Elizabeth (Muzzy) Wulfsberg, played in the orchestra from 1976 to 1994. As pictured here, he also plays the Norwegian Hardanger fiddle.

10.41 Frank Hanson, second trumpet, and Linda Kimball, principal horn, 2008. One of several married couples in the orchestra, Frank and Linda were music faculty members at UW–Whitewater, commuting nearly 50 miles one way for decades to play in the MSO and Wisconsin Chamber Orchestra. Frank played in the MSO from 1988 to 2022. Linda joined the horn section in 1987, became principal in 2004, and retired in 2023, though she still continues to play frequently as a substitute.

10.42 Elisabeth (Lisel) Ellenwood, viola, 2000. Lisel, who trained at the Eastman School of Music, joined the MSO in 1996. She also commutes from Whitewater and teaches in the fine public school string program in Oregon, Wisconsin.

10.43 Anthony (Tony) di Sanza, principal percussion, 2009. Tony joined the MSO in 1999, the year he arrived in Madison to become a percussion teacher at the University.

10.44 Diedre Buckley, viola, 2010. Diedre has been a member of the orchestra since 1997. Like several MSO players, she is also a member of the Wisconsin Chamber Orchestra.

10.45 Ross Gilliland, bass, 2007. Ross played in the MSO during the 2000s.

10.46 Stephanie Jutt, principal flute, 2009. Stephanie, who, since retiring from UW–Madison, commutes from New York City to play in the orchestra, joined the University faculty and the MSO in 1991. Her chamber ensemble Bach Dancing and Dynamite Society is acclaimed both for the quality of its performances and for its eclectic, sometimes whimsical programming.

10.47 Christopher Dozoryst, principal viola, 2017. Chris joined the MSO in 2007. This was a publicity photo taken before his performance of *Harold in Italy* with the orchestra.

10.48 Carol Rosing, contrabassoon and bassoon, 2003. Carol first played in the orchestra in 1989. She maintains a busy schedule, playing in several orchestras and teaching at UW–Whitewater, UW–Oshkosh, and Beloit College.

10.49 Suzanne Beia, co-concertmaster, 2009. Suzanne joined the orchestra in 1995, shortly after she came to Madison to join the Pro Arte Quartet. She has been co-concertmaster since 2010, frequently stepping forward to lead the string section when Naha Greenholtz is absent. She also serves as concertmaster of the Wisconsin Chamber Orchestra.

10.50 Renata Hornik, viola, 2005. Renata joined the MSO in 2004. She also plays assistant principal viola in the Fox Valley Symphony Orchestra.

10.51 Leanne Kelso, associate concertmaster, 2017. Leanne first joined the MSO in 1993 and then won the associate job in 1999. She also teaches at UW–Whitewater and performs with the Wisconsin Chamber Orchestra and the Madison Bach Musicians.

10.52 Karen Beth Atz, principal harp, 2001. The MSO has had only four music directors in nearly a hundred years ... but it has had only *three* principal harpists. Karen joined the orchestra in 1978, taking over from her former teacher, Margaret Rupp Cooper, who had joined the orchestra for its first concert in 1926 when she was still in eighth grade. Karen retired in 2017, and the current harpist, Johanna Weinholts, won the principal chair the next season.

10.53 Fred Shrank, principal bass, 2011. Fred (1952–2019) joined the orchestra in 1977 and became principal bass in 1982, retiring in 2016. He worked as a music educator for many years at Sun Prairie and Madison West High Schools.

10.55 Margaret (Maggie) Darby Townsend, cello, 2010. Maggie joined the MSO in 2002. Her day job is working for the UW–Madison Institute for Research on Poverty.

10.54 Rictor Noren, viola, 2000. Rictor performed with the MSO during the late 1990s and 2000s.

10.56 Alexis Carreon, viola, 2006. Alexis joined the orchestra as a musician and as personnel manager in 2005. In 2016, she also took on an administrative post as the MSO's office manager.

The *A* That Lasts a Hundred Years

With an inhale that
has taken centuries
of study,
the oboe keeps
its appointment as
tamer of chaos,
sentry of overtones,
marshal of tune

Delivers a bell of tone,
settling the silk of
an *A* out over the stage,
onto the waiting shoulders
of the house,
as we settle into
a tonality for
the next opus,
the next shimmer
of century

Notes to Chapter 10

1. *CT* 9/30/1998, 29, 35.
2. Prager seems to have instituted opening the season with the *Banner* as a tradition during World War II.
3. Email from Erika Nikrenz, April 14, 2024.
4. Interview with John DeMain, 6/14/2024.
5. As I remember it, the final and "best" solution was to have the unsightly concrete block back wall of the stage serving as the sound reflector at the back of the orchestra. This was hidden from view only by a sheer fabric scrim, which we were strictly forbidden to touch.
6. Acoustic Dimensions (Mamaronk, NY), "Preliminary Acoustical Review of the Orpheum Theatre," July 2, 1996. (document from the MSO Archives). DeMain noted that one of the engineers summed it up by saying, "We can get you from a 3 to a 5, but never to a 10."
7. Document from the MSO Archives.
8. Interview with Terry Haller, 5/24/2019.
9. Pat Schneider and Chris Murphy, "Frautschi gives $50M for arts here," *CT* 9/27/998. Just a personal note of admiration here: Though the Frautschis donated nearly all of the money for this project, there has never been any consideration of naming the facility after themselves; it has been "Overture" since the beginning.
10. Kevin Lynch, "Overture exterior gets go-ahead," *CT* 5/31/2001, 1B-2B. Of course, Madison being Madison, this became a highly political issue, with charges of classism and racism launched at the Overture Foundation over the next few years, and countless calls for this money to be spent on other civic needs. There was also resistance from business owners on the block, including a long and spirited defense from Jeff Stanley, who owned Dotty Dumplings Dowry, a wonderful burger joint on North Fairchild Street, and from his neighbor, Jack Miller of Miller's Eats & Treats.
11. Interview with Rick Mackie, 4/18/2024.
12. Interview with Sharon Stark, 4/23/2024.
13. Michael Allsen, "Lock, stock pavilion, and barrel," *WSJ* 9/19/2004, G1, G8. I will note that I was not responsible for the rather unfortunate headline! (My proposed title, without the egregious pun, was "Have orchestra, will travel.")
14. Watts, who passed away in 2023, appeared on six different MSO programs between 1991 and 2011. He is remembered fondly by members of the orchestra, both for his awesome playing and his geniality.
15. James Oestreich, "Critic's Notebook: Everything's Up to Date in Madison, in Tune with Its New Overture Hall," *New York Times* 11/23/2004.
16. Interview with Terry Haller, 5/24/2019. The Overture Foundation did, however, ultimately pay for the necessary reinforcement of the stage to bear the substantial extra weight of the organ.
17. Haller notes that the decision to engage the German firm was in part a "happy accident" having to do with currency exchange rates in the early 2000s. (Interview with Terry Haller, 5/24/2019.)
18. John DeMain interview with Phillip Gainsley, for the podcast, "Let's Talk About Music!" January 7, 2024: https://www.podomatic.com/.../2024-01-07T07_24_44-08_00, accessed 2/8/2024.

19 Interview with Samuel Hutchison, 2/17/24. Hutchison notes that "you *feel* the note rather than hear it." I can attest to this, having played Strauss's *Also sprach Zarathustra* with the MSO in September 2006—a work whose opening "sunrise" fanfare begins with a long-held pedal C from the organ.

20 The orchestra's first concertmaster, Marie Endres, was only 24 when she took a leadership role and led the string section until 1960. See Lindsay Christians, "Young Canadian concertmaster, 26, to lead Madison Symphony," *CT* 9/15/2011, 12.

21 Interview with Rick Mackie, 4/18/2024.

22 Interview with Rick Mackie, 4/18/2024. According to Mackie, most of the group's initial repertoire came from a large collection of arrangements collected by his father. The orchestra is still quite active in New Orleans. During his time in Madison, he helped start another revival group, the Hyperion Oriental Fox-Trot Orchestra.

23 Interview with Rick Mackie, 4/18/2024

24 Interview with Rick Mackie, 4/18/2024. As noted at the end of Chapter 9, DeMain clearly valued his relationship with Mackie as well.

25 Interview with Ann Bowen, 4/25/2024.

26 Interview with Beverly Simone, 4/17/2024.

27 *Hear the Angel Voices: Christmas with the Madison Symphony Chorus*, Madison Symphony Chorus, Beverly Taylor, director, Ion Records compact disc, 2010.

28 Interview with Rose Heckenkamp-Busch, 5/15/2024.

29 Mackie notes with some pride that some nervous board members wanted to cancel "three or four" programs due to the financial downturn. However, he assured them that, given the reserve funds, this would not be necessary. In the end, it was necessary to cut only one of the nine programs. (Interview with Rick Mackie, 4/18/2024.)

30 Note that John DeMain already had a relationship with Adams and his music, having conducted the premiere of his opera *Nixon in China* in Houston in 1987. The works were: the *Violin Concerto* (2000, with violinist Robert McDuffie), *On the Transmigration of Souls* (2011), *Doctor Atomic Symphony* (2014), and *The Chairman Dances* (2023).

31 Harbison is, of course, something of a local celebrity: he summers every year in nearby Token Creek. The works were: *The Flight into Egypt* (2000, with the Madison Symphony Chorus), *The Great Gatsby Suite* (2010), and *The Most Often Used Chords* (2019).

32 The Naughton twins grew up in the Madison area, and both were winners of various youth competitions with the MSO before going on to careers as soloists and duo-pianists.

33 Spivakov played twice with the MSO. On the first occasion (January 2003), he was not only the soloist in Mozart's second violin concerto, he was also the guest conductor, giving a truly memorable reading of the Tchaikovsky fifth symphony. Maestro Spivakov still stands in the memory of many veteran players as one of our all-time favorite guest conductors.

34 Arlo Guthrie's appearance in January 2001 marks one of those very rare occasions in which the program annotator actually had an impact on the program. When I wrote program notes for the booklet—with very little information to go by—I talked about one of my favorite Guthrie songs, the epic talking blues *Alice's Restaurant*, which he would "of course" be playing. At the Friday night dress rehearsal, I found, to my embarrassment, that the song was nowhere to be found on the program. Before the Saturday show, I knocked on his dressing room door and fessed up to my mistake, which he assured me was certainly not a big deal. Then, after intermission, he

held up the booklet and announced that: "Well, it says in this here program, which was written by an *expert*, that I'm actually doing *Alice's Restaurant* ... so I guess I'd better." He then launched into an impromptu, nearly full-length version of the song!

35   Interview with Rick Mackie, 4/18/2024.

36   These awards were endowed by Marian Bolz and Evelyn Steenbock.

37   The curriculum has been designed by Carnegie Hall's Weill Music Institute. The sonic impact of over a thousand kids hooting away on recorders, while being accompanied by a full symphony orchestra, is simply amazing!

38   See Michelle A. Kaebisch and Shannon E. Lobdell, *HeartStrings*[SM]: *A Guide to Music Therapy-Informed Community Engagement for Symphony Orchestras.* (Madison: Madison Symphony Orchestra Inc., 2011).

39   John DeMain interview with Phillip Gainsley, for the podcast, "Let's Talk About Music!" January 7, 2024. This production cost over $400,000, close to what *Shining Brow* had cost a decade earlier. DeMain jokingly noted that it set an unrealistically high standard for opera productions to follow in Overture Hall!

40   Interview with John DeMain, 6/14/2024.

41   Interview with Greg Zelek, 4/22/2024.

42   Interview with Rose Heckenkamp-Busch, 5/15/2024.

43   Interview with Naha Greenholtz, 5/12/2024.

44   Interview with Naha Greenholtz, 5/12/2024.

45   Interview with Kyle Knox, 4/25/2024.

46   Interview with Kyle Knox, 4/25/2024.

47   Interview with Kyle Knox, 4/25/2024.

CHAPTER 11

The Madison Symphony Orchestra and the Future

I had originally titled this final chapter "The Madison Symphony Orchestra and the Next Hundred Years." As I thought about it, however, the sheer audacity of that title began to wear on me. I am relatively confident that if Sigfrid Prager and members of the 1926 Madison Civic Symphony were somehow transported into the audience for one of the orchestra's concerts in Overture Hall today, they would recognize it as the same sort of program and musicmaking they were engaged in back in 1926. I assume that they would be impressed to find out that their enterprise was still functioning and functioning very well a century later ... though some of them may have been dismayed to find out every member of this Madison Symphony Orchestra was being paid to play! However, I am not so sure that my own imagination could conceive of what a Madison Symphony Orchestra concert might look and sound like in 2125, so instead I will confine my speculation to the nearer future.

Robert Reed

During the summer of 2022, the Madison Symphony Orchestra hired Robert Alan Reed as executive director. Reed grew up in Louisville, Kentucky, and remembers being inspired as a fourth grader when he attended a youth concert by the Louisville Symphony Orchestra. The next day he walked into the band room at school and told the band director that he wanted to join. When asked what instrument he was going to play, Robert pointed to a clarinet, which he had

11.01 Robert Reed, 2023.

remembered seeing at the concert. He was eventually able to get lessons through a program offered by the University of Louisville; in auditioning for this scholarship, he remembers that he left his music in his locker at school and instead of canceling the audition played for the next 30 minutes without music. He was offered lessons all the way through high school and eventually excelled as a clarinetist. Reed talks about developing a thick skin early on, being an African American child growing up in the inner city, whose interests were "symphonic music, books, the arts, and school." He endured teasing and bullying—according to Reed, "I felt disowned by my own community, and not welcomed by other communities. Despite all these challenges and many tears, I was still determined to pursue music, as I could not imagine a life without it." Reed also excelled in math and science classes in high school, and his parents, knowing that he would probably be the only one of his siblings to get a college degree, fully expected him to go into engineering. Though they were not at all thrilled by his decision to go into music, he pointed out that it was really his decision to make, since they were not paying for any of his college education. Reed graduated from the Cincinnati College-Conservatory of Music with a degree in music performance in 1987, with a further master's degree in music performance in 1989.

While studying in Cincinnati, Reed began to be aware of what kind of sacrifices he would have to make to be a professional symphonic clarinetist, and he began to think about a Plan B. This was to become an arts administrator. In 1989–90 he was one of eight selected to become an Orchestra Management Fellow, a fellowship sponsored by the American Symphony Orchestra League. He had postings with the New York Philharmonic, the Florida West Coast Symphony, and the Houston Symphony Orchestra that year, but remembers that most administrators he worked with fully expected him to fail. In fact, over the course of 32 successful years of orchestra management before coming to Madison, he has still faced discrimination: "I have had orchestra representatives tell me that I am not the 'right type' for their orchestra, headhunters refusing to consider me for positions despite my being highly qualified, being regularly mistaken for the security guy, and feeling alone and not accepted." Over the course of 32 years, Reed had a peripatetic career that is relatively standard for those in arts administration: many jobs, some of them only for a season or two. Before coming to Madison, and beginning in 1990, Reed worked for orchestras in San Jose, California, Louisville (his hometown), Nashville, Buffalo, Tulsa, an interim position as executive director of the San Francisco Symphony Orchestra, Jackson, Mississippi, Kansas City, and non-orchestra positions at the Lincoln Theater in Washington, DC, and the Tucson multicultural arts project, and the Pittsburgh Symphony Orchestra. Directly before coming to Madison, Reed had longer tenures at two orchestras in Texas: in Corpus Christi and Plano. He seems to have every intention of staying in Madison until his retirement. Writing in 2022,[1] Reed said that

> I am a truly blessed and happy man! At 58, I know who I am. I know what I am excellent at, and what I'm capable of doing. I know what cities would be a good fit for me to reside in, and what cities I need to avoid. I know how to say no. Strangely enough, I was offered a job with another arts organization a month before Madison but I declined the job because the Madison Symphony Orchestra was the job that felt right to me and worth waiting for.[2]

Ebullient and upbeat, Reed has proven himself to be an effective chief administrator for the MSO and a fine representative to the community for the orchestra. Surveying the last two years, he points with pride to the community concerts as an initiative he started. He notes that "there are a lot of folks who might not feel welcome in the traditional setting in Overture Hall—or who just don't know anything about the Madison Symphony Orchestra—and this is a way to meet them where they are." He also mentions the "MSO at the Movies" series that started this year successfully with the nearly sold-out *Pixar in Concert*™ program. Regarding the all-Mexican show in May, he notes that "we made some really nice connections there that we will certainly go back to in the future."[3]

Challenges and Opportunities

In 2025 the MSO faces many challenges, most of them shared by other orchestras and performing arts organizations across the country. Though many trends predated the onset of Covid-19, the pandemic shutdown of 2020–2022 has been a primary factor, causing many larger and smaller orchestras less financially sound than the MSO to suspend operations completely. For example, the San Antonio Symphony formally suspended operations in 2021, after 83 seasons.[4] It is no secret that the MSO's audience is aging: one need only survey all of the gray heads at a typical Sunday matinee. And a certain proportion of the audience has simply not come back following the pandemic, partly because some people justifiably feel unsafe in a large crowd. Subscriptions, once the lifeblood of the MSO's budget, are at relatively low levels. Where the MSO had nearly 5000 season subscribers in the heady seasons following the opening of Overture Hall, it now regularly has about 2400. This is a trend that predated the pandemic and has been seen by nearly all performing arts organizations across the country, as fewer people are willing to commit in advance to an entire season of events. It now it seems that post-pandemic ticket buyers are more likely to buy single tickets, often in the week before the show, than they are to invest in a subscription series. However, it is not all bad news, as single ticket sales have rebounded to fill the gap. Overall ticket sales (subscriptions plus single tickets) have in fact rebounded well past the 2019 level: again, part of a national trend.[5] As unpredictable as this new reality may be for the MSO marketing staff, it is the reality that we live with, and the MSO's marketing is designed to embrace it.

The other part of the revenue stream, development/fundraising, has also faced challenges. One trend seen nationwide is that wealth that formerly might have gone to support arts organizations is now more likely to be passed on to younger family members, whose charitable support often leans toward social justice issues and poverty. However, while MSO certainly has many very generous donors, it has managed to avoid the dependence on a few "deep-pocket" donors that has spelled disaster for other arts organizations, as in the example of Opera Pacific discussed in Chapter 9.

Diversity, equity, and inclusion (DEI) might be a political hot button in some circles, but as League of American Orchestras (LAO) president Simon Woods said during a May 2024 visit to Madison, for orchestras like the MSO, fostering DEI efforts "is not just a moral issue, it is a big-time business issue."[6] Addressing this comes on several fronts for the MSO. The diversity of the orchestra itself is pretty low, at about the rate of 1.8% musicians of color reported nationwide by the LAO. As with most orchestras, diversity efforts are hampered by the tradition of blind auditions. However, there is a clear tradition of inviting in an ethnically diverse range of soloists and guest conductors over the years. Diversity has also been a welcome addition to the MSO's repertoire. As discussed in Chapter 10, recent seasons have seen a welcome infusion of works by composers of color and women; the days where the subscription repertoire was entirely music by "dead white guys" seem to be gone forever. Of course, the "big-time business issue" alluded to by Woods concerns ticket sales: that is, can the MSO attract a younger and more ethnically diverse audience? It is common knowledge that the proportion of white people—traditionally the core of a symphony orchestra's audience—as part of the total American population is declining, from nearly 85% in 1965 to a projected 46% in 2065, with most of the difference being taken up by a larger proportion of Asian/Pacific Islander and Hispanic Americans.[7] In May 2024, the MSO made a concerted and largely successful effort to attract a large Mexican American audience with an all-Mexican program, with works by Moncayo, Ponce, and Revueltas, with a Mexican piano soloist, Jorge Osorio, and a closing set featuring the famed Mariachi los Camperos. The MSO even took the unusual step of printing the program notes in both English and Spanish. To be sure, one all-Mexican program in 98 seasons is merely a start, but it was an encouraging start. Another effort to reach out to more diverse audiences is a series of free community concerts that started in 2022–23, bringing the orchestra into ethnically diverse neighborhoods in south Madison and elsewhere.

In order to survive and thrive in the future, the MSO must also try to attract younger audiences. The millennial generation, those born between 1981 and 1996, are set to overtake the baby boomers (born between 1946 and 1964) as the largest U.S. adult generation.[8] As described in the previous chapter, the MSO does a fine job of engaging with children and teens, but starting this past season it has also begun an "MSO at the Movies" series. These shows, which combine film with a live performance of the orchestral film score, are designed to be family-friendly. Next season, the orchestra will expand its movie offerings to two. With an eye on a tech-savvy younger audience, the MSO has also dramatically expanded its online offerings and its presence on social media networks. providing, for example, preconcert video features by DeMain, our soloists, MSO marketing consultant Sebastian Jimenez, and me, as well as entertaining "musicology moments" by Steve Kurr (a series sponsored by the MSOL). The orchestra clearly plans to expand its online presence significantly in the years to come.

Climate change will certainly have an impact on Madison in the coming century. The states surrounding the Great Lakes will likely become havens for Americans fleeing environmentally deteriorating parts of the country. Madison and other midwestern cities will almost undoubtedly see dramatic increases in population, with the possibility of the population of the Madison metro area rising to over a million in the relatively near future. One of my final conversations in preparing this book was with Jeff Bauer, a member of the board for the past six years, and of the Madison Symphony Chorus since he moved to town eight years ago. Jeff has an impressive background in economics, meteorological science, and medical technology, but he defines himself as a "futurist"—as someone who uses data to forecast alternative futures.[9] His prediction of a million-person Madison, for example, greatly exceeds the more modest growth numbers predicted by governmental agencies. Bauer suggests that, because of the tremendous growth potential in Madison itself, the MSO is one of a small minority of American orchestras that "can look forward to the future with optimism." In fact, he feels that the potential is there for the Madison Symphony Orchestra to join the first rank of American orchestras, and for Madison to become an arts destination for the nation. Of course, achieving this vision would involve tremendous changes and the will to make them, but Bauer feels very strongly that it is in the "realm of the possible," given the extraordinary history of community support for classical music in Madison.[10]

The orchestra itself may also evolve. The MSO is currently among the finest "per-service" orchestras in the country. Once again, this has been, in part, the result of blind auditions instituted by John DeMain in 1994. As I discussed in Chapter 10, most of the members of the orchestra who have joined since that time are mostly professional musicians who make their living playing music. A few of the respondents on the orchestra survey in the spring of 2024 suggested the next logical step is a transition to a "core orchestra" approach where a defined core of players become full-time salaried employees of the orchestra, including insurance and retirement benefits that are currently out of reach for most part-time musicians. This typically comes with a specified number of services that the core musicians need to play, which would undoubtedly result in a dramatic expansion of the season. To cite the example of a relatively close peer of the MSO that has a core orchestra, the Fort Wayne Philharmonic: this orchestra is performing over 40 distinct programs in 2024–25, including several pops programs—some of them repeated multiple times in multiple locations—as well as various "run-out" concerts, youth concerts, a chamber series, and movie shows very much like what the MSO has done recently. By comparison, the MSO will play about two dozen distinct programs next season, including its performances for the Madison Opera. Nearly doubling the number of programs would come with a tremendous increase in operational costs for the orchestra, and it would likely be a hardship for some musicians who remain on per-service contracts. In a conversation with Mark Bridges, MSO cellist and current president of the orchestra players committee, Mark noted that while many orchestra members supported a move to a core orchestra, he acknowledged that the transition would be "challenging." Speaking for the administration, Robert Reed said that "the time was not yet right for this discussion." For his part, DeMain points to the fact that while he feels that the MSO is *the* symphony orchestra of Madison, there is actually a second thriving orchestra in town, the Wisconsin Chamber Orchestra, with its popular Concerts on the Square series in the summer and a classical series during the season. He feels strongly that as long as the WCO maintains a separate identity, it will be nearly impossible to transition to a core orchestra.[11]

Of course, the most important decision the orchestra needs to make in the next couple of years is a new music director. This orchestra has been very fortunate over the last century in its choice of music directors, and also fortunate in their longevity in the job, which has led to continued stability and growth: Prager served for 21 years, Heermann for 14, Johnson for 33, and DeMain will have rounded out 32 years by the close of 2025–26. The MSO must choose someone with the conducting chops and musical skills needed to continually improve the quality of performances by the MSO and the Madison Symphony Chorus, but who also has the personality and vision needed to represent the orchestra to the community. There is currently a search committee of 12 people working on the conductor search, including representatives from the orchestra, and rather than issuing an open invitation to anyone interested and qualified, the committee has taken the approach of inviting candidates of particular interest. The orchestra will bring in three guest conductors in 2024–25 and four more in 2025–26. While the MSO hopes to have a music director named at the end of the 2025–26 season, given the importance of this decision, it may go on to a third year ... or as long as it needs to. According to Reed: "We have the luxury that John isn't going anywhere, and neither is Kyle Knox, so we have highly competent conductors to cover concerts."

Looking Toward the 100th Season

As I wrap up work on this book in June 2024, the hundredth season is still well over a year away. However, an active committee, co-chaired by Elaine Mischler and Derrick Smith, has already been at work since January 2022 on plans for the centennial season celebration, with several brainstorming sessions before then. They recently presented their plans to the executive committee of the board, and I sat down with Mischler to talk about how the MSO will celebrate its hundredth season. The season will start off with a pair of non-subscription concerts on September 19 and 20, 2025. The first program will be a classical one, featuring an MSO favorite such as Olga Kern, followed by a celebratory dinner. On September 20, the MSO will present a more innovative program featuring Cirque de la Symphonie, a group that brings the spirit of the world-famous Cirque du Soleil to orchestra programs. According to their website:

Artists include the most amazing veterans of exceptional cirque programs throughout the world—aerial flyers, acrobats, contortionists, dancers, jugglers, balancers, and strongmen. Each performance is professionally choreographed to classical masterpieces and popular contemporary music in collaboration with the maestro.[12]

The season itself will open with a concert featuring Mahler's transcendent *Symphony No. 2 (Resurrection)*, directed by Maestro DeMain. To close the season in May 2026, the orchestra and chorus will perform a newly composed piece by one of America's leading composers, Jake Heggie. Heggie, familiar to Madison Opera audiences for his *The End of the Affair* (2005) and *Dead Man Walking* (2014), has been commissioned to write a "major, 50-minute work" on a libretto by Gene Scheer, a work that may include some of our community partners like the Madison Opera, the Mount Zion Gospel Choir, and the Madison Children's Choirs. The subject matter may include our county's 250th anniversary as well as the MSO Centennial. To wrap up the celebrations on June 13 and 14, 2026, there will be a two-day community "open house" using the entire Overture Center, with performances by MSO members, an instrument "petting zoo," talks on the orchestra's history, and a Sunday afternoon orchestra performance—with all events free to the public.

The celebrations will certainly build on MSO's "brand," with everything from airport kiosks to bus wraps. During the season there are plans for community concerts in neighborhoods in Dane County, as well as school concerts by small groups from the MSO and a series of public lectures on the orchestra's history. According to Mischler,

> Our idea is not only to celebrate our past, but importantly, we must look to the future. We want to engage the community in many types of music and activities and to build our audience for the future.[13]

Notes to Chapter 11

1. Interview with Robert Reed, 6/11/2024.
2. This quote, and much of the foregoing background on Reed, comes from a self-introduction he published in 2022 for MSO patrons in the orchestra's newsletter: Robert A. Reed, "My Symphony Story," *The Score* (Fall 2022): 10–11.
3. Interview with Robert Reed, 6/10/2024.
4. Gus Bova, "The Life, Death, and Life of San Antonio's Symphony," *The Texas Observer* 3/15/2023, https://www.texasobserver.org/san-antonio-symphony-philharmonic-union-following-a-nine-month-labor-largest-city-without-a-symphony. In this case, the pandemic came on the heels of a nine-month strike by musicians, and years of issues between musicians and the board. In 2022, musicians of the former orchestra reformed as the San Antonio Philharmonic.
5. "Report: Attendance at Orchestras is Starting to Reach Prepandemic Levels, Despite some Declines," *Symphony* News Brief: March 14, 2024: https://symphony.org/report-attendance-at-orchestras-starting-to-reach-prepandemic-levels-despite-some-declines/, accessed 6/10/2024.
6. Simon Wood, presentation to MSO board members, 5/21/2024. The League of American Orchestras (LAO) is the successor to the American Symphony Orchestra League (ASOL). See also League of American Orchestras, *Making the Case for Equity, Diversity, and Inclusion in Orchestras* (New York City: League of American Orchestras, 2024).
7. Pew Research Center, "10 demographic trends shaping the U.S. and the world in 2016." https://www.pewresearch.org/short-reads/2016/03/31/10-demographic-trends-that-are-shaping-the-u-s-and-the-world/, accessed 6/8/2024.
8. Pew Research Center, "10 demographic trends."
9. Among his many publications is Jeffrey C. Bauer, *Upgrading Leadership's Crystal Ball: Five Reasons Why Forecasting Must Replace Predicting and How to Make Strategic Change in Business and Public Policy* (Boca Raton, FL: Productivity Press, 2013).
10. Interview with Jeff Bauer, 6/13/2024.
11. Interview with John DeMain, 6/13/2024. DeMain notes that there were serious discussions about bringing the two orchestras together under a single management following the unexpected death of WCO's longtime music director, David Lewis Crosby, in 1998, but in the end, WCO decided to maintain its distinct identity.
12. "Cirque de la Symphonie," https://www.cirquedelasymphonie.com/, accessed 6/20/2024.
13. Interview with Elaine Mischler, 6/20/2024.

Photos and Images: Sources and Permissions

Note: *WSJ* = *Wisconsin State Journal*; *CT* = *Capital Times*

Cover photos and Preface

Madison Civic Symphony, 1926. Used by permission, MSO Archives.
Madison Symphony Orchestra, 2023. Photo by Peter Rodgers, used by permission.
Allsen head shot. Photo by Katrin Talbot, used by permission.
MSO Low Brass with DeMain. From personal collection of the author.

Chapter 1

1.01 - UW School of Music Digital Commons.
1.02 - *WSJ* 8/24/1870, 4. Used by permission Capital Newspapers.
1.03a-1.06 - Wikimedia Commons.
1.07 - Public domain image from *Gallery of Players: The Illustrated American*, ed. Maxwell Hall (New York: Lorillard Spencer, 1895): 65.
1.08 - Image WHI 83363, used by permission, Wisconsin Historical Society.
1.09 - Photo used by permission, foundphotographs.com.
1.10 - Photo used by permission, Tim Denee.
1.11 - Image WHI 98333, used by permission, Wisconsin Historical Society.
1.12 - Image WHI 17374, used by permission, Wisconsin Historical Society.
1.13-1.14 - UW-Madison School of Music Digital Commons.
1.15 - *WSJ* 3/11/1874, 2. Used by permission Capital Newspapers.
1.16-1.17 - UW-Madison School of Music Digital Commons.
1.18 - Image WHI 22543, used by permission, Wisconsin Historical Society.
1.19 - *WSJ* 2/14/1917, 5; *WSJ* 2/18/1917, 4. Used by permission Capital Newspapers.

Chapter 2

2.01 - From personal collection of the author.
2.02 - 2.03 - Used by permission, MSO Archives.
2.04 - *WSJ* 12/23/1943,1/*WSJ* 10/7/1947,1. Used by permission, Capital Newspapers.
2.05 - Used by permission, MSO Archives.
2.06 - Wikimedia Commons.
2.07 - Used by permission, MSO Archives.
2.08 - Image WHI 57047, used by permission, Wisconsin Historical Society.
2.09 - Image WHI 55538, used by permission, Wisconsin Historical Society.
2.10 - Used by permission, MSO Archives.

2.11 - *WSJ* 6/3/1932, 1. Used by permission, Capital Newspapers.
2.12 - Used by permission, MSO Archives.
2.13 - *WSJ* 5/1/1943, 1. Used by permission, Capital Newspapers.
2.14 - 2.17 - Photos by Nathan Moy, used by permission.
2.18 - Public domain image from Baas's papers in the WHS Archives.
2.19 - Image WHI 74512, used by permission, Wisconsin Historical Society.
2.20 - *WSJ* 2/4/1930, 8. Used by permission Capital Newspapers.
2.21 - Image WHI 67436, used by permission, Wisconsin Historical Society.
2.22 - 2.23 - Used by Permission, Wisconsin Music Archives.

Chapter 3

3.01 - Used by permission, MSO Archives.
3.02 - Public domain illustration from the journal *Bühne und Welt* 10/1 (1907–8), p. 185
3.03-3.06 - Wikimedia Commons.
3.07 - IMSLP Commons.
3.08-3.09 - Wikimedia Commons.
3.10-3.11 - Used by permission, MSO Archives.
3.12 - Used by permission, Luther Memorial Church.
3.13 - Photo by the author.
3.14 - Used by permission, Bradley Short (Hanks family).
3.15 - *Chicago Daily News*, 12/12/1931. (This newspaper has since gone out of business.)
3.16 - Used by permission, MSO Archives.
3.17 - Image WHI 120123, used by permission, Wisconsin Historical Society.
3.18 - Used by permission, MSO Archives.
3.19 - From personal collection of the author.
3.20 - *WSJ* 4/25/1954, 10. Used by permission, Capital Newspapers.

Chapter 4

4.01–4.02 - Used by permission, MSO Archives.
4.03 - *CT* 11/29/1942, 8. Used by permission, Capital Newspapers.
4.04 - UW-Madison Digital Commons.
4.05-4.06 - Used by permission, MSO Archives.
4.07 - Wikimedia Commons.
4.08-4.10 - Used by permission, MSO Archives.
4.11 - Image WHI 133235, used by permission, Wisconsin Historical Society.
4.12 - Image WHI 72559, used by permission, Wisconsin Historical Society.
4.13 - Image WHI 67421, used by permission, Wisconsin Historical Society.

4.14 - Image WHI 92520, used by permission, Wisconsin Historical Society.
4.15-4.16 - Used by permission, MSO Archives.
4.17 - Image WHI 75513, used by permission, Wisconsin Historical Society.
4.18 - Photo by the author.
4.19 - Used by permission, MSO Archives.
4.20 - Image WHI 138739, used by permission, Wisconsin Historical Society.
4.21 - Photo by Katrin Talbot, used by permission.

Chapter 5

5.01 - Wikimedia Commons.
5.02-5.12 - Used by permission, Heermann family.
5.13 - Used by permission, Interlochen Center for the Arts.
5.14a-5.14b - Used by permission, Heermann family.
5.15 - UW-Madison Digital Commons.
5.16 - *Charleston Daily Mail* 5/3/1936, 58. Used by permission, the *Charleston Gazette-Mail*.
5.17-5.20 - Used by permission, Heermann family.

Chapter 6

6.01-6.02 - Used by permission, MSO Archives.
6.03 - Used by permission, New York Public Library.
6.04-6.07 - Used by permission, MSO Archives.
6.08 - Wikimedia Commons.
6.09 - Used by permission, MSO Archives.
6.10 - Wikimedia Commons.
6.11-6.13 - Used by permission, MSO Archives.
6.14 - *WSJ* 3/30/1941, 1. Used by permission, Capital Newspapers.
6.15 - Image WHI 88359, used by permission, Wisconsin Historical Society.
6.16 - Used by permission, Monona Terrace.
6.17 - Used by permission, MSO Archives.
6.18 - *CT* 1/10/1970, 21. Used by permission, Capital Newspapers.
6.19 - Image WHI 106457, used by permission, Wisconsin Historical Society.
6.20a-6.20b - Used by permission, MSO Archives.
6.21 - Photo by David Sandell, (*CT* 9/30/1970), used by permission, Wisconsin Historical Society.
6.22a-6.25 - Used by permission, MSO Archives.
6.26 - Photo by Katrin Talbot, used by permission.
6.27 - Photo by the author.
6.28 - Photo by Katrin Talbot, used by permission.

Chapter 7

7.01-7.05 - Used by permission, Johnson family.!
7.06 - Used by permission, Heermann family.
7.07 - *Cincinnati Post*, 1951 (This newspaper has since gone out of business.)
7.08-7.16 - Used by permission, Johnson family.
7.17 - UW-Madison Digital Commons.
7.18 - Used by permission, Johnson family.
7.19 - Photo by the author.
7.20 - Photo by the author, used by permission, Johnson family.

Chapter 8

8.01-8.05 - Used by permission, MSO Archives.
8.06 - *CT* 4/22/1993, 49. Used by permission, Capital Newspapers.
8.07 - Used by permission, Daron Hagen.
8.08-8.09c - Used by permission, MSO Archives.
8.10 - *WSJ* 5/15/1994, 1. Used by permission, Capital Newspapers.
8.11 - Photo by Katrin Talbot, used by permission.
8.12-8.13 - Used by permission, MSO Archives.
8.14 - Photo by Peter Rodgers, used by permission.
8.15 - Used by permission, Terry Haller.
8.16 - Wikimedia Commons.
8.17a-8.19 - Photos by Katrin Talbot, used by permission.
8.20 - From personal collection of the author.

Chapter 9

9.01 - Used by permission, John DeMain.
9.02 - Used by permission, Youngstown Playhouse.
9.03-9.04 - Wikimedia Commons.
9.05 - Used by permission, John DeMain.
9.06-9.07 - Used by permission, Houston Grand Opera Archives.
9.08 - Wikimedia Commons.
9.09 - Used by permission, Houston Grand Opera Archives.
9.10-9.11 - Used by permission, John DeMain.
9.12-9.13 - Used by permission, MSO Archives.
9.14 - Photo by Peter Rodgers, used by permission.

Chapter 10

10.01-10.03 - Photos by Katrin Talbot, used by permission.
10.04a-10.06 - Used by permission, MSO Archives.
10.07 - Used by permission, Sharon Stark.

10.08 - Photo by Peter Rodgers, used by permission.
10.09-10.10 - Used by permission, MSO Archives.
10.11 - Photo by Katrin Talbot, used by permission.
10.12 - Photo by Peter Rodgers, used by permission.
10.13a - Used by permission, Lisa Bressler (MSO cellist).
10.13b - Used by permission, Elisabeth Duessen (MSO violist).
10.13c - Used by permission, Rob Rickman (MSO bassist).
10.13d - Used by permission, Linda Kimball (MSO hornist).
10.14-10.16 - Photos by Katrin Talbot, used by permission.
10.17 - Photo by the author.
10.18 - Used by permission, Lisa Bressler (MSO cellist).
10.19 - Photo by Peter Rodgers, used by permission.
10.20 - Wikimedia Commons.
10.21 - Photo by Peter Rodgers, used by permission.
10.22 - Photo by Rose Heckenkamp-Busch, used by permission.
10.23 - Photo by Peter Rodgers, used by permission.
10.24-10.57 - Photos and poem by Katrin Talbot, used by permission.

Chapter 11
11.01 - Photo by Peter Rodgers, used by permission.

Bibliography

A) Interviews and Personal Communications

Aley, Anne (former director, UW Summer Music Clinic). Email correspondence with the author, 4/4/2021.

Anklan, LeAnne (executive director of the Cincinnati Chamber Orchestra). Phone conversation with the author, 1/25/2021.

Bauer Jeff. Interview by the author, 6/13/2024.

Bielefeld, Betty. Interview by the author, 5/1/2019.

Bolz, Marian. Interview by the author, 6/22/2018.

Borsuk, Gerald. Interview by the author, 6/20/2000.

Bowen, Ann. Interview with the author, 4/25/2024.

Bruno-Videla, Lucio. Email correspondence with the author, 8/14-16/2001.

Chatman, Stephen. Email correspondence with the author, 10/6/2022.

Crow, James and Ann. Interview with the author, 9/19/2000.

DeMain, John. Interview with the author, 6/5/2000.

_____. Interview with the author, 6/14/2024.

_____. Interview with Phillip Gainsley, for the podcast, "Let's Talk About Music!" 1/7/2024: https://www.podomatic.com/.../2024-01-07T07_24_44-08_00, accessed 2/8/2024.

Douma, Walter. Interview with the author, 5/23/2019.

Iltis, Ted. Interview with the author, 7/31/2000.

Greenholtz, Naha. Interview by the author, 5/12/2024.

Greive, Tyrone and Janet. Interview with the author, 11/29/2022.

Haller, Terry. Email correspondence with the author, 6/12/2024.

_____. Interview by the author, 5/24/2019.

Hay, Helen. Interview with the author, 6/17/2000.

Heckenkamp-Busch, Rose. Interview with the author, 5/15/2024.

Heermann Neal, Paulita. Phone conversations with the author, 3/27/2021 and 10/20/2021.

Heermann Neal, Paulita and Peter Neal. Interview with the author, 10/16/2020.

Huthchison, Samuel. Interview with the author, 2/1/2024.

Johnson, Carl and Barbara Westfahl. Interview by the author, 10/14/2022.

Johnson, Roland. Interview by the author, 8/10/2000.

_____. Interview by the author, 8/15/2004.

Knox, Kyle. Interview by the author, 4/25/2024.

Kretschman, Karen and David. Interview by the author, 10/22/2022.

Libecap, Nuggie (Springfield Symphony Orchestra). Email correspondence with the author, 3/3/2021.

Lottridge, Richard. Interview with the author, 6/3/2019.

Madden, Sandra. Interview by the author, 4/11/2023.

Mackie, Rick. Interview by the author, 4/18/2024.

McClure, Patricia (volunteer historian, West Virginia Symphony Orchestra). Email correspondence with the author, 2/27/2021.

Michell, Brian (Archivist, Houston Grand Opera), Email correspondence with the author, 6/3/2024.

Mischler, Elaine. Interview by the author, 6/20/2024.

Moy, Nathan. Email correspondence with the author, 11/13/2019.

Neal, Peter. Email correspondence with the author, 3/12/2021

Nikrenz, Erika. (Eroica Trio). Email correspondence with the author, 4/14/2024

Palmer, Robert. Interview by the author, 3/22/2022.

Reed, Robert. Interview by the author, 6/11/2024.

Schneider, Barbara. Email correspondence with the author, 6/17/2024.

Shook, George. Email correspondence with the author, 10/22/2019.

Shook, George and Nancy. Interview with the author, 1/17/2023.

Simone, Beverly. Phone conversations with the author, 4/17/2024.

Skornicka, Joel. Interview by the author, 5/8/2019.

Stark, Sharon. Interview by the author, 4/23/2024.

Talbot, Katrin. Email correspondence with the author, 2/3/2021.

Vich, Beverly (Houston Grand Opera), Email correspondence with the author, 6/3/2024.

Walzinger, Stefanie. Email correspondence with the author, 1/5-7/2022.

Wood, Simon (League of American Orchestras). Presentation to MSO board members, 5/21/2024.

Zelek, Greg. Interview by the author, 4/22/2024.

B) Newspapers (Accessed primarily through newspapers.com.)

Appleton Post-Crescent (Appleton, Wisconsin).

Bangor Daily Whig and Courier (Bangor, Maine).

Birmingham News (Birmingham, Alabama).

Birmingham Post-Herald (Birmingham, Alabama).

The Boston Globe (Boston, Massachusetts).

The Bridgeport Post (Bridgeport, Connecticut).

The Bristol Herald-Courier (Bristol, Tennessee).

Bühne und Welt (Berlin, Germany).

Capital Times (CT – Madison, Wisconsin).

The Capital Journal (Salem, Oregon).

The Central New Jersey Home News (New Brunswick, New Jersey).

Charleston Daily Mail (Charleston, West Virginia).

Charleston Gazette (Charleston, West Virginia).

Chattanooga Daily Times (Chattanooga, Tennessee).

Chicago Tribune (Chicago, Illinois).

Cincinnati Enquirer (Cincinnati, Ohio).

Cincinnati Post (Cincinnati, Ohio).

Cincinnati Times-Star (Cincinnati, Ohio).

Cleveland Plain dealer (Cleveland, Ohio).

The Courier-Journal (Louisville, Kentucky).

Dayton Daily News (Dayton, Ohio).

Detroit Free Press (Detroit, Michigan).

Evening Star (Washington, DC).

Hamilton Daily News (Hamilton, Ohio).

Indianapolis Star (Indianapolis, Indiana).

Isthmus (Madison, Wisconsin).

Janesville Daily Gazette (Janesville, Wisconsin).

Johnson City Press (Johnson City, Tennessee).

Johnson City Staff-News (Johnson City, Tennessee).

The Key Outpost (Key West Naval Station, Florida).

Daily Freeman (Kingston, New York).

La Crosse Tribune (La Crosse, Wisconsin).

Milwaukee Daily Sentinel (Milwaukee, Wisconsin).

Minneapolis Star (Minneapolis, Minnesota).

Minneapolis Tribune (Minneapolis, Minnesota).

Montgomery Advertiser (Montgomery, Alabama).

Musical Courier (New York City, New York).

The Musical Gazette (Boston, Massachusetts).

New York Daily News (New York City, New York).

New York Times (New York City, New York).

Newsday (Melville, New York).

Oklahoma State Register (Guthrie, Oklahoma).

Port Clinton Daily News (Port Clinton, Ohio).

The Raleigh News and Observer (Raleigh, North Carolina).

Rock Island Argus (Rock Island, Illinois).

The Sheboygan Press (Sheboygan, Wisconsin).

Springfield News-Sun (Springfield, Ohio).

Die Stimme (Berlin, Germany).

Tagliches Cincinnatier Volksblatt (Cincinnati, Ohio).

The Texas Observer (San Antonio, Texas).

The Toledo Blade (Toledo, Ohio).

Traverse City Record Eagle (Traverse City, MI).

Variety (Los Angeles, California).

Wisconsin Argus (Madison, Wisconsin).

Wisconsin State Journal (*WSJ* – Madison, Wisconsin).

Youngstown Vindicator (Youngstown, Ohio).

C) Documents

"A Listing of All the Musicians of the Cleveland Symphony Orchestra." www.stokowski.org/Cleveland_Orchestra_Musicians_List.htm, accessed 11/5/2020.

Acoustic Dimensions (Mamaronk, New York). "Preliminary Acoustical Review of the Orpheum Theatre," July 2, 1996. From the MSO Archives.

J. MICHAEL ALLSEN

Alexius Baas Papers. From the Wisconsin State Historical Society Archives.

Biographical note on Walter Heermann. From the MSO Archives.

Board Minutes for the Madison Community Music Committee, Madison Civic Music Association [MCMA], and Madison Symphony Orchestra [MSO], 1922-2024. From the MSO Archives.

"Citation to Marie A. Endres at Milton College Commencement, June 6, 1965," From the *Wisconsin Music Archives* [WMA] *Marie Endres Collection.*

Documents accessed on ancestry.com.

Documents accessed in the Carnegie Hall Performance History Database. https://www.carnegiehall.org/About/History/Performance-History-Search.

Focus: WHA Television Community Outreach 12 (December 1979). From the *WMA Olive Endres Collection.*

Golden, Joseph. *Hunger Amid Plenty: The Quest for Cultural Space in Madison, Wisconsin.* From the MSO Archives.

Heermann Scrapbooks. A collection of 13 dated scrapbooks, containing programs, photos, newspaper clippings, letters, and more, documenting over 60 years of Walter Heermann's career. They are currently held by his daughter, Paulita Heermann Neal.

Information from the Cincinnati Symphony Orchestra repertoire database.

Jennings, Evelyn. Typescript history of the MSOL Symphony Singers. Provided by Ms. Jennings.

Johnson Memoir. A collection of several manuscript and typescript documents compiled by Johnson, mostly between 1994 and 2003. From the *Johnson Papers.*

Johnson Papers. Five uncataloged bins of Roland and Arline Johnson's papers, programs, photographs, clippings, musical scores and manuscripts, and more, collectively owned by their children, Carl Johnson and Karen Kretschman.

Letter from A. Kunrad Kvam to Alexander R. Graham and Stella Kayser, 3/2/1946. From the MSO Archives.

Letter from Charles V. Seastone to Roland Johnson, 4/25/1972. From the MSO Archives.

Letter from Col. L. A. Fuller to Sgt. Walter Heermann, 2/17/1919. From the *Heermann Scrapbooks.*

Letter from George Shook to the family of Roland Johnson, 6/7/2012. Shared by Prof. Shook with the author.

Letter from Joel Skornicka to John Urich (Madison City Planning Department), 10/27/1975. From the MSO Archives.

Letter from Otto Festge to Marie Endres, 2/22/1967. From the *WMA Marie Endres Collection*.

Letter from Percy Grainger to Alexander Graham, 11/28/1941. From the MSO Archives.

Letter from several members of the Madison Civic Chorus, addressed to "the members of the Board of Vocational and Adult Education, and the Board of Directors, Madison Civic Music Association," 5/16/1946. From the MSO Archives.

Letter from Sigfrid Prager to Florence Anderson, 9/28/1947. From the MSO Archives.

Letter from Sigfrid Prager to Helen Marting Supernaw, March 1972. Printed in *MCMA50*, 7–8.

Letter from Sigfrid Prager to Marie Endres, 4/23/1930. From the *WMA Marie Endres collection*.

Letter from Walter Heermann to Roland and Arline Johnson, 12/7/1961. From *Johnson Papers*.

Letters from Leon Perssion (10/23/37) and Eugene M. Juster (10/25/37) to Sigfrid Prager. From the MSO Archives.

Letters from Sigfrid Prager to Grace Schumpert, 5/17/1937, 5/27/1941, and 12/28/1941. From the *Johnson Papers*.

Madison String Sinfonia programs for April 1943 and April 1945. From the Wisconsin Music Archives, Marie Endres collection.

"Memoir: Gilbert Ross." *University of Michigan Faculty History Project*. http://faculty-history.dc.umich.edu/faculty/gilbert-ross/memoir, accessed 12/14/2021.

Memorandum: Helen Hay to the MCMA board, 3/10/1964. From the MSO Archives.

Memorandum: John Reel to the MCMA board, 1/27/1969. From the MSO Archives.

Paul Haugan, May 23, 1955 – July 28, 2012. Biography compiled by Paul's family. Copy provided by Paul's sister, Judith Ryan.

Press Release, Madison Symphony Orchestra, 11/10/1993. From the MSO Archives.

Tyrone Greive, Approved professional narrative pages for *Marquis Who's Who*, dated 2/22/2019. Provided by Dr. Greive.

University of Wisconsin School of Music Bulletin 1903–1904. From the *William Kerr Collection* in the University Archives. digitalcommons.usu.edu/kerr_applications, accessed 8/2/2021.

WMA Jerzy Bojanowski Collection. https://www.library.wisc.edu/music/home/collections/wisconsin-music-archives/jerzy-bojanowski-collection-c-1932-1960/, accessed 12/18/2019

WPA Federal Music Project (Wisconsin), Records 1936-41. Wisconsin Historical Society Library microfilm P46092.

D) Recordings

Beethoven, Ludwig van. *Missa Solemnis*. Nine 78 RPM discs. Sandra Cortez, soprano; Mari Barova, alto; Maximilian Schmelter, tenor; Harry Swanson, bass; Marie Endres, soloviolin; Madison Civic Chorus and Symphony; University Chorus; Dr. Sigfrid Prager, conductor, Live performance, 5/23/1948. From the MSO Archives. [NOTE: There is also a digitized version on CD in the MSO Archives, and excerpts are available streaming at http://www.allsenmusic.com/HISTORY/Recordings.html.]

Hagen, Daron. *Shining* Brow. Two CD discs. Libretto by Paul Muldoon. Buffalo Philharmonic and Chorus; JoAnn Falletta, conductor. [Hong Kong:] Naxos Digital Stereo 8.669020–21, 2009.

Hagen, Oskar. *Concerto Grosso*. One 33 RPM disc. Madison Civic Symphony; Walter Heermann, conductor. Live performance, 10/31/1950 (U.S. premiere). [NOTE: The original recording is held in the Wisconsin Music Archives, but there is a digitized version on CD in the MSO Archives. [This recording is available streaming at http://www.allsenmusic.com/HISTORY/Recordings.html.]

Handel, George Frideric. *Messiah*, aria "Why Do the Nations So Furiously Rage Together." One 78 RPM disc. Alexius Baas, baritone; Madison Civic Symphony; Sigfrid Prager, conductor. Live performance, 12/22/1941. From the MSO Archives. [NOTE: This recording is available streaming at http://www.allsenmusic.com/HISTORY/Recordings.html.]

Hanks, Sybil Anne. *The Compositions of Sybil Anne Hanks*. Two 33 RPM LP discs. Members of the Madison Civic Symphony and Chorus; Walter

Heermann, conductor, live performance, 4/29/1955 Copies in both the MSO Archives and the Wisconsin Music Archives. [NOTE: There is also a digitized version of extracts on CD, and excerpts are available streaming at http://www.allsenmusic.com/HISTORY/Recordings.html.]

Haydn Mozart Schubert. One CD disc. Ellsworth Snyder, piano; Roland Johnson, conductor. Madison, Wisconsin: [n.p.], ca. 2001.

Hear the Angel Voices: Christmas with the Madison Symphony Chorus. One CD disc. Madison Symphony Chorusl Beverly Taylor, director. [Madison, Wisconsin]: Ion Records compact disc, 2010

Heermann Trio. Three 78 RPM discs from 1929. Brunswick 4229: *Arabesque in E Major* and *Arabesque in G Major*; Brunswick 4153: *An Old Italian Love Song* and *Andalusian Caprice*; Brunswick 4228; *Dalvisa (Song of The Dale)* and *Pierrette (Air De Ballet)*. From www.discogs.com/artist/6926406-Heermann-Trio, accessed 3/6/2021.

Mount, William Sidney. *The Cradle of Harmony: William Sidney Mount's Violin & Fiddle Music*. One 33 RPM LP disc. New York City: Folkways Records LP 33379, 1975.

Schuller, Gunther. *Orchestral Works*. One CD disc. Radio Philharmonic of Hannover, conducted by Gunther Schuller. Boston, Massachusetts: GM Recordings GM2059CD, 1998.

Vaughan Williams, Ralph. *Dona nobis pacem*. One 33 RPM LP disc Vera Weikel Adams, soprano; Bert Jahr, bass; Madison Civic Symphony and Chorus; Walter Heermann, conductor. Live performance, 3/27/1955. From the MSO Archives.

Verdi, Giuseppe. *Requiem*. Two 33 RPM LP discs Bettina Bjorksten, soprano; Audrey Paul, alto; Warren Crandall, tenor; Robert Tottingham, bass; Madison Civic Symphony and Chorus; Walter Heermann, conductor. Live performance, 3/14/1950. From the MSO Archives. [NOTE: The discs are incorrectly dated "Feb. 1953."]

Vivaldi, Antonio. *Gloria*. One 33 RPM LP disc. Genevieve Gersbach, soprano; Tina Baird, alto; Madison Civic Symphony and Chorus; Walter Heermann, conductor. Live performance, 3/15/1956. From the MSO Archives.

E) Printed and Online Sources

"Affiliate Artists." *Wikipedia*. https://en.wikipedia.org/wiki/Affiliate_Artists, accessed 6/1/2024.

Allsen, J. Michael. *75 Years of the Madison Symphony Orchestra, 1926–2001: Chronicle, Repertoire, and Soloists*. Madison, Wisconsin: Madison Symphony Orchestra, 2002. [Available at http://www.allsenmusic.com/HISTORY/Chronicle.html.]

_____. "Program Notes." *Madison Symphony Orchestra Program Book, May 14, 1994*.

_____. "Program Notes." *Madison Symphony Orchestra Program Book, September 22-24, 2025*.

_____. "Program Notes." *Madison Symphony Orchestra Program Book, May 9-11, 2025*.

"American Singers Return from Germany: Food Conditions There Reported by Robert Henry Perkins and George Walker." *Musical America* XXVI, No. 9 (June 30, 1917).

Anderson, Eleanor. *Madison Opera and Guild, 25 Years. 1962–63 - 1987: A Silver Jubilee.* Madison, Wisconsin: The Madison Opera, 1987

Arion Choral Society History Committee. *The History of the Liederkranz of the City of New York and of the Arion, New York, 1847 to 1947, Compiled During the Centennial Year of the Liederkranz, 1947.* New York City: Drechsel Printing Company, 1948.

Barker, John W. *The Pro Arte Quartet: A Century of Musical Adventure on Two Continents.* Rochester, New York: University of Rochester Press, 2017.

Barton, Albert O. "Ole Bull and his Wisconsin Contacts." *The Wisconsin Magazine of History* 7/4 (June 1924).

"Battle of Baxter Springs." *Wikipedia*. https://en.wikipedia.org/wiki/Battle_of_Baxter_Springs, accessed 8/17/2020.

Bauer Jeffrey C. *Upgrading Leadership's Crystal Ball: Five Reasons Why Forecasting Must Replace Predicting and How to Make Strategic Change in Business and Public Policy.* Boca Raton, Florida: Productivity Press, 2013.

Beaumont, Anthony. "Busoni, Ferruccio." *Grove Music Online*, www.oxfordmusiconline, accessed 12/31/2019.

Bennee, Tim. Blog post on S. C. Campbell. In the Facebook *Theatre History* group. https://www.facebook.com/theatrehistory/posts/sherwood-abraham-coan-who-performed-under-the-stage-name-sc-campbell-was-concede/2813496985439284/, accessed 8/24/2021.

Benser, Caroline Cepin. "Ottokar Čadek." *The Encyclopedia of Alabama*. http://encyclopediaofalabama.org/article/h-3022, accessed 1/23/2023.

Beresford, Hattie. "Moguls and Mansions: Max C. Fleischmann." *Montecito Journal*. [n.d.]. http://www.digitaleditiononline.com/publication/?i=26368&article_id=263857, accessed 1/21/2023.

Bernas, Richard. "Johnson, Thor." *Grove Music Online*. www.oxfordmusiconline, accessed 2/27/2021.

Bernhard, Michael, ed. *Lexicon Musicum Latinum Medii Aevi* [*Dictionary of Medieval Latin Musical Terminology to the End of the 15th* Century]. Munich: Bayerischen Akademie der Wissenschaften, 2006.

Berry, Paul. *Brahms Among Friends: Listening, Performance, and the Rhetoric of Allusion*. New York City: Oxford University Press, 2014.

Bindas, Kenneth J. *All of This Music Belongs to the Nation: The WPA's Federal Music Project and American Society*. Knoxville, Tennessee: University of Tennessee Press, 1995.

Brooks, William. "Strakosch, Maurice." *Grove Music Online*. www.oxfordmusiconline, accessed 9/1/2021.

Brunner, Gerhard. "Scherchen, Hermann." *Grove Music Online*. www.oxfordmusiconline, accessed 1/21/2023.

Burwell, Fred. Blog post "A Writing Family, Pt.4: My Great Aunt Florence Bennett." *Fred Burwell: Writing*. https://fredburwell.com/2012/05/18/a-writing-family-pt-4-my-great-aunt-florence-beckett-bennett/, accessed 5/8/2020.

Byrne, Robert. Review of *Die Nibelungen (1924)* [DVD release]. *The Moving Image: The Journal of the Association of Moving Image Archivists* 13, No. 2 (Fall 2013).

"Camp Sheridan." *Encyclopedia of Alabama*. http://www.encyclopediaofalabama.org/article/h-3733, accessed 2/21/2021.

Cecil, George. "Berlin." *The English Illustrated Magazine* (July 1907).

Censo general de población, edification, comercio é industrias de la cuidad de Buenos Aires, capital federal de la República conmemorativo del primer centenario de la Revolución de Mayo, 1810–1910. Buenos Aires: Compañia Sud-Americana de Billets de Banco, 1910.

Chybowski, Julia J. "Becoming the 'Black Swan' in Mid-Nineteenth Century America: Elizabeth Taylor Greenfield's Early Life and Debut Concert Tour." *Journal of the American Musicological Society* 67 (2014).

_____. "Greenfield, Elizabeth Taylor." *Grove Music Online*. www.oxfordmusiconline, accessed 9/1/2021.

Cincinnati Symphony Orchestra. *Cincinnati Symphony Orchestra: Centennial Portraits*. Cincinnati: Cincinnati Symphony Orchestra, 1994.

Cirque de la Symphonie. https://www.cirquedelasymphonie.com/. accessed 6/20/2024.

Clive, Peter. *Brahms and His World: A Biographical Dictionary*. Lanham, Maryland: Scarecrow, 2006.

Cobbett, W. W. and John Moran. "Heermann, Hugo," *Grove Music Online*, accessed 2/15/2021.

"College-Conservatory of Music: History." *University of Cincinnati, College-Conservatory of Music*. https://ccm.uc.edu/overview/history.html, accessed 3/7/2021.

Cook, Susan C., ed. *A Century of Making Music: A Documentary Scrapbook of the University of Wisconsin–Madison School of Music*. Madison, Wisconsin: University of Wisconsin–Madison School of Music, 1995.

Copeland, Robert. "May Festival (Cincinnati)," *Grove Music Online*. www.oxfordmusiconline, accessed 3/5/2021.

"Dadmun, Royal (vocalist: baritone vocal)." *Discography of American Historical Recordings*. https://adp.library.ucsb.edu/index.php/talent/detail/28809/Dadmun_Royal_vocalist_baritone_vocal, accessed 12/21/2019.

"A Daughter of the Gods." *Wikipedia*. https://en.wikipedia.org/wiki/A_Daughter_of_the_Gods, accessed 6/10/2024.

DeMain, John and Greg Hettsmannberger. *An American Conductor: Working with My Heros—The Life and Music of John DeMain*. (Madison: University of Wisconsin Press, 2025). [NOTE: Publication of Maestro DeMain's memoir was still in process as of February 2025. I am very grateful to him for sharing an unpublished draft.]

Dizeckes, John. *Opera in America: A Cultural History*. New Haven, Connecticut: Yale University Press, 1993.

Dupuis, Robert. *Bunny Berigan: Elusive Legend of Jazz*. Baton Rouge, Louisiana: Louisiana State University Press, 1993.

Dynkins, Dale. "Program Note, *Symphonic Suite*." *Orchestralist*. http://www.orchestralist.net/olist/registry/ol/Dale_Dykins.php, accessed 3/10/2021.

"Edward Alsworth Ross." *Wikipedia*. https://en.wikipedia.org/wiki/Edward_Alsworth_Ross, accessed 12/14/2021.

Epstein, Dena J., H. Wiley Hitchcock, and Polly Carder. "Root, George Frederick." *Grove Music Online*. www.oxfordmusiconline, accessed 9/1/2021.

Essert, Paul, Richard Layman, Eric Walke, et al. *Madison Maennerchor: 150 Years*. Madison, Wisconsin: Madison Maennerchor, 2002.

"Esther Dale." *Wikipedia*. https://en.wikipedia.org/wiki/Esther_Dale, accessed 1/16/2020.

Feldman, Jim. *The Buildings of the University of Wisconsin*. Madison, Wisconsin: The University Archives, 1997.

Fifield, Christopher. "Bruch, Max." *Grove Music Online*. www.oxfordmusiconline, accessed 12/31/2019.

"Florodora." *Wikipedia*. https://en.wikipedia.org/wiki/Florodora, accessed 12/9/2022.

"From the Archives: Queen City Connections." *Crescendo*. https://crescendo.interlochen.org/story/archives-queen-city-connection, accessed 3/10/2021.

Garden State Theatre Organ Society. "Ashley B. Miller." https://gstos.org/artists/ashley-miller/, accessed 9/23/2020.

Gerloff, Barbara K. *Pastiche: A History of Music Hall and the School of Music, University of Wisconsin–Madison*. Madison, Wisconsin: University of Wisconsin Board of Regents, 1985.

Glocer, Silvia. "Sigfrid Prager." *Proyecto Culturas interiors*. http://culturasinteriores.ffyh.unc.edu.ar/ifi002.jsp?pidf=TT2DDWBBD&po=DB, accessed 7/1/2020.

Gough, Peter. *Sounds of the New Deal: The Federal Music Project in the West*. Urbana, Illinois: University of Illinois Press, 2015.

Griesinger, David. "Brilliant Resurrection of Schuller Piece." *The Boston Musical Intelligencer* 3/27/2011. https://www.classical-scene.com/2011/03/27/schuller-piece/, accessed 3/11/2021.

"Guy Watson Taylor." *Prabook*. prabook.com/web/guy.watson.taylor/466659, accessed 3/2/2021.

"Habilitation." *Wikipedia*. https://en.wikipedia.org/wiki/Habilitation, accessed 2/7/2024.

Hagen, Daron. *Duet with the Past: A Composer's Memoir*. Jefferson, North Carolina: McFarland & Company, 2019.

Haugen, Einar and Camilla Cai. *Ole Bull: Norway's Romantic Musician and Cosmopolitan Patriot*. Madison, Wisconsin: University of Wisconsin Press, 1993.

"Helene Billing Wurlitzer." *Wikipedia*. https://en.wikipedia.org/wiki/Helene_Billing_Wurlitzer, accessed 1/16/2023.

Hildebrandt, Edith W. "Music Memory Contests." *The School Review* 30/4 (April 1922).

Historical Society of Wisconsin. "Bach, Christopher (1835–1927)." *Dictionary of Wisconsin History*. https://www.wisconsinhistory.org/Records/Article/CS5082, accessed 11/19/2022'

———. "Historical Essay: Ada Bird (1859–1914)." *Dictionary of Wisconsin History*. https://wisconsinhistory.org/Records/Article/CS5461, accessed 9/20/2021.

———. "Historical Essay: William Boeppler (1863–1928)." *Dictionary of Wisconsin History*. https://www.wisconsinhistory.org/Records/Article/CS5591, accessed 12/12/2019.

———. "Painting: *Sunrise on Lake Monona*." *Dictionary of Wisconsin History*. https://wisconsinhistory.org/Records/Image/IM102418, accessed 3/192021.

Gill, Bernhard. *Many Masks: a Life of Frank Lloyd Wright*. New York: Random House, Inc., 1987.

Gilliland, Norman. "Famed Norwegian Violinist Ole Bull's Madison Years." *Wisconsin Life*, www.wisconsinlife.org, accessed 10/17/18

Granados, Enrique. *Two Transcriptions by Gilbert Ross and Sigfrid Prager: 1. Anoranza and 2. La maja y el ruiseñorm, from the Opera "Goyescas"* [sheet music]. New York City: G. Schirmer, 1930.

Grymes James A. *Violins of Hope: Instruments of Hope and Liberation in Mankind's Darkest Hour*. New York City: Harper Perennial, 2014.

Haynes, Nathaniel Smith. *History of the Disciples of Christ in Illinois, 1819–1914*. Cincinnati, Ohio: Standard Publishing Company, 1914.

Heath, Charles V. "Wisconsin's Good Neighbor: Maestro Diego 'Jimmy' Innes and the Wisconsin WPA Symphony Orchestra." *The Wisconsin Magazine of History* 100 (Winter 2016–17).

Heermann, Hugo. *Meine Lebenserinnerungen*. Ed. Günther Ewig. Heilbronn, Germany: Stadtbücherei Heilbronn, 1994.

"HGO's History." *Houston Grand Opera*. https://www.houstongrandopera.org/about, accessed 6/3/204.

Hibberd, Howard. *Caravaggio*. New York City: Taylor & Francis, 1983.

"History of the Chorus." *The Philharmonic Chorus of Madison*. www.philharmonicchorusofmadison.org/history, accessed 10/22/2020.

"History of the Sewaunee Summer Music Festival." *Sewaunee Summer Music Festival*. https://ssmf.sewanee.edu/about-us/, accessed 1/31/2023.

Holliday, Thomas. *Falling Up: The Days and Nights of Carlisle Floyd: the Authorized Biography*. Syracuse, New York: Syracuse University Press, 2012.

James, Bryan W. *One Hundred Years of Orchestra at the University of Wisconsin–Madison*. Madison, Wisconsin: University of Wisconsin–Madison School of Music, [1996].

"Johnson City." *Tennessee Encyclopedia*. https://tennesseeencyclopedia.net/entries/johnson-city/, accessed 1/10/2023.

"Johnson City Blues." http://www.stateoffranklin.net/johnsons/oldtime/jcblues/jcblues.htm, accessed 1/11/2023.

"Johnson City Sessions." *Wikipedia*. https://en.wikipedia.org/wiki/Johnson_City_sessions, accessed 1/10/2023.

"Johnson City, Tennessee." *Wikipedia*. https://en.wikipedia.org/wiki/Johnson_City,_Tennessee, accessed 1/10/2023.

Katzman, Michael M. "Louis Katzman: His Musical Life and Times." *Association for Recorded Sound Collections Journal* 24, no. 2 (2014).

Kaebisch, Michelle A. and Shannon E. Lobdell. *HeartStrings^{SM}: A Guide to Music Therapy-Informed Community Engagement for Symphony Orchestras*. Madison: Madison Symphony Orchestra, 2011.

Kaufman, Charles H., *Music in New Jersey, 1655–1860: A Study of Musical Activity and Musicians in New Jersey from Its First Settlement to the Civil War*. Rutherford, New Jersey: Fairleigh Dickinson University Press, 1981.

"Kenley Players." *Wikipedia*. https://en.wikipedia.org/wiki/Kenley_Players, accessed 5/30/2024.

"Kenley Players History: Timeline." *The Kenley Players: America's Most Exciting Summer Theatre*. http://www.kenleyplayershistory.com/timeline.htm, accessed 6/15/2024.

Koegel, John. *Music in German Immigrant Theater: New York, 1840–1940*. Rochester: University of Rochester Press, 2007.

Kutsch, Karl-Josef and Leo Riemens. *Großes Sängerlexikon*, 4th edition. Munich, Germany: Saur, 2003: Bd. 4.

La Follette, Isobel Bacon. "Early History of the Wisconsin Executive Residence." *The Wisconsin Magazine of History* 21/2 (December 1937).

Lamson, Lisa. "Performance Venues." *Encyclopedia of Milwaukee*, https://emke.uwm.edu/entry/performance-venues/, accessed 12/18/2019.

League of American Orchestras. *Making the Case for Equity, Diversity, and Inclusion in Orchestras.* New York City: League of American Orchestras, 2024.

Levitan, Stuart D. *Madison in the Sixties.* Madison, Wisconsin: Wisconsin Historical Society Press, 2018.

_____ *Madison: The Illustrated Sesquicentennial History, Volume 1: 1856-1931.* Madison, Wisconsin: University of Wisconsin Press, 2006.

"Madison Area Technical College." *Wikipedia.* https://en.wikipedia.org/wiki/Madison_Area_Technical_College, accessed 1/31/2023.

Madison Civic Music Association [Eleanor Anderson]. *A History of the Madison Civic Music Association: The First Fifty Years, 1925–1975* (Madison: Madison Civic Music Association, 1975) [MCMA50].

"Madison Opera: History." *Madison Opera.* https://www.madisonopera.org/history/, accessed 6/17/2024.

"The Making of *Shining Brow.*" *Madison Opera Program Book: Shining Brow World Premiere* [4/21/1993].

May, Thomas. *The John Adams Reader: Essential Writings on an American Composer.* Prompton Plains, New Jersey: Amadeus Press, 2006.

McCarthy, Kevin M. *Christmas in Florida.* Sarasota, Florida: Pineapple Press, 2000.

McWilliams, J. C. *Were I But His Own Wife* [sheet music]. St. Louis, Missouri: Balmer & Weber, 1855.

Mills, Marion. "Select Salutes Arline Johnson, Woman of the Month." *Madison Select.* (May 1975).

"Milwaukee Turners: History." *Milwaukee Turners.* https://www.milwaukeeturners.org/history, accessed 6/17/2024.

"Mission and History." *West Virginia Symphony Orchestra.* https://wvsymphony.org/missionhistory, accessed 2/28/2021.

Metzger, Alfred. "Giacomo Minkowski Returned from Europe." *Pacific Coast Musical Review* 41/19 (2/4/1922)

Mollenoff, David V. *Madison: The Formative Years.* 2nd edition. Madison, Wisconsin: University of Wisconsin Press, 2003.

Mollenhoff, David V., and Mary Jane Hamilton. *Frank Lloyd Wright's Monona Terrace: The Enduring Power of a Civic Vision.* Madison, Wisconsin: University of Wisconsin Press, 1999.

Mondolo, Maria. "Ernesto Drangosch: vida y obra." *Musica Classica en la Argentina*. http://www.musicaclasicaargentina.com/drangosch/index.htm, accessed 12/19/2019.

Morgan, Kenneth. *Fritz Reiner: Maestro and Martinet*. Urbana, Illinois: University of Chicago Press, 2010.

"New York City Opera." *Wikipedia*. https://en.wikipedia.org/wiki/New_York_City_Opera, accessed 6/15/2025.

"Nixon In China." *Wikipedia*. https://en.wikipedia.org/wiki/Nixon_in_China, accessed 6/4/2024

Oja, Carol J. *Making Music Modern: New York in the 1920s*. Oxford: Oxford University Press, 2000.

Orlando, Vincent A. *An Historical Study of the Origins and Development of the College of Music of Cincinnati*. D.E. dissertation: Teachers College of the University of Cincinnati, 1946.

"Peter Herman Adler." *Wikipedia*. https://en.wikipedia.org/wiki/Peter_Herman_Adler, accessed 5/31/2024.

Pew Research Center. "10 demographic trends shaping the U.S. and the world in 2016." https://www.pewresearch.org/short-reads/2016/03/31/10-demographic-trends-that-are-shaping-the-u-s-and-the-world/, accessed 6/8/2024.

Pincus, Andrew. *Scenes from Tanglewood*. Boston, Massachusetts: Northeastern University Press, 1989.

Prager, Sigfrid. *Comments on Anton Dvorák, Symphony No.5 From the New World, Opus 9*. New York City: Edwin F. Kalmus, [1945].

_____. *Comments on César Franck, Symphony in D minor*. New York: Edwin F. Kalmus, [1945].

_____. *The Message of Song, for Unison Chorus*, words by John Mael [sheet music].Chicago, Illinois: H.T. FitzSimons Company, 1932.

Reed, Robert A. "My Symphony Story." *The Score* (Fall 2022).

"Report: Attendance at Orchestras is Starting to Reach Prepandemic Levels, Despite some Declines." *Symphony News Brief*: 3/14/2024. https://symphony.org/report-attendance-at-orchestras-starting-to-reach-prepandemic-levels-despite-some-declines/, accessed 6/10/2024.

Rosen, Carole. "Goossens family; (3) Sir (Aynsley) Eugene Goossens." *Grove Music Online*. www.oxfordmusiconline, accessed 2/27/2021.

Ross, Gilbert. "The Auer Mystique." *Michigan Quarterly Review* 14 (1975).

Rosser, Annetta. *An Offering of Song: 48 Songs in English for Medium to High Voice* [sheet music]. Madison, Wisconsin: Gilbert Publications, 1977.

Scherchen, Hermann. *Lehrbuch des Dirigierens*. Leipzig, Germany: J. J. Weber, 1929. See also: Hermann Scherchen. *Handbook of Conducting*. Translated by M. D. Calvocoressi. Oxford, England: Oxford University Press, 1933

Schippers, Thomas. "Scherchen Familie: 1. Hermann." *Die Music in Geschichte und Gegenwart, Personenteil*. Kassel, Germany: Bahrenreiter-Verlag, 1999.

Schuller, Gunther. *A Life in Pursuit of Music and Beauty*. Rochester, New York: University of Rochester Press, 2011.

_____. "Program Note: Cello Concerto." https://www.wisemusicclassical.com/work/32626/Concerto-for-Cello-and-Orchestra--Gunther-Schuller/, accessed 3/10/2021.

Schumann, Ferdinand. "Brahms and Clara Schumann." *The Musical Quarterly* 2 (1916).

Schwarz, Boris. "Joseph Joachim and the Genesis of Brahms's Violin Concerto." *The Musical Quarterly* 69 (1983).

Scott, Derek B. *German Operetta on Broadway and in the West End, 1900–1940*. Cambridge, England: Cambridge University Press, 2019.

Shanet, Howard. *Philharmonic: A History of New York's Orchestra*. New York City: Doubleday, 1975.

Shenk, Joshua Wolf. *Lincoln's Melancholy: How Depression Challenged a President and Fueled His Greatness*. New York City: Houghton Mifflin Harcourt, 2006.

"Sigfrid Prager. *The Monochord as an Instrument and as a System*. Read in Madison on January 10, 1948, at a meeting of the Western section of the Midwest Chapter." *Journal of the American Musicological Society* 1, No. 3 (Autumn, 1948).

"Stefanie Walzinger Interview." *Sheet Music Singer*. https://www.sheetmusicsinger.com/zz-stefanie-walzinger-interview/, accessed 12/9/2021.

Stockhem, Michel. "Ysaÿe, Eugène(-Auguste)." *Grove Music Online*. www.oxfordmusiconline, accessed 2/27/2021.

"Storm Bull." *Wikipedia*. https://en.wikipedia.org/wiki/Storm_Bull, accessed 3/12/2019.

Surface, Karalee. "The Milwaukee Symphony Orchestra." *Encyclopedia of Milwaukee.* https://emke.uwm.edu/entry/milwaukee-symphony-orchestra/, accessed 11/20/2019.

"Third Wisconsin Cavalry: Regimental History." *Second Wisconsin Volunteer Infantry.* http://www.secondwi.com/wisconsinregiments/third_wisconsin_cavalry.htm, accessed 8/17/2021.

Thomas, Louis Russell. *A History of the Cincinnati Symphony Orchestra to 1931.* Ph.D. dissertation: University of Cincinnati, 1972.

Thompson, Abbey E. *Revival, Revision, Rebirth: Handel Opera in Germany, 1920–1930.* Master's thesis: University of North Carolina at Chapel Hill, 2006.

Weingartner, Felix. *Eine Künstlerfart nach Südamerika: Tagebuch Juni-November 1920.* Vienna: Hugo Heller, 1921.

Wierzbicki, James. "Traditional Values in a Century of Flux: The Music of Feliks Łabuński (1892–1979)." *Polish Music Journal* IV/1 (Summer 2001).

Wilhelmi, A. "Kritik: Konzert." *Die Musik* 5, No. 9 (February 1906).

"Wisconsin Chamber Orchestra: History." *Wisconsin Chamber Orchestra.* https://wcoconcerts.org/meet-the-wco/history, accessed 12/10/2023.

Youngerman, Henry C. "Theatre Buildings in Madison Wisconsin 1836–1900." *The Wisconsin Magazine of History* 30/3 (July 1947).

Index of Composers and Musical Works

This is an index to nearly 750 musical works cited either directly or indirectly, sorted by composer. Wherever possible, I have identified works that are indirectly cited here. Where identification is impossible, I have used "unspecified." - JMA

Adamo, Mark
   Little Women, 425, 433.
Adams, John
   The Chairman Dances, 336, 421, 443 n. 30.
   Doctor Atomic Symphony, 421, 443 n. 30.
   Nixon in China, 385, 386-87, 443 n. 30.
   On the Transmigration of Souls, 398, 421, 443 n. 30.
   Short Ride in a Fast Machine, 336.
   Violin Concerto, 396, , 421, 443 n. 30.
Albéniz, Isaac
   Jota Aragonaise (orch. Prager), 133.
Anonymous/Traditional
   Witness (traditional black spiritual), 161.
Auber, Daniel
   Fra diavolo, 17.
Baas, Alexius
   The Building of the Ship, 99 n.65.
   Flag of our Fathers (A Tribute to Madison), 64, 66, 68, 77.
   Latin masses, 99 n. 65.
   Nature Hymn, 170.
   O How Fair, How Pure Thy World, 65, 66, 68.
   Recessional, 170.
Bach, Christopher
   Turner March, 34.
Bach, Jan
   Gala Fanfare, 336.
Bach, Johann Sebastian
   Brandenburg Concerto No. 1, 277, 288, 365, 367, 382.
   Brandenburg Concerto No. 2, 190, 365, 367.
   Brandenburg Concerto No. 4, 365.
   Brandenburg Concerto No. 5, 121, 131, 190, 216, 277, 365.
   Brandenburg Concerto No. 6, 216, 219.
   Concerto for Violin and Oboe, 279, 431.
   Concerto for Two Violins, 63, 92.
   Concerto No.5 for Keyboard, 95, 160.
   Freue dich, erlöste Schar (Cantata BWV 30), 121.
   Fugue from The Musical Offering (orch. Walter Heermann), 166.
   Gottes Zeit ist die allerbeste Zeit (Cantata BWV 106), 121, 229.
   Die Himmel erzählen die Ehre Gottes (Cantata BWV 76), 121.
   Jesu, Joy of Man's Desiring (from Cantata BWV 147), 230.
   Komm, süsser Tod (chorale, orch. Walter Heermann), 166, 230.
   Lobet Gott in seinen Reichen (Cantata BWV 11), 121.
   Magnificat, 166, 188, 281.
   Mass in B minor, 188, 272, 281, 282, 351.
   O ewiges Feuer, O Ursprung der Liebe (Cantata BWV 34), 167.
   Orchestral Suite No. 2, 82, 92.
   Orchestral Suite No. 3, 36, 121.
   St. Matthew Passion, 188, 281, 282
   Singet den Herrn (Motet No. 1), 282.
   unspecified, 170.
   Weinachtsoratorium (Christmas Oratorio), 58, 70, 94, 188, 281, 326.
   Wenn wir in höchsten Nöten sein (chorale prelude), 141.
   Wie schön leuchtet der Morgenstern (Cantata BWV 1), 314.
Bach/Gounod
   Ave Maria, 327.
Bales, Richard
   American Design: National Gallery Suite No. 3, 250.
Balfe, Michael William
   The Bohemian Girl, 6, 16-17, 43 n. 55.

Barber, Samuel
   Adagio for Strings, 170, 232, 397.
   Die Natali, 250.
   Knoxville, Summer of 1915, 170, 307.
   Medea, 309.
   Piano Concerto, 396.
Barlow, Wayne
   Rhapsody for Oboe and Orchestra: The Winter's Past, 250 .
Barroso, Ary
   Aquarela do Brasil, 155.
Bartók, Béla
   Bluebeard's Castle, 336-37.
   Concerto for Orchestra, 250, 337.
   Dance Suite, 362.
   Piano Concerto No. 3, 250.
   unspecified, 112.
Bax, Arnold
   Symphony No. 6, 153.
Beethoven, Ludwig van
   Choral fantasy, 153.
   Egmont (incidental music), 171.
   Fidelio, 321.
   Leonore Overture No. 3, 134, 166.
   Missa solemnis, 76, 136, 160-61, 163-64, 168, 192 n. 31, 193 n.32, 193 n. 38, 249, 419, 431.
   Piano Concerto No. 1, 291, 377.
   Piano Concerto No. 2, 117-18, 382.
   Piano Concerto No. 3, 107, 171.
   Piano Concerto No. 4, 153.
   Piano Concerto No. 5 "Emperor", 291, 404.
   Piano Sonata in C minor, Op. 13 "Pathétique", 31.
   Piano Sonata in G Major, Op. 49, No. 2, 30.
   Piano Trio, Op. 70, No. 1, 205.
   Symphony No. 1, 214, 358, 421.
   Symphony No. 2, 54, 56, 421.
   Symphony No. 3 "Eroica", 63, 421.
   Symphony No. 4, 36, 421.
   Symphony No. 5, 421.
   Symphony No. 6, 421.
   Symphony No. 7, 421.
   Symphony No. 8, 229, 421.
   Symphony No. 9, xxi, 58, 282, 307, 334, 355, 359, 361, 367, 421.
   Triple Concerto, 364, 365, 397-98.
   unspecified, 128, 170, 202.
   Violin Concerto, 15, 92, 203.
Bellini, Vincenzo
   Norma, 6.
   La sonnambula, 16, 17, 43 n. 62.
Berg, Alban
   Lulu Suite, 250.
   Wozzeck: Three Excerpts, 337.
Berlin, Irving
   Annie Get Your Gun, 385.
   White Christmas, 304.
Berlioz, Hector
   Harold in Italy, 278, 439.
Bernstein, Leonard
   A Quiet Place, 350, 370 n. 31, 377, 385, 386.
   Candide, 250.
   Chichester Psalms, 250, 281, 282, 357.
   Serenade (after Plato's Symposium), 431.
   Trouble in Tahiti, 386.
   West Side Story, 250, 387.
Berold, William
   Little Rose Bud, 301.
Bizet, Georges
   L'Arlesienne Suite No. 1, 230.
   L'Arlesienne Suite No. 2, 52, 53, 55.
   Carmen, 17, 69, 79, 81, 99 n. 59, 104, 152, 261, 263, 318, 405.
   Carmen Suite No. 2, 55, 67.
Blitzstein, Marc
   Regina, 385.
Boccherini, Luigi
   Cello Concerto in B-flat Major, 157.
Boieldieu, François-Adrien
   Le calife de Bagdad, 26.
   La dame blanche, 67.
Boito, Arrigo
   Mefistofele, 112, 182, 370.
Borodin, Alexander
   In the Steppes of Central Asia, 63.
   Polovtsian Dances from "Prince Igor", 68, 121.
Bowers, Robin Hood
   A Daughter of the Gods (film score), 33.
Bradbury, William

Esther, the Beautiful Queen, 12.
Brahms, Johannes
 Alto Rhapsody, 167, 170, 282.
 Ein deutsches Requiem (German Requiem), 170, 172, 281, 282, 352, 419.
 Double Concerto, 92, 170, 212, 216-17, 230, 364.
 Hungarian Dance No. 5, 55, 98 n.55.
 Liebeslieder-Walzer, 107, 282.
 Nänie, 107, 170.
 Piano Concerto No. 1, 153, 170.
 Piano Concerto No. 2, 131, 153, 170.
 Piano Quartet in G minor, 198.
 Piano Quintet Op. 34, 131.
 Schicksalslied, 107, 230.
 Symphony No. 1, 170, 235, 248, 352, 421.
 Symphony No. 2, 170, 421.
 Symphony No. 3, 170, 421.
 Symphony No. 4, 170, 421.
 unspecified, 128, 202.
 Variations on a Theme by Haydn, 63.
 Violin Concerto, 83, 198, 203, 216, 237 n. 3, 338.
Britten, Benjamin
 Festival Te Deum, 282, 307.
 Noyes Fludde, 261.
 Owen Wingrave, 388.
 Peter Grimes, 307, 357-58.
 Rejoice in the Lamb, 282.
 Saint Nicholas, 281.
 War Requiem, 250, 282, 289.
Brubeck, Chris
 Affinity: Concerto for Guitar and Orchestra, 421.
Bruch, Max
 Schön Ellen, 107.
 Violin Concerto No. 1, 15, 203.
Bruckner, Anton
 Intermezzo for String Quintet, 186.
 Te Deum, 282.
Burleigh, Cecil
 Evangeline, 64, 66.
 Fairy Sailing, 15.
 Two Sketches from the Orient, 65, 66.
 Violin Concerto Op. 60, 15, 34.

Busoni, Ferruccio
 Piano Concerto (with final chorus for male voices), 153.
Byrd, William
 The Music Master of 1952, 330 n. 30.
Cadman, Charles Wakefield
 Call me No More, 54, 63, 64.
 The garden of mystery, 110
Cain, Noble
 Evangeline, 230.
Carpenter, John Alden
 Don't Ceäre, 54, 63 64.
Casella, Alfredo
 unspecified, 112.
Catán, Daniel
 Florencia en al Amazonas, 425-26.
 Suite from "Florencia en al Amazonas", 421.
Chatman, Stephen
 3 A.M. on Capitol Square, 251, 256.
 Crimson Dream, 256.
 Occasions, 251, 256.
Chausson, Ernest
 Poéme, 3.
Chopin, Frédéric
 Piano Concerto No. 2, 382.
 Polonaise in E-flat Major, 131.
Cimarosa/Benjamin
 Oboe Concerto, 367.
Clyne, Anna
 This Midnight Hour, 422.
Coleman, Valerie
 Umoja, 422.
Copland, Aaron
 Appalachian Spring, 250, 396.
 Fanfare for the Common Man, 250.
 In the Beginning, 250, 282.
 Preamble to a Solemn Event, 334.
 Rodeo, 250, 307.
Corelli, Archangelo
 "Christmas" Concerto, Op. 8, No. 6, 278, 323.
Corigliano, John
 Chaconne from "The Red Violin", 421, 431.
 Gazebo Dances, 396, 421.
 Pope's Concert from "The Red Violin", 421.
 Promenade Overture, 336.

Crane Robert
    Cino, 251.
    Exsequiarum Ordo: In Memoriam Berlioz, 251.
    Fanfare for Christmas, 251.
Dawson, William Levi
    Negro Folk Symphony, 421.
De Koven, Reginald
    The Mandarin, 13.
    Robin Hood, 12.
Debussy, Claude
    Deux arabesques, 219, 241 n. 66.
    Pelléas et Mélisande, 317.
    Prelude to "The Afternoon of a Faun", 63.
    The Prodigal Son, 82.
    Rêverie (orch. Sigfrid Prager), 132.
    unspecified, 112, 128.
    unspecified song, 316.
Delibes, Léo
    Lakme, 82.
Delius, Frederick
    Piano Concerto, 129.
    The Walk to the Paradise Garden, 288, 347.
Dello Joio, Norman
    Song of Affirmation, 315.
Diamond, David
    Young Joseph, 307.
DiChiera, David
    Four Sonnets of Edna St. Vincent Millay, 362.
Dobson, Tom
    Yasmin, 54, 64.
Donizetti, Gaetano
    Don Pasquale, 17.
    La favorite, 6.
    Lucia di Lammermoor, 3, 17.
Douglas, William
    Annie Laurie, 152.
Drangosch, Ernesto
    Piano Concerto in E Major, 108.
Drdla, Frantisek
    Souvenir, 30.
Dupont, Gabriel
    unspecified, 112.
Dumler, Martin
    Missa latreutrica, 230.

Dvorák, Antonin
    Symphony No. 9 "From the New World", 67, 134, 149, n. 97, 350, 423.
Dvorak, Raymond
    Canto Buffo: a Singer's March, 170, 193 n. 47.
    The Cataract of Lodore, 170, 193 n. 47.
Dykins, Dale
    Symphonic Suite, 235.
Elgar, Edward
    Cello Concerto, 350.
    Enigma Variations, 423.
    The Music Makers, 282.
    Nimrod from "Enigma Variations", 388.
Endres, Olive
    The Canticle of Judith, 96.
    Divergent Moods, 96.
    Latin liturgical music, 95.
    Magnificat, 96.
    Prelude and Fugue for Three Clarinets, 96.
    Violin Sonata in A, 95, 100 n. 97.
Eppert, Carl
    The Argonauts of '49, 65, 67.
Fauré, Gabriel
    Requiem, 282, 355.
Ferroni, Vincenzo
    Spanish Rhapsody, 63.
Finney, Ross Lee
    String Quartet No. 8, 316.
Flotow, Friedrich von
    Martha, 17, 19, 34, 82, 112.
Floyd, Carlisle
    The Passion of Jonathan Wade, 385, 386.
    Susannah, 385.
    Willie Stark, 385.
Foss, Lukas
    Baroque Variations, 250.
    The Jumping Frog of Calaveras County, 188, 261, 316, 330 n. 30.
    Parable of Death, 315.
    Quintets for Orchestra, 336.
Franck, César
    Le chasseur maudit, 34.
    Symphonic Variations, 121, 153.
    Symphony in D minor, 134, 149 n. 97, 347.

Franklin, Cary John
   The Very Last Green Thing, 358.
Friml, Rudolf
   The Vagabond King, 385.
Gaines, Samuel Richard
   Out Where the West Begins, 65.
Gates, Crawford
   Lake Songs, 337, 339.
Gaul, Harvey
   I Hear America Singing, 65.
Gershwin, George
   An American in Paris, 250.
   Concerto in F, 117-18, 181.
   Cuban Overture, 250.
   Porgy and Bess, 161-62, 383-85, 387, 389.
   Rhapsody in Blue, 64, 65-66, 131, 250.
Giannini, Vittorio
   Canticle of the Martyrs, 171.
Gilbert and Sullivan
   H.M.S. Pinafore, 17, 19, 22.
   The Mikado, 17, 19, 22, 29.
   Patience, 19.
   Pirates of Penzance, 19.
Ginastera, Alberto
   Variaciones concertantes, 382.
Glass, Philip
   Akhnaten, 385.
   Galileo Galilei, 425.
   The Making of the Representative for Planet Eight, 385.
Glazunov, Alexander
   Symphony No. 3, 211.
Gluck, Christoph Willibald von
   Alceste, 248.
Godard, Benjamin
   Berceuse, 30.
Godfrey, D.
   Waterloo Polka, 26.
Goldmark, Carl
   Die Königen von Saba, 112.
Golijov, Osvaldo
   Three songs for Soprano and Orchestra, 421.
Gould, Morton
   New China March, 153.
   Pavane, 250.

Gounod, Charles
   Faust, 17, 79-80, 105.
   Près du fleuve étranger, 121.
   La reine de Saba, 53.
Grainger, Percy
   Colonial Song, 155.
   The Lads of Wamphray, 155, 191 n. 8.
   Mock Morris, 54.
   unspecified, 129.
Granados, Enrique
   Goyescas, transcriptions by Gilbert Ross and Sigfrid Prager, 15, 43 n. 51, 149, n. 92.
   Spanish Suite (orch. Prager), 132.
Greene, Clarence
   Johnson City Blues, 300.
Grieg, Edvard
   Landkjenning (Land Sighting), 115.
   Olaf Trygvason, 229.
   Piano Concerto, 10, 229.
   Sigurd Jorsfalar, 77.
Griffes, Charles Tomlinson
   The Pleasure-Dome of Kubla Khan, 166, 216.
Guthrie, Arlo
   Alice's Restaurant, 443-44 n. 34.
Hadley, Henry
   In Bohemia, 211.
   Silhouettes, 64.
Hagen, Daron
   The Antient Concert, 346.
   Bandanna, 346.
   Forward!, 336, 362-63.
   Heliotrope, 336, 372 n.27.
   Joyful Music, 336, 337.
   Shining Brow, xiii, xxi, 291, 298, 321, 328, 334, 336, 341, 343-46, 348, 350, 351, 372 n. 23-24, 370 n. 31, 370 n. 34-36, 370 n. 41, 405, 416.
   Taliesin: Choruses from "Shining Brow", 362.
   Vera of Las Vegas, 346.
Hagen, Oskar
   Choral Rhapsody in the Romantic Style, 155, 156.
   Concerto Grosso, 157, 170, 181-182, 194 n. 71.
   Violin Sonata in G Major, 157.

Handel, George Frideric
  Acis et Galatea, 317.
  Concerto grosso, Op. 6, No. 12, 365.
  Coronation Anthem No. 1 (Zadok the Priest), 404.
  Giulio Cesare, 192, n. 26.
  Israel in Egypt, 282.
  Judas Maccabeus, 58, 67.
  Messiah, 3, 58-59, 73, 88, 158, 164, 166, 180, 193 n. 56, 281, 292, 304, 321, 326, 330 n. 22.
  Organ Concerto, Op. 4 No. 4, 131.
  Serse, 161.
  Solomon, 367.
  unspecified, 170.
Hanks, Sybil
  Concertino for three saxophones, 119, 182.
  The Creation, 119, 182.
  Decoration Day Hymn, 65, 66, 119, 170, 182.
  Meditation (orchestra), 65, 66, 68, 82, 119.
  Meditation for Cello and Piano, 183, 184, 232.
  Our Washington, 65, 66, 119.
  Theme with Variations for Winds, 183.
  Three Preludes for Piano, 119.
  Quiet My Heart, 119, 170, 182.
  Rondo in Old style for Violin and Piano, 119, 182-83.
Hanson, Howard
  Symphony No. 1, "Nordic", 153.
Harbison, John
  The Flight into Egypt, 421, 443 n. 31.
  Great Gatsby Suite, 421, 443 n. 31.
  The Most Often Used Chords, 421, 443 n. 31.
  Overture: Michael Kohlhaas, 337.
Harris, Roy
  Symphony No. 3 in One Movement, 250.
Haydn, Franz Joseph
  The Creation, 25, 58, 158, 281, 282.
  Die Jahreszeiten (The Seasons), 106-07.
  Missa in tempori belli ("Timpani" Mass), 166, 188, 282.
  Sinfonia Concertante for Oboe, Bassoon, Violin and Cello, 92, 288, 431.
  Symphony No. 31, 215.
  Trumpet Concerto, 185.
  unspecified, 170.
  Violin Concerto No. 4, 431.
Heggie, Jake
  Dead Man Walking, 389, 425, 452.
  The End of the Affair, 425, 452.
  work commissioned to celebrate the MSO's 100th season, 452.
Herman, Jerry
  Hello, Dolly!, 385.
Heermann, Victor
  Drei Lieder, 200.
Herbert, Victor
  American Rhapsody, 212.
  Babes in Toyland, 358, 385.
  Canzonetta, 30.
Higdon, Jennifer
  blue cathedral, 421.
  Fanfare Ritmico, 421.
  Loco, 421.
Hindemith, Paul
  There and Back, 330 n. 30.
  Symphony "Mathis der Maler", 362, 396.
Hodkinson, Sydney
  Vox Populous, 382.
Hofmann, Heinrich
  Das Märchen von der schönen Melusina, 121.
Hoiby, Lee
  The Tides of Sleep, 251.
  Music for a Celebration, 251.
Holst, Gustav
  The Planets, 250.
Honegger, Arthur.
  Christmas Cantata, 188, 282.
  King David, 168, 249, 281, 282, 315, 316, 318.
  Jeanne d'Arc au bûcher, 282.
Hosmer, Lucius
  Northern Rhapsody, 212.
Humperdinck, Engelbert
  Hansel und Gretel, 262, 358.
Huppertz, Gottfried,
  Metropolis (film score), 146 n. 21.
  Siegfried (film score), 109, 146 n. 21.
Ibert, Jacques
  Flute Concerto, 189.

Iturbi, José
   Fantasy for Piano and Orchestra, 214.
Ives, Charles
   Largo, 395.
   Three places in New England, 250.
   The Unanswered Question, 250, 337.
Joachim, Joseph
   unspecified, 202.
   Violin Concerto No. 2 in the Hungarian Style, 203.
Johansen, Gunnar
   Piano Concerto No. 2, 153, 337.
Johnson, Roland
   Have Mercy on Me, O Lord, 310.
   It was a Lover and his Lass, 310, 311, 331 n. 40.
   One Perfect Love, 310.
   Prelude for Flute and Piano, 310.
   Quartet for Flute, Oboe, Clarinet, and Bassoon, 310, 312, 331 n. 40.
   Song for Orchestra with Mezzo-soprano, Op. 1, 310, 312-13, 331 n. 40.
   Stopping by the Woods on a Snowy Evening, 310, 327.
   Trio for Flute, Viola, and Cello, 310.
Jongen, Joseph
   Symphonie concertante for Organ and Orchestra, 405.
Joplin, Scott
   Treemonisha, 385.
Katzman, Louis
   Sonatique, 31.
Kern and Hammerstein
   Show Boat, 385, 387.
Kernis, Aaron
   Too Hot Toccata, 421.
Key, Francis Scott.
   The Star-Spangled Banner, 130, 153, 239 n. 29, 334, 357, 397.
Khachaturian, Aram
   Piano Concerto, 307.
King, Hial Bancroft
   Future Shock, 250, 294 n. 10.
Kodály, Zoltán
   Suite from "Háry János", 170, 355.

Krenek, Ernst
   Eleven Transparencies, 315.
   unspecified, 129.
Kreutz, Arthur
   Music for Orchestra in Two Movements, 128-29.
Kreutzer, Conradin
   Das Nachtrager in Granada, 27.
Kroll, William
   Banjo and Fiddle, 365.
Labunski, Felix
   Canto di aspirazione, 250, 294 n. 7.
   Salut à Paris: Ballet Suite, 250, 294 n. 7.
Lauridsen, Morten
   unspecified, 409.
Lees, Benjamin
   Passacaglia for Orchestra, 396.
Lehár, Franz
   The Merry Widow, 258.
Leoncavallo Ruggero
   I pagliacci, 3, 105.
   March Viva l'America, 11.
Lerner and Loewe
   Brigadoon, 358, 377.
   Camelot, 379.
   My Fair Lady, 385.
Leshnoff, Jonathan
   Rush for Orchestra, 422.
Liebermann, Lowell
   Flute Concerto, 336.
Ligeti, György
   Atmosphères, 251-52.
Liszt, Franz
   Fantasie über Ungarische Volksmelodien, 112.
   Gondoliera from "Venezia e Napoli", 131.
   Hungarian March from the "Damnation of Faust", 54.
   Piano Concerto No. 1, 350.
   Les préludes, 3, 112, 134, 143, 230.
Litolff, Henry
   Concerto symphonique No. 4, 3.
Loesser, Frank
   The Most Happy Fella, 377.
Lortzing, Albert
   Czar und Zimmermann, 19.

Luckhardt, Hilmar
   Chorale Prelude No. 1, 153.
Luening, Otto and Vladimir Ussachevsky
   Concerted Piece for Tape Recorder and Orchestra, 251, 256.
Luke, Ray
   Symphonic Dialogues for Violin, Oboe, and Orchestra, 250, 279-80.
Lumbye, Hans Christian
   Drømmebilleder, 27.
MacDowell, Edward
   As told at Sunset, from "Woodland Sketches", 63, 64, 67, 78.
   Piano Concerto No. 2, 95,160.
   To a Waterlily, from "Woodland Sketches", 63, 64.
MacPherson, Christina
   Waltzing Matilda, 152.
Martin, Frank
   Concerto for Seven Winds, Timpani, Percussion, and Strings, 288, 367.
Mahler, Gustav
   the "Mahler Cycle", 361, 373 n. 57, 406, 421.
   Symphony No. 1, 357, 361-62, 421.
   Symphony No. 2, 355, 362, 421, 452.
   Symphony No. 3, 207, 362.
   Symphony No. 4, 362, 421, 432.
   Symphony No. 5, 362, 396, 421.
   Symphony No. 8, 373 n. 57, 406.
   Symphony No. 9, 421.
Marcello, Alessandro
   Oboe Concerto, in C minor, 367.
Marsalis, Wynton
   Violin Concerto, 422.
Mascagni, Pietro
   Cavalleria rusticana, 82, 105, 172, 261, 319.
Massenet, Jules
   Eve, 58.
   Manon, 253, 263.
   Scenes napolitaines, 30.
Massing, Francis
   Der Peter in der Fremde, 17-18, 19.
McWilliams, J. C.
   Where I But His Own Wife, 5, 40 n. 16.

Mendelssohn, Felix
   Abscheislied der Zugvögel, 5.
   Elijah, 69, 76, 180, 281, 282, 351, 371 n. 3.
   Die erste Walpugisnacht (*The First Walpurgis Night*), 58.
   A Midsummer Night's Dream, 6, 115, 121, 405.
   Octet, 315.
   Die Primel, 121.
   Ruy Blas Overture, 30.
   St. Paul, 3.
   Symphony No. 3 "Scottish", 405.
   Symphony No. 4 "Italian", 230, 423.
   Violin Concerto in E minor, 15, 203, 365, 431.
Mennin, Peter
   Folk Overture, 308.
Menotti, Gian Carlo
   Amahl and the Night Visitors, 376, 380.
   Amelia Goes to the Ball, 263.
   The Consul, 317.
   Help, Help, the Globolinks!, 262.
   The Medium, 377.
   The Telephone, 377.
Meyerbeer, Giacomo
   Le prophète, 6.
Mihaud, Darius
   La creation du monde, 261.
   Protée, 307.
   Suite Provençale, 170.
Miller, Ashley
   Rhapsody for String Orchestra, 151, 155.
Mills, Charles H.
   The Wreck of the Hesperus, 56, 57, 64, 66.
Mollincone, Henry
   Starbird, 385.
Moniuszko, Stanisław
   Mazurka from "Halka", 153
Monteverdi, Claudio
   Il combattimento di Tancredi e Clorinda, 382.
   Lamento d'Arianna (orch. Carl Orff), 170.
Montgomery, Jessie
   Coincident Dances, 422.
Moore, Douglas
   The Ballad of Baby Doe, 188, 261, 263.
Moran, Robert
   Desert of Roses, 385.

Morgan, B. Q.
  Hornpipe for String Instruments, 55, 64, 66.
Morley, Thomas
  Now is the month of Maying, 121.
Morse, Woolson
  Dr. Syntax, 12-13.
Moszkowski, Moritz
  Moszkowskiana, 30.
Mozart, Wolfgang Amadeus
  Ave verum corpus, 357.
  Bassoon Concerto, 288.
  La Clemenza di Tito, 382.
  Cosi fan tutte, 172, 188, 263, 317.
  Coronation Mass, 188, 282.
  Don Giovanni, 6, 78, 230.
  Flute Concerto No. 1, 325.
  Mass in C minor "Great", 281, 323.
  Missa Longa, K.262, 90.
  Oboe Concerto, 367-68.
  Piano Concerto No. 22, 214.
  Piano Concerto No. 23, 95, 160, 256.
  Piano Concerto No. 27, 325.
  Le nozze di Figaro (The Marriage of Figaro), 26, 63, 261, 382.
  Der Schauspieldirektor (The Impressario), 263.
  Requiem, 281, 282.
  Sinfonia Concertante for Violin and Viola, 92, 156.
  Sinfonia Concertante for Violin, Cello, Oboe, and Bassoon, 185.
  Symphony No. 29, 382.
  Symphony No. 40, 134.
  Violin Concerto No. 2, 443 n. 33.
  Violin Concerto No. 4, 92.
  Violin Concerto No. 5, 365.
  Die Zauberflöte (The Magic Flute), 350, 358 382.
Mozart spurious works
  Sinfonia Concertante for Oboe, Clarinet, Bassoon, and Horn, 166, 184-85, 288.
  Twelfth Mass, 27.
Müller, Christian Gottlieb
  Potpourri: Gay Fellows, 27.
Murray, James R.
  Away in a Manger, 318.

Symphony No. 39, 235.
Mussorgsky, Modest
  Boris Gudenov, 182.
  Pictures at an Exhibition (orch. Maurice Ravel), 347.
Nahirniak, Taras.
  Hodie Christus, 363.
  Night Dances, 405, 421.
Nicolai, Otto
  Die lustigen Weiber von Windsor, 121
Offenbach, Jacques
  The Tales of Hoffmann, 104, 145 n. 8.
Orff, Carl
  Carmina Burana, 172, 282, 296 n. 63, 419.
  Catulli carmina, 282, 296 n. 63.
  Die Kluge, 172.
  Der Sänger in der Vorwelt, 282.
  Trionfo de Afrodite, 296, n. 63.
O'Neill, Charles
  Romance, 65, 66, 69.
  Suite Symphonique, 65, 66, 69.
Ott, David
  Concerto for Two Cellos and Orchestra, 336.
Paganini, Niccolo
  unspecified, 202.
Paine, John Knowles
  The Tempest, 63, 64.
Parker, Horatio
  A Song of Times, 63, 64.
Pärt, Arvo
  Cantus in Memory of Benjamin Britten, 337.
Penderecki, Krzysztof
  Threnody for the Victims of Hiroshima, 252.
Pergolesi, Giovanni Battista
  The Music Master, 309, 330 n. 30.
  La serva padrona, 316.
Persichetti, Vincent
  String Quartet No. 3, 316.
  Symphony No. 3, 315.
Piazzolla, Astor
  Four Seasons of Buenos Aires, 421, 431.
  Maria de Buenos Aires, 385, 387.
Piston, Walter
  Prelude and Allegro for Organ and Strings, 308.

Planquette, Robert
   Les cloches de Corneville (*The Chimes of Normandy*), 19.
Popper, David
   Requiem for Three Cellos and Orchestra, 157-58.
Porter, Cole
   Can-Can, 379.
Poulenc, Francis
   Concert Champetre, 323.
   Concerto for Organ, Strings, and Timpani, 307.
   La voix humaine (*The Human Voice*), 261.
   Gloria, 250, 282.
   Stabat Mater, 396.
Powell, John
   Natchez on the Hill, 230.
Powell, Laurence
   Keltic Legend, 65, 66.
Prager, Sigfrid
   Mendota (unfinished symphonic poem?), 133.
   The Message of Song, 65, 67, 68, 78, 133.
   Pale Moon, an Indian Love Song, 65, 67, 133.
   Sicania, 104, 132.
   Symphonic Suite, Op. 17, 64, 67, 123, 128, 131, 132-33.
Price, Florence
   Symphony No. 3, 421.
Prokofiev, Sergei
   Alexander Nevsky (film score), 351-52.
   Piano Concerto No. 3, 250, 307.
   Romeo and Juliet, 396.
   Symphony No. 5, 423.
   Violin Concerto No. 2, 431.
Puccini, Giacomo
   La Bohème, 188, 260-61, 316, 321, 325.
   Gianni Schicchi, 261.
   Madama Butterfly, 79, 81, 82, 334.
   Suor Angelica, 309, 330 n. 30.
   Tosca, 188.
   Turandot, 425, 444 n. 39.
Purcell, Henry
   Dido and Aeneas, 330 n. 30.
Purdy/Beck.
   On Wisconsin!, 368, 374 n. 65.

Puts, Kevin
   Contact, 422.
   Inspiring Beethoven, 421.
Rachmaninoff, Sergei
   Piano Concerto No. 2, 95, 160.
   Rhapsody on a theme of Paganini, 253.
   Symphony No. 2, 350.
Ravel, Maurice
   Alborada del gracioso, 250.
   Bolero, 63, 214.
   Daphnis et Chlöe, Suite No. 2, 250.
   Introduction and Allegro, 395.
   Piano Concerto for the Left Hand, 250.
   Piano Concerto in G Major, 235.
Respighi, Ottorino
   Lauda per la Natività del Signore, 281-82.
   Pines of Rome, 396.
Revueltas, Silvestre
   La noche de las Mayas, 421.
Riegger, Wallingford
   Dance Rhythms, 248, 250.
   Symphony No. 3, 315.
Rimsky-Korsakov, Nikolai
   Dance of the Tumblers, 230.
   Flight of the Bumblebee, 230.
   Scheherazade, 63, 288, 347, 423.
   Snegourochka, 152.
Robbins, Chandler
   Forest Festival, 16, 24-25.
Robinson, Avery
   Water Boy, 54, 64.
Rogers and Hammerstein
   Carousel, 385.
Rodgers and Laurents
   Do I Hear a Waltz?, 379.
Root, George F.
   The Haymakers, 4, 40 n. 10.
Rorem, Ned
   Mallet Concerto, 421
Rossini, Gioacchino
   Mosè in Egitto, 317.
   Otello, 6.
   Semiramide, 6.
   Stabat mater, 6, 172.

Rouse, Christopher
   Flute Concerto, 336
   The Infernal Machine, 336
   Rapture, 421
Rusch, Milton
   unspecified, 128
Rutter, John
   Requiem, 355
Saint-Saëns, Camille
   Carnival of the Animals, 153, 291
   Danse macabre, 92, 180, 296 n. 48
   Samson et Dalila, 58, 69, 79, 81, 160, 182
   Symphony No. 3 "Organ", 404
   Violin Concerto No. 3, 15, 55, 215
Schaeffer, Pierre
   unspecified *musique concrète* works, 314
Schmidt and Jones
   The Fantasticks, 377
Schnyder, Daniel
   Charlie Parker's Yardbird, 425
Schoenberg, Arnold
   Pierrot lunaire, 313
   String Quartet No. 2, 395
Schubert, Franz
   Symphony No. 8 "Unfinished", 211
   unspecified, 170
   unspecified four-hand piano works, 314
Schuller, Gunther
   Cello Concerto, 236, 244 n. 120
   Concerto for String Quartet and Orchestra, 288, 336, 337, 347
   A Dramatic Overture, 336
   Fanfare for brass instruments, 250
   Meditation (a.k.a. Symphonic Study), 308-09
   Music for a Celebration: A Fantasy on National Themes, 336
   Seven studies on themes of Paul Klee, 250
   Vertige d'Eros, 250-51
Schuman, William
   A Free Song, 308
   Henry VIII (incidental music), 170
   New England Triptych, 170
Schumann, Robert
   Liederkreis, 205-06

   Symphony No. 1, 382p
   Zigeunerleben, 106
Schütz, Heinrich
   Historia von der Geburt Jesu Christ, 188, 281
Scriabin, Alexander
   Poem of Ecstasy, 250
Shostakovich, Dimitri
   Concerto for Piano, Trumpet, and Strings, 250
   Symphony No. 5, 350
   Symphony No. 10, 396.
   Violin Concerto No. 1, 431
Sibelius, Jean
   Finlandia, 56
   The Swan of Tuonela, 118
   Symphony No. 2, 166, 170
   Violin Concerto, 92, 303
Sinding, Christian
   The Rustle of Spring, 77
Skilton, Charles Sanford
   Two Indian Songs, 212
Smetana, Bedřich
   The Bartered Bride, 79, 81, 83, 104, 145 n. 8, 330 n. 30
Snodgrass, Louise Harrison
   Fair Sailing, 236, 243 n. 119
Sondheim, Stephen
   Sweeney Todd, 385
Sousa, John Philip
   El Capitan, 13, 385
   The Stars and Stripes Forever, 30
   U.S. Artillery March, 212
Spears, Gregory
   Fellow Travelers, 388, 426
Spenser, Willard
   The Little Tycoon, 19
Spohr, Louis
   unspecified, 202
Stevens, John
   Adagio for Strings, 370
   Jubilare!, 396-97,
Stothart, Herbert
   The Cancelled Cook, 19

Strakosch, Maurice
   Nightingale Woodland Sketch, 6
   Nocturne, 6
   Young America Galop, 6
Strauss, Johann II
   An der schönen, blauen Donau (On the Beautiful Blue Danube), 27
   Die Fledermaus, 121, 188, 249, 253, 258, 262, 291, 294 n. 14, 323
   Kaiser Walzer (Emperor Waltzes), 180
Strauss, Richard
   Alpine Symphony, 207, 421
   Also sprach Zarathustra, 421, 443, n. 19
   Ariadne auf Naxos, 17
   Death and Transfiguration, 144, 421
   Don Juan, 421
   Don Quixote, 278, 421
   Enoch Arden, 232
   Ein Heldenleben, 421
   Oboe Concerto, 367
   Salome, 426
   Till Eulenspiegel's Merry Pranks, 211, 421
   Violin Sonata in E-flat Major, 206
Stravinsky, Igor
   Apollon Musagéte, 338
   Le chant de rossignol, 250
   Concertino for Twelve Instruments, 338
   Firebird Suite, 351, 421
   Petroushka, 250, 362, 396, 421
   Pulcinella, 250, 253
   Rite of Spring, 421, 423
   Symphony of Psalms, 307
Stokes, Eric
   Of the Badlands – Parables, 383
Stuart, Leslie
   Florodora, 13
Stucky, Steven
   Symphony, 421
Suppé, Franz von
   Dichter und Bauer (Poet and Peasant), 28, 32, 34
   Morning, Noon, and Night in Vienna, 180
Taussig, Karl
   Gypsy Fantasy (orch. Ilona Eibenschütz)

Taylor, Deems
   The Chambered Nautilus, 230
Tchaikovsky, Peter Ilych
   1812 Overture, 3, 112, 153
   Capriccio Italien, 216
   The Nutcracker, 185
   Piano Concerto No. 1, 166-67, 213, 291
   Pourquoi, 54
   Romeo and Juliet, 134, 248
   Serenade, 350
   Serenade (art song), 54
   Symphony No. 5, 63
   unspecified, 202
   Violin Concerto, 278
Thomson, Virgil
   The Seine at Night, 308
Thompson Randall
   Alleluia, 166, 404
Tippett, Michael
   Fantasia Concertante on a Theme of Corelli, 365
   New Year, 385
Torke, Michael
   Jasper, 363
   Verdant Music, 337
Tower, Joan
   Fanfare for the Uncommon Woman, 336
Van Alstyne, Egbert
   My Sunbeam, 13.
Vaughan Williams, Ralph
   Dona nobis pacem, 194 n. 71
   Five Mystical Songs, 282
   Flos campi, 278
   Oboe Concerto, 307
   On Wenlock Edge, 395
   Riders to the Sea, 316
   Serenade to Music, 250, 282, 307
   Symphony No. 2 "A London Symphony", 213
   Wasps Overture, 405
Verdi, Giuseppe
   Aïda, 188, 263, 292, 317, 334
   Don Carlo, 161
   Ernani, 6, 334
   Falstaff, 188, 261-62
   La forza del destino, 318

Macbeth, 334
Otello, 314
Il trovatore, 6, 26, 79, 81, 105
La traviata, 79, 81, 123, 188, 258, 263
Requiem, 58, 69, 97 n. 24, 172, 188, 194 n. 71, 281, 282, 323, 332 n. 75, 347, 370 n. 37, 419
Vieuxtemps, Henri
Violin Concerto No. 4, 92
Violin Concerto No. 5, 350
Villa-Lobos, Heitor
Bachianas Brasilieras No. 5, 307
Vitali, Tomaso
Chaconne in G minor, 128, 202
Vivaldi, Antonio
Concerto for Bassoon and Cello, 288
Concerto for Oboe in C Major, 367
Concerto for Two Trumpets, 185
Concertos "The Four Seasons", 365, 431
Gloria, 194 n. 71
Voelker, George
A Hunt in the Black Forest, 69
Vuillermoz, Emile
Jardin d'amour, 54.
Wagner, Richard
Der fliegender Holländer, 131
Lohengrin, 34, 103, 112
Die Meistersinger von Nürnberg, 52, 63, 78, 317, 338
Parsifal, 225
The "ring cycle," 109, 338.
 Das Rheingold, 34, 338
 Die Walküre, 211, 338
 Sigfried, 338
 Götterdämmerung, 133-34, 152, 338
Tannhaüser, 78, 112, 152, 350
Tristan und Isolde, 167
unspecified, 128, 214-15
Walker, George
Lyric for Strings, 421
Wallace, Stewart
Kaddish from "Harvey Milk", 362
Where's Dick?, 385

Wallace, William Vincent
Maritana, 17
Walton, William
Belshazzar's Feast, 282
Viola Concerto, 396
Weber, Carl Maria von
Bassoon Concerto, 288
Clarinet Concertino, 55, 57
Euryanthe, 215
Der Freischütz, 121, 213
Invitation to the Dance (arr. Felix Weingartner), 216, 217
Oberon, 171
Polacca brilliant (orch. Franz Liszt), 153
Webern, Anton
Passacaglia, Op. 1, 297 n. 70
Weingartner, Felix
Phantasiebilder, 107
Serenade, 107
songs, 107
Symphony No. 1, 107-08
Weisberg, Arthur
Concerto for Oboe, Bassoon, and Strings, 363
White, Clarence Cameron
arrangements of Black spirituals, 230
Whithorne, Emerson
Pell Street from "Chinatown", 64
Wick, Frederick
Norwegian Folk Songs, 77
Rustic Norwegian Dance, 77
Wolf-Ferrari, Ermanno
I gioielli della Madonna, 112
Zwillich, Ellen Taafe
Celebration for Orchestra, 396

General Index

Note: Page numbers followed by *i* refer to photos or graphic illustrations. Page numbers followed by *t* refer to tables. Page numbers followed by *n* and a number refer to end-of-chapter notes.

A

"The *A* That Lasts a Hundred Years" (Talbot poem), 441
Ada Bird Society, 43n66
Adagio for Strings (Barber), 397–98
Adams, Bert, 262
Adams, Charles K., 23, 72
Adams, John, 386, 398, 421
Adler, Peter Herman, 380, 380*i*
administrative staff development (MCMA), 283–86
administrative staff development (MSO), 414–19
Alabama Quartet, 315–16, 316*i*
Alberti, Achille, 20
Aley, John, 411, 434*i*
all-Brahms program (1994), 352
Allen, Steve, 258
all-Mexican program, 449
Allsen, Mike, xvi, 370*i*
all-Wagner program (1937), 69
all-Wagner program (1975), 283
all-Wagner program (1983), 338
amateur choirs, early Madison groups, 1–3.
   See also Madison Civic Chorus; Madison Symphony Chorus American composers.
   See also local composers
   early Civic Symphony performances, 57, 63–67, 64–65*t*
   FMP promotion, 124
   John DeMain's support, 385–86
   Madison Opera support, 425–26
   MSO programming in 1980s and 1990s, 336–37
   Roland Johnson's support, 250–51, 252, 305, 307–8
   Thor Johnson's support in Cincinnati, 212
American Federation of Musicians
   collective bargaining representation, 413–14
   FMP relationship with, 125, 126

Music Performance Trust Fund, 180, 270, 271, 413
American Girl, 401
American Musicological Society, 134
American Society of Composers, Authors, and Producers, 179
American Symphony Orchestra League, 179
Anderson, Eleanor, 262–63, 283
Anderson, Florence, 60, 175*i*, 178
Anderson, Jess, 352
Anderson, Leroy, 258
Anderson, Marian, 76, 384
Andresen, Daniel, 284
Andrew, Jon, 283
Anello, John-David, 130
Appleton Vocational School, 159–160
Arion Choral Society, 112
Army musicians in the MCM, 151–52
Arrau, Claudio, 76, 254, 255
Arroyo, Martina, 334, 337
Arts Ball, 360
Artz, Elsie, 301
Arvold, William V., 125, 128
ASCAP Award for Service to Contemporary Music, 252*i*
Askins, David, 257
Assembly Hall (University of Wisconsin), 23
Atkins, Chet, 336
Atz, Karen Beth, 440*i*
Aubert, Henri, 171
auditions under DeMain, 353, 412, 450
"Auditorium Wars," 264–68
Auer, Leopold, 14–15
Augustana College, 364–65
Austin, George, 401, 407
autographed drum heads, 84–86, 85*i*
   avant-garde works under DeMain, 382
   avant-garde works under Johnson, 251–52
Ax, Emanuel, 337, 422
Axley, Katharine Hartman, 58, 66, 83

B

Baas, Alexius
   account of Prager's decision to move to Madison, 113–15
   biography, 87–88, 88i
   as *Capital Times* correspondent, 83, 87, 248
   compositions performed, 64t, 65t, 66, 68, 78, 170
   letters from Prager, 140–41
   as local choral director, 70, 78, 87, 116
   Missa Solemnis review in 1947, 161
   photo with Civic Chorus, 1931, 56i
   review of 1949 concert, 167–68
   vocal performances, 115
   work with opera, 80, 81
Baas, Evelyn, 161
babysitting money, 179–180, 270
Bach, Christopher, 28, 33–34
Bach, John L., 67, 69, 70, 127
Bach Dancing and Dynamite Society, 438i
Badura-Skoda, Paul, 255
Bailey, Zuill, 422
ballet, 32, 80, 83, 405
Ballweg, Diane Endres, 409
Balshaw, Paul, 261–62
Bareuther, August, 27, 28
Barnett, Henry, 315, 316i
Barova, Mari, 81, 86, 161
Barrère, Georges, 300
Barrows, John, 287
Barrymore Theatre, 98n38
Bartell, Gerald, 334
Bartley, Linda, 435i
Baskerville, Inez, 325–26
Bass, John Quincy, 219
Bassermann, Fritz, 197i
Basso, Robert, 278
Bauer, Harold, 72
Bauer, Jeff, 449–450
Baxter Springs, battle of, 24
Becker, David, 347, 373n53
Becker, Hugo, 197i, 198, 205
Becknell, Arthur, 255, 260, 281, 289–290, 323, 355
Becknell, Nancy, 275, 360

Beia, Suzanne, 413, 424, 430, 439i
Bell, Joshua, 337, 422
Bencriscutto, Frank, 189i
Bennett, Florence, 22, 30–31, 49, 88–89, 115
Bentz Quartet, 156
Berenguer, Manuel, 11
Beresina, Theodore, 212
Berg, Alban, 313
Berigan, Bernard "Bunny," 31
Berkey, Ruth, 376
Bermudez, Alvaro, 428
Bernstein, Leonard
   "big break" story, 213
   DeMain's work with, 350, 386, 386i, 387
   as guest conductor in Cincinnati, 216, 234–35, 235i
   as inspiration for DeMain's Mahler cycle, 361
   Johnson's Tanglewood audition for, 307
   as mentor to music director candidates, 349, 350
   support of *Shining Brow* opera, 345
Bertram, Carl, 159
Beyond the Score series, 423–24
Bianconi, Philippe, 422
Bielefeld, Betty, 77, 181, 189i, 189–190, 190i
Bielefeld, George, 189
Biere, Josh, xivi, 412
Bird, Ada, 20–21, 23, 34
Bishop, Anna, 16
Bishop, Louisa, 16
Bishop's Bay, 358–59
Bjorksten, Bettina, 171, 255
Black Mountain College, 304–5
Black Swan, 6i, 6–7
Blatz, Emil, 129
Blatz Bandshell, 129i, 129–130
Bleid, Frank C., 48
blind auditions under DeMain, 353, 412, 450
Blind Lemon Jefferson, 300
Bloodgood, Katherine, 3
Bloodgood, Robert, 160
Blum, Martha, 275, 278, 434i
Blum, Richard, 278, 434i
Bodanzky, Artur, 112

Bodebeder, Sheila. *See* Heermann, Martha Amelia Sheila (Bodebeder, a.k.a. Sheila O'Day)
Boehm, Thomas, 325
Boeppler, William [Wilhelm], 120
Bojanowski, Jerzy, 130
Bolet, Jorge, 337
Bolognini, Ennio, 152
Bolz, Eugenie Mayer, 176, 176*i*, 178, 340
Bolz, Marian
 changes to Women's Committee, 178
 on Coliseum pops concerts, 258
 on music director search committee, 348
 Opera in the Park idea, 426
 Overture organ project involvement, 406–7
 tenure as MCMA board president, 339–340, 340*i*
Bonci, Alessandro, 72
Boniface, George C. Jr., 13
bonus payments, 270, 271
Borge, Victor, 258
Borsuk, Gerald
 1948 concert performance, 160
 on friction over musician pay, 180
 on performance flaws under Heermann, 181
 photo, 118*i*
 on Prager as composer, 132
 private lessons with Prager, 117–18
 Wisconsin Symphony Orchestra performance, 131
Boston Bar Association Orchestra, 356
Boston Festival Orchestra, 3, 35*t*
Boston Stars, 20
Boulanger, Nadia, 94
Boulez, Pierre, 314
Bowen, Ann, 411, 416*i*, 416–17, 418*i*, 419
Bowen, Glenn, 275
Bowers, Robert Hood, 33
Bowman, Charlie, 300
Brahms, Johannes, 198–99, 228
Brahms compositions, Heermann's favor for, 170
Bravo Broadway, 423
Bredin, Elias, 2

Bressler, Lisa, 422*i*
Brey, Carter, 422
Brice, Carol, 161*i*, 161–62
Bricken, Carl, 154
Bridges, Mark, 450
Brightman, Sarah, 426
Brion, Keith, 336
Bristol, Frederick E., 12
Broadway
 Bertha Waltzinger's career, 13
 Carol Brice's career, 161
 DeMain's experience, 387
 Kenley Players from, 379
 Porgy and Bess, 384
brochures, 174
Brock, Karl, 260
Brodt, Cecil, 50, 53
Bronfman, Yefim, 422
Brown, Louise, 263
Brown Bag Concerts, 253, 254*i*
Browning, John, 255, 363
Brubeck, Chris, 421
Bruch, Max, 104, 105*i*, 132
Brunswick, Mark, 305
Bryant, Anita, 379
Buchhauser, Thomas, 324
Buckley, Diedre, 438*i*
Buckley, Richard, 358
Buehl, Wendy, 411
Buehler, Elizabeth, 21*i*, 48, 115
Bull, Alexander, 10
Bull, Ole, 7–10, 9*i*
Bull, Sara Chapman (Thorp), 8–9, 9*i*
Bull, Storm (i), 10
Bull, Storm (ii), 10–11
Burke, William, 26–27
Burleigh, Cecil, 15, 37, 66, 132
Burns, Laura, 424
Burrows, Mrs. M. E., 16
Burton Opera Company, 17
Burwell, Fred, 99*n*71
Busoni, Ferruccio, 104, 105*i*
Byrd, William C., 309

C

Čadek, Ottokar, 315, 319
Callas, Maria, 314
Cameron (Cameron-Fix), Cynthia, 288, 297n74, 399, 435i
Camp Sheridan, 209
Campanari, Giuseppe, 3
Campbell, S. C., 16–17
Campbell and Castle's English Opera Troupe, 16–17
Canadian Brass, 336
Capital Times
    account of Prager's decision to move to Madison, 113–15
    Arline Johnson tribute, 321
    coverage of first Civic Symphony concert, 54–55
    "Know Your Symphony Orchestra" series, 274, 410
    MCMA's relationship with, 82–84
    Prager biography, 102
    report of Prager detention rumor, 117
Capitol Theater
    conversion to civic auditorium, 266i, 266–67, 334
    MCMA concerts 1928–29, 60
    orchestra, 30, 31, 32
    preservation in Overture Project, 406
Captain Kangaroo, 256
Carlton, Julian, 345
Carman, David, 171
Carreon, Alexis, 417, 418i, 419, 440i
Carroll, Diahann, 336
Carter, Eleanor, 178
Carter, Elliot, 382
Carter, John, 130
Casadesus, Richard, 94
Casals, Pablo, 238n20
Cass, Betty, 138
Castle, William, 16–17
Cello Concerto (Schuller), 236
centennial season celebration, 451–52
Central High School Auditorium
    first Civic Symphony concert, 53–54
    first Civic Symphony rehearsal, 51–52

    limitations, 253, 253i, 280, 280i, 335
    periods as MCMA's primary venue, 173, 174, 253
    Roland Johnson's moves away from, 253–54
Central Madison Committee, 266
Chang, Sarah, 387, 422
Channing, Carol, 385
Charleston Music Festival, 213, 229–230
Chase, Allen, 275
Chatman, Stephen, 256–57
Chen, Chelsea, 428
Chen, Margaret, 407
Cheney, Mamah, 345
Chicago Bach Chorus, 120–21
Chicago Civic Opera, 121
Chicago Civic Orchestra, 37, 39t, 75
Chicago College of Music, 197
Chicago Festival Opera Company, 79–80, 81
Chicago Opera Company, 17
Chicago Singverein, 120, 120i, 121
Chicago Symphony Orchestra
    Beyond the Score series, 423
    Chicago Bach Chorus association, 120
    Lottridge's participation, 286–87
    Madison Orchestral Association sponsorship, 36, 37, 39t
    origins, 34
    Stock Pavilion concerts, 75
choral music, early amateur groups in Madison, 1–3. *See also* Madison Civic Chorus; Madison Symphony Chorus
Choral Rhapsody in the Romantic Style (Hagen), 155, 156
Christopher Bach's Orchestra, 28, 33–34
Christy, Margaret, 315, 316i, 319
Chung, Kyung-Wha, 255
Church, Richard, 65, 78, 82, 228, 232, 348
church choirs, early groups in Madison, 1–2
cimbasso, 369
Cincinnati Art Museum concert, 219, 219i
Cincinnati Chamber Orchestra, 215, 221
Cincinnati Conservatory of Music, 221
Cincinnati Little Symphony, 212–13, 220i, 220–21, 309
Cincinnati Summer Orchestra, 212, 218

Cincinnati Symphony Orchestra
    conductors, 207, 210–12
    Heermann brothers join, 204, 206–7
    Hugo Heermann as concertmaster of, 197, 203, 204
    Madison Orchestral Association sponsorship, 36–37, 39t
Cirque de la Symphonie, 451–52
City Hall
    early opera productions, 16–17
    early touring performances in, 6, 8
    local musical society concerts, 25–28
    Madison Musical Union concerts in, 3–4
civic auditorium
    early recognition of need, 49, 264
    history of debates over, 264–68
    Madison Civic Center, 266–67, 327–28, 334–35
    Wright's design, 174, 264, 267–68
Civic Music Festivals, 67–70, 68i
Civic Music ideal, 180
Civic Music Notes (newsletter), 175
Clara Schumann Orchestra, 35t
Clark, Paul, 50
Cliburn, Van, 76, 254, 255, 255i
Clyne, Anna, 422
Cole, Robert, 190, 275, 287, 289
Coleman, Valerie, 422
College of Music of Cincinnati
    Heermann's teaching career, 165, 213, 221–24
    Roland Johnson's studies, 302–3
    Roland Johnson's work for, 307–9
College Orchestra, College of Music of Cincinnati
    Roland Johnson's direction, 306, 307–9
    Walter Heermann's direction, 213, 221–22, 224
Collins, Judy, 336
Comet, Catherine, 347i, 347–48
Compositions for Cooking (book), 177
The Compositions of Sybil Ann Hanks (recording), 119
Concert for Planet Earth, 387
Concert Grosso (Hagen), 157, 170, 181–82

Concert on the Green, 336, 358–59, 359i, 360, 423
Concertino for Three Saxophones and Piano (Hanks), 183
concertmasters of the MCS/MSO
    Gilbert Ross (1926), 15, 44n50
    Marie Endres (1927–60), 22, 42n50, 89, 91–93, 156, 172, 276, 443n20
    Shirley Reynolds (1950–51 temporary replacement), 93
    Mary Perssion (1960–63), 276
    Annetta Rosser (1963–64, 1965–66), 276, 277i
    Won-Mo Kim (1964–65), 277–78
    Miriam Schneider (1966–69), 276–77, 277i, 278i
    Martha Blum (1969–70), 278
    Thomas Moore (1970–75, 1976–77), 278i, 278–79
    Norman Paulu (1975–76, 1977–89), 279–80, 279i
    Tyrone Greive (1989–2010), 280, 363–66, 364i
    concertmaster search (2010–11), 412–13
    Naha Greenholz (2011–present), 280, 413, 429–31, 430i
Concerts on the Square, 401, 451
Concordia Society, 26
Congregational Church, 3, 10
Conlon, Hazel, 69
Contemporary Music Symposiums, 307–8, 315
Conti, Bill, 358
Cook, Winifred, 252i, 278i, 285
Cooke, Rosa, 16
Coolidge, Elizabeth Sprague, 154
Cooper, Earl, 270
Cooper, Margaret Rupp, 52, 160, 166, 182, 440i
Copland, Aaron, 305
"core orchestra" approach, 450–51
Corigliano, John, 421
Cornfield, Dorothy, 152, 161
Cortez, Sandra, 161
Coughlin, "Roundy," 86
Covid pandemic, 366, 367–68, 414, 415, 447–48
Cowan, Ken, 428

"cradle of harmony" fiddle, 15
Crain, Jon, 262
Crandall, Warren, 249, 260, 261i
The Creation (Hanks), 183
Creatore, Giuseppi, 20
Creitz, Lowell, 275, 278, 278i, 279
Crooks, Richard, 130, 300
Crosby, David Lewis, 323–24, 453n11
Crow, Ann, 185, 186, 186i, 187, 284, 323
Crow, James
    on Heermann's leadership, 181
    on Johnson's initial impact, 248
    on musician pay debate, 180
    friendship with Johnsons, 323, 326
    profile of musical contributions, 185–87, 186i
    role in board debate on regular admission fees, 272
Cui, Yumian, 418i, 419
Culp, Siegmund, 218
Cushing, Rex, 80

D

Dadmun, Royal, 109–10
Dale, Esther, 53, 54i, 55, 132
Dane County Coliseum, 254, 258, 273
Dane County Music Festival, 68
Dane County Youth Building, 249i, 254, 258
Daniels, Ray, 161
A Daughter of the Gods (film), 32–33, 33i
Davies, Dennis Russell, 378, 381, 382
Davis, Esther, 229
Dawson, William Levi, 421
de Mille, Agnes, 305
de Vermond, Kai, 80
De Voe, May, 12
"Decade by Decade" series, 395–96
Decoration Day Hymn (Hanks), 65t, 68, 170, 182
Dee, John, 363
DeMain, Barbara Dittman, 387–88, 388i, 403, 403i
DeMain, Dominic, 376
DeMain, Jennifer, 388, 388i
DeMain, John
    Ann Stanke's work with, 292
    early life, 376i, 376–78, 377i
    guest conducting during HGO tenure, 387–88
    guest conducting during MSO tenure, 389–390
    Houston Grand Opera directorship, 162, 349, 351, 382–87
    inaugural season and early years with MSO, 357–363
    initial impact on MSO, 275, 352–57
    invitations to Johnson to conduct, 325
    Juilliard experience and later fellowships, 378–382
    marriage and family life, 387–88, 388i
    MSO 75th anniversary programming, 395–97
    as music director candidate, 349–351
    NOA lifetime achievement award, 390
    opinion on core orchestra approach, 450–51
    Oscar Mayer Theatre comments, 399
    Overture Hall development role, 401, 402–3, 403i
    as pianist, 377, 378, 382
    pictured with Roland Johnson, 353i, 434i
    retirement plans and legacy, 390–92
    work with Carol Brice, 162
    work with Civic Chorus, 290
DeMain, Nancy, 376, 376i
Dethier, Édouard, 303
Detroit Symphony Orchestra, 36, 39t
Devanny, Michael, 207, 208
"Development of the Song" lectures, 111
Deverient, Elisa, 35t
DeVoe, Maude, 82
di Sanza, Anthony (Tony), 438i
Diamond, David, 344
DiChiera, David, 362
Dichter, Mischa, 255
Dichter, Misha, 337
Dick, Lois, 249, 260, 261i, 262
Dickenson, Jean, 130
Dickson, Donald, 130
Die Fledermaus (J. Strauss), 1962 performance, 249, 259, 291
Dill, Amanda, 418i, 419

diversity, equity, and inclusion, 448–49
Domingo, Placido, 387, 388
Dominik, Shirley, 189*i*
Donath, Helen, 362
Dooley, Meranda, 418*i*, 419
Doppmann, William, 253*i*, 255
Double Concerto (Brahms), 216–17, 230*i*, 231
Doudna, William, 83, 136, 161
Douma, Walter, 322
Downs, Warren, 436*i*
Dozoryst, Christopher, 424, 439*i*
Dragonette, Jessica, 130
dramatic sopranos, 371*n*6
Drangosch, Ernesto, 108, 108*i*
Dressler, William, 8
Druckenmiller, William, 183
drum head signatures, 84–86, 85*i*
DuCombles cello, 234
Duncan, Isadora, 35*t*
Dunner, Leslie, 357
Duveneck, Frank, 224
Dvorak, Raymond, 170, 193*n*47
Dykema, Peter, 1
Dykins, Dale, 235
Dykstra, Clarence, 154

E

Eames, Henry, 20
early classical music in Madison
   amateur choirs, 1–3
   local orchestras and bands, 23–32
   Madison Musical Union, 3–4
   Madison Orchestral Association, 15, 34–38, 39*t*
   Monona Lake Assembly, 18–20
   noteworthy local musicians, 12–15
   opera, operetta, and musical comedy, 16–18, 19*t*
   schools and conservatories, 20–23
   touring performers, 4–11, 16–17, 32–34, 35*t*
East Side Civic Chorus, 67, 69, 70
East Tennessee Normal School, 299, 301
Eastwood Theater, 67, 98*n*38
Effron, Sigmund, 217, 222
Ehnes, James, 422

Ellenwood, Elisabeth (Lisel), 438*i*
Ellis, Viola, 113
Elman, Mischa, 72, 226
Elsner, Carmen, 248, 260
Encore School for Strings, 430
endowment fund, 342–43, 415
Endres, Amelia (Schneyer), 91
Endres, Marie
   biography, 91–94, 94*i*, 96*i*
   as Civic Symphony concertmaster, 42*n*50, 276, 443*n*20
   final performance, 172
   in Hanks recording, 182
   Haydn *Sinfonia* performance, 185
   Missa Solemnis recording, 164
   recollection of Bennett-Prager incident, 89
   recruiting to Civic Symphony by, 53
   Wisconsin School of Music connection, 22
Endres, Mathias Aloisus, 91
Endres, Olive, 94*i*, 95–96, 96*i*
Endres-Kountz, Emma, 48, 94*i*, 94–95, 160
Eppert, Carl, 67
Eroica Trio, 397–98
Erolle, Ralph, 319
Ersland, Lawrence, 53
Ersland, Peter, 141
Euterpean Society, 25–27
extravaganzas, 67–79, 68*i*
Exxon/NEA/ Affiliate Artists fellowship, 381–82

F

Fair Sailing (Snodgrass), 236
Fairbanks Symphony Orchestra, 367
Fairchild's Hall, 5, 10
"Fairy Operatta of *Forest Festival*," 24–25
Falk, Clara, 10
Falk, Louis, 10
Fall Pops programs, 336
Fall Youth Concerts, 257
Falletta, JoAnn, 357
Falletti, Mona, 176, 176*i*
Fandrich, Walter, 324
Farell, Marita, 160
farewell concert recording (1948), 163–64

Farrell, Eileen, 76, 77, 254, 255, 283
Fauchald, Nora, 77
Faulhaber, Charles, 183
Faulhauber, Charles, 246
Faust (Gounod), 79–80, 80*i*
Federal Music Project (FMP), 124–131
Federal Project One, 124
Feghali, José, 350
Feige, Jean, 285, 340
Felder, Harvey, 357
Feltsman, Vladimir, 337, 422
Fennell, Frederick, 227
Fenske, Viola, 272
Ferrill, Floyd, 56
Festge, Otto, 94, 265
Festival of the Lakes, 338–39
Ficcocelli, Michael, 376
Fiedler, William, 230
Final Forte, 391, 424
finances. *See also* fundraising activities
 changing ticket sales trends, 447–48
 endowment fund, 342–43
 leading to 1994 reorganization, 341–42
 for Madison Civic Symphony's founding, 50
 Madison Vocational School agreement, 59–62
 MCMA budget growth from 1960, 333
 musician compensation, 56
 for Overture Project, 401, 407, 408–9
 for *Shining Brow* project, 344–45
Findlan, Rosie, 348
Fine Arts Trio (Wheeler conservatory), 22
Fink, Marc, 348, 366–68
Fiol, Chris, 418*i*, 419
First Methodist Episcopal Church, 35*t*
Fischer, Lois, 255, 261
Fischer, Walter, 104, 105*i*
Fischer-Niemann, Karl, 78, 86, 128
Fisk Jubilee Singers, 131
Flag of Our Fathers (Baas), 64*t*, 68, 78
Flagstad, Kirsten, 307
Fleischmann, Stephen, 395
Fleischmann Foundation, 313, 331*n*42
Flindt, Emil, 31, 32
Floyd, Carlisle, 385*i*, 385–86

Foley, Madeline, 170
Fontanna, Arlene, 380
Forrester, Maureen, 255, 337
Foster, Marvin, 178, 283
Fountain, Robert, 355
Fox Valley Symphonette, 160
Fox Valley Symphony Orchestra, 160
Frank Lloyd Wright Foundation, 344, 345
Frautschi, Pleasant Rowland, 400*i*, 401, 407, 442*n*9
Frautschi, W. Jerome (Jerry), 400*i*, 401, 404, 407, 442*n*9
"Freeway Philharmonic," 411
Fried, Miriam, 337
Friends of the Overture Concert Organ, 408–9, 428
Frost, William, 373*n*50
Fuller Opera House
 Armory's advantages, 34
 early opera productions, 19*t*
 early touring orchestra concerts, 35*t*
 house orchestra, 29–30
 Nitschke's role, 28
 opening, 11, 23
fundraising activities. *See also* finances
 Concert on the Green, 336, 358, 360
 by Madison Symphony Orchestra League, 359–360
 pops concerts, 177, 258, 272
 youth program with Captain Kangaroo, 256
Furtwängler, Wilhelm, 210, 307
Fusaro, Lisa, 419
Futterer, Roger and Marie, 163–64

G

Gabrilowitsch, Ossip, 72
Gadski, Johanna, 2*i*, 72
Gale, Nettie, 20
Galli-Curci, Amelita, 11, 11*i*, 76
Galway, James, 337, 351
Garbousova, Raya, 255, 364
Garcia Huerta, Maria Isabella Moeller, 199
Garner Park, 426
Garvin, Bradley, 343*i*
Gary, John, 258

Gates, Crawford, 337, 339
Gaylan, Diana, 130
"General Bernstein at the Battle of Parkersburg" (drawing), 234–35, 235*i*
George, Florence, 130
George, Harrison, 8
Gerhardt, Alban, 422
German immigrants
    to Argentina, 106
    choral groups, 2, 27, 70, 78. *See also* Madison Maennerchor
    composers, 17–18
    early orchestra organizers, 27, 28–29
    musical influence in Cincinnati, 206
Gershwin, George, 31, 65–66, 66*i*, 383–84
Gershwin, Ira, 383
Gialamas, Candy, 358
Gibson, Michel, 160
Giddings, Thaddeus, 226
A Gift from Madison (E. Hegland poem), 136–37
Gilad, Yehuda, 431–32
Gilbert, Dale, 171
Gill, Vince, 426
Gilliland, Ross, 438*i*
Giunta, Joseph, 349, 350
Glazer, Frank, 130
Glocer, Silvia, 145–46*n*15
Gockley, David, 382–83, 383*i*, 384
Godfrey, Arthur, 379
Goerlich, Herman, 218*i*
Goldberg, Beatrice, 175*i*
Goldberg, Jennifer, 417, 418*i*, 419
Golden, Joseph, 400
Goldman, Sherwin, 384
Golijov, Osvaldo, 421
Gonzo, Carroll, 262
Goodall, Nicholas, 10
Goodman, Benny, 258, 324
Goodson, Howard, 316–17
Goossens, Eugene
    career overview, 240*n*43
    Cincinnati Little Symphony direction, 221
    impact on Walter Heermann's career, 211, 213, 214, 215
    role in Emil Heermann's demotion, 217

Gordon, David, 418*i*, 419
Gordon, E. B., 48, 55
Gorno, Romeo, 218
Götterdämmerung (Wagner), Prager's orchestration, 133*i*, 133–34
Göttingen Handel Festival, 155
Gottschalk, Louis Moreau, 41*n*18
Gould, Morton, 252*i*
Governor's Mansion Inn, 9
Grace Episcopal Church, 19*t*, 22
Graham, Alexander
    acceptance of Kvam resignation, 158
    beginning of relationship with MCMA, 59
    correspondence with Carl Bertram, 159–160
    friendship with Prager, 62, 269
    Grainger's letter to, 142
    MCMA funding proposal to city council, 61
    photo, 60*i*
Graham, Larry, 378
Grainger, Ella Bird, 154*i*
Grainger, Percy
    appearance with Wisconsin Symphony Orchestra, 129
    appearances with Madison Civic Symphony, 154–55, 191*n*8
    autographed photo to Heermann, 191*n*7, 205
    Hoch Conservatory studies, 205
    pictured with Pragers, 154*i*
    tribute to Prager, 142, 191*n*7
Grammy Award for *Porgy and Bess*, 162, 384–85
Graves, Denyce, 422
Greeley, H. P., 38
Green Mountain Boys, 4–5
Greene, Clarence, 300
Greenfield, Elizabeth Taylor, 6*i*, 6–7
Greenholtz, Naha, 280, 413, 422, 429–433, 430*i*
Greenwood, Lee, 426
Greive, Janet, 326, 363–66, 364*i*
Greive, Tyrone, 280, 326–27, 363–66, 364*i*, 399, 412
Grieg Chorus, 2
Grieg Men's Choir, 67, 69, 70, 87
Griffith, D. W., 33
Grove, Jill, 362
Grüss, Blanche, 376

Grüss, Hermann, 376
guest conductors in Madison
    in DeMain's first season, 357–58
    diversity in, 448
    favorites, 421, 443n33
    impact on orchestra, 288, 347–48, 357
    during Johnson's recovery from heart attack, 323–24
    for youth programs, 373n53
Gunderson, E. N., 68
Gunlaugson, Christine, 139
Gunsaulus, Frank, 75
Guthrie, Arlo, 423, 443–44n33
Gutiérrez, Horacio, 337, 363, 378, 422

H

Hadelich, Augustin, 422
Hadley, Henry, 211
Haenel, Frederick, 234
Haenel cello, 233i, 234
Hagen, Beatrice, 156, 157, 276, 276i
Hagen, Daron, 337, 343–45, 344i, 346, 362
Hagen, Holger, 191n13
Hagen, Oskar, 155–57, 156i, 170, 181–82, 192n26
Hagen, Thyra, 156
Hagen, Uta, 156i, 191n13
Hahn, Hilary, 363, 422
Hall, Gustavus, 8
Haller, Terry
    on Monona Terrace plans, 268
    on music director search committee, 348
    on Overture Hall development, 400–401
    Overture organ project involvement, 406–7
    recollections about 1994 reorganization, 341–42
    service as MSO president, 361i
    on *Shining Brow* project, 343, 344–45
Hall-Tompkins, Kelly, 422
Hambrecht, George, 59, 60, 60i
Hambrecht, Otto, 122
Hamburg Steinway grand piano, 403, 403i, 404
Hamelin, Marc-Andre, 422
Handbook of Conducting (Scherchen), 313
Hanke, Dorothy, 318, 318i
Hanke, Julius, 318, 318i
Hanke, Oscar, 13–14
Hanks, Lucien (Louis) Mason, 118
Hanks, Mary Vilas, 118
Hanks, Sybil
    biographic profile, 118–19
    compositions performed, 65t, 66, 68, 83, 170
    death in Argentina, 141
    recorded performances of works, 119, 182–84
Hansen, Ann, 183
Hanson, Frank, 437i
Hanson, George, 349, 350–51
Hanvey, Katelyn, 418i, 419, 424
Harbison, John, 337, 421, 443n31
Hardy, Cora, 231–32, 234
Harrell, Linda, 422
Harrell, Lynn, 337
Harry Potter films, 426
Harth, Sidney, 255, 365
Hartman, Marvin, 84–87
Harvey, Vivien, 231
Hastreiter, Helen, 3
Haugan, Paul, 348, 368i, 368–370, 370i
Have Mercy on Me, O Lord (Johnson), 310, 311
Haverly's Minstrels, 17
Hay, Helen, 187, 284, 285
Haywood, Lorna, 337
Hear the Angel Voices CD, 420
Hearts of the World (film), 33
HeartStrings program, 425
Heatherton, Joey, 379
Heck, Irma, 161
Heckenkamp-Busch, Rose, 420, 428–29, 429i
Heermann, Bella, 199i, 201, 201i, 202, 225
Heermann, Eileen, 224
Heermann, Emil
    arrest during World War I, 207–8
    career overview, 200
    childhood photos, 199i, 205i
    demotion with Cincinnati orchestra, 217
    emigration to U.S., 206
    family life in Cincinnati, 224
    joins Cincinnati Symphony Orchestra, 204
    Madison performances, 167, 232
    photo, 201i

photos with Walter, 211*i*, 230*i*
Roland Johnson's studies with, 301–2
as soloist, 216, 231
as teacher, 221, 222–24, 227, 228
U.S. performances with Hugo, 202
Heermann, Hugo, 197*i*, 197–204, 199*i*, 210, 238n16
Heermann, Isabella (Garcia Huerta), 199, 201, 225
Heermann, Maja, 199*i*, 200, 201*i*, 202, 205*i*, 225
Heermann, Martha Amelia Sheila (Bodebeder) (a.k.a. Sheila O'Day), 224
Heermann, Norbert, 199*i*, 201, 201*i*, 202, 204, 205*i*, 224–25
Heermann, Victor Hugo, 199*i*, 200, 201*i*, 205*i*
Heermann, Walter
   1950s concerts and changes to MCS, 169–174
   age difference from Prager, 162
   charcoal sketch, 215*i*
   childhood photos, 199*i*, 205*i*
   departure from Cincinnati, 217
   as director versus Prager, 180–81
   family life in Cincinnati, 224–25
   father's life and career, 197–204
   first Madison visit, 37
   Interlochen photos, 226*i*, 227*i*
   legacy, 234–36
   life in Madison, 231–32, 233
   Madison performances, 167
   Marie Endres's musical relationship with, 93
   move to U.S., 202
   moves to professionalize orchestra, 179–180
   name change following emigration, 201
   opening season as director, 165–69
   opportunities to conduct in Cincinnati, 212–16
   other musical work in Cincinnati, 218–224
   performance on Hanks recording, 183, 184
   photo with Joan Taliaferro, 171*i*
   photo with Norbert, 201*i*
   photos with Emil, 211*i*, 230*i*
   Prager's role in recruiting, 165, 348
   quality of performances under, 180–84
   relationship with MCMA board, 234, 269
   retirement and final years, 233–34
   Roland Johnson's relationship with, 222, 231, 233, 302, 306
   role in Roland Johnson's hiring, 233, 246–47
   selection as MCMA music director, 164–65
   as soloist, 216, 217, 231
   Springfield Symphony Orchestra direction, 223, 230–31
   as teacher, 165, 213, 221–24, 226–29, 232
   use of Prager's *Messiah* cuts, 59
   World War I Army service, 208*i*, 208–10
   youth and emigration to U.S., 204–6
Heermann Quartet, 197, 197*i*, 198, 218*i*
Heermann Trio, 218–19, 229
Heggie, Jake, 452
Hegland, Ellen, 136
Hegyi, Julius, 322
Heiberg, Tania, 257
Heifetz, Jascha, 72
Heizer, Ruth, 70
Heldentenors, 240n51, 371n6
Helseth, Tine Thing, 422
Henderson, Skitch, 258
Henze, Hans Werner, 314
Herbert, Victor, 207
Hess, William, 231
Hettmannsberger, Greg, 376
Hetzler, Mark, 428
Heyward, DuBose, 383
Higdon, Jennifer, 421
Hildebrandt, Edith, 47, 48
Hill, Douglas, 324
Hillis, Lois E. (Newhall), 5
Hillis, Margaret, 324, 347
Hillis, William D., 5
A History of the Madison Civic Music Association (Anderson), 283
Hoch Conservatory, 197, 205
Hockney, David, 425
Hodkinson, Sydney, 382
Hoebig, Desmond, 363
Hoffman, Edward, 8
holiday concerts
   choral traditions, 420

costume tradition, 410*i*
   under DeMain, 358, 423, 423*i*
   under Johnson, 361
   under Prager, 59, 70
Holiday Spectacular, 358, 363, 423
Hollander, Lorin, 255, 337
Holmquest, Barbara, 231
Homecoming Concert of 1907, 72
Honeysucker, Robert, 326
Hooley's Opera House, 4, 27, 35*t*
Horncastle, Henry, 8
Hornik, Renata, 439*i*
Horowitz, Robert, 340
Horowitz, Vladimir, 378
Horton, Hope, 361
Hotel Loraine, 174, 177
Hotter, Hans, 307
Hottmann, David, 255, 261
Hough, Stephen, 378
Houston Grand Opera, 162, 349, 351, 382–83
Howe, Julia Ward, 10
Hoyt, Marika Fischer, 436*i*
Huber, Billie, 212
Huddleston, Patricia, 316
Humphrey, Doris, 305
Humphreys, Siegfried "Sigi," 234–35, 243n117
hundredth season celebration, 451–52
Hungarian Court Orchestra, 35*t*
Hungarian Dance No. 5 (Brahms), 63
Hunger Amid Plenty report, 400
Hunt Quartet, 424
Hunter, Elizabeth, 90*i*
Hunter, John Patrick, 321
Hutchison, Samuel, 404, 406–7, 408*i*, 408–9, 422, 427
Hutton, Eileen, 80
Hymes-Bianci, Janna, 357

I

Iltis, Ted, 143, 343, 348
immigrant groups, music's importance, 2
influenza epidemic, 209
Innes, Diego "James," 131
Instituto Superior de Música de la Universidad Nacional del Litoral, 140

Interlochen Arts Camp, 165
Interlochen National Music Camp, 226*i*, 226–28, 227*i*, 315
Irons, Jeremy, 387
Irving, Bill, 370*i*
Isserlis, Steven, 422, 422*i*
It Was a Lover and His Lass (Johnson), 310, 311, 311*i*
Iturbi, José, 214

J

J. F. Crow Institute for the Study of Evolution, 186
"Jackies" band, 75
Jacobs, Arnold, 368
Jacobs, Paul, 427
Jaffe, Willy, 22
Jalowitz, Heinrich, 304
James, Ralph, 90*i*, 355
Janis, Byron, 378
Jansky, Helen, 90*i*
Japan International Volunteer Center, 325–26
jazz music, 31, 47, 65–66
Jefferson, Blind Lemon, 300
Jencks, Frederick, 81
Jennings, Evelyn, 360
Jepson, Helen, 130
jigsaw puzzle, 177, 177*i*
Jimenez, Sebastian, 449
Joachim, Joseph, 198
Jobim, Antonio Carlos, 387
Johannesen, Grant, 337, 382
Johansen, Gunnar, 129, 153, 153*i*, 171, 255, 337
Johnson, Anna Laura Christine Dahl, 299, 300
Johnson, Arline Hanke
   Madison Civic Opera Workshop formation, 249, 259
   opera revival under, 249, 259–263, 320
   overview of life and career, 318–321, 319*i*
   teaching career and marriage, 316–17
Johnson, Carl, 298, 302, 317, 324
Johnson, Carl Albert, 298–99, 300
Johnson, David, 70
Johnson, James Weldon, 183
Johnson, Leonore, 68, 80, 83

Johnson, Roland
   1962 photo, 322*i*
   arrival in Madison, 246–49
   assessment of Heermann's tenure, 181
   Civic Chorus work, 280–82
   collaborations with Gunnar Johansen, 153
   on College of Music faculty, 307–9
   comments on Stock Pavilion, 74
   as composer, 309–13
   early life, 298–301, 302*i*
   Heermann's relationship with, 222, 231, 233, 302, 306
   legacy, 327–28
   life in Madison and outside engagements, 321–24
   Lottridge's assessment, 288
   music studies in Cincinnati, 301–3
   Navy service, 303–5
   opera revival under, 249, 259–263
   pictured with Arline, 317*i*, 320*i*
   pictured with John DeMain, 353*i*, 434*i*
   postwar graduate study, 305–7
   programming changes in 1960s and 1970s, 250–53, 255
   retirement and final years, 324–27, 346–48, 351–52, 397, 397*i*
   role in realizing *Shining Brow*, 328, 343–44
   Stock Pavilion concerts, 76
   studies with Hermann Scherchen, 313*i*, 313–14
   on University of Alabama faculty, 314–17, 316*i*
   venue changes under, 253–54
   youth concerts, 255–57
Johnson, Thor, 211–12, 215, 227
Johnson Carl, 232
Johnson City (TN), 299–300
Jones, Jack, 379
Jones, Paul, 116*i*
Jones, Sam, 141
Jones, Samuel, 255, 261, 334
Jones-Iltis, Josephine, 160
Journal of the American Musicological Society, 134
Jubilare! (Stevens), premiere, 325, 396–97

Juilliard School of Music, 303, 378–380, 427, 430, 432, 433
Julian, Augusta, 348
Jutsum, John, 435*i*
Jutt, Stephanie, 190, 438*i*

K

Kaebisch, Michelle, 425
Kahlson, Erik, 246
Kainer, Eden, 434*i*
Kains, Sherwood, 221
Karp, Howard, 255
Katzman, Louis, 31
Kay, Richard, 364
Kayser, Stella, 178
Keeshan, Bob, 256
Kellerman, Annette, 32–33
Kelly, Minnie, 29
Kelm, Linda, 338
Kelso, Leanne, 430, 439*i*
Kemp, Edwin, 80
Kenley, John, 379*i*, 379–380
Kenley Players, 379–380
Kern, Olga, 422, 451
Kernis, Aaron Jay, 421
Kids from Wisconsin, 428
Kiley, Leon, 166
Kim, Benny, 363
Kim, Won-Mo, 277–78
Kimball, Linda, 437*i*
Kimball, Norman, 53
Kincaid, William, 190
Kirkpatrick, Donald, 166, 184*i*, 184–85, 189*i*
Kirkpatrick, Fern, 185, 185*i*
Kirkpatrick, Neal, 184, 184*i*
Kirkpatrick, R. Bruce, 184
Kirkpatrick, Robert, 183, 184, 184*i*
Kirkpatrick, Vernon, 184, 184*i*
Kirkpatrick, Wendell, 184, 184*i*
Kirksmith, Karl, 216
Kirschnereit, Matthias, 403, 403*i*
Kjentvet, Lisa, 418*i*, 419, 424
Klais, Philipp, 407–8, 408*i*
Klieforth, Max, 53

"Know Your Symphony Orchestra" series, 274, 410
Knox, Kyle, 417, 429–433
Koch, Erwin, 53
Kockritz, Hubert, 214, 215, 227
Kolisch, Rudolf, 278, 305
Kombrink, Ilona, 255, 334
Korean War, 180
Korst, Robert, 200, 225
Koss, Herman, 129
Kountz, Frederick, 94, 95
Koussevitsky, Serge, 210, 307
Kowalski, James, 185
Kraggerud, Henning, 422
Krenek, Ernst, 129, 305
Kretschman, Katie, 370*i*
Kretschmann, David, 298
Kretschmann, Karen, 262, 298, 321, 322, 326
Kreutz, Arthur, 121, 126, 129
Kronenberg, Ferdinand Y., 265*i*
Kucinski, Leo, 363
Kunwald, Ernst, 207, 239*n*29
Kurr, Steve, 449
Kvam, Arnold Kunrad, 59, 157–59, 158*i*, 355

L

La Scala Orchestra, 34, 35*t*, 72
Labunski, Felix, 309*i*, 309–10, 311
The Lads of Wamphray (Grainger) premiere, 155, 191*n*8
Lake Songs (Gates), 339
Lakes, Gary, 338
Lakeside Quartet, 233*i*
Lamy, Andy, 431
Lange, Robert, 340
Lansing, Egbert, 8
Laredo, Jamie, 433
Laredo, Ruth, 337
large-scale programs under Prager, 67–79, 68*i*
Larrocha, Alicia de, 255, 337
Latimer, James, 275, 324, 324*i*
Laube, Nathan, 422
Lauridsen, Morten, 409
Lavine, Karl, 424, 435*i*

Law Park, 264, 266
Lawrence, Arthur, 387
Lawrence, Marjorie, 76, 133, 152, 152*i*
lectures by Prager, 111, 113, 119, 122–23, 135, 139, 140
Lehman, Otto, 16
Lehmann, Lotte, 130
Lehmann, Philip, 323
Lehrbuch des Dirigierens (Scherchen), 313
Leighton, Mary, 214
Leonard, Erwin, 53
Leonardi, Giovanni, 6
Leoncavallo, Ruggero, 11, 35*t*, 72
Lesnoff, Jonathan, 422
Leutscher, Harold, 81
Levenson, Harry, 246
Leventhal, Sharan, 257
Levine, Rhoda, 380
Lewis, John, 40*n*13
Lewis, Ken, 378
Liebenberg, Donald, 183
Liederkranz, 2
Link Up, 424
Lippi, Isabella, 413
Little, Minnie, 3
Livingston, Peter, 403, 403*i*
local composers. *See also individual entries*
    Alexius Baas, 87–88
    Cecil Burleigh, 132
    early Civic Symphony performances, 63, 64–65*t*, 66–67
    Heermann's regard for, 170
    Hilmar Luckhardt, 155
    Olive Endres, 95–96
    Oskar Hagen, 155–57
    Roland Johnson's support, 250–51
    Stephen Chatman, 256–57
    Sybil Hanks, 118–19, 182–83
Lockington, David, 362
London Symphony Orchestra, 34, 35*t*, 72
Looking at Music (TV series), 140
Loraine Hotel, 254, 272
Los Angeles Master Chorale, 409
Los Indios Tabajaras, 258

Lottridge, Richard, 275, 286–88, 287i, 335, 347
Loyanich, Peter Paul, 166–67
Luckhardt, Hilmar, 155
Lueders, John, 23, 27, 28
Luening, Otto, 251, 251i
Lui, Huy, 430
Luminaria, 429
Luther Memorial Church choir, 115–16, 116i
Lyford, Ralph, 212
Lynn, Lytta, 32
Lyons, Daniel, 290, 419, 420

M

Maazel, Lorin, 129, 384
MacDonald, William, 8
Mackie, Richard, 286, 341, 391, 402–3, 406–7, 414–16, 415i
Madden, Sandra, 327, 340–41, 341i, 361, 416, 419
Maddy, Joseph, 226
Maderna, Bruno, 314
Madey, Marjorie, 261
Madison Area Technical College, 348, 418–19.
   See also Madison Vocational School
Madison Art Center, 395
Madison Baroque Chorus, 93, 94
Madison Brass Band, 26
Madison Choral Union, 35t
Madison Civic Ballet, 68, 80
Madison Civic Band, 61
Madison Civic Center, 266–67, 327–28, 334–35
Madison Civic Chorus
   1931 photo, 56i
   Ann Stanke's management, 291
   concerts of the 1930s, 62
   developments in 1960s and 1970s, 280–82
   founding, 46, 56
   growth under Johnson, 249
   guest conductors, 347
   Heermann's inaugural season with, 166–68
   Heermann's rebuilding efforts, 172
   inaugural season, 56–58
   Johnson's legacy, 328, 333
   Kvam conflict, 157–59
   large-scale programs under Prager, 67–79, 68i
   Messiah performances, 58–59. *See also* *Messiah* performances
   name change in 1983, 274
   post–World War II programs, 160–61, 163–64
   programming changes in 1960s and 1970s, 250–53, 255
   rehearsal photo with Heermann, 169i
   selected musician profiles from Heermann era, 188
   selected musician profiles from Johnson era, 289–290
   selected musician profiles from Prager era, 89–91, 90i
   venue changes under Johnson, 253–54
   World War II impact on, 152, 157i
Madison Civic Music Association
   administrative staff development, 283–86
   board's evolving oversight role, 178–79, 269–270
   budget growth 1960–1980, 333
   civic auditorium advocacy, 49, 264, 267
   Civic Chorus beginnings, 56–59
   Civic Symphony beginnings, 50–56
   concerts of the 1930s, 62–67, 64–65t
   dissolution in 1990s, 341–42
   early concerns about losing Prager, 60, 61, 122
   end of free concerts, 271–73
   formation, 46–50
   impact on Madison Orchestral Association, 38
   James Crow's board service, 186
   large-scale programs under Prager, 67–79, 68i
   major changes in 1960s and 1970s, 245
   opera productions in 1930s, 79–82, 259
   organizational changes in 1990s, 339–343
   post–World War II administrative growth, 174–78
   post–World War II programs, 160–62
   relations with local press, 82–84

securing Johnson's successor, 346–352
selected musician profiles from 1920s and
    1930s, 84–96
selected musician profiles from Heermann
    era, 184–190
selected musician profiles from Johnson
    era, 286–293
UW music school's participation ban, 57
Vocational School support, 59–62
Women's Committee, 176–78, 179
World War II years, 151–57
Madison Civic Opera, 260, 263, 334–35. *See also*
    Madison Opera; opera
Madison Civic Opera Guild
    early productions and growth, 260–63
    Johnson's legacy, 328
    name changes, 260, 263
    origins, 245, 259, 320
    Robert Tottingham's membership, 188,
        261–62
Madison Civic Opera Workshop, 249, 259, 259i
Madison Civic Symphony (MCS). *See also*
    Madison Symphony Orchestra (MSO)
    1950s concerts and changes under
        Heermann, 169–174
    concerts of the 1930s, 62–67, 64–65t
    early programs, 55
    first performance, 15, 53–55, 54i
    first rehearsals, 38, 51
    founding, 46, 50–53
    growing professionalism in 1960s, 270–71,
        333
    Heermann's inaugural season with, 165–68
    jigsaw puzzle, 177, 177i
    Johnson's initial impact, 248–49, 249i
    large-scale programs under Prager, 67–79,
        68i
    name change in 1966, 273–74
    Prager's inaugural season, 53–56
    programming changes in 1960s and 1970s,
        250–53, 255
    rehearsal photo with Heermann, 169i
    selected musician profiles from Heermann
        era, 184–190

selected musician profiles from Johnson
    era, 286–88, 290–93
selected musician profiles from Prager era,
    84–87, 88–89, 91–96
venue changes under Johnson, 253–54
Wisconsin School of Music connection,
    21–22
World War II years, 151–57
Madison Community Music Committee, 47–48
Madison Concert Orchestra, 126–27, 131, 171,
    179
Madison Maennerchor
    appearances with local orchestras, 27, 29,
        34
    Baas's direction, 78, 87, 116
    Civic Chorus members from, 56
    civic music festival participation, 67, 69, 70
    founding, 2, 70
    Massing's leadership, 18
    Prager's direction, 56, 60, 78, 115–16
Madison Musical Academy, 27
Madison Musical Society, 27–28
Madison Musical Union, 3–4, 4i, 27
Madison Opera. *See also* Madison Civic
    Opera Guild
    Ann Stanke's work with, 291–92
    DeMain's orchestra direction, 358
    Johnson's contributions, 328
    name change to, 260, 263
    in Overture Hall grand opening, 405
    programming in 21st century, 425i, 425–26
    programming in 1980s and 1990s, 339
    reorganization as separate entity, 341–42
    Shining Brow, 328, 343–46
Madison Opera Chorus, 325
Madison Opera Guild, 82, 283
Madison Orchestral Association, 4, 15, 34–38,
    39t, 49
Madison Philharmonic Society, 25
Madison String Sinfonia, 93–94
Madison Summer Theatre, 29
Madison Symphony Chorus
    continued improvement, 419–420
    holiday traditions, 420, 423

initial changes under DeMain, 355–57
Overture Hall staging for, 402
selected current musician profiles, 428–29, 429*i*
A Madison Symphony Christmas, 423
Madison Symphony Orchestra (MSO). *See also* Madison Civic Symphony (MCS)
   50th anniversary season, 282–83
   75th anniversary season, 395–97
   administrative growth, 414–19, 415*i*, 416*i*, 418*i*
   amateur to professional evolution, 409–14
   centennial season planning, 451–52
   Civic Symphony renamed in 1966, 273–74
   concerts of 21st century, 420–26
   concerts of the 1980s and 1990s, 336–39
   developments in 1960s and 1970s, 274–280
   future challenges and opportunities, 447–452
   holiday traditions, 410*i*
   initial changes under DeMain, 352–55
   Johnson's legacy, 327, 333
   move to Oscar Mayer Theatre, 334–35
   musical response to September 11 attacks, 397–98
   Overture Hall development, 398–406, 401*i*, 405*i*
   Reed's leadership, 445–47
   reorganization in 1994, 342
   securing Johnson's successor, 346–352
   selected current musician profiles, 427–28, 429–433, 434–440*i*
   selected musician profiles, 1980s into 2000s, 363–370, 434–440*i*
   selected musician profiles from Johnson era, 286–88, 290–93
Madison Symphony Orchestra Foundation, 343, 415
Madison Symphony Orchestra League (MSOL), 176, 178, 179, 359–60. *See also* Women's Committee
Madison Vocational School (Madison Area Technical College)
   end of MSO connection with MATC, 418–19

   financial support for MCMA established, 59–62
   Heermann retirement arrangement, 233, 246
   Heermann's work, 231–32
   Johnson's work, 321–22
   MCMA administrative spaces in, 62, 285–86
   MCMA director decision role, 164–65
   Prager's work, 116
Madison Vocational School Music Festival, 68–69
Mael, John, 133
Magnes, Frances, 231
Mahler, Gustav, 362*i*
Mahler cycle, 361–62, 406, 421
Main, Anna, 26
Majestic Theater orchestra, 30, 32
Mancini, Henry, 336
Marcel, Lucille, 107, 107*i*
Marcus, Adele, 378
Mariachi los Camperos, 449
Marietta Sherman Orchestra, 88–89
Marsalis, Wynton, 387, 422
Masonic Temple Auditorium
   Heermann's inaugural season in, 165–66, 167*i*
   large-scale programs in, 69
   as MCMA's primary venue 1937 to 1953, 173
Massing, Francis, 18, 18*i*
Massing, Francis (Franz), 2
master agreement, 287, 413
"Masterworks of Opera" lectures, 140
Matrose, Rosetta, 167
May Festivals
   Charleston, 229–230
   Cincinnati, 206, 229
   University Choral Union, 2*i*, 3
Mayer, Oscar G., 267
Mayer, Robert, 366
McAdoo, James, 75
McAllister, Roy, 315, 319
McCrady, Edward, 322
McDuffie, Robert, 363, 422

McKinley, J. H., 3
Mears, S. E., 69
Meditation for Cello and Piano (Hanks), 65*t*, 83, 183
Meekhof, Lindsey, 418*i*, 419
Meeks, John, 49
Meisle, Kathryn, 130
Melba, Nellie, 72
Melchior, Lauritz, 214, 215
Melton, James, 130
Memphis Symphony Orchestra, 217
Mengelberg, Willem, 112
MERIT program, 95
Merman, Ethel, 379
Merriman, Nan, 167, 167*i*, 170
Mesa, Thomas, 422
The Message of Song (Prager), 65*t*, 68, 133
Messer, Joyce, xvi, 370*i*, 411, 411*i*
Messiah performances
    Baas recording, 88
    conducted by Johnson in Tokyo, 326, 326*i*
    under Heermann's directorship, 166, 172–73
    Johnson's changes, 281
    Johnson's direction during Navy service, 304
    Kvam conflict, 158
    as Madison Civic Chorus tradition, 58–59
    at new Coliseum, 273
    Prager era recording, 164
    as University Choral Union's opening concert, 3
Messner, Robert, 183
Mester, Jorge, 379
Meyn, Heinrich, 3
Michaels, Ria, 340
Midori, 422
Midwinter Matinees, 336
Miller, Ashley B., 151–52
Miller, George, 56
Miller, Jack, 442n10
Miller, Mitch, 258, 258*i*
Mills, Charles H., 56, 57, 66
Milton College, 94
Milwaukee A Capella Chorus, 120

Milwaukee Philharmonic Orchestra, 123
Minneapolis Symphony Orchestra
    early Madison performances, 34, 35*t*
    Madison Orchestral Association sponsorship, 36, 37, 39*t*, 75
Mintz, Shlomo, 422
Mischler, Elaine, 409, 451, 452
Mischler, Nicholas, 409
Missa Solemnis (Beethoven)
    1947 performance, 160–61, 249
    Prager's farewell concert, 76, 136, 162*i*, 162–64, 249
Mitby, Norman, 322
monochord, 102–3, 134
Monona, Olivia, 13–14
Monona Lake Assembly
    brief consideration as civic auditorium, 264
    early touring orchestra concerts, 35*t*
    summer music programs, 18–20
    Waltzinger's 1895 performance, 13, 20
Monona Terrace, 264–65, 268, 268*i*
Monroe, Lucy, 130
Montgomery, Jessie, 422
Moody Blues, 426
Moore, E. C., 160
Moore, Thomas, 275, 278*i*, 279, 412
Morales, Ricardo, 431
Moran, Thomas, 41n35
Morgan, Andrew, 357
Morgan, B. Q., 48, 55, 59, 66
Morgan, Rick, 411, 437*i*
Morin, Henri, 20
Morino, Vincenzo, 7
Morphy, Edwin, 29
Morris, Mark, 334–35
Morrissey, Louise, 90*i*
Moser, Arcenia, 188*i*, 260
Moser, Karlos, 160, 260
Motte, Adelina, 16
Mount, William Sidney, 15
movie theater orchestras, 28, 29–33
Moy, Nathan, 84
Mozart Club
    in 1930s music festivals, 67, 69, 70

in 1949 Spring Music Festival, 167, 167*i*
Baas's direction, 87
founding, 2
photo, 56*i*
State Capitol concerts in 1925, 49
Mozart oboe concerto, 367–68
MSO at the Movies, 447, 449
Mt. Zion Gospel Choir, 423*i*
Mueller, Harry, 229
Muldoon, Paul, 344*i*, 344–45, 346
Munch, Charles, 243n117
"Music at War" remembrance (Prager), 105–6
music director search committees, 348, 351, 451
music festivals
  MCMA sponsored, 67–70, 68*i*
  University sponsored, 161, 163, 167–68
"Music for You" series, 128
Music Hall (University of Wisconsin), 23, 24*i*
Music Memory Contests, 47–48
"Music of the Allied Nations" program, 155
Music Performance Trust Fund, 180, 270, 271, 413
music therapy, 425
"Music Under the Stars" series, 129–130
musical comedy, 13, 17, 32
musician compensation
  benefits of repeat programs for, 253–54
  in Cincinnati during Heermann's tenure, 218
  collective bargaining representation, 413–14
  early MCMA proposal, 56
  Endres's stipend, 92, 179
  growth in 1960s, 270–71
  growth under Heermann, 179–180, 270
  master agreement, 287, 413
  with move to Oscar Mayer Theatre, 335
musique concrète, 314
Muth, Mark, 125

N

Nahirniak, Taras, 363
Naret-Konig, Johann, 197*i*
national anthem, 155
Naughton, Christina, 422
Naughton, Michelle, 422

Nazi regime, 117, 201, 225
Neal, Paulita Heermann, 196, 224, 227, 232
Neal, Peter, 227, 232, 233*i*, 234
Neighborhood Family Concerts (Cincinnati), 212
Neighborhood Family Concerts (Madison), 257
Nelson, Daniel, 263, 263*i*, 334
Nelson, Marie, 161
Nelsova, Zara, 255, 364
Nero, Peter, 258
New Leviathan Oriental Fox-Trot Orchestra, 415
New Madison Choral Society, 159
new music under Johnson, 250–51
New Orpheum Theater orchestra, 30, 31, 32
New Symphony Orchestra, 112
New York City Opera, 380–81, 393n17
New York Philharmonic, 36, 39*t*, 75–76
New York String Seminar, 430, 433
New York Symphony Orchestra, 34, 35*t*
newsletter, 175
newspapers. *See also Capital Times; Wisconsin State Journal*
  Kvam conflict coverage, 158–59
  MCMA's relationship with, 82–84
  Overture grand opening coverage, 403–4
  Prager letters, 139, 140
  on Prager's retirement, 136–37
NEXUS, 363
Niemeyer, Ken, 348
Nikisch, Arthur, 72
Nikrenz, Erika, 398
Nitschke, Charles, 19*t*, 28–29, 29*i*, 99n64
Nitschke Orchestra, 28–29
Nixon, Richard, 386
Nixon in China (Adams), 386–87
Nolan Terrace, 268
Nono, Luigi, 314
Nordica, Lillian, 72
Noren, Rictor, 440*i*
Norwegian immigrants, 2, 7, 10, 70–78
Norwegian Sangarfests, 70–78, 78*i*
Nowlin, Patrick, 436*i*
Nureyev, Rudolf, 338
Nutcracker (Tchaikovsky) near-disaster, 187

O

O'Brien, Jack, 384
O'Connor, Mark, 422
Odana Road offices, 417–18
O'Day, Sheila. *See* Heermann, Martha Amelia Sheila (Bodebeder, a.k.a. Sheila O'Day)
Oelkers, Casey, 416, 418*i*, 419
Oestreich, James R., 405
Ohlsson, Garrick, 337, 422
O'Keefe, Margaret, 326
Oklahoma City Symphony, 279–280
Oldham-Baas, Evelyn, 56, 87
Olin Park, 265–66
Olin Park Auditorium, 264. *See also* Monona Lake Assembly
Olive Endres, 95–96
Oliveira, Elmar, 337
Olivera, Elmar, 363
Ollmann, Kurt, 362
Olsen, Broderick, 378
One Perfect Love (Johnson), 310
O'Neill, Charles, 66, 69
opera. *See also* Madison Opera
   Ann Stanke's work with, 291–92
   Bertha Waltzinger's career, 12–13
   in Cincinnati, 212
   concert versions under Heermann, 173
   early Madison performances, 16–18, 19*t*
   John DeMain's experience, 349, 351, 376–77, 382–87
   Olivia Monona's career, 13–14
   Prager's early introduction to, 103–4
   Prager's lectures, 139, 140
   Prager's MCMA productions in 1930s, 79–82, 259
   revival under Johnsons, 249, 259–263, 320, 328
   Robert Tottingham's local contributions, 188
   touring orchestras with, 32
   at University of Alabama, 316–17
Opera in the Park, 325, 425*i*, 426
Opera Integration Committee, 341
Opera Omaha, 387
Opera Pacific, 389
Opera Project, 380
operetta, 17, 19*t*, 22, 112
Orchestra Galas, 174, 177, 272
orchestra library, 417, 418
Organizational Structure Committee, 341–42
Orgelbau Klais, 407
O'Riley, Christopher, 422
Orphean Brothers, 26
Orpheum Theater, 30, 60, 399–400
Orquestra Filharmonica de Punilla, 139
Ortel, Jo, 395
Ortiz, Cristina, 255, 337
Oscar Mayer Theatre
   improvements for performers, 287
   Johnson's efforts for, 327–28
   naming of, 267
   opening of, 334–35
   preservation in Overture Project, 401*i*, 406
   shortcomings, 398–99
Osorio, Jorge, 449
Otterson, Margaret, 49, 81, 111, 166, 182, 183
Otto, Miriam, 227
outdoor programs
   Concert on the Green, 336, 358–59, 359*i*
   at Monona Terrace, 268
   Opera in the Park, 325, 425*i*, 426
   under Roland Johnson, 253, 254*i*
Overn, Joanna, 260, 261*i*, 343
Overture Concert Organ, 403–4, 405, 406–9, 407*i*, 409*i*, 427–28
Overture Foundation, 401–2, 407
Overture Hall
   community response, 405, 420–21
   grand opening, 403–5
   improvements for performers, 405*i*, 405–6, 420–21
   planning and construction, 398–406, 401*i*, 442n9, 442n10

P

Pach, Ernst, 218, 218*i*
Paderewski, Ignacy, 72, 76
Page, Carolann, 343*i*
Page, Tom, 386

Pale Moon, An Indian Love Song (Prager), 133
Palmer, Robert
    comments on Opera Guild and MCMA, 259–260
    as MCMA manager, 269, 286, 286*i*, 327
    resignation, 340
    success in bringing in guest musicians, 337
Park, Alyssa, 350
Parkening, Christopher, 363
Parker, Fletcher, 2, 23, 23*i*
Parker, Jon Kimura, 363
Parkway Theatre, 60, 80, 81
Parkway Theatre orchestra, 30, 32, 32*i*
parlor concerts, 3
Parnell, Cleo, 129
Parnell, Clyde, 129
Parodi, Teresa, 6, 6*i*, 16
Paton, John, 260
Paton, Marion, 260
Patras, Leona, 183, 185, 189*i*
Patti, Adelina, 7, 41n18
Patti, Amalia, 6, 6*i*, 16, 41n18
Patti, Carlotta, 41n18
Patti, Sandy, 426
Paul, James, 324
Paulu, Catherine, 279*i*, 279–280, 366
Paulu, Norman, 279*i*, 279–280, 412
P.D.Q. Bach, 423
Pearcy, Hiram, 435*i*
Pellage, Henry, 23–24
Pelli, Cesar, 400*i*, 402
Perlman, Itzhak, 338, 338*i*
Perssion, Mary, 93, 276, 276*i*
Pesel, Yella, 305
Peters, Henry, 183, 249, 260, 275
Peters, William Wesley, 265–66
Petratta, Josephine, 183
Phelps, Margaret, 183
Philharmonic Chorus, 95, 159, 172
Philips, William, 80
Piazza, Marguerite, 258
Piazzolla, Astor, 421
Pickart, Margaret, 249
Pine, Rachel Barton, 422
Pixar in Concert™, 424, 447

Pleasant Company, 401
Pollak, Ignaz, 8
pops concerts
    of 1980s and 1990s, 336
    changes under Johnson, 249, 254, 258
    as fundraisers for orchestra, 177, 258, 272
    under Heermann, 172
    later discontinuance, 422–23
Potter, Emma, 390
Poulenc, Francis, 261, 310
Pouliot, Blake, 422
Powell, Laurence, 31, 66
Prager, Frances (Silva). *See* Silva (Prager), Frances
Prager, Sigfrid
    1931 portrait, 50*i*
    appointment as MCMA's first music director, 50–51
    appreciation for Susan Seastone, 48
    Baas's friendship with, 88
    Civic Chorus leadership, 56–59
    comments on assembling Civic Symphony, 51–52, 53
    as composer and arranger, 132–34
    compositions performed, 64t, 65t, 68, 128, 131
    as director versus Heermann, 180–81
    early life, 101–6
    farewell concert, 76, 136, 162*i*, 162–64
    financial support from vocational school established, 59–62
    at first Civic Symphony concert, 54*i*
    first visits to Madison, 110–13
    Germany visit in 1934, 116–17
    Gilbert Ross's musical relationship with, 15
    Grainger's connection with, 154–55
    incident with Florence Bennett, 89
    Kvam conflict with, 59, 157–59
    letters to Grace Schumpert, 90–91, 99n79
    Madison Maennerchor direction, 56, 60, 78, 115–16
    Marie Endres's musical relationship with, 92–93
    New York City residence, 109–13
    as opera director, 79–82, 259

as performer, 104, 109–10, 131–32
personality and legacy, 141–44, 159, 181, 192n26, 269
photo with Civic Chorus, 1931, 56i
pictured with Graingers, 154i
pictured with Marjorie Lawrence, 152i
post–World War I move to Argentina, 106–9
post–World War II programs, 160–62
relocation to Madison for MCMA, 113–19
retirement and final years, 135–141, 162–64, 283
Rhapsody in Blue performance, 65–66
role in recruiting Heermann, 165, 348
visits sponsored by Wisconsin School of Music, 21–22, 111, 112–13
Wisconsin Symphony Orchestra direction, 67, 82, 123–131
work in Chicago and Sheboygan, 120–23, 128
World War II years, 151–57
writings and lectures, 134–35
Pre-College Institute, 365
Prelude for Flute and Piano (Johnson), 310
premiered works in Madison
during DeMain's tenure, 362–63, 421
during Heermann's tenure, 119, 170
by Johnson in retirement, 325
during Johnson's tenure, 153, 250–51, 257, 292, 337, 346, 347
during Prager's tenure, 67, 68, 83, 119, 132–33, 155
Presber, Hedwig, 203, 237–38n12
Preucil, William, 430
Prévost, Germain, 154
Price, Florence, 421
Priebe, Arthur, 415
printed programs, 174–75
Pro Arte Quartet
arrival in 1939, 153–54
MSO concertmasters from, 278–79, 413
Schuller's *Concerto for String Quartet and Orchestra* premiere, 288, 337, 347
professionalization of MSO, 411–14. *See also* musician compensation
publications (MCMA), 174–75

publicity (MCMA), 174–75
Putnam, Anthony, 267
Puts, Kevin, 421, 422

Q

Quartet for Flute, Oboe, Clarinet, and Bassoon (Johnson), 310, 312
Quesnel, Albert, 72
Quiet My Heart (Hanks), 182

R

Raab, Emil, 316i
Rabin, Marvin, 323
Rachmaninoff, Sergei, 76
radio broadcasts
Heermann's experience, 219, 220
Madison concert in 1921, 37
Messiah performances, 166
under Roland Johnson, 253
Sangarfests, 78, 85
railroads' impact on early Madison music scene, 5–6, 16
Raimond, Josephine, 139–140
Raitt, John, 379
Ramey, Samuel, 370i
Rands, Bernard, 344
Reardon, John, 255, 262
recordings
The Compositions of Sybil Ann Hanks, 119, 182–84
Concert Grosso (Hagen), 181–82
of Heermann-led concerts, 181–84
Messiah featuring Baas aria, 88
Missa Solemnis 1948 performance, 163–64
Red Cedar Symphony Orchestra, 234
Reed, Robert
career overview, 445–47
first concert attendance, 368
on future needs, 450, 451
in organization chart, 418i, 419
Reel, John R., 284–85
Regan, Alice, 203
Reiner, Fritz, 210–11
Reményi, Edouard, 20
"Resident Companies Gala," 405

Reuter-Foss, Kitt, 268, 327, 337
Revueltas, Silvestre, 421
Reynolds, Shirley, 93
Rhapsodie Quartet, 424–25
Rhapsody in Blue (Gershwin), 65–66
Rhodes, John P., 216, 309
Rhythm and Booms, 426
Ribaupierre, André de, 170, 218
Ricci, Ruggiero, 255, 337
Rieck, Alan, 290, 355, 355*i*, 357
Riley, Edwin, 378, 380
Riley, Marcia, 380
Ring Cycle (Wagner), 338
Robbins, Chandler, 24–25
Robbins, Jerome, 387
Robbins, Tom, 340
Roberts, Henry, 265
Roberts, Mary, 387
Robida, Craig, 419
Robinson, Rene, 423*i*
Rodgers, Margaret, 319
Rodgers, Peter, 416, 418*i*, 419
Rodriguez, Santiago, 337
Roebuck, Don, 260, 261*i*
Rogers, Samuel, 156, 157
Rolston, Shauna, 350
Romero, Angel, 337
Rondo in Old Style for Violin and Piano (Hanks), 182
Roosevelt, Theodore, 33
Rosen, Nathaniel, 337
Rosing, Carol, 439*i*
Ross, Edward Alsworth, 14, 42n45, 42n47
Ross, Gilbert, 14*i*, 14–15, 37, 55, 132
Ross, Hugh, 307
Ross, Lanny, 130
Ross, Rosamond, 14, 14*i*
Rosser, Annetta, 276, 277*i*
Roth, Franz, 7, 8
Rouse, Christopher, 421
Royal Opera (Berlin), 103
Rudel, Julius, 380–81
Rusch, Milton, 128
Russian Ballet Company, 224
Russian Symphony Orchestra, 36

S

sacred concerts, early Madison performances, 1–2
Saengerfest, 78
Safford, Hattie, 8
Salerno, Lawrence, 86, 127
Salerno-Sonnenberg, Nadja, 422
Samson and Delilah (Saint-Saëns), 81
Samuels, Homer, 11, 11*i*
San Francisco Symphony Orchestra, 161
Sandoval, Arturo, 363
Sangarfests, 70–78, 85
Sant'Ambrosio, Sara, 422
Sauchuck, Emmett, 418*i*, 419
saxophone players at first Civic Symphony rehearsal, 51
Schacht, Alice, 249
Schaeffer, Pierre, 314
Schatz, Hilmar, 314
Scheer, Gene, 452
Scherchen, Hermann, 313*i*, 313–14
Schmelter, Maximilian, 161
Schneider, Miriam, 276–77, 277*i*, 278*i*
Schoenberg, Arnold, 313
schools, programming for, 36, 47–48, 256, 360, 424
Schreiber, Louis, 7–8
Schroeder, Hans, 203
Schuller, Gunther
  Cello Concerto written for Heermann, 236
  commission for College Orchestra, 308
  as MSO guest conductor, 288, 347
  MSO performances of works by, 250, 288, 337
  Roland Johnson's friendship with, 305, 305*i*, 330n24
Schulze, Elizabeth, 358
Schumann, Clara, 197, 198, 228
Schumann, Ferdinand, 198
Schumann-Heink, Ernestine, 11, 72
Schumpert, Grace, 89–91, 90*i*, 99n79, 143
Schwantner, Joseph, 344
Schwarzkopf, Elisabeth, 307
Scolten, Adrian, 55

search committees, 348, 351, 451
Searle, Humphrey, 314
season subscriptions
    double performances, 253–54, 335, 361
    early recognition of needs beyond, 50
    early venues, 60
    falling levels, 448
    Overture Hall's impact, 420
    pricing for the first time, 272–73
    program expansion in 1980s, 336
    triple performances, 391, 420–21
Seastone, Charles, 48, 143, 192*n*26
Seastone, Susan B., 48, 50, 51, 55, 56, 59
Second Vienna School, 313
Sedgewick, A., 16
Seguin, Edward, 16
September 11 attacks, 397–98
Serkin, Peter, 422
Severinsen, Doc, 336
Sewaunee Summer Music Center, 322–23, 323*i*
Seybold, Rick, 370*i*
Shahan, Gil, 422
Shapey, Ralph, 367
Shaw, Robert, 307
Sheboygan Civic Chorus, 81, 82, 123, 128
Shickele, Peter, 423
Shifrin, David, 337
Shining Brow (Hagen and Muldoon), 328, 343*i*, 343–46, 350
Shook, George, 76, 280–81, 289*i*, 289–290
Shook, Nancy, 289*i*, 289–290
Shrank, Fred, 440*i*
Sidlin, Murry, 357, 362
Sid's Serenaders, 32
Siegel, Jeffrey, 426
Siegfried (film), 109
Silva (Prager), Frances
    death reported, 141
    Germany visit in 1934, 117
    marriage and move to Madison, 111–12
    photos, 111*i*, 154*i*
    retirement, 138–39
    vocal performances, 67, 115, 120
Simone, Beverly, 348

Singakademie (Buenos Aires), 106–8
Sirucek, Jerry, 366
Skaats, William, 16
Skornicka, Joel, 263, 267
Skroch, Benjamin, xvi, 412
Sliester, Terry, 370*i*
Smith, Derrick, 451
Smith, Greg, 411, 436*i*
Smith, James, 432
Snell, Grace, 88*i*
Snodgrass, Louise Harrison, 236
Snyder, Ellsworth, 325
Soglin, Paul, 266–67
Sokol, Michael, 343*i*
Sokoloff, Nikolai, 130
Sokolov, Nikolai, 124
Solzhenitzen, Ignat, 363
Sonatique incident, 31
Sondheim, Stephen, 387
Song for Orchestra with Mezzo-soprano (Johnson), 310, 312–13
Sorenson, Sterling, 83
Sousa, John Philip, 75
South Shore Music Circus, 379
Southeastern Composers Forum, 315
Spalding, Albert, 130, 300
Spenser, Jennie Mae, 3
Spiering String Quartet, 20
Spivakov, Vladimir, 422, 443*n*33
Spring Music Festival (UW), 161, 163, 167–68
Springfield (Ohio) Symphony Orchestra
    Heermann brothers' performance with, 217
    Roland Johnson's work with, 306
    Walter Heermann's direction, 165, 223, 230–31
St. Clair, Carl, 421
St. James Catholic Church, 94, 95
St. Paul Chamber Orchestra, 381–82
St. Paul Symphony Orchestra, 35*t*
Stack, Edward, 70
staff development (MCMA), 283–86
Staines, Agnes, 3
Stanke, Ann
    concerns about Overture organ, 407

friendship with Johnsons, 323, 325, 326
overview of contributions, 290–93, 291*i*
pictured with Madison Symphony Chorus, 355*i*
regard for Beverly Taylor, 356
role in Civic Opera's first productions, 260, 291–92
Stanke, Ernest, 290, 291, 323, 324
Stanke, Mildred, 185, 291
Stanley, Jeff, 442*n10*
Stanley, Tamera, 423*i*
Stanley Quartet, 15
Stark, Sharon, 403, 403*i*
Starker, Janos, 364, 422
The Star-Spangled Banner, 155
State Capitol concerts in 1925, 49
Steber, Eleanor, 262
Steenbock, Evelyn, 257
Steenbock Awards Program, 257
Steffens, Leo, 232, 255, 278
Steinway grand piano, 403, 403*i*, 404
Stevens, John, 325, 396*i*, 396–97
Stewart, Rose, 3
Still, Ray, 366
Stock, Frederick, 73
Stock Pavilion. *See* University Stock Pavilion
Stockhausen, Karlheinz, 314
Stokes, Eric, 382
Stokowski, Leopold, 203, 204, 207, 239*n28*
Stopping by a Woods on a Snowy Evening (Johnson), 310, 327
Strakosch, Maurice, 6, 6*i*, 41*n18*
Strand Theater orchestra, 30, 31, 32
Stránsky, Josef, 112
Straus, Marshall, 160
Strauss, Richard, 205–6
Stravinsky, Igor, 94
string section reorganization, 353–54
Stuart Walker Company, 212
Stub, Valborg, 20
Stucky, Steven, 421
subscriptions. *See* season subscriptions
Sullivan, Louis, 345
Summer Musical Institute, 304–5

Sunrise on Lake Monona (painting), 41–42*n35*
Supernaw, Helen Marting, 49, 51, 175, 175*i*, 176, 179, 283–84
Swanson, Harry, 161
Swarthout, Gladys, 130
Swiss Bell Ringers, 5
Sydney Rosenfeld Opera Company, 17
Symphonic Suite op. 17 (Prager), 132–33
Symphony at Sunset, 423
Symphony Showhouse, 360
Symphony Singers, 360
Symphony Soup, 361, 424
Szigeti, Joseph, 279
Szpinalski, George, 67, 128, 276

T

Taft, Anna Sinton, 207
Talbot, Katrin, 186–87, 433, 434*i*
Taliaferro, Joan, 171*i*
Taliesin, 345, 372*n24*
Tanglewood Festival, 307
task-specific focal dystonia, 432
Taylor, Beverly, 290, 355–57, 356*i*, 419–420, 429
Taylor, Christopher, 422
Taylor, Guy, 231
Taylor, Kathy, 388, 418, 437*i*
Taylor, Latanya, 423*i*
Teatro Colón, 108*i*, 108–9
Tebaldi, Renata, 314
Tecco, Romuald, 380
television broadcasts, 140, 252–53, 391, 424
Temple of Music (Milwaukee), 129*i*, 129–130
Texas Opera Theater, 382–83
theater orchestras, 28, 29–33
Theme with Variations for Winds (Hanks), 183
Theodore Thomas Orchestra, 28, 34, 35*t*, 36
Third Wisconsin Cavalry, 24, 44*n72*
Thomas, John Charles, 130
Thomas, Theodore, 28, 206
Thomson, Virgil, 305
Thorp, Amelie, 8, 9
Thorp, Joseph G., 8
Three Preludes for Piano (Hanks), 182–83
ticket sales, introduction of, 271–73

To the Charter Members (poem), 137
Tocco, James, 255
Tofani, Dave, 378
Toledo Symphony Orchestra, 95
Torke, Michael, 337, 363
Torno, Laurent, 246
Totenberg, Roman, 152, 160, 191n3
Tottingham, Robert
    in 1962 *Die Fledermaus* performance, 249
    career overview, 188
    as Falstaff, 188i, 261–62
    in Opera Guild's first *La Bohème*, 260, 261i
    in Prager's last spring concert, 160
    as principal trumpet in symphony, 185
touring opera companies, 16–17
touring orchestras, 32–34, 35t, 75–76
touring performers in Madison's early music history, 4–11
Tower, Joan, 421
Townell, Eric, 347, 358, 373n53
Towner, Robert, 260, 261i
Townsend, Margaret (Maggie) Darby, 440i
Tozzi, Giorgio, 379
Trachte, Meta, 161
Traver, Berniece, 178, 283, 284
Trio for Flute, Viola, and Cello (Johnson), 310
Trotter, Thomas, 405, 422
trumpet players at first Civic Symphony rehearsal, 51–52
Tucker, Richard, 76, 254, 255
Tune, Tommy, 379
Turner Hall, 19t, 29, 34, 35t
Turn-Vereine, 34, 45n102
Tuthill, Burnet, 221

U

University Armory
    early touring orchestra concerts, 35t
    history as concert venue, 72–73
    Madison Orchestral Association events in, 34, 36, 39t, 73
    Messiah concert in 1894, 3
    origins, 71i, 71–72
University Choral Union, 2–3
University Field House, 68–69
University of Alabama, 314–17, 319
University of Chicago Contemporary Ensemble, 367
University Opera, 260
University Orchestra, 29, 30i
University Stock Pavilion
    history as concert venue, 73–77
    large-scale programs in, 67
    Madison Orchestral Association concerts, 37
    Prager's farewell concert, 76, 136, 162i, 163–64
    Roland Johnson's use, 254
Up Close and Musical program, 424
Upshaw, Dawn, 422
Urrey, Frederick, 326
Ussachevsky, Vladimir, 251i
UW Spring Music Festival, 167–68
UW Summer Music Clinic, 165, 228, 232
UW–Madison Piano Quartet, 278
UW–Madison School of Music
    Ada Bird's tenure, 20
    Beverly Taylor's work, 356
    featured musicians in Roland Johnson's programs, 255
    founding, 22–23
    Gilbert's leadership, 171
    Heermann's work with, 232
    Nitschke's employment with, 28, 29
    Prager's work with, 119, 122, 139
    prohibition of civic music participation, 57
    representation in Roland Johnson's orchestra, 275, 286, 287, 365, 366
    start of Pro Arte Quartet residency, 153–54

V

Valley Civic Music Association, 160
Valley Symphony Orchestra, 160
Van Bergen's Hall, 24, 26
Varèse, Edgard, 112
Varga, Lazlo, 364
Varian, Charlotte, 8
Varsik, John, 183

vaudeville, 13
Vaughan, Sarah, 258
Vaughan Williams, Ralph, 314
Velie, Lester, 66, 83, 102
Verrett, Shirley, 255
"Vienna, City of Music" program, 249
Vienna Lady Orchestra, 35*t*
Vilas, William F., 118, 119
violin players at first Civic Symphony rehearsal, 52
Violins of Hope, 277
Virrecke, Charles, 16
Vogts, Harry, 53, 55, 57
Vogts, Henry, 53
Vollstedt, Siegfried, 127
von Rhein, John, 346

W

Wadsworth, Stephen, 345, 386
Wahler, Viola, 70
Wahlin, William, 183
Walker, George, 421
Walker, George P., 110*i*, 110–11, 112–13, 115, 120
Walker, Stuart, 220
Walker, William, 258
Wallace, Stewart, 362
Walter, Bruno, 213
Waltzinger, Bertha, 12*i*, 12–13, 20
Walzinger, Stefanie, 42*n*45
War Song Jubilee of 1898, 72
Ward, Lane, 50, 53
Ward, Viola, 176, 178, 179
Ward-Brodt Music Company, 50, 53
Watts, André, 404, 422, 442*n*14
Weber, Jeanette Daggett, 29
Webern, Anton, 313
Weingartner, Felix, 107*i*, 107–8, 210
Weinholts, Johanna, 440*i*
Weisberg, Arthur, 363
Wellerstein, Alisa, 422
Wellesz, Egon, 314
West High School Auditorium, 69
West Side Story revival, 387
Westbrook-Geha, Mary, 326
Western, Lucie, 80

Westlund, Vernon, 246
"What to Listen For in Music" (UW course), 232
Wheeler, Fletcher, 22, 34
Wheeler School of Music and Dramatic Arts, 22, 89
Whitaker, Donald, 185, 275, 284
White, G. Laurenz (Glenn), 127
White, Warren, 16
Whitty, Brian, 370*i*
Wick, Frederick, 77
Wild, Earl, 255, 337
Williams, Bob, 166
Williams, Gail, 363
Williams, Thomie Prewett, 218–19, 229
Williams, Tom, 377
Willie Stark (Floyd), 385–86
Willner, Anna, 103*i*, 104, 111
Wilson, Ransom, 337
Winston, Margaret, 343
Wisconsin Chamber Orchestra, 401, 406, 413, 439*i*, 451, 453*n*11
Wisconsin Conservatory of Music, 20
Wisconsin School of Music
    Endres sisters' work with, 93, 95
    Florence Bennett's work with, 89
    founding and early leadership, 20–22
    Prager's work with, 21–22, 111, 112–13, 115
Wisconsin State Journal
    column on Prager's retirement, 136
    Kronenberg auditorium design image, 265*i*
    MCMA's relationship with, 82–84
    Messiah performance review, 58
    Overture grand opening article, 403–4
    Prager's "Music at War" remembrance in, 105–6
    Prager's *Rhapsody in Blue* defense, 65–66
    typical MCMA program coverage, 83
Wisconsin Sunday School Assembly, 18. *See also* Monona Lake Assembly
Wisconsin Symphony Orchestra, 67, 82, 123–131
Wisconsin Union Theater, 263
Wisconsin Youth Symphony Orchestras, 432
Wittwer, Herman, 53
Woerpel, Marvin, 343
Women's Committee. *See also* Madison

Symphony Orchestra League (MSOL)
   fundraising activities, 177, 256, 258, 272
   origins and evolution, 176–78, 179
   volunteer administrative work, 269
Wong, Randall, 362
Woods, Simon, 448
Woollen, Robert, 166
Works Progress Administration, 124
Worland, Gayle, 376
World War I, 105–6, 109, 207–8
World War II
   impact on FMP, 125
   impact on MCMA festivals, 78–79
   impact on musician recruiting, 151–52
   MCMA programming during, 152–57
   Pro Arte Quartet residency, 154
World's Columbian Exposition, 28
The Wreck of the Hesperus (cantata), 56, 57
Wright, Frank Lloyd, 174, 264, 267–68, 343–44, 345
Wright, Gordon, 367, 374n64
Wright, Margaret, 301
Wuerl, Adolf J., 123
Wulfsberg, Rolf, 411, 437i
Wunderle, Carl, 218, 218i, 219i
Wurlitzer, Helene, 303

Y

Yang, Joyce, 422
Yeiser, Frederick, 213–14, 216–17
Yorkville Theater, 109, 109i, 111, 112, 113
Young People's Matinees, 171–72
Youngstown Vindicator, 377
youth concerts
   under DeMain, 358
   under Heermann, 171–72, 214, 256
   Heermann's Cincinnati experience, 214
   under Prager, 171, 255–56
   under Roland Johnson, 255–57
   since 2000, 424
youth programming, 36, 47–48, 256, 360, 424
Ysaÿe, Eugène, 37, 72, 209, 210, 226, 240n38
Ysaÿe, Gabriel, 226
Yuletide Festival of Song (1913), 72
Yuletide Music Festival, 70

Z

Zelek, Greg, 409, 409i, 422, 427i, 427–28
Zerler, Ruth, 183
Ziebarth, Gertrude, 70
Ziegfeld, Florenz, 202
Ziffrin, Marilyn, 143–44
Zor Shrine Chanters, 160, 167, 167i, 193–94n56
Zukerman, Eugenia, 337
Zukerman, Pinchas, 255, 422

Printed in the United States
by Baker & Taylor Publisher Services